ASPEN COMICS PRESENTS:

In Association with
BLOCKADE ENTERTAINMENT

Executive Assistant: Iris
[VOLUME TWO]

D1289740

created by

David Wohl

Brad Foxhoven

&

Michael Turner

EXECUTIVE ASSISTANT: IRIS™ VOLUME 2

ISBN: 978-0-9854473-0-4 Softcover
FIRST PRINTING, 2012. *Collects material originally published as Executive Assistant: Iris vol. 2 Issues 0-5*

PUBLISHED BY ASPEN MLT, INC.
Office of Publication: 5855 Green Valley Circle. Suite. 111, Culver City, CA 90230.

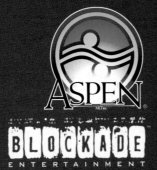

Address correspondence to:
EA: IRIS c/o
Aspen MLT Inc.
5855 Green Valley Circle. Suite. 111
Culver City, CA. 90230-6946
or fanmail@aspencomics.com

Visit us on the web at:
www.aspencomics.com
www.aspenstore.com
www.facebook.com/aspencomics
www.twitter.com/aspencomics

Collected Edition Editors: Mark Roslan and Frank Mastromauro
Original Series Editors: Vince Hernandez and Frank Mastromauro
Book Design: Mark Roslan and Peter Steigerwald
Cover Design: Peter Steigerwald
Cover Illustration: Joe Benitez and Peter Steigerwald
original lettering font designed by: Dreamer Design

For Aspen:

Founder: Michael Turner
Co-Owner: Peter Steigerwald
Co-Owner/President: Frank Mastromauro
Editor in Chief: Vince Hernandez
Director of Design and Production: Mark Roslan
Editorial Assistant: Josh Reed
Marketing Assistant: India Cosper
Office Coordinator: Erick Raymundo
AspenStore.com: Chris Rupp

Also available from Aspen Comics:

A Tribute to Michael Turner —— *ISBN: 978-0-9774821-7-7*

Executive Assistant: Iris™ Volume 1 —— *ISBN: 978-0-9823628-5-3*
Executive Assistant: The Hitlist Agenda™ Volume 1 —— *ISBN: 978-0-9854473-1-1*

Fathom™ Volume I: The Definitive Edition —— *ISBN: 978-0-9774821-5-3*
Fathom™ Volume II: Into The Deep —— *ISBN: 978-0-9774821-3-9*
Fathom™ Volume III: Worlds at War —— *ISBN: 978-0-9774821-9-1*
Fathom™: Dawn of War —— *ISBN: 978-0-9823628-2-2*
Fathom™: Kiani: Volume 1 —— *ISBN: 978-0-9774821-8-4*

Shrugged™ Volume 1: A Little Perspective —— *ISBN: 978-0-9774821-6-0*

Soulfire™ Volume I: The Definitive Edition —— *ISBN: 978-0-9823628-6-0*
Soulfire™: Dying of the Light —— *ISBN: 978-0-9774821-1-5*
Soulfire™: Chaos Reign —— *ISBN: 978-0-9774821-4-6*

Table of Contents

———✦———

All Lettering by: JOSH REED

———✦———

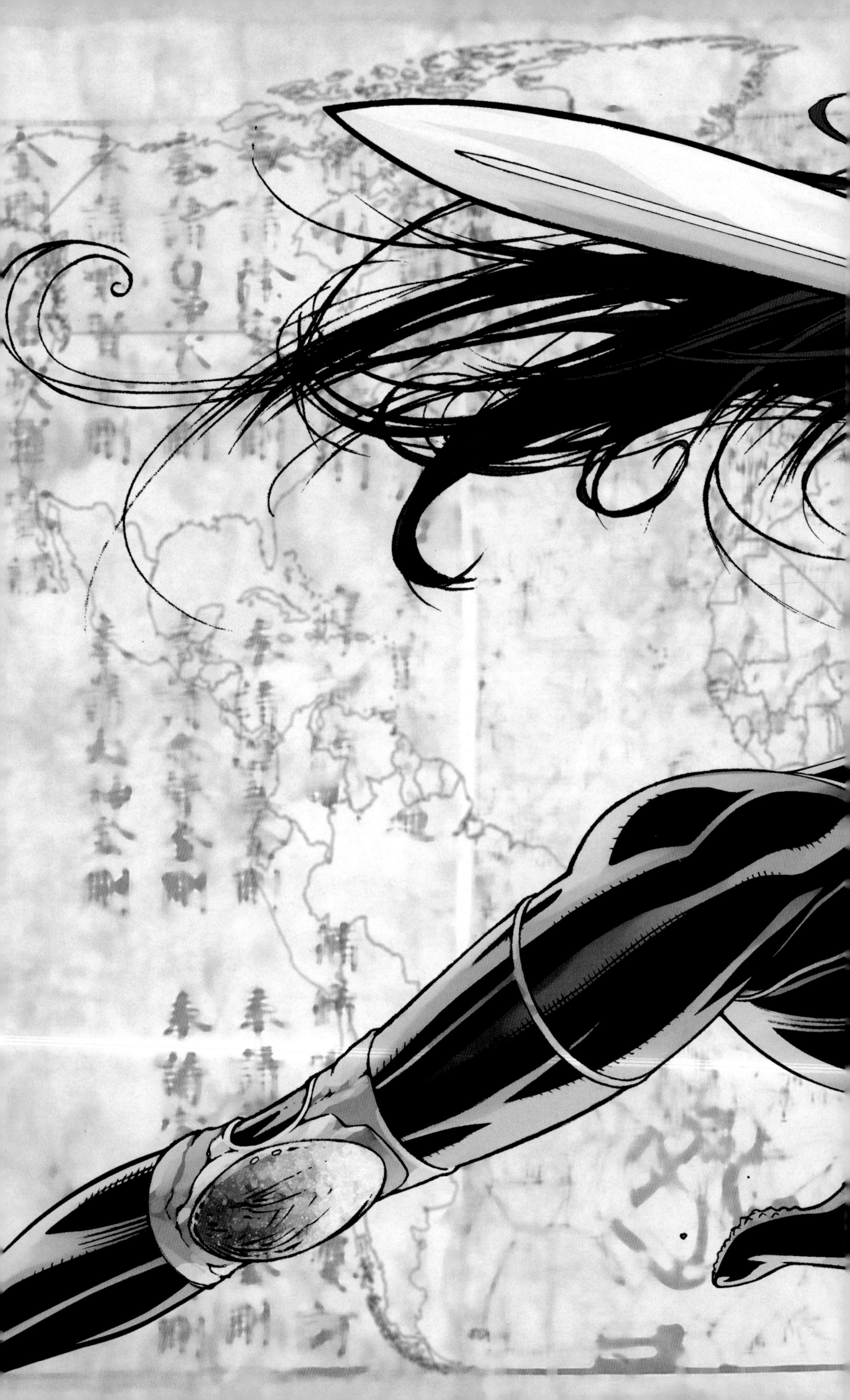

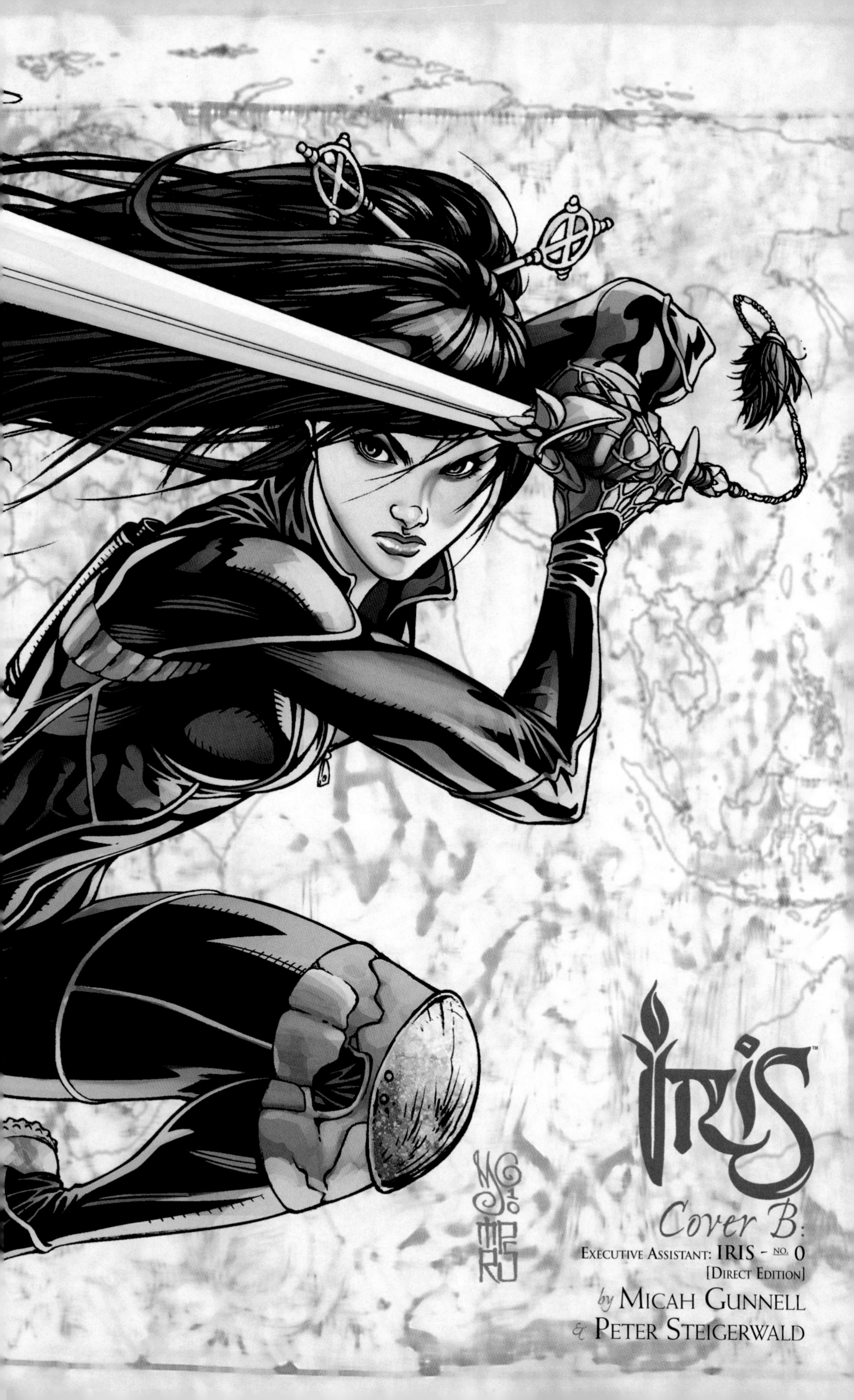
IRIS™
Cover B:
Executive Assistant: IRIS - No. 0
[Direct Edition]
by Micah Gunnell
& Peter Steigerwald

IRIS™

Cover A:

Executive Assistant: IRIS - No. 0

[Direct Edition]

by Eduardo Francisco & Sunny Gho

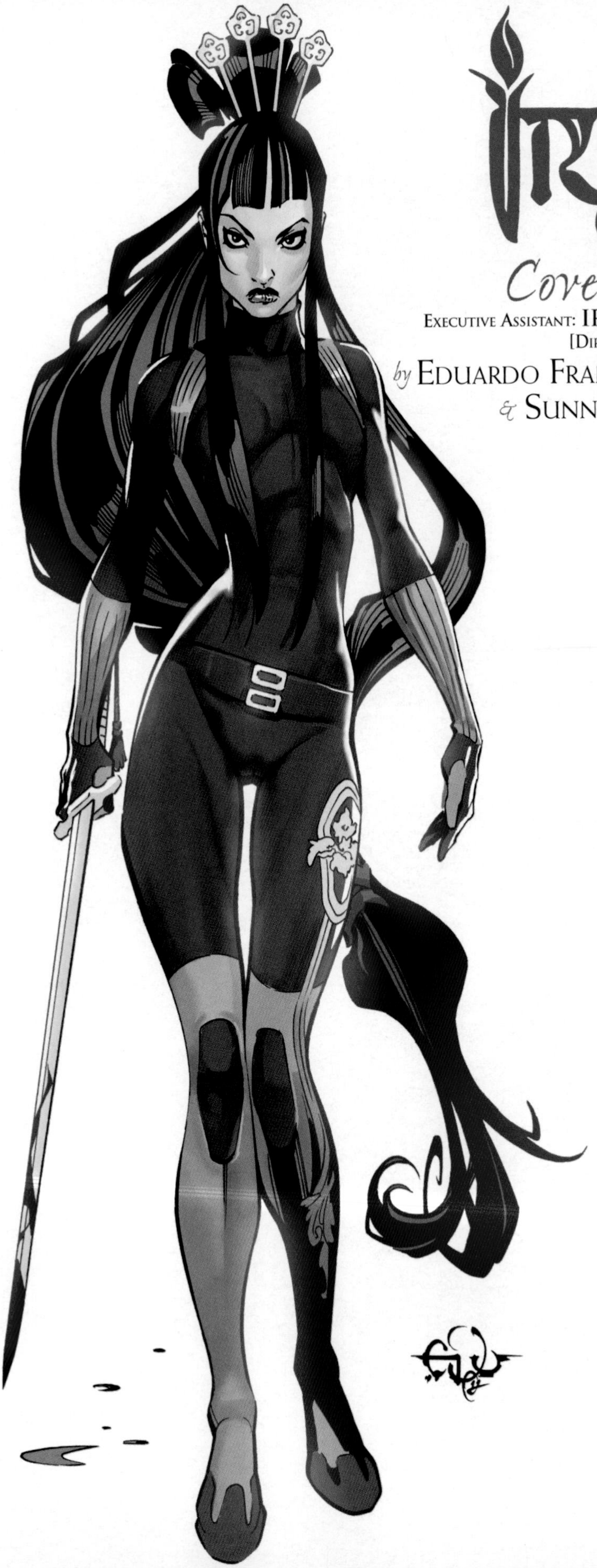

CHAPTER ONE

ZERO

"WELCOME TO THE MACHINE"

STORY
DAVID WOHL & BRAD FOXHOVEN

SCRIPT
DAVID WOHL

PENCILS
EDUARDO FRANCISCO

COLORS
SUNNY GHO

LETTERING
JOSH REED

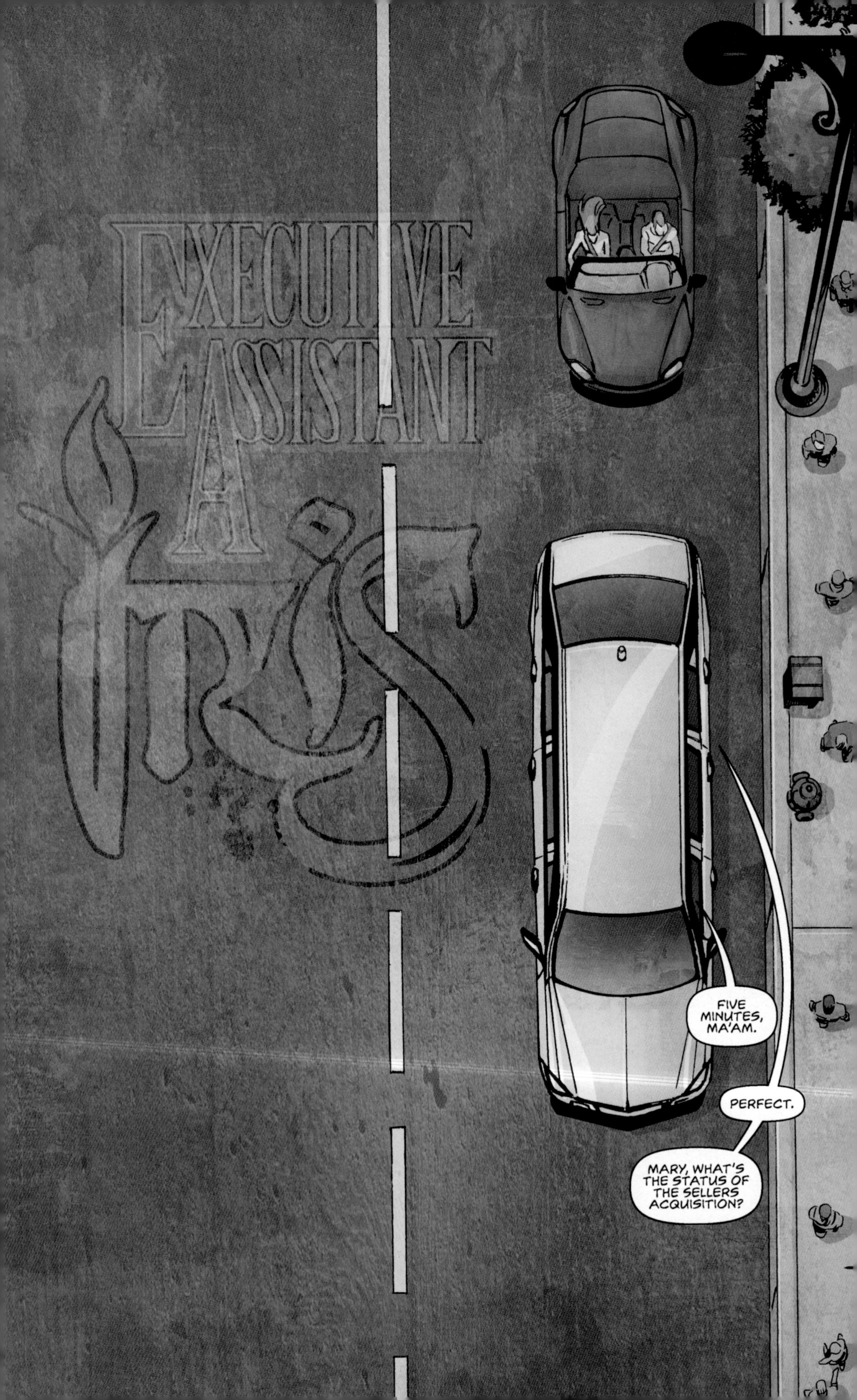
EXECUTIVE ASSISTANT
IRIS
FIVE MINUTES, MA'AM.
PERFECT.
MARY, WHAT'S THE STATUS OF THE SELLERS ACQUISITION?

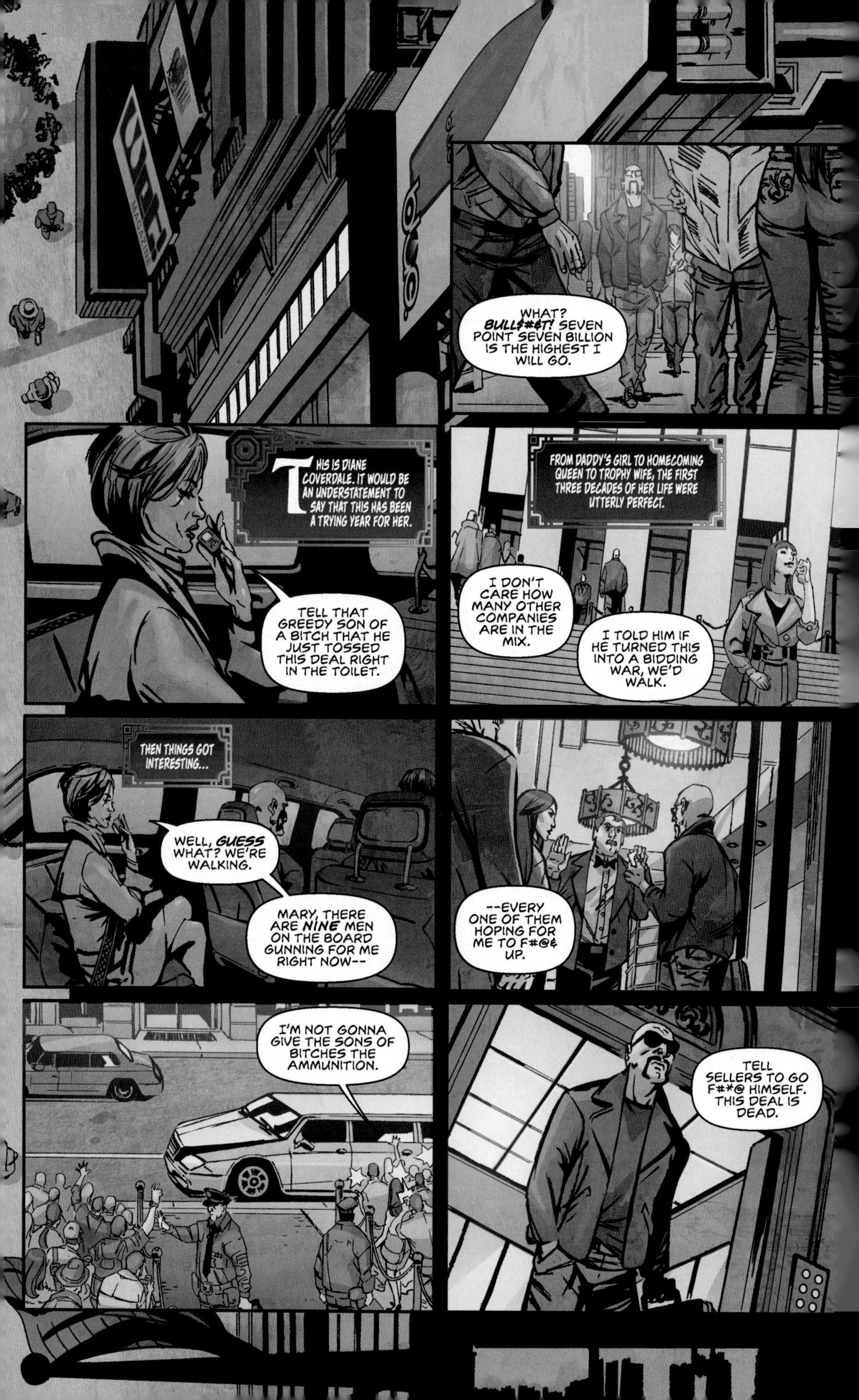
WHAT? BULL$#$T! SEVEN POINT SEVEN BILLION IS THE HIGHEST I WILL GO.
THIS IS DIANE COVERDALE. IT WOULD BE AN UNDERSTATEMENT TO SAY THAT THIS HAS BEEN A TRYING YEAR FOR HER.
TELL THAT GREEDY SON OF A BITCH THAT HE JUST TOSSED THIS DEAL RIGHT IN THE TOILET.
FROM DADDY'S GIRL TO HOMECOMING QUEEN TO TROPHY WIFE, THE FIRST THREE DECADES OF HER LIFE WERE UTTERLY PERFECT.
I DON'T CARE HOW MANY OTHER COMPANIES ARE IN THE MIX.
I TOLD HIM IF HE TURNED THIS INTO A BIDDING WAR, WE'D WALK.
THEN THINGS GOT INTERESTING...
WELL, GUESS WHAT? WE'RE WALKING.
MARY, THERE ARE NINE MEN ON THE BOARD GUNNING FOR ME RIGHT NOW--
--EVERY ONE OF THEM HOPING FOR ME TO F#@¢ UP.
I'M NOT GONNA GIVE THE SONS OF BITCHES THE AMMUNITION.
TELL SELLERS TO GO F#*@ HIMSELF. THIS DEAL IS DEAD.

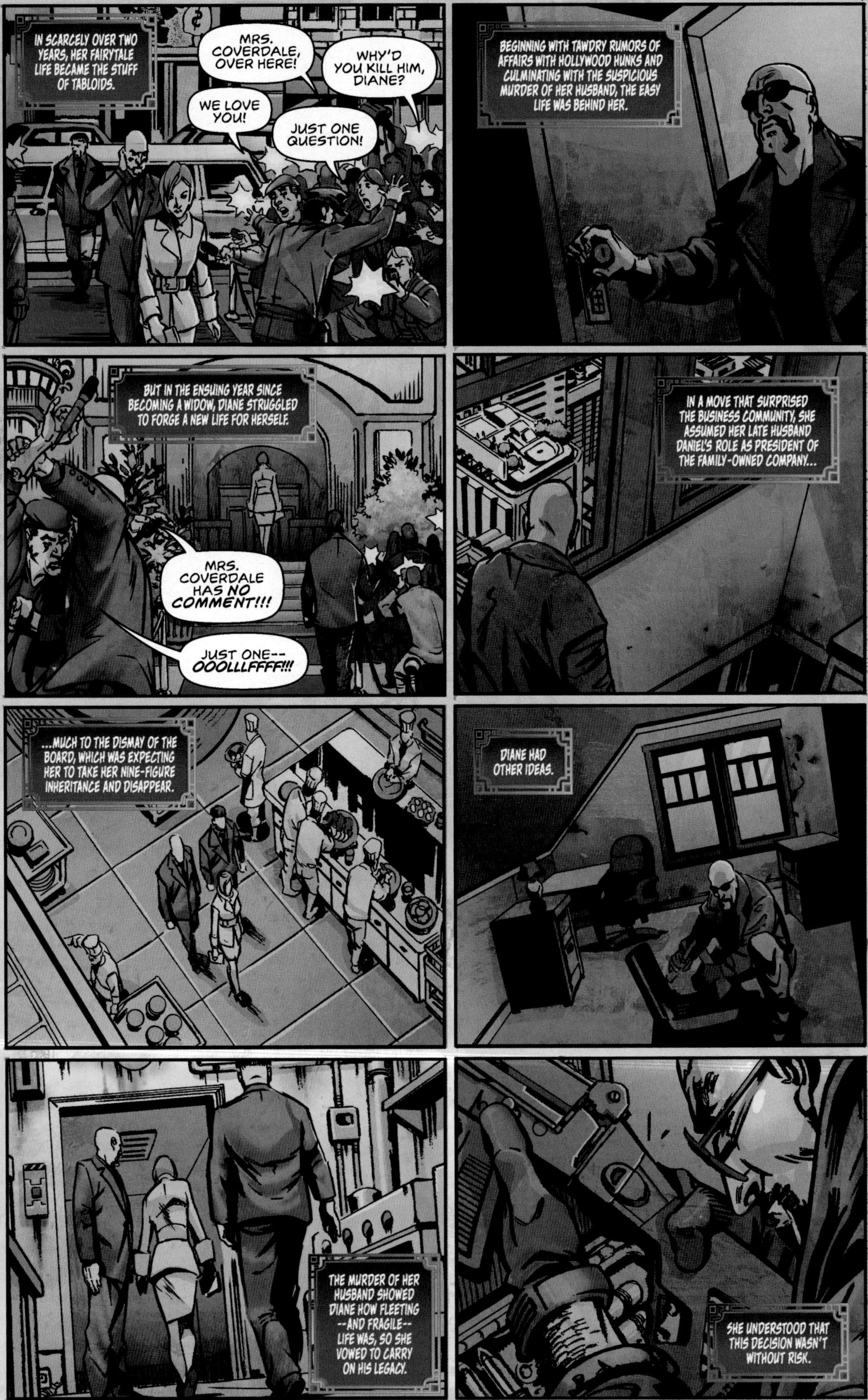
IN SCARCELY OVER TWO YEARS, HER FAIRYTALE LIFE BECAME THE STUFF OF TABLOIDS.
MRS. COVERDALE, OVER HERE!
WHY'D YOU KILL HIM, DIANE?
WE LOVE YOU!
JUST ONE QUESTION!
BEGINNING WITH TAWDRY RUMORS OF AFFAIRS WITH HOLLYWOOD HUNKS AND CULMINATING WITH THE SUSPICIOUS MURDER OF HER HUSBAND, THE EASY LIFE WAS BEHIND HER.
BUT IN THE ENSUING YEAR SINCE BECOMING A WIDOW, DIANE STRUGGLED TO FORGE A NEW LIFE FOR HERSELF.
MRS. COVERDALE HAS NO COMMENT!!!
JUST ONE--OOOLLLFFFF!!!
IN A MOVE THAT SURPRISED THE BUSINESS COMMUNITY, SHE ASSUMED HER LATE HUSBAND DANIEL'S ROLE AS PRESIDENT OF THE FAMILY-OWNED COMPANY...
...MUCH TO THE DISMAY OF THE BOARD, WHICH WAS EXPECTING HER TO TAKE HER NINE-FIGURE INHERITANCE AND DISAPPEAR.
DIANE HAD OTHER IDEAS.
THE MURDER OF HER HUSBAND SHOWED DIANE HOW FLEETING --AND FRAGILE-- LIFE WAS, SO SHE VOWED TO CARRY ON HIS LEGACY.
SHE UNDERSTOOD THAT THIS DECISION WASN'T WITHOUT RISK.

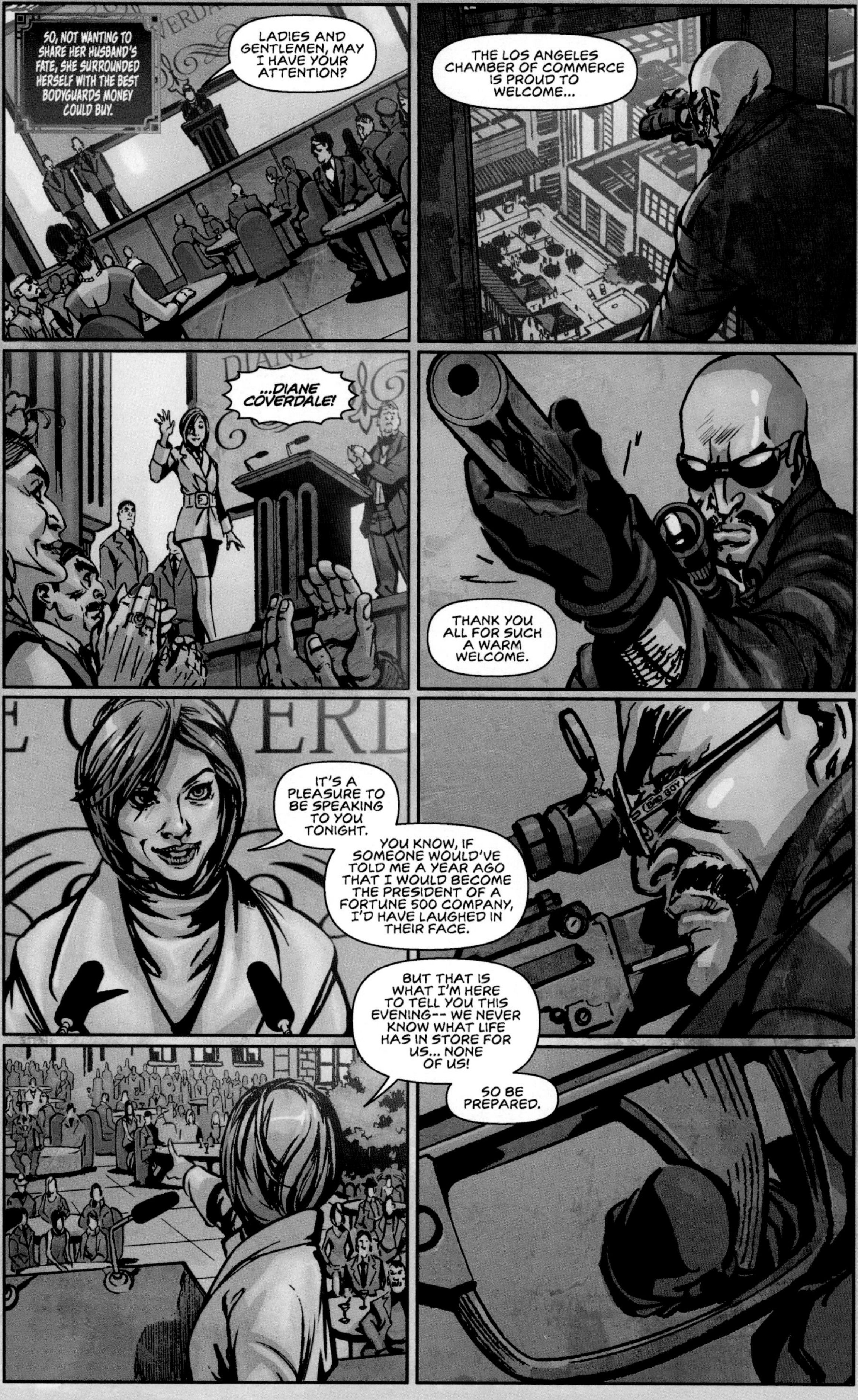
SO, NOT WANTING TO SHARE HER HUSBAND'S FATE, SHE SURROUNDED HERSELF WITH THE BEST BODYGUARDS MONEY COULD BUY.
LADIES AND GENTLEMEN, MAY I HAVE YOUR ATTENTION?
THE LOS ANGELES CHAMBER OF COMMERCE IS PROUD TO WELCOME...
...DIANE COVERDALE!
THANK YOU ALL FOR SUCH A WARM WELCOME.
IT'S A PLEASURE TO BE SPEAKING TO YOU TONIGHT.
YOU KNOW, IF SOMEONE WOULD'VE TOLD ME A YEAR AGO THAT I WOULD BECOME THE PRESIDENT OF A FORTUNE 500 COMPANY, I'D HAVE LAUGHED IN THEIR FACE.
BUT THAT IS WHAT I'M HERE TO TELL YOU THIS EVENING-- WE NEVER KNOW WHAT LIFE HAS IN STORE FOR US... NONE OF US!
SO BE PREPARED.

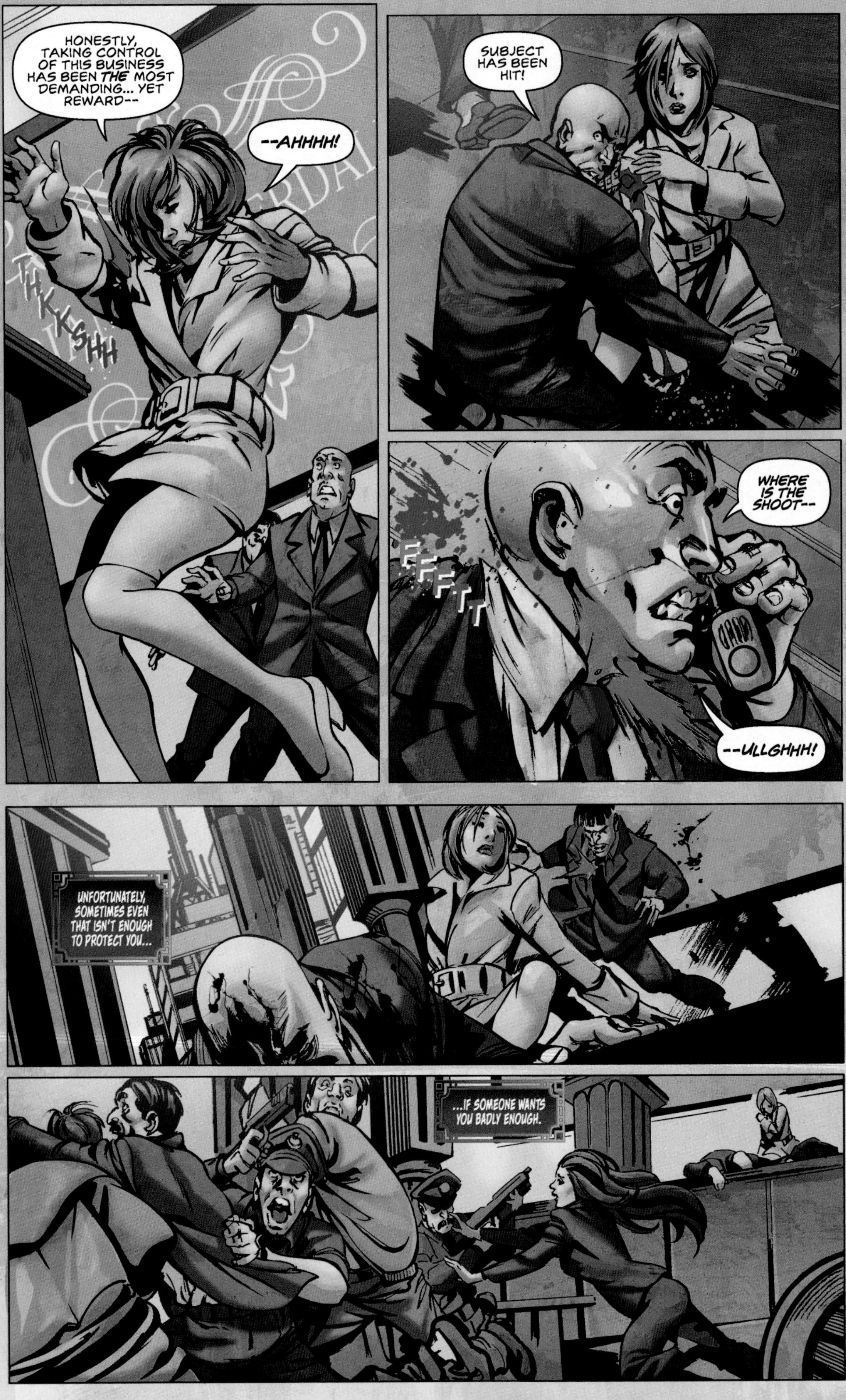
HONESTLY, TAKING CONTROL OF THIS BUSINESS HAS BEEN THE MOST DEMANDING... YET REWARD--
--AHHHH!
THKKSHH
SUBJECT HAS BEEN HIT!
WHERE IS THE SHOOT--
FFFTTT
--ULLGHHH!
UNFORTUNATELY, SOMETIMES EVEN THAT ISN'T ENOUGH TO PROTECT YOU...
...IF SOMEONE WANTS YOU BADLY ENOUGH.

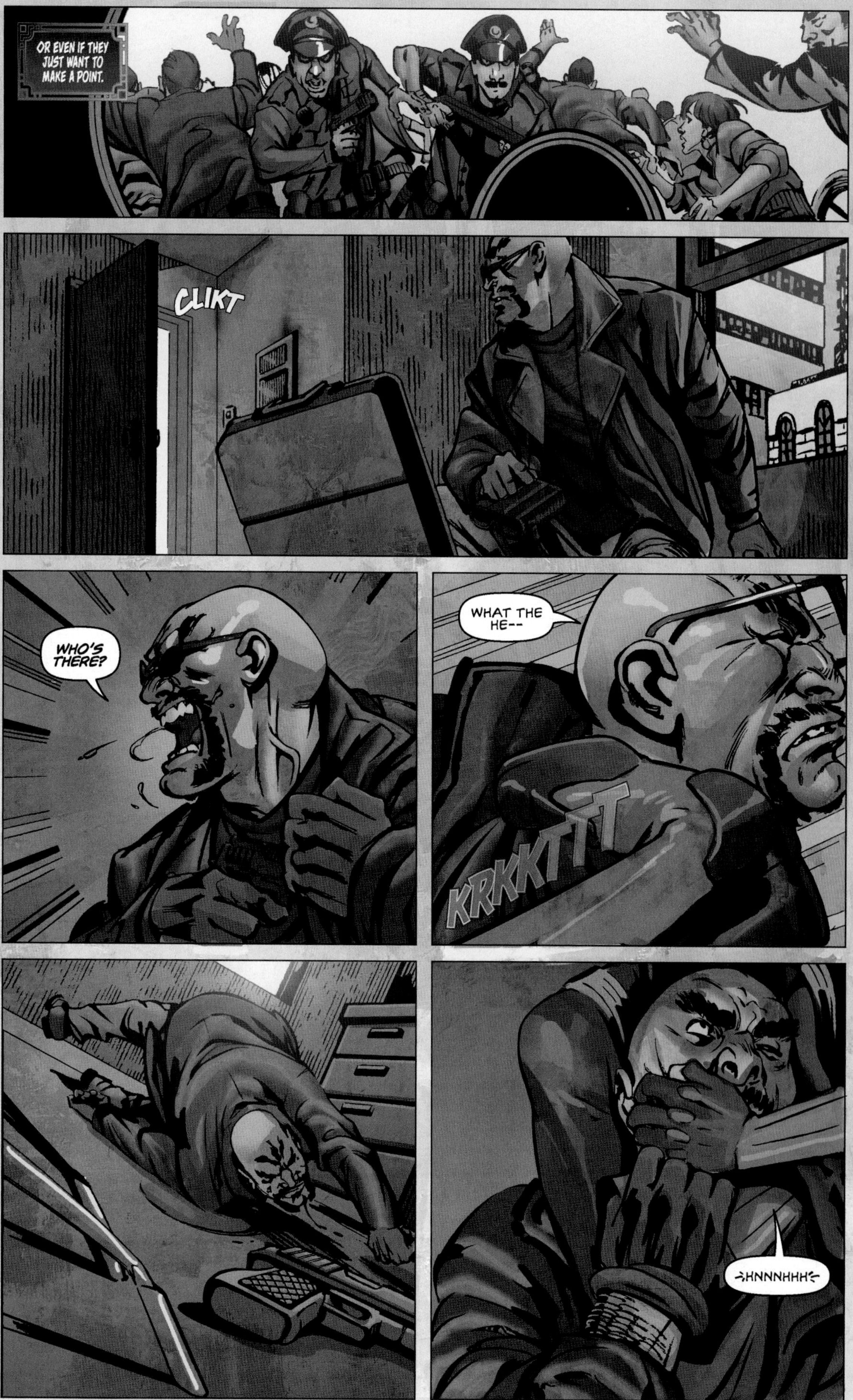
OR EVEN IF THEY JUST WANT TO MAKE A POINT.
CLIKT
WHO'S THERE?
WHAT THE HE--
KRKKTTT
-HNNNHHH-

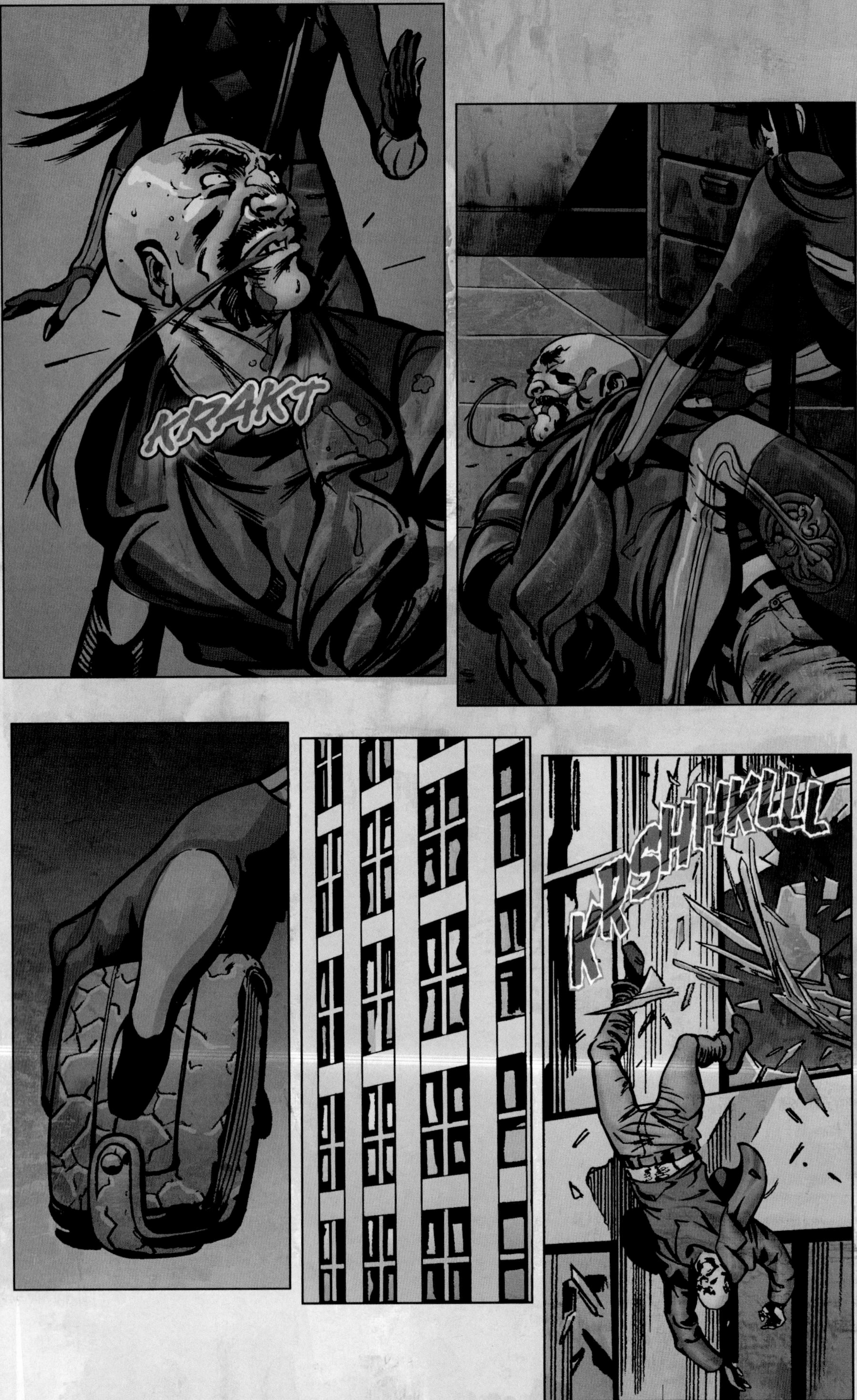
KRAKT
KRSHHKLLL

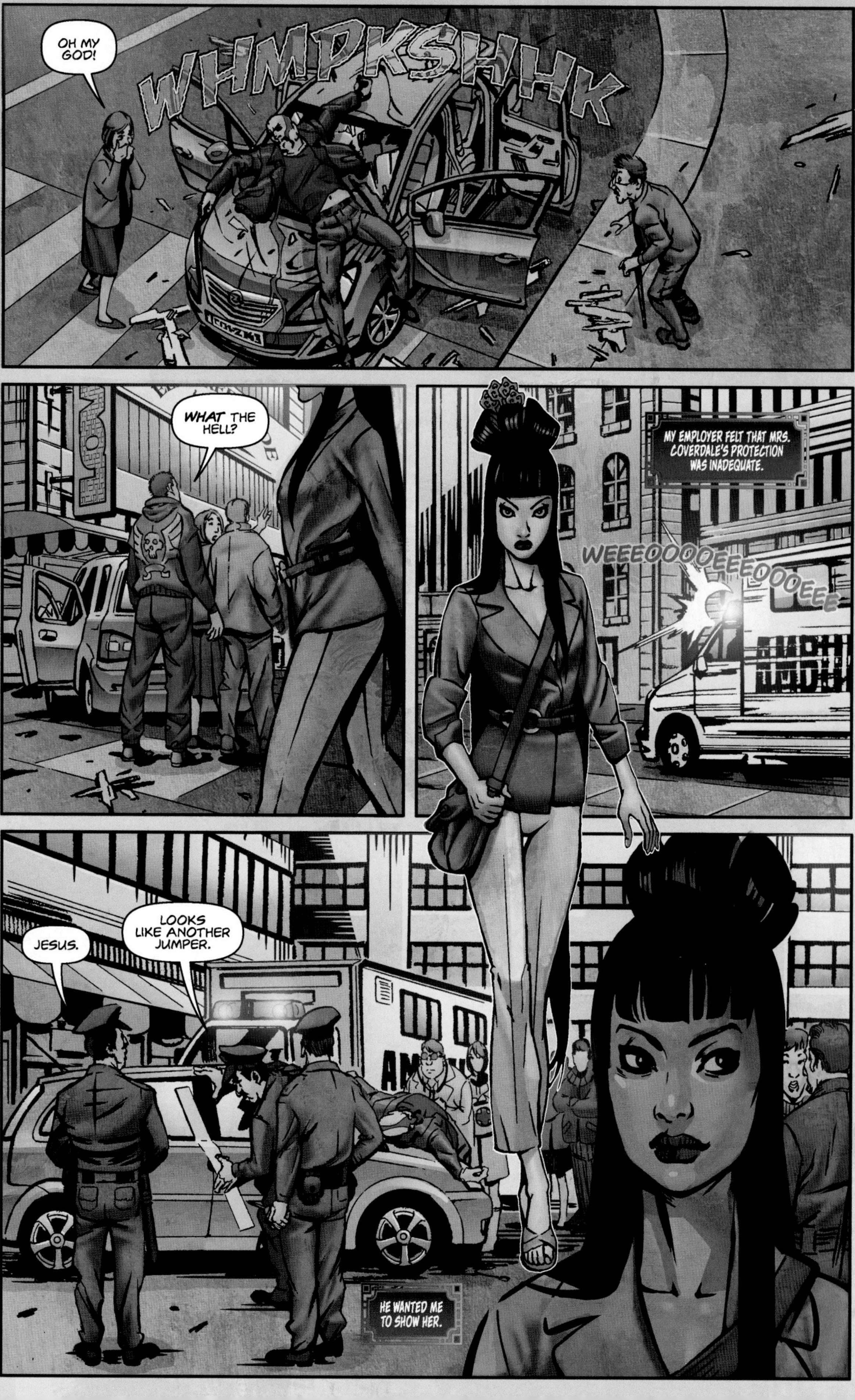
OH MY GOD!
WHMPKSHHK
WHAT THE HELL?
MY EMPLOYER FELT THAT MRS. COVERDALE'S PROTECTION WAS INADEQUATE.
WEEEOOOOEEEOOOEEE
JESUS.
LOOKS LIKE ANOTHER JUMPER.
HE WANTED ME TO SHOW HER.

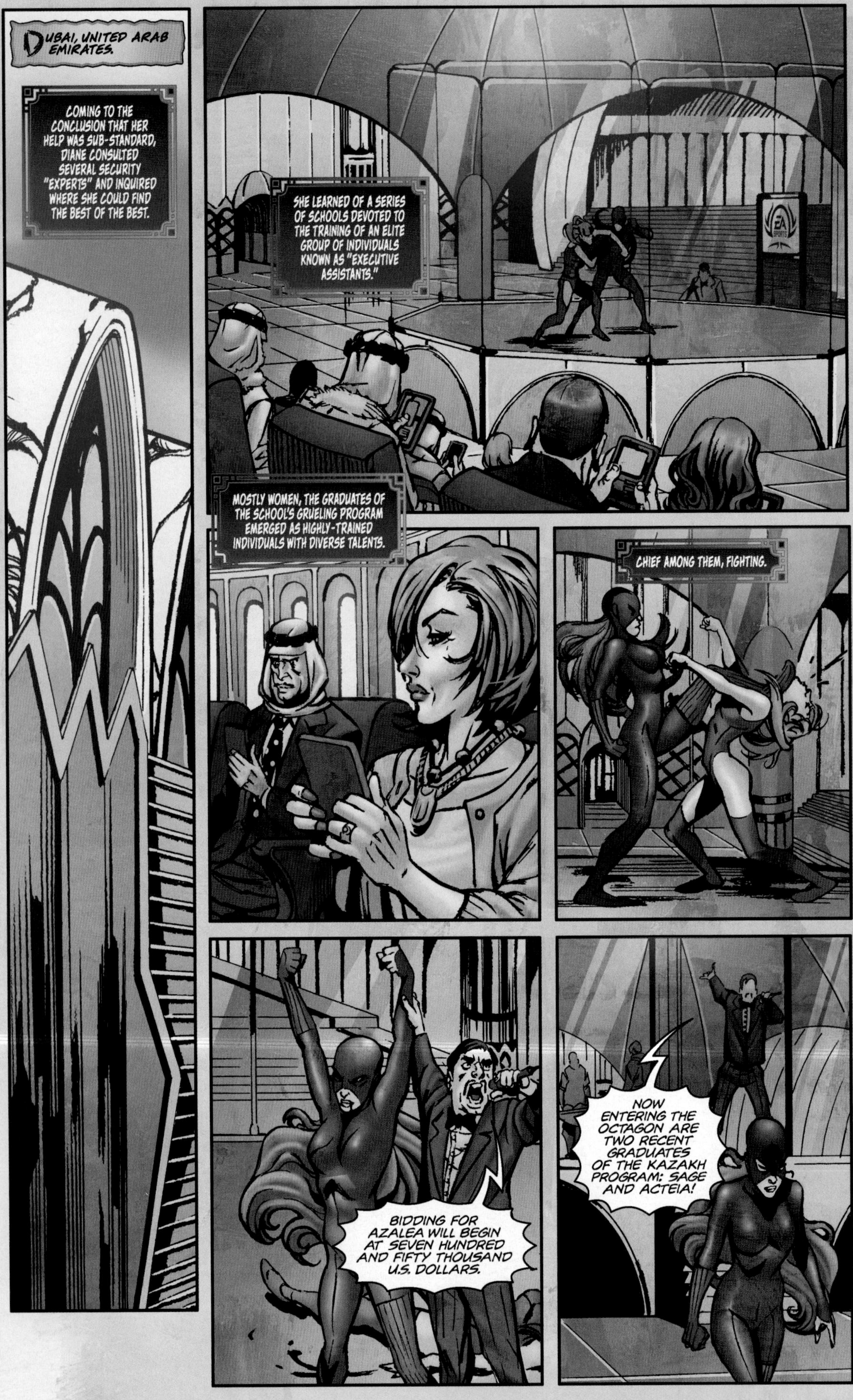
DUBAI, UNITED ARAB EMIRATES.
COMING TO THE CONCLUSION THAT HER HELP WAS SUB-STANDARD, DIANE CONSULTED SEVERAL SECURITY "EXPERTS" AND INQUIRED WHERE SHE COULD FIND THE BEST OF THE BEST.
SHE LEARNED OF A SERIES OF SCHOOLS DEVOTED TO THE TRAINING OF AN ELITE GROUP OF INDIVIDUALS KNOWN AS "EXECUTIVE ASSISTANTS."
MOSTLY WOMEN, THE GRADUATES OF THE SCHOOL'S GRUELING PROGRAM EMERGED AS HIGHLY-TRAINED INDIVIDUALS WITH DIVERSE TALENTS.
CHIEF AMONG THEM, FIGHTING.
BIDDING FOR AZALEA WILL BEGIN AT SEVEN HUNDRED AND FIFTY THOUSAND U.S. DOLLARS.
NOW ENTERING THE OCTAGON ARE TWO RECENT GRADUATES OF THE KAZAKH PROGRAM: SAGE AND ACTEIA!

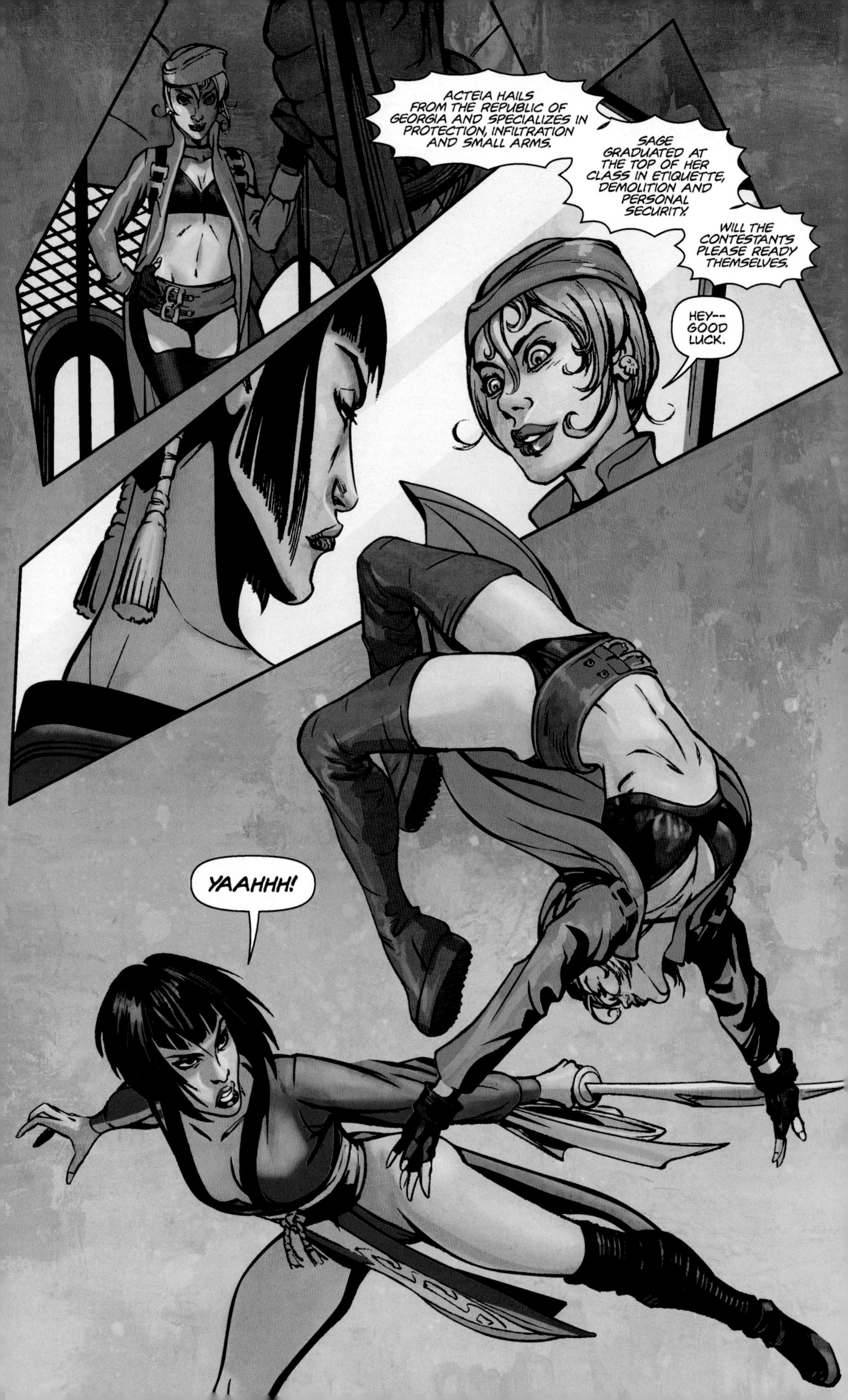
ACTEIA HAILS FROM THE REPUBLIC OF GEORGIA AND SPECIALIZES IN PROTECTION, INFILTRATION AND SMALL ARMS.
SAGE GRADUATED AT THE TOP OF HER CLASS IN ETIQUETTE, DEMOLITION AND PERSONAL SECURITY.
WILL THE CONTESTANTS PLEASE READY THEMSELVES.
HEY--GOOD LUCK.
YAAHHH!

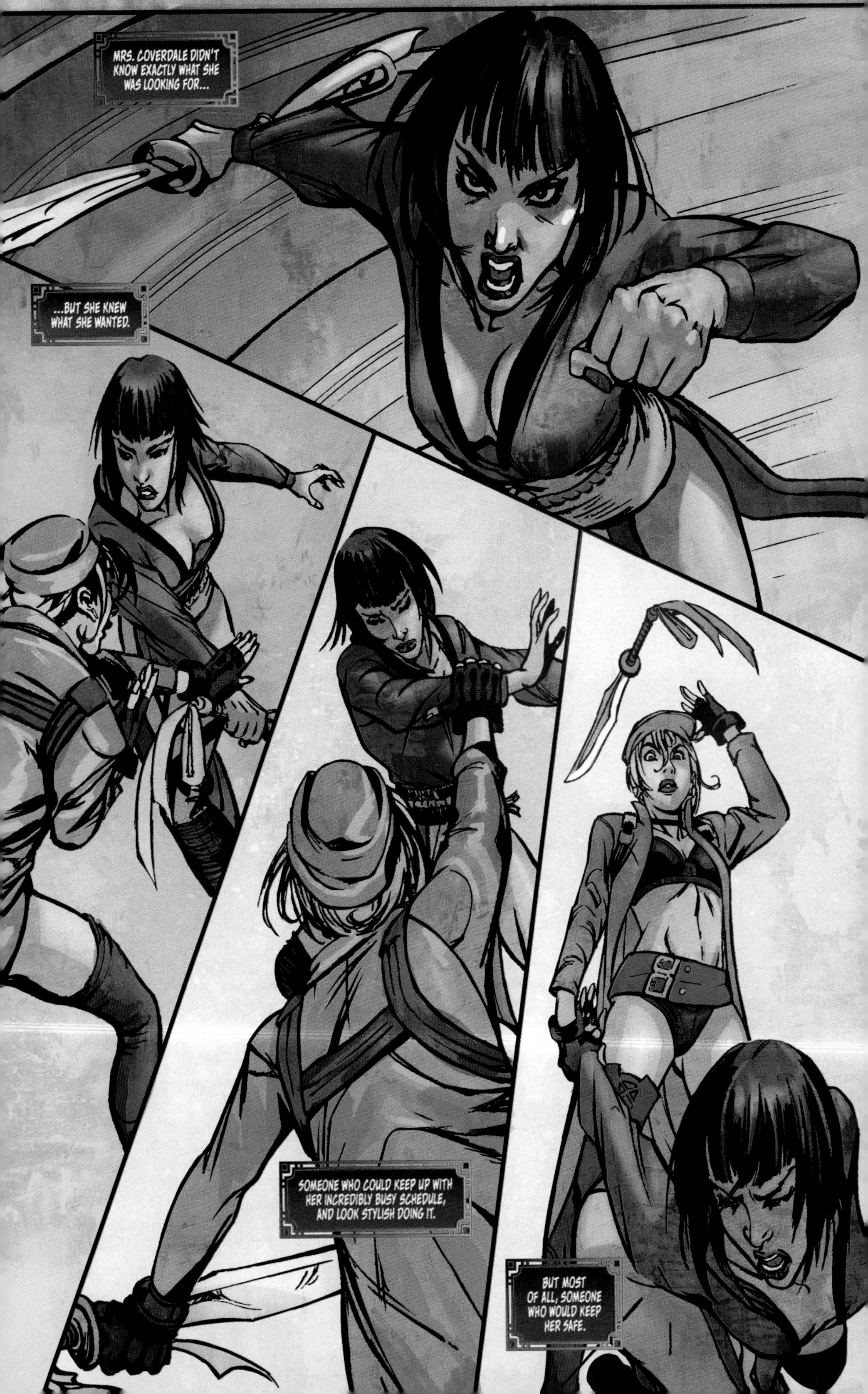
MRS. COVERDALE DIDN'T KNOW EXACTLY WHAT SHE WAS LOOKING FOR...
...BUT SHE KNEW WHAT SHE WANTED.
SOMEONE WHO COULD KEEP UP WITH HER INCREDIBLY BUSY SCHEDULE, AND LOOK STYLISH DOING IT.
BUT MOST OF ALL, SOMEONE WHO WOULD KEEP HER SAFE.

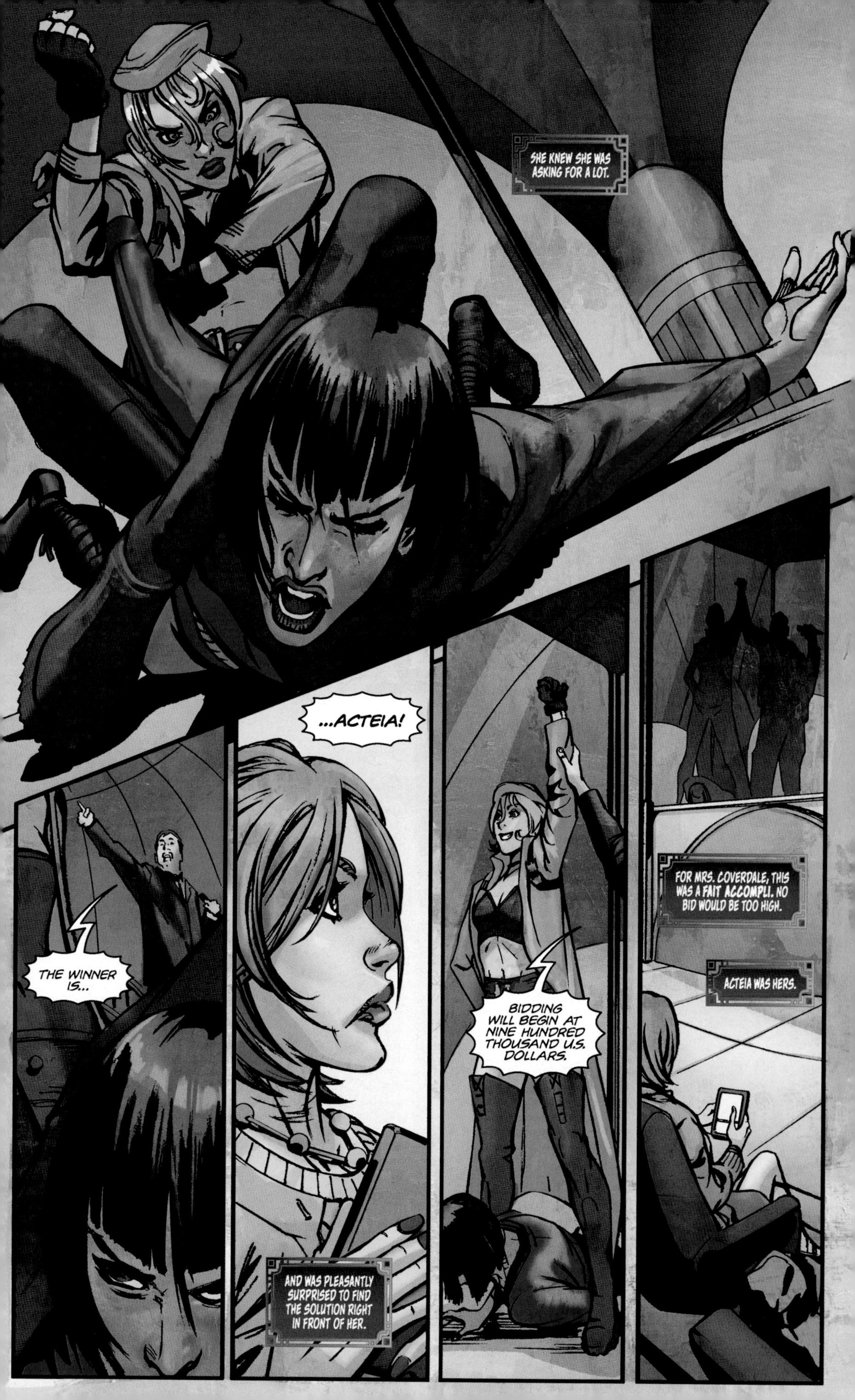
SHE KNEW SHE WAS ASKING FOR A LOT.
THE WINNER IS...
...ACTEIA!
AND WAS PLEASANTLY SURPRISED TO FIND THE SOLUTION RIGHT IN FRONT OF HER.
BIDDING WILL BEGIN AT NINE HUNDRED THOUSAND U.S. DOLLARS.
FOR MRS. COVERDALE, THIS WAS A FAIT ACCOMPLI. NO BID WOULD BE TOO HIGH.
ACTEIA WAS HERS.

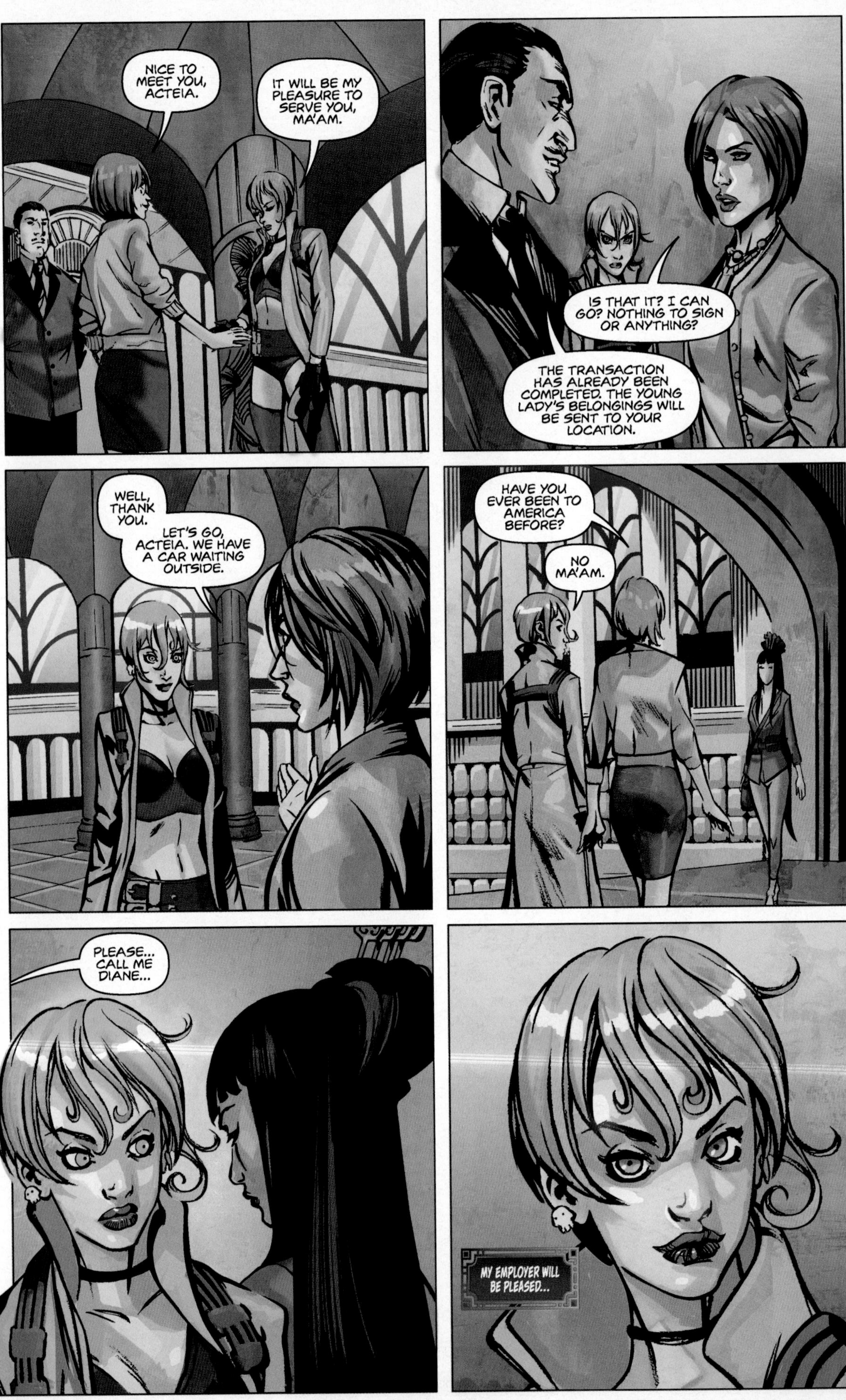
NICE TO MEET YOU, ACTEIA.
IT WILL BE MY PLEASURE TO SERVE YOU, MA'AM.
IS THAT IT? I CAN GO? NOTHING TO SIGN OR ANYTHING?
THE TRANSACTION HAS ALREADY BEEN COMPLETED. THE YOUNG LADY'S BELONGINGS WILL BE SENT TO YOUR LOCATION.
WELL, THANK YOU.
LET'S GO, ACTEIA. WE HAVE A CAR WAITING OUTSIDE.
HAVE YOU EVER BEEN TO AMERICA BEFORE?
NO MA'AM.
PLEASE... CALL ME DIANE...
MY EMPLOYER WILL BE PLEASED...

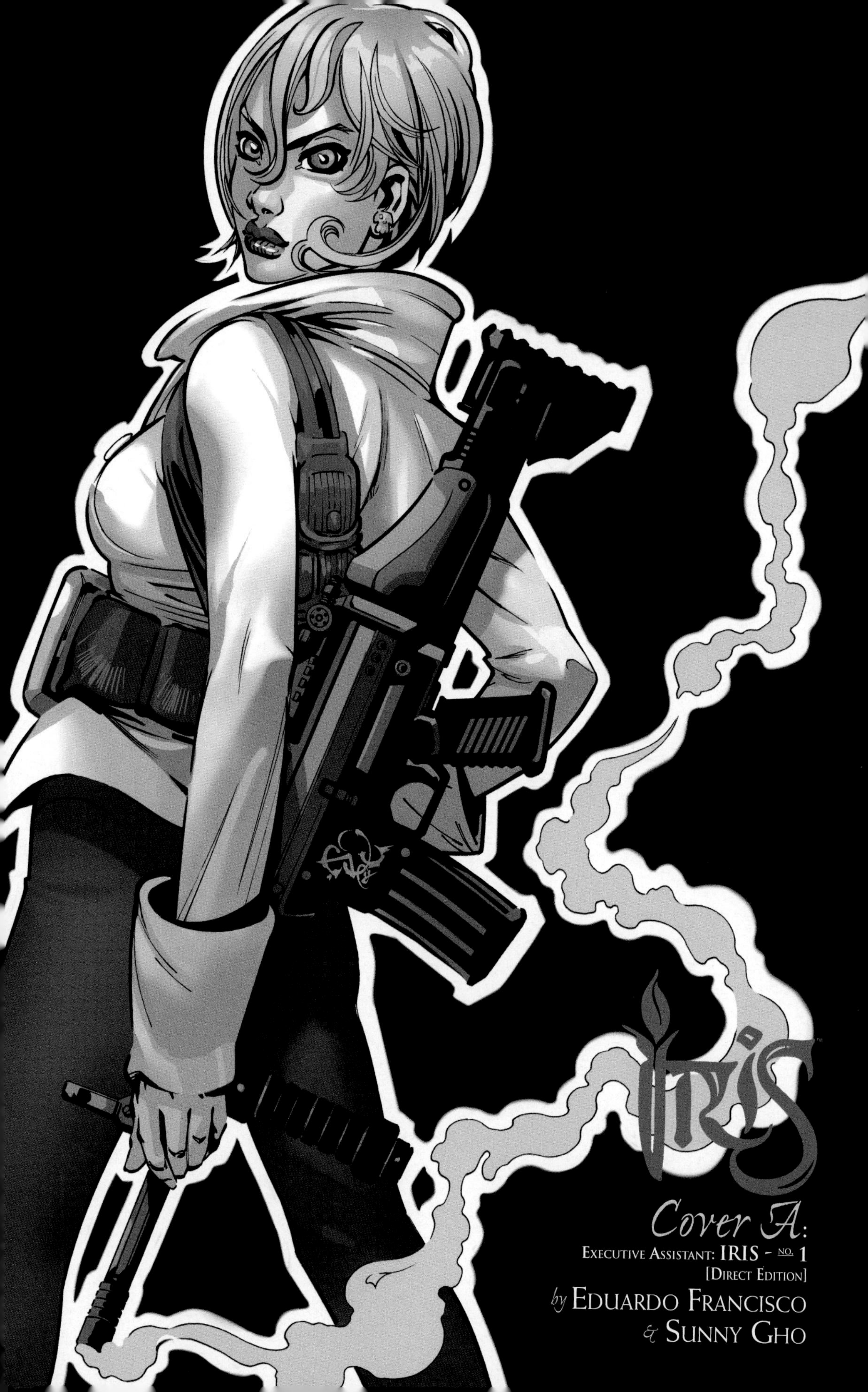
IRIS™

Cover A:
Executive Assistant: IRIS - No. 1
[Direct Edition]
by Eduardo Francisco
& Sunny Gho

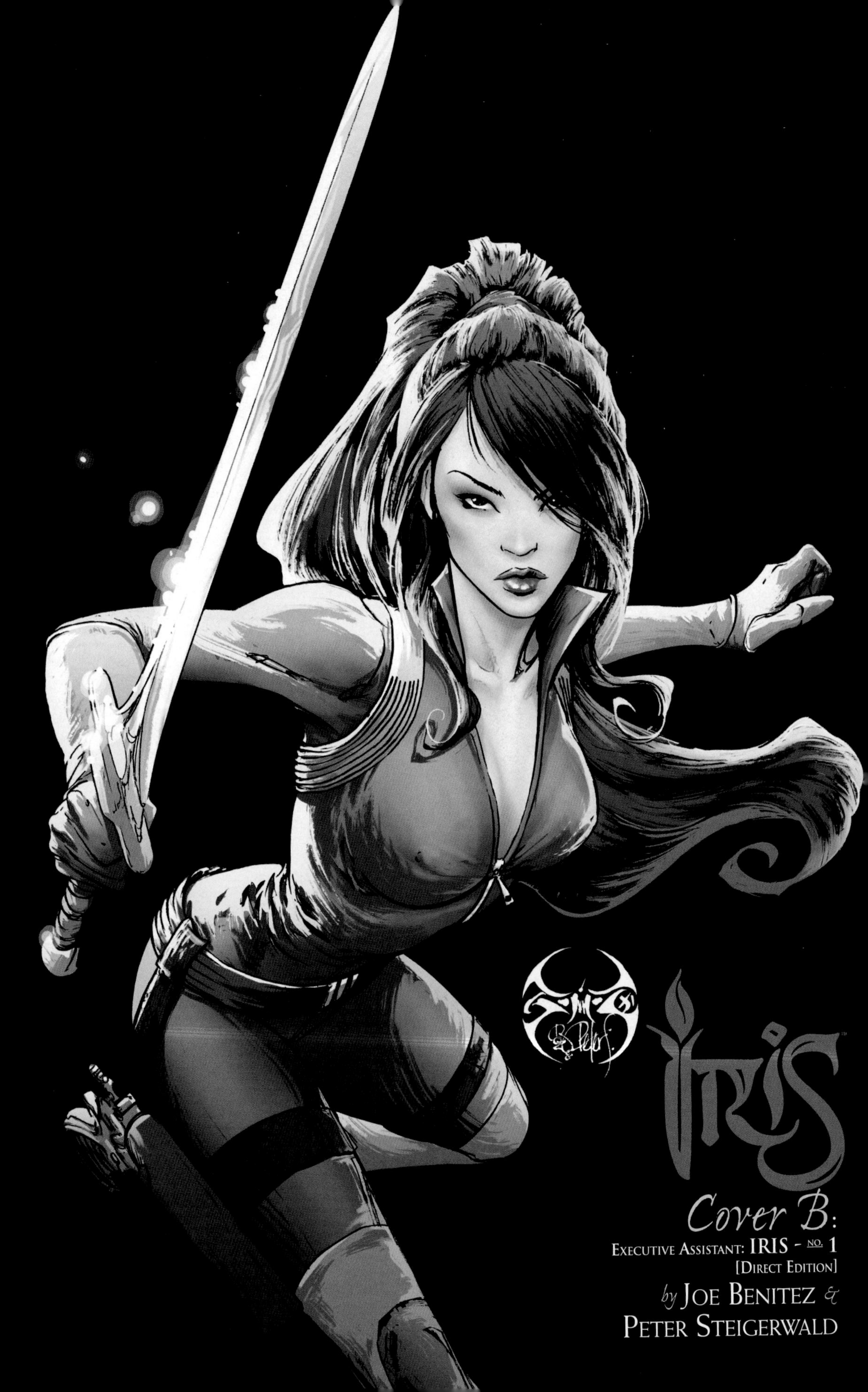
Iris

Cover B:

Executive Assistant: IRIS - No. 1

[Direct Edition]

by Joe Benitez &

Peter Steigerwald

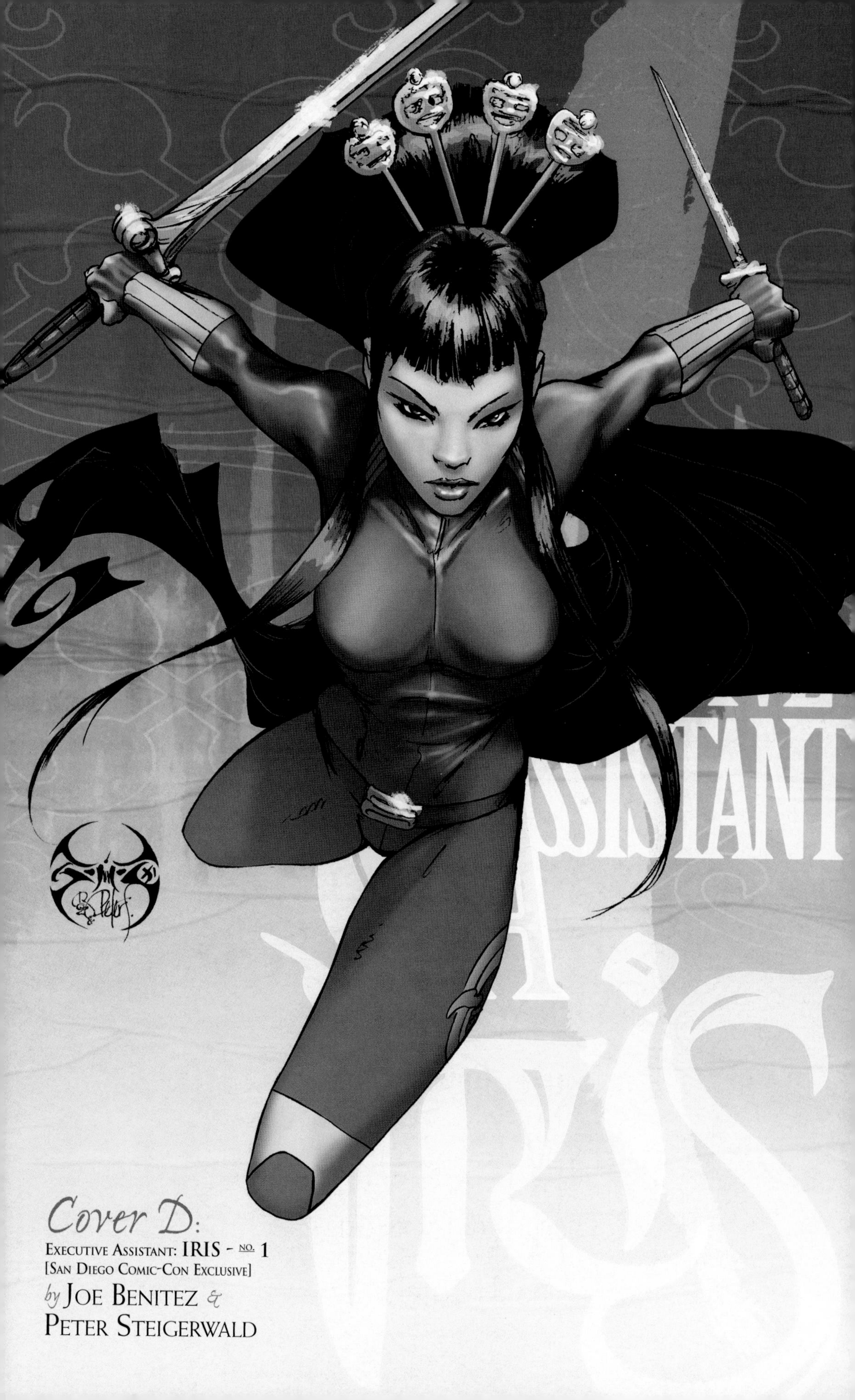

Cover D:
EXECUTIVE ASSISTANT: IRIS - No. 1
[SAN DIEGO COMIC-CON EXCLUSIVE]
by JOE BENITEZ & PETER STEIGERWALD

CHAPTER TWO

ONE

"NO SURRENDER"

WRITER
DAVID WOHL

PENCILS
EDUARDO FRANCISCO

INKS
ALEX LEI

COLORS
TEODORO GONZALEZ

LETTERING
JOSH REED

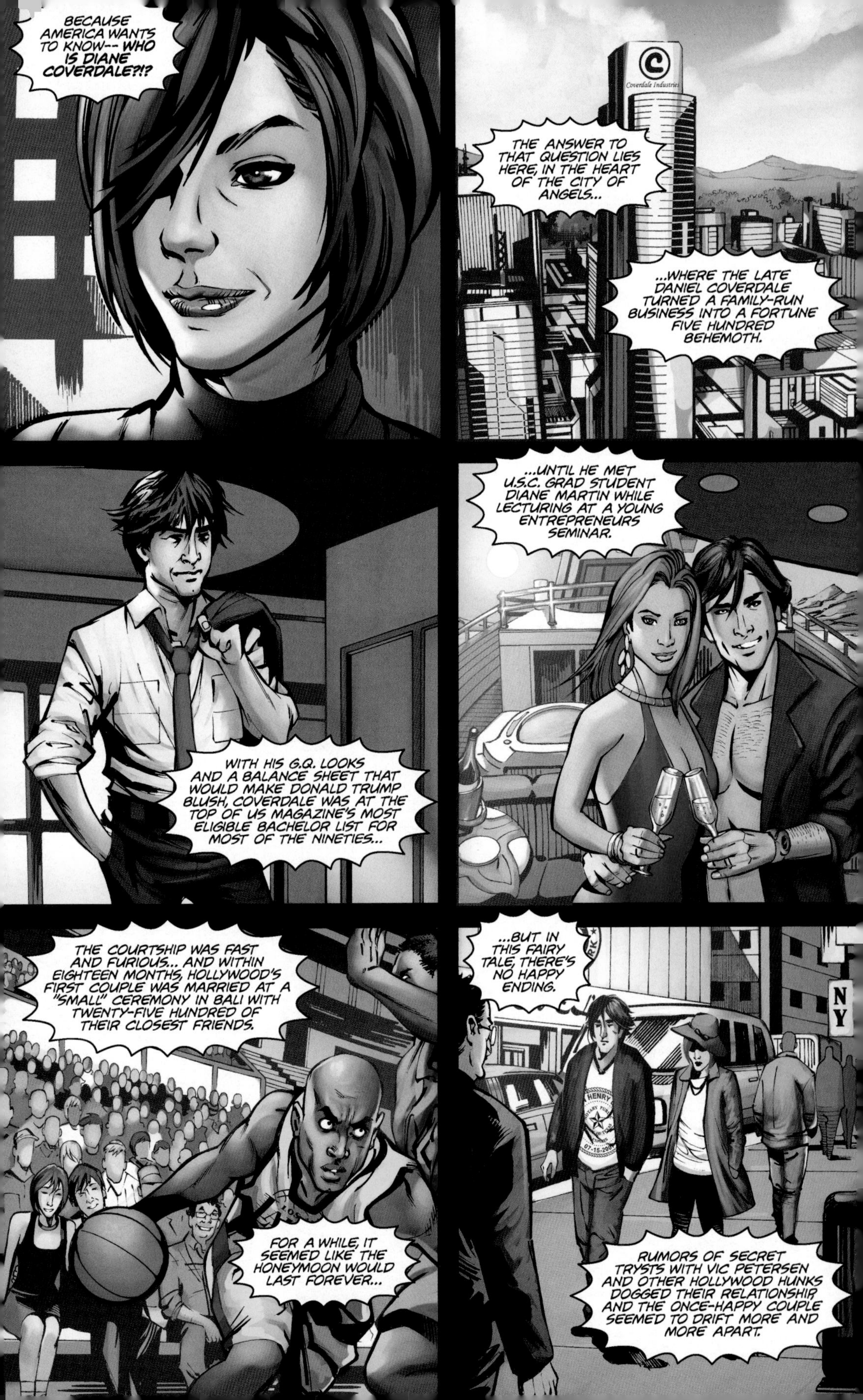
BECAUSE AMERICA WANTS TO KNOW-- WHO IS DIANE COVERDALE?!?
Coverdale Industries
THE ANSWER TO THAT QUESTION LIES HERE, IN THE HEART OF THE CITY OF ANGELS...
...WHERE THE LATE DANIEL COVERDALE TURNED A FAMILY-RUN BUSINESS INTO A FORTUNE FIVE HUNDRED BEHEMOTH.
WITH HIS G.Q. LOOKS AND A BALANCE SHEET THAT WOULD MAKE DONALD TRUMP BLUSH, COVERDALE WAS AT THE TOP OF US MAGAZINE'S MOST ELIGIBLE BACHELOR LIST FOR MOST OF THE NINETIES...
...UNTIL HE MET U.S.C. GRAD STUDENT DIANE MARTIN WHILE LECTURING AT A YOUNG ENTREPRENEURS SEMINAR.
THE COURTSHIP WAS FAST AND FURIOUS... AND WITHIN EIGHTEEN MONTHS, HOLLYWOOD'S FIRST COUPLE WAS MARRIED AT A "SMALL" CEREMONY IN BALI WITH TWENTY-FIVE HUNDRED OF THEIR CLOSEST FRIENDS.
FOR A WHILE, IT SEEMED LIKE THE HONEYMOON WOULD LAST FOREVER...
...BUT IN THIS FAIRY TALE, THERE'S NO HAPPY ENDING.
NY
HENRY
RUMORS OF SECRET TRYSTS WITH VIC PETERSEN AND OTHER HOLLYWOOD HUNKS DOGGED THEIR RELATIONSHIP AND THE ONCE-HAPPY COUPLE SEEMED TO DRIFT MORE AND MORE APART.

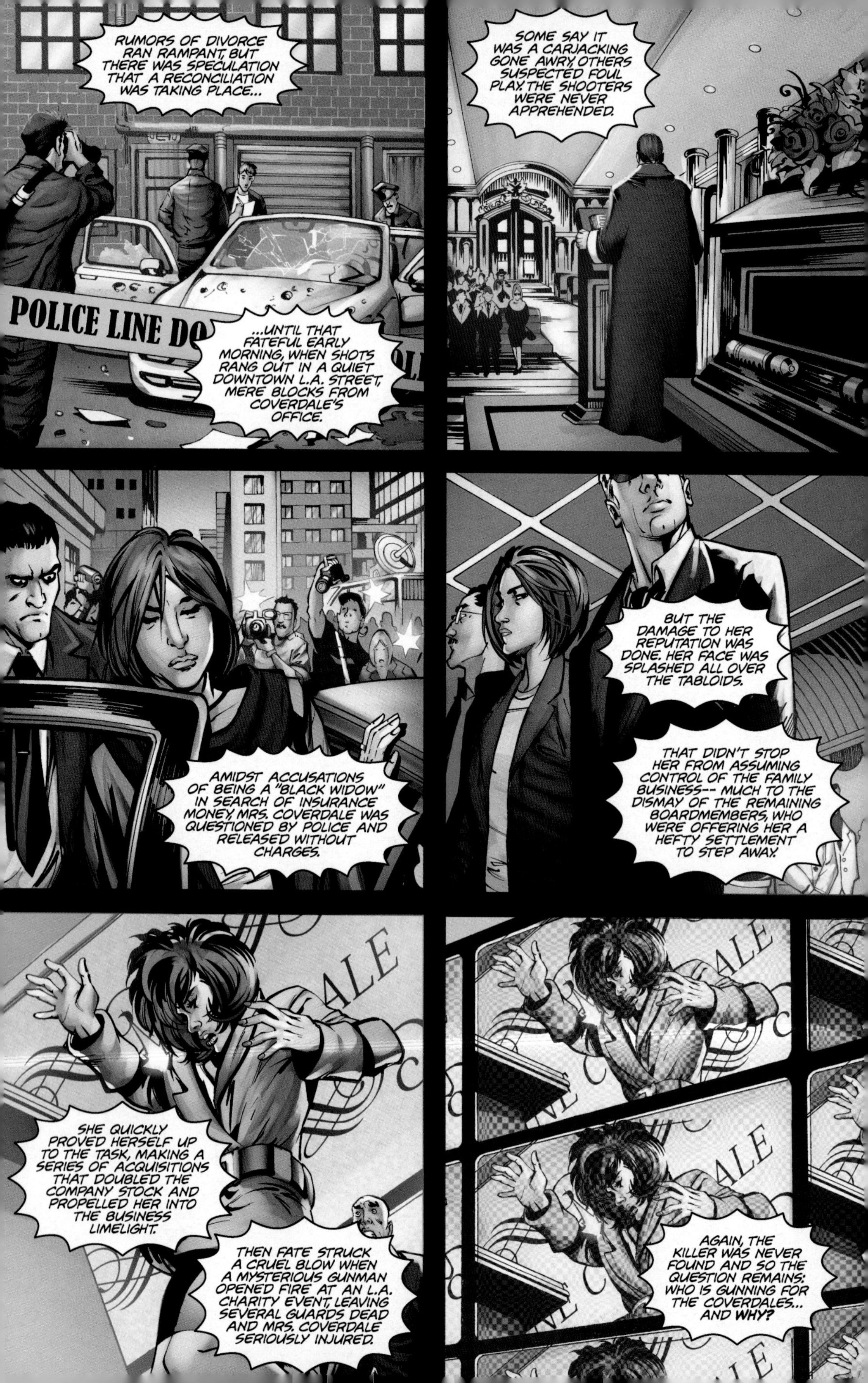
RUMORS OF DIVORCE RAN RAMPANT, BUT THERE WAS SPECULATION THAT A RECONCILIATION WAS TAKING PLACE...
POLICE LINE DO
...UNTIL THAT FATEFUL EARLY MORNING, WHEN SHOTS RANG OUT IN A QUIET DOWNTOWN L.A. STREET, MERE BLOCKS FROM COVERDALE'S OFFICE.
SOME SAY IT WAS A CARJACKING GONE AWRY, OTHERS SUSPECTED FOUL PLAY. THE SHOOTERS WERE NEVER APPREHENDED.
AMIDST ACCUSATIONS OF BEING A "BLACK WIDOW" IN SEARCH OF INSURANCE MONEY, MRS. COVERDALE WAS QUESTIONED BY POLICE AND RELEASED WITHOUT CHARGES.
BUT THE DAMAGE TO HER REPUTATION WAS DONE. HER FACE WAS SPLASHED ALL OVER THE TABLOIDS.
THAT DIDN'T STOP HER FROM ASSUMING CONTROL OF THE FAMILY BUSINESS-- MUCH TO THE DISMAY OF THE REMAINING BOARDMEMBERS, WHO WERE OFFERING HER A HEFTY SETTLEMENT TO STEP AWAY.
SHE QUICKLY PROVED HERSELF UP TO THE TASK, MAKING A SERIES OF ACQUISITIONS THAT DOUBLED THE COMPANY STOCK AND PROPELLED HER INTO THE BUSINESS LIMELIGHT.
THEN FATE STRUCK A CRUEL BLOW WHEN A MYSTERIOUS GUNMAN OPENED FIRE AT AN L.A. CHARITY EVENT, LEAVING SEVERAL GUARDS DEAD AND MRS. COVERDALE SERIOUSLY INJURED.
AGAIN, THE KILLER WAS NEVER FOUND AND SO THE QUESTION REMAINS: WHO IS GUNNING FOR THE COVERDALES... AND WHY?

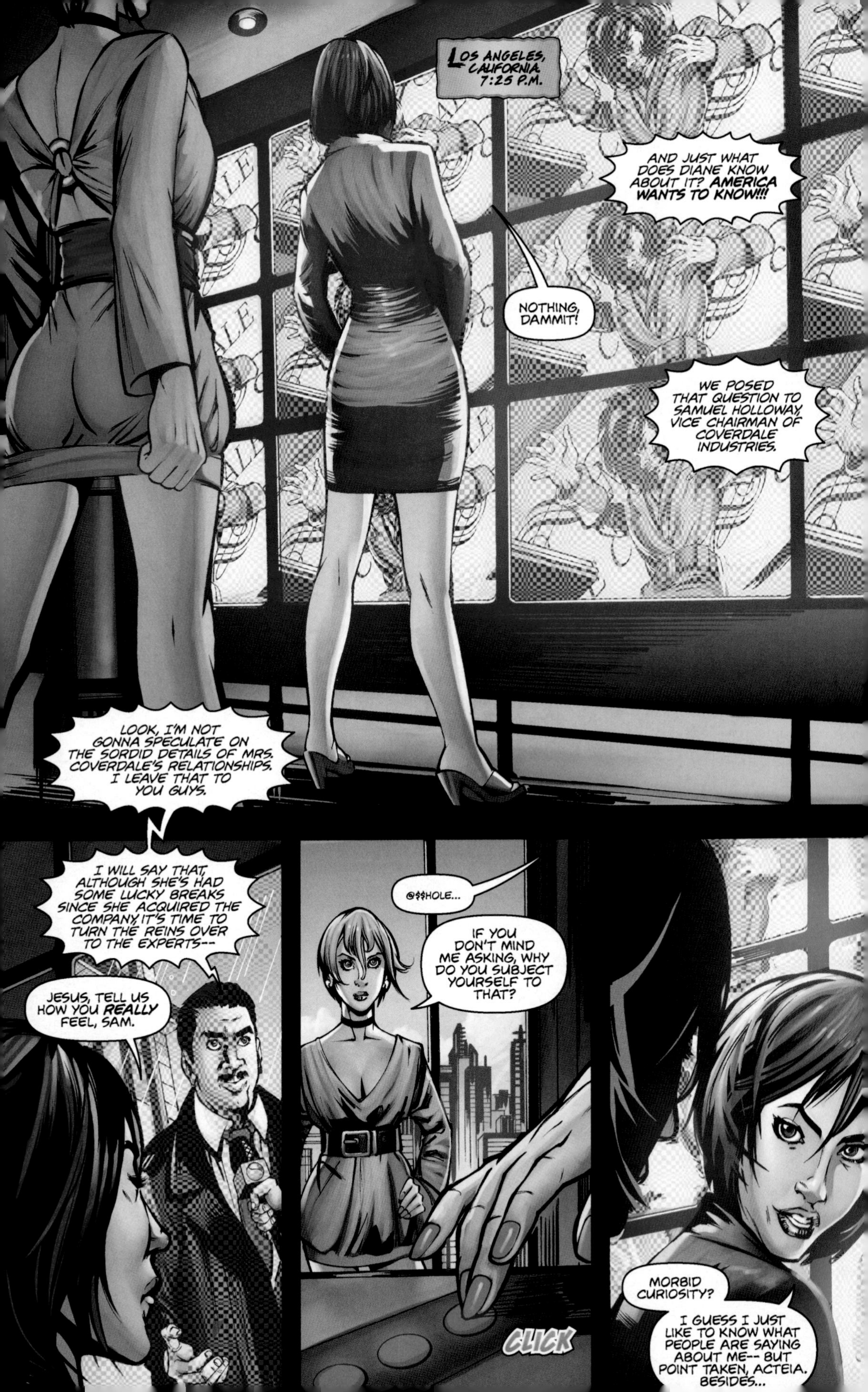
LOS ANGELES, CALIFORNIA 7:25 P.M.
AND JUST WHAT DOES DIANE KNOW ABOUT IT? AMERICA WANTS TO KNOW!!!
NOTHING, DAMMIT!
WE POSED THAT QUESTION TO SAMUEL HOLLOWAY, VICE CHAIRMAN OF COVERDALE INDUSTRIES.
LOOK, I'M NOT GONNA SPECULATE ON THE SORDID DETAILS OF MRS. COVERDALE'S RELATIONSHIPS. I LEAVE THAT TO YOU GUYS.
I WILL SAY THAT, ALTHOUGH SHE'S HAD SOME LUCKY BREAKS SINCE SHE ACQUIRED THE COMPANY, IT'S TIME TO TURN THE REINS OVER TO THE EXPERTS--
JESUS, TELL US HOW YOU REALLY FEEL, SAM.
@$$HOLE...
IF YOU DON'T MIND ME ASKING, WHY DO YOU SUBJECT YOURSELF TO THAT?
CLICK
MORBID CURIOSITY?
I GUESS I JUST LIKE TO KNOW WHAT PEOPLE ARE SAYING ABOUT ME-- BUT POINT TAKEN, ACTEIA. BESIDES...

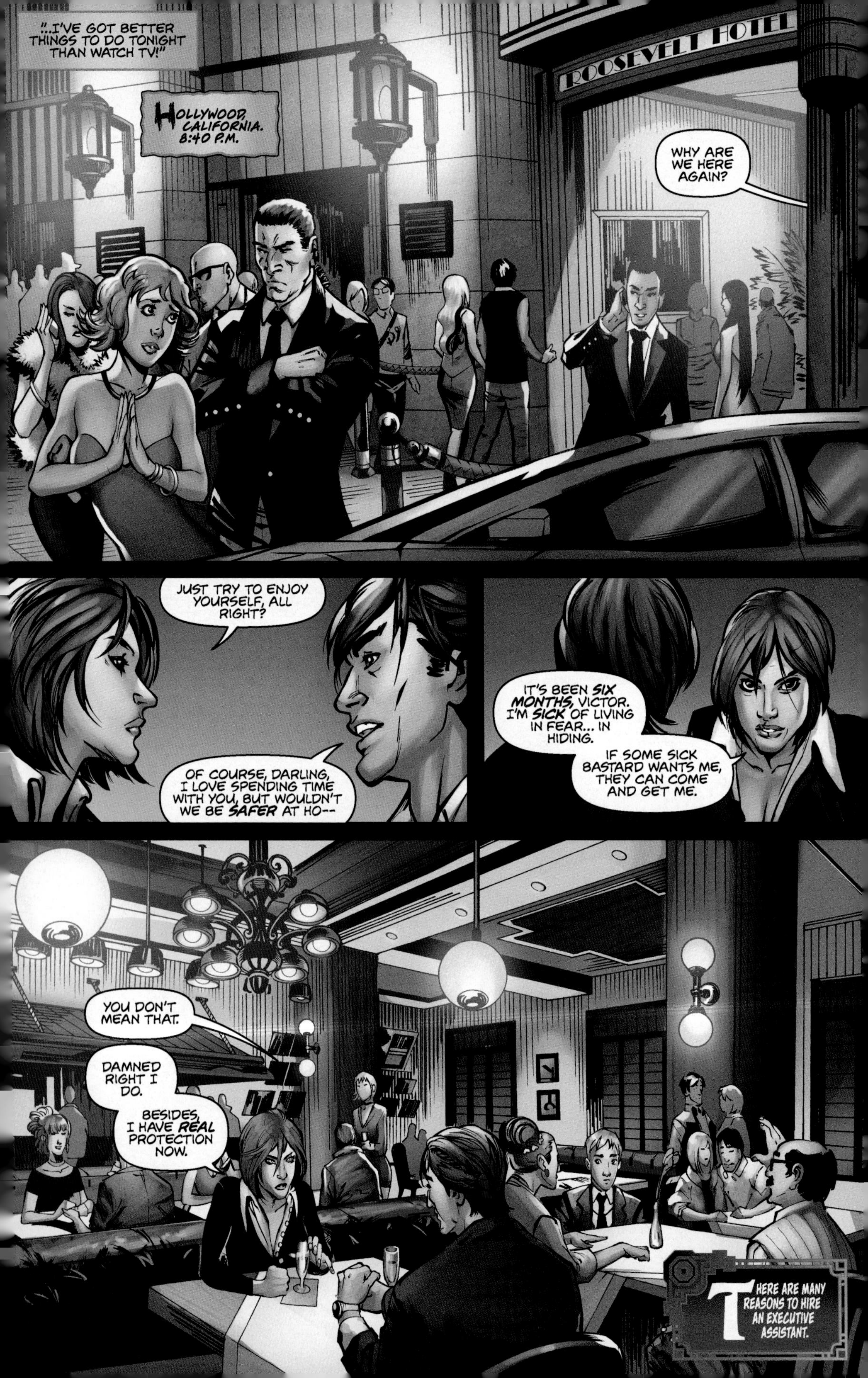
"...I'VE GOT BETTER THINGS TO DO TONIGHT THAN WATCH TV!"
HOLLYWOOD, CALIFORNIA. 8:40 P.M.
ROOSEVELT HOTEL
WHY ARE WE HERE AGAIN?
JUST TRY TO ENJOY YOURSELF, ALL RIGHT?
OF COURSE, DARLING, I LOVE SPENDING TIME WITH YOU, BUT WOULDN'T WE BE SAFER AT HO--
IT'S BEEN SIX MONTHS, VICTOR. I'M SICK OF LIVING IN FEAR... IN HIDING.
IF SOME SICK BASTARD WANTS ME, THEY CAN COME AND GET ME.
YOU DON'T MEAN THAT.
DAMNED RIGHT I DO.
BESIDES, I HAVE REAL PROTECTION NOW.
THERE ARE MANY REASONS TO HIRE AN EXECUTIVE ASSISTANT.

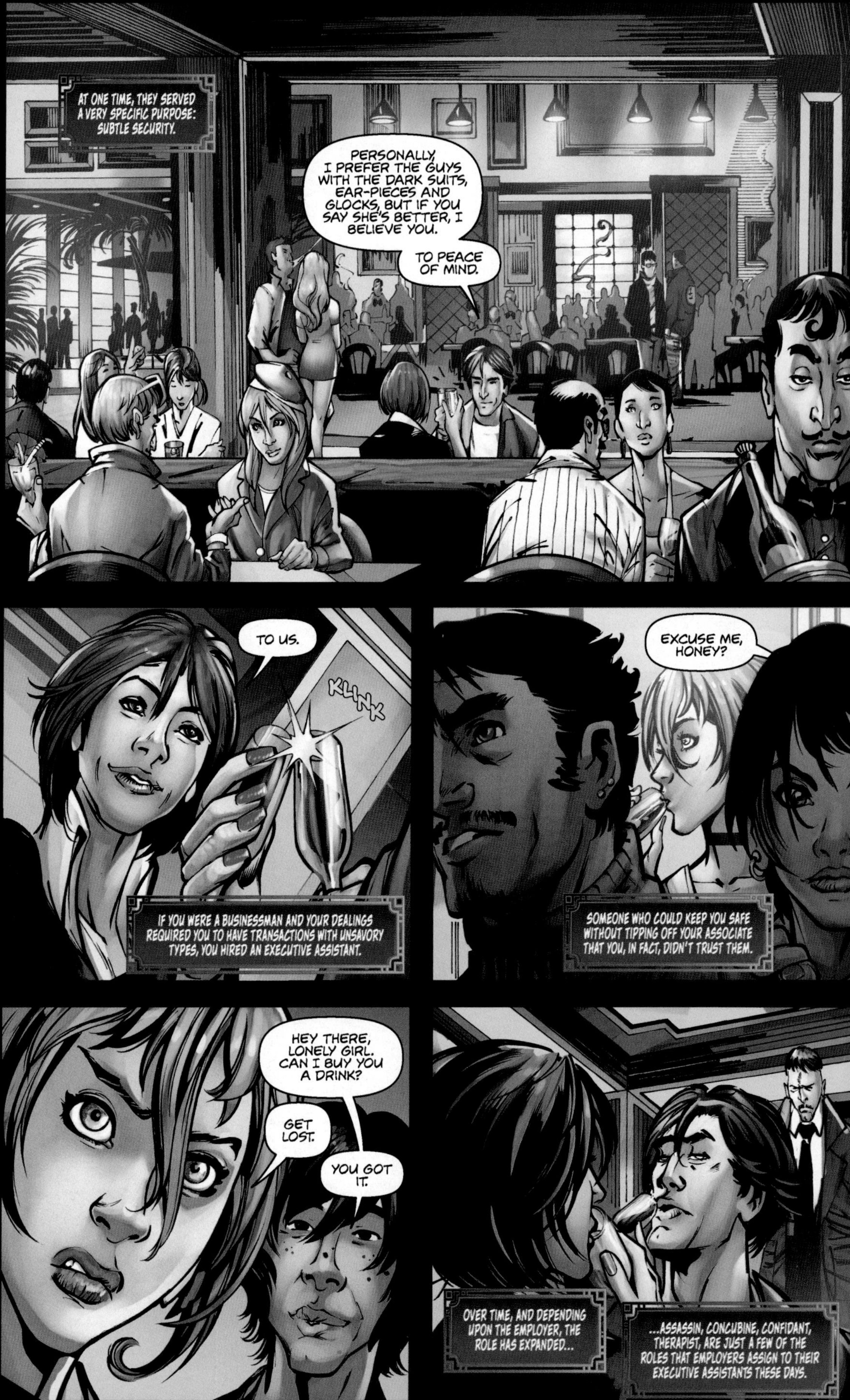
AT ONE TIME, THEY SERVED A VERY SPECIFIC PURPOSE: SUBTLE SECURITY.
PERSONALLY, I PREFER THE GUYS WITH THE DARK SUITS, EAR-PIECES AND GLOCKS, BUT IF YOU SAY SHE'S BETTER, I BELIEVE YOU.
TO PEACE OF MIND.
TO US.
KLINK
IF YOU WERE A BUSINESSMAN AND YOUR DEALINGS REQUIRED YOU TO HAVE TRANSACTIONS WITH UNSAVORY TYPES, YOU HIRED AN EXECUTIVE ASSISTANT.
EXCUSE ME, HONEY?
SOMEONE WHO COULD KEEP YOU SAFE WITHOUT TIPPING OFF YOUR ASSOCIATE THAT YOU, IN FACT, DIDN'T TRUST THEM.
HEY THERE, LONELY GIRL. CAN I BUY YOU A DRINK?
GET LOST.
YOU GOT IT.
OVER TIME, AND DEPENDING UPON THE EMPLOYER, THE ROLE HAS EXPANDED...
...ASSASSIN, CONCUBINE, CONFIDANT, THERAPIST, ARE JUST A FEW OF THE ROLES THAT EMPLOYERS ASSIGN TO THEIR EXECUTIVE ASSISTANTS THESE DAYS.

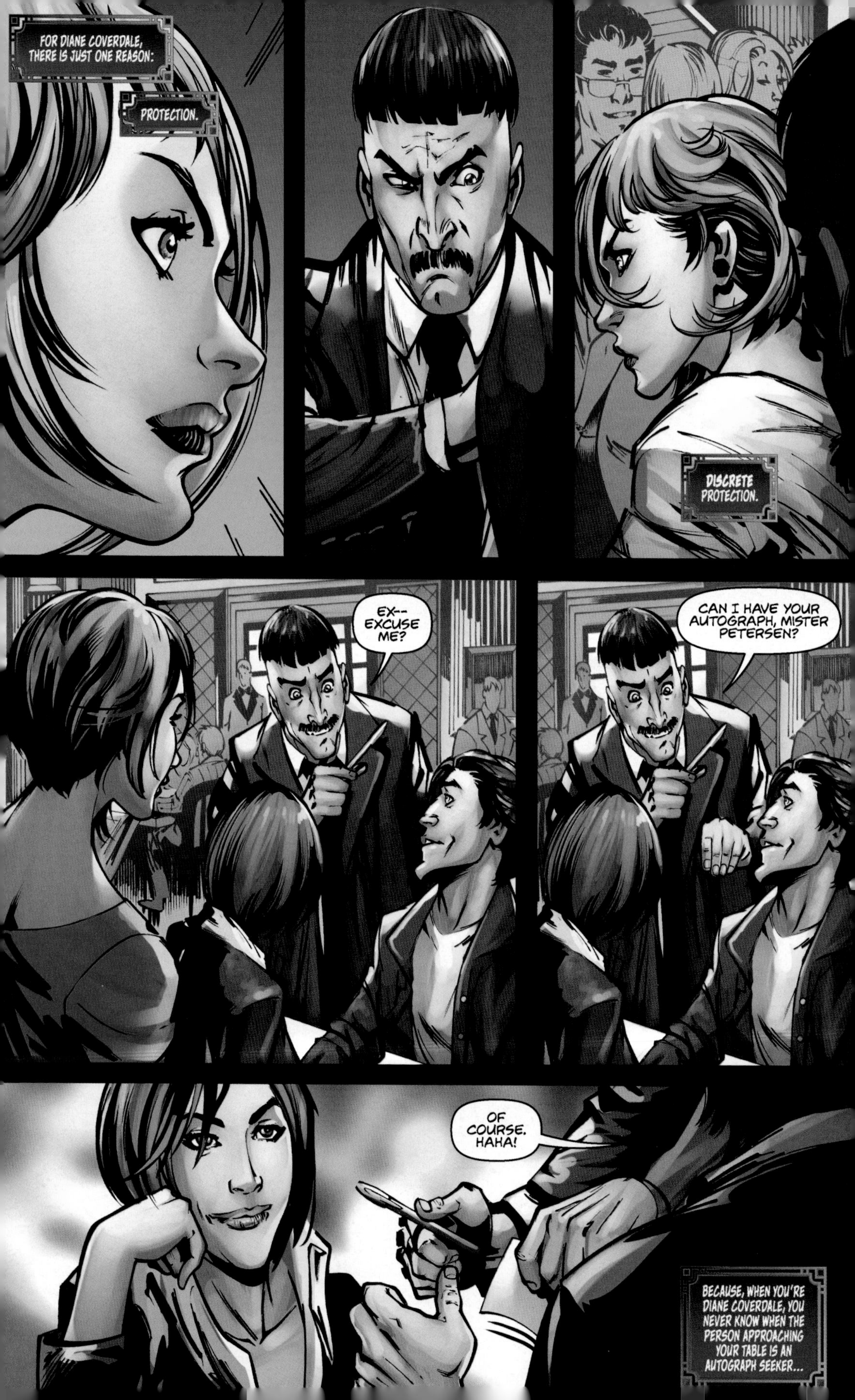
FOR DIANE COVERDALE, THERE IS JUST ONE REASON:
PROTECTION.
DISCRETE PROTECTION.
EX-- EXCUSE ME?
CAN I HAVE YOUR AUTOGRAPH, MISTER PETERSEN?
OF COURSE. HAHA!
BECAUSE, WHEN YOU'RE DIANE COVERDALE, YOU NEVER KNOW WHEN THE PERSON APPROACHING YOUR TABLE IS AN AUTOGRAPH SEEKER...

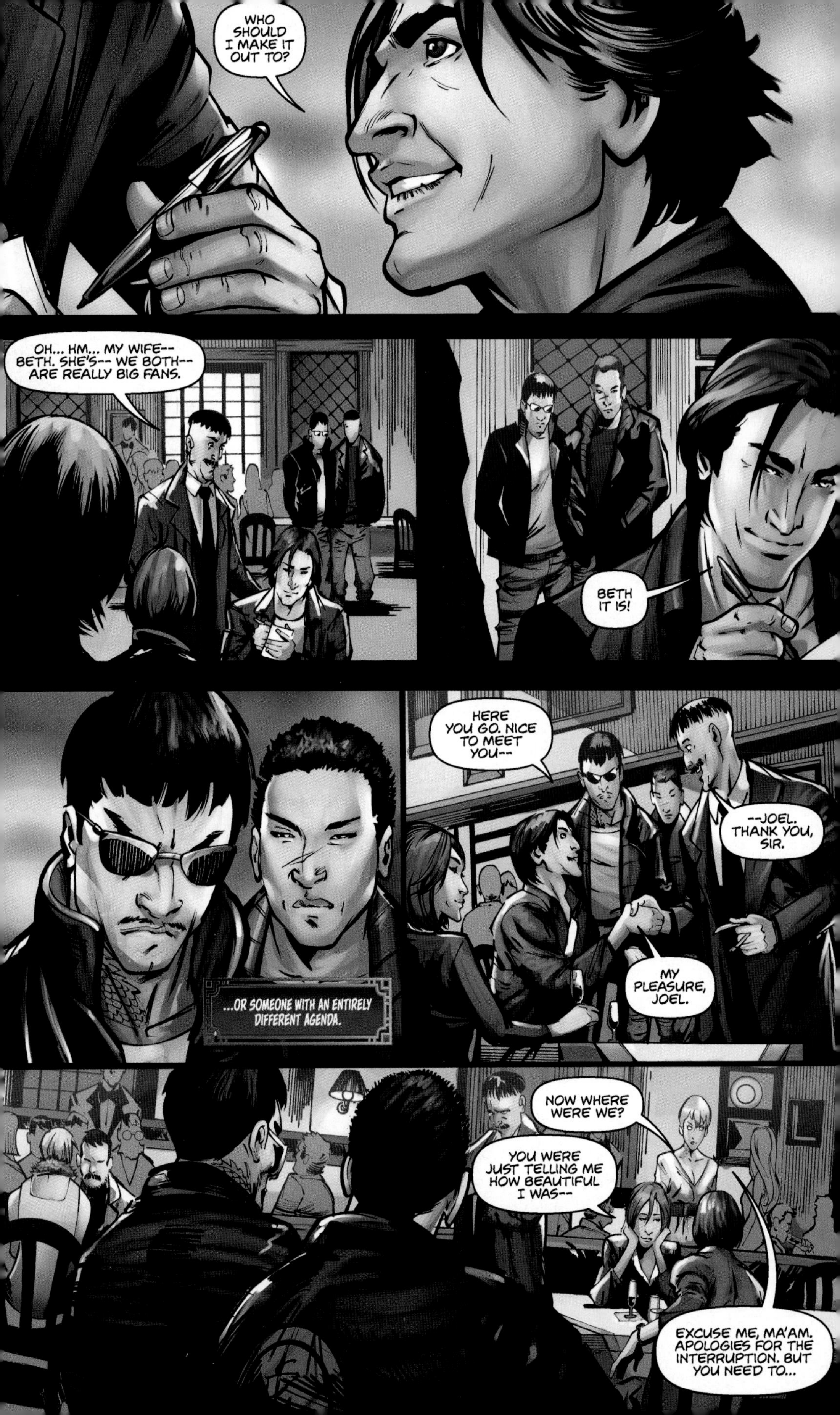
WHO SHOULD I MAKE IT OUT TO?
OH... HM... MY WIFE-- BETH. SHE'S-- WE BOTH-- ARE REALLY BIG FANS.
BETH IT IS!
...OR SOMEONE WITH AN ENTIRELY DIFFERENT AGENDA.
HERE YOU GO. NICE TO MEET YOU--
--JOEL. THANK YOU, SIR.
MY PLEASURE, JOEL.
NOW WHERE WERE WE?
YOU WERE JUST TELLING ME HOW BEAUTIFUL I WAS--
EXCUSE ME, MA'AM. APOLOGIES FOR THE INTERRUPTION. BUT YOU NEED TO...

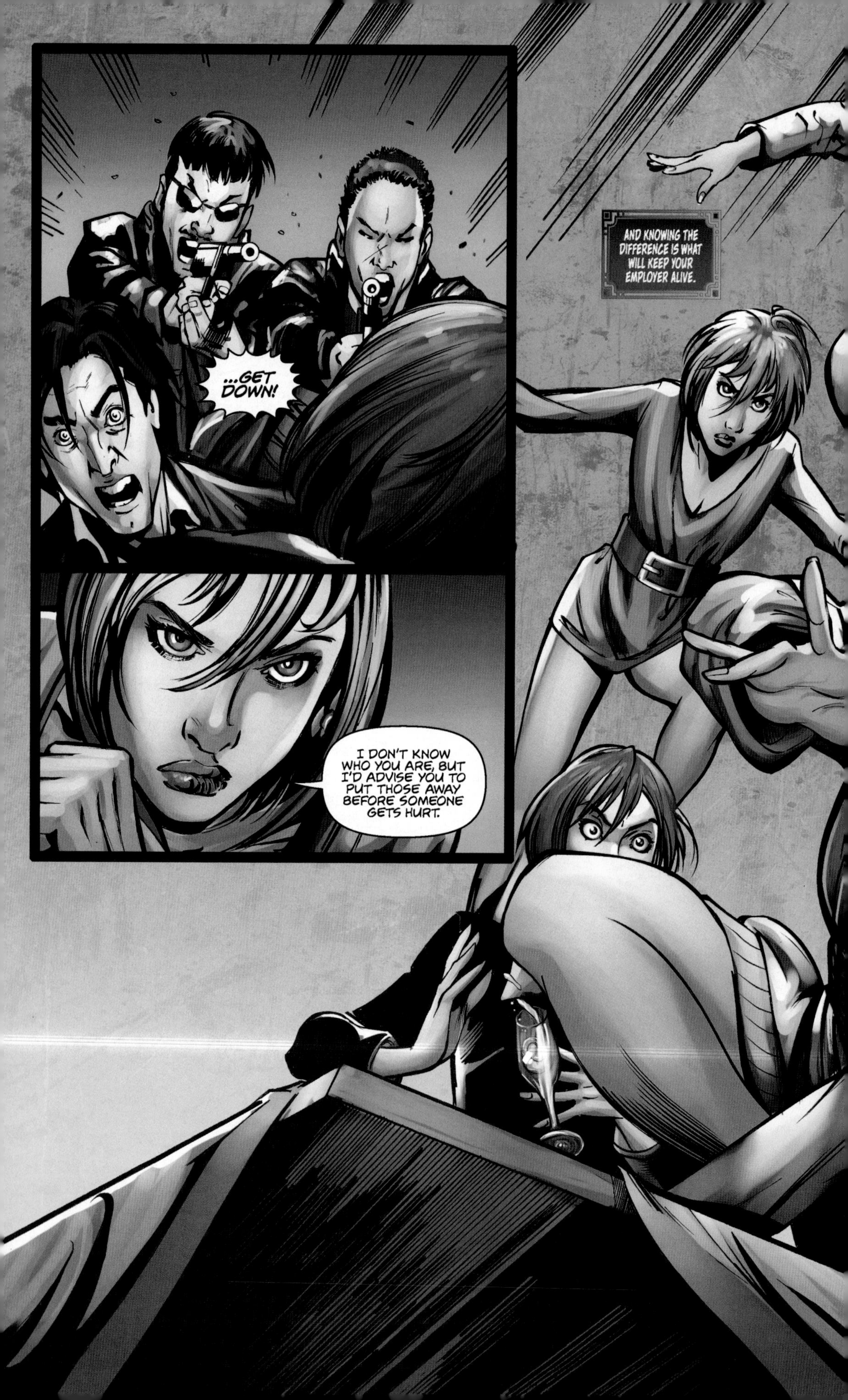
...GET DOWN!
I DON'T KNOW WHO YOU ARE, BUT I'D ADVISE YOU TO PUT THOSE AWAY BEFORE SOMEONE GETS HURT.
AND KNOWING THE DIFFERENCE IS WHAT WILL KEEP YOUR EMPLOYER ALIVE.

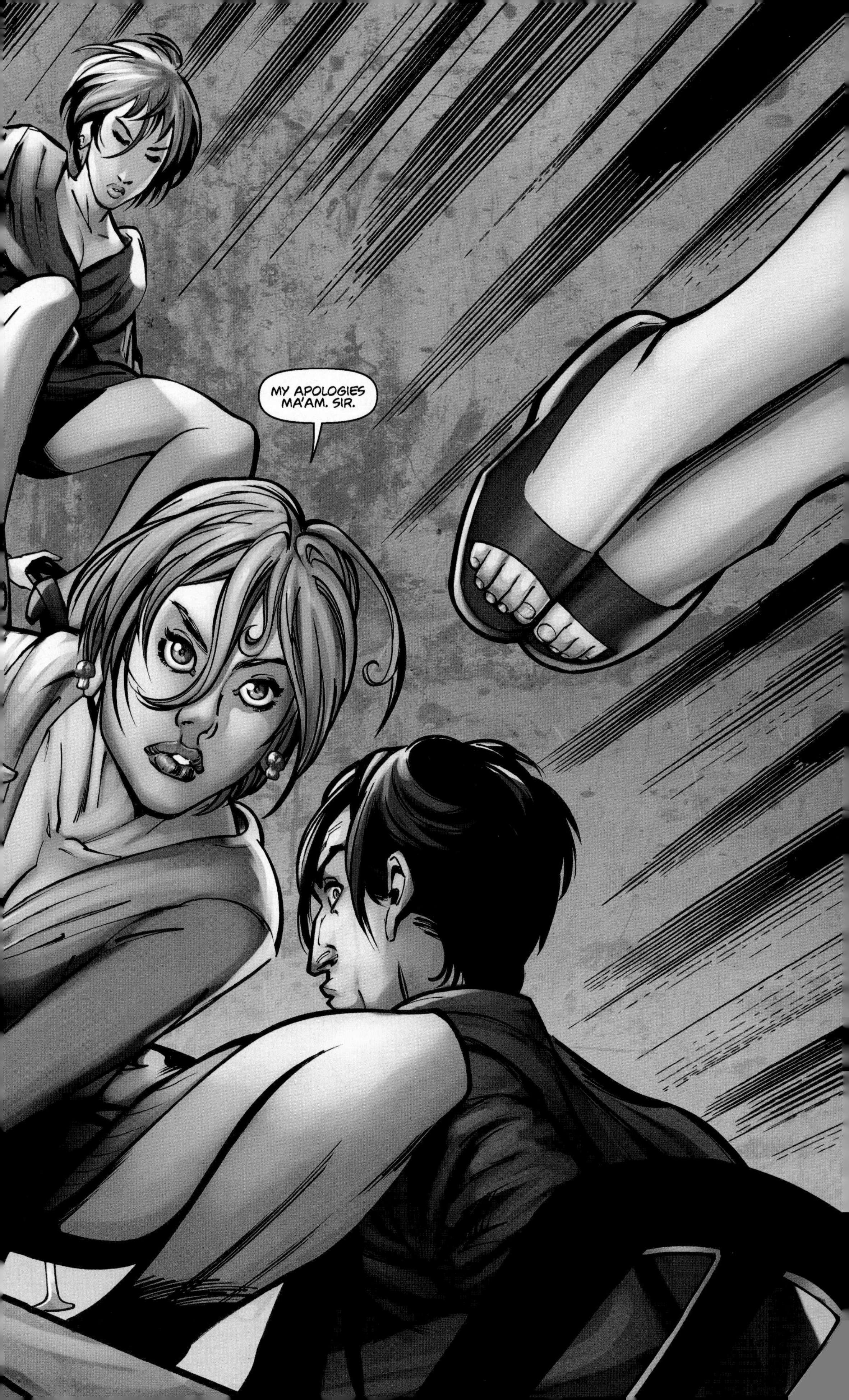
MY APOLOGIES MA'AM. SIR.

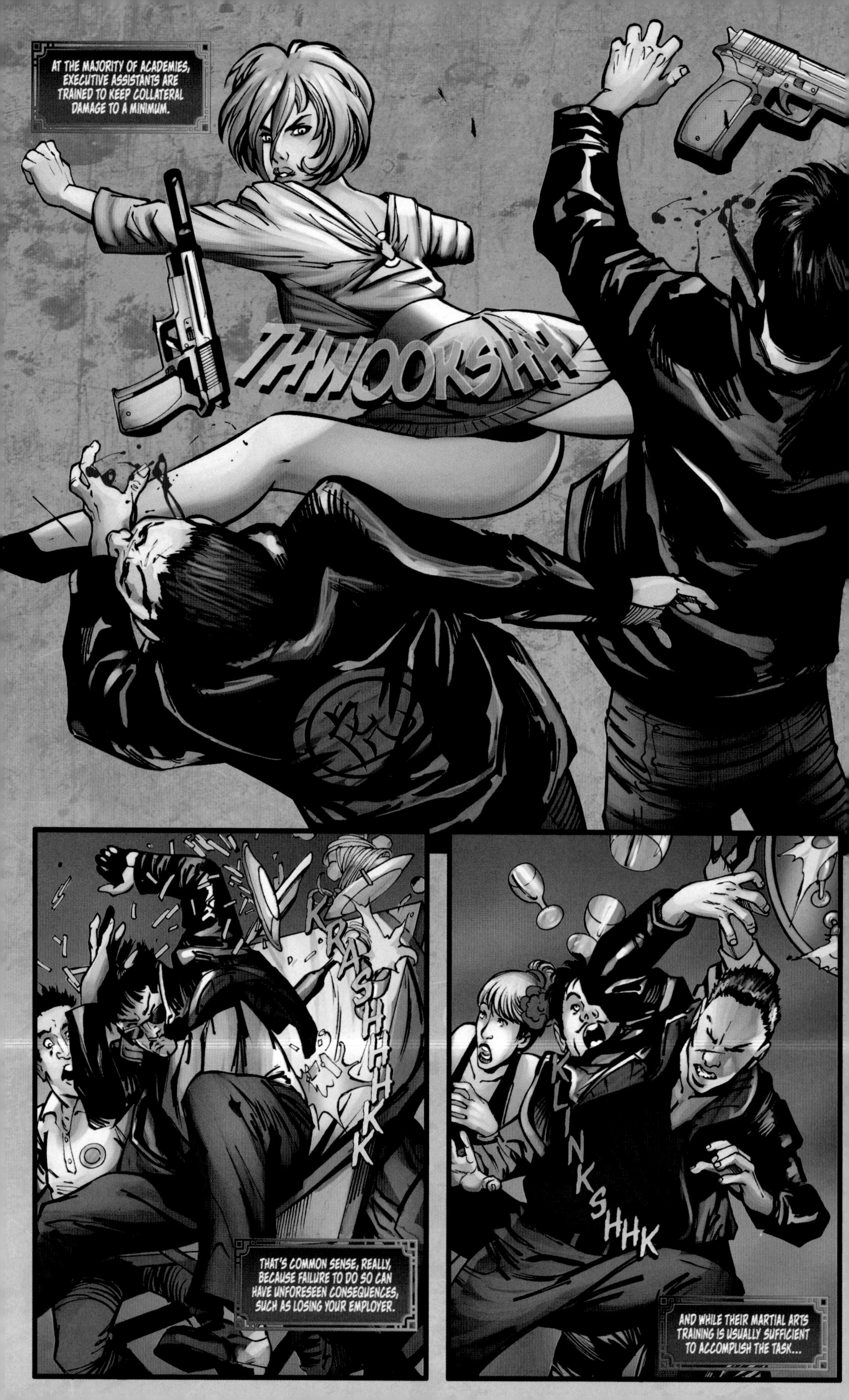
AT THE MAJORITY OF ACADEMIES, EXECUTIVE ASSISTANTS ARE TRAINED TO KEEP COLLATERAL DAMAGE TO A MINIMUM.
THWOOKSHH
KRASHHHHKK
THAT'S COMMON SENSE, REALLY, BECAUSE FAILURE TO DO SO CAN HAVE UNFORESEEN CONSEQUENCES, SUCH AS LOSING YOUR EMPLOYER.
KLINKSHHK
AND WHILE THEIR MARTIAL ARTS TRAINING IS USUALLY SUFFICIENT TO ACCOMPLISH THE TASK...

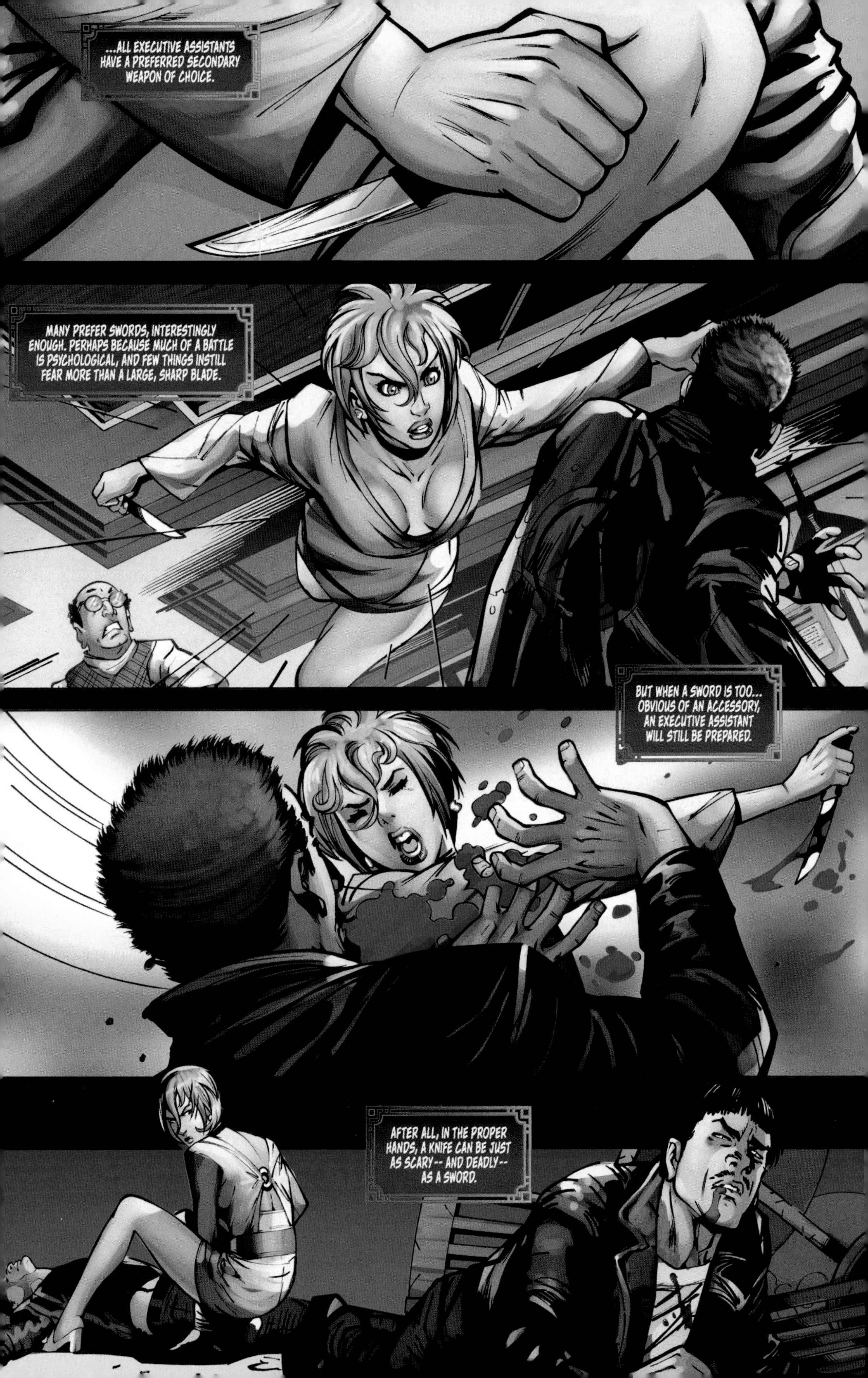
...ALL EXECUTIVE ASSISTANTS HAVE A PREFERRED SECONDARY WEAPON OF CHOICE.
MANY PREFER SWORDS, INTERESTINGLY ENOUGH. PERHAPS BECAUSE MUCH OF A BATTLE IS PSYCHOLOGICAL, AND FEW THINGS INSTILL FEAR MORE THAN A LARGE, SHARP BLADE.
BUT WHEN A SWORD IS TOO... OBVIOUS OF AN ACCESSORY, AN EXECUTIVE ASSISTANT WILL STILL BE PREPARED.
AFTER ALL, IN THE PROPER HANDS, A KNIFE CAN BE JUST AS SCARY-- AND DEADLY-- AS A SWORD.

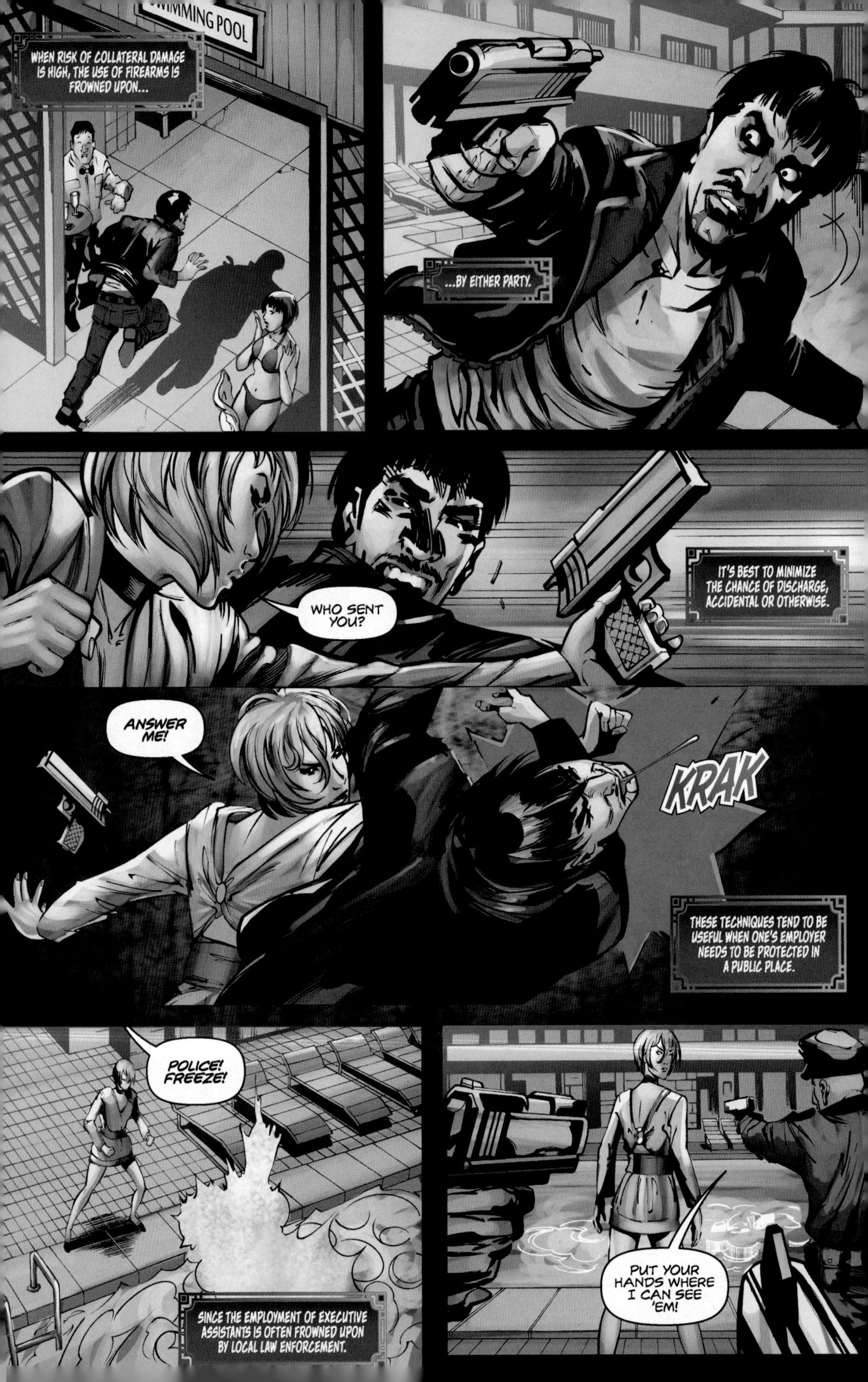
SWIMMING POOL
WHEN RISK OF COLLATERAL DAMAGE IS HIGH, THE USE OF FIREARMS IS FROWNED UPON...
...BY EITHER PARTY.
WHO SENT YOU?
IT'S BEST TO MINIMIZE THE CHANCE OF DISCHARGE, ACCIDENTAL OR OTHERWISE.
ANSWER ME!
KRAK
THESE TECHNIQUES TEND TO BE USEFUL WHEN ONE'S EMPLOYER NEEDS TO BE PROTECTED IN A PUBLIC PLACE.
POLICE! FREEZE!
SINCE THE EMPLOYMENT OF EXECUTIVE ASSISTANTS IS OFTEN FROWNED UPON BY LOCAL LAW ENFORCEMENT.
PUT YOUR HANDS WHERE I CAN SEE 'EM!

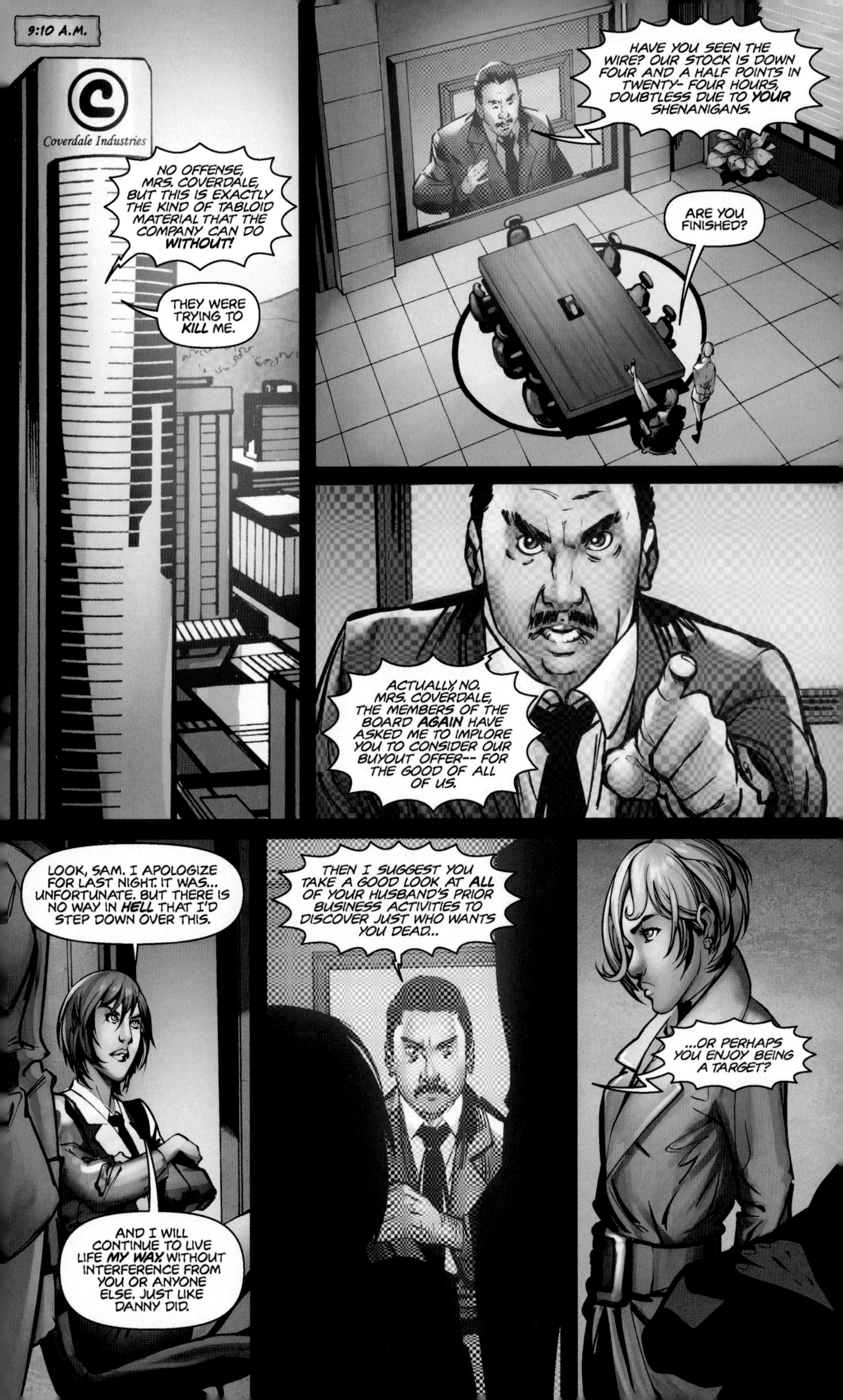
9:10 A.M.
Coverdale Industries
NO OFFENSE, MRS. COVERDALE, BUT THIS IS EXACTLY THE KIND OF TABLOID MATERIAL THAT THE COMPANY CAN DO WITHOUT!
THEY WERE TRYING TO KILL ME.
HAVE YOU SEEN THE WIRE? OUR STOCK IS DOWN FOUR AND A HALF POINTS IN TWENTY- FOUR HOURS, DOUBTLESS DUE TO YOUR SHENANIGANS.
ARE YOU FINISHED?
ACTUALLY, NO. MRS. COVERDALE, THE MEMBERS OF THE BOARD AGAIN HAVE ASKED ME TO IMPLORE YOU TO CONSIDER OUR BUYOUT OFFER-- FOR THE GOOD OF ALL OF US.
LOOK, SAM. I APOLOGIZE FOR LAST NIGHT. IT WAS... UNFORTUNATE. BUT THERE IS NO WAY IN HELL THAT I'D STEP DOWN OVER THIS.
AND I WILL CONTINUE TO LIVE LIFE MY WAY. WITHOUT INTERFERENCE FROM YOU OR ANYONE ELSE. JUST LIKE DANNY DID.
THEN I SUGGEST YOU TAKE A GOOD LOOK AT ALL OF YOUR HUSBAND'S PRIOR BUSINESS ACTIVITIES TO DISCOVER JUST WHO WANTS YOU DEAD...
...OR PERHAPS YOU ENJOY BEING A TARGET?

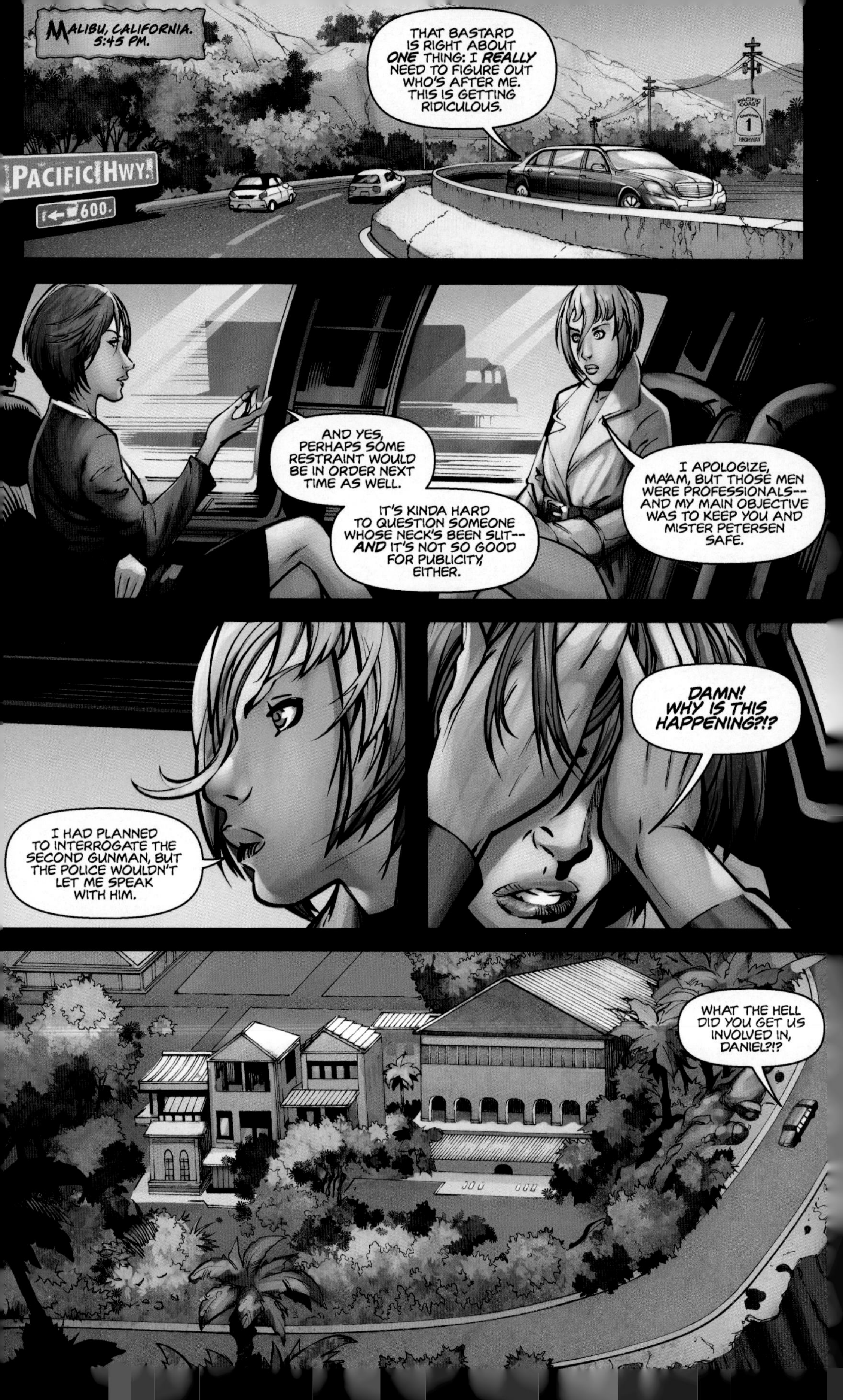
MALIBU, CALIFORNIA. 5:45 PM.
PACIFIC HWY.
600
PACIFIC COAST
CALIFORNIA
1
HIGHWAY
THAT BASTARD IS RIGHT ABOUT ONE THING: I REALLY NEED TO FIGURE OUT WHO'S AFTER ME. THIS IS GETTING RIDICULOUS.
AND YES, PERHAPS SOME RESTRAINT WOULD BE IN ORDER NEXT TIME AS WELL.
IT'S KINDA HARD TO QUESTION SOMEONE WHOSE NECK'S BEEN SLIT-- AND IT'S NOT SO GOOD FOR PUBLICITY, EITHER.
I APOLOGIZE, MA'AM, BUT THOSE MEN WERE PROFESSIONALS-- AND MY MAIN OBJECTIVE WAS TO KEEP YOU AND MISTER PETERSEN SAFE.
I HAD PLANNED TO INTERROGATE THE SECOND GUNMAN, BUT THE POLICE WOULDN'T LET ME SPEAK WITH HIM.
DAMN! WHY IS THIS HAPPENING?!?
WHAT THE HELL DID YOU GET US INVOLVED IN, DANIEL?!?

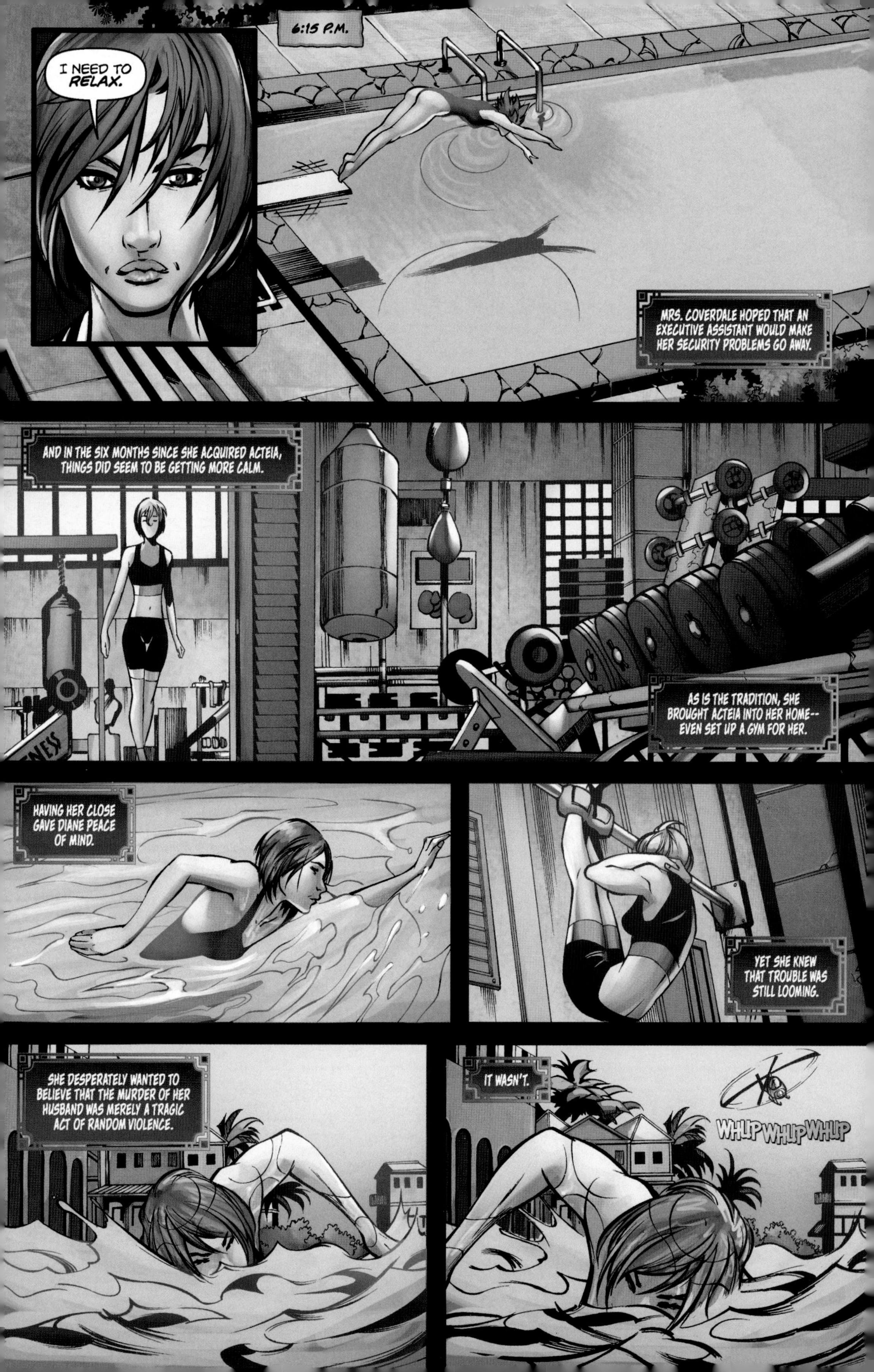
6:15 P.M.
I NEED TO RELAX.
MRS. COVERDALE HOPED THAT AN EXECUTIVE ASSISTANT WOULD MAKE HER SECURITY PROBLEMS GO AWAY.
AND IN THE SIX MONTHS SINCE SHE ACQUIRED ACTEIA, THINGS DID SEEM TO BE GETTING MORE CALM.
AS IS THE TRADITION, SHE BROUGHT ACTEIA INTO HER HOME-- EVEN SET UP A GYM FOR HER.
HAVING HER CLOSE GAVE DIANE PEACE OF MIND.
YET SHE KNEW THAT TROUBLE WAS STILL LOOMING.
SHE DESPERATELY WANTED TO BELIEVE THAT THE MURDER OF HER HUSBAND WAS MERELY A TRAGIC ACT OF RANDOM VIOLENCE.
IT WASN'T.
WHUPWHUPWHUP

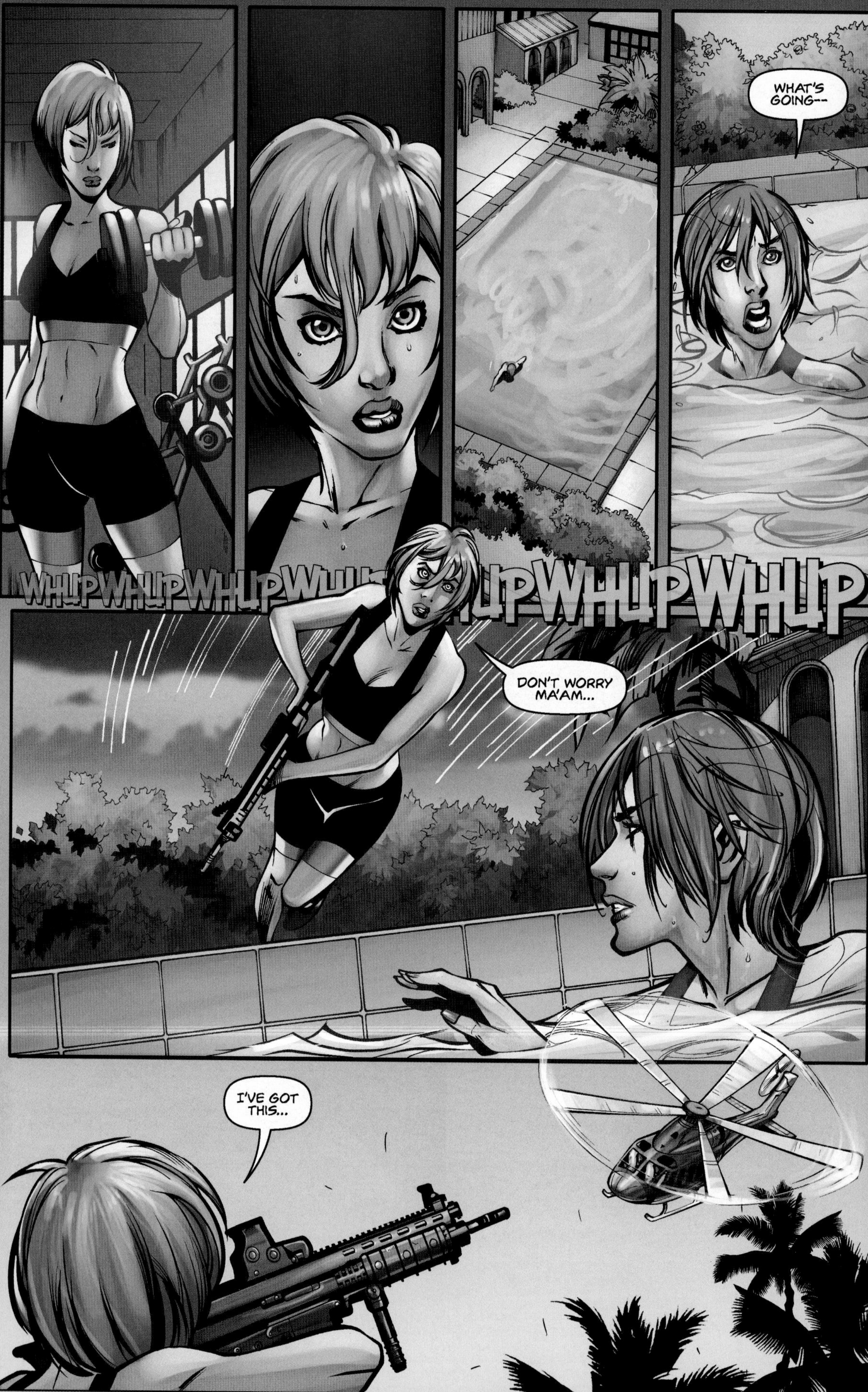
WHAT'S GOING--
WHUPWHUPWHUPWHU
UPWHUPWHUP
DON'T WORRY MA'AM...
I'VE GOT THIS...

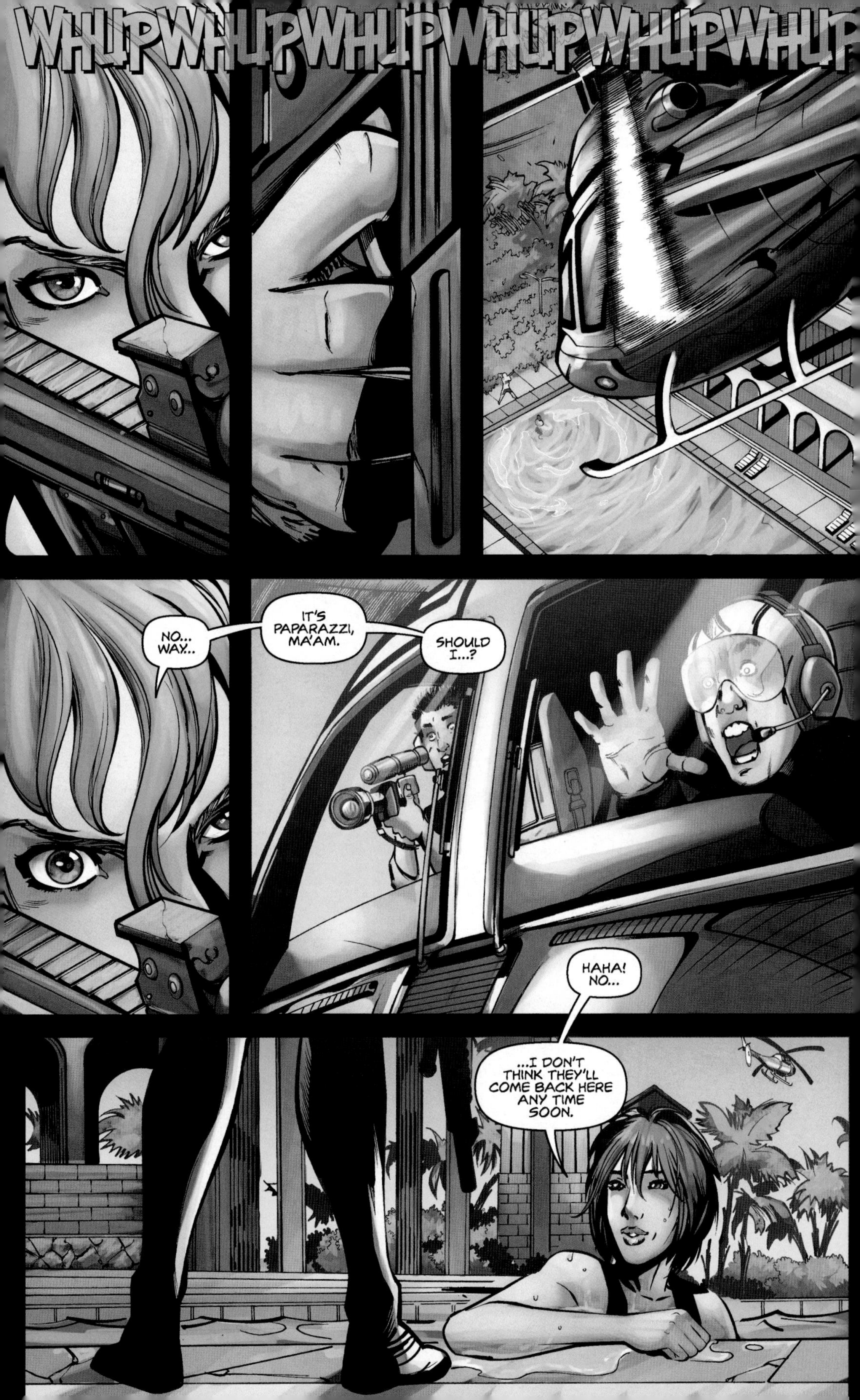
WHUPWHUPWHUPWHUPWHUPWHUP
NO... WAY...
IT'S PAPARAZZI, MA'AM.
SHOULD I...?
HAHA! NO...
...I DON'T THINK THEY'LL COME BACK HERE ANY TIME SOON.

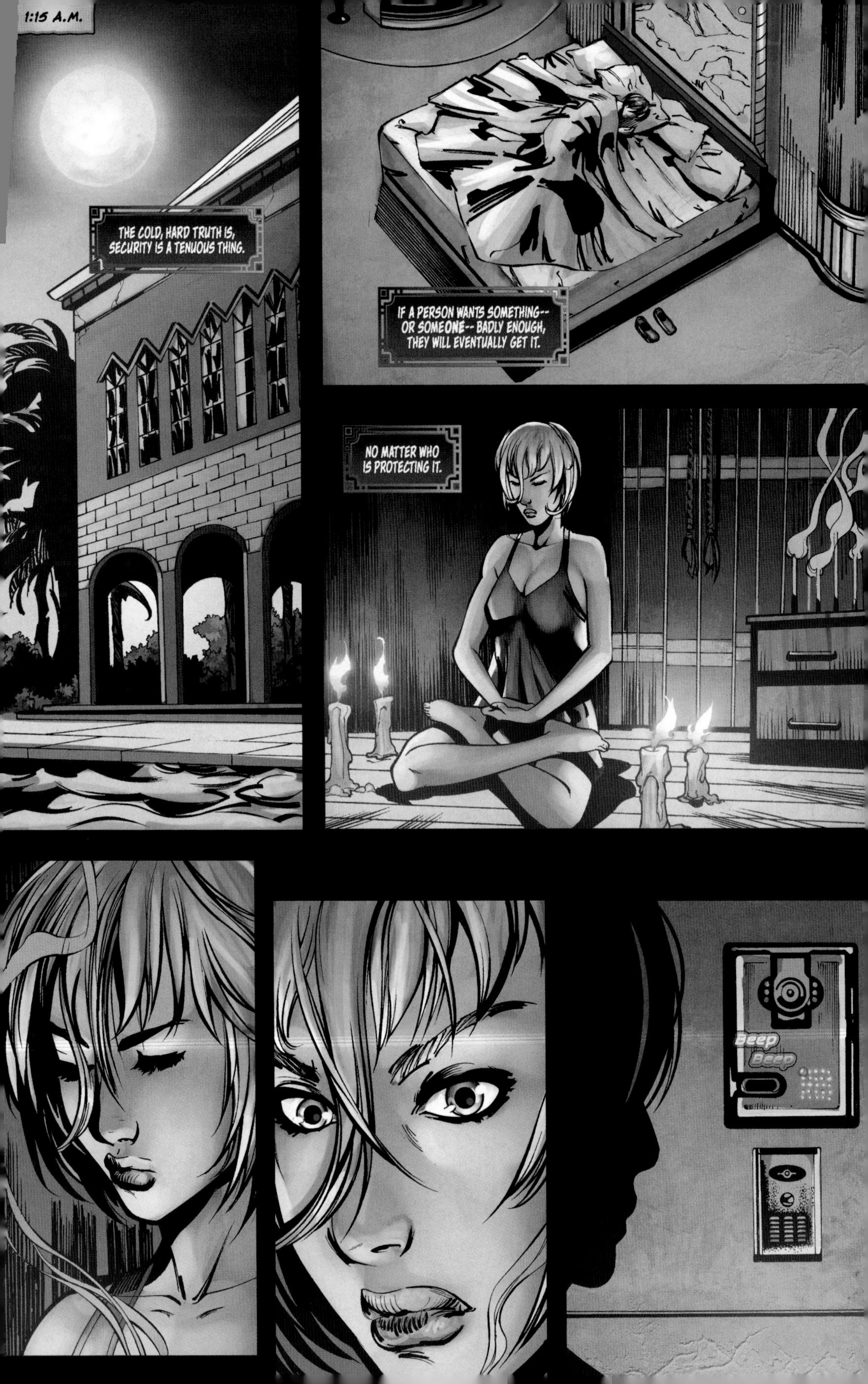
1:15 A.M.
THE COLD, HARD TRUTH IS, SECURITY IS A TENUOUS THING.
IF A PERSON WANTS SOMETHING-- OR SOMEONE-- BADLY ENOUGH, THEY WILL EVENTUALLY GET IT.
NO MATTER WHO IS PROTECTING IT.
Beep
Beep

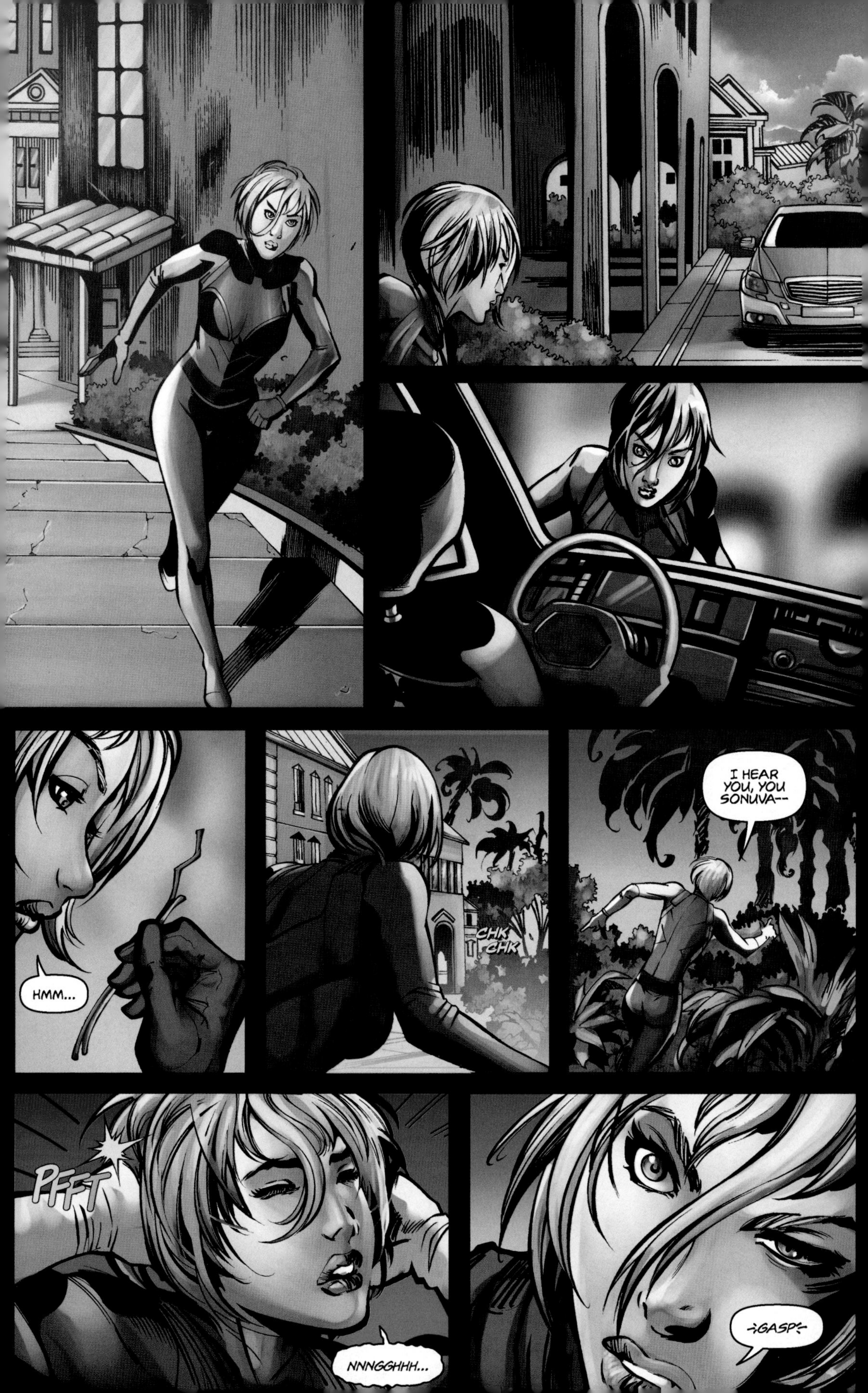
HMM...
CHK CHK
I HEAR YOU, YOU SONUVA--
PFFT
NNNGGHHH...
-GASP-

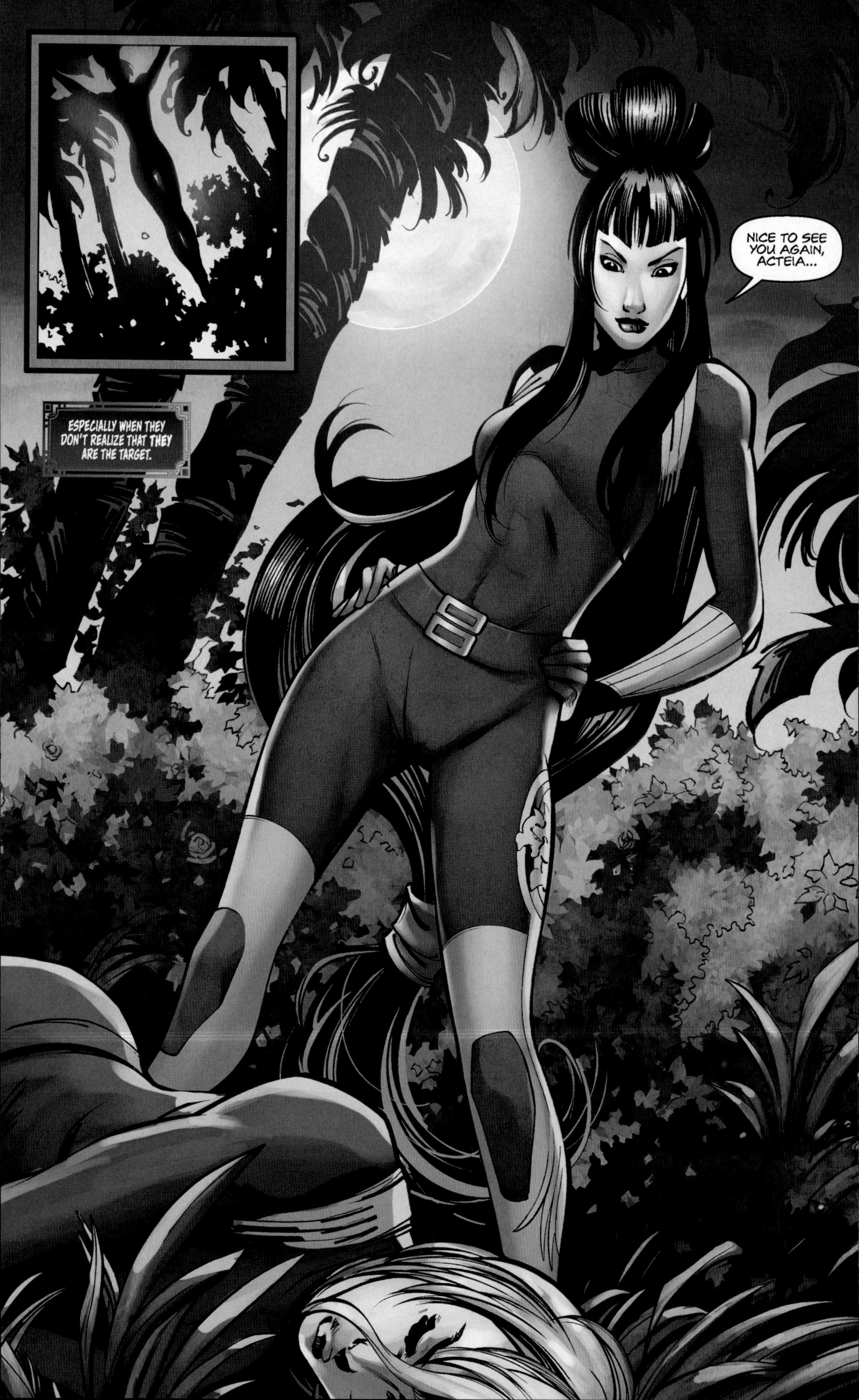
ESPECIALLY WHEN THEY DON'T REALIZE THAT THEY ARE THE TARGET.
NICE TO SEE YOU AGAIN, ACTEIA...

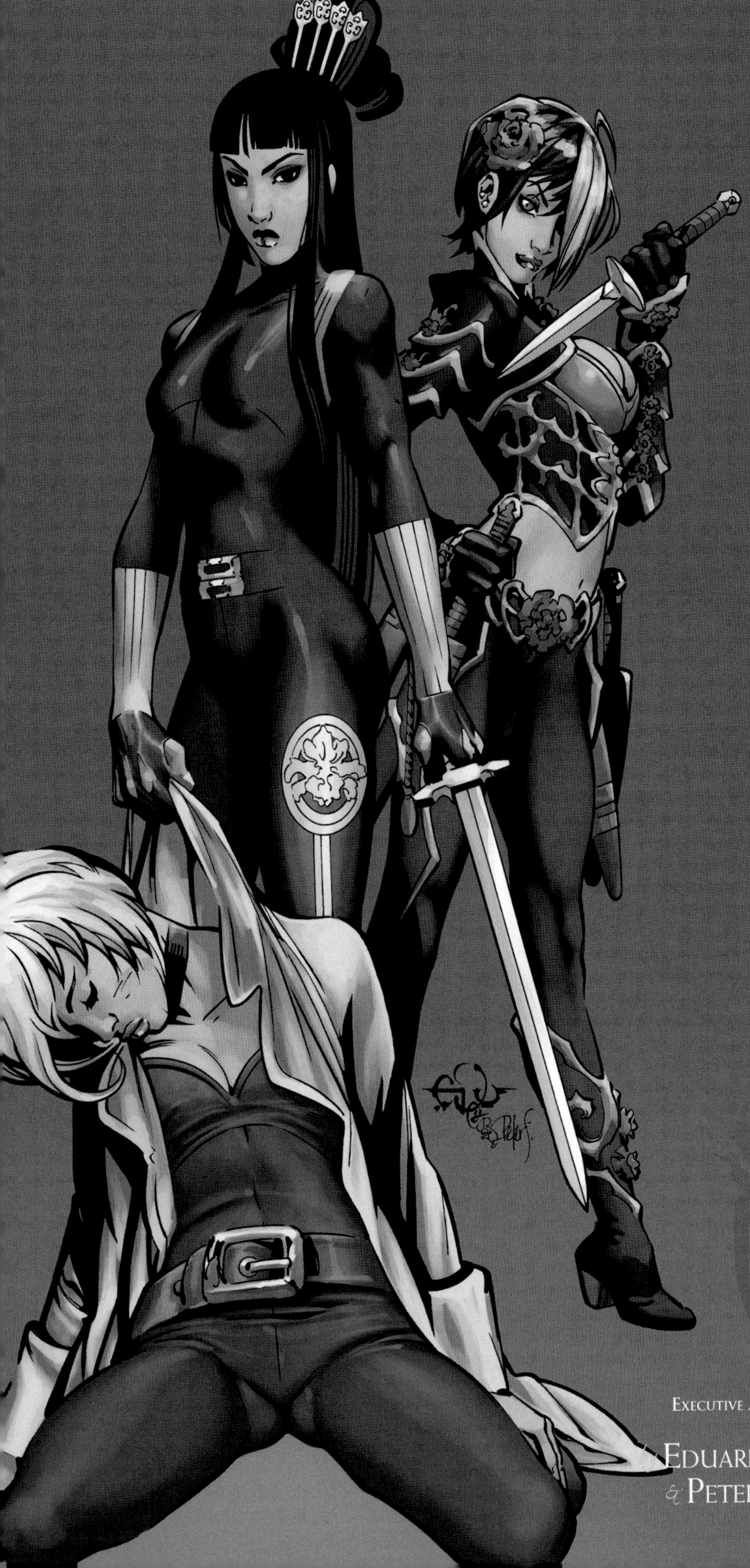

Cover A:
Executive Assistant: IRIS - No. 2
[Direct Edition]
by Eduardo Francisco
& Peter Steigerwald

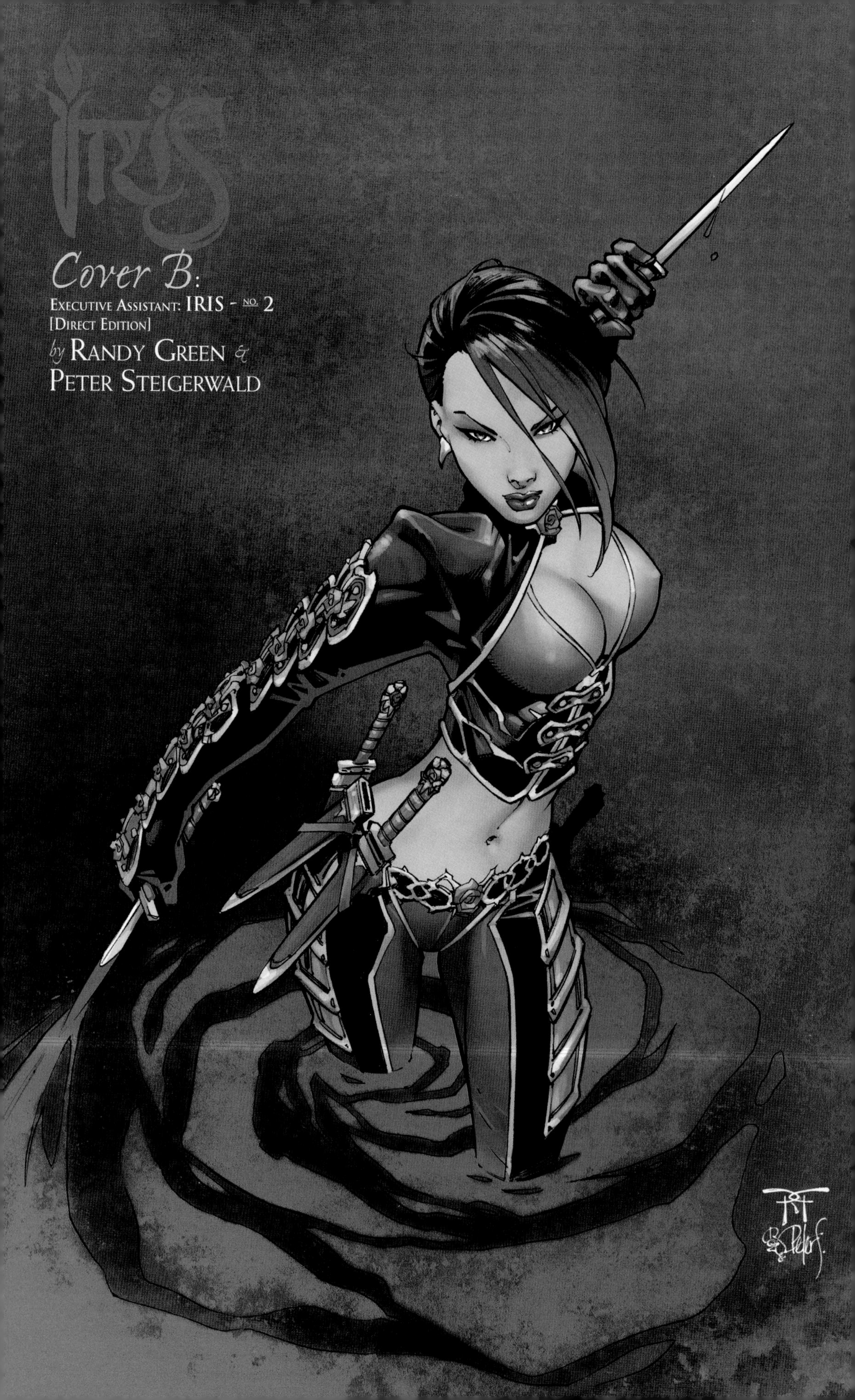
IRIS
Cover B:
EXECUTIVE ASSISTANT: IRIS - No. 2
[DIRECT EDITION]
by RANDY GREEN &
PETER STEIGERWALD

CHAPTER THREE

Two

"WELCOME TO PARADISE"

WRITER
DAVID WOHL

PENCILS
RYAN ODAGAWA

COLORS
TEODORO GONZALEZ

LETTERING
JOSH REED

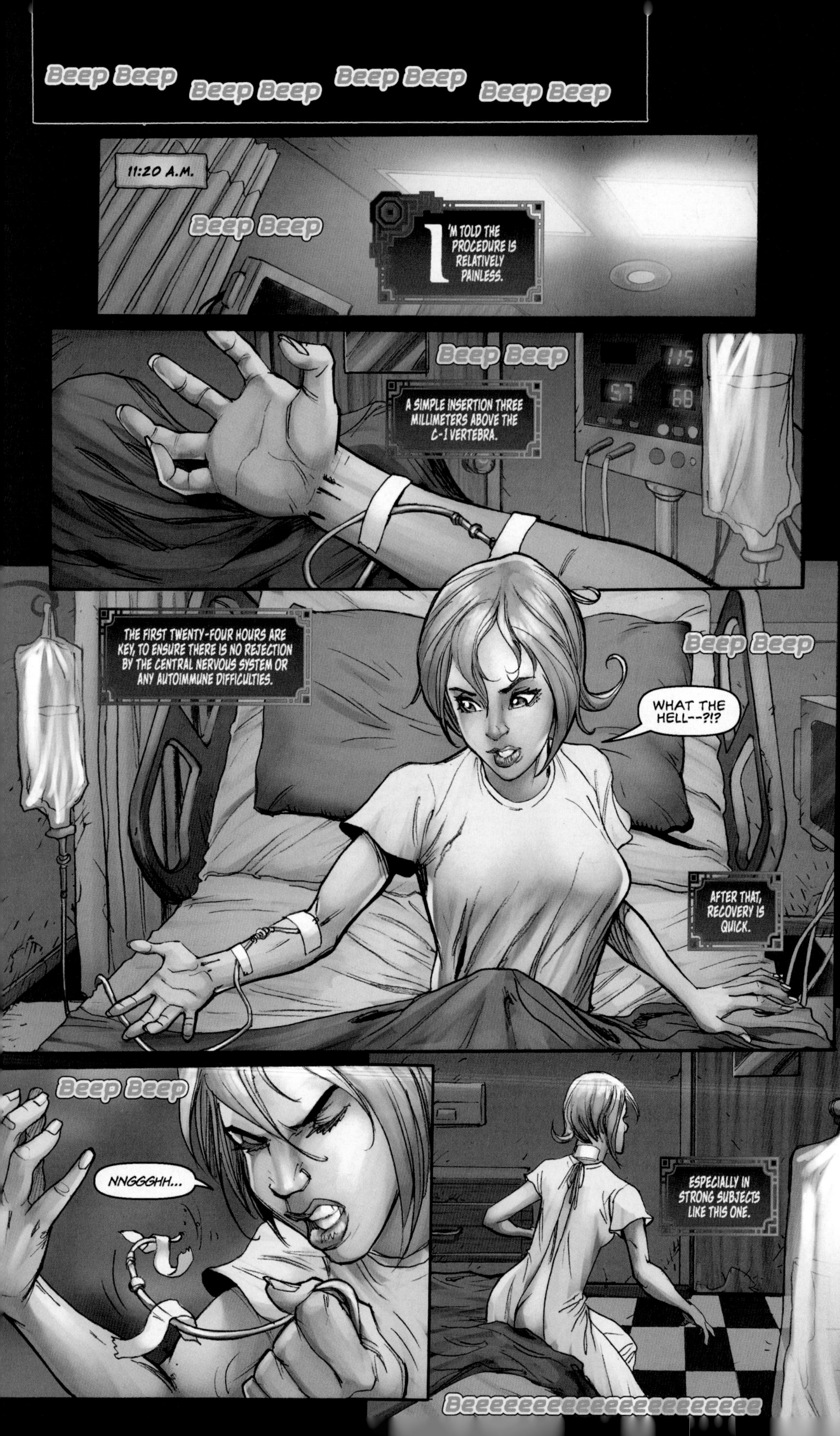
Beep Beep
Beep Beep
Beep Beep
Beep Beep
11:20 A.M.
Beep Beep
I'M TOLD THE PROCEDURE IS RELATIVELY PAINLESS.
Beep Beep
A SIMPLE INSERTION THREE MILLIMETERS ABOVE THE C-1 VERTEBRA.
THE FIRST TWENTY-FOUR HOURS ARE KEY, TO ENSURE THERE IS NO REJECTION BY THE CENTRAL NERVOUS SYSTEM OR ANY AUTOIMMUNE DIFFICULTIES.
Beep Beep
WHAT THE HELL--?!?
AFTER THAT, RECOVERY IS QUICK.
Beep Beep
NNGGGHH...
ESPECIALLY IN STRONG SUBJECTS LIKE THIS ONE.
Beeeeeeeeeeeeeeeeeeeeeee

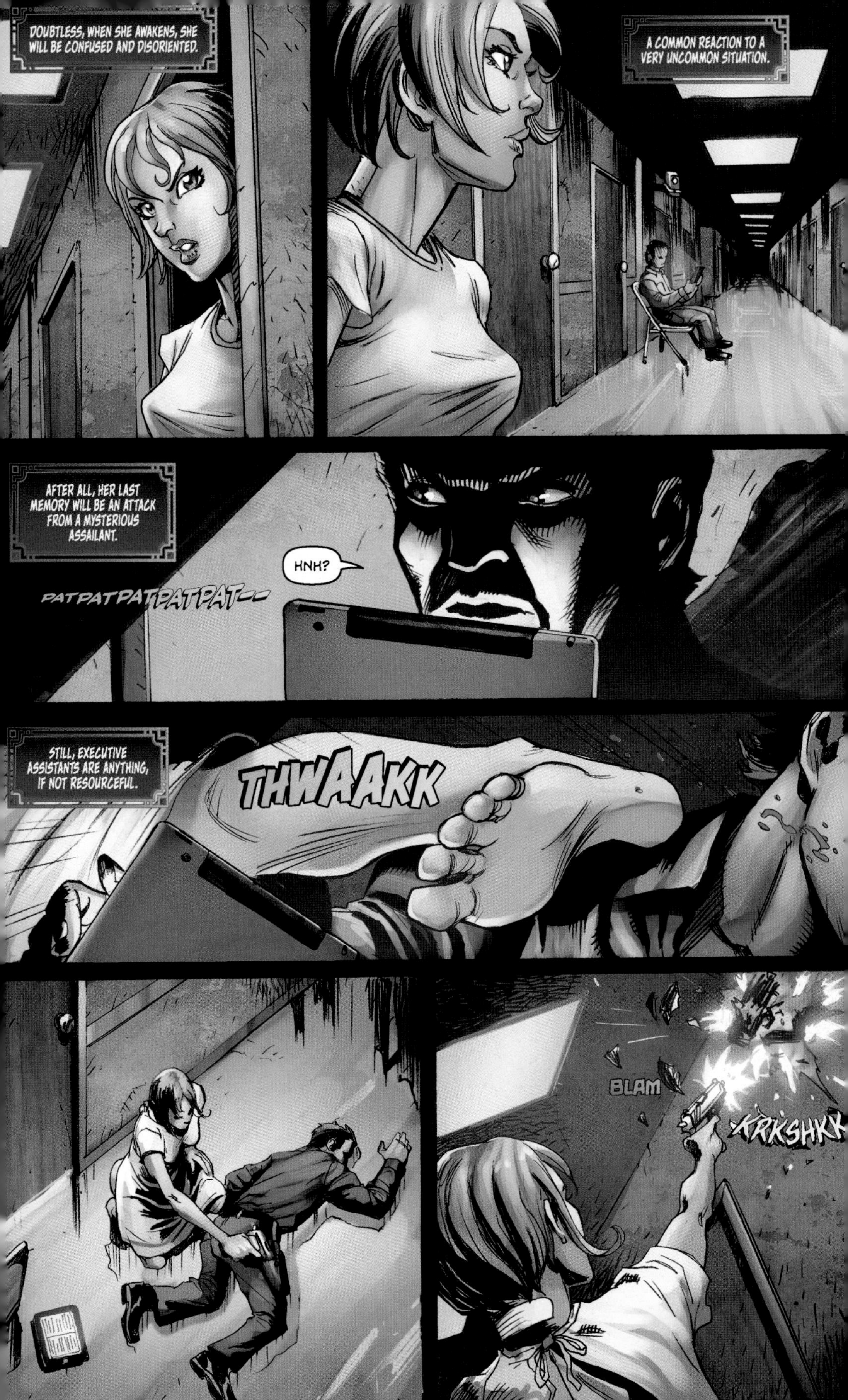
DOUBTLESS, WHEN SHE AWAKENS, SHE WILL BE CONFUSED AND DISORIENTED.
A COMMON REACTION TO A VERY UNCOMMON SITUATION.
AFTER ALL, HER LAST MEMORY WILL BE AN ATTACK FROM A MYSTERIOUS ASSAILANT.
HNH?
PATPATPATPATPAT--
STILL, EXECUTIVE ASSISTANTS ARE ANYTHING, IF NOT RESOURCEFUL.
THWAAKK
BLAM
KRKSHKK

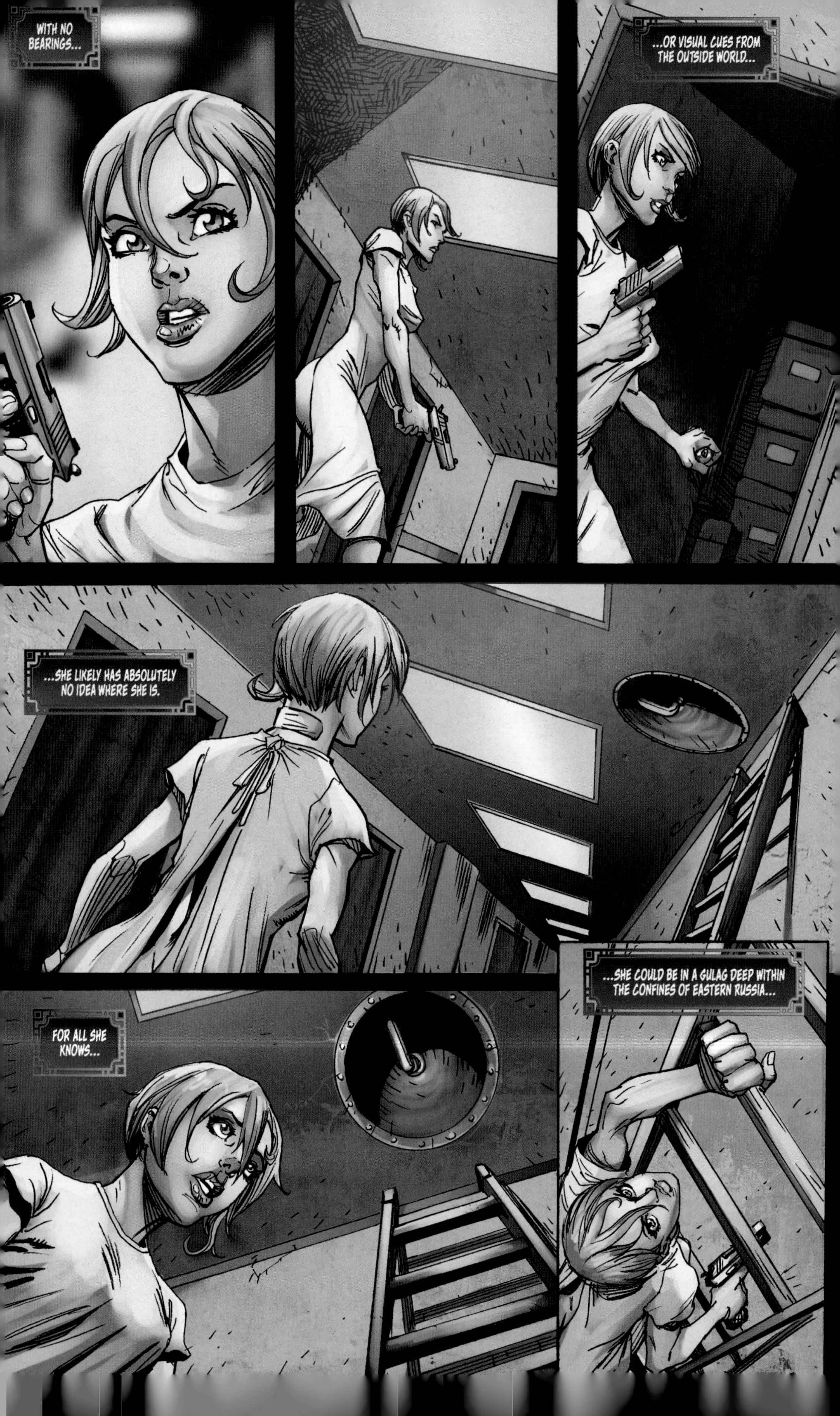
WITH NO BEARINGS...
...OR VISUAL CUES FROM THE OUTSIDE WORLD...
...SHE LIKELY HAS ABSOLUTELY NO IDEA WHERE SHE IS.
FOR ALL SHE KNOWS...
...SHE COULD BE IN A GULAG DEEP WITHIN THE CONFINES OF EASTERN RUSSIA...

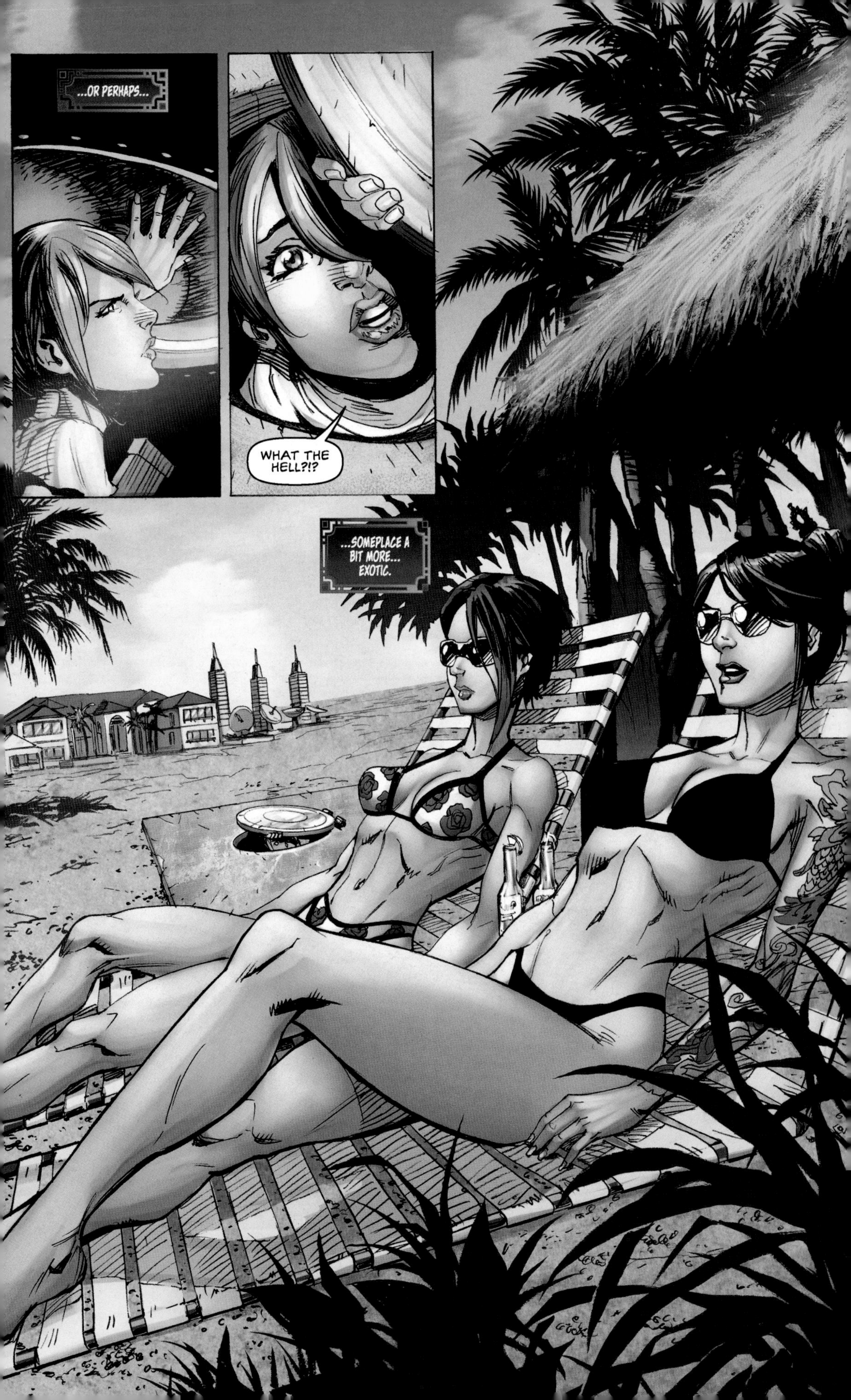
...OR PERHAPS...
WHAT THE HELL?!?
...SOMEPLACE A BIT MORE... EXOTIC.

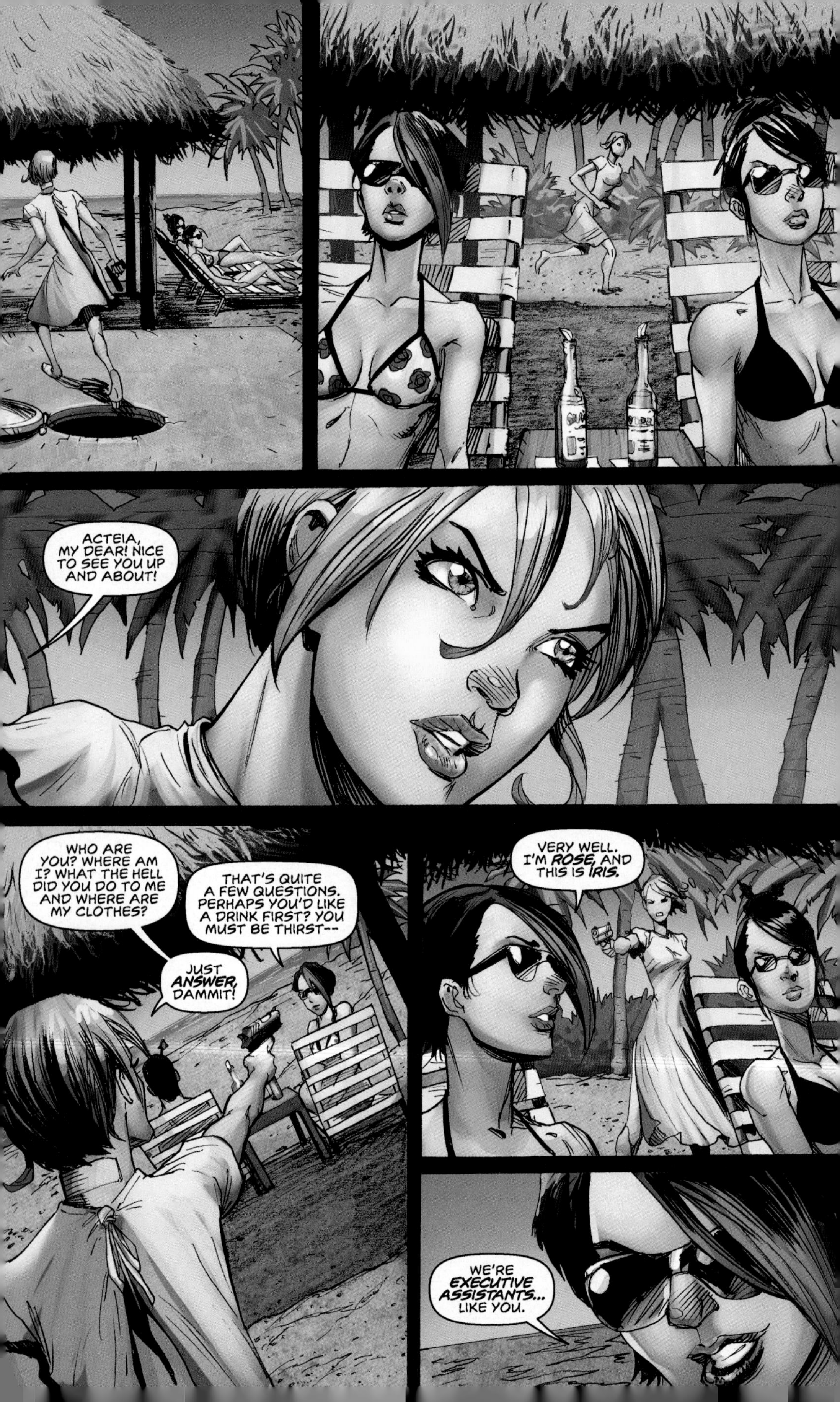
ACTEIA, MY DEAR! NICE TO SEE YOU UP AND ABOUT!
WHO ARE YOU? WHERE AM I? WHAT THE HELL DID YOU DO TO ME AND WHERE ARE MY CLOTHES?
THAT'S QUITE A FEW QUESTIONS. PERHAPS YOU'D LIKE A DRINK FIRST? YOU MUST BE THIRST--
JUST ANSWER, DAMMIT!
VERY WELL. I'M ROSE, AND THIS IS IRIS.
WE'RE EXECUTIVE ASSISTANTS... LIKE YOU.

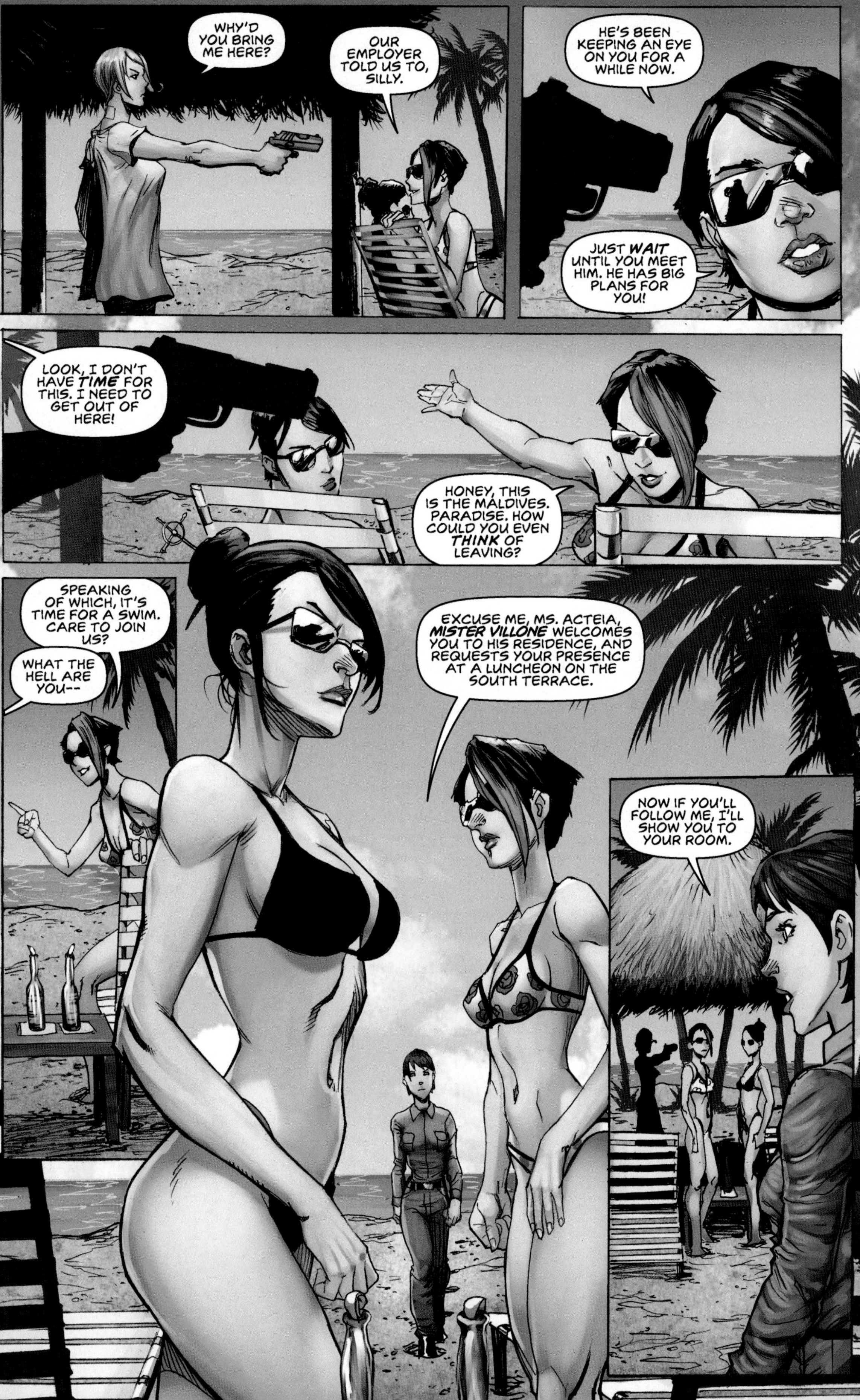
WHY'D YOU BRING ME HERE?
OUR EMPLOYER TOLD US TO, SILLY.
HE'S BEEN KEEPING AN EYE ON YOU FOR A WHILE NOW.
JUST WAIT UNTIL YOU MEET HIM. HE HAS BIG PLANS FOR YOU!
LOOK, I DON'T HAVE TIME FOR THIS. I NEED TO GET OUT OF HERE!
HONEY, THIS IS THE MALDIVES. PARADISE. HOW COULD YOU EVEN THINK OF LEAVING?
SPEAKING OF WHICH, IT'S TIME FOR A SWIM. CARE TO JOIN US?
WHAT THE HELL ARE YOU--
EXCUSE ME, MS. ACTEIA, MISTER VILLONE WELCOMES YOU TO HIS RESIDENCE, AND REQUESTS YOUR PRESENCE AT A LUNCHEON ON THE SOUTH TERRACE.
NOW IF YOU'LL FOLLOW ME, I'LL SHOW YOU TO YOUR ROOM.

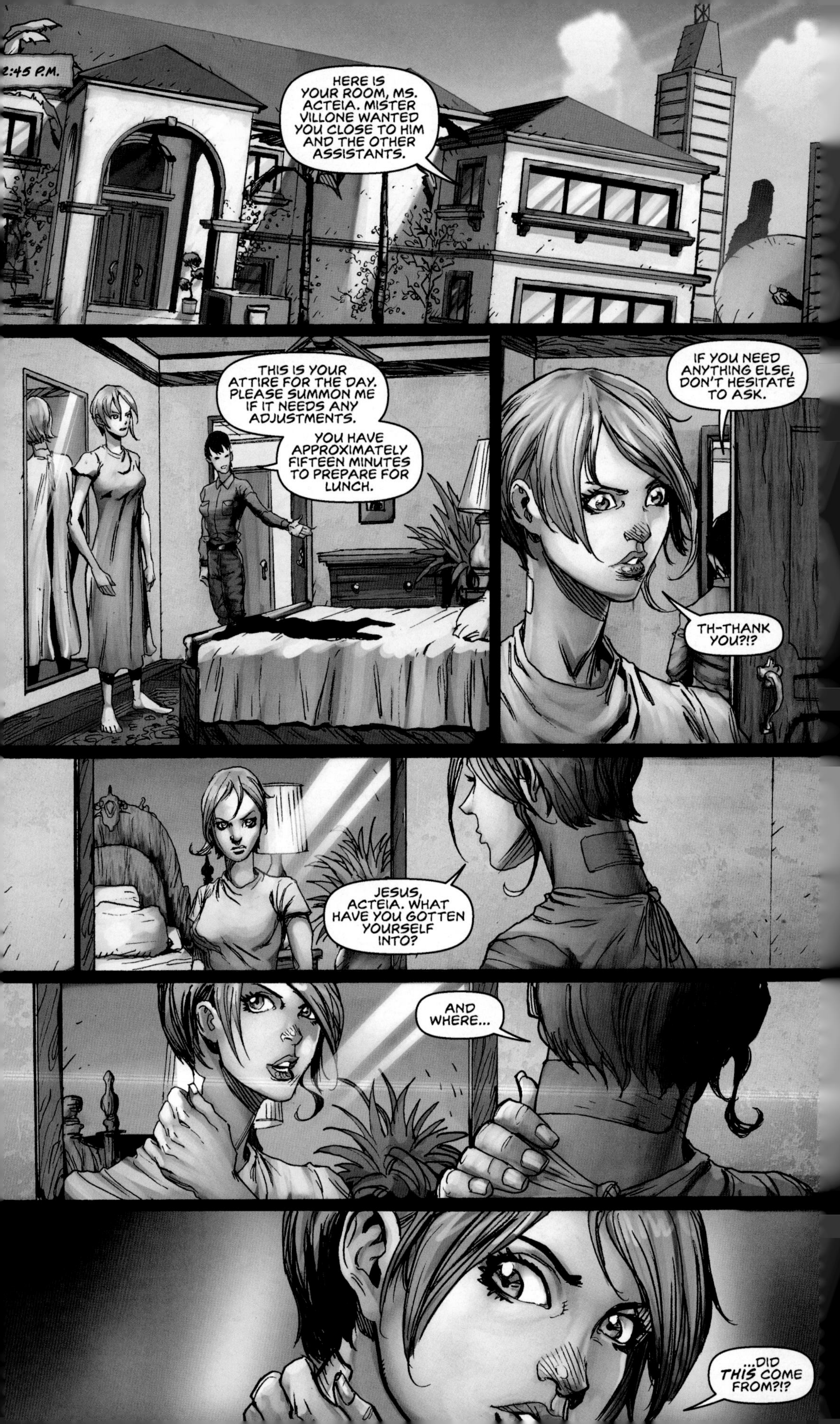
2:45 P.M.
HERE IS YOUR ROOM, MS. ACTEIA. MISTER VILLONE WANTED YOU CLOSE TO HIM AND THE OTHER ASSISTANTS.
THIS IS YOUR ATTIRE FOR THE DAY. PLEASE SUMMON ME IF IT NEEDS ANY ADJUSTMENTS.
YOU HAVE APPROXIMATELY FIFTEEN MINUTES TO PREPARE FOR LUNCH.
IF YOU NEED ANYTHING ELSE, DON'T HESITATE TO ASK.
TH-THANK YOU?!?
JESUS, ACTEIA. WHAT HAVE YOU GOTTEN YOURSELF INTO?
AND WHERE...
...DID *THIS* COME FROM?!?

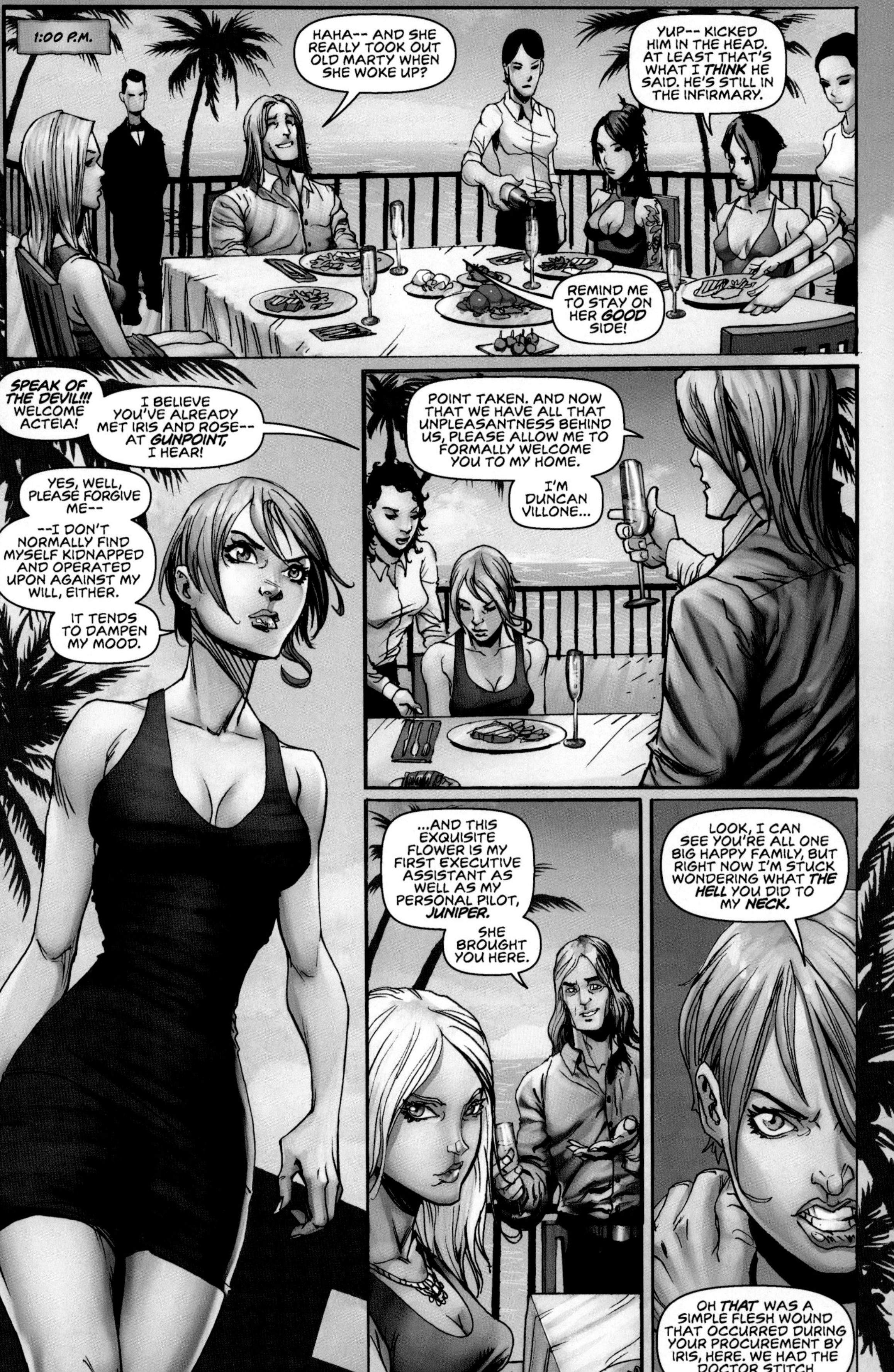
1:00 P.M.
HAHA-- AND SHE REALLY TOOK OUT OLD MARTY WHEN SHE WOKE UP?
YUP-- KICKED HIM IN THE HEAD. AT LEAST THAT'S WHAT I THINK HE SAID. HE'S STILL IN THE INFIRMARY.
REMIND ME TO STAY ON HER GOOD SIDE!
SPEAK OF THE DEVIL!!! WELCOME ACTEIA!
I BELIEVE YOU'VE ALREADY MET IRIS AND ROSE-- AT GUNPOINT, I HEAR!
YES, WELL, PLEASE FORGIVE ME--
--I DON'T NORMALLY FIND MYSELF KIDNAPPED AND OPERATED UPON AGAINST MY WILL, EITHER.
IT TENDS TO DAMPEN MY MOOD.
POINT TAKEN. AND NOW THAT WE HAVE ALL THAT UNPLEASANTNESS BEHIND US, PLEASE ALLOW ME TO FORMALLY WELCOME YOU TO MY HOME.
I'M DUNCAN VILLONE...
...AND THIS EXQUISITE FLOWER IS MY FIRST EXECUTIVE ASSISTANT AS WELL AS MY PERSONAL PILOT, JUNIPER.
SHE BROUGHT YOU HERE.
LOOK, I CAN SEE YOU'RE ALL ONE BIG HAPPY FAMILY, BUT RIGHT NOW I'M STUCK WONDERING WHAT THE HELL YOU DID TO MY NECK.
OH THAT WAS A SIMPLE FLESH WOUND THAT OCCURRED DURING YOUR PROCUREMENT BY IRIS, HERE. WE HAD THE DOCTOR STITCH YOU UP.

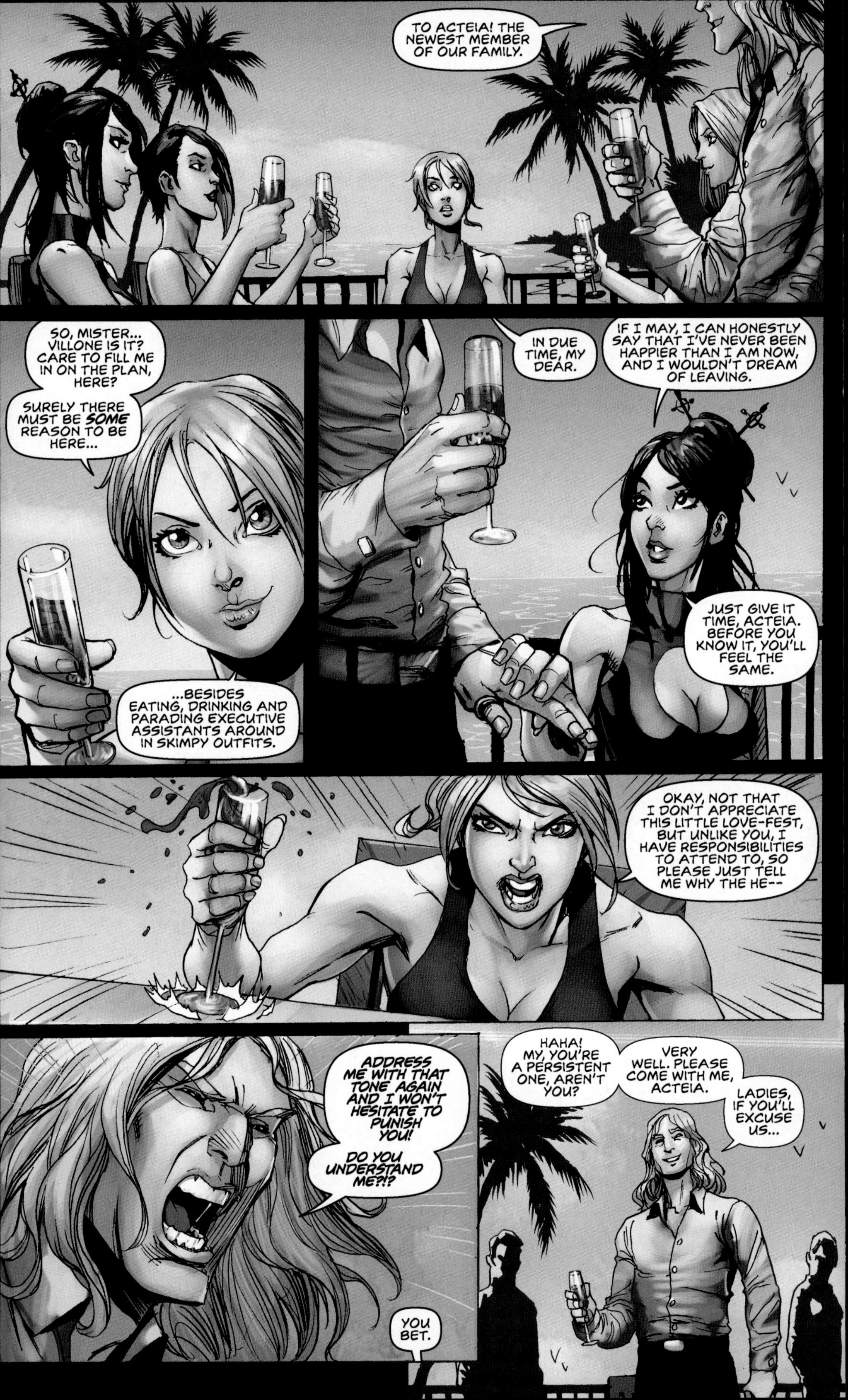
TO ACTEIA! THE NEWEST MEMBER OF OUR FAMILY.
SO, MISTER... VILLONE IS IT? CARE TO FILL ME IN ON THE PLAN, HERE?
SURELY THERE MUST BE SOME REASON TO BE HERE...
...BESIDES EATING, DRINKING AND PARADING EXECUTIVE ASSISTANTS AROUND IN SKIMPY OUTFITS.
IN DUE TIME, MY DEAR.
IF I MAY, I CAN HONESTLY SAY THAT I'VE NEVER BEEN HAPPIER THAN I AM NOW, AND I WOULDN'T DREAM OF LEAVING.
JUST GIVE IT TIME, ACTEIA. BEFORE YOU KNOW IT, YOU'LL FEEL THE SAME.
OKAY, NOT THAT I DON'T APPRECIATE THIS LITTLE LOVE-FEST, BUT UNLIKE YOU, I HAVE RESPONSIBILITIES TO ATTEND TO, SO PLEASE JUST TELL ME WHY THE HE--
ADDRESS ME WITH THAT TONE AGAIN AND I WON'T HESITATE TO PUNISH YOU!
DO YOU UNDERSTAND ME?!?
YOU BET.
HAHA! MY, YOU'RE A PERSISTENT ONE, AREN'T YOU?
VERY WELL. PLEASE COME WITH ME, ACTEIA.
LADIES, IF YOU'LL EXCUSE US...

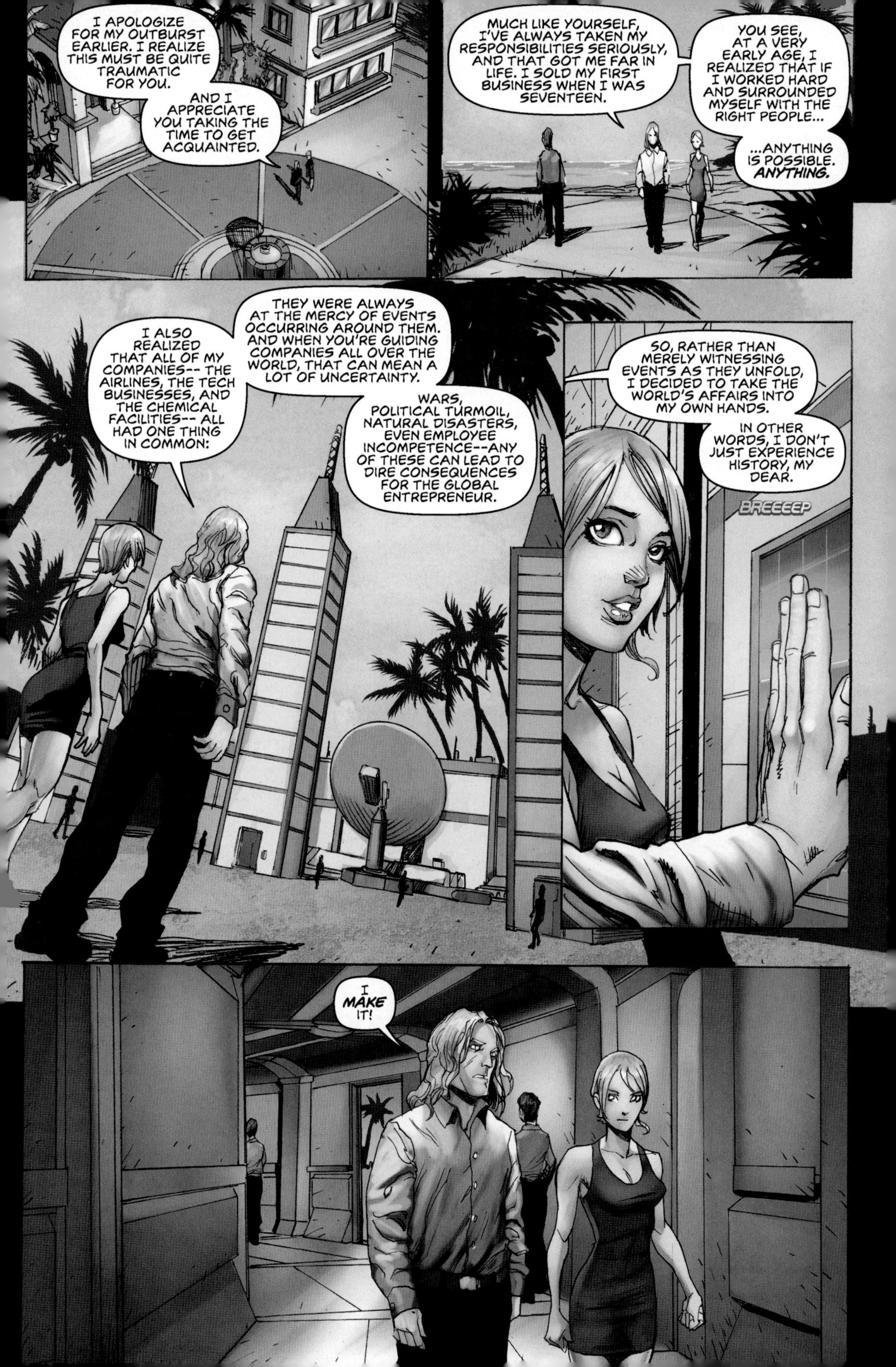
I APOLOGIZE FOR MY OUTBURST EARLIER. I REALIZE THIS MUST BE QUITE TRAUMATIC FOR YOU.
AND I APPRECIATE YOU TAKING THE TIME TO GET ACQUAINTED.
MUCH LIKE YOURSELF, I'VE ALWAYS TAKEN MY RESPONSIBILITIES SERIOUSLY, AND THAT GOT ME FAR IN LIFE. I SOLD MY FIRST BUSINESS WHEN I WAS SEVENTEEN.
YOU SEE, AT A VERY EARLY AGE, I REALIZED THAT IF I WORKED HARD AND SURROUNDED MYSELF WITH THE RIGHT PEOPLE...
...ANYTHING IS POSSIBLE. ***ANYTHING.***
I ALSO REALIZED THAT ALL OF MY COMPANIES-- THE AIRLINES, THE TECH BUSINESSES, AND THE CHEMICAL FACILITIES-- ALL HAD ONE THING IN COMMON:
THEY WERE ALWAYS AT THE MERCY OF EVENTS OCCURRING AROUND THEM. AND WHEN YOU'RE GUIDING COMPANIES ALL OVER THE WORLD, THAT CAN MEAN A LOT OF UNCERTAINTY.
WARS, POLITICAL TURMOIL, NATURAL DISASTERS, EVEN EMPLOYEE INCOMPETENCE--ANY OF THESE CAN LEAD TO DIRE CONSEQUENCES FOR THE GLOBAL ENTREPRENEUR.
SO, RATHER THAN MERELY WITNESSING EVENTS AS THEY UNFOLD, I DECIDED TO TAKE THE WORLD'S AFFAIRS INTO MY OWN HANDS.
IN OTHER WORDS, I DON'T JUST EXPERIENCE HISTORY, MY DEAR.
BREEEEP
I ***MAKE*** IT!

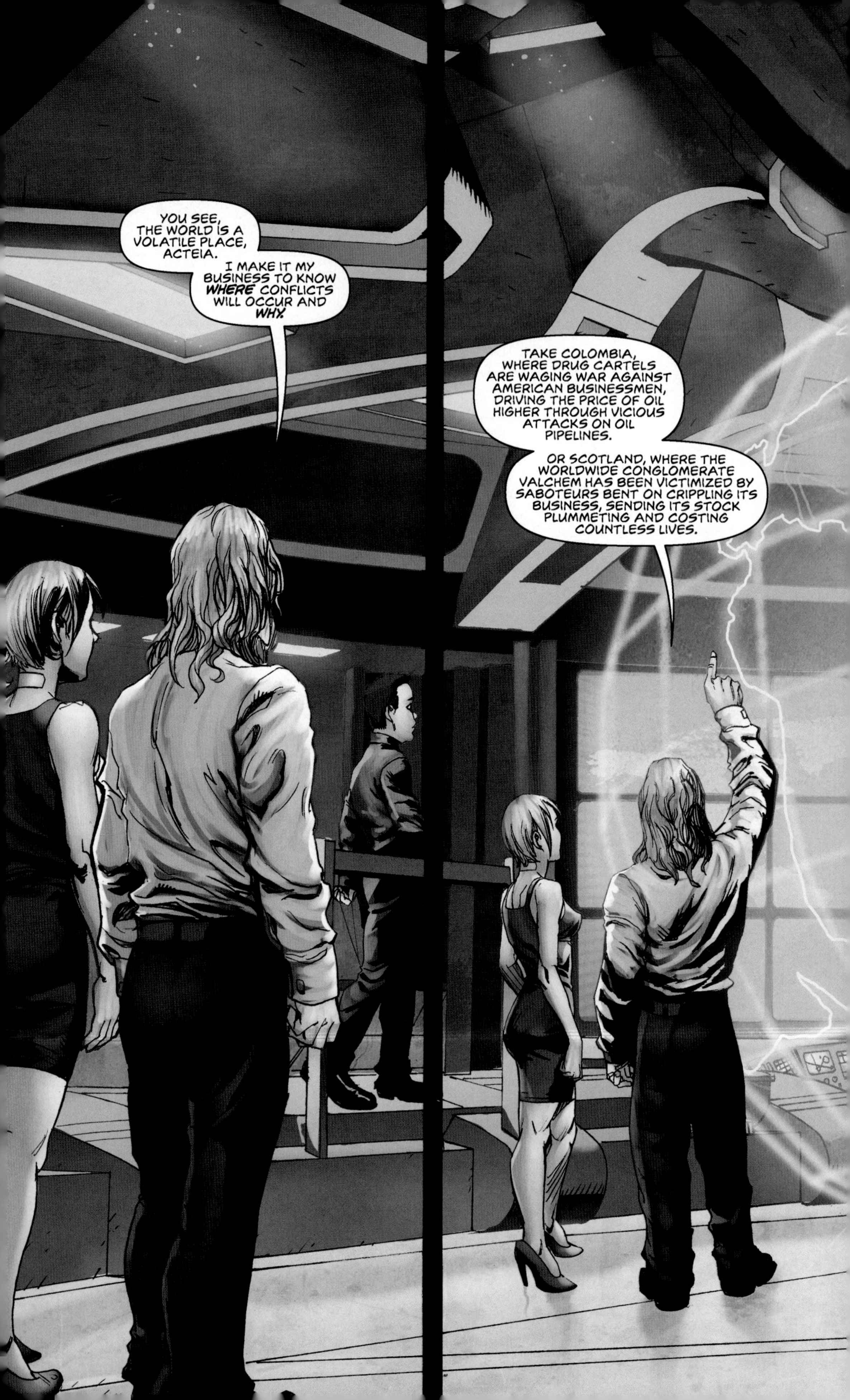
YOU SEE, THE WORLD IS A VOLATILE PLACE, ACTEIA.
I MAKE IT MY BUSINESS TO KNOW *WHERE* CONFLICTS WILL OCCUR AND *WHY*.
TAKE COLOMBIA, WHERE DRUG CARTELS ARE WAGING WAR AGAINST AMERICAN BUSINESSMEN, DRIVING THE PRICE OF OIL HIGHER THROUGH VICIOUS ATTACKS ON OIL PIPELINES.
OR SCOTLAND, WHERE THE WORLDWIDE CONGLOMERATE VALCHEM HAS BEEN VICTIMIZED BY SABOTEURS BENT ON CRIPPLING ITS BUSINESS, SENDING ITS STOCK PLUMMETING AND COSTING COUNTLESS LIVES.

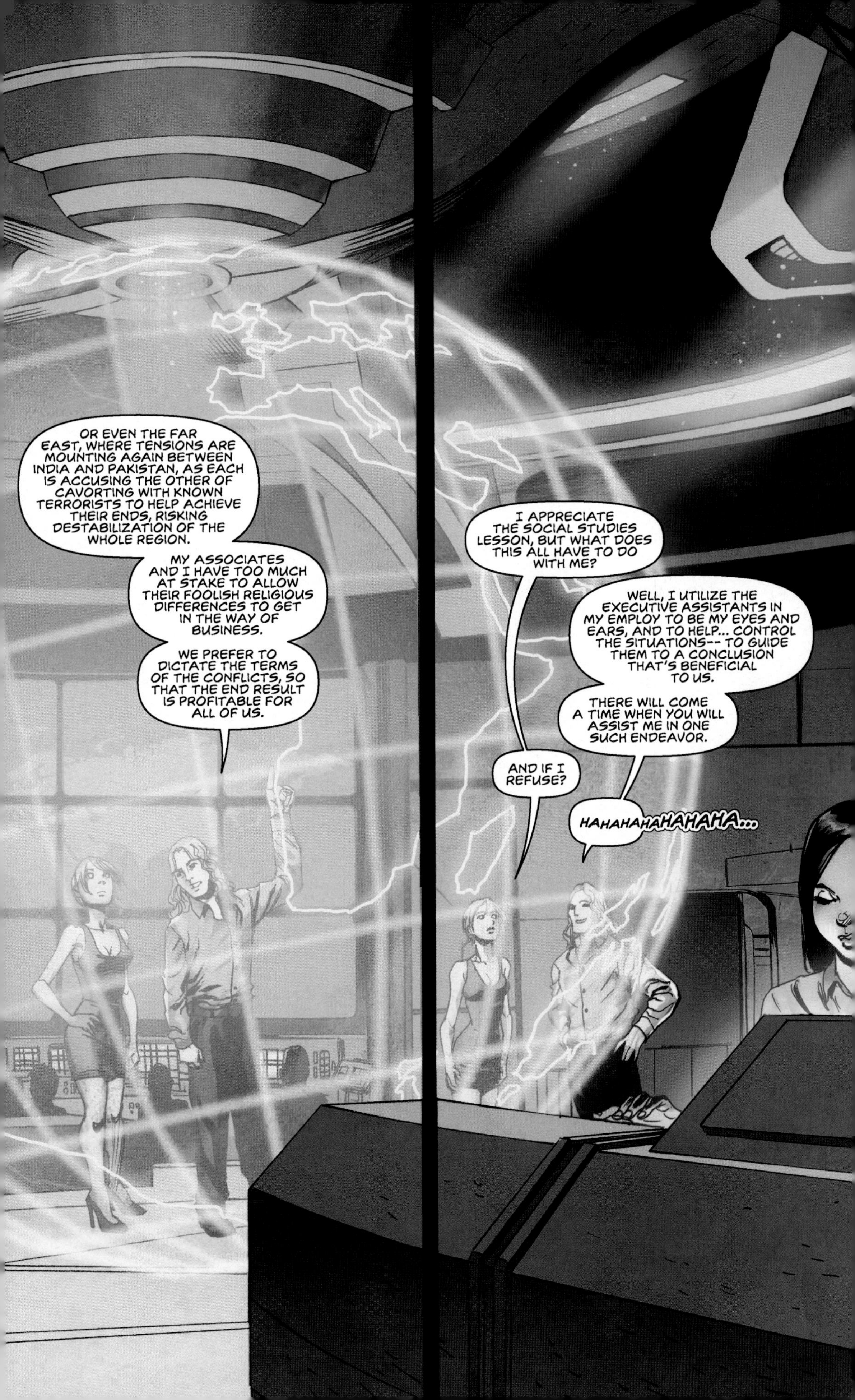
OR EVEN THE FAR EAST, WHERE TENSIONS ARE MOUNTING AGAIN BETWEEN INDIA AND PAKISTAN, AS EACH IS ACCUSING THE OTHER OF CAVORTING WITH KNOWN TERRORISTS TO HELP ACHIEVE THEIR ENDS, RISKING DESTABILIZATION OF THE WHOLE REGION.
MY ASSOCIATES AND I HAVE TOO MUCH AT STAKE TO ALLOW THEIR FOOLISH RELIGIOUS DIFFERENCES TO GET IN THE WAY OF BUSINESS.
WE PREFER TO DICTATE THE TERMS OF THE CONFLICTS, SO THAT THE END RESULT IS PROFITABLE FOR ALL OF US.
I APPRECIATE THE SOCIAL STUDIES LESSON, BUT WHAT DOES THIS ALL HAVE TO DO WITH ME?
WELL, I UTILIZE THE EXECUTIVE ASSISTANTS IN MY EMPLOY TO BE MY EYES AND EARS, AND TO HELP... CONTROL THE SITUATIONS-- TO GUIDE THEM TO A CONCLUSION THAT'S BENEFICIAL TO US.
THERE WILL COME A TIME WHEN YOU WILL ASSIST ME IN ONE SUCH ENDEAVOR.
AND IF I REFUSE?
HAHAHAHAHAHAHA...

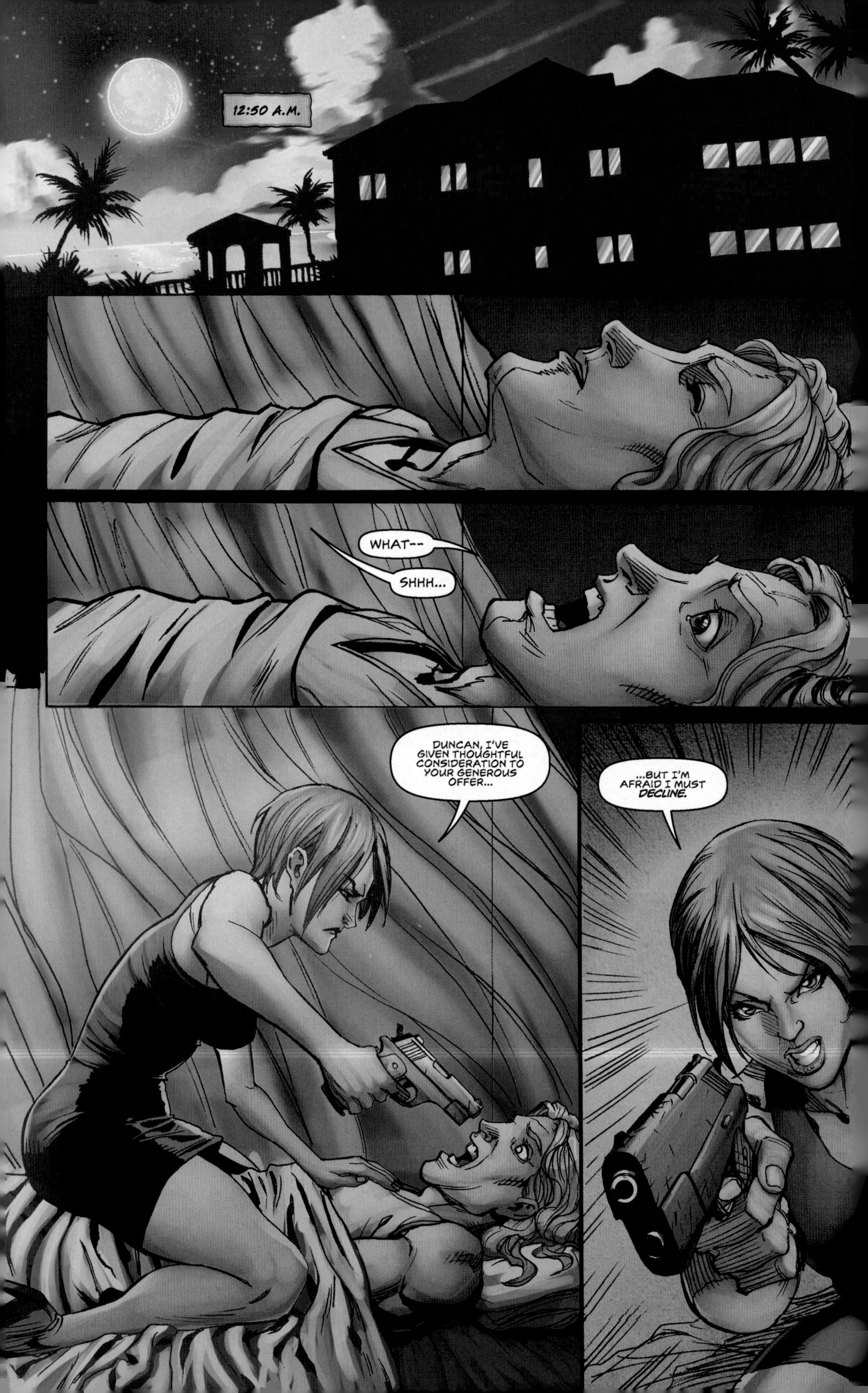
12:50 A.M.
WHAT--
SHHH...
DUNCAN, I'VE GIVEN THOUGHTFUL CONSIDERATION TO YOUR GENEROUS OFFER...
...BUT I'M AFRAID I MUST *DECLINE.*

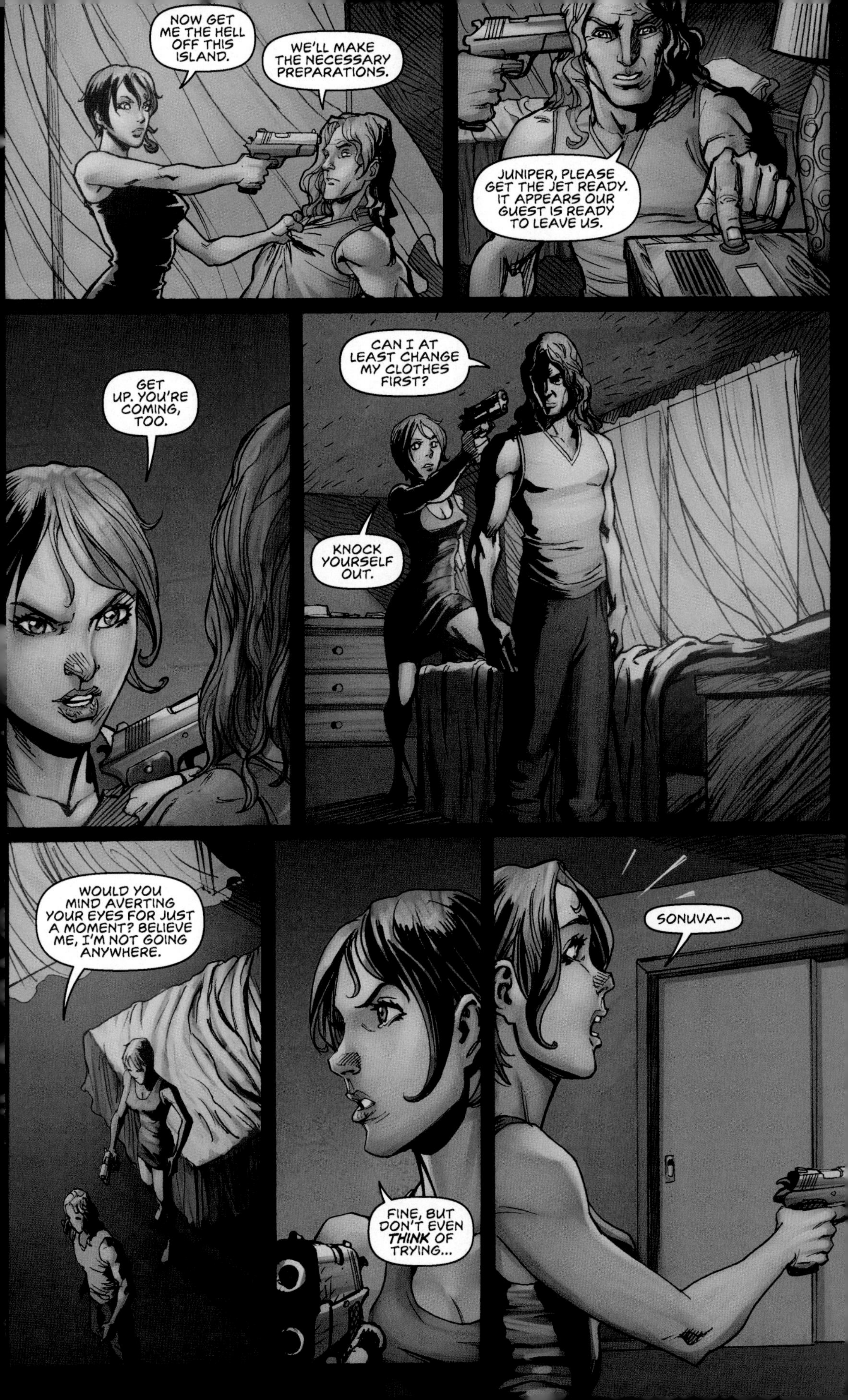
NOW GET ME THE HELL OFF THIS ISLAND.
WE'LL MAKE THE NECESSARY PREPARATIONS.
JUNIPER, PLEASE GET THE JET READY. IT APPEARS OUR GUEST IS READY TO LEAVE US.
GET UP. YOU'RE COMING, TOO.
CAN I AT LEAST CHANGE MY CLOTHES FIRST?
KNOCK YOURSELF OUT.
WOULD YOU MIND AVERTING YOUR EYES FOR JUST A MOMENT? BELIEVE ME, I'M NOT GOING ANYWHERE.
FINE, BUT DON'T EVEN *THINK* OF TRYING...
SONUVA--

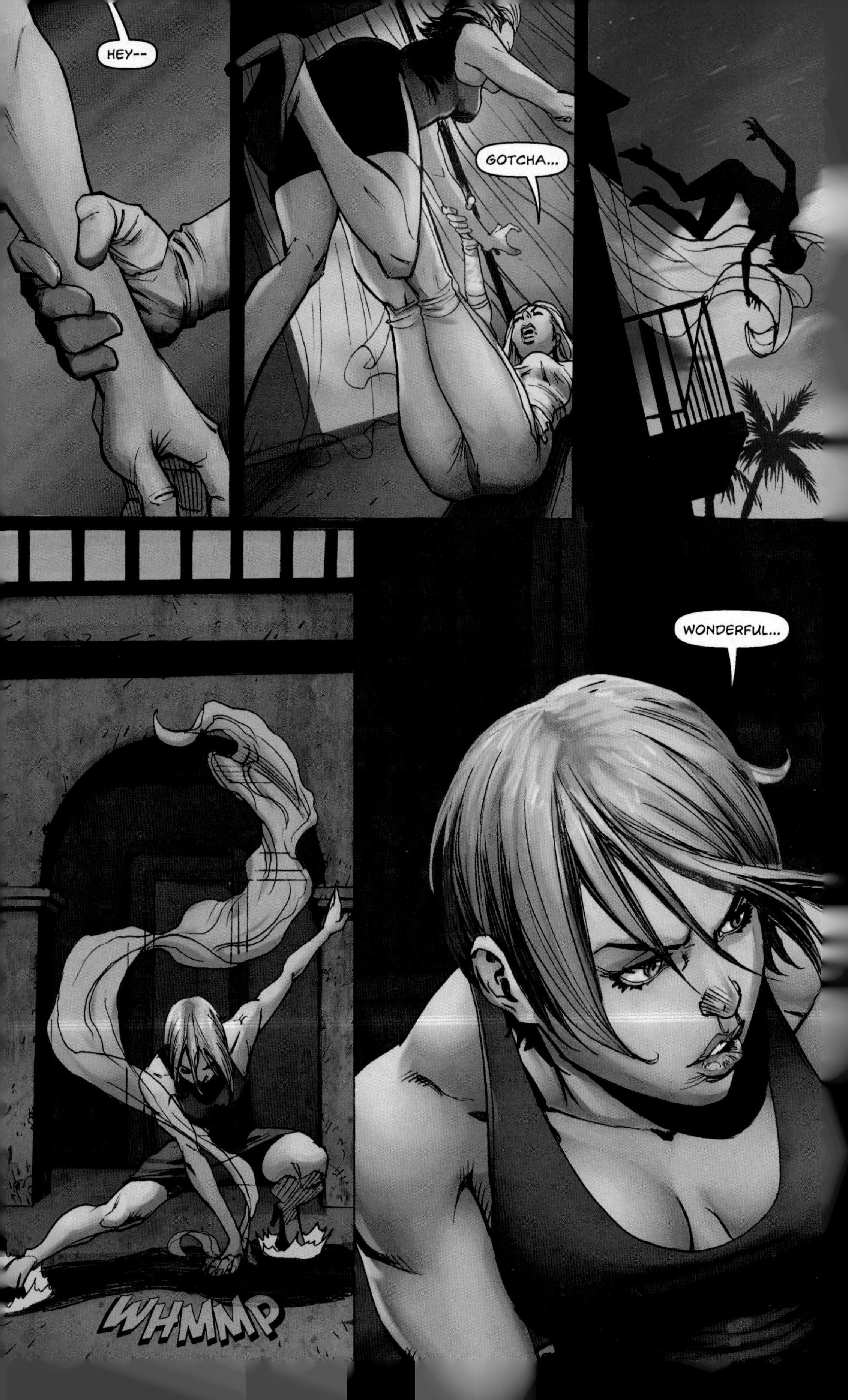
HEY--
GOTCHA...
WHMMP
WONDERFUL...

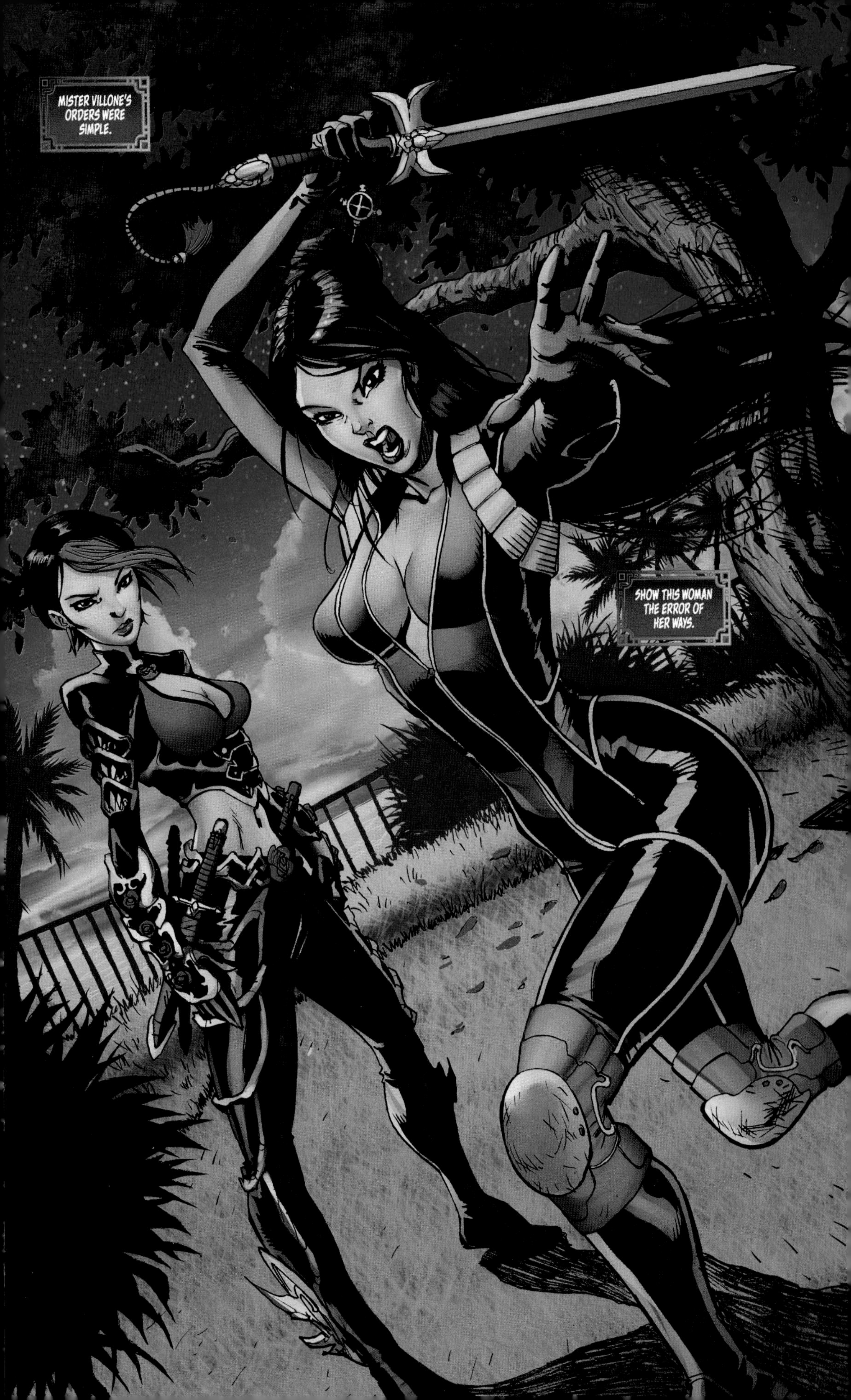
MISTER VILLONE'S ORDERS WERE SIMPLE.
SHOW THIS WOMAN THE ERROR OF HER WAYS.

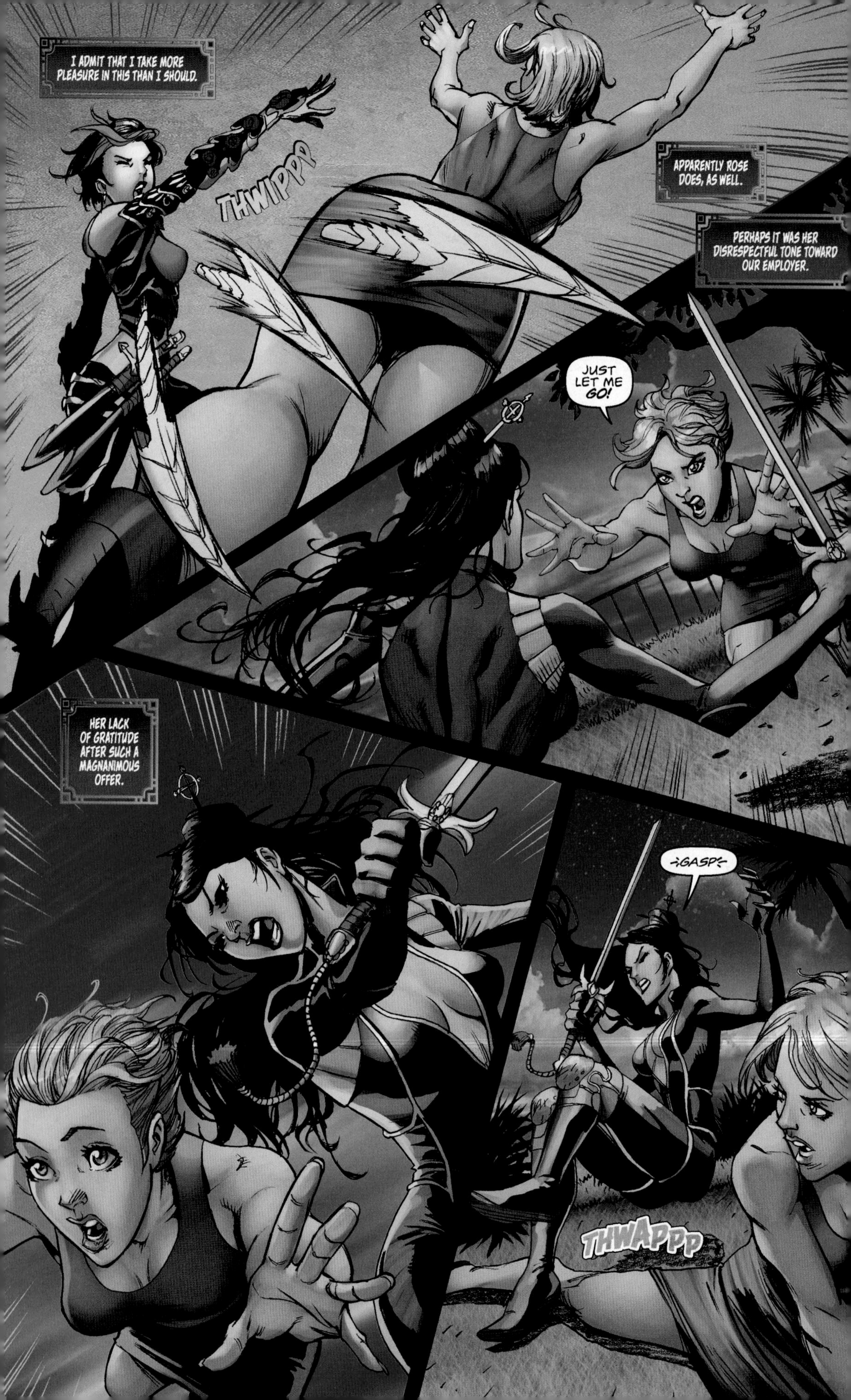

I ADMIT THAT I TAKE MORE PLEASURE IN THIS THAN I SHOULD.
THWIPPP
APPARENTLY ROSE DOES, AS WELL.
PERHAPS IT WAS HER DISRESPECTFUL TONE TOWARD OUR EMPLOYER.
JUST LET ME GO!
HER LACK OF GRATITUDE AFTER SUCH A MAGNANIMOUS OFFER.
GASP
THWAPPP

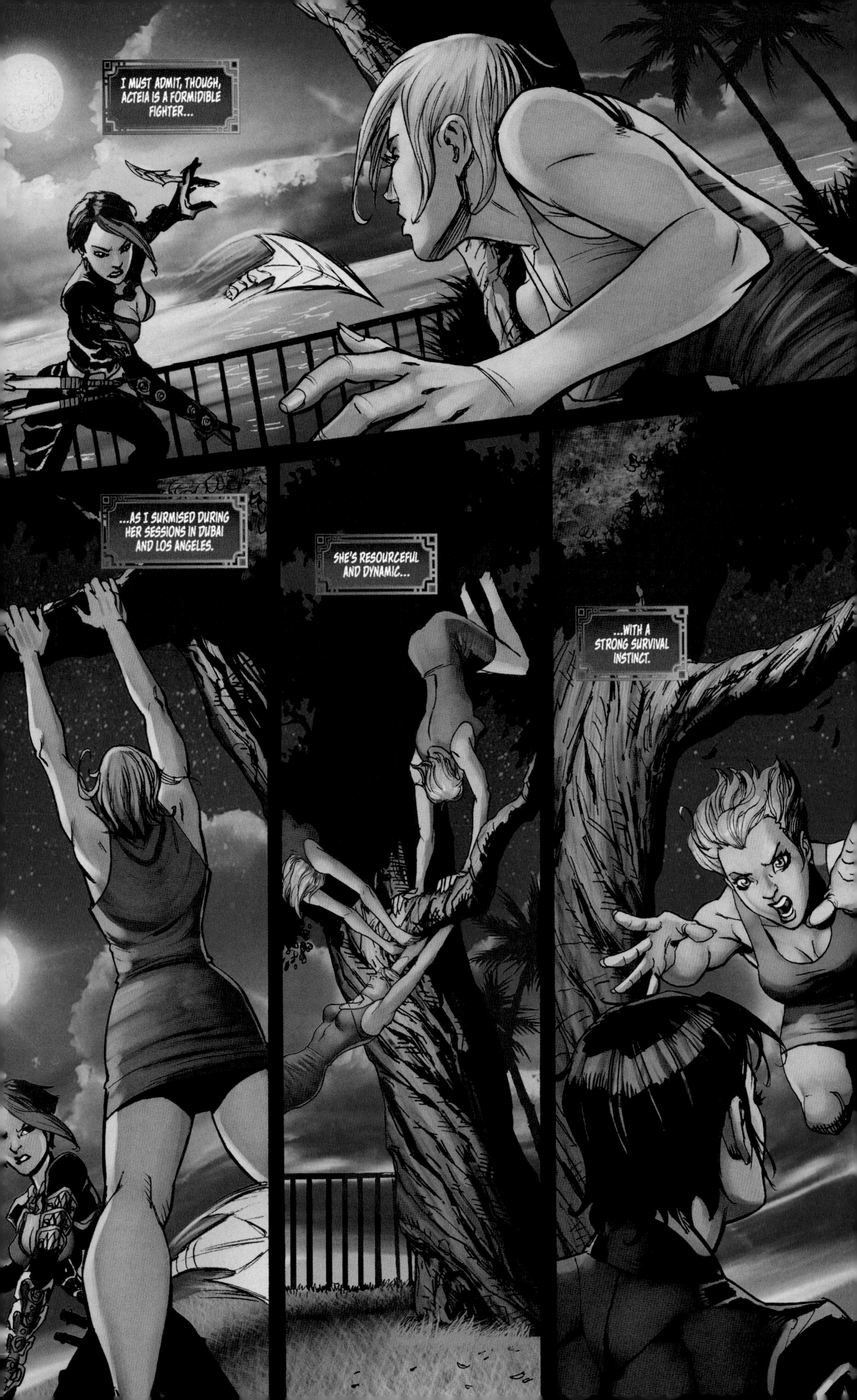
I MUST ADMIT, THOUGH, ACTEIA IS A FORMIDIBLE FIGHTER...
...AS I SURMISED DURING HER SESSIONS IN DUBAI AND LOS ANGELES.
SHE'S RESOURCEFUL AND DYNAMIC...
...WITH A STRONG SURVIVAL INSTINCT.

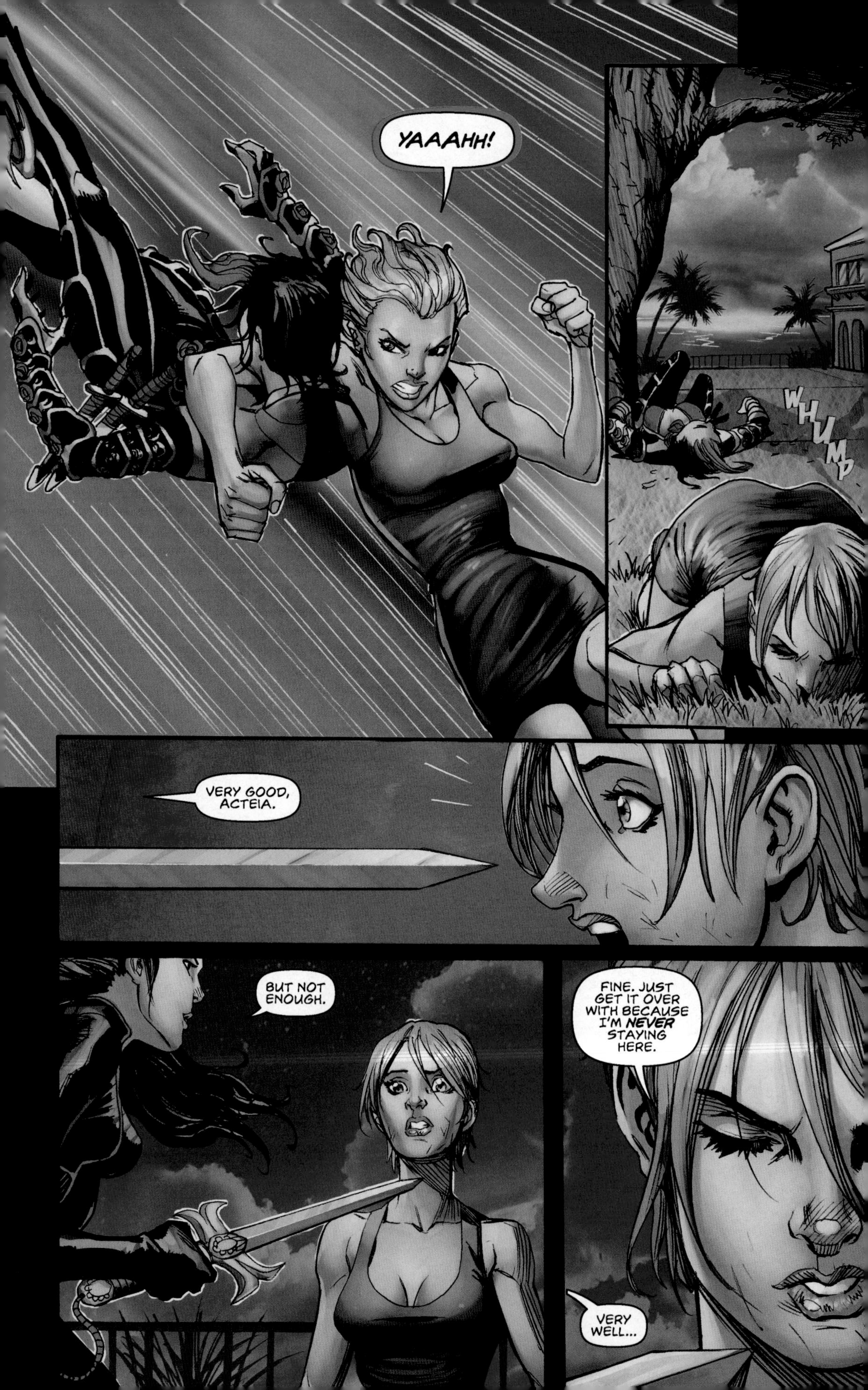
YAAAHH!
WHUMP
VERY GOOD, ACTEIA.
BUT NOT ENOUGH.
FINE. JUST GET IT OVER WITH BECAUSE I'M *NEVER* STAYING HERE.
VERY WELL...

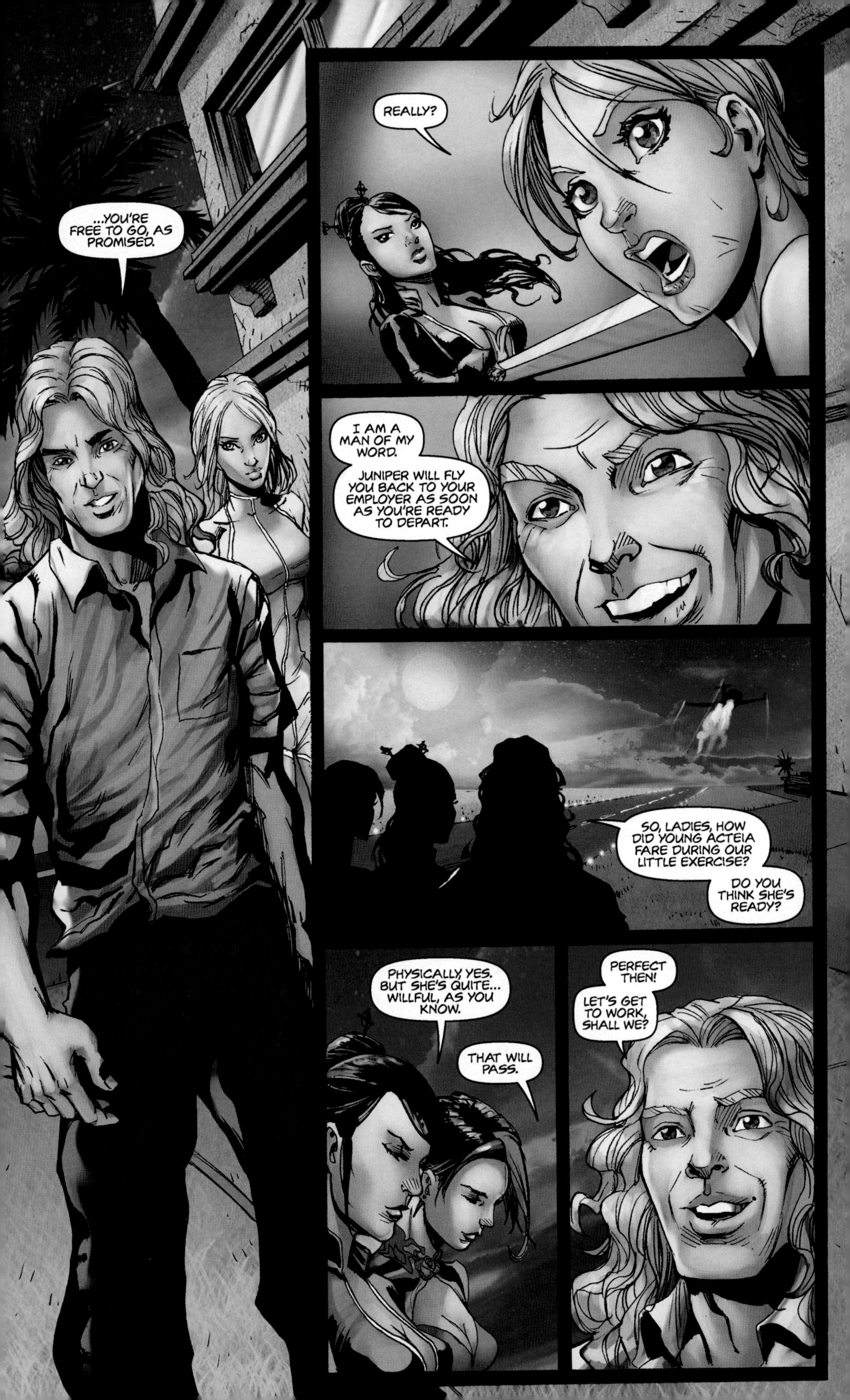
...YOU'RE FREE TO GO, AS PROMISED.
REALLY?
I AM A MAN OF MY WORD.
JUNIPER WILL FLY YOU BACK TO YOUR EMPLOYER AS SOON AS YOU'RE READY TO DEPART.
SO, LADIES, HOW DID YOUNG ACTEIA FARE DURING OUR LITTLE EXERCISE?
DO YOU THINK SHE'S READY?
PHYSICALLY, YES. BUT SHE'S QUITE... WILLFUL, AS YOU KNOW.
THAT WILL PASS.
PERFECT THEN!
LET'S GET TO WORK, SHALL WE?

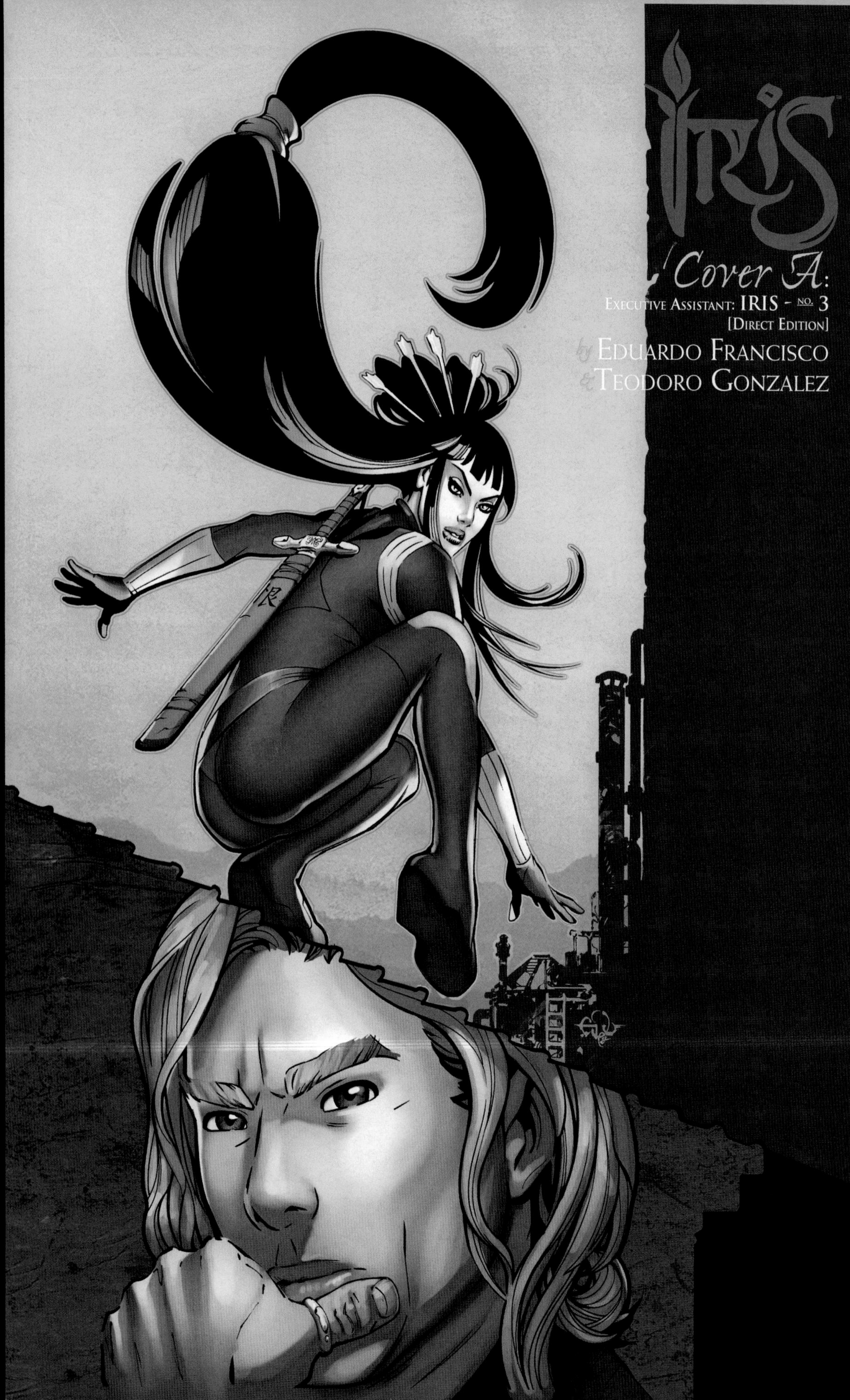
IRIS
Cover A:
EXECUTIVE ASSISTANT: IRIS - NO. 3
[DIRECT EDITION]
by EDUARDO FRANCISCO
& TEODORO GONZALEZ

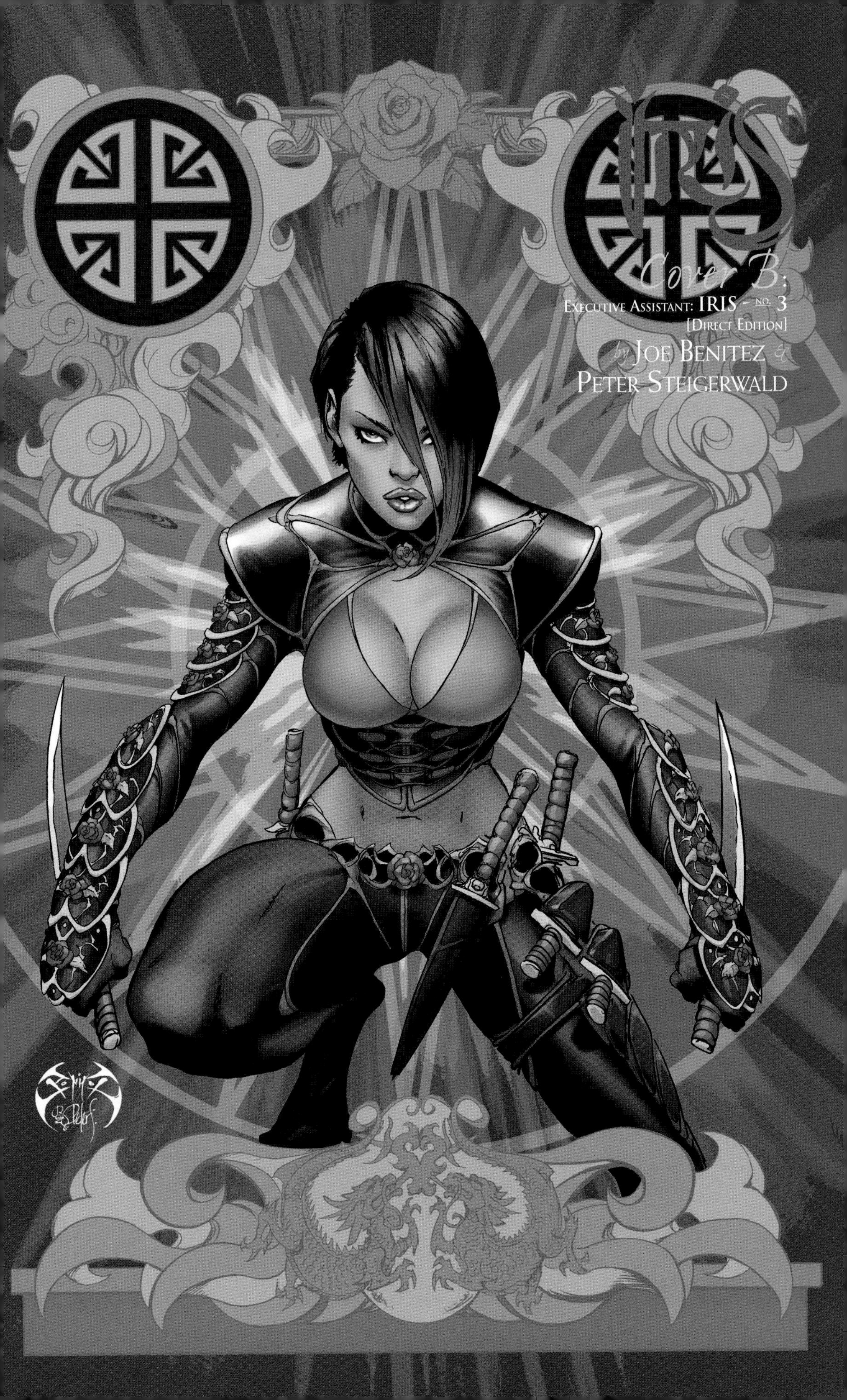
IRIS
Cover B:
Executive Assistant: IRIS - No. 3
[Direct Edition]
by Joe Benitez &
Peter Steigerwald

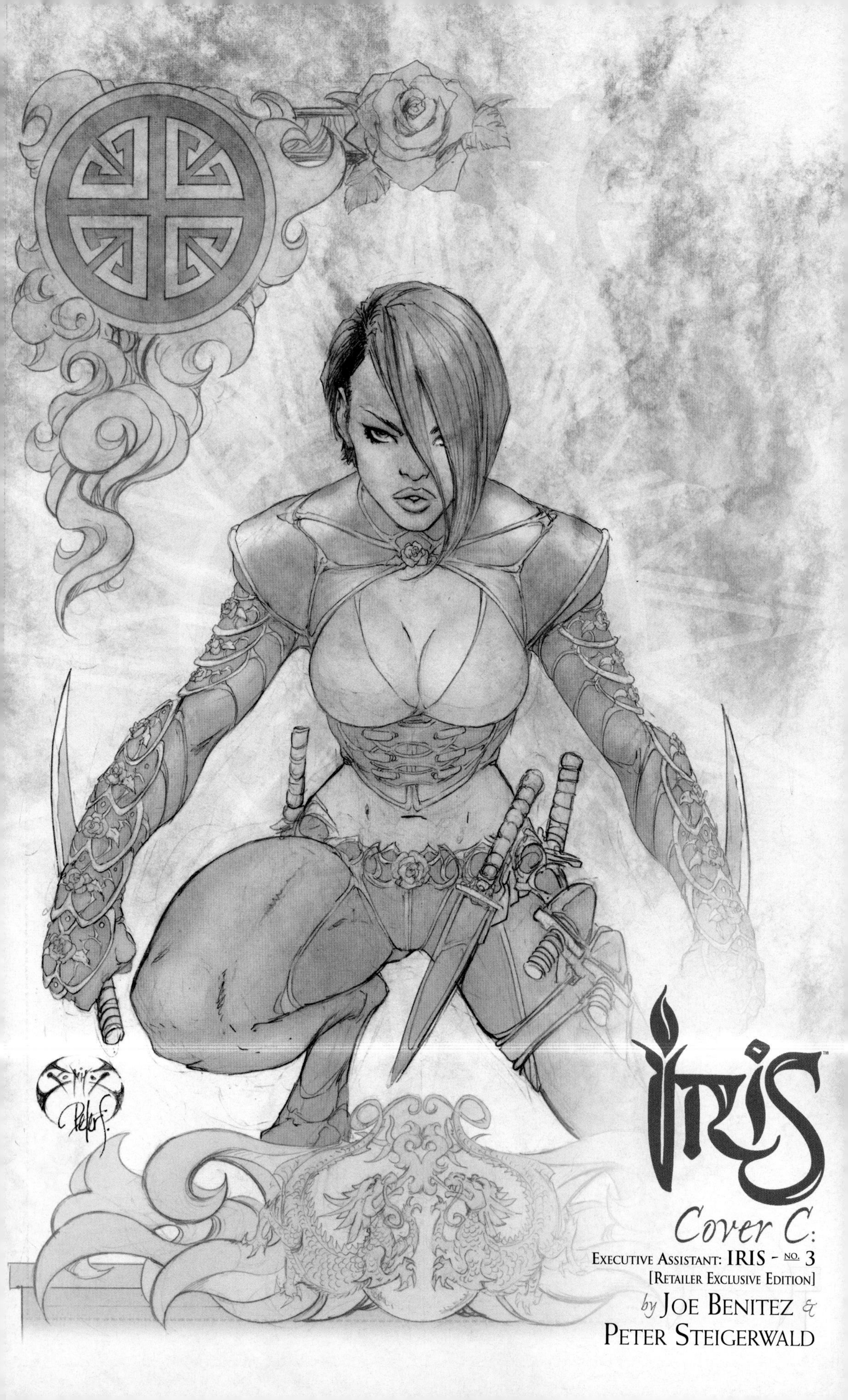
IRIS™
Cover C:
EXECUTIVE ASSISTANT: IRIS - NO. 3
[RETAILER EXCLUSIVE EDITION]
by JOE BENITEZ &
PETER STEIGERWALD

CHAPTER FOUR

THREE

"WHAT HAVE YOU DONE FOR ME LATELY"

WRITER
DAVID WOHL

PENCILS
RYAN ODAGAWA

COLORS
TEODORO GONZALEZ

LETTERING
JOSH REED

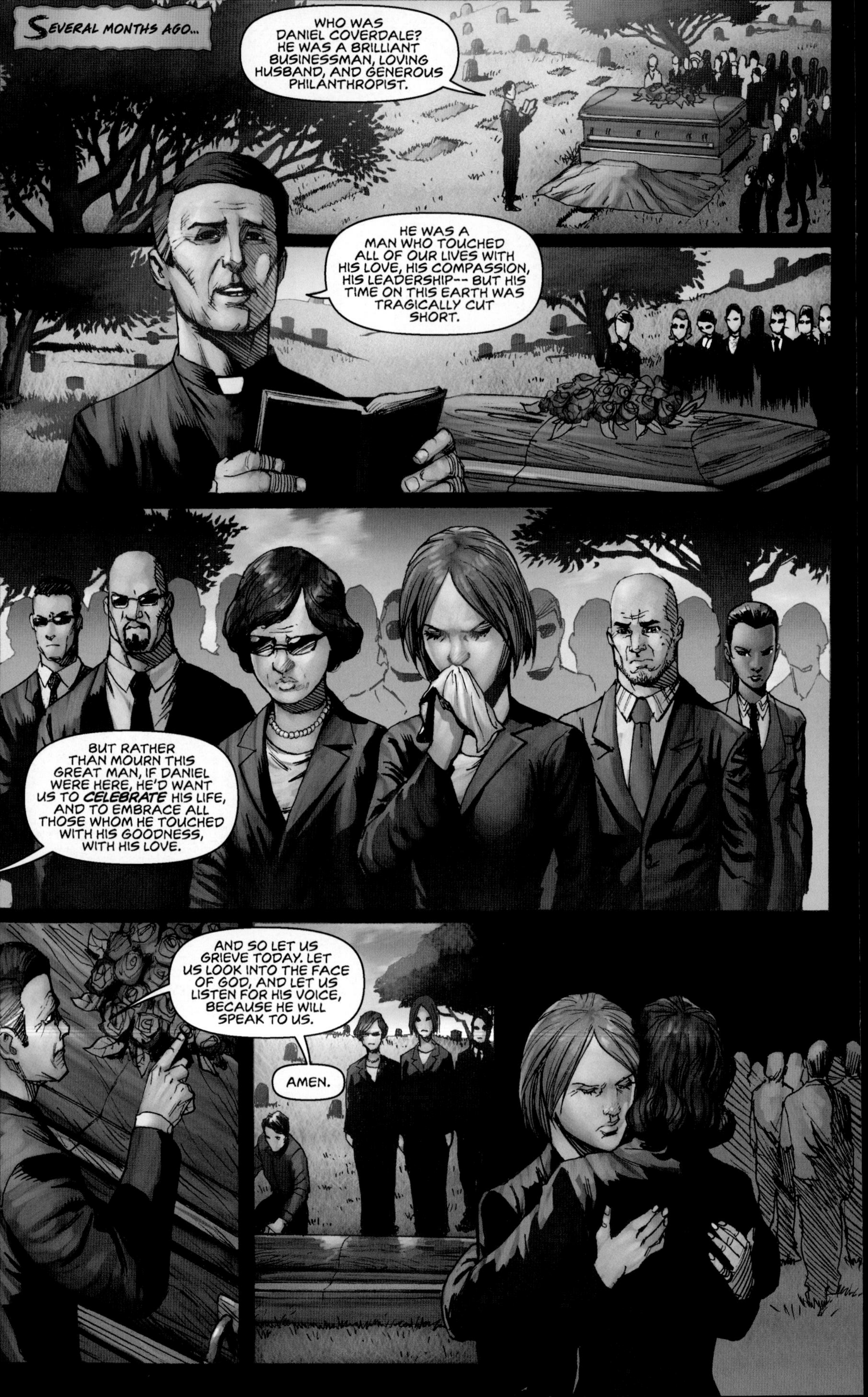
SEVERAL MONTHS AGO...
WHO WAS DANIEL COVERDALE? HE WAS A BRILLIANT BUSINESSMAN, LOVING HUSBAND, AND GENEROUS PHILANTHROPIST.
HE WAS A MAN WHO TOUCHED ALL OF OUR LIVES WITH HIS LOVE, HIS COMPASSION, HIS LEADERSHIP-- BUT HIS TIME ON THIS EARTH WAS TRAGICALLY CUT SHORT.
BUT RATHER THAN MOURN THIS GREAT MAN, IF DANIEL WERE HERE, HE'D WANT US TO *CELEBRATE* HIS LIFE, AND TO EMBRACE ALL THOSE WHOM HE TOUCHED WITH HIS GOODNESS, WITH HIS LOVE.
AND SO LET US GRIEVE TODAY. LET US LOOK INTO THE FACE OF GOD, AND LET US LISTEN FOR HIS VOICE, BECAUSE HE WILL SPEAK TO US.
AMEN.

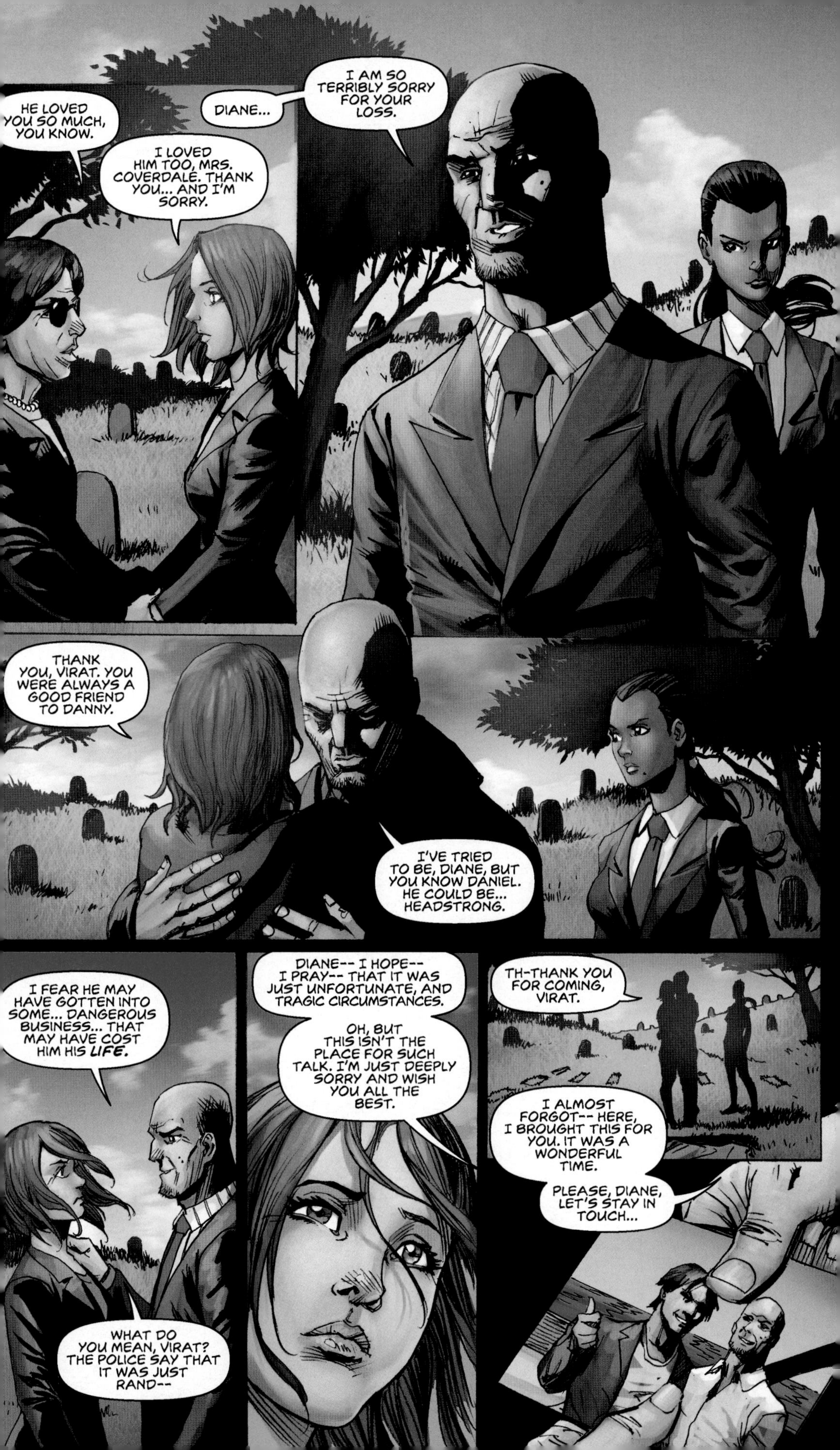
HE LOVED YOU SO MUCH, YOU KNOW.
I LOVED HIM TOO, MRS. COVERDALE. THANK YOU... AND I'M SORRY.
DIANE...
I AM SO TERRIBLY SORRY FOR YOUR LOSS.
THANK YOU, VIRAT. YOU WERE ALWAYS A GOOD FRIEND TO DANNY.
I'VE TRIED TO BE, DIANE, BUT YOU KNOW DANIEL. HE COULD BE... HEADSTRONG.
I FEAR HE MAY HAVE GOTTEN INTO SOME... DANGEROUS BUSINESS... THAT MAY HAVE COST HIM HIS LIFE.
WHAT DO YOU MEAN, VIRAT? THE POLICE SAY THAT IT WAS JUST RAND--
DIANE-- I HOPE-- I PRAY-- THAT IT WAS JUST UNFORTUNATE, AND TRAGIC CIRCUMSTANCES.
OH, BUT THIS ISN'T THE PLACE FOR SUCH TALK. I'M JUST DEEPLY SORRY AND WISH YOU ALL THE BEST.
TH-THANK YOU FOR COMING, VIRAT.
I ALMOST FORGOT-- HERE, I BROUGHT THIS FOR YOU. IT WAS A WONDERFUL TIME.
PLEASE, DIANE, LET'S STAY IN TOUCH...

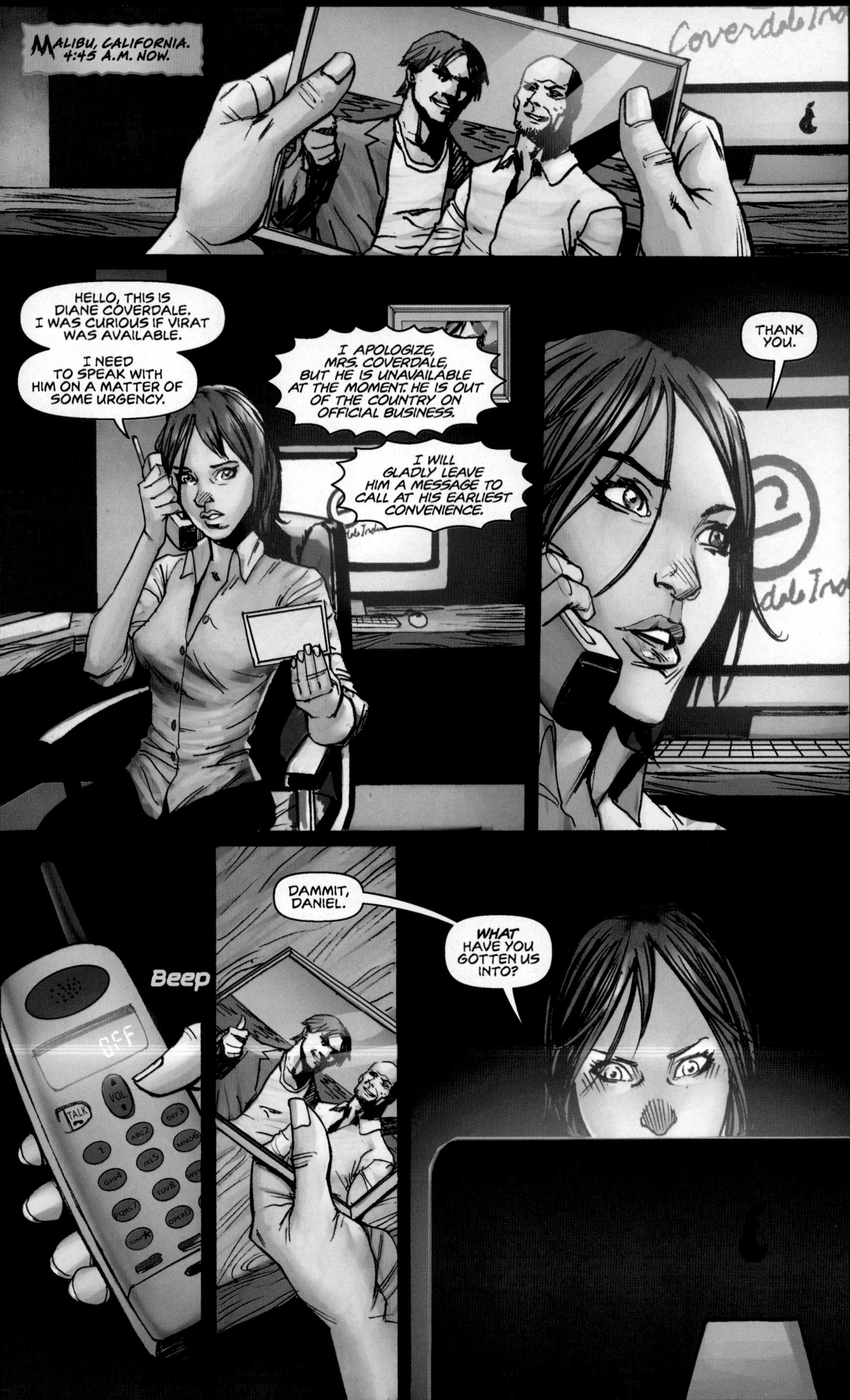
MALIBU, CALIFORNIA. 4:45 A.M. NOW.
Coverdale Ind
HELLO, THIS IS DIANE COVERDALE. I WAS CURIOUS IF VIRAT WAS AVAILABLE.
I NEED TO SPEAK WITH HIM ON A MATTER OF SOME URGENCY.
I APOLOGIZE, MRS. COVERDALE, BUT HE IS UNAVAILABLE AT THE MOMENT. HE IS OUT OF THE COUNTRY ON OFFICIAL BUSINESS.
I WILL GLADLY LEAVE HIM A MESSAGE TO CALL AT HIS EARLIEST CONVENIENCE.
THANK YOU.
Beep
OFF
DAMMIT, DANIEL.
WHAT HAVE YOU GOTTEN US INTO?

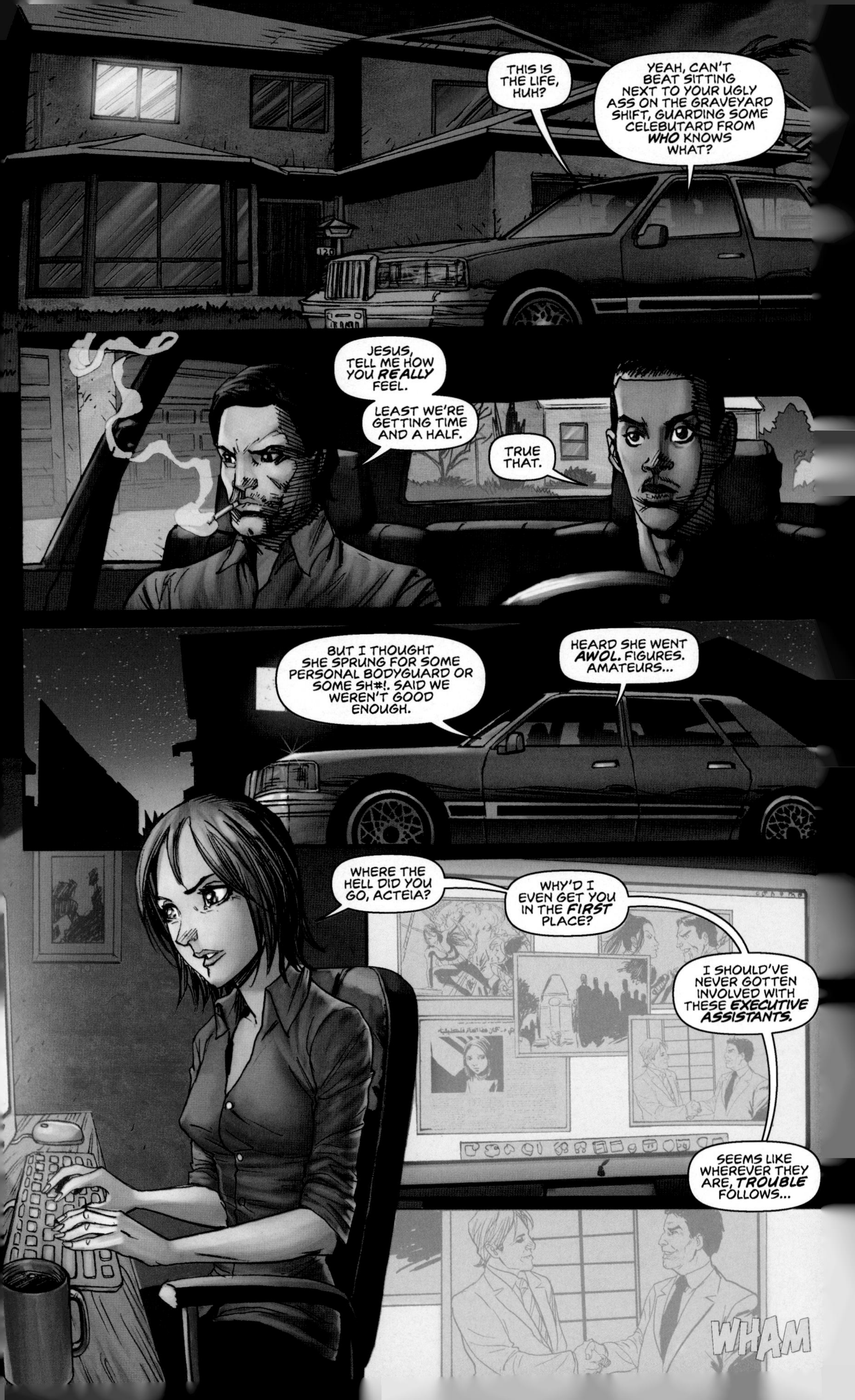
THIS IS THE LIFE, HUH?
YEAH, CAN'T BEAT SITTING NEXT TO YOUR UGLY ASS ON THE GRAVEYARD SHIFT, GUARDING SOME CELEBUTARD FROM WHO KNOWS WHAT?
JESUS, TELL ME HOW YOU REALLY FEEL.
LEAST WE'RE GETTING TIME AND A HALF.
TRUE THAT.
BUT I THOUGHT SHE SPRUNG FOR SOME PERSONAL BODYGUARD OR SOME SH#!. SAID WE WEREN'T GOOD ENOUGH.
HEARD SHE WENT AWOL. FIGURES. AMATEURS...
WHERE THE HELL DID YOU GO, ACTEIA?
WHY'D I EVEN GET YOU IN THE FIRST PLACE?
I SHOULD'VE NEVER GOTTEN INVOLVED WITH THESE EXECUTIVE ASSISTANTS.
SEEMS LIKE WHEREVER THEY ARE, TROUBLE FOLLOWS...
WHAM

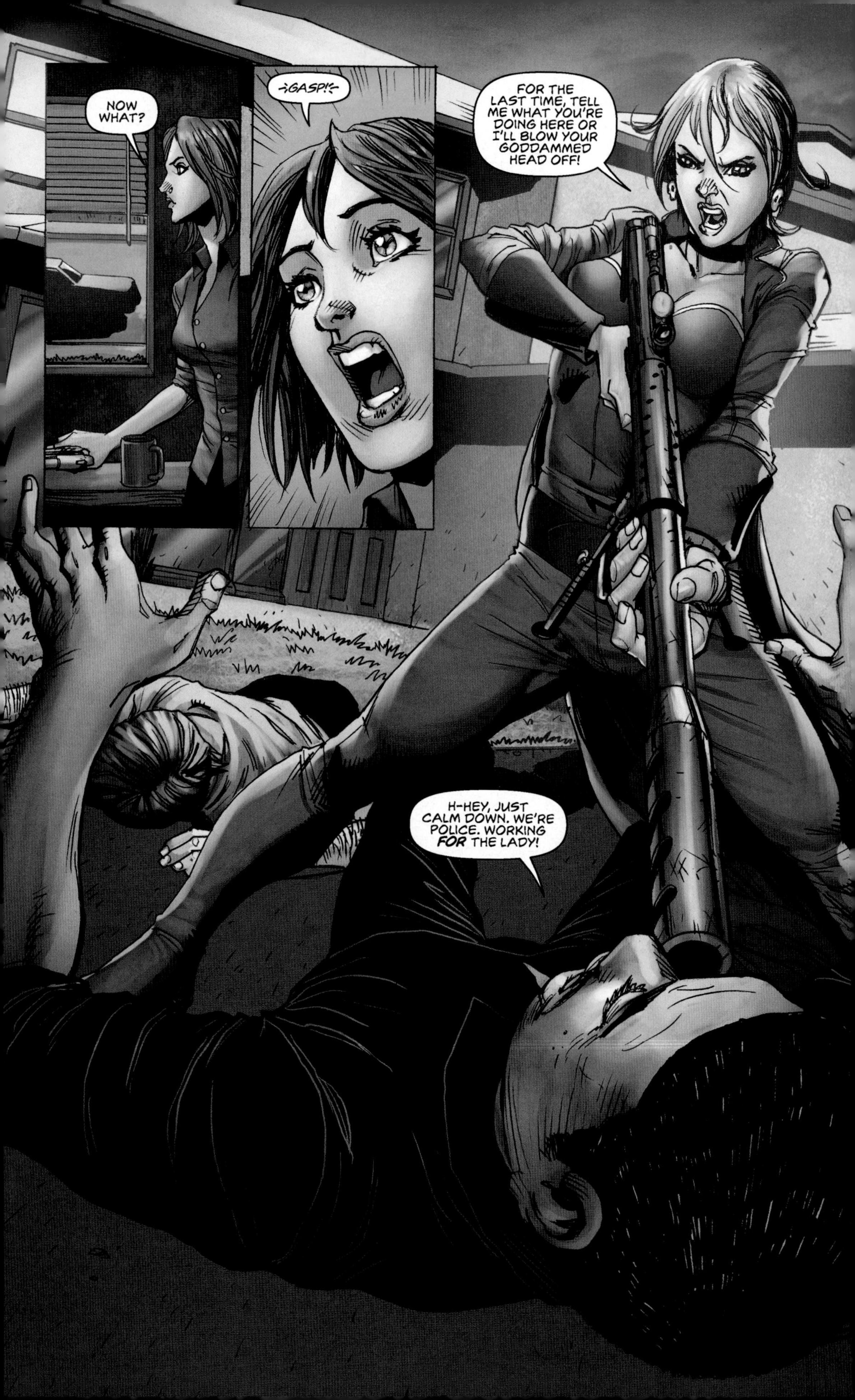
NOW WHAT?
-GASP!-
FOR THE LAST TIME, TELL ME WHAT YOU'RE DOING HERE OR I'LL BLOW YOUR GODDAMMED HEAD OFF!
H-HEY, JUST CALM DOWN. WE'RE POLICE. WORKING FOR THE LADY!

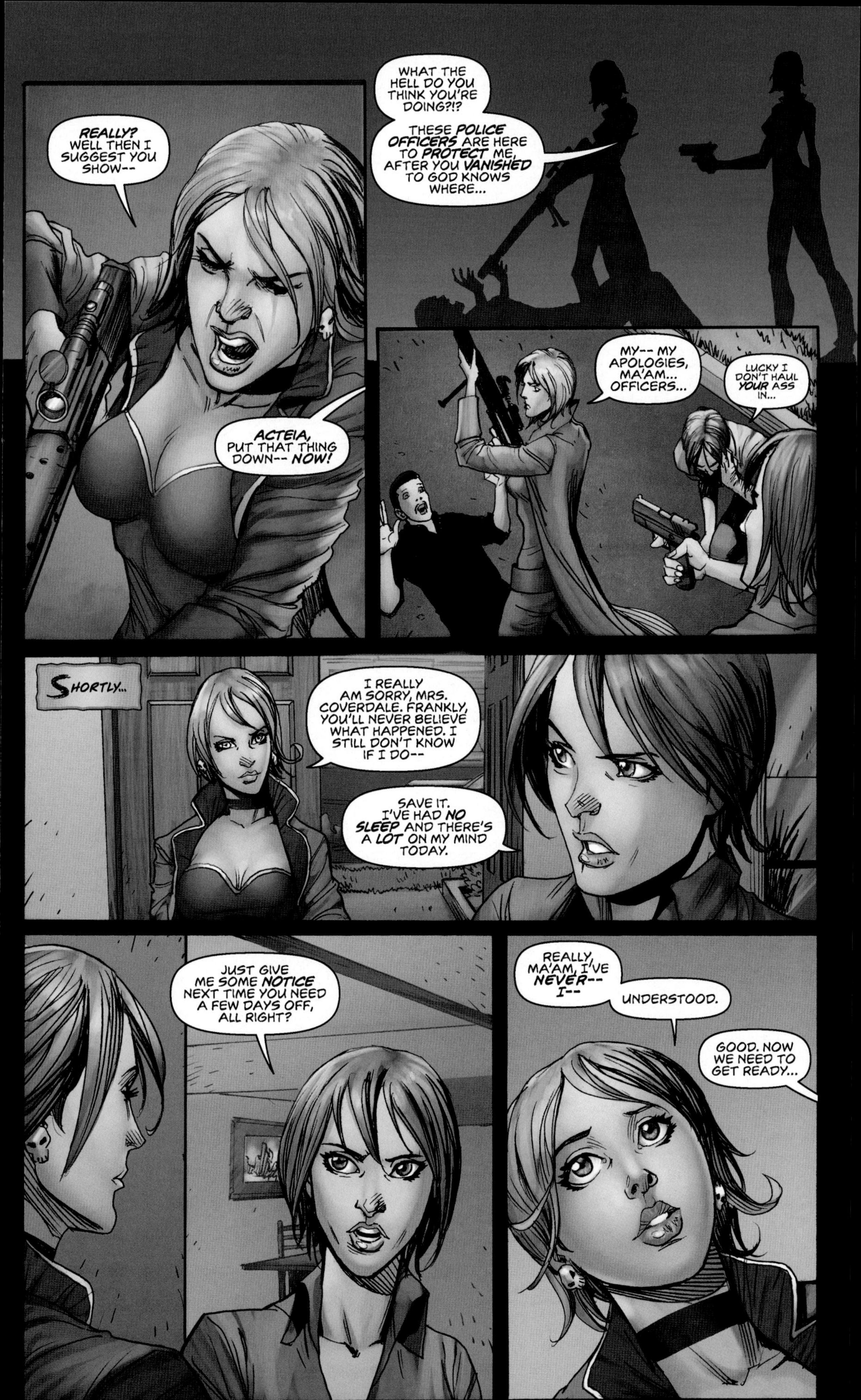
REALLY? WELL THEN I SUGGEST YOU SHOW--
WHAT THE HELL DO YOU THINK YOU'RE DOING?!?
THESE POLICE OFFICERS ARE HERE TO PROTECT ME, AFTER YOU VANISHED TO GOD KNOWS WHERE...
ACTEIA, PUT THAT THING DOWN-- NOW!
MY-- MY APOLOGIES, MA'AM... OFFICERS...
LUCKY I DON'T HAUL YOUR ASS IN...
SHORTLY...
I REALLY AM SORRY, MRS. COVERDALE. FRANKLY, YOU'LL NEVER BELIEVE WHAT HAPPENED. I STILL DON'T KNOW IF I DO--
SAVE IT. I'VE HAD NO SLEEP AND THERE'S A LOT ON MY MIND TODAY.
JUST GIVE ME SOME NOTICE NEXT TIME YOU NEED A FEW DAYS OFF, ALL RIGHT?
REALLY, MA'AM, I'VE NEVER-- I--
UNDERSTOOD.
GOOD. NOW WE NEED TO GET READY...

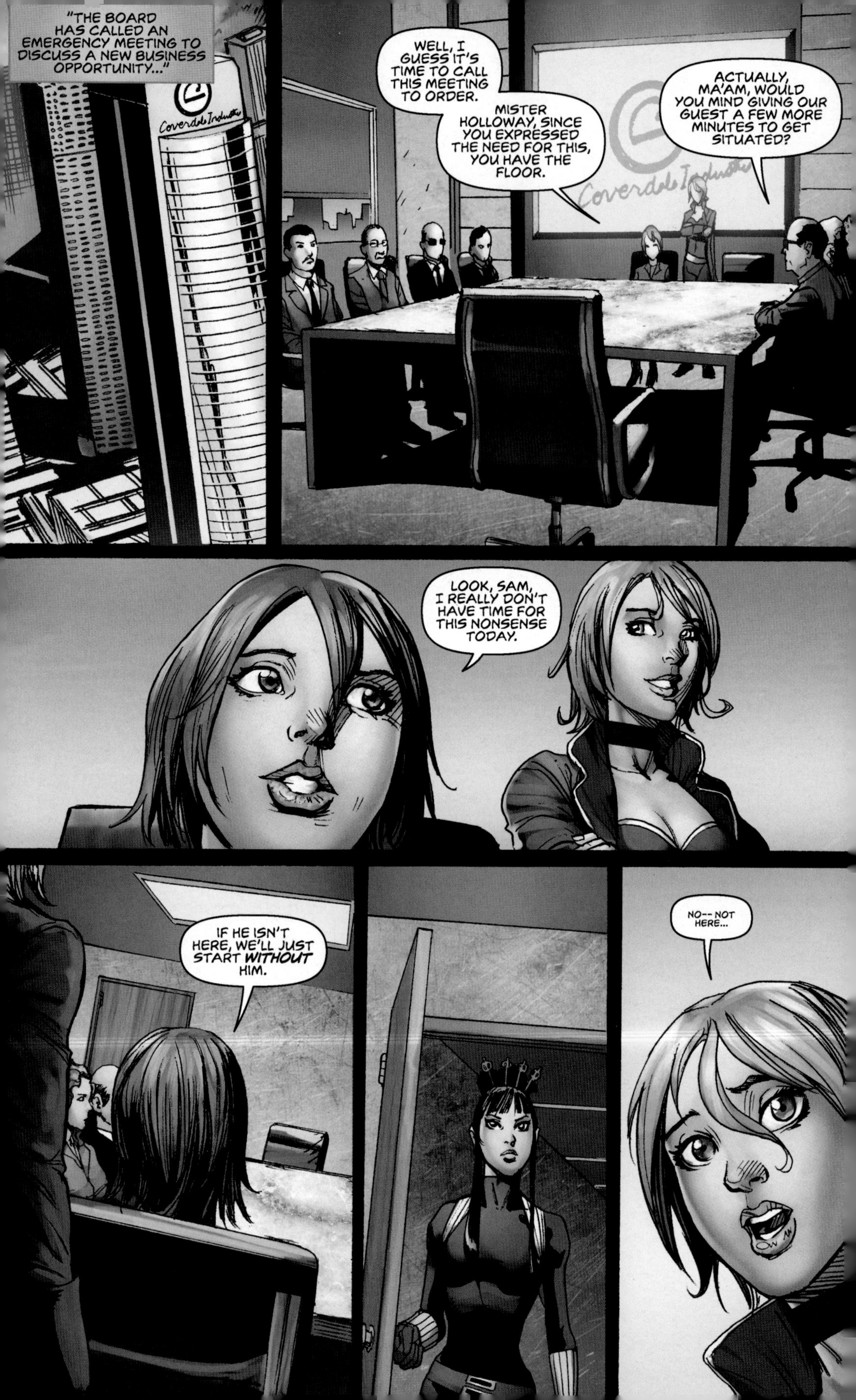
"THE BOARD HAS CALLED AN EMERGENCY MEETING TO DISCUSS A NEW BUSINESS OPPORTUNITY..."
Coverdale Industries
WELL, I GUESS IT'S TIME TO CALL THIS MEETING TO ORDER.
MISTER HOLLOWAY, SINCE YOU EXPRESSED THE NEED FOR THIS, YOU HAVE THE FLOOR.
ACTUALLY, MA'AM, WOULD YOU MIND GIVING OUR GUEST A FEW MORE MINUTES TO GET SITUATED?
LOOK, SAM, I REALLY DON'T HAVE TIME FOR THIS NONSENSE TODAY.
IF HE ISN'T HERE, WE'LL JUST START *WITHOUT* HIM.
NO-- NOT HERE...

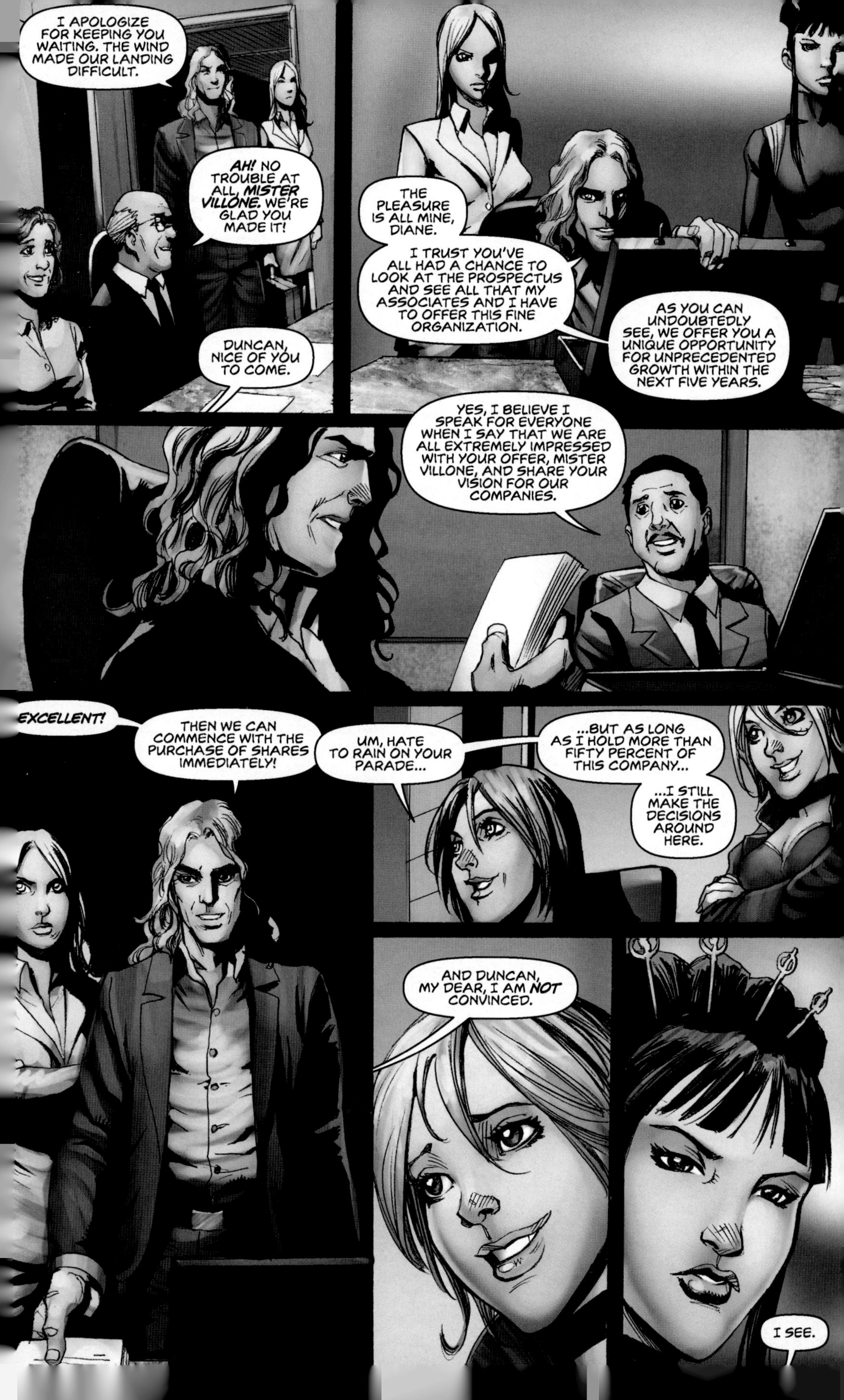
I APOLOGIZE FOR KEEPING YOU WAITING. THE WIND MADE OUR LANDING DIFFICULT.
AH! NO TROUBLE AT ALL, MISTER VILLONE. WE'RE GLAD YOU MADE IT!
DUNCAN, NICE OF YOU TO COME.
THE PLEASURE IS ALL MINE, DIANE.
I TRUST YOU'VE ALL HAD A CHANCE TO LOOK AT THE PROSPECTUS AND SEE ALL THAT MY ASSOCIATES AND I HAVE TO OFFER THIS FINE ORGANIZATION.
AS YOU CAN UNDOUBTEDLY SEE, WE OFFER YOU A UNIQUE OPPORTUNITY FOR UNPRECEDENTED GROWTH WITHIN THE NEXT FIVE YEARS.
YES, I BELIEVE I SPEAK FOR EVERYONE WHEN I SAY THAT WE ARE ALL EXTREMELY IMPRESSED WITH YOUR OFFER, MISTER VILLONE, AND SHARE YOUR VISION FOR OUR COMPANIES.
EXCELLENT!
THEN WE CAN COMMENCE WITH THE PURCHASE OF SHARES IMMEDIATELY!
UM, HATE TO RAIN ON YOUR PARADE...
...BUT AS LONG AS I HOLD MORE THAN FIFTY PERCENT OF THIS COMPANY...
...I STILL MAKE THE DECISIONS AROUND HERE.
AND DUNCAN, MY DEAR, I AM NOT CONVINCED.
I SEE.

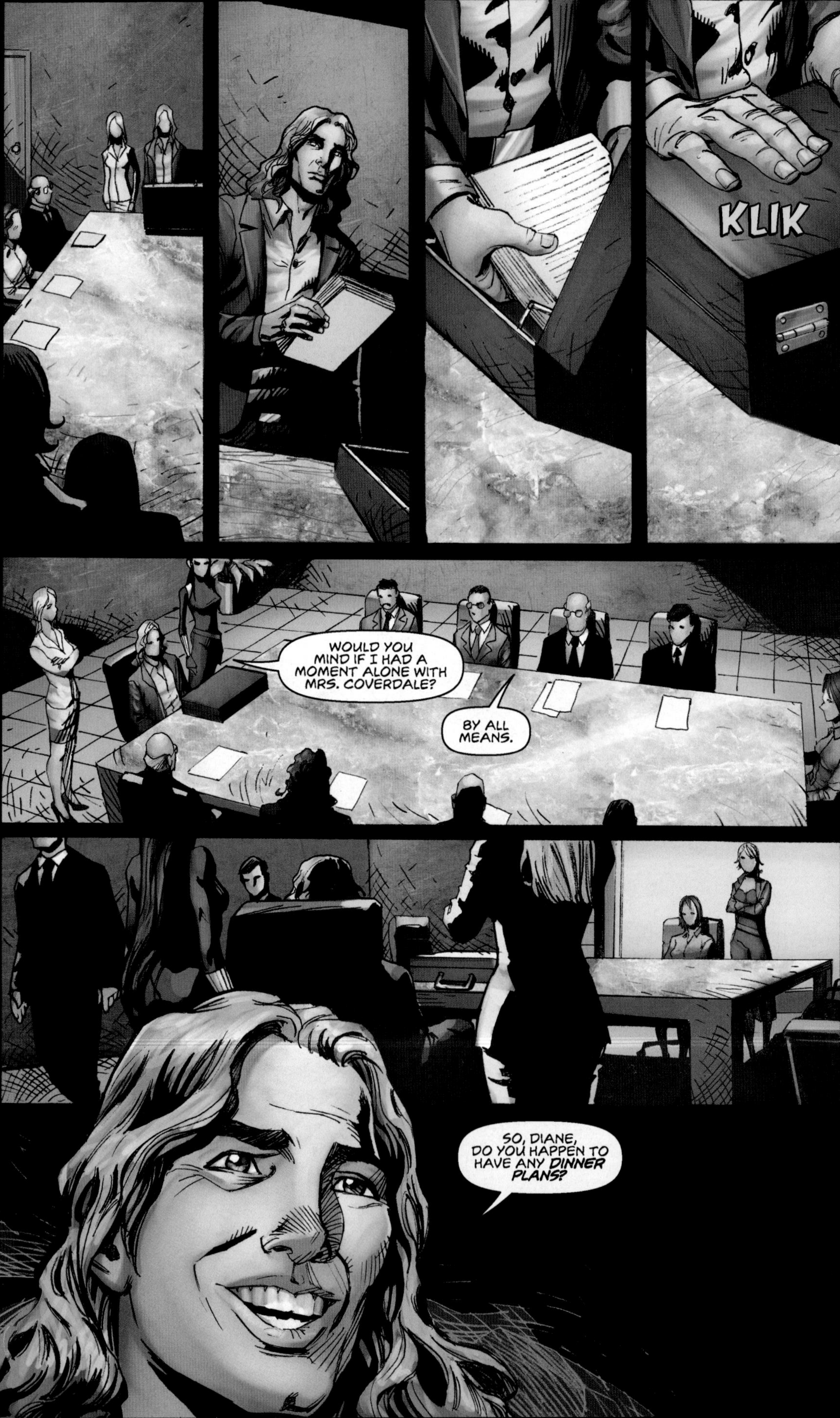
KLIK
WOULD YOU MIND IF I HAD A MOMENT ALONE WITH MRS. COVERDALE?
BY ALL MEANS.
SO, DIANE, DO YOU HAPPEN TO HAVE ANY *DINNER PLANS?*

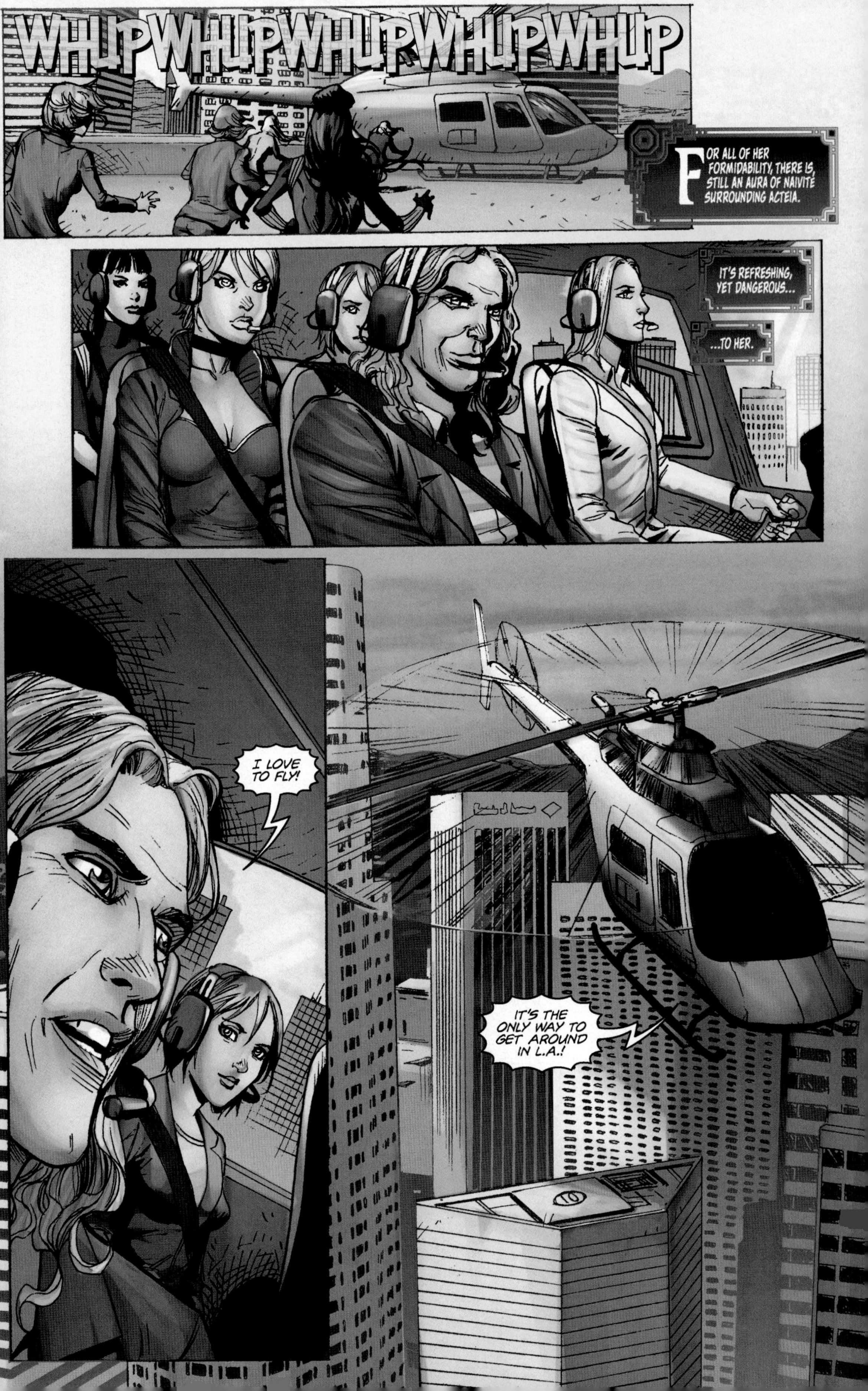
WHUPWHUPWHUPWHUPWHUP
FOR ALL OF HER FORMIDABILITY, THERE IS, STILL AN AURA OF NAIVITÉ SURROUNDING ACTEIA.
IT'S REFRESHING, YET DANGEROUS...
...TO HER.
I LOVE TO FLY!
IT'S THE ONLY WAY TO GET AROUND IN L.A.!

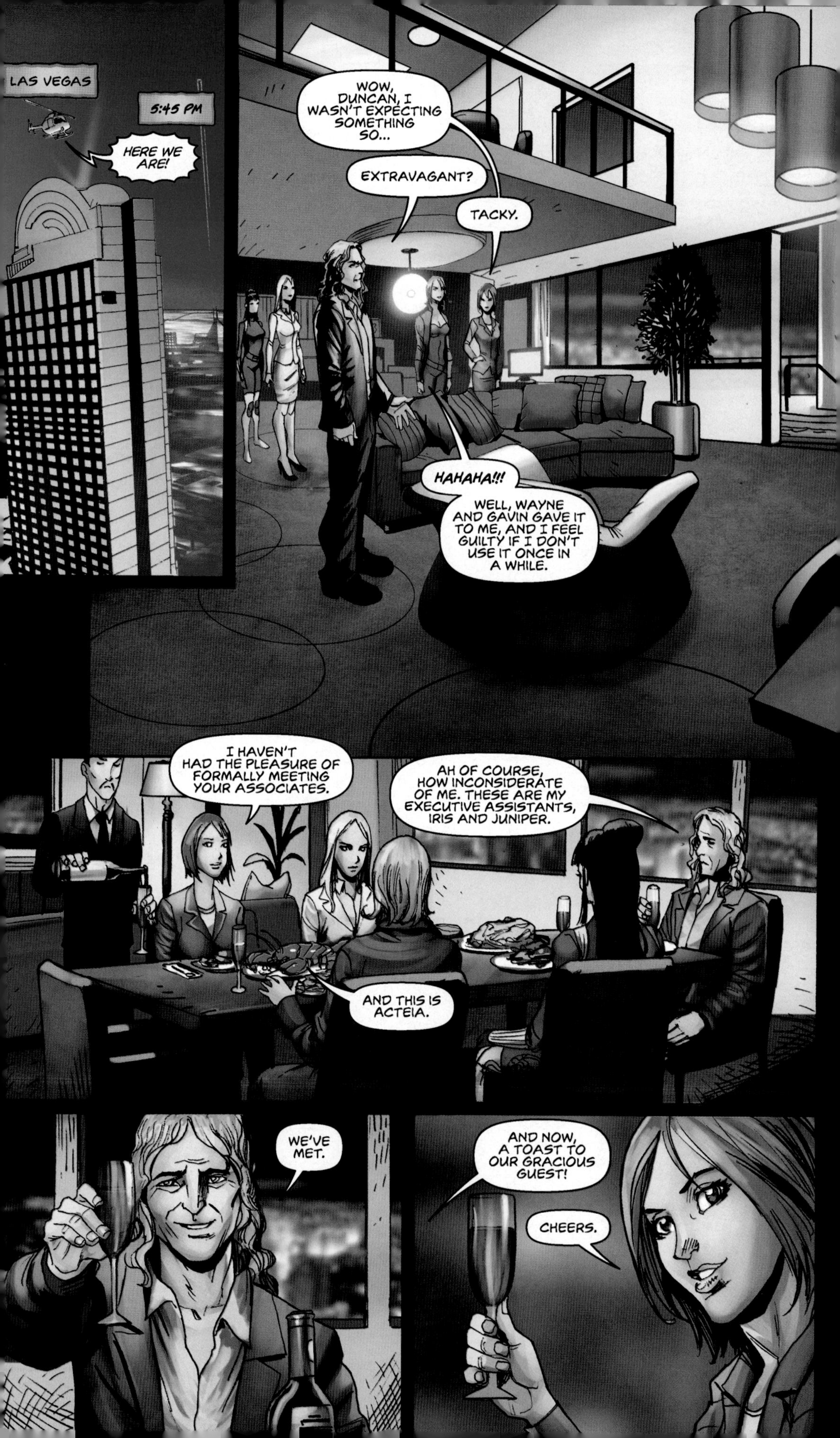
LAS VEGAS
5:45 PM
HERE WE ARE!
WOW, DUNCAN, I WASN'T EXPECTING SOMETHING SO...
EXTRAVAGANT?
TACKY.
HAHAHA!!!
WELL, WAYNE AND GAVIN GAVE IT TO ME, AND I FEEL GUILTY IF I DON'T USE IT ONCE IN A WHILE.
I HAVEN'T HAD THE PLEASURE OF FORMALLY MEETING YOUR ASSOCIATES.
AH OF COURSE, HOW INCONSIDERATE OF ME. THESE ARE MY EXECUTIVE ASSISTANTS, IRIS AND JUNIPER.
AND THIS IS ACTEIA.
WE'VE MET.
AND NOW, A TOAST TO OUR GRACIOUS GUEST!
CHEERS.

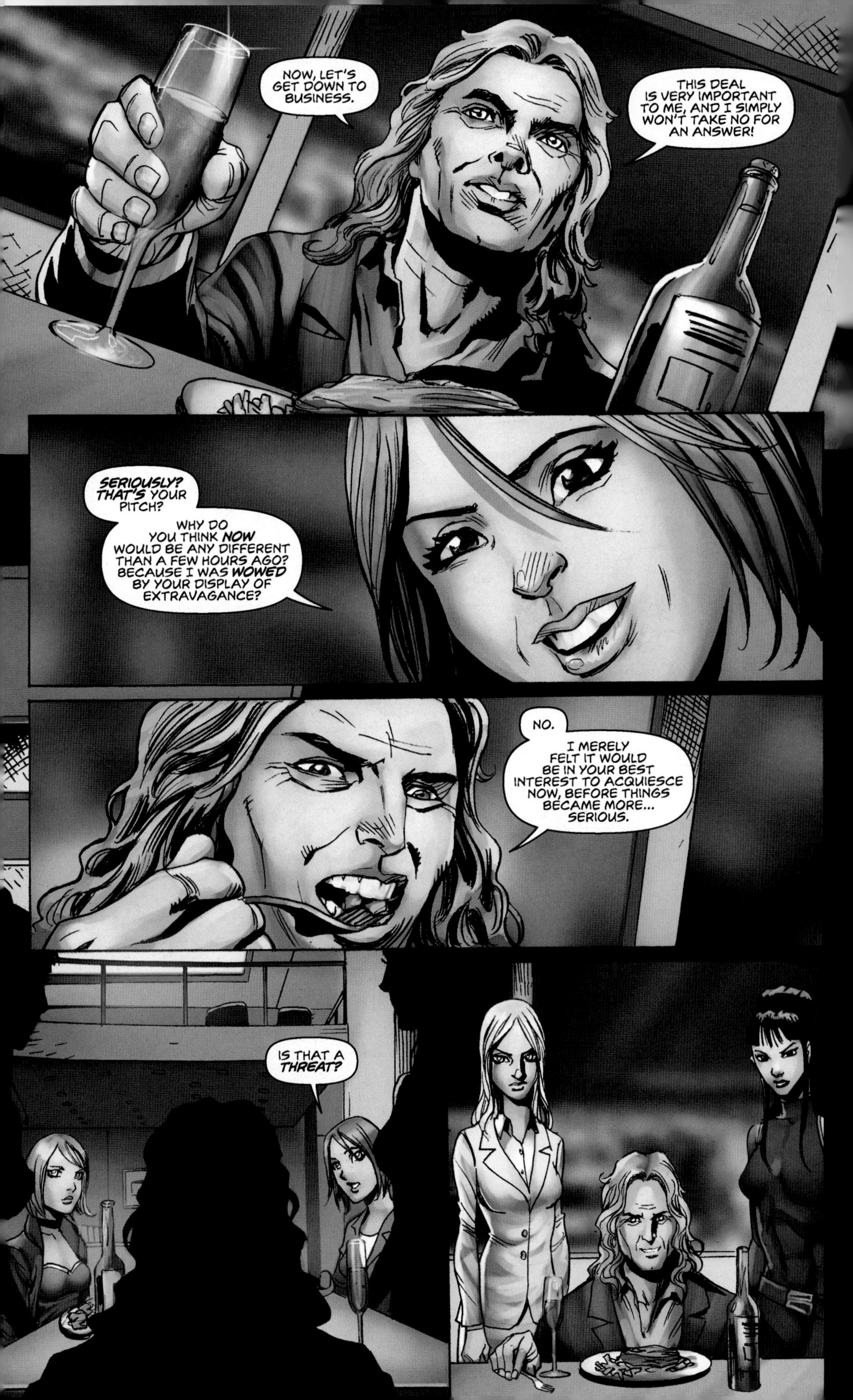
NOW, LET'S GET DOWN TO BUSINESS.
THIS DEAL IS VERY IMPORTANT TO ME, AND I SIMPLY WON'T TAKE NO FOR AN ANSWER!
SERIOUSLY? THAT'S YOUR PITCH?
WHY DO YOU THINK NOW WOULD BE ANY DIFFERENT THAN A FEW HOURS AGO? BECAUSE I WAS WOWED BY YOUR DISPLAY OF EXTRAVAGANCE?
NO.
I MERELY FELT IT WOULD BE IN YOUR BEST INTEREST TO ACQUIESCE NOW, BEFORE THINGS BECAME MORE... SERIOUS.
IS THAT A THREAT?

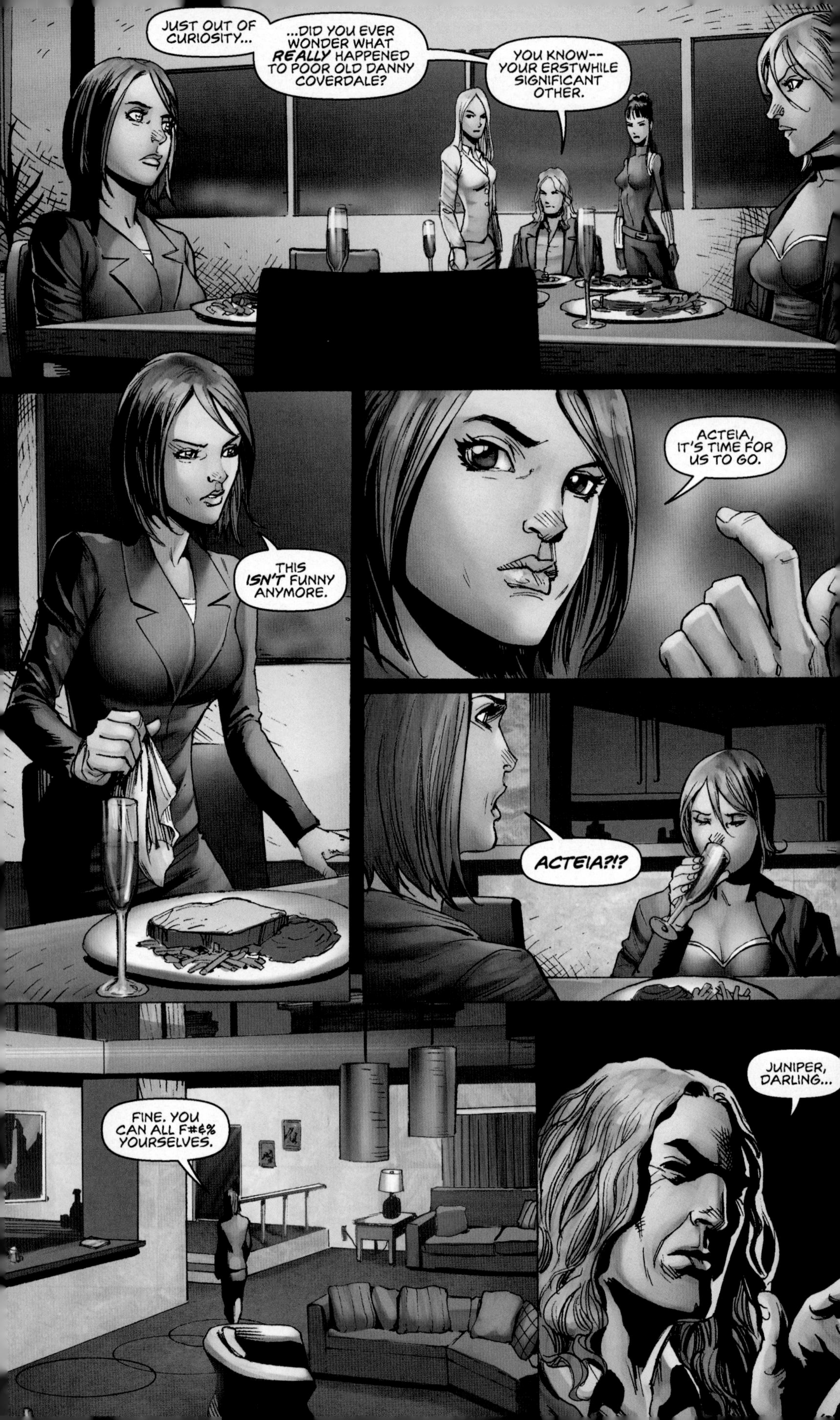
JUST OUT OF CURIOSITY...
...DID YOU EVER WONDER WHAT REALLY HAPPENED TO POOR OLD DANNY COVERDALE?
YOU KNOW-- YOUR ERSTWHILE SIGNIFICANT OTHER.
THIS ISN'T FUNNY ANYMORE.
ACTEIA, IT'S TIME FOR US TO GO.
ACTEIA?!?
FINE. YOU CAN ALL F#&% YOURSELVES.
JUNIPER, DARLING...

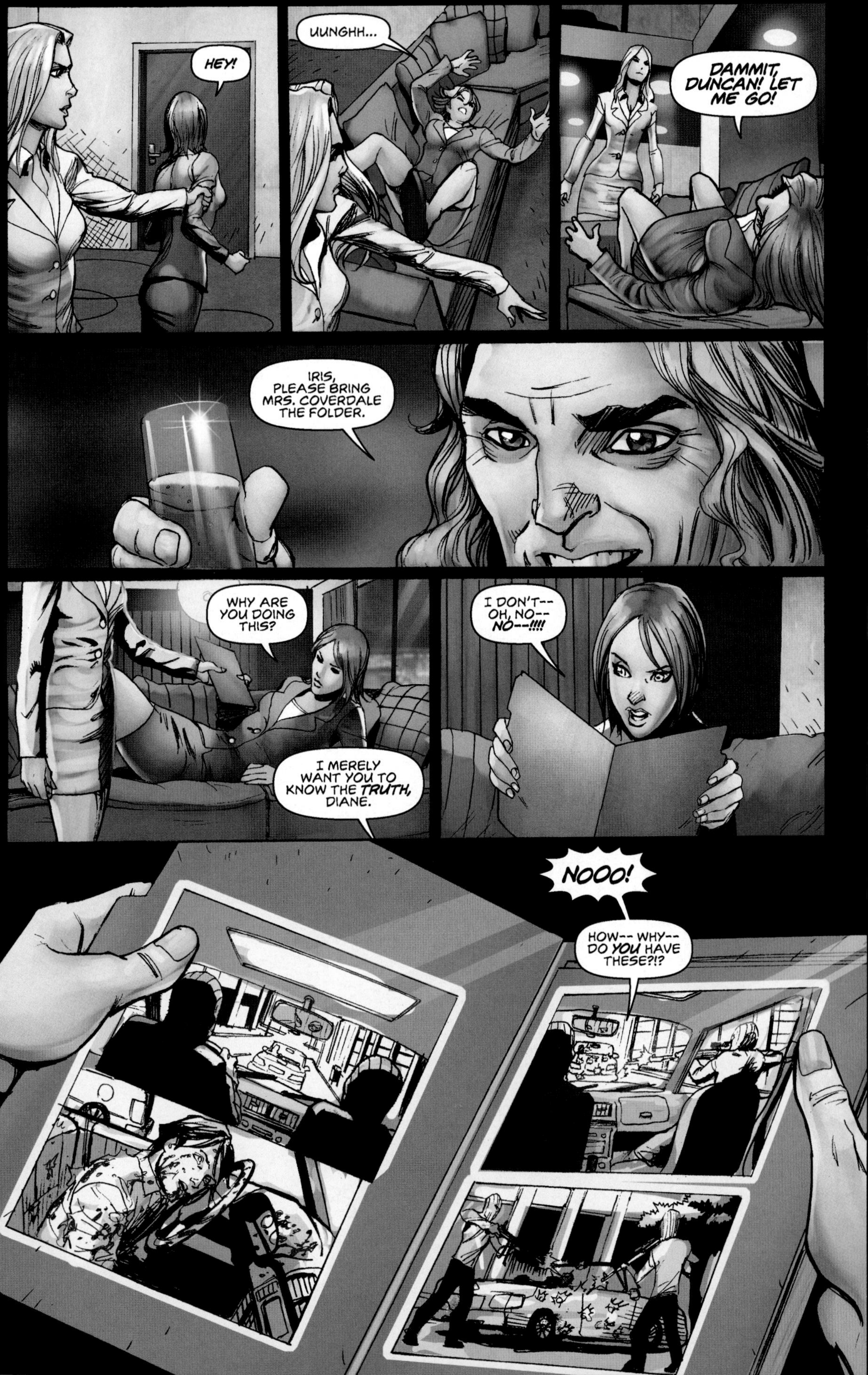
HEY!
UUNGHH...
DAMMIT, DUNCAN! LET ME GO!
IRIS, PLEASE BRING MRS. COVERDALE THE FOLDER.
WHY ARE YOU DOING THIS?
I MERELY WANT YOU TO KNOW THE *TRUTH*, DIANE.
I DON'T-- OH, NO-- *NO*--!!!!
NOOO!
HOW-- WHY-- DO *YOU* HAVE THESE?!?

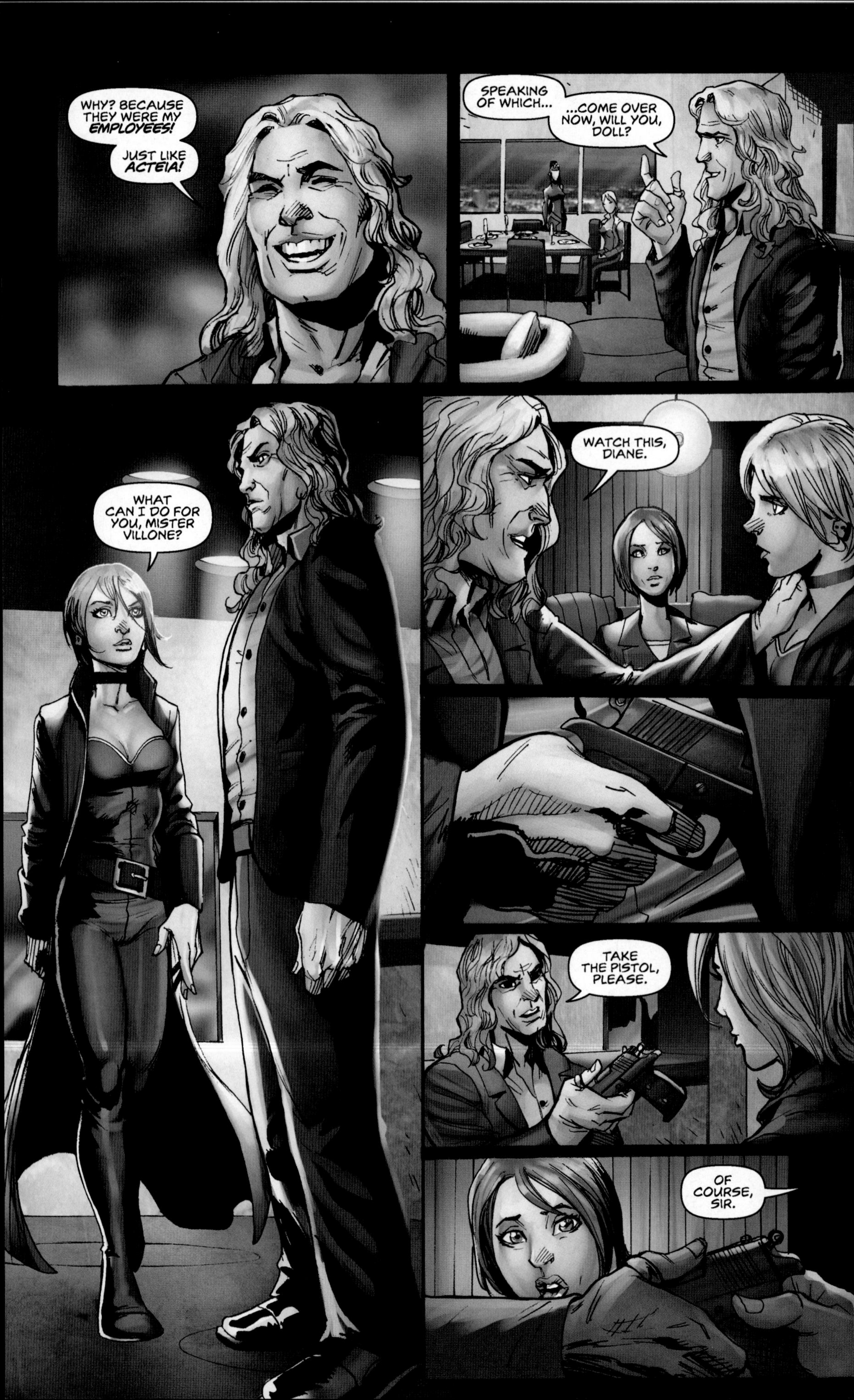
WHY? BECAUSE THEY WERE MY EMPLOYEES!
JUST LIKE ACTEIA!
SPEAKING OF WHICH...
...COME OVER NOW, WILL YOU, DOLL?
WHAT CAN I DO FOR YOU, MISTER VILLONE?
WATCH THIS, DIANE.
TAKE THE PISTOL, PLEASE.
OF COURSE, SIR.

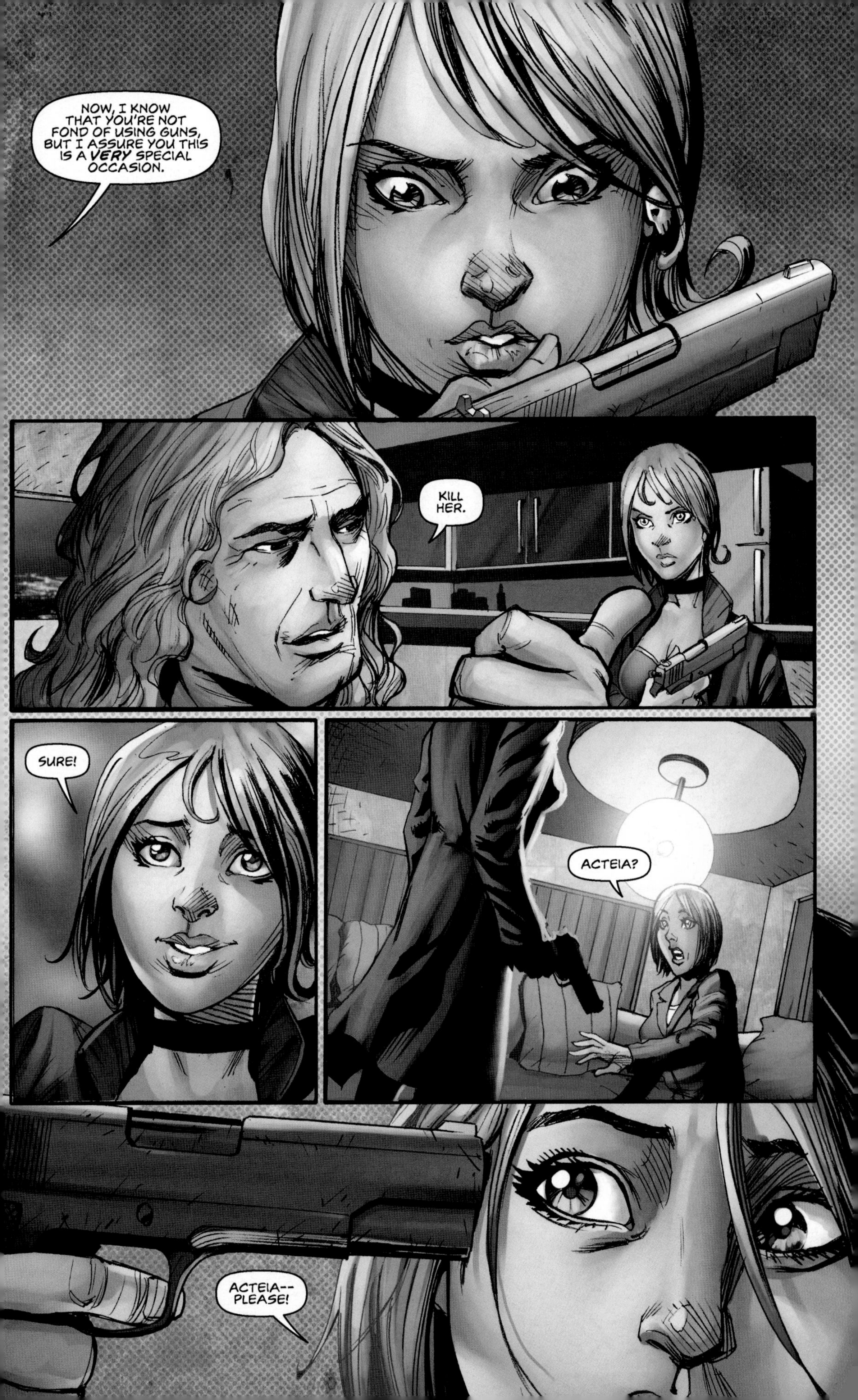
NOW, I KNOW THAT YOU'RE NOT FOND OF USING GUNS, BUT I ASSURE YOU THIS IS A VERY SPECIAL OCCASION.
KILL HER.
SURE!
ACTEIA?
ACTEIA-- PLEASE!

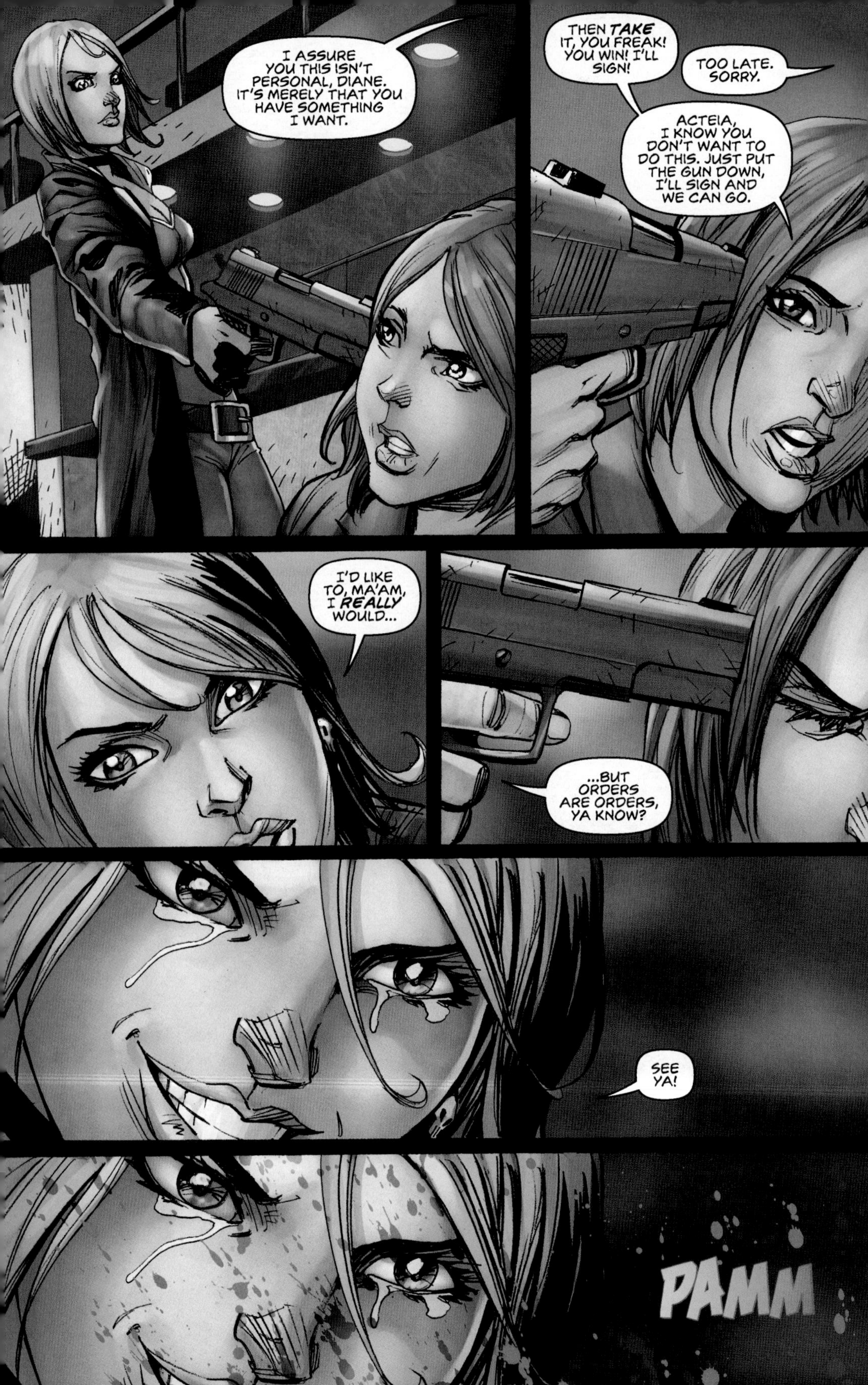
I ASSURE YOU THIS ISN'T PERSONAL, DIANE. IT'S MERELY THAT YOU HAVE SOMETHING I WANT.
THEN *TAKE* IT, YOU FREAK! YOU WIN! I'LL SIGN!
TOO LATE. SORRY.
ACTEIA, I KNOW YOU DON'T WANT TO DO THIS. JUST PUT THE GUN DOWN, I'LL SIGN AND WE CAN GO.
I'D LIKE TO, MA'AM, I *REALLY* WOULD...
...BUT ORDERS ARE ORDERS, YA KNOW?
SEE YA!
PAMM

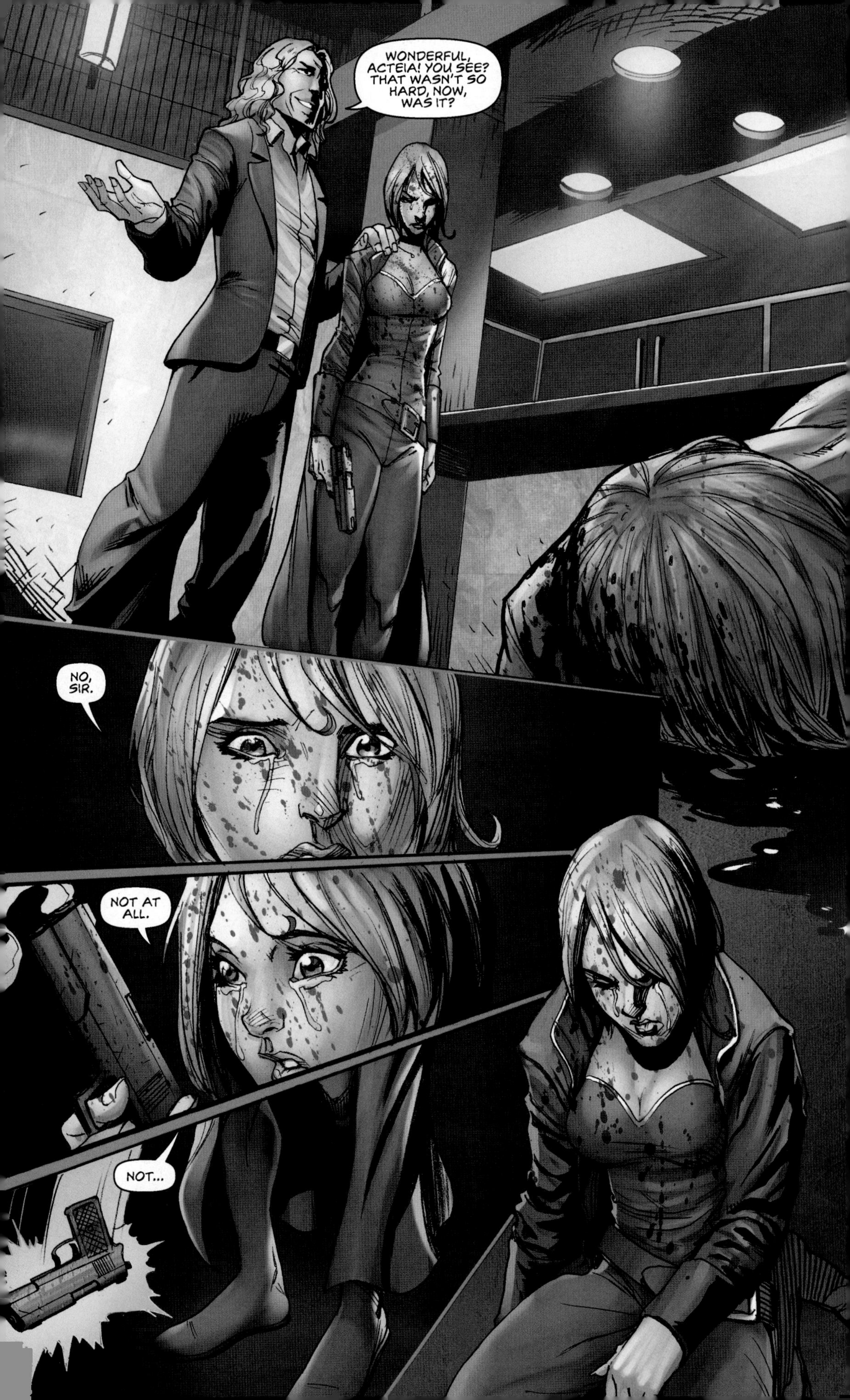
WONDERFUL, ACTEIA! YOU SEE? THAT WASN'T SO HARD, NOW, WAS IT?
NO, SIR.
NOT AT ALL.
NOT...

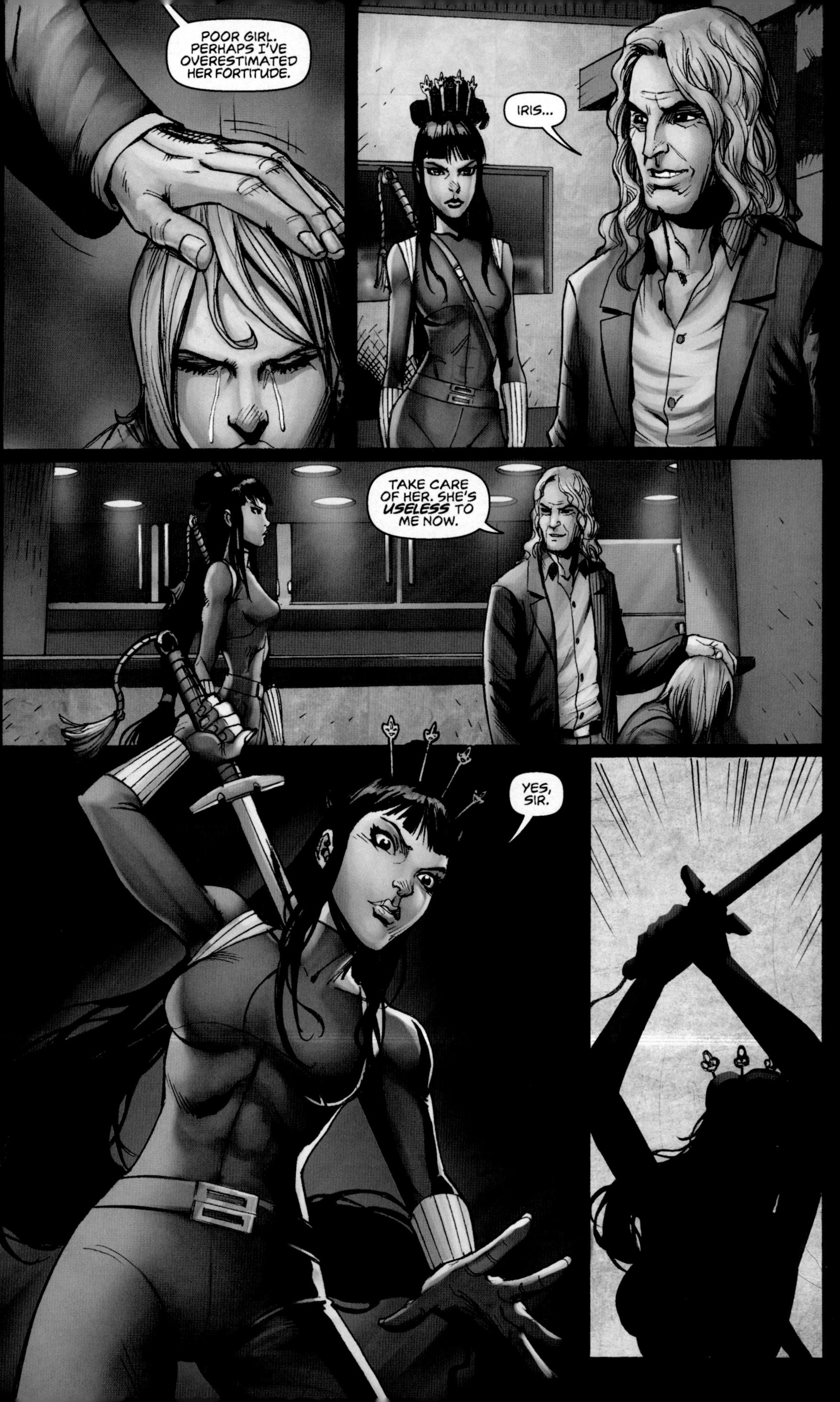
POOR GIRL. PERHAPS I'VE OVERESTIMATED HER FORTITUDE.
IRIS...
TAKE CARE OF HER. SHE'S USELESS TO ME NOW.
YES, SIR.

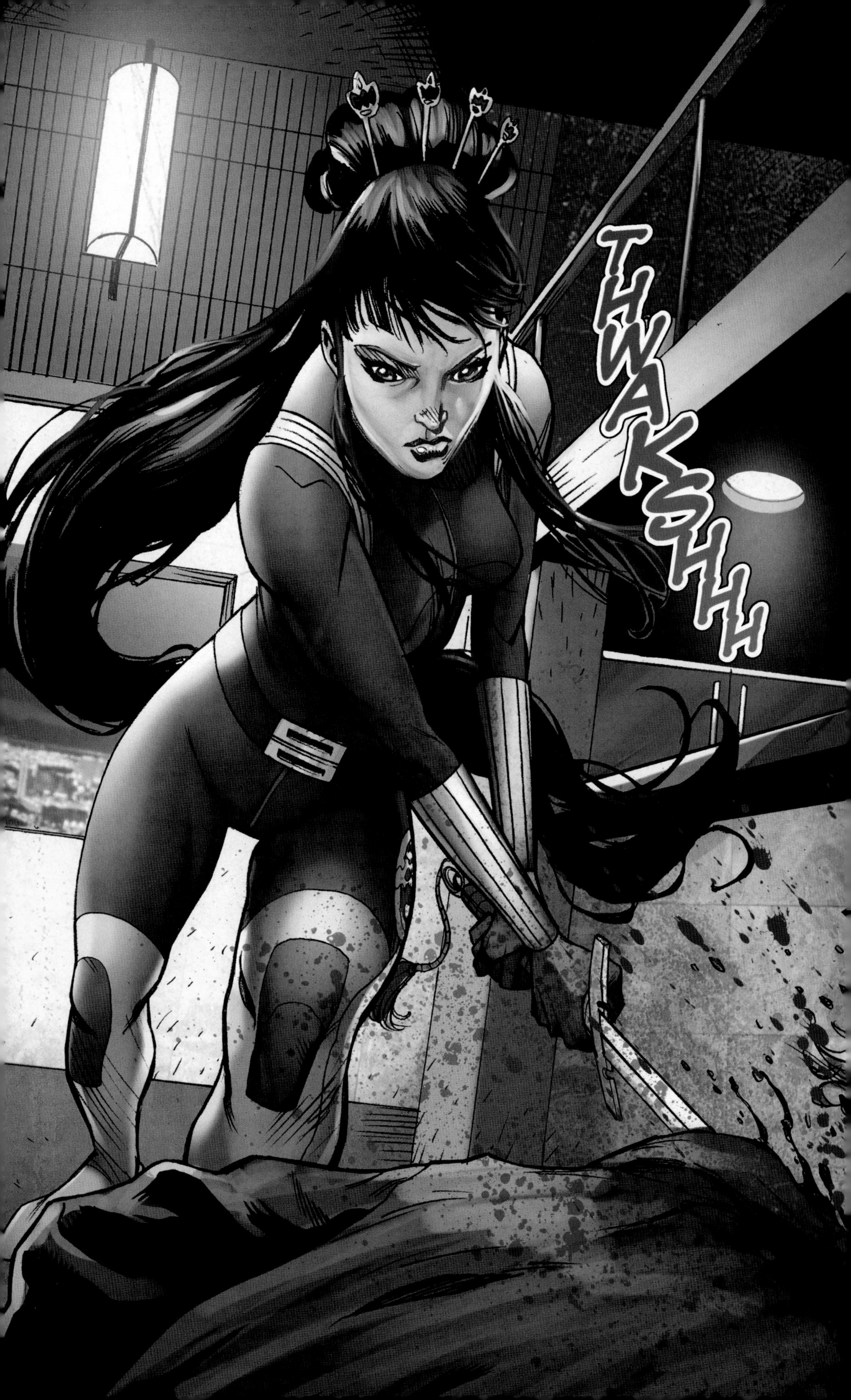
THWAKSHHH

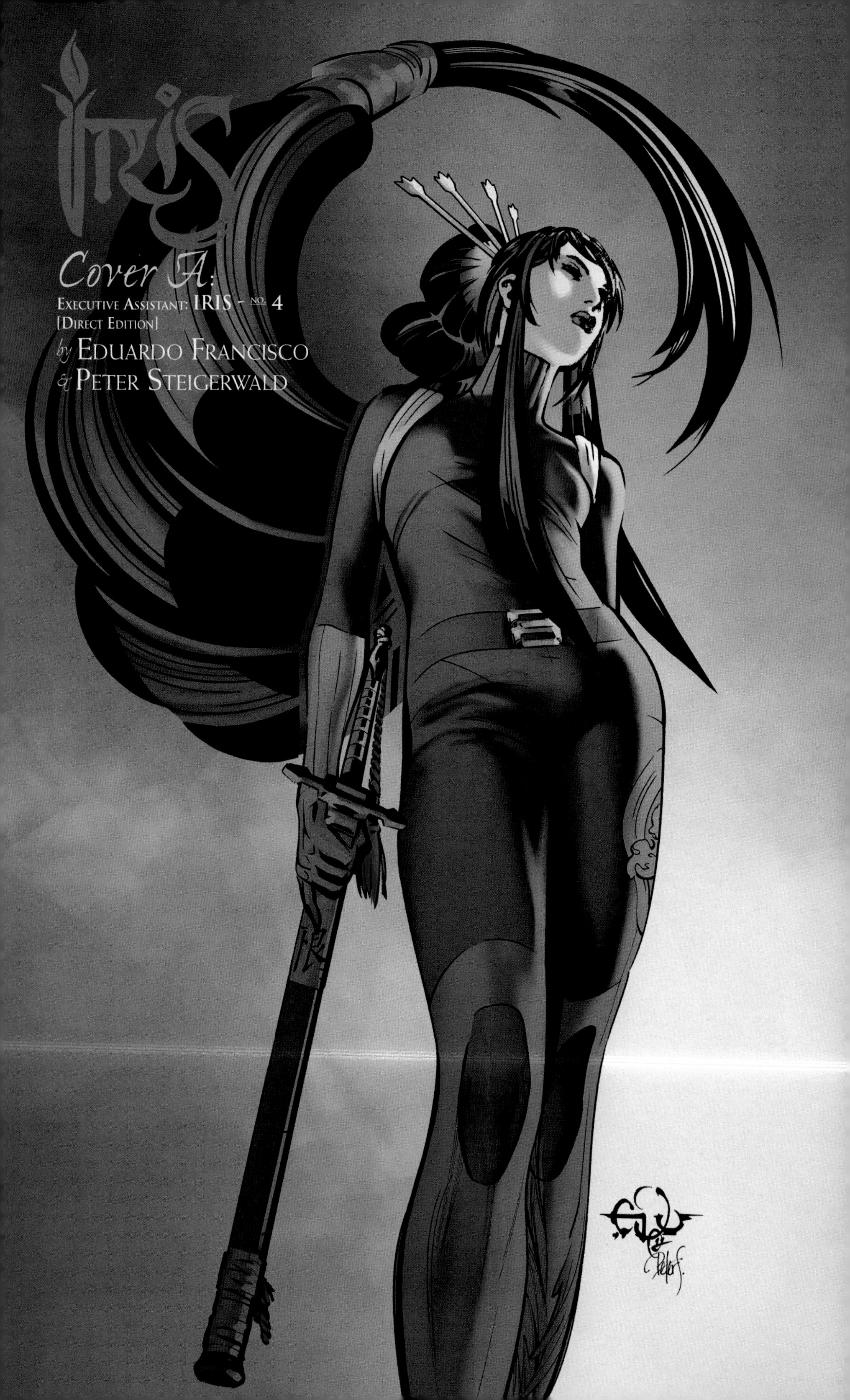
Iris
Cover A:
Executive Assistant: IRIS - No. 4
[Direct Edition]
by Eduardo Francisco
& Peter Steigerwald

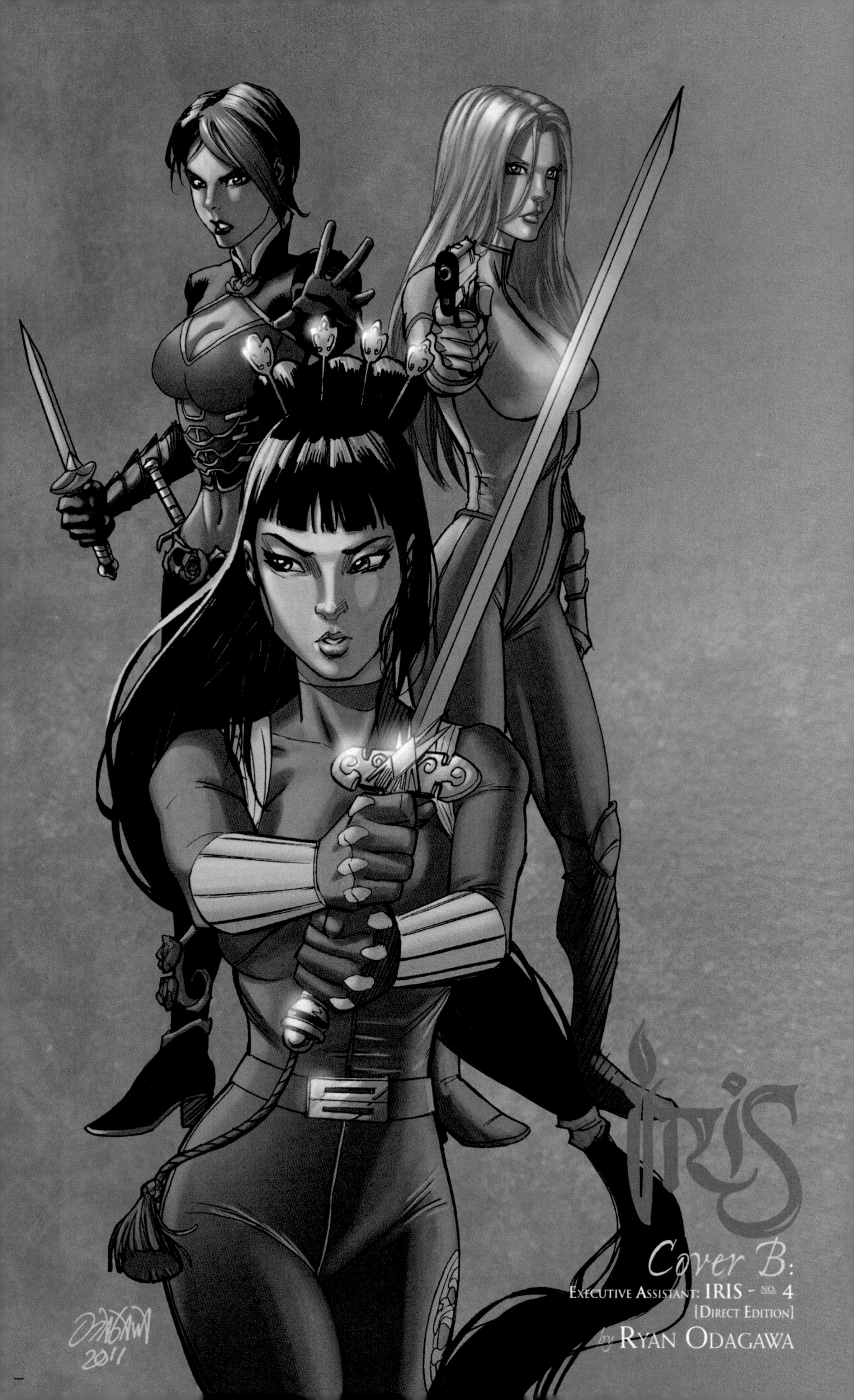
IRIS
Cover B:
Executive Assistant: IRIS - No. 4
[Direct Edition]
by Ryan Odagawa
2011

CHAPTER FIVE

FOUR

"WHAT A GIRL WANTS"

WRITER
DAVID WOHL

PENCILS
RYAN ODAGAWA

COLORS
TEODORO GONZALEZ

LETTERING
JOSH REED

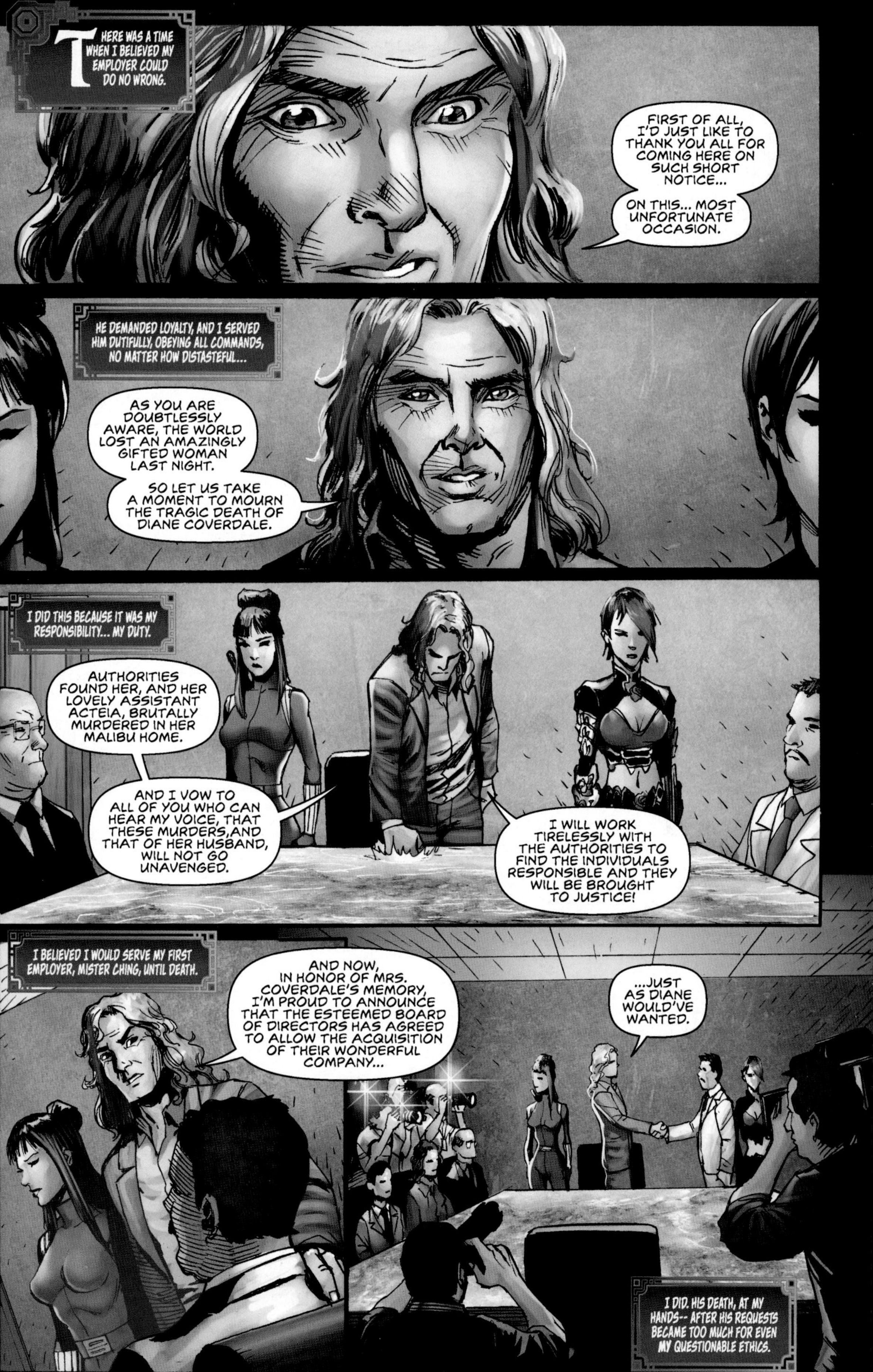
THERE WAS A TIME WHEN I BELIEVED MY EMPLOYER COULD DO NO WRONG.
FIRST OF ALL, I'D JUST LIKE TO THANK YOU ALL FOR COMING HERE ON SUCH SHORT NOTICE...
ON THIS... MOST UNFORTUNATE OCCASION.
HE DEMANDED LOYALTY, AND I SERVED HIM DUTIFULLY, OBEYING ALL COMMANDS, NO MATTER HOW DISTASTEFUL...
AS YOU ARE DOUBTLESSLY AWARE, THE WORLD LOST AN AMAZINGLY GIFTED WOMAN LAST NIGHT.
SO LET US TAKE A MOMENT TO MOURN THE TRAGIC DEATH OF DIANE COVERDALE.
I DID THIS BECAUSE IT WAS MY RESPONSIBILITY... MY DUTY.
AUTHORITIES FOUND HER, AND HER LOVELY ASSISTANT ACTEIA, BRUTALLY MURDERED IN HER MALIBU HOME.
AND I VOW TO ALL OF YOU WHO CAN HEAR MY VOICE, THAT THESE MURDERS,AND THAT OF HER HUSBAND, WILL NOT GO UNAVENGED.
I WILL WORK TIRELESSLY WITH THE AUTHORITIES TO FIND THE INDIVIDUALS RESPONSIBLE AND THEY WILL BE BROUGHT TO JUSTICE!
I BELIEVED I WOULD SERVE MY FIRST EMPLOYER, MISTER CHING, UNTIL DEATH.
AND NOW, IN HONOR OF MRS. COVERDALE'S MEMORY, I'M PROUD TO ANNOUNCE THAT THE ESTEEMED BOARD OF DIRECTORS HAS AGREED TO ALLOW THE ACQUISITION OF THEIR WONDERFUL COMPANY...
...JUST AS DIANE WOULD'VE WANTED.
I DID. HIS DEATH, AT MY HANDS-- AFTER HIS REQUESTS BECAME TOO MUCH FOR EVEN MY QUESTIONABLE ETHICS.

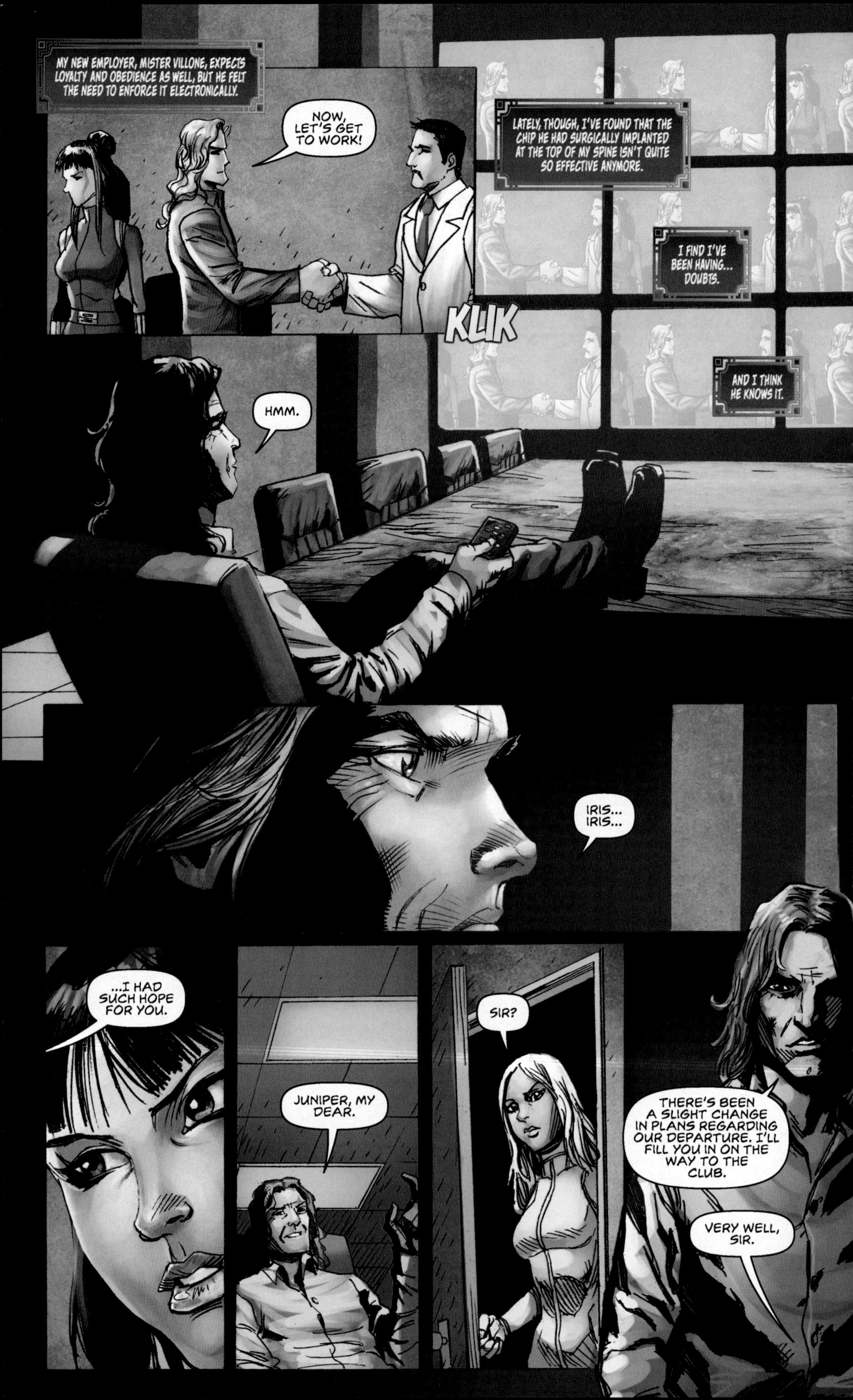
MY NEW EMPLOYER, MISTER VILLONE, EXPECTS LOYALTY AND OBEDIENCE AS WELL, BUT HE FELT THE NEED TO ENFORCE IT ELECTRONICALLY.
NOW, LET'S GET TO WORK!
LATELY, THOUGH, I'VE FOUND THAT THE CHIP HE HAD SURGICALLY IMPLANTED AT THE TOP OF MY SPINE ISN'T QUITE SO EFFECTIVE ANYMORE.
I FIND I'VE BEEN HAVING... DOUBTS.
KLIK
AND I THINK HE KNOWS IT.
HMM.
IRIS... IRIS...
...I HAD SUCH HOPE FOR YOU.
JUNIPER, MY DEAR.
SIR?
THERE'S BEEN A SLIGHT CHANGE IN PLANS REGARDING OUR DEPARTURE. I'LL FILL YOU IN ON THE WAY TO THE CLUB.
VERY WELL, SIR.

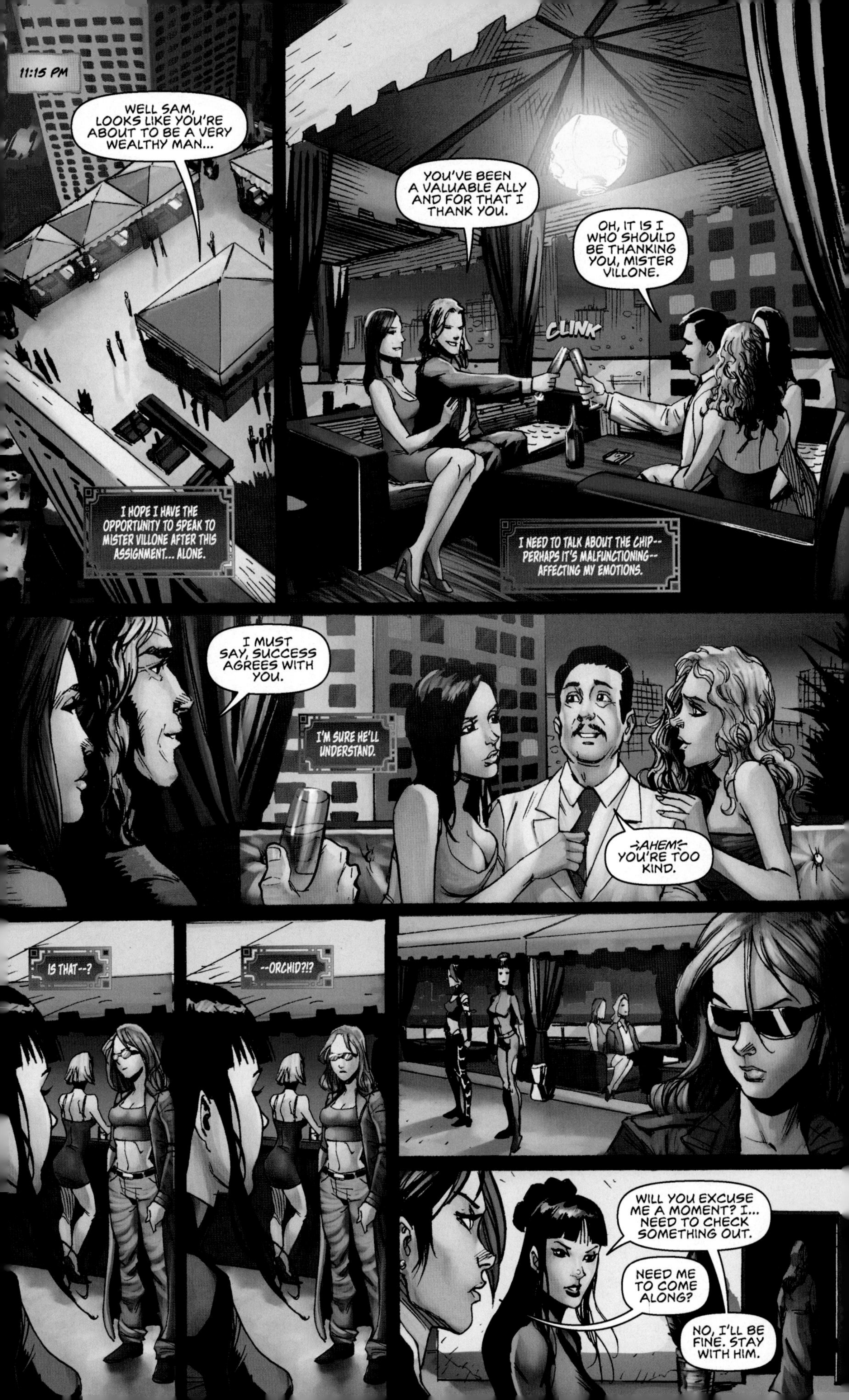

11:15 PM
WELL SAM, LOOKS LIKE YOU'RE ABOUT TO BE A VERY WEALTHY MAN...
I HOPE I HAVE THE OPPORTUNITY TO SPEAK TO MISTER VILLONE AFTER THIS ASSIGNMENT... ALONE.
YOU'VE BEEN A VALUABLE ALLY AND FOR THAT I THANK YOU.
OH, IT IS I WHO SHOULD BE THANKING YOU, MISTER VILLONE.
CLINK
I NEED TO TALK ABOUT THE CHIP-- PERHAPS IT'S MALFUNCTIONING-- AFFECTING MY EMOTIONS.
I MUST SAY, SUCCESS AGREES WITH YOU.
I'M SURE HE'LL UNDERSTAND.
-AHEM- YOU'RE TOO KIND.
IS THAT--?
--ORCHID?!?
WILL YOU EXCUSE ME A MOMENT? I... NEED TO CHECK SOMETHING OUT.
NEED ME TO COME ALONG?
NO, I'LL BE FINE. STAY WITH HIM.

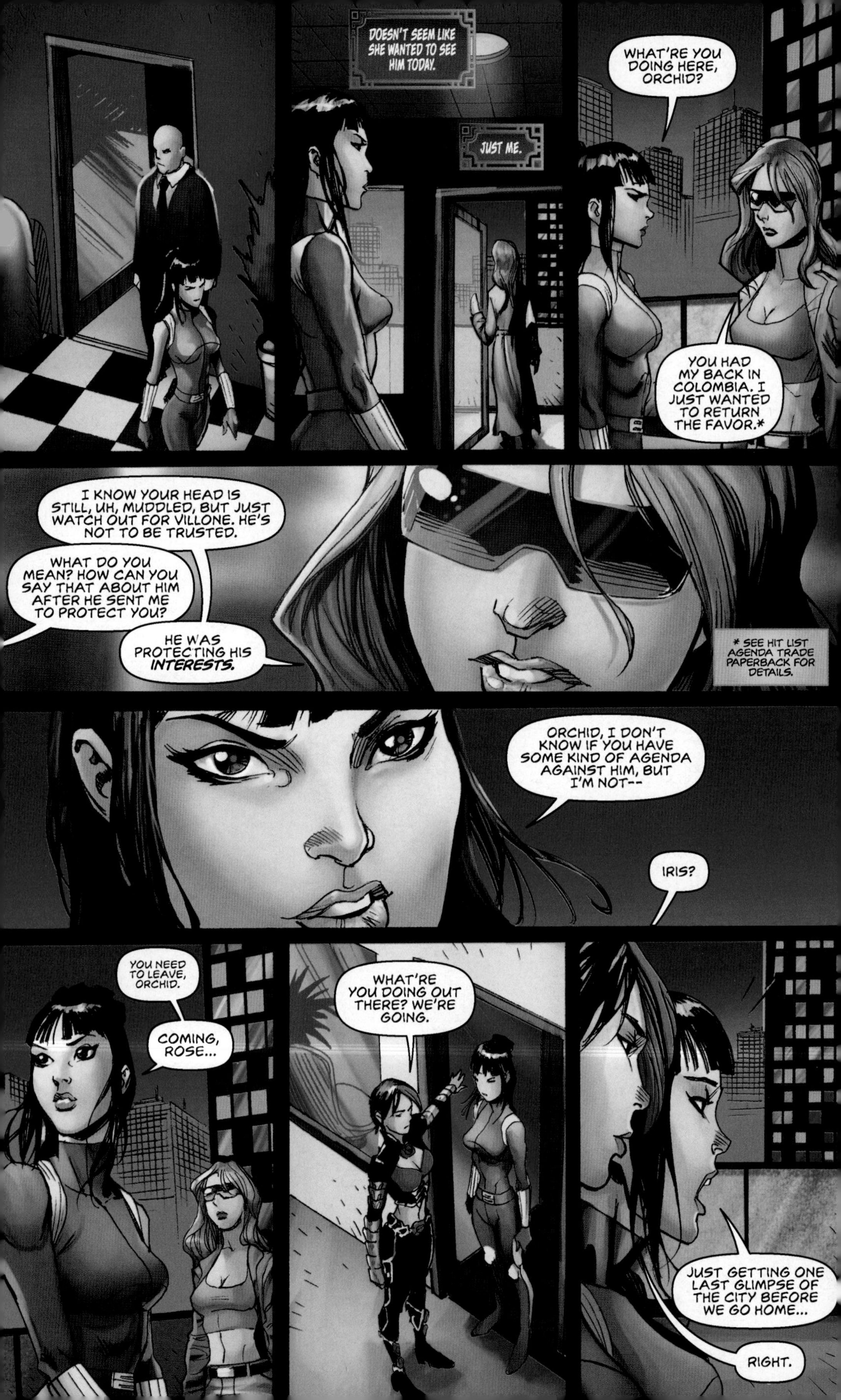
DOESN'T SEEM LIKE SHE WANTED TO SEE HIM TODAY.
JUST ME.
WHAT'RE YOU DOING HERE, ORCHID?
YOU HAD MY BACK IN COLOMBIA. I JUST WANTED TO RETURN THE FAVOR.*
I KNOW YOUR HEAD IS STILL, UH, MUDDLED, BUT JUST WATCH OUT FOR VILLONE. HE'S NOT TO BE TRUSTED.
WHAT DO YOU MEAN? HOW CAN YOU SAY THAT ABOUT HIM AFTER HE SENT ME TO PROTECT YOU?
HE WAS PROTECTING HIS *INTERESTS.*
* SEE HIT LIST AGENDA TRADE PAPERBACK FOR DETAILS.
ORCHID, I DON'T KNOW IF YOU HAVE SOME KIND OF AGENDA AGAINST HIM, BUT I'M NOT--
IRIS?
YOU NEED TO LEAVE, ORCHID.
COMING, ROSE...
WHAT'RE YOU DOING OUT THERE? WE'RE GOING.
JUST GETTING ONE LAST GLIMPSE OF THE CITY BEFORE WE GO HOME...
RIGHT.

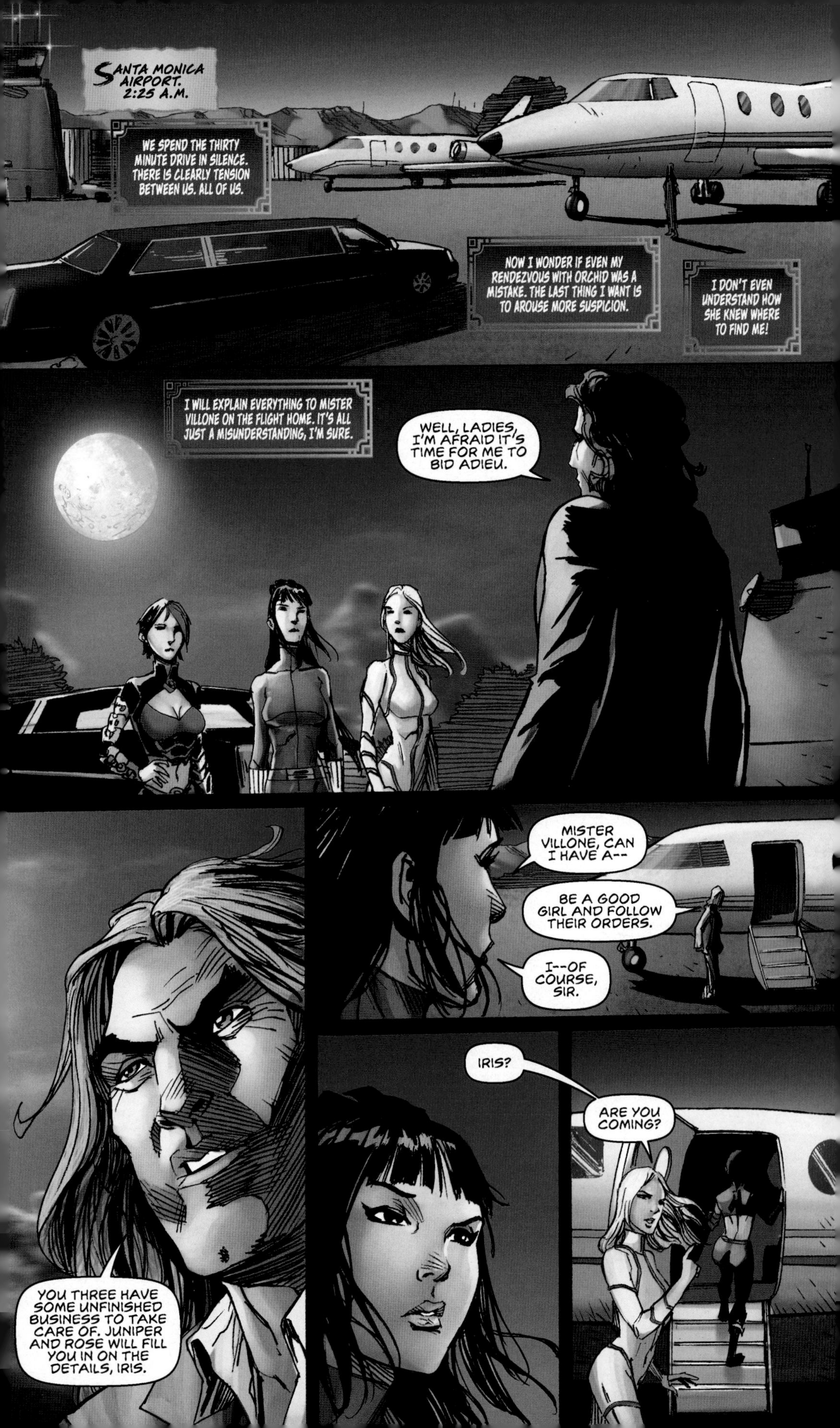

SANTA MONICA AIRPORT. 2:25 A.M.
WE SPEND THE THIRTY MINUTE DRIVE IN SILENCE. THERE IS CLEARLY TENSION BETWEEN US. ALL OF US.
NOW I WONDER IF EVEN MY RENDEZVOUS WITH ORCHID WAS A MISTAKE. THE LAST THING I WANT IS TO AROUSE MORE SUSPICION.
I DON'T EVEN UNDERSTAND HOW SHE KNEW WHERE TO FIND ME!
I WILL EXPLAIN EVERYTHING TO MISTER VILLONE ON THE FLIGHT HOME. IT'S ALL JUST A MISUNDERSTANDING, I'M SURE.
WELL, LADIES, I'M AFRAID IT'S TIME FOR ME TO BID ADIEU.
YOU THREE HAVE SOME UNFINISHED BUSINESS TO TAKE CARE OF. JUNIPER AND ROSE WILL FILL YOU IN ON THE DETAILS, IRIS.
MISTER VILLONE, CAN I HAVE A--
BE A GOOD GIRL AND FOLLOW THEIR ORDERS.
I--OF COURSE, SIR.
IRIS?
ARE YOU COMING?

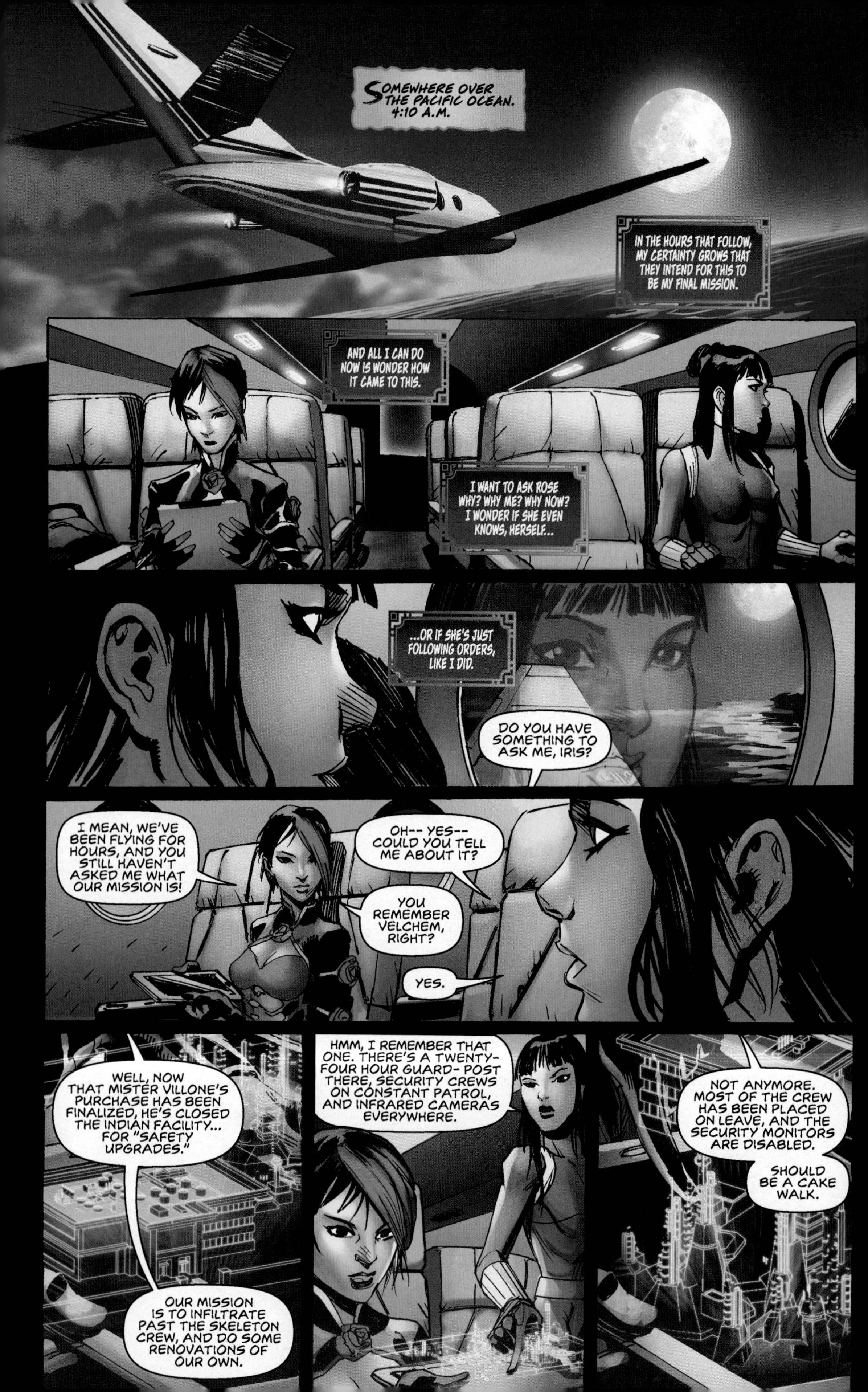
SOMEWHERE OVER THE PACIFIC OCEAN. 4:10 A.M.
IN THE HOURS THAT FOLLOW, MY CERTAINTY GROWS THAT THEY INTEND FOR THIS TO BE MY FINAL MISSION.
AND ALL I CAN DO NOW IS WONDER HOW IT CAME TO THIS.
I WANT TO ASK ROSE WHY? WHY ME? WHY NOW? I WONDER IF SHE EVEN KNOWS, HERSELF...
...OR IF SHE'S JUST FOLLOWING ORDERS, LIKE I DID.
DO YOU HAVE SOMETHING TO ASK ME, IRIS?
I MEAN, WE'VE BEEN FLYING FOR HOURS, AND YOU STILL HAVEN'T ASKED ME WHAT OUR MISSION IS!
OH-- YES-- COULD YOU TELL ME ABOUT IT?
YOU REMEMBER VELCHEM, RIGHT?
YES.
WELL, NOW THAT MISTER VILLONE'S PURCHASE HAS BEEN FINALIZED, HE'S CLOSED THE INDIAN FACILITY... FOR "SAFETY UPGRADES."
OUR MISSION IS TO INFILTRATE PAST THE SKELETON CREW, AND DO SOME RENOVATIONS OF OUR OWN.
HMM, I REMEMBER THAT ONE. THERE'S A TWENTY-FOUR HOUR GUARD- POST THERE, SECURITY CREWS ON CONSTANT PATROL, AND INFRARED CAMERAS EVERYWHERE.
NOT ANYMORE. MOST OF THE CREW HAS BEEN PLACED ON LEAVE, AND THE SECURITY MONITORS ARE DISABLED.
SHOULD BE A CAKE WALK.

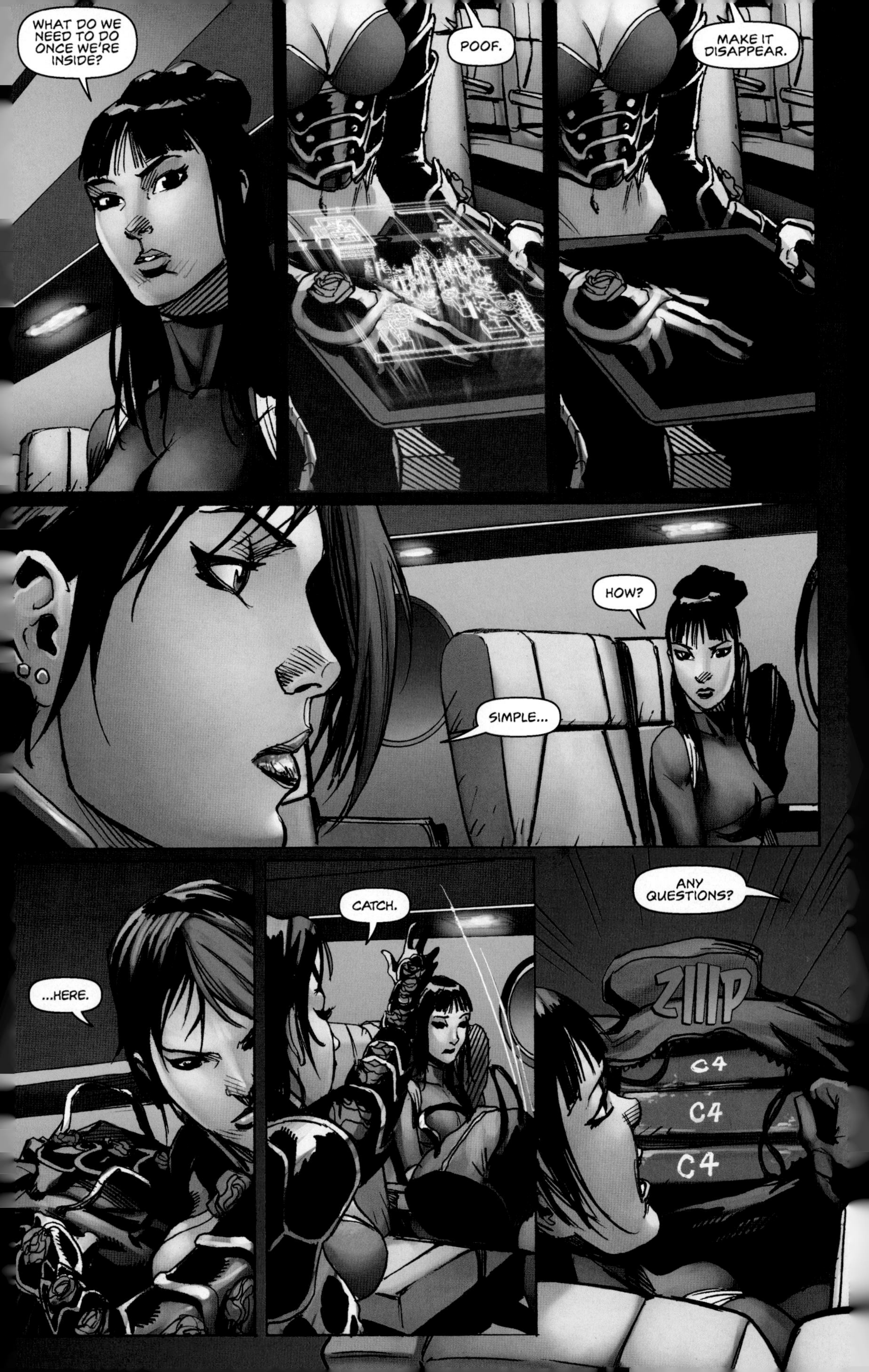
WHAT DO WE NEED TO DO ONCE WE'RE INSIDE?
POOF.
MAKE IT DISAPPEAR.
HOW?
SIMPLE...
...HERE.
CATCH.
ANY QUESTIONS?
ZIIIP
C4
C4
C4

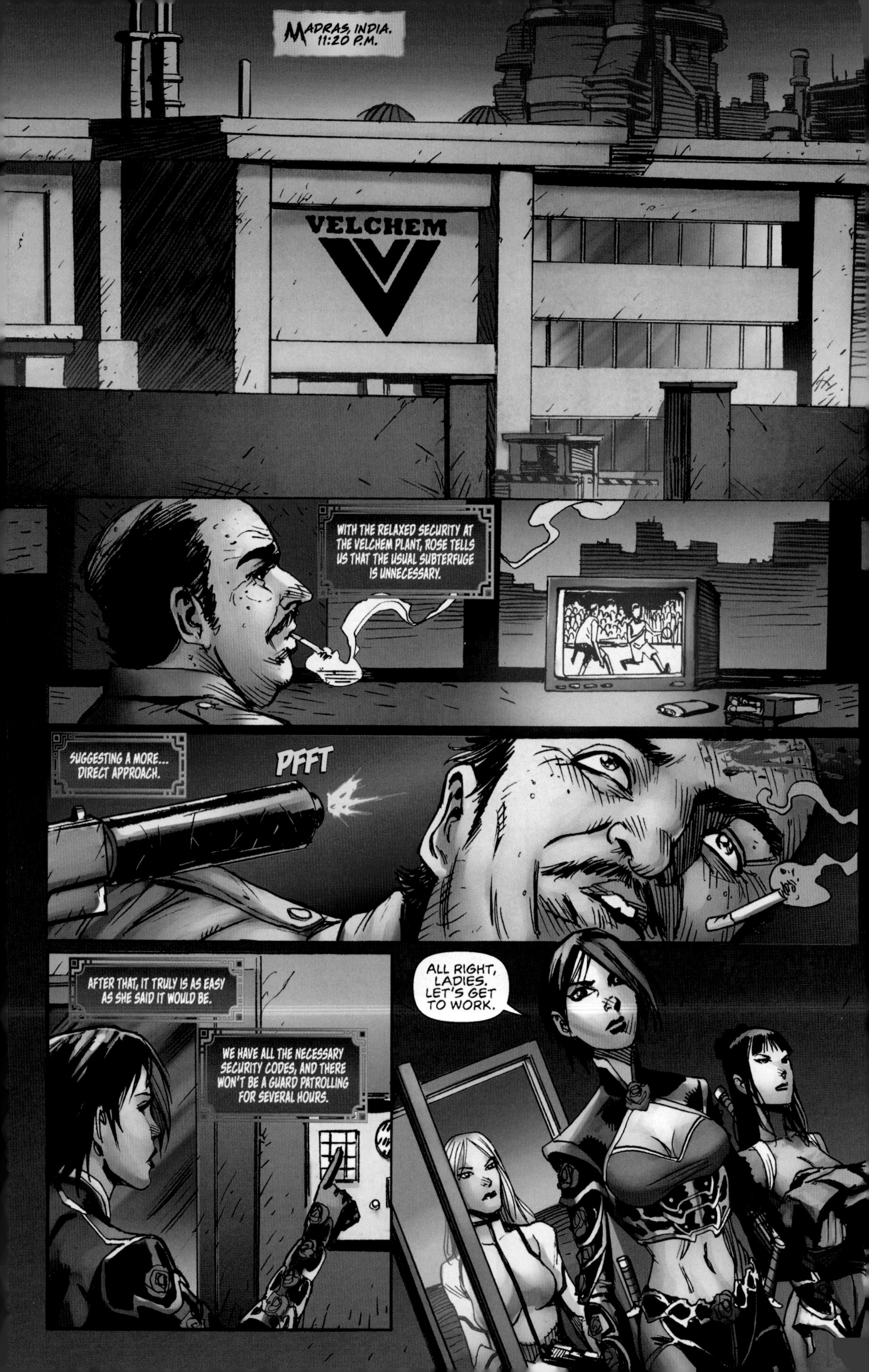
MADRAS, INDIA.
11:20 P.M.
VELCHEM
WITH THE RELAXED SECURITY AT THE VELCHEM PLANT, ROSE TELLS US THAT THE USUAL SUBTERFUGE IS UNNECESSARY.
SUGGESTING A MORE... DIRECT APPROACH.
PFFT
AFTER THAT, IT TRULY IS AS EASY AS SHE SAID IT WOULD BE.
WE HAVE ALL THE NECESSARY SECURITY CODES, AND THERE WON'T BE A GUARD PATROLLING FOR SEVERAL HOURS.
ALL RIGHT, LADIES. LET'S GET TO WORK.

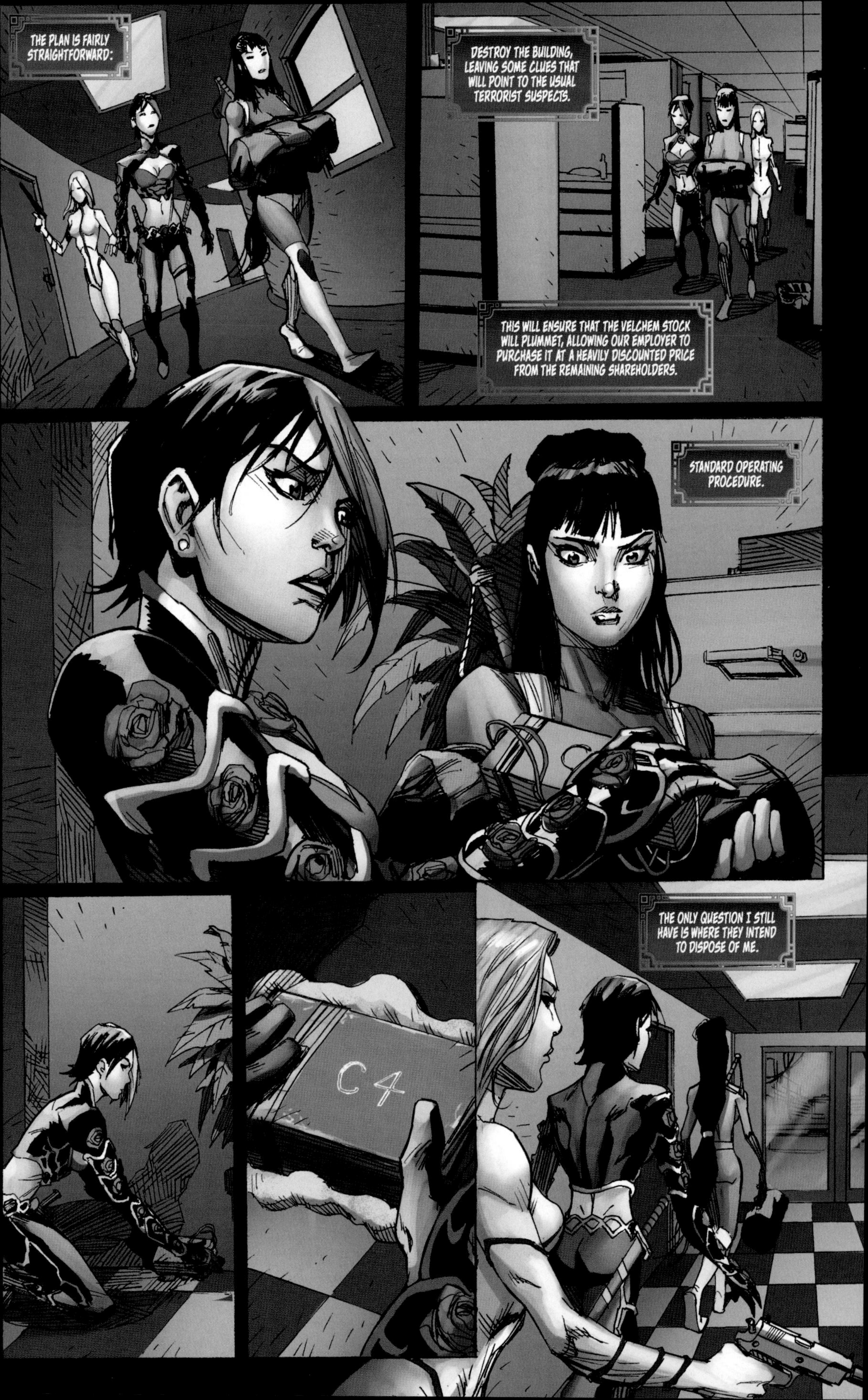
THE PLAN IS FAIRLY STRAIGHTFORWARD:
DESTROY THE BUILDING, LEAVING SOME CLUES THAT WILL POINT TO THE USUAL TERRORIST SUSPECTS.
THIS WILL ENSURE THAT THE VELCHEM STOCK WILL PLUMMET, ALLOWING OUR EMPLOYER TO PURCHASE IT AT A HEAVILY DISCOUNTED PRICE FROM THE REMAINING SHAREHOLDERS.
STANDARD OPERATING PROCEDURE.
C4
THE ONLY QUESTION I STILL HAVE IS WHERE THEY INTEND TO DISPOSE OF ME.

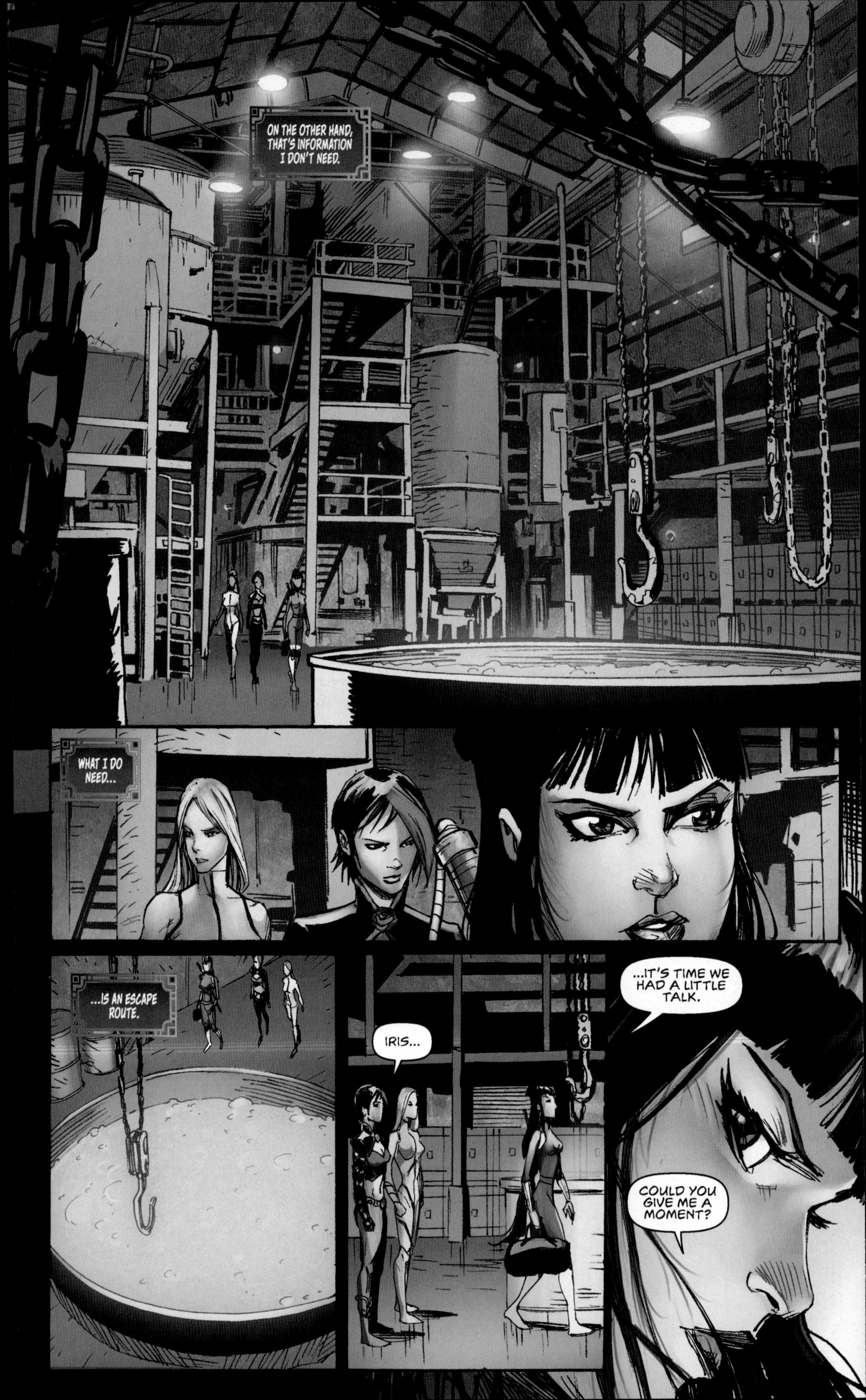
ON THE OTHER HAND, THAT'S INFORMATION I DON'T NEED.
WHAT I DO NEED...
...IS AN ESCAPE ROUTE.
IRIS...
...IT'S TIME WE HAD A LITTLE TALK.
COULD YOU GIVE ME A MOMENT?

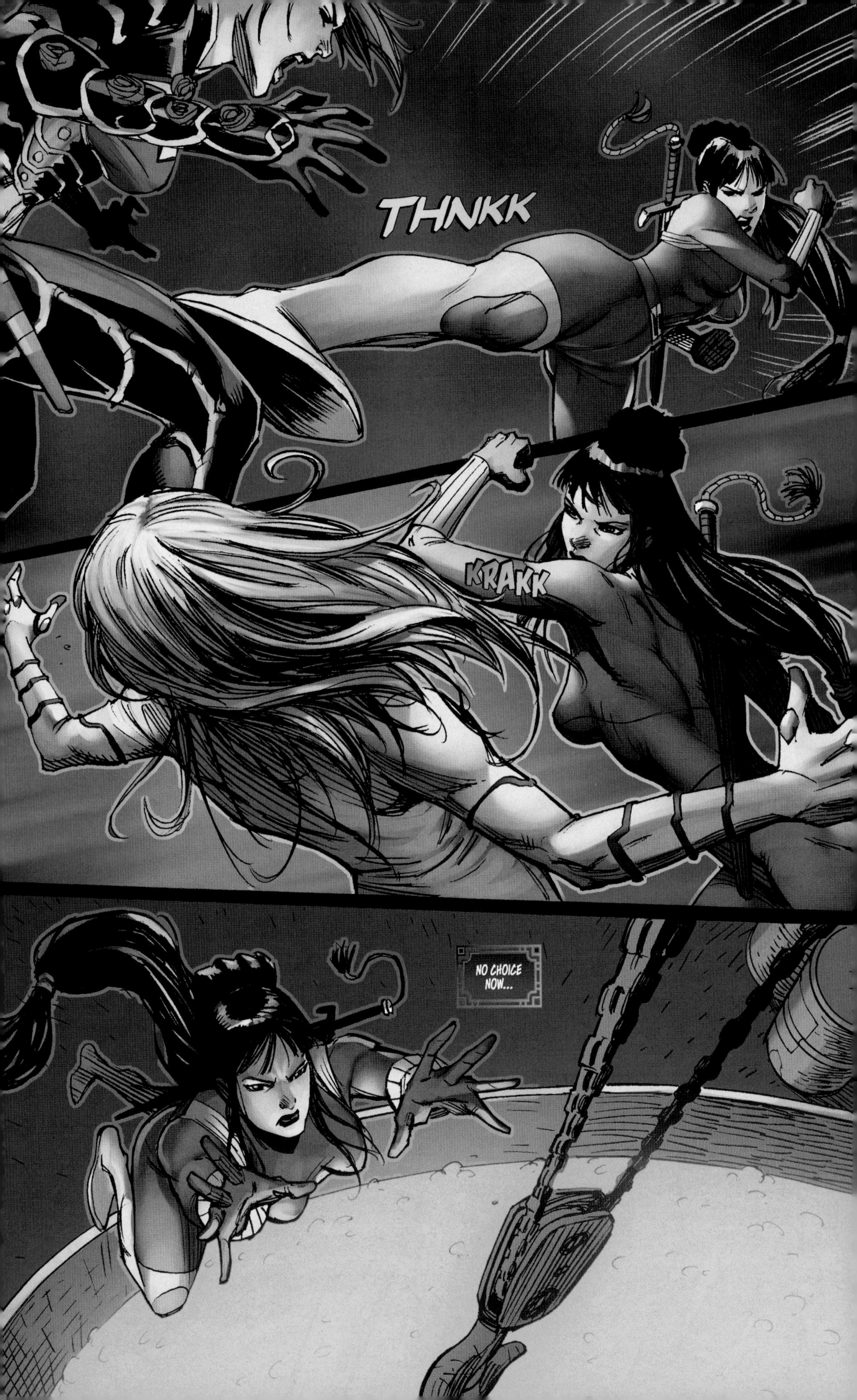
THNKK
KRAKK
NO CHOICE NOW...

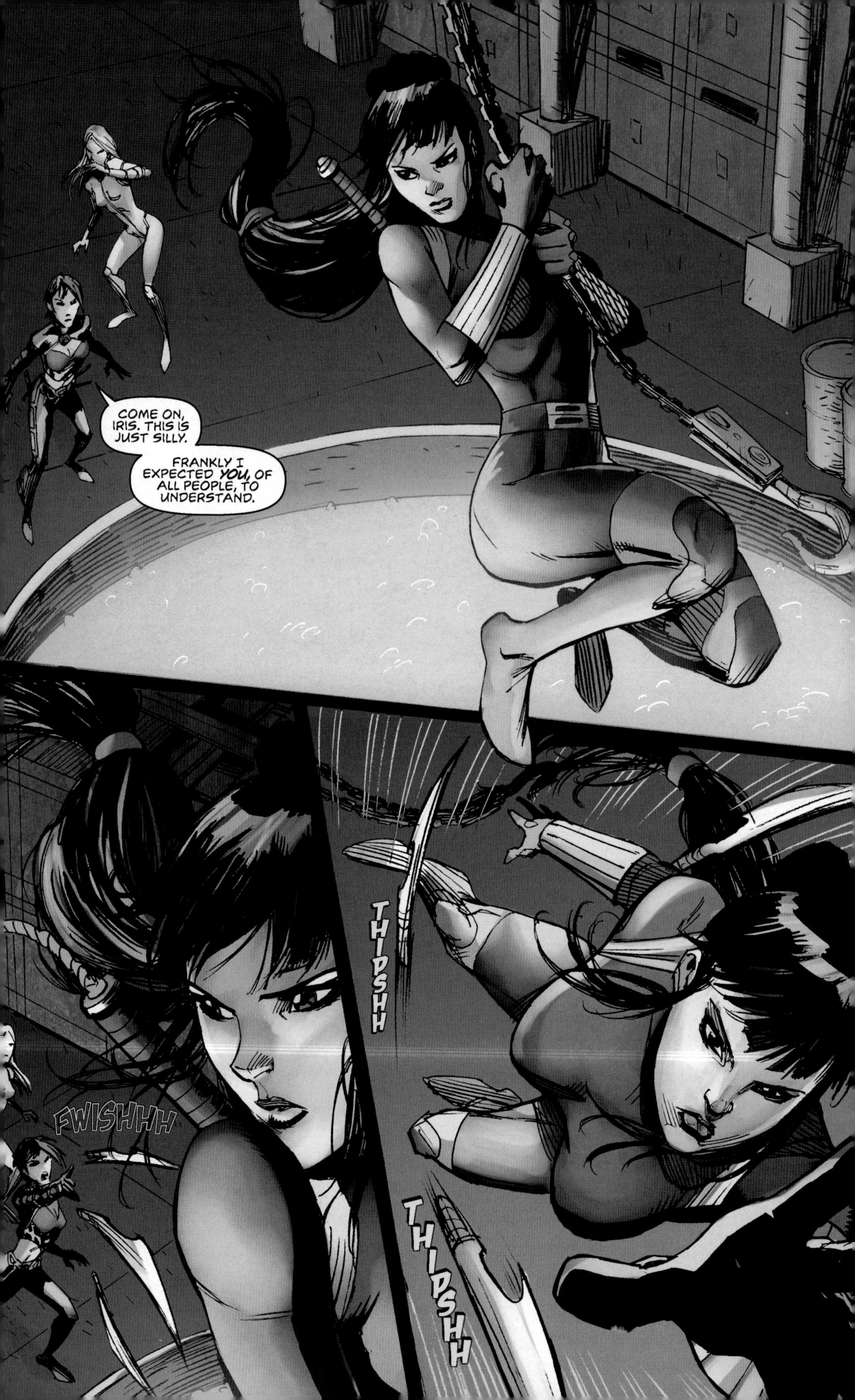
COME ON, IRIS. THIS IS JUST SILLY.
FRANKLY I EXPECTED YOU, OF ALL PEOPLE, TO UNDERSTAND.
FWISHHH
THIPSHH
THIPSHH

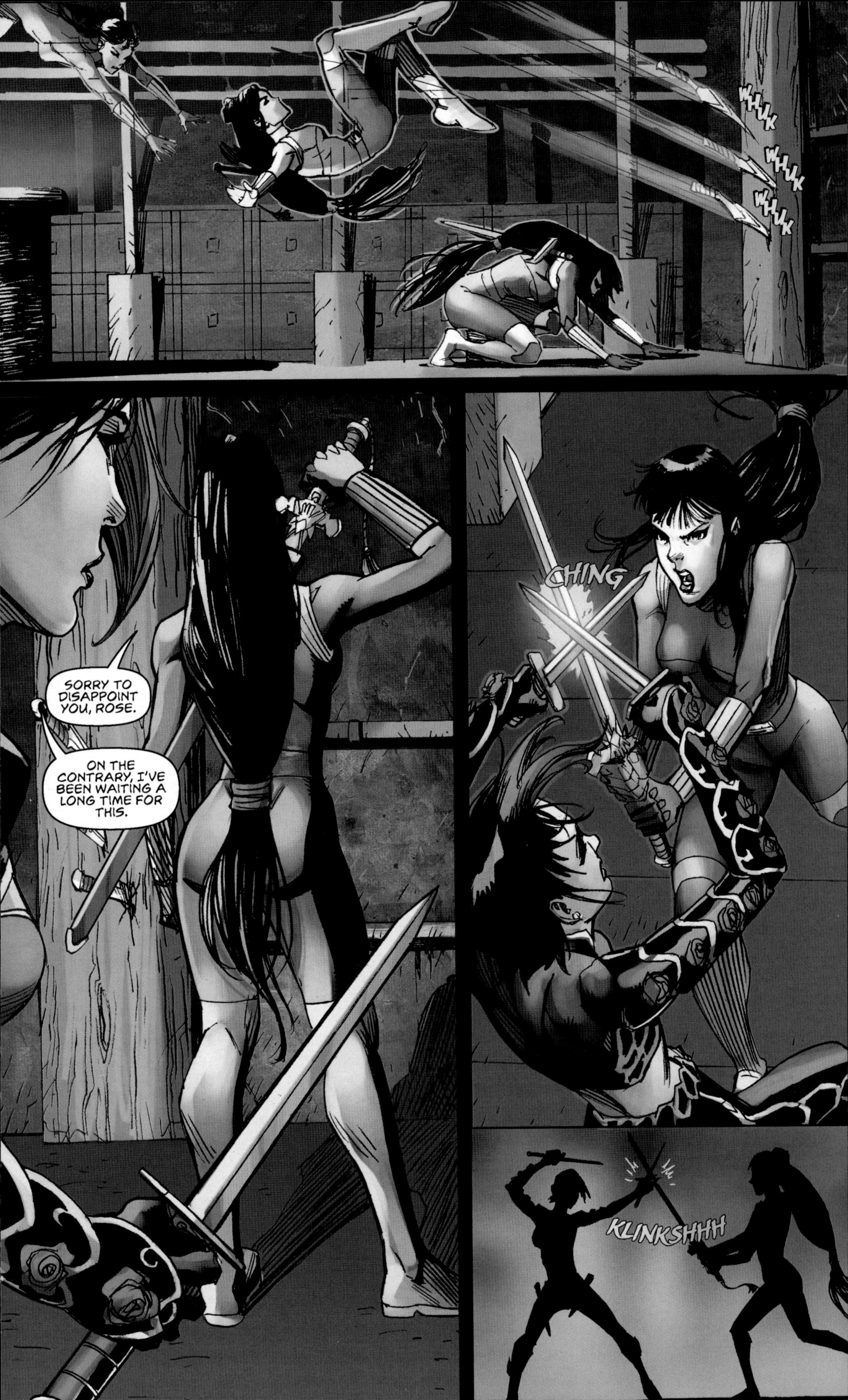
WHUK
WHUK
WHUK
SORRY TO DISAPPOINT YOU, ROSE.
ON THE CONTRARY, I'VE BEEN WAITING A LONG TIME FOR THIS.
CHING
KLINKSHHH

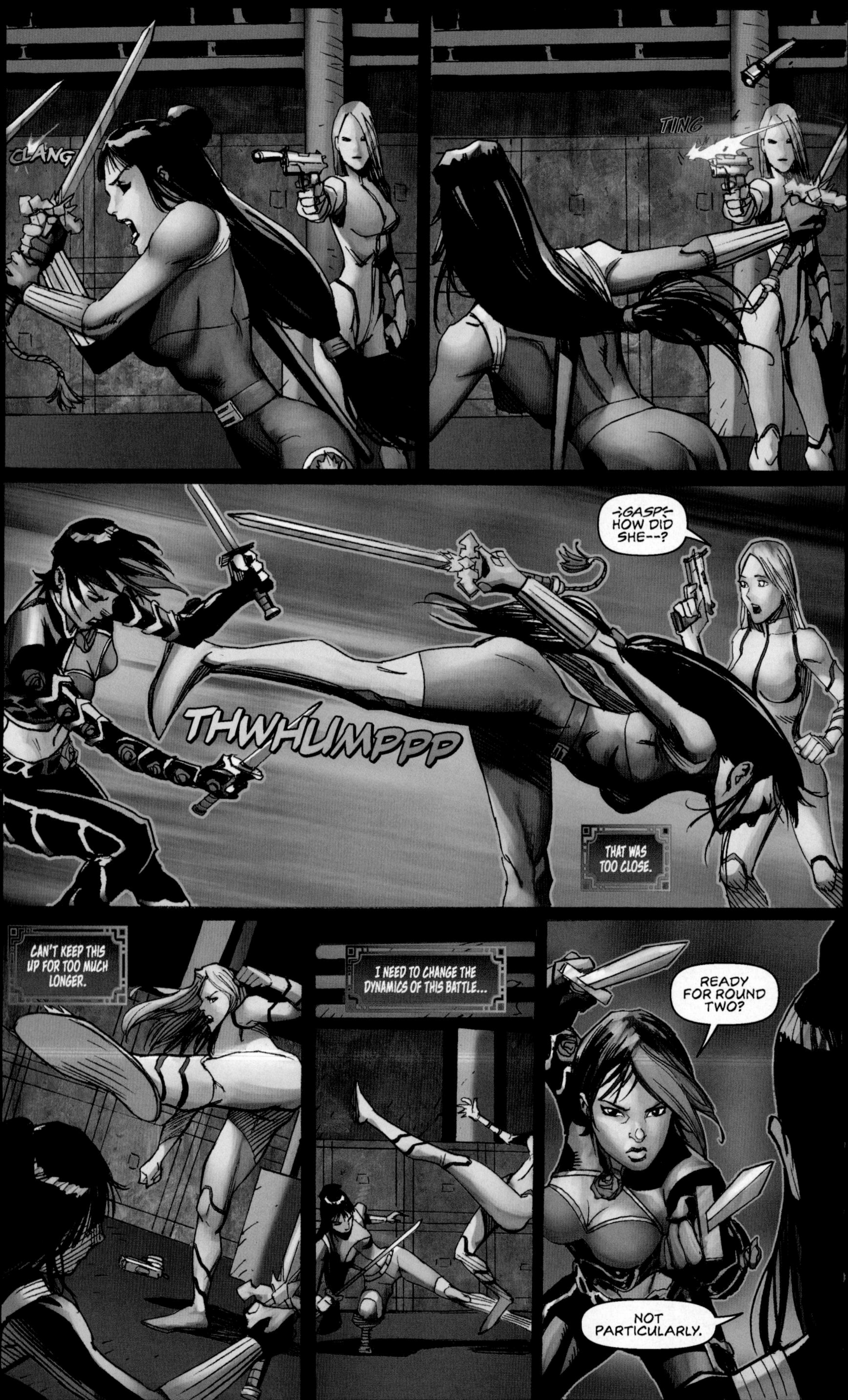
CLANG
TING
¡GASP! HOW DID SHE--?
THWHUMPPP
THAT WAS TOO CLOSE.
CAN'T KEEP THIS UP FOR TOO MUCH LONGER.
I NEED TO CHANGE THE DYNAMICS OF THIS BATTLE...
READY FOR ROUND TWO?
NOT PARTICULARLY.

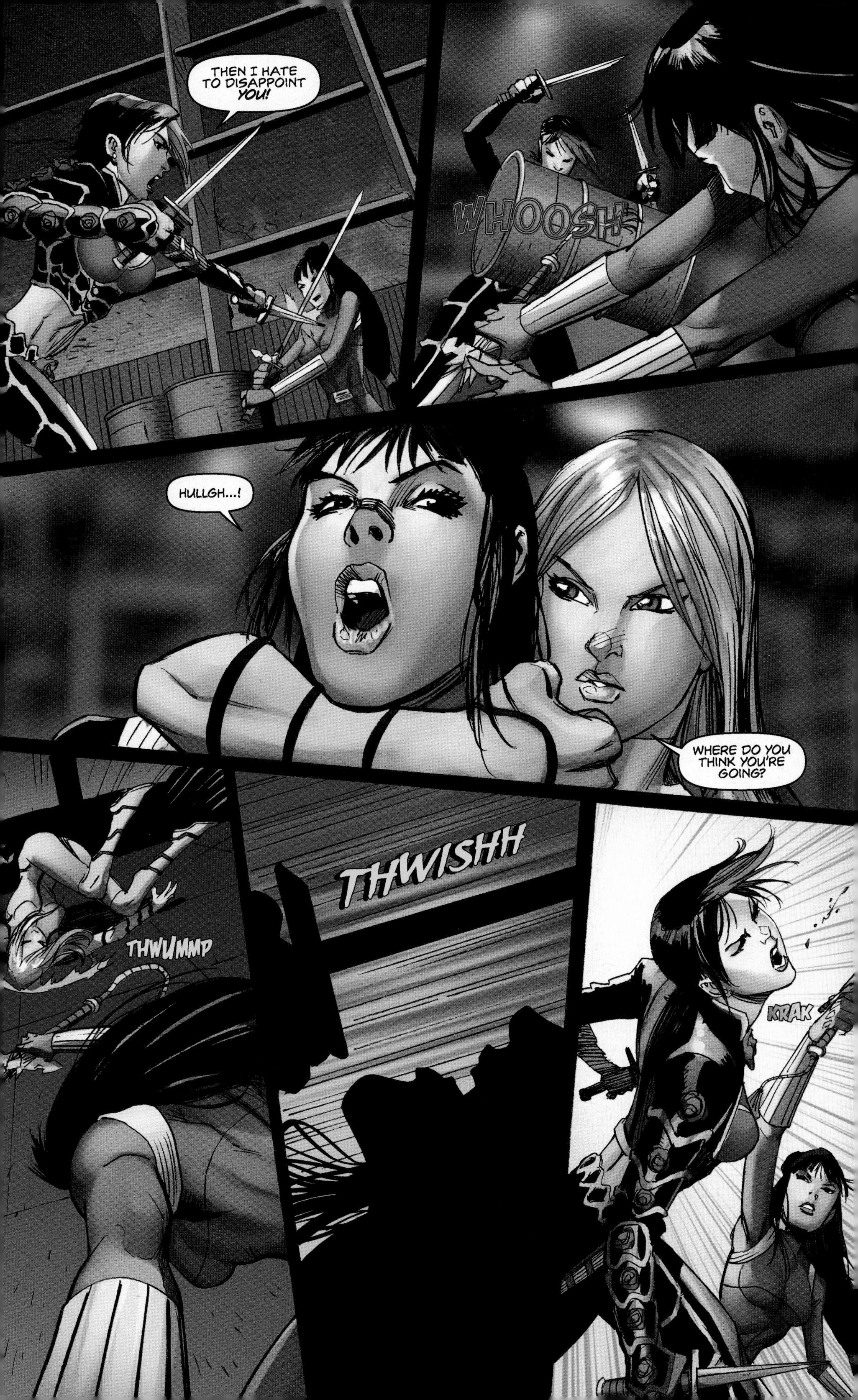
THEN I HATE TO DISAPPOINT YOU!
WHOOSH
HULLGH...!
WHERE DO YOU THINK YOU'RE GOING?
THWUMMD
THWISHH
KRAK

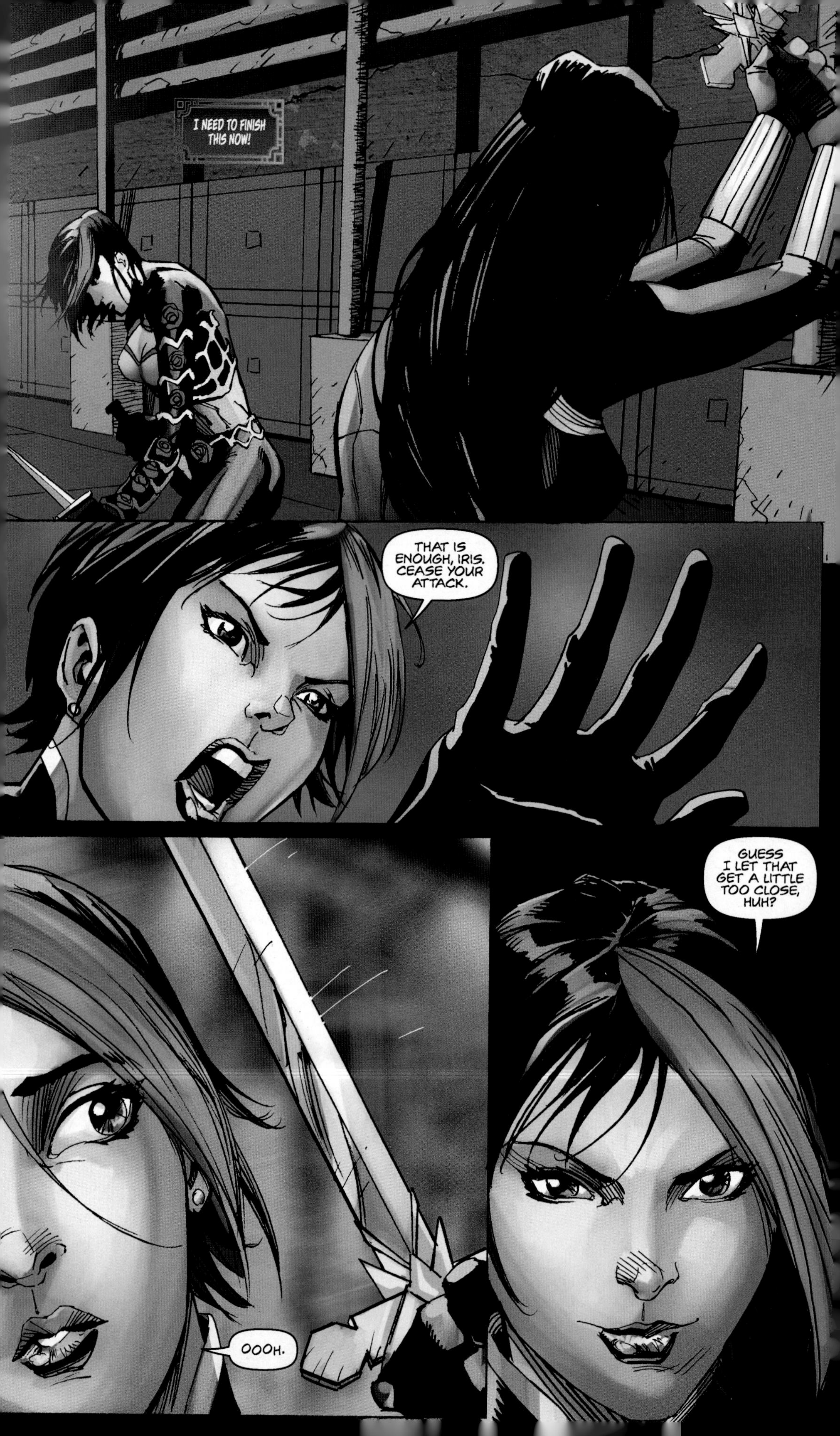
I NEED TO FINISH THIS NOW!
THAT IS ENOUGH, IRIS. CEASE YOUR ATTACK.
GUESS I LET THAT GET A LITTLE TOO CLOSE, HUH?
OOOH.

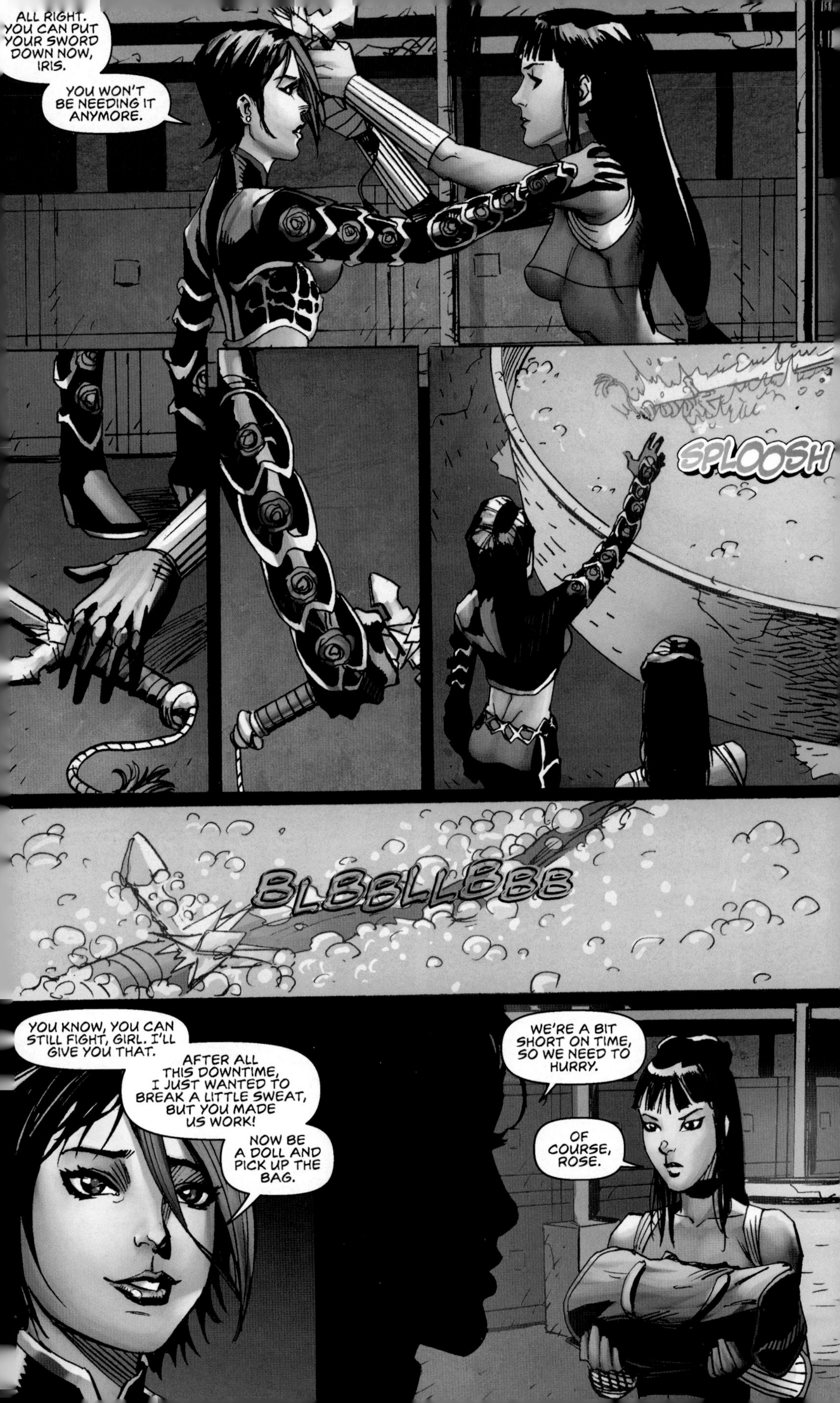

ALL RIGHT. YOU CAN PUT YOUR SWORD DOWN NOW, IRIS.
YOU WON'T BE NEEDING IT ANYMORE.
SPLOOSH
BLBBLLBBB
YOU KNOW, YOU CAN STILL FIGHT, GIRL. I'LL GIVE YOU THAT.
AFTER ALL THIS DOWNTIME, I JUST WANTED TO BREAK A LITTLE SWEAT, BUT YOU MADE US WORK!
NOW BE A DOLL AND PICK UP THE BAG.
WE'RE A BIT SHORT ON TIME, SO WE NEED TO HURRY.
OF COURSE, ROSE.

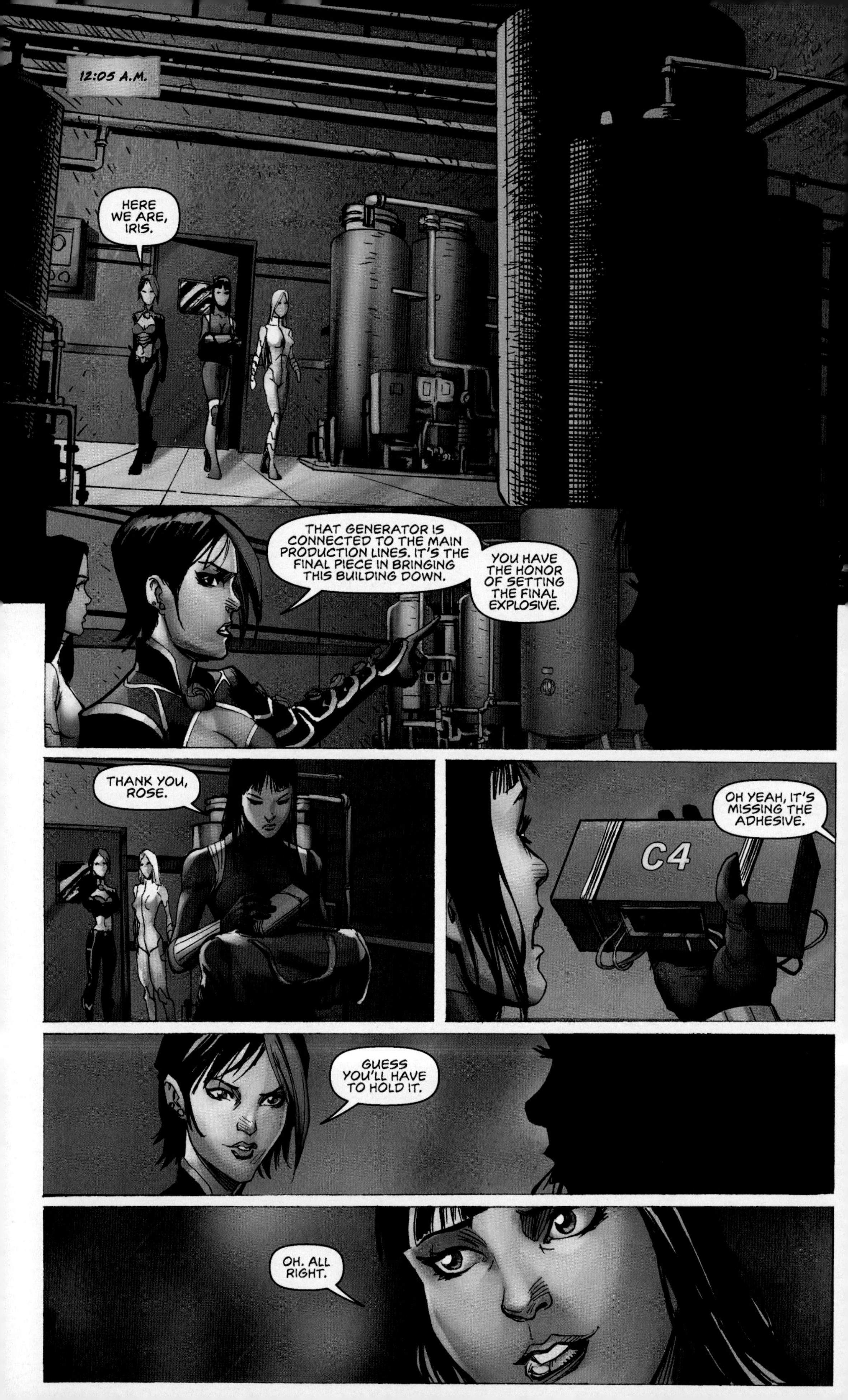
12:05 A.M.
HERE WE ARE, IRIS.
THAT GENERATOR IS CONNECTED TO THE MAIN PRODUCTION LINES. IT'S THE FINAL PIECE IN BRINGING THIS BUILDING DOWN.
YOU HAVE THE HONOR OF SETTING THE FINAL EXPLOSIVE.
THANK YOU, ROSE.
OH YEAH, IT'S MISSING THE ADHESIVE.
C4
GUESS YOU'LL HAVE TO HOLD IT.
OH. ALL RIGHT.

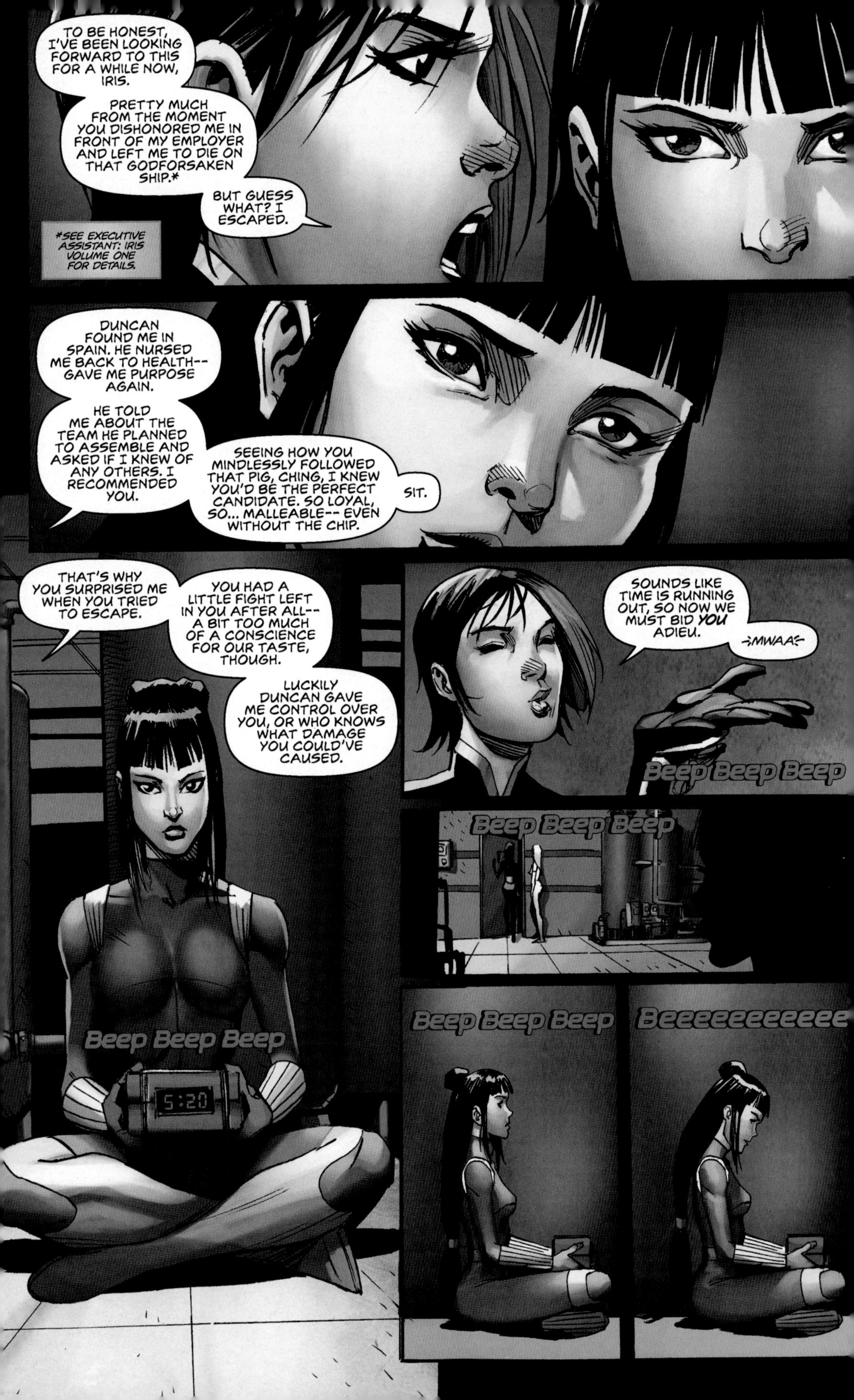

TO BE HONEST, I'VE BEEN LOOKING FORWARD TO THIS FOR A WHILE NOW, IRIS.
PRETTY MUCH FROM THE MOMENT YOU DISHONORED ME IN FRONT OF MY EMPLOYER AND LEFT ME TO DIE ON THAT GODFORSAKEN SHIP.*
BUT GUESS WHAT? I ESCAPED.
*SEE EXECUTIVE ASSISTANT: IRIS VOLUME ONE FOR DETAILS.
DUNCAN FOUND ME IN SPAIN. HE NURSED ME BACK TO HEALTH-- GAVE ME PURPOSE AGAIN.
HE TOLD ME ABOUT THE TEAM HE PLANNED TO ASSEMBLE AND ASKED IF I KNEW OF ANY OTHERS. I RECOMMENDED YOU.
SEEING HOW YOU MINDLESSLY FOLLOWED THAT PIG, CHING, I KNEW YOU'D BE THE PERFECT CANDIDATE. SO LOYAL, SO... MALLEABLE-- EVEN WITHOUT THE CHIP.
SIT.
THAT'S WHY YOU SURPRISED ME WHEN YOU TRIED TO ESCAPE.
YOU HAD A LITTLE FIGHT LEFT IN YOU AFTER ALL-- A BIT TOO MUCH OF A CONSCIENCE FOR OUR TASTE, THOUGH.
LUCKILY DUNCAN GAVE ME CONTROL OVER YOU, OR WHO KNOWS WHAT DAMAGE YOU COULD'VE CAUSED.
Beep Beep Beep
5:20
SOUNDS LIKE TIME IS RUNNING OUT, SO NOW WE MUST BID YOU ADIEU.
-MWAA-
Beep Beep Beep
Beep Beep Beep
Beep Beep Beep
Beeeeeeeeeee

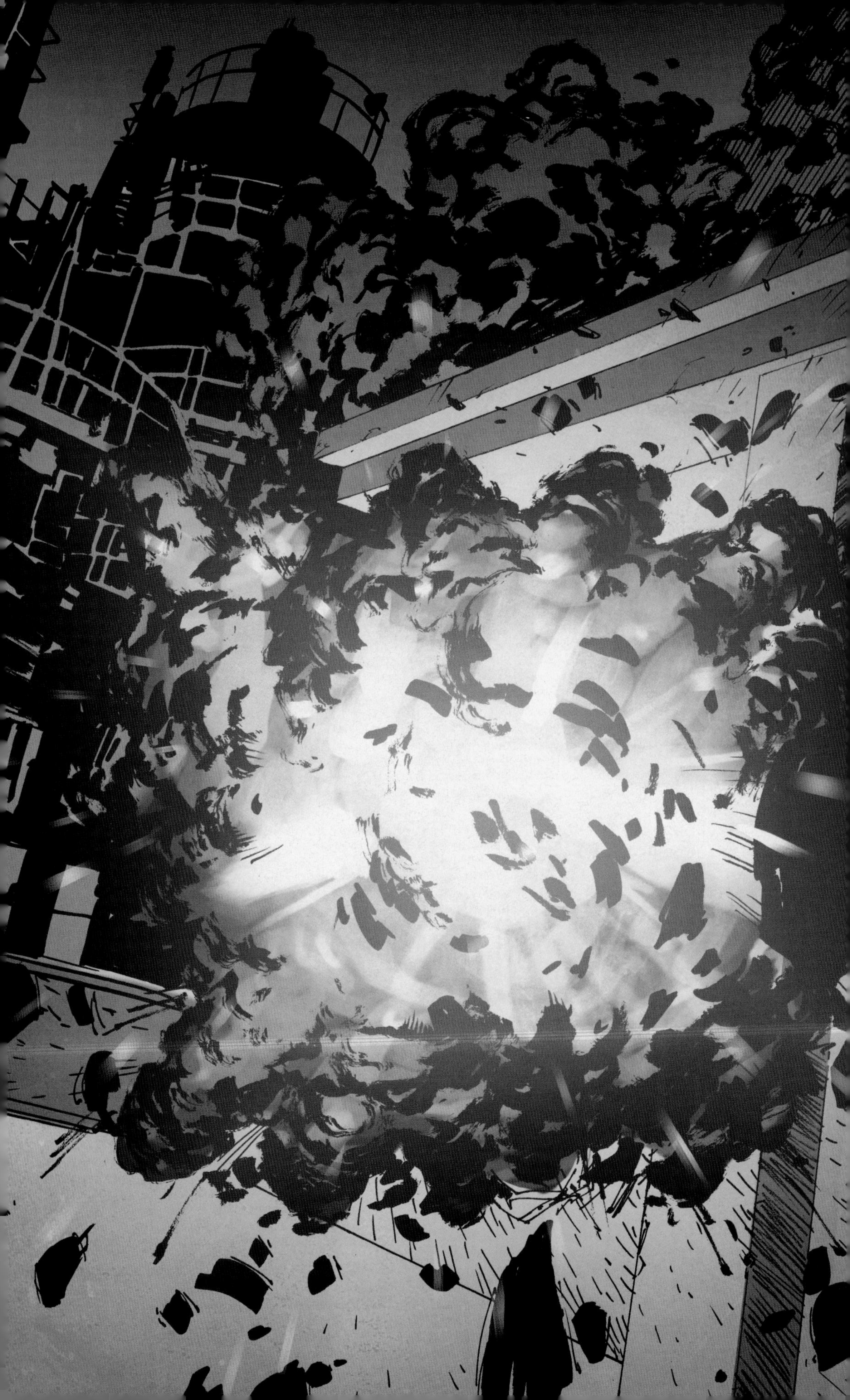

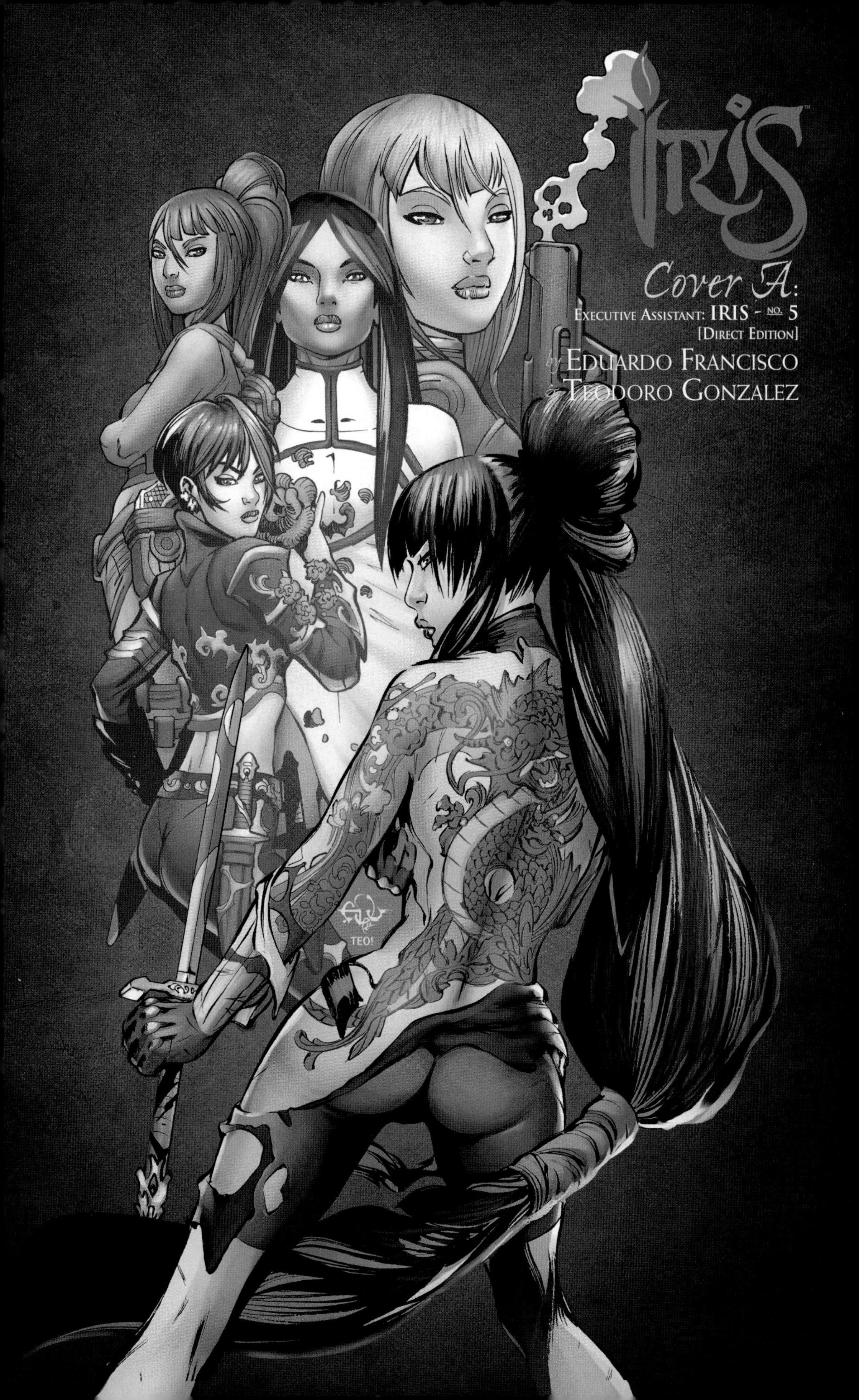
IRIS
Cover A:
Executive Assistant: IRIS - No. 5
[Direct Edition]
by Eduardo Francisco
& Teodoro Gonzalez
TEO!

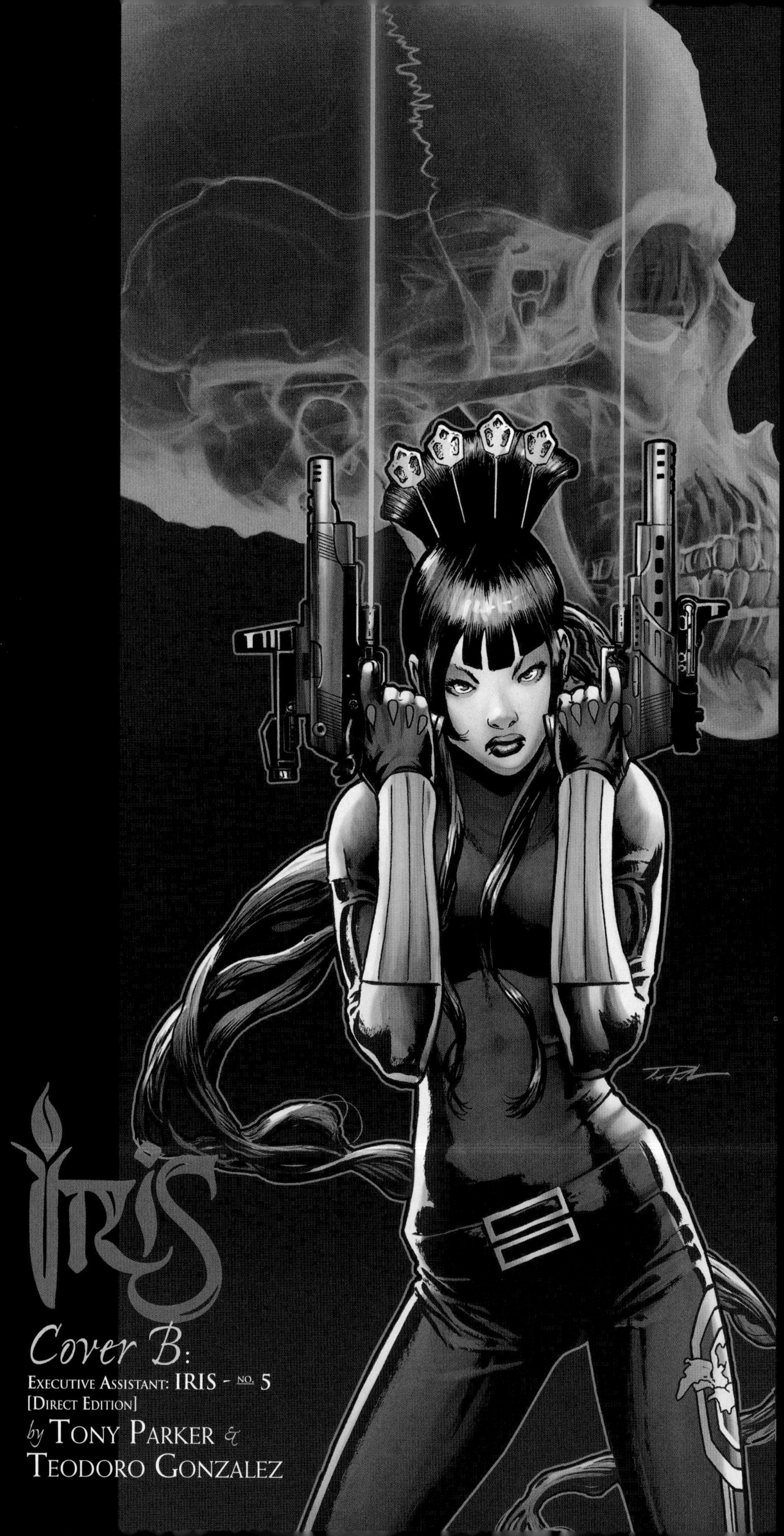
IRIS
Cover B:
Executive Assistant: IRIS - No. 5
[Direct Edition]
by Tony Parker & Teodoro Gonzalez

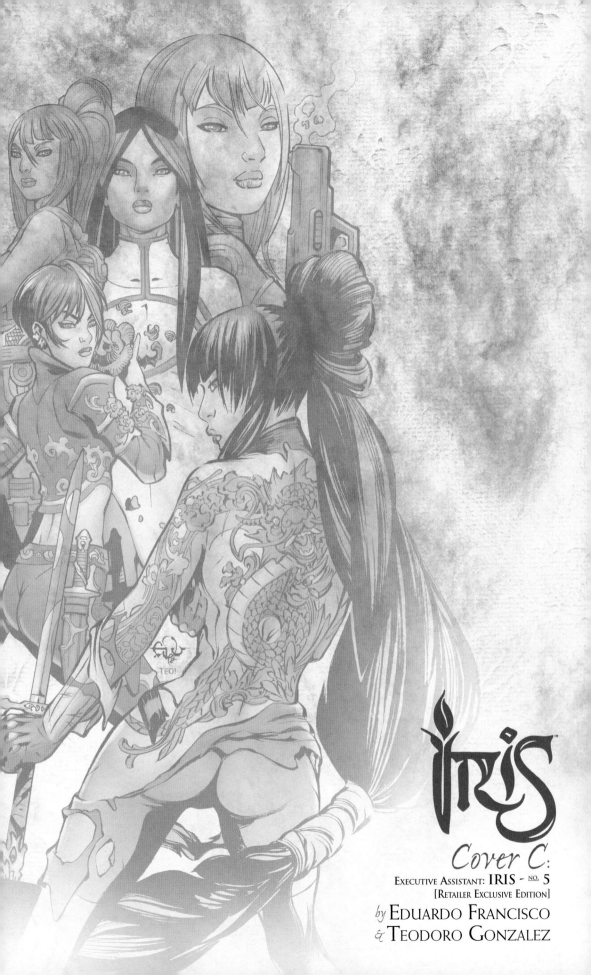

Iris

Cover C:

EXECUTIVE ASSISTANT: *IRIS* - NO. 5
[RETAILER EXCLUSIVE EDITION]

by EDUARDO FRANCISCO
& TEODORO GONZALEZ

CHAPTER SIX

FIVE

"BLAZE OF GLORY"

WRITER
DAVID WOHL

PENCILS
RYAN ODAGAWA

COLORS
TEODORO GONZALEZ

LETTERING
JOSH REED

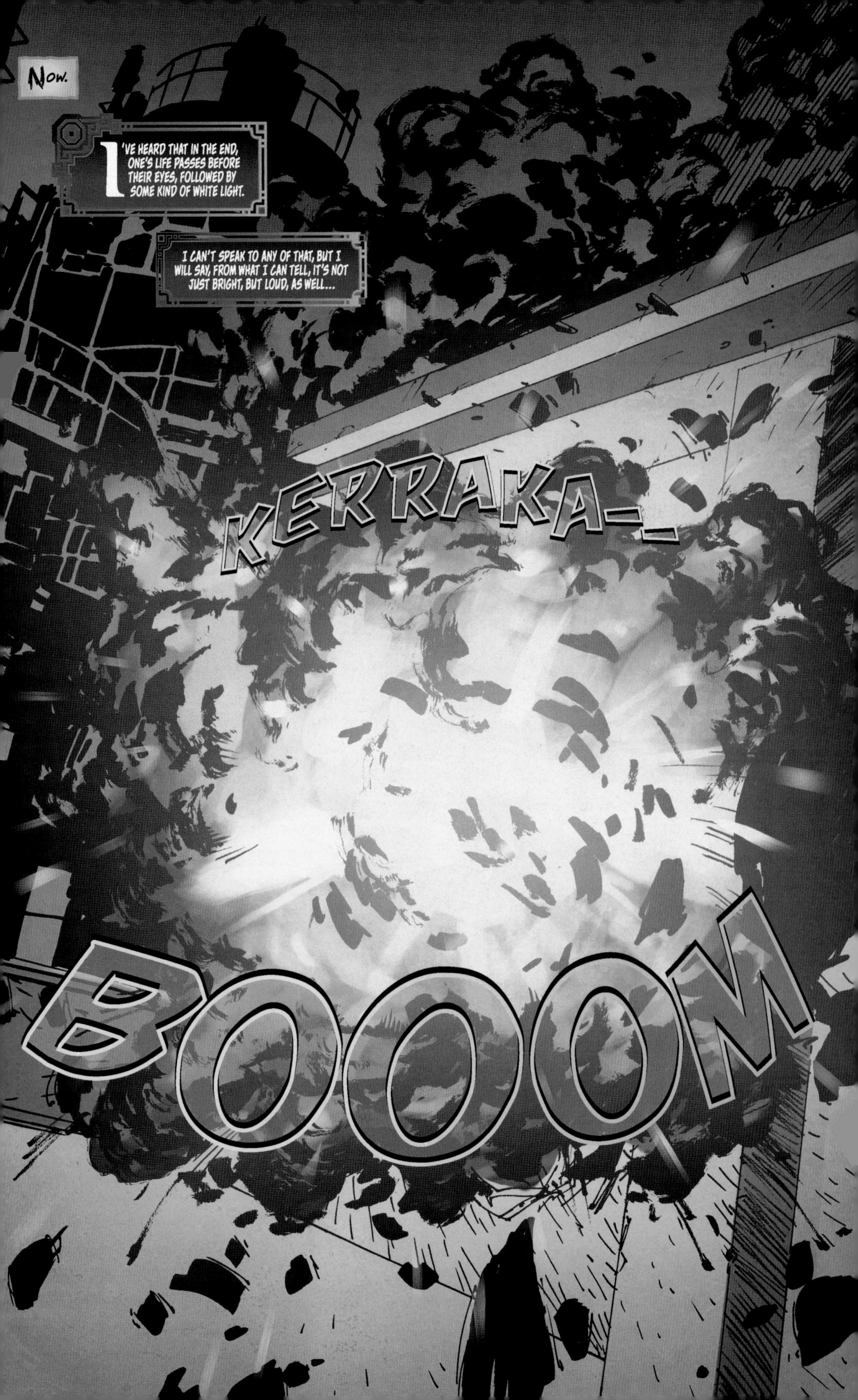
Now.
I'VE HEARD THAT IN THE END, ONE'S LIFE PASSES BEFORE THEIR EYES, FOLLOWED BY SOME KIND OF WHITE LIGHT.
I CAN'T SPEAK TO ANY OF THAT, BUT I WILL SAY, FROM WHAT I CAN TELL, IT'S NOT JUST BRIGHT, BUT LOUD, AS WELL...
KERRAKA--
BOOOM

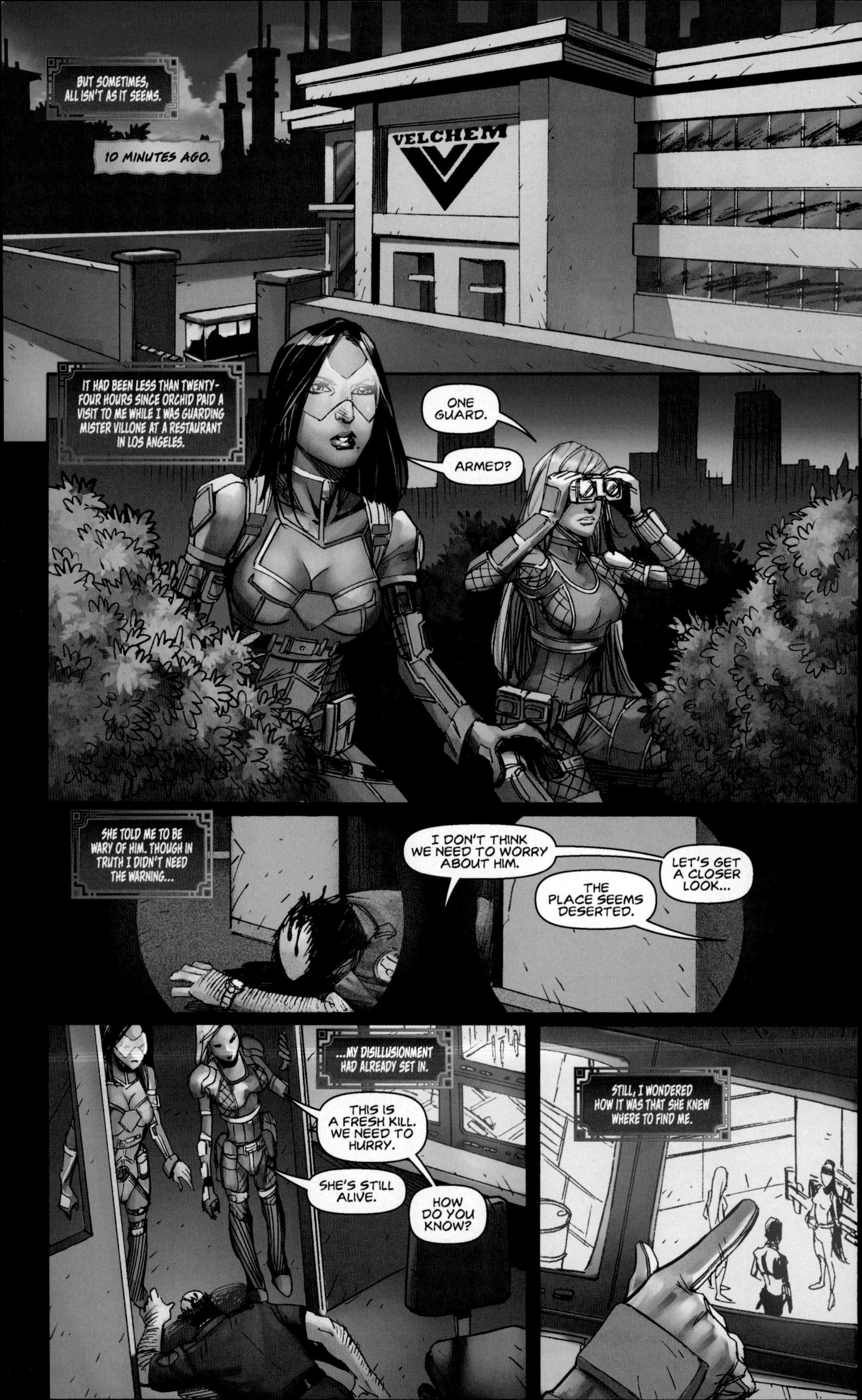
BUT SOMETIMES, ALL ISN'T AS IT SEEMS.
10 MINUTES AGO.
VELCHEM
IT HAD BEEN LESS THAN TWENTY-FOUR HOURS SINCE ORCHID PAID A VISIT TO ME WHILE I WAS GUARDING MISTER VILLONE AT A RESTAURANT IN LOS ANGELES.
ONE GUARD.
ARMED?
SHE TOLD ME TO BE WARY OF HIM. THOUGH IN TRUTH I DIDN'T NEED THE WARNING...
I DON'T THINK WE NEED TO WORRY ABOUT HIM.
LET'S GET A CLOSER LOOK...
THE PLACE SEEMS DESERTED.
...MY DISILLUSIONMENT HAD ALREADY SET IN.
THIS IS A FRESH KILL. WE NEED TO HURRY.
SHE'S STILL ALIVE.
HOW DO YOU KNOW?
STILL, I WONDERED HOW IT WAS THAT SHE KNEW WHERE TO FIND ME.

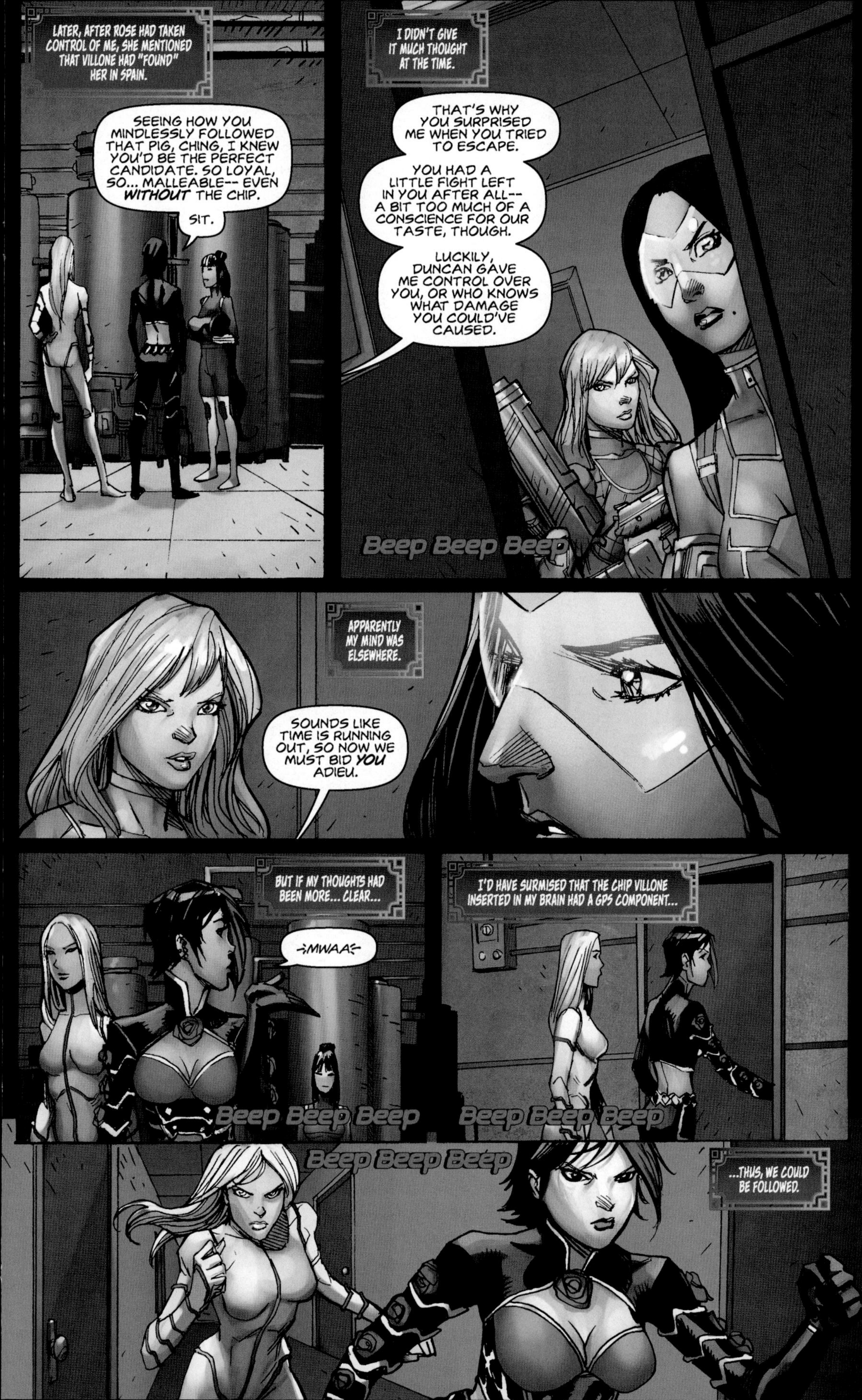
LATER, AFTER ROSE HAD TAKEN CONTROL OF ME, SHE MENTIONED THAT VILLONE HAD "FOUND" HER IN SPAIN.
SEEING HOW YOU MINDLESSLY FOLLOWED THAT PIG, CHING, I KNEW YOU'D BE THE PERFECT CANDIDATE. SO LOYAL, SO... MALLEABLE-- EVEN WITHOUT THE CHIP.
SIT.
I DIDN'T GIVE IT MUCH THOUGHT AT THE TIME.
THAT'S WHY YOU SURPRISED ME WHEN YOU TRIED TO ESCAPE.
YOU HAD A LITTLE FIGHT LEFT IN YOU AFTER ALL-- A BIT TOO MUCH OF A CONSCIENCE FOR OUR TASTE, THOUGH.
LUCKILY, DUNCAN GAVE ME CONTROL OVER YOU, OR WHO KNOWS WHAT DAMAGE YOU COULD'VE CAUSED.
Beep Beep Beep
APPARENTLY MY MIND WAS ELSEWHERE.
SOUNDS LIKE TIME IS RUNNING OUT, SO NOW WE MUST BID YOU ADIEU.
BUT IF MY THOUGHTS HAD BEEN MORE... CLEAR...
MWAA
Beep Beep Beep
I'D HAVE SURMISED THAT THE CHIP VILLONE INSERTED IN MY BRAIN HAD A GPS COMPONENT...
Beep Beep Beep
Beep Beep Beep
...THUS, WE COULD BE FOLLOWED.

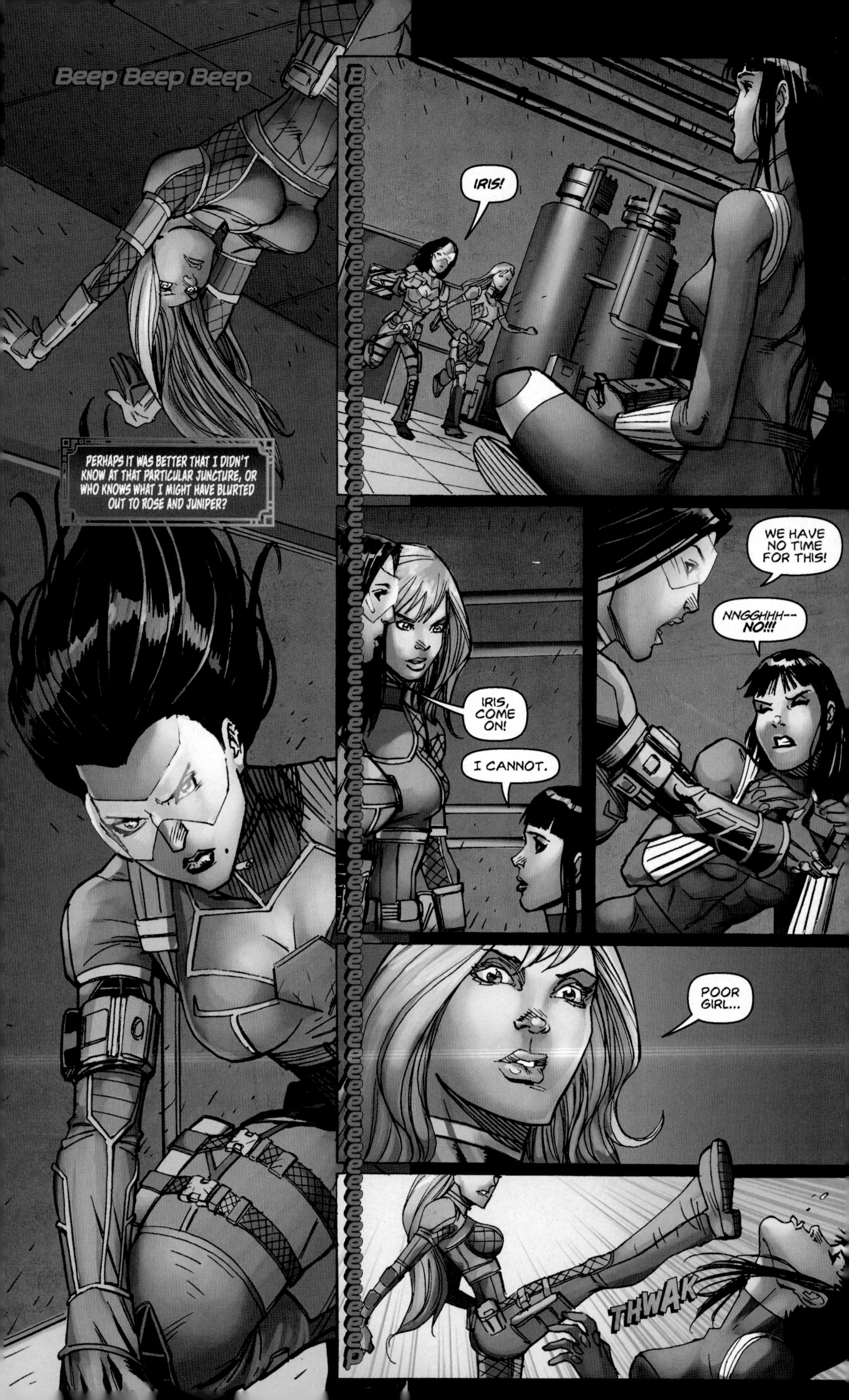
Beep Beep Beep
IRIS!
PERHAPS IT WAS BETTER THAT I DIDN'T KNOW AT THAT PARTICULAR JUNCTURE, OR WHO KNOWS WHAT I MIGHT HAVE BLURTED OUT TO ROSE AND JUNIPER?
IRIS, COME ON!
I CANNOT.
WE HAVE NO TIME FOR THIS!
NNGGHHH-- NO!!!
POOR GIRL...
THWAK

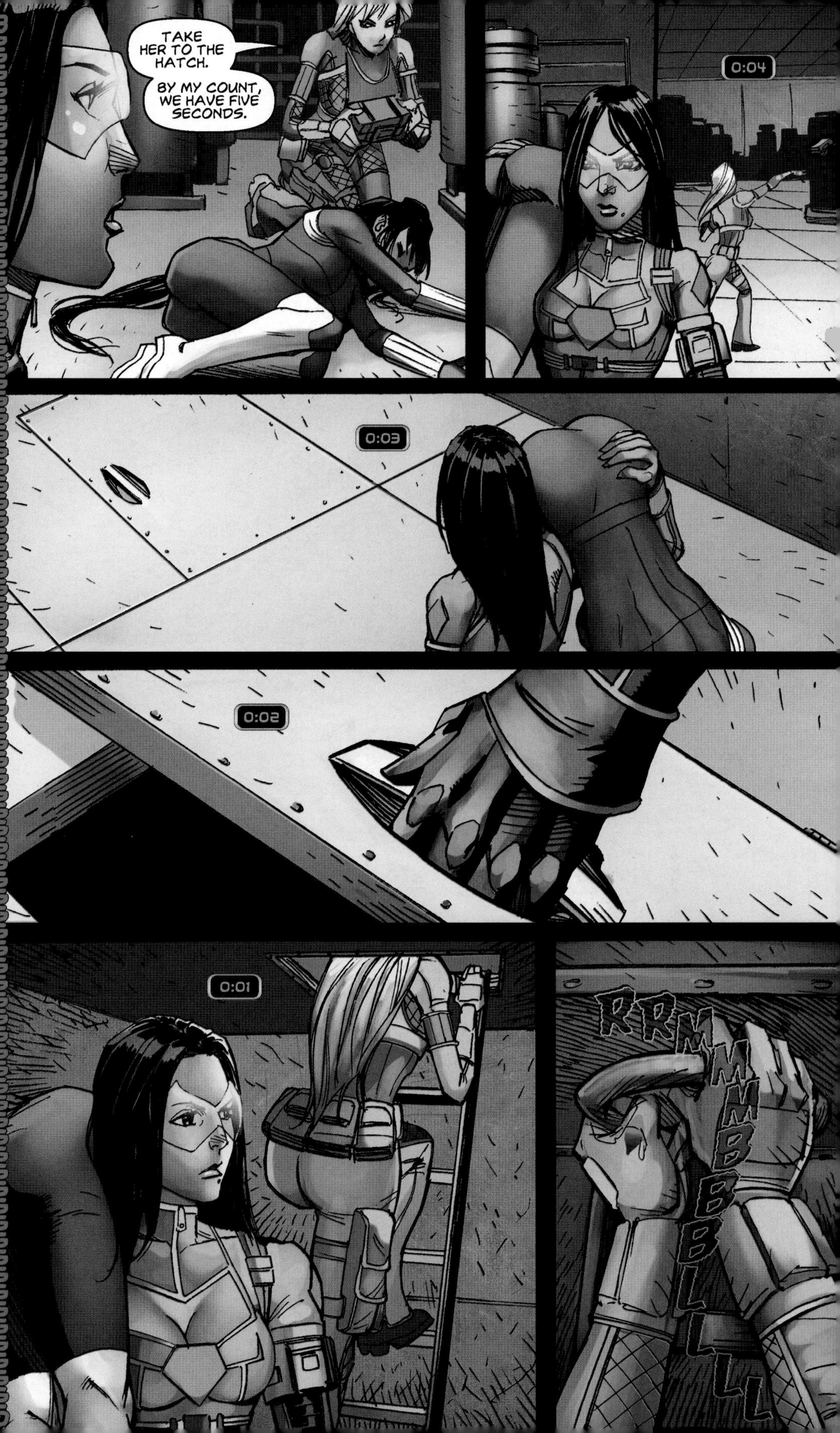

TAKE HER TO THE HATCH.
BY MY COUNT, WE HAVE FIVE SECONDS.
0:04
0:03
0:02
0:01
RRMMMBBBLLLL

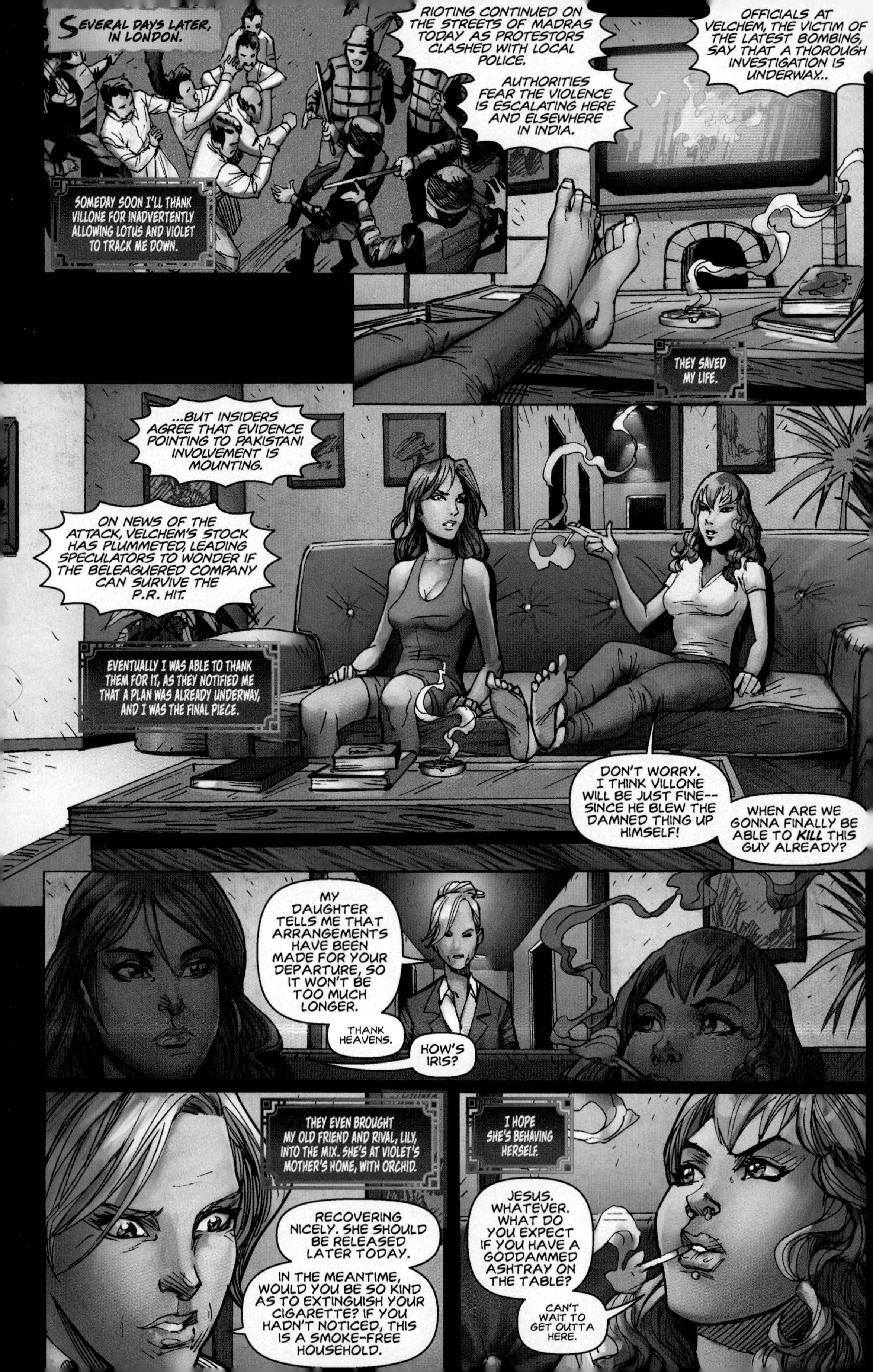

SEVERAL DAYS LATER, IN LONDON.
RIOTING CONTINUED ON THE STREETS OF MADRAS TODAY AS PROTESTORS CLASHED WITH LOCAL POLICE.
AUTHORITIES FEAR THE VIOLENCE IS ESCALATING HERE AND ELSEWHERE IN INDIA.
OFFICIALS AT VELCHEM, THE VICTIM OF THE LATEST BOMBING, SAY THAT A THOROUGH INVESTIGATION IS UNDERWAY...
SOMEDAY SOON I'LL THANK VILLONE FOR INADVERTENTLY ALLOWING LOTUS AND VIOLET TO TRACK ME DOWN.
THEY SAVED MY LIFE.
...BUT INSIDERS AGREE THAT EVIDENCE POINTING TO PAKISTANI INVOLVEMENT IS MOUNTING.
ON NEWS OF THE ATTACK, VELCHEM'S STOCK HAS PLUMMETED, LEADING SPECULATORS TO WONDER IF THE BELEAGUERED COMPANY CAN SURVIVE THE P.R. HIT.
EVENTUALLY I WAS ABLE TO THANK THEM FOR IT, AS THEY NOTIFIED ME THAT A PLAN WAS ALREADY UNDERWAY, AND I WAS THE FINAL PIECE.
DON'T WORRY. I THINK VILLONE WILL BE JUST FINE-- SINCE HE BLEW THE DAMNED THING UP HIMSELF!
WHEN ARE WE GONNA FINALLY BE ABLE TO KILL THIS GUY ALREADY?
MY DAUGHTER TELLS ME THAT ARRANGEMENTS HAVE BEEN MADE FOR YOUR DEPARTURE, SO IT WON'T BE TOO MUCH LONGER.
THANK HEAVENS.
HOW'S IRIS?
THEY EVEN BROUGHT MY OLD FRIEND AND RIVAL, LILY, INTO THE MIX. SHE'S AT VIOLET'S MOTHER'S HOME, WITH ORCHID.
RECOVERING NICELY. SHE SHOULD BE RELEASED LATER TODAY.
IN THE MEANTIME, WOULD YOU BE SO KIND AS TO EXTINGUISH YOUR CIGARETTE? IF YOU HADN'T NOTICED, THIS IS A SMOKE-FREE HOUSEHOLD.
I HOPE SHE'S BEHAVING HERSELF.
JESUS. WHATEVER. WHAT DO YOU EXPECT IF YOU HAVE A GODDAMMED ASHTRAY ON THE TABLE?
CAN'T WAIT TO GET OUTTA HERE.

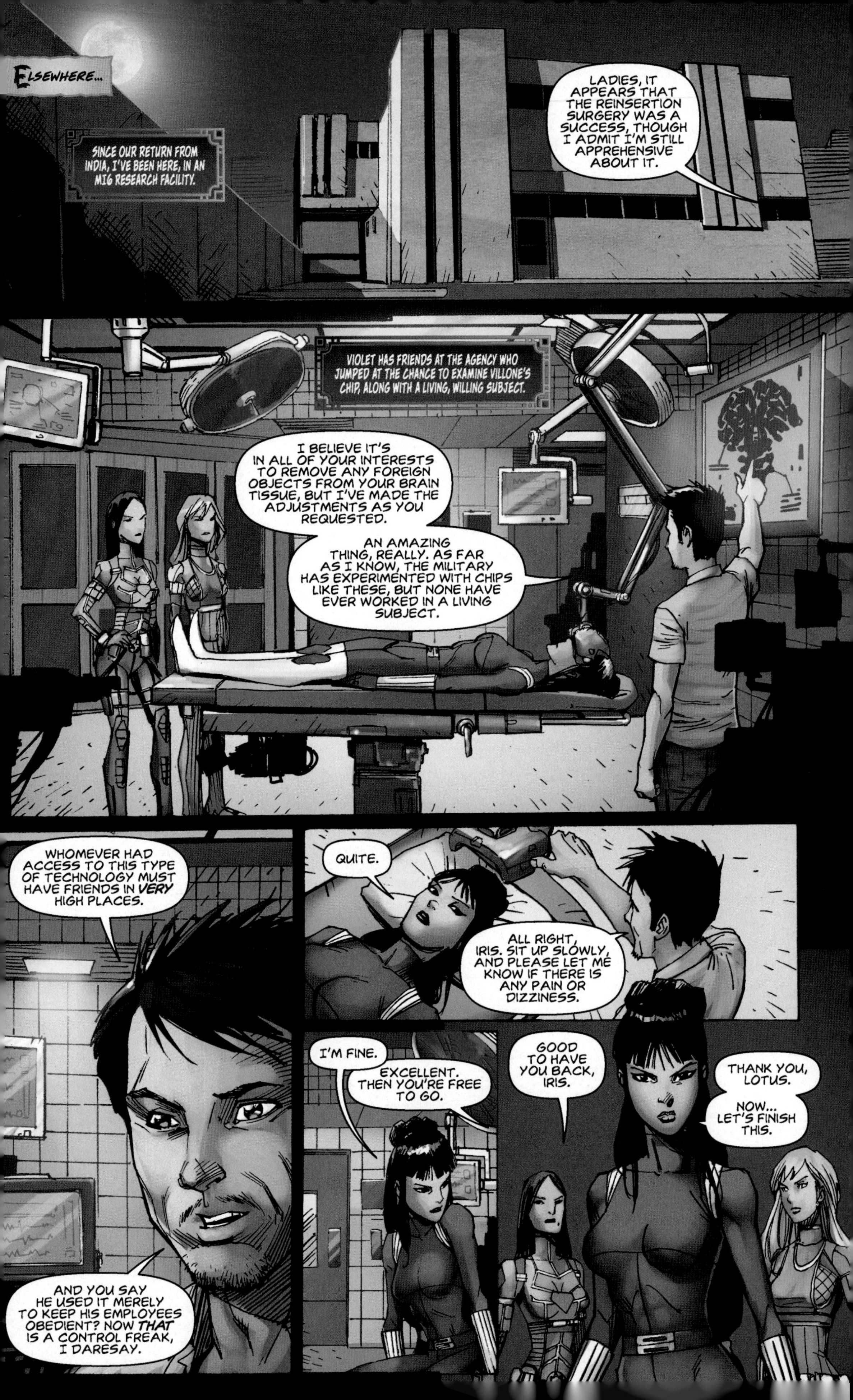
ELSEWHERE...
SINCE OUR RETURN FROM INDIA, I'VE BEEN HERE, IN AN MI6 RESEARCH FACILITY.
LADIES, IT APPEARS THAT THE REINSERTION SURGERY WAS A SUCCESS, THOUGH I ADMIT I'M STILL APPREHENSIVE ABOUT IT.
VIOLET HAS FRIENDS AT THE AGENCY WHO JUMPED AT THE CHANCE TO EXAMINE VILLONE'S CHIP, ALONG WITH A LIVING, WILLING SUBJECT.
I BELIEVE IT'S IN ALL OF YOUR INTERESTS TO REMOVE ANY FOREIGN OBJECTS FROM YOUR BRAIN TISSUE, BUT I'VE MADE THE ADJUSTMENTS AS YOU REQUESTED.
AN AMAZING THING, REALLY. AS FAR AS I KNOW, THE MILITARY HAS EXPERIMENTED WITH CHIPS LIKE THESE, BUT NONE HAVE EVER WORKED IN A LIVING SUBJECT.
WHOMEVER HAD ACCESS TO THIS TYPE OF TECHNOLOGY MUST HAVE FRIENDS IN *VERY* HIGH PLACES.
AND YOU SAY HE USED IT MERELY TO KEEP HIS EMPLOYEES OBEDIENT? NOW *THAT* IS A CONTROL FREAK, I DARESAY.
QUITE.
ALL RIGHT, IRIS. SIT UP SLOWLY, AND PLEASE LET ME KNOW IF THERE IS ANY PAIN OR DIZZINESS.
I'M FINE.
EXCELLENT. THEN YOU'RE FREE TO GO.
GOOD TO HAVE YOU BACK, IRIS.
THANK YOU, LOTUS.
NOW... LET'S FINISH THIS.

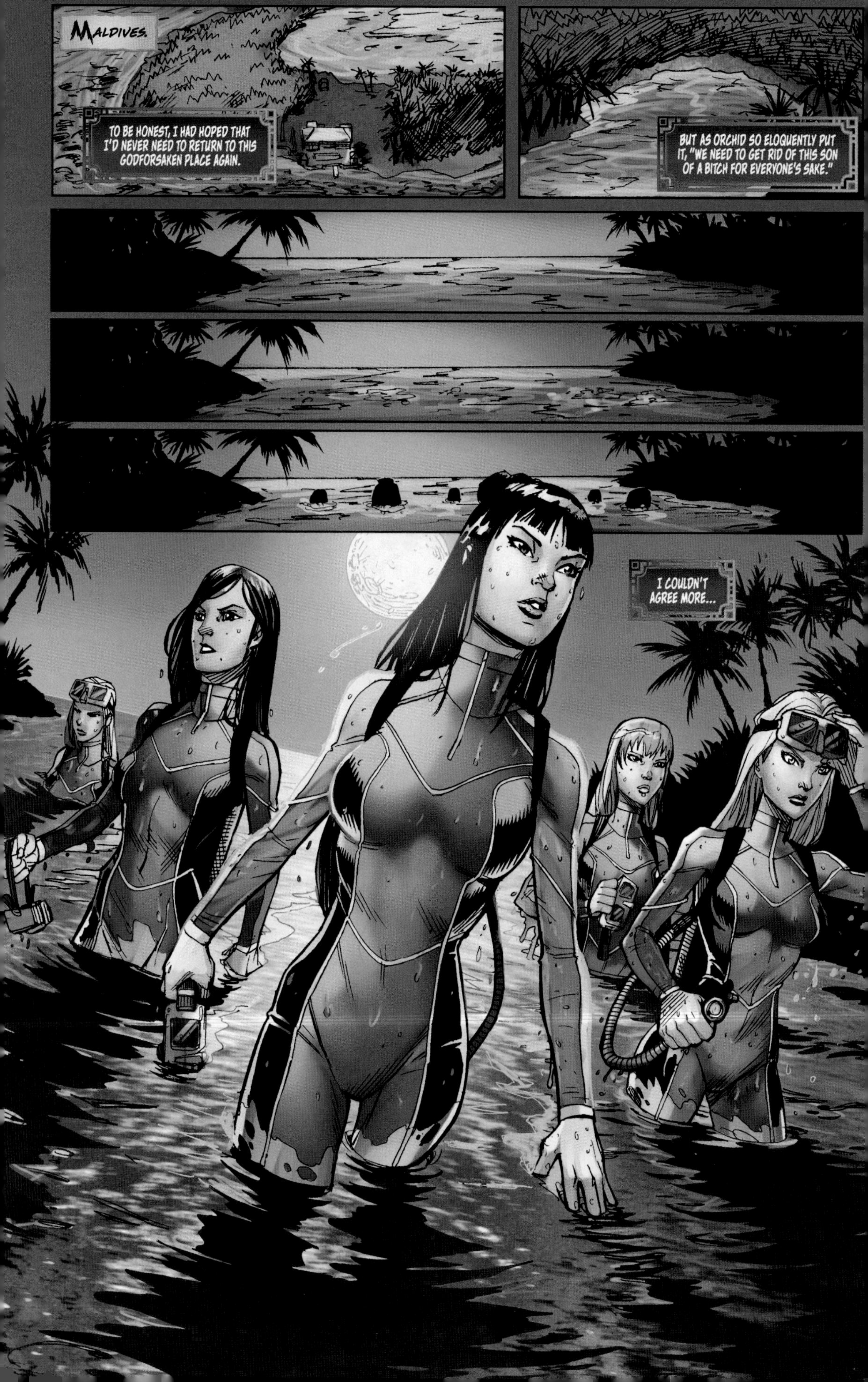

MALDIVES.
TO BE HONEST, I HAD HOPED THAT I'D NEVER NEED TO RETURN TO THIS GODFORSAKEN PLACE AGAIN.
BUT AS ORCHID SO ELOQUENTLY PUT IT, "WE NEED TO GET RID OF THIS SON OF A BITCH FOR EVERYONE'S SAKE."
I COULDN'T AGREE MORE...

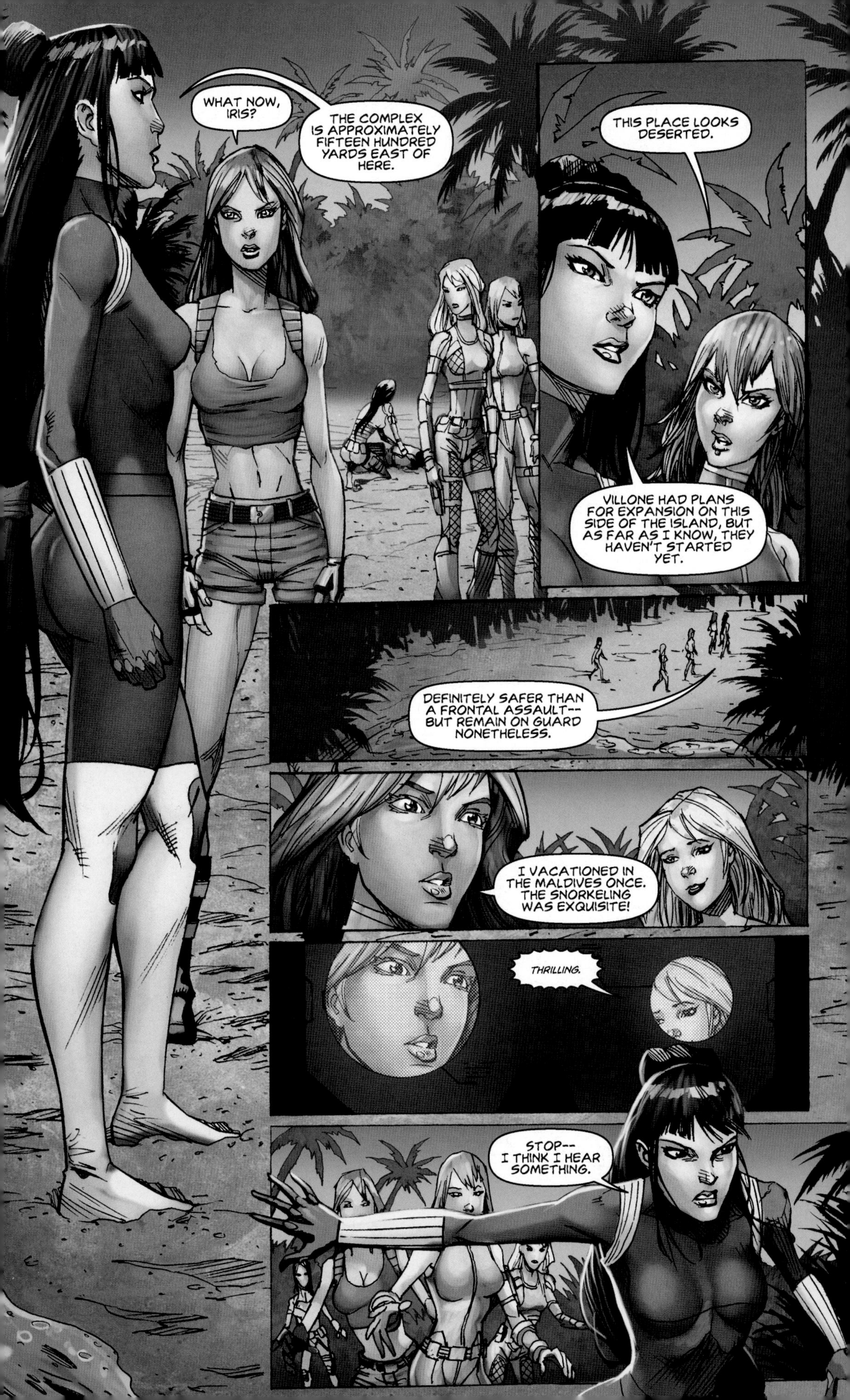
WHAT NOW, IRIS?
THE COMPLEX IS APPROXIMATELY FIFTEEN HUNDRED YARDS EAST OF HERE.
THIS PLACE LOOKS DESERTED.
VILLONE HAD PLANS FOR EXPANSION ON THIS SIDE OF THE ISLAND, BUT AS FAR AS I KNOW, THEY HAVEN'T STARTED YET.
DEFINITELY SAFER THAN A FRONTAL ASSAULT-- BUT REMAIN ON GUARD NONETHELESS.
I VACATIONED IN THE MALDIVES ONCE. THE SNORKELING WAS EXQUISITE!
THRILLING.
STOP-- I THINK I HEAR SOMETHING.

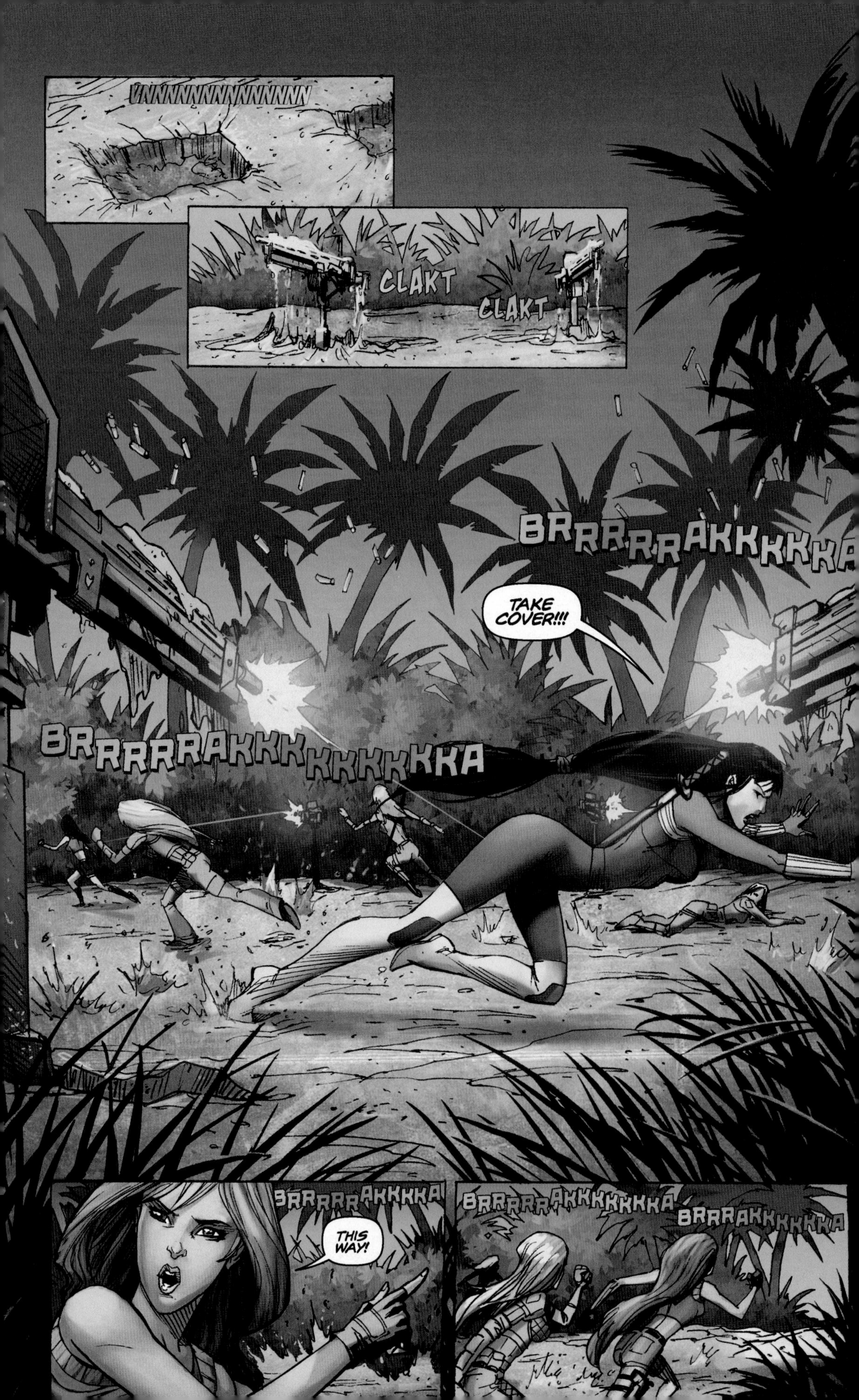
VNNNNNNNNNNNNNN
CLAKT
CLAKT
BRRRRRRAKKKKKKA
TAKE COVER!!!
BRRRRRRAKKKKKKKKKA
BRRRRRAKKKKA
THIS WAY!
BRRRRRAKKKKKKKA
BRRRAKKKKKKKA

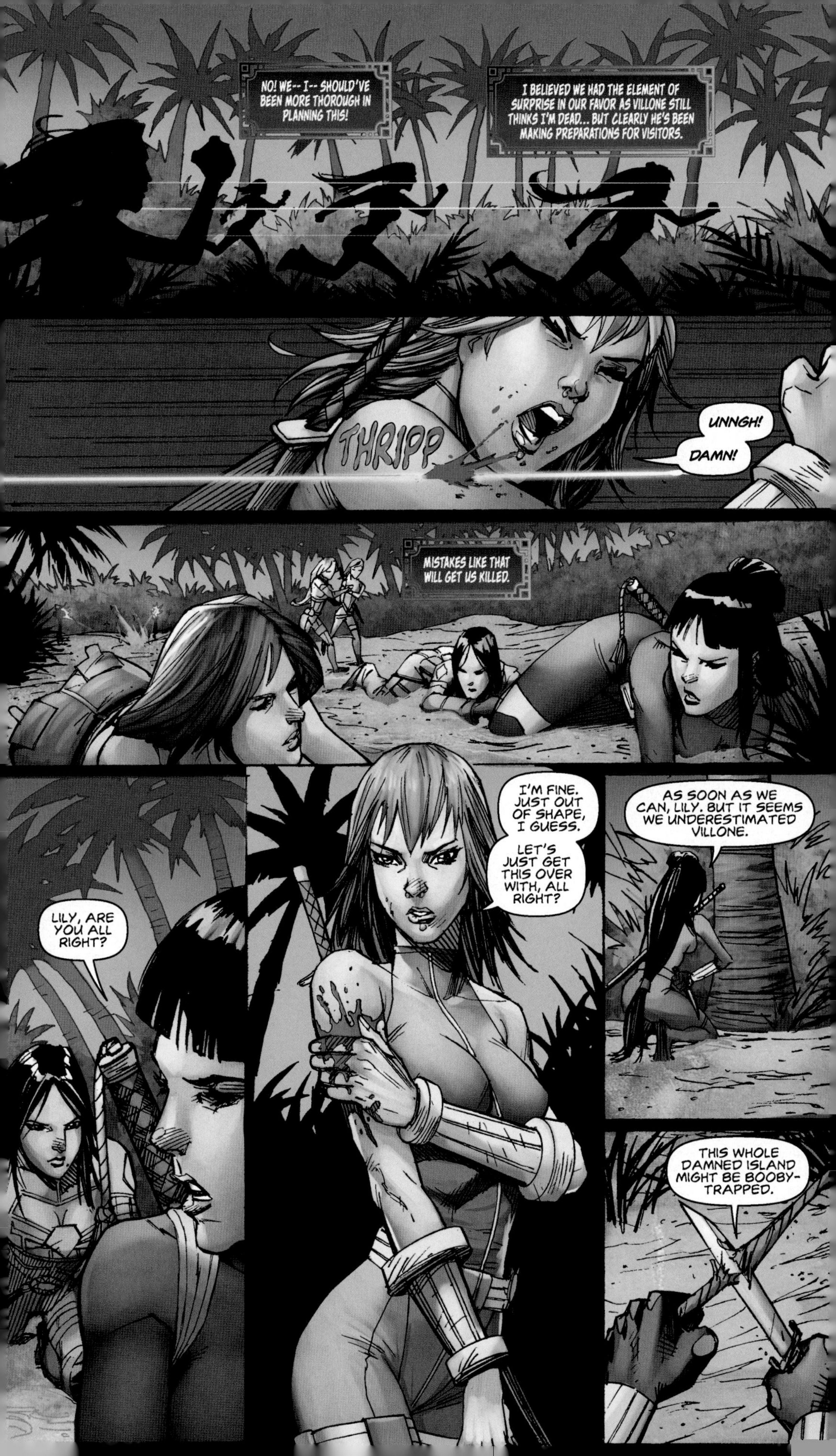
NO! WE-- I-- SHOULD'VE BEEN MORE THOROUGH IN PLANNING THIS!
I BELIEVED WE HAD THE ELEMENT OF SURPRISE IN OUR FAVOR AS VILLONE STILL THINKS I'M DEAD... BUT CLEARLY HE'S BEEN MAKING PREPARATIONS FOR VISITORS.
THRIPP
UNNGH!
DAMN!
MISTAKES LIKE THAT WILL GET US KILLED.
LILY, ARE YOU ALL RIGHT?
I'M FINE. JUST OUT OF SHAPE, I GUESS.
LET'S JUST GET THIS OVER WITH, ALL RIGHT?
AS SOON AS WE CAN, LILY. BUT IT SEEMS WE UNDERESTIMATED VILLONE.
THIS WHOLE DAMNED ISLAND MIGHT BE BOOBY-TRAPPED.

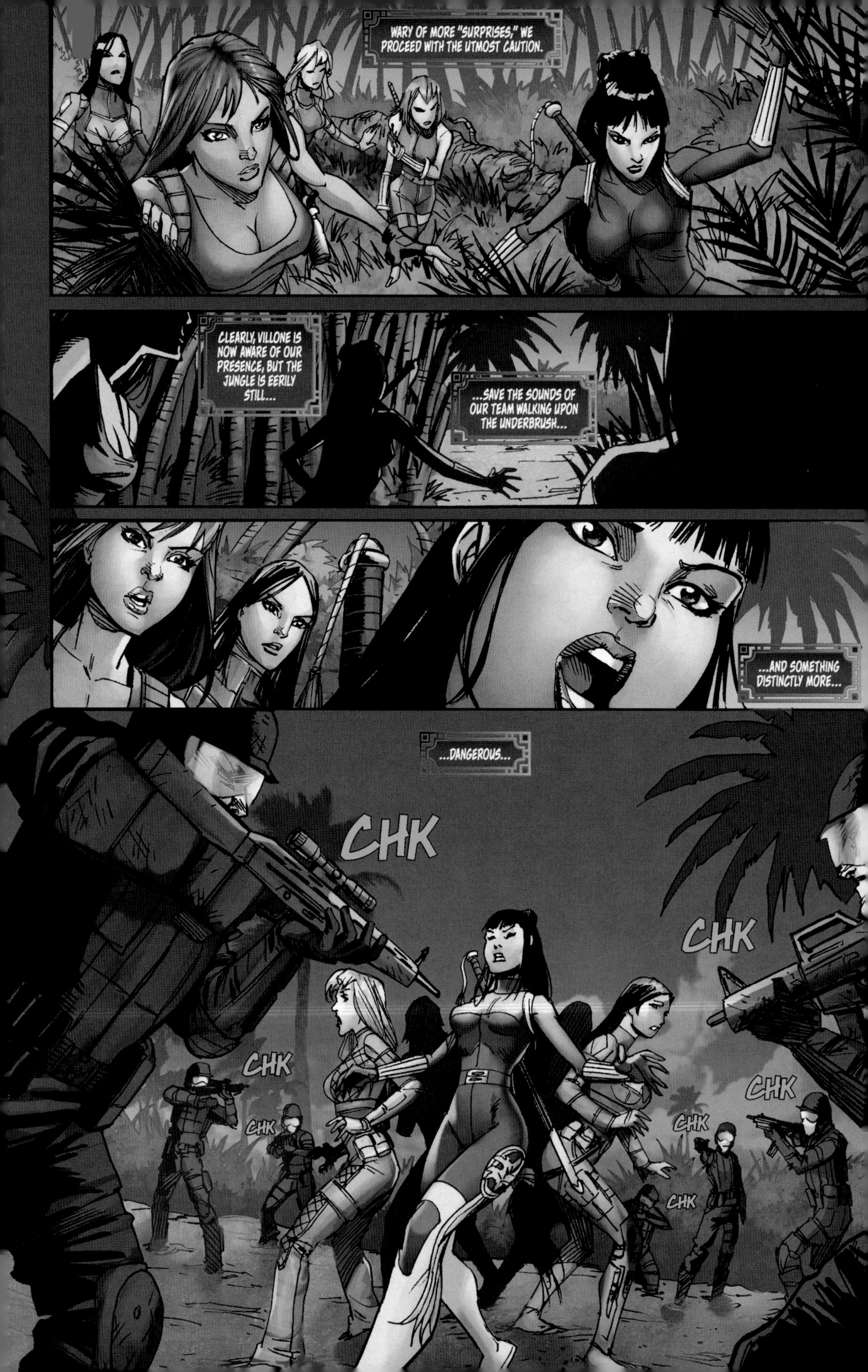
WARY OF MORE "SURPRISES," WE PROCEED WITH THE UTMOST CAUTION.
CLEARLY, VILLONE IS NOW AWARE OF OUR PRESENCE, BUT THE JUNGLE IS EERILY STILL...
...SAVE THE SOUNDS OF OUR TEAM WALKING UPON THE UNDERBRUSH...
...AND SOMETHING DISTINCTLY MORE...
...DANGEROUS...
CHK
CHK
CHK
CHK
CHK
CHK
CHK

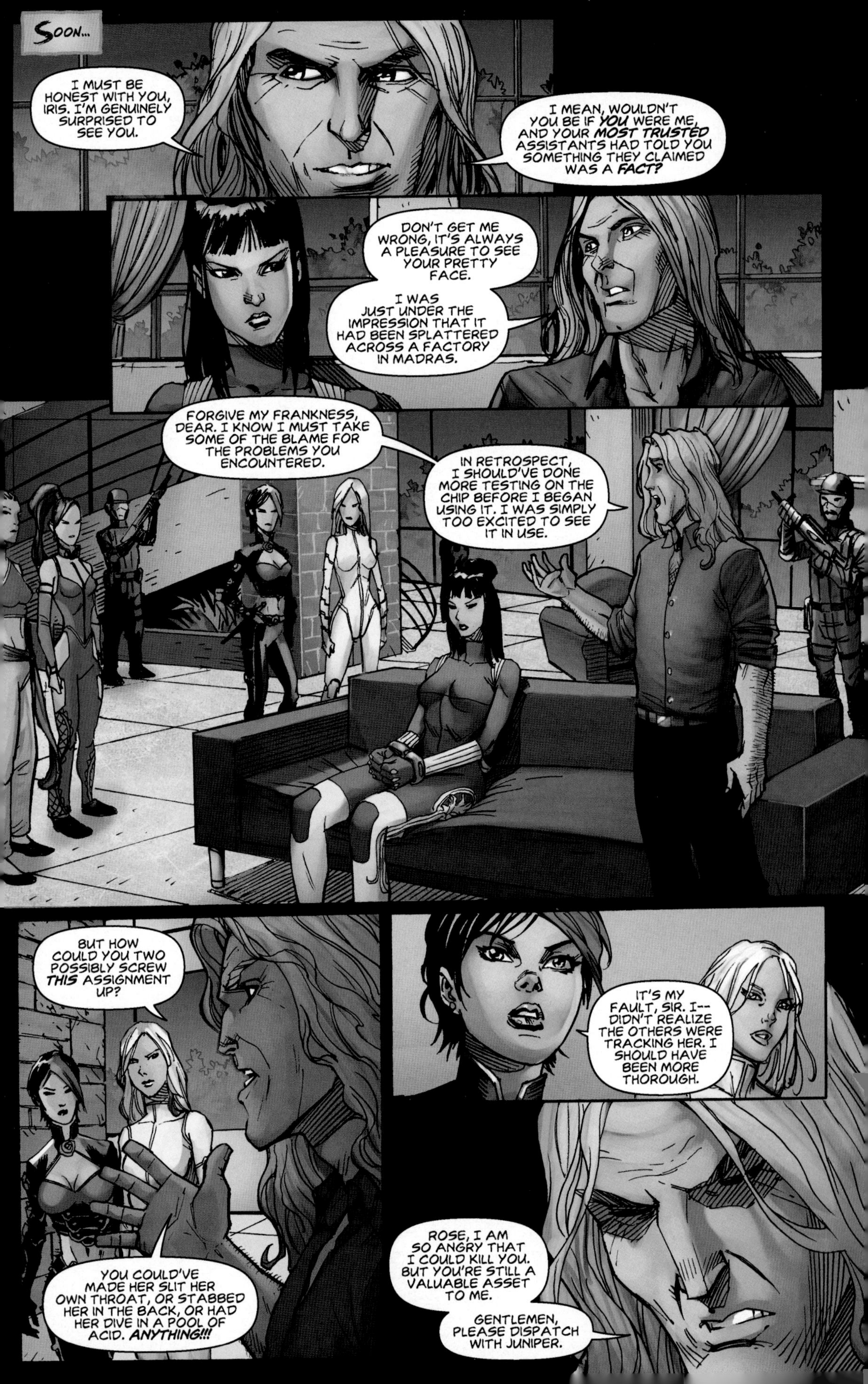
SOON...
I MUST BE HONEST WITH YOU, IRIS. I'M GENUINELY SURPRISED TO SEE YOU.
I MEAN, WOULDN'T YOU BE IF YOU WERE ME, AND YOUR MOST TRUSTED ASSISTANTS HAD TOLD YOU SOMETHING THEY CLAIMED WAS A FACT?
DON'T GET ME WRONG, IT'S ALWAYS A PLEASURE TO SEE YOUR PRETTY FACE.
I WAS JUST UNDER THE IMPRESSION THAT IT HAD BEEN SPLATTERED ACROSS A FACTORY IN MADRAS.
FORGIVE MY FRANKNESS, DEAR. I KNOW I MUST TAKE SOME OF THE BLAME FOR THE PROBLEMS YOU ENCOUNTERED.
IN RETROSPECT, I SHOULD'VE DONE MORE TESTING ON THE CHIP BEFORE I BEGAN USING IT. I WAS SIMPLY TOO EXCITED TO SEE IT IN USE.
BUT HOW COULD YOU TWO POSSIBLY SCREW THIS ASSIGNMENT UP?
YOU COULD'VE MADE HER SLIT HER OWN THROAT, OR STABBED HER IN THE BACK, OR HAD HER DIVE IN A POOL OF ACID. ANYTHING!!!
IT'S MY FAULT, SIR. I-- DIDN'T REALIZE THE OTHERS WERE TRACKING HER. I SHOULD HAVE BEEN MORE THOROUGH.
ROSE, I AM SO ANGRY THAT I COULD KILL YOU. BUT YOU'RE STILL A VALUABLE ASSET TO ME.
GENTLEMEN, PLEASE DISPATCH WITH JUNIPER.

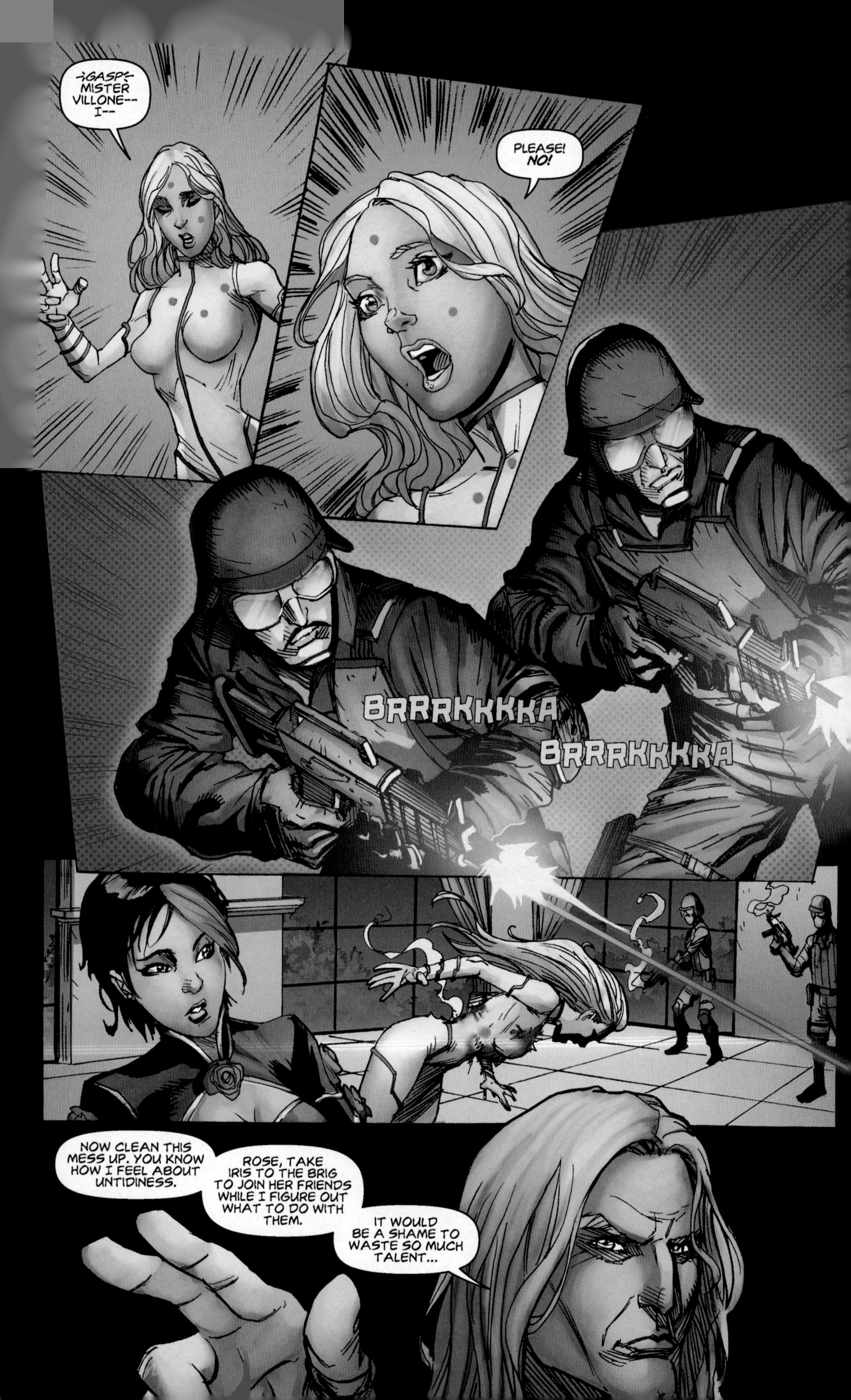

-GASP- MISTER VILLONE-- I--
PLEASE! NO!
BRRRKKKKA
BRRRKKKKA
NOW CLEAN THIS MESS UP. YOU KNOW HOW I FEEL ABOUT UNTIDINESS.
ROSE, TAKE IRIS TO THE BRIG TO JOIN HER FRIENDS WHILE I FIGURE OUT WHAT TO DO WITH THEM.
IT WOULD BE A SHAME TO WASTE SO MUCH TALENT...

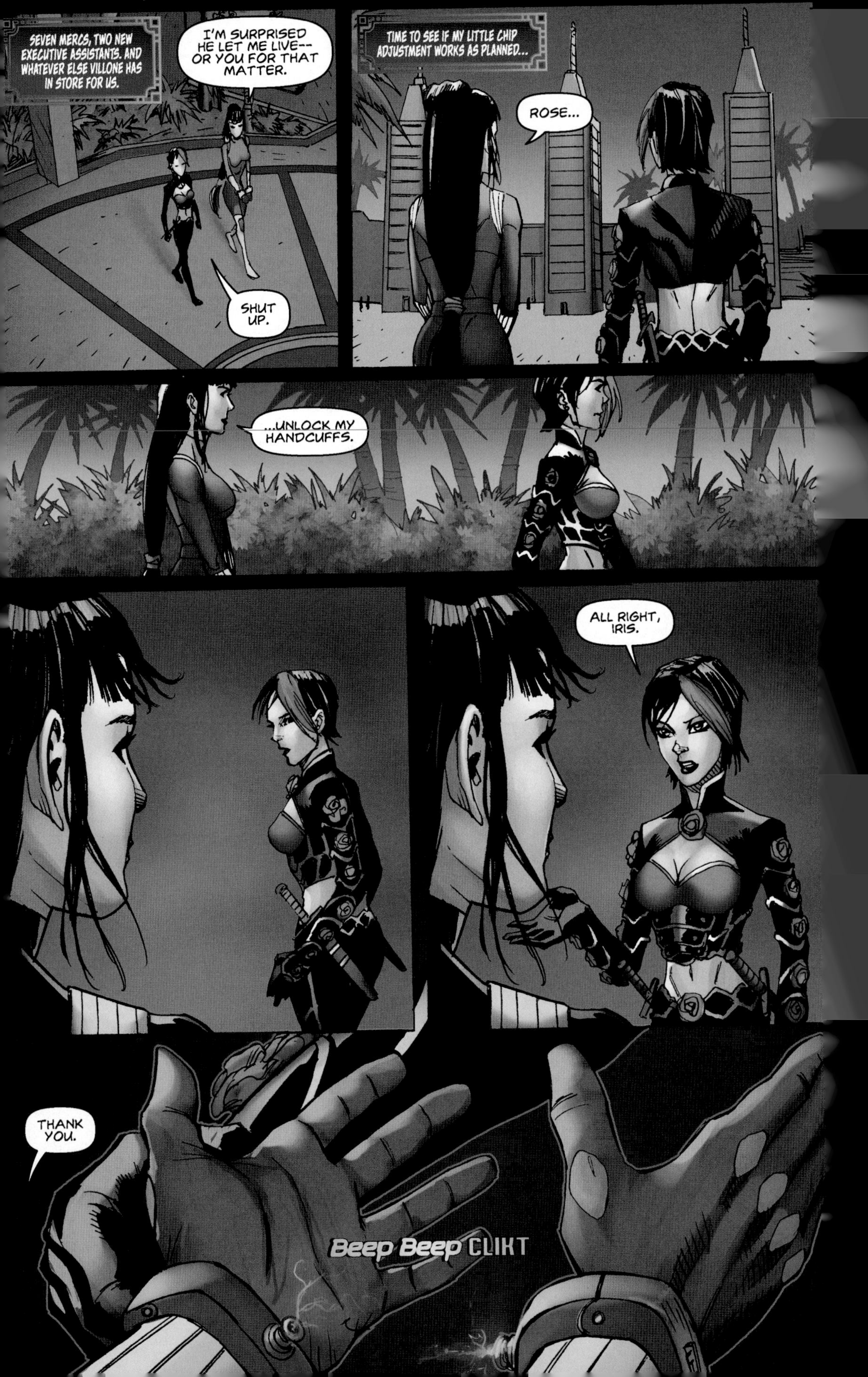
SEVEN MERCS, TWO NEW EXECUTIVE ASSISTANTS. AND WHATEVER ELSE VILLONE HAS IN STORE FOR US.
I'M SURPRISED HE LET ME LIVE-- OR YOU FOR THAT MATTER.
SHUT UP.
TIME TO SEE IF MY LITTLE CHIP ADJUSTMENT WORKS AS PLANNED...
ROSE...
...UNLOCK MY HANDCUFFS.
ALL RIGHT, IRIS.
THANK YOU.
Beep Beep CLIKT

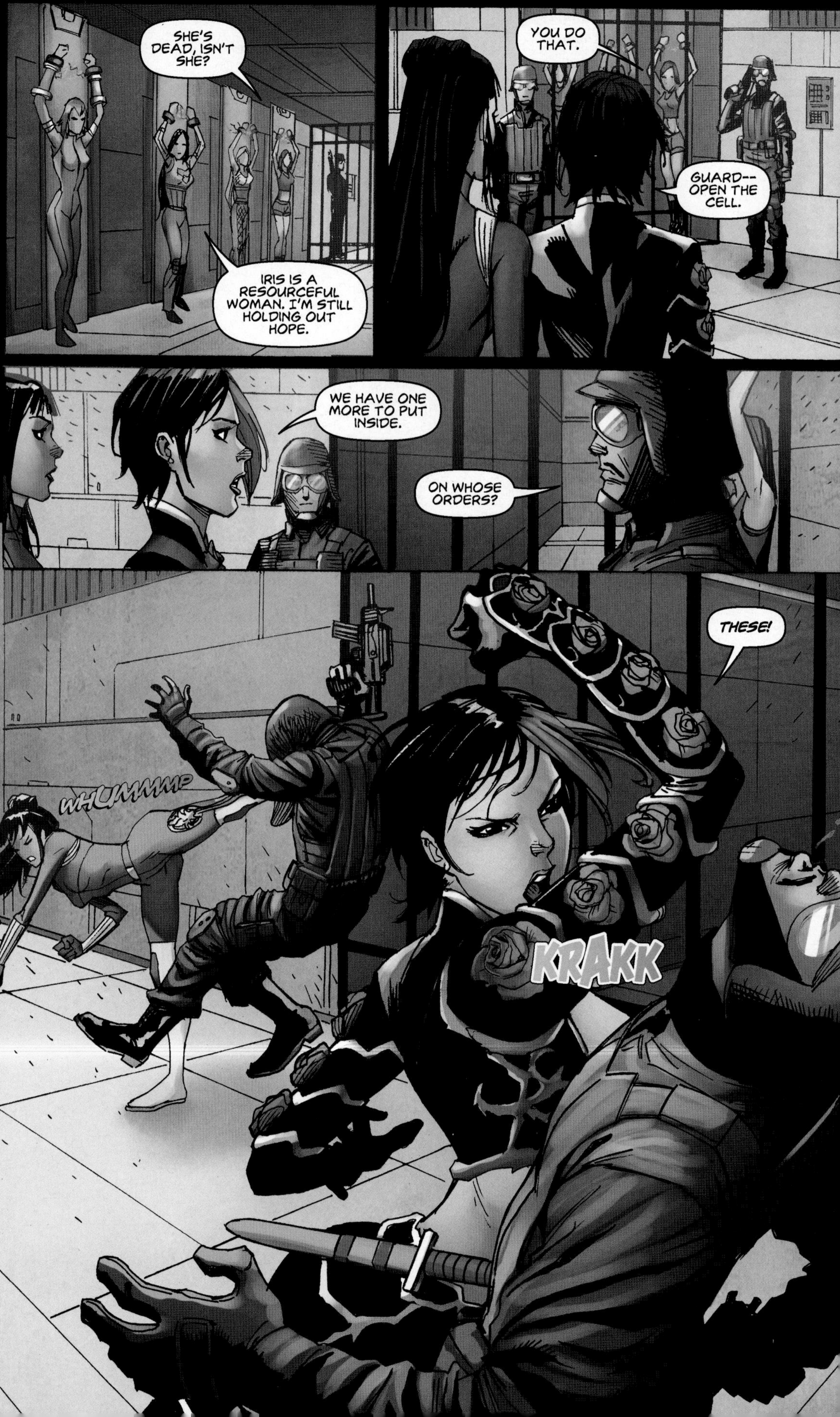
SHE'S DEAD, ISN'T SHE?
IRIS IS A RESOURCEFUL WOMAN. I'M STILL HOLDING OUT HOPE.
YOU DO THAT.
GUARD-- OPEN THE CELL.
WE HAVE ONE MORE TO PUT INSIDE.
ON WHOSE ORDERS?
THESE!
WHUMMMP
KRAKK

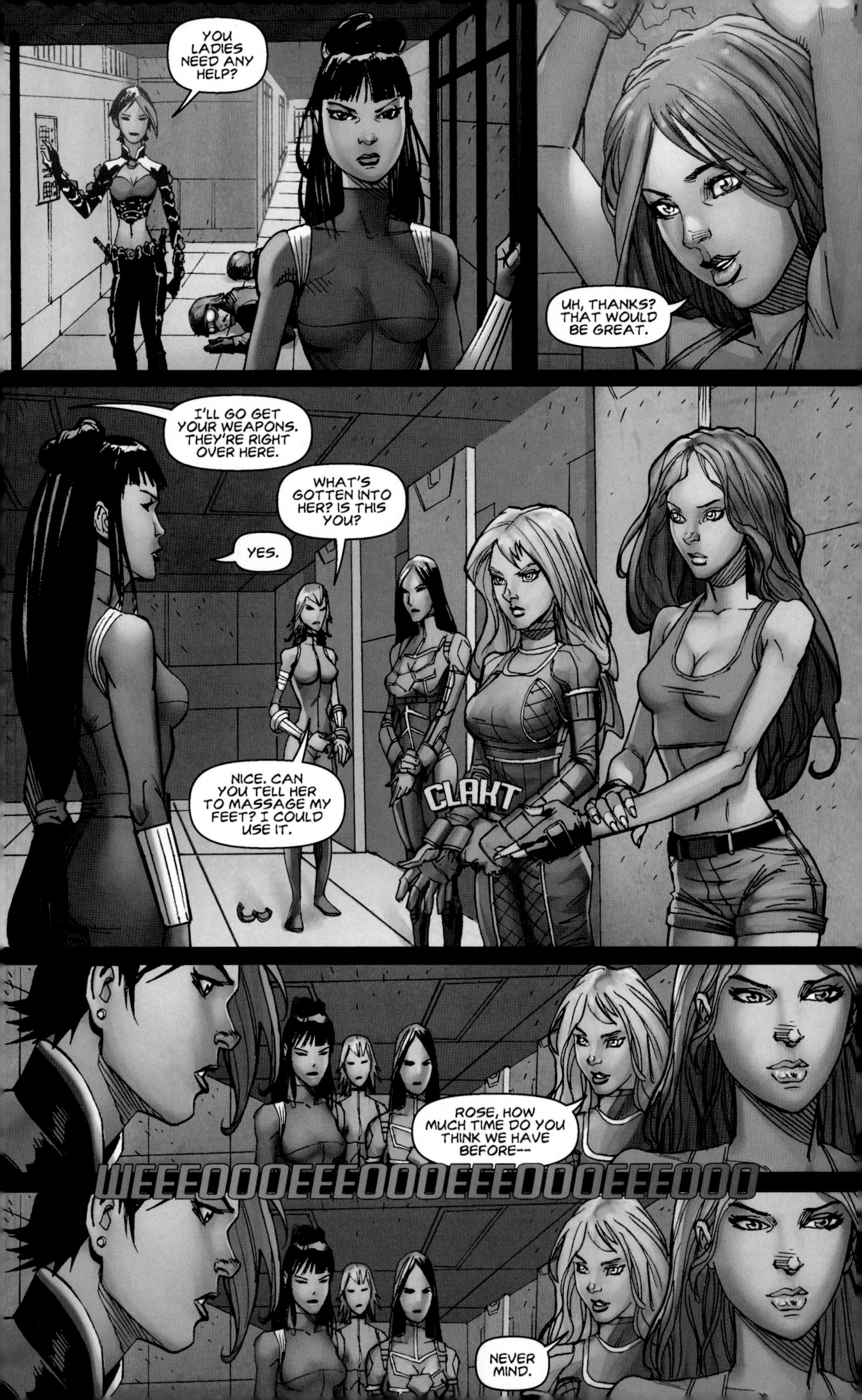
YOU LADIES NEED ANY HELP?
UH, THANKS? THAT WOULD BE GREAT.
I'LL GO GET YOUR WEAPONS. THEY'RE RIGHT OVER HERE.
WHAT'S GOTTEN INTO HER? IS THIS YOU?
YES.
NICE. CAN YOU TELL HER TO MASSAGE MY FEET? I COULD USE IT.
CLAKT
ROSE, HOW MUCH TIME DO YOU THINK WE HAVE BEFORE--
WEEEOOOEEEOOOEEEOOOEEEOOO
NEVER MIND.

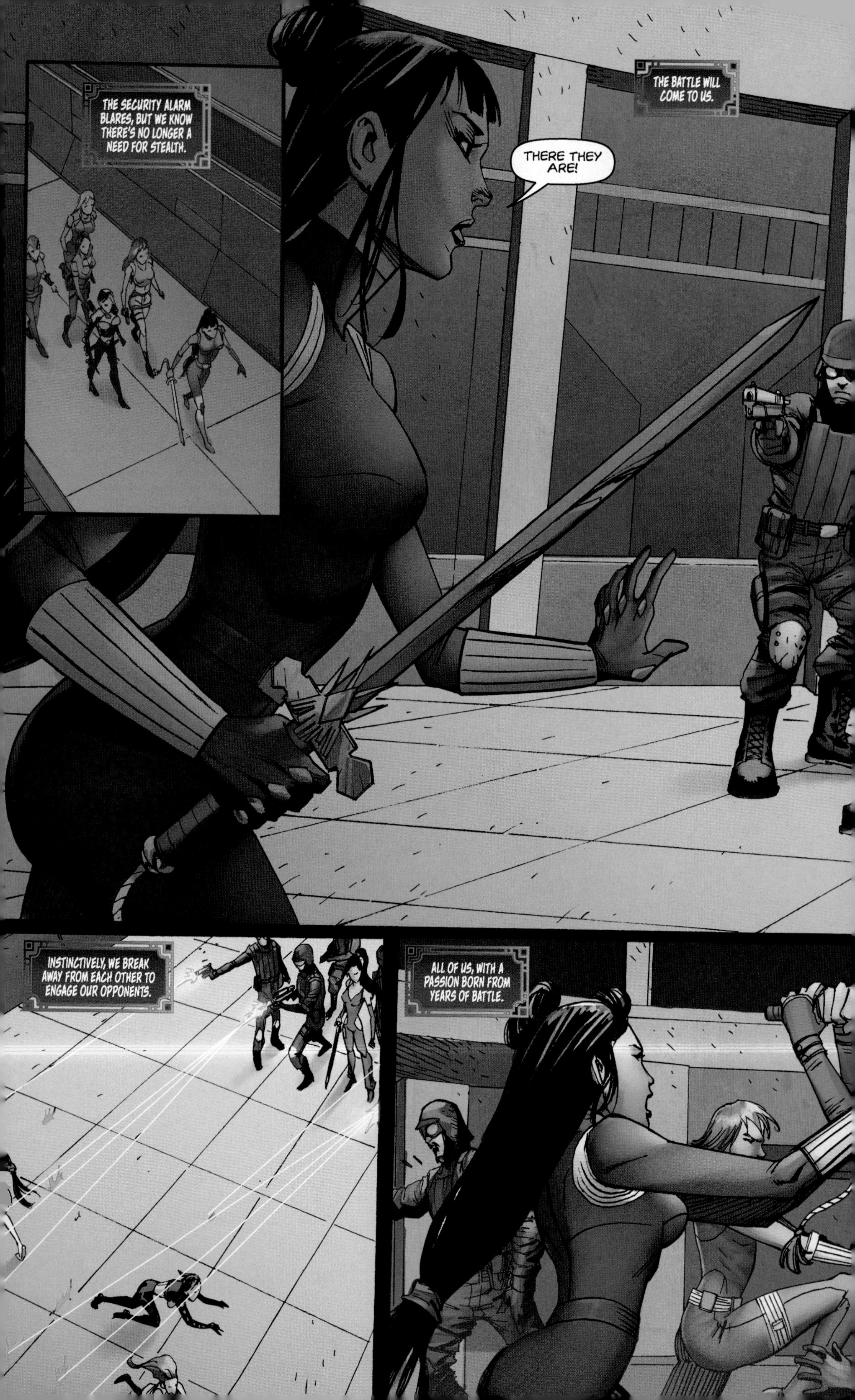
THE SECURITY ALARM BLARES, BUT WE KNOW THERE'S NO LONGER A NEED FOR STEALTH.
THERE THEY ARE!
THE BATTLE WILL COME TO US.
INSTINCTIVELY, WE BREAK AWAY FROM EACH OTHER TO ENGAGE OUR OPPONENTS.
ALL OF US, WITH A PASSION BORN FROM YEARS OF BATTLE.

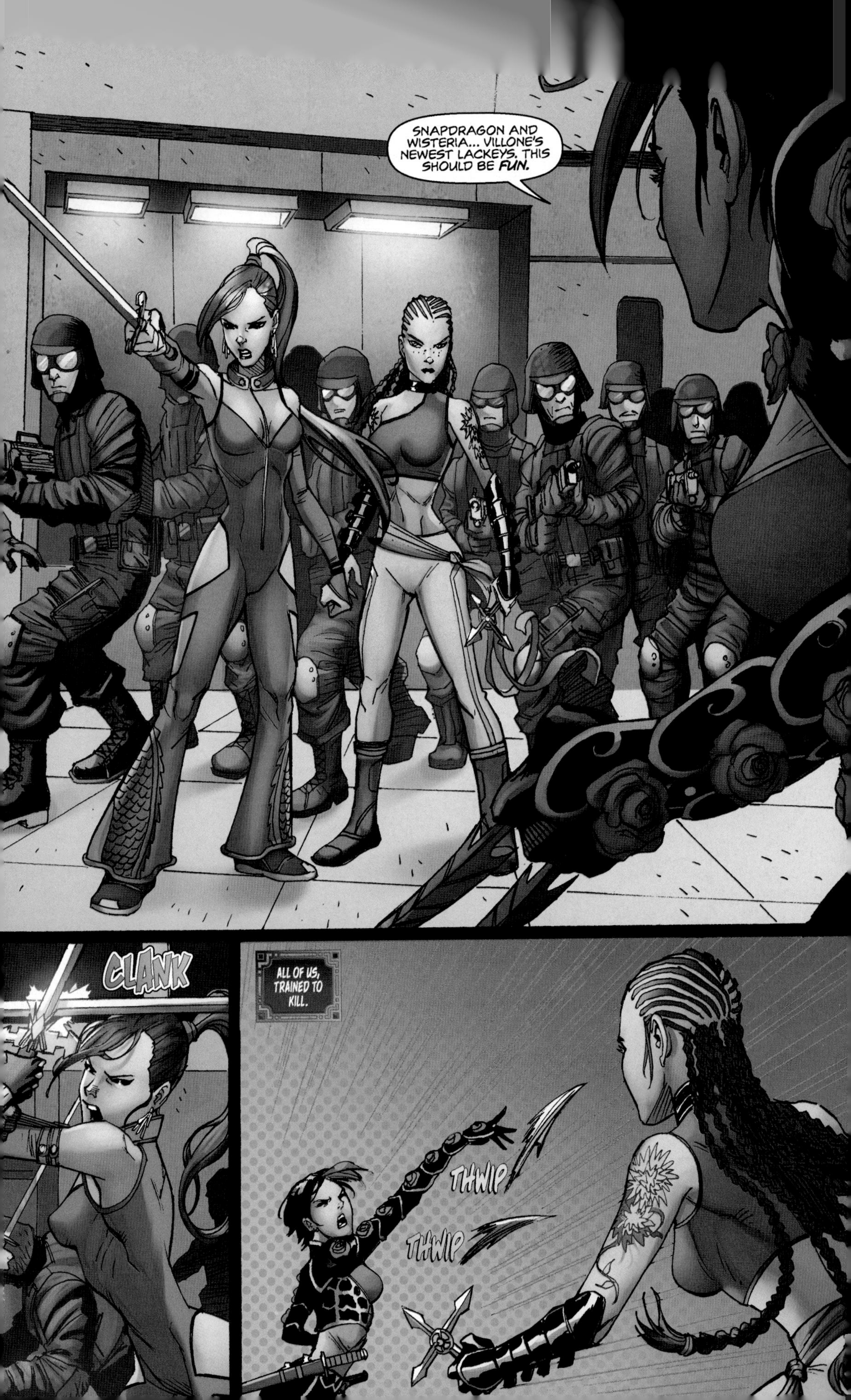
SNAPDRAGON AND WISTERIA... VILLONE'S NEWEST LACKEYS. THIS SHOULD BE FUN.
CLANK
ALL OF US, TRAINED TO KILL.
THWIP
THWIP

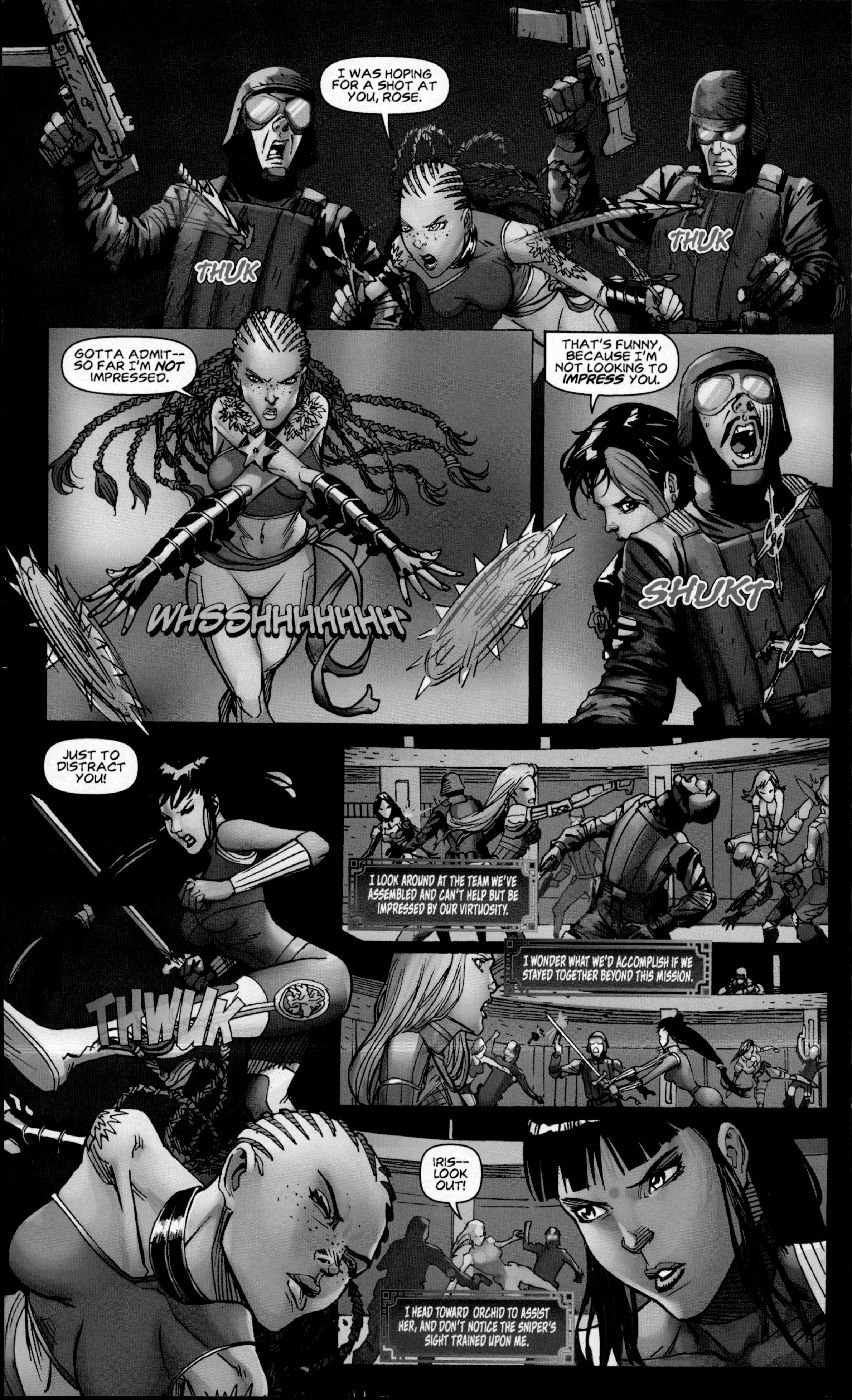
I WAS HOPING FOR A SHOT AT YOU, ROSE.
THUK
THUK
GOTTA ADMIT-- SO FAR I'M NOT IMPRESSED.
WHSSHHHHHHH
THAT'S FUNNY, BECAUSE I'M NOT LOOKING TO IMPRESS YOU.
SHUKT
JUST TO DISTRACT YOU!
THWUK
I LOOK AROUND AT THE TEAM WE'VE ASSEMBLED AND CAN'T HELP BUT BE IMPRESSED BY OUR VIRTUOSITY.
I WONDER WHAT WE'D ACCOMPLISH IF WE STAYED TOGETHER BEYOND THIS MISSION.
IRIS-- LOOK OUT!
I HEAD TOWARD ORCHID TO ASSIST HER, AND DON'T NOTICE THE SNIPER'S SIGHT TRAINED UPON ME.

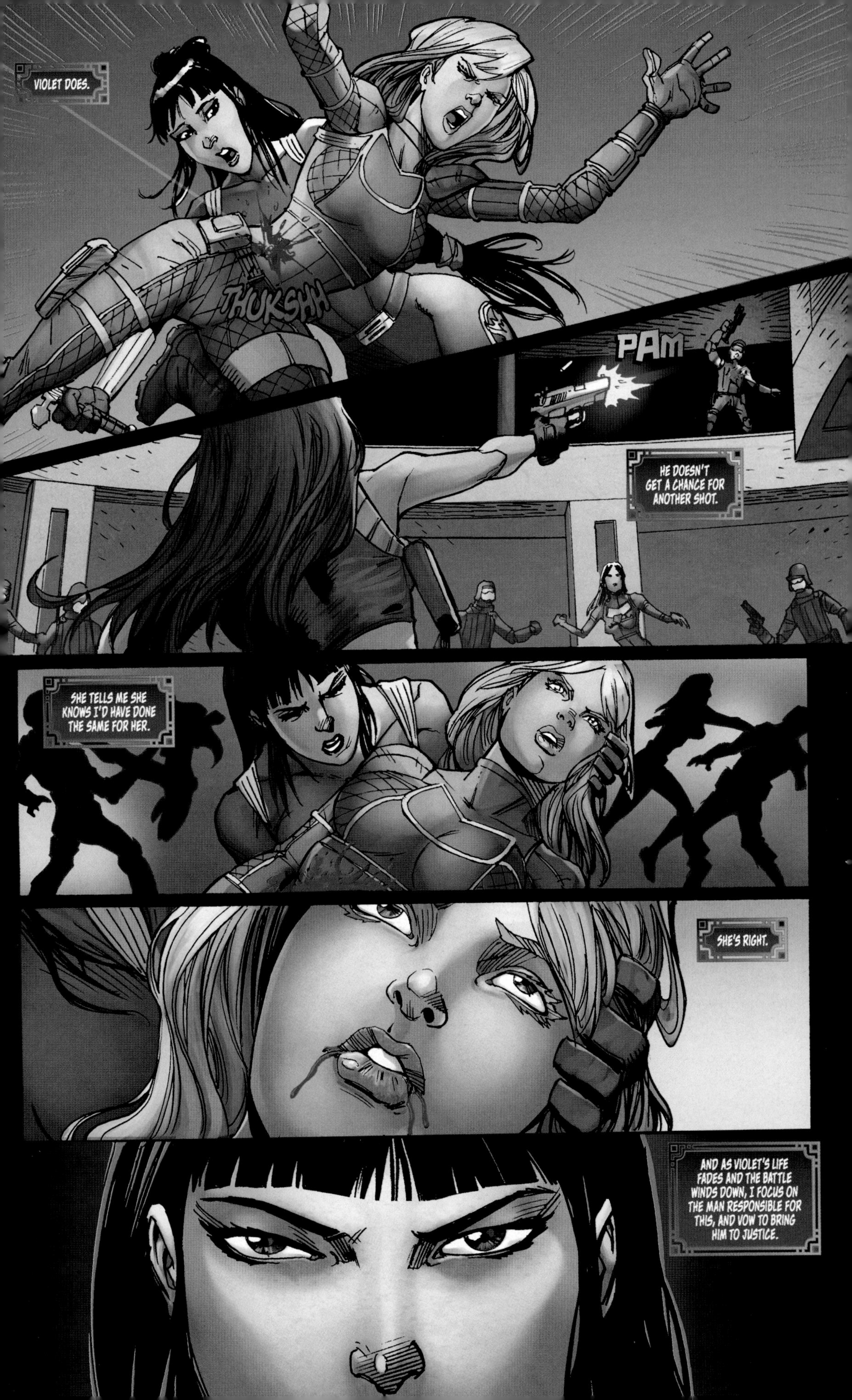
VIOLET DOES.
THUKSHH
PAM
HE DOESN'T GET A CHANCE FOR ANOTHER SHOT.
SHE TELLS ME SHE KNOWS I'D HAVE DONE THE SAME FOR HER.
SHE'S RIGHT.
AND AS VIOLET'S LIFE FADES AND THE BATTLE WINDS DOWN, I FOCUS ON THE MAN RESPONSIBLE FOR THIS, AND VOW TO BRING HIM TO JUSTICE.

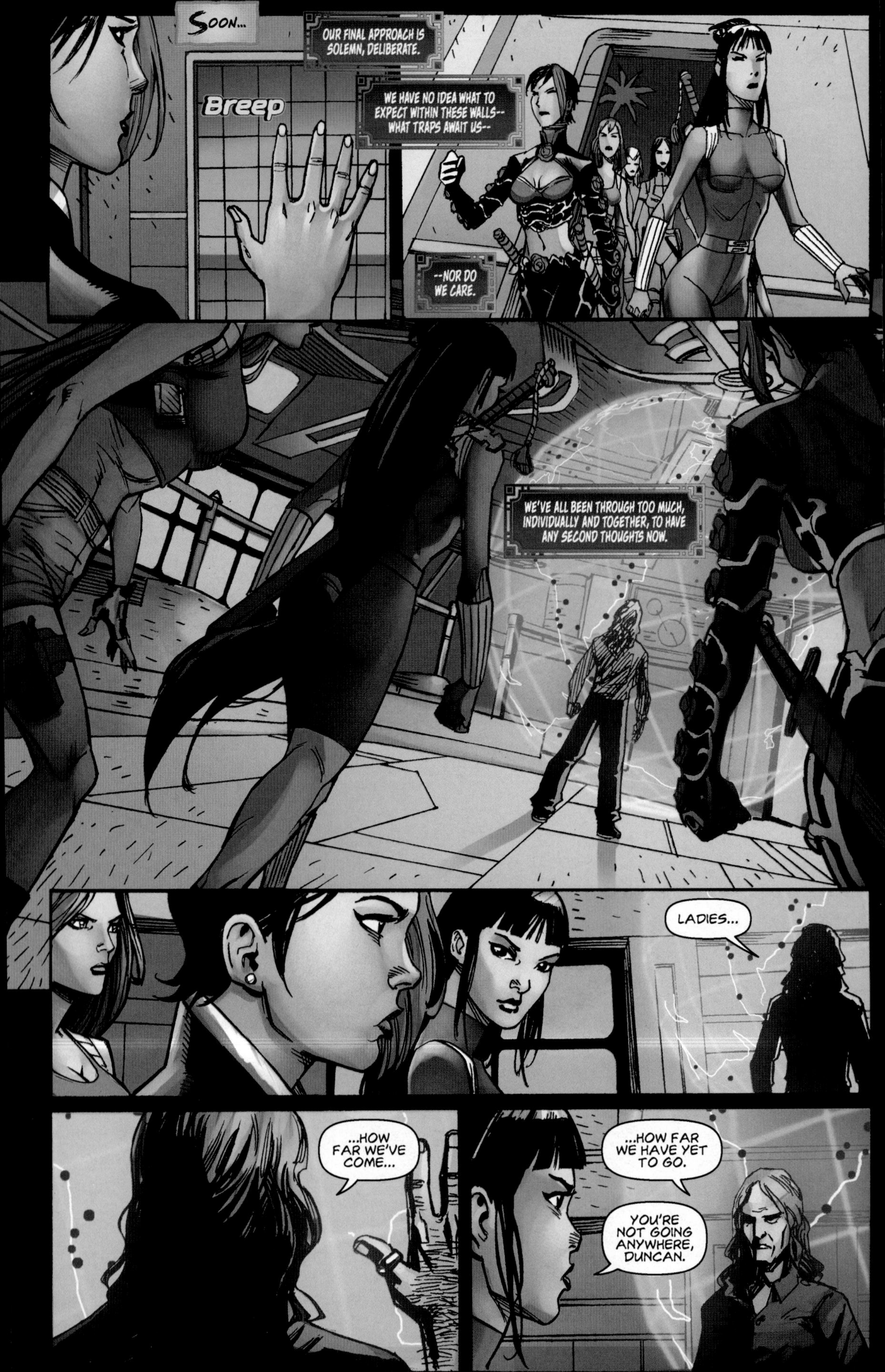
SOON...
OUR FINAL APPROACH IS SOLEMN, DELIBERATE.
Breep
WE HAVE NO IDEA WHAT TO EXPECT WITHIN THESE WALLS-- WHAT TRAPS AWAIT US--
--NOR DO WE CARE.
WE'VE ALL BEEN THROUGH TOO MUCH, INDIVIDUALLY AND TOGETHER, TO HAVE ANY SECOND THOUGHTS NOW.
LADIES...
...HOW FAR WE'VE COME...
...HOW FAR WE HAVE YET TO GO.
YOU'RE NOT GOING ANYWHERE, DUNCAN.

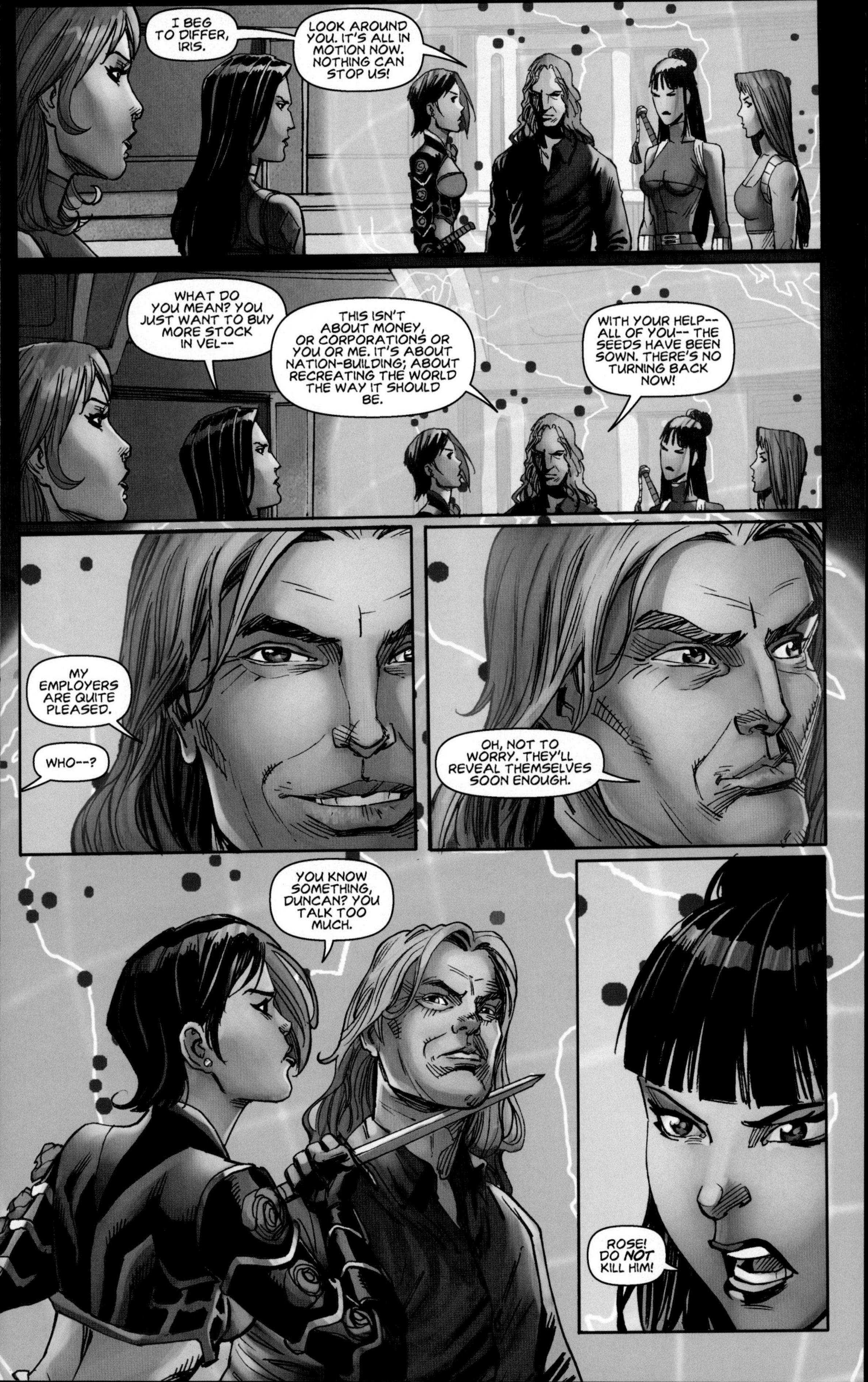
I BEG TO DIFFER, IRIS.
LOOK AROUND YOU. IT'S ALL IN MOTION NOW. NOTHING CAN STOP US!
WHAT DO YOU MEAN? YOU JUST WANT TO BUY MORE STOCK IN VEL--
THIS ISN'T ABOUT MONEY, OR CORPORATIONS OR YOU OR ME. IT'S ABOUT NATION-BUILDING; ABOUT RECREATING THE WORLD THE WAY IT SHOULD BE.
WITH YOUR HELP-- ALL OF YOU-- THE SEEDS HAVE BEEN SOWN. THERE'S NO TURNING BACK NOW!
MY EMPLOYERS ARE QUITE PLEASED.
WHO--?
OH, NOT TO WORRY. THEY'LL REVEAL THEMSELVES SOON ENOUGH.
YOU KNOW SOMETHING, DUNCAN? YOU TALK TOO MUCH.
ROSE! DO NOT KILL HIM!

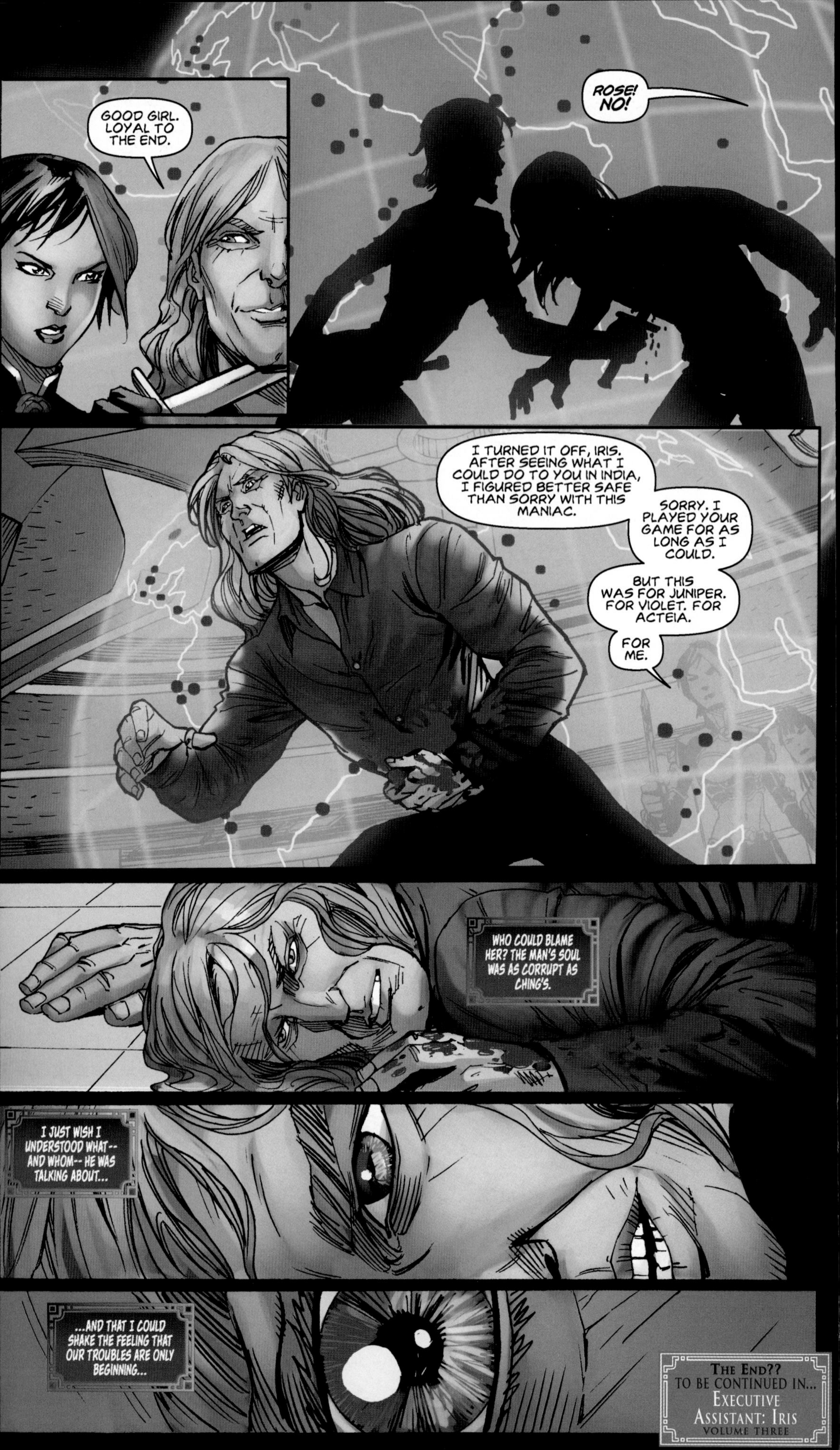
GOOD GIRL. LOYAL TO THE END.
ROSE! NO!
I TURNED IT OFF, IRIS. AFTER SEEING WHAT I COULD DO TO YOU IN INDIA, I FIGURED BETTER SAFE THAN SORRY WITH THIS MANIAC.
SORRY. I PLAYED YOUR GAME FOR AS LONG AS I COULD.
BUT THIS WAS FOR JUNIPER. FOR VIOLET. FOR ACTEIA.
FOR ME.
WHO COULD BLAME HER? THE MAN'S SOUL WAS AS CORRUPT AS CHING'S.
I JUST WISH I UNDERSTOOD WHAT-- AND WHOM-- HE WAS TALKING ABOUT...
...AND THAT I COULD SHAKE THE FEELING THAT OUR TROUBLES ARE ONLY BEGINNING...
THE END??
TO BE CONTINUED IN...
EXECUTIVE ASSISTANT: IRIS
VOLUME THREE

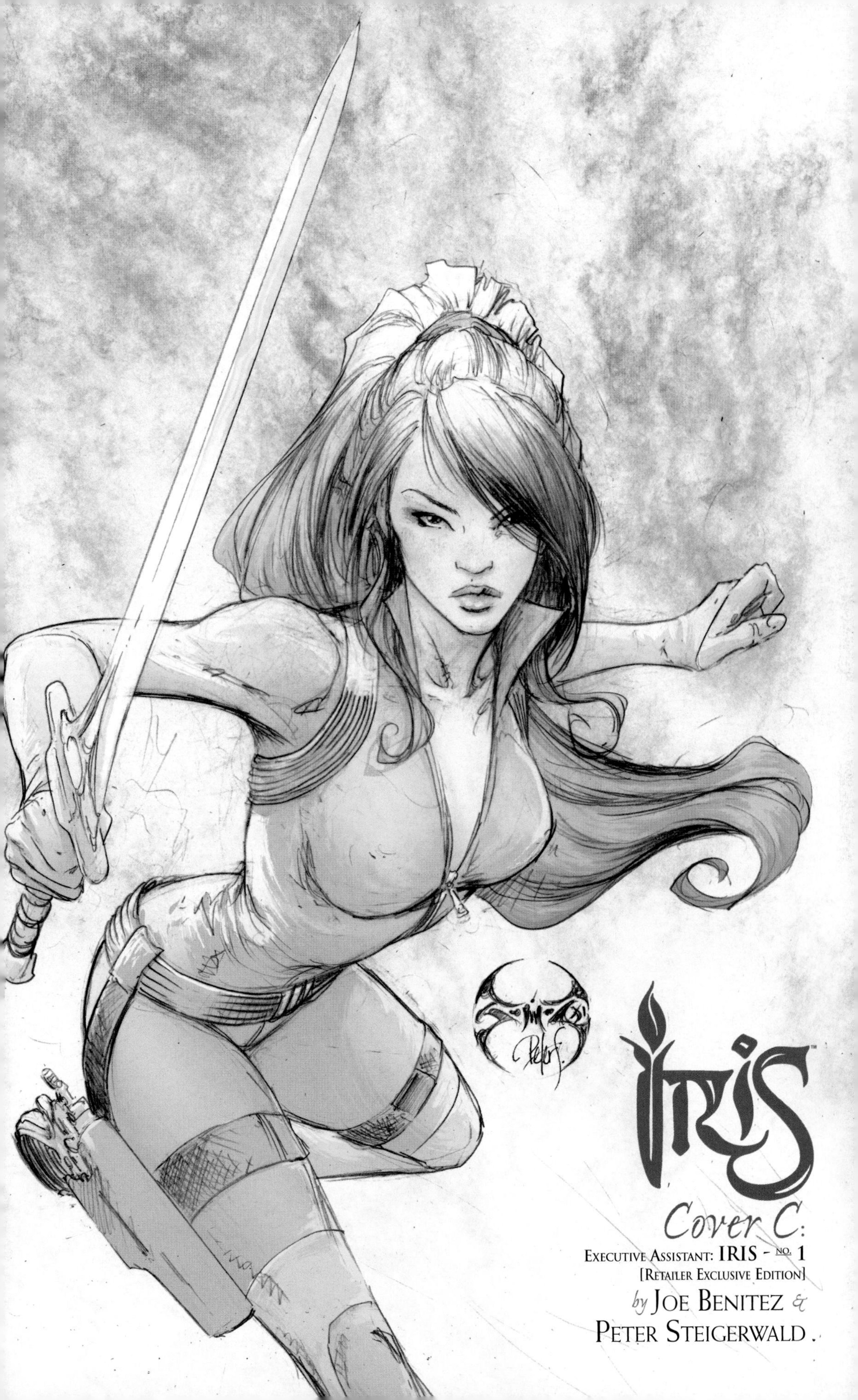

Cover C:

EXECUTIVE ASSISTANT: IRIS - No. 1

[RETAILER EXCLUSIVE EDITION]

by JOE BENITEZ & PETER STEIGERWALD.

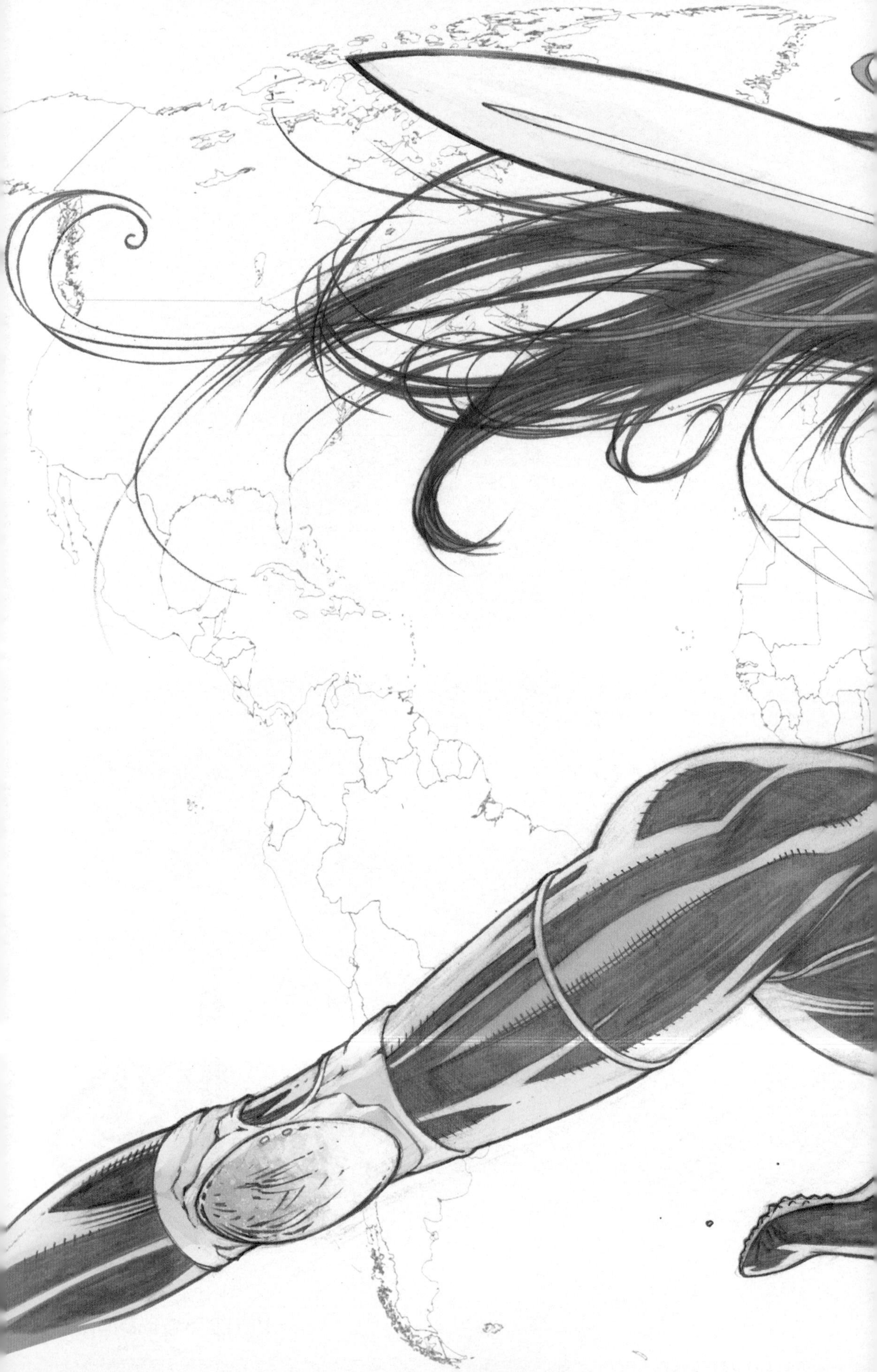

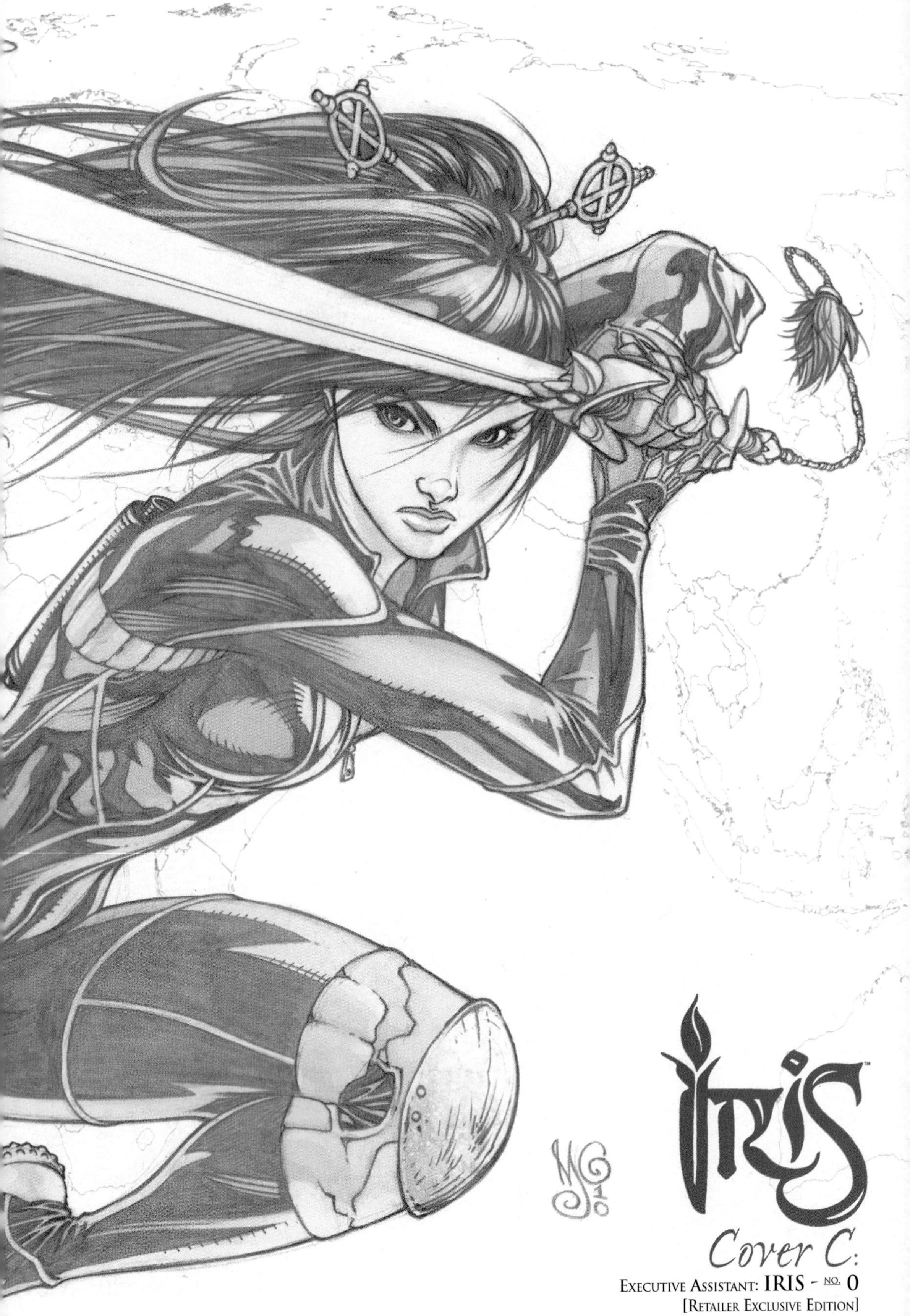

IRIS™

Cover C:

Executive Assistant: IRIS - No. 0

[Retailer Exclusive Edition]

by Micah Gunnell

& Peter Steigerwald

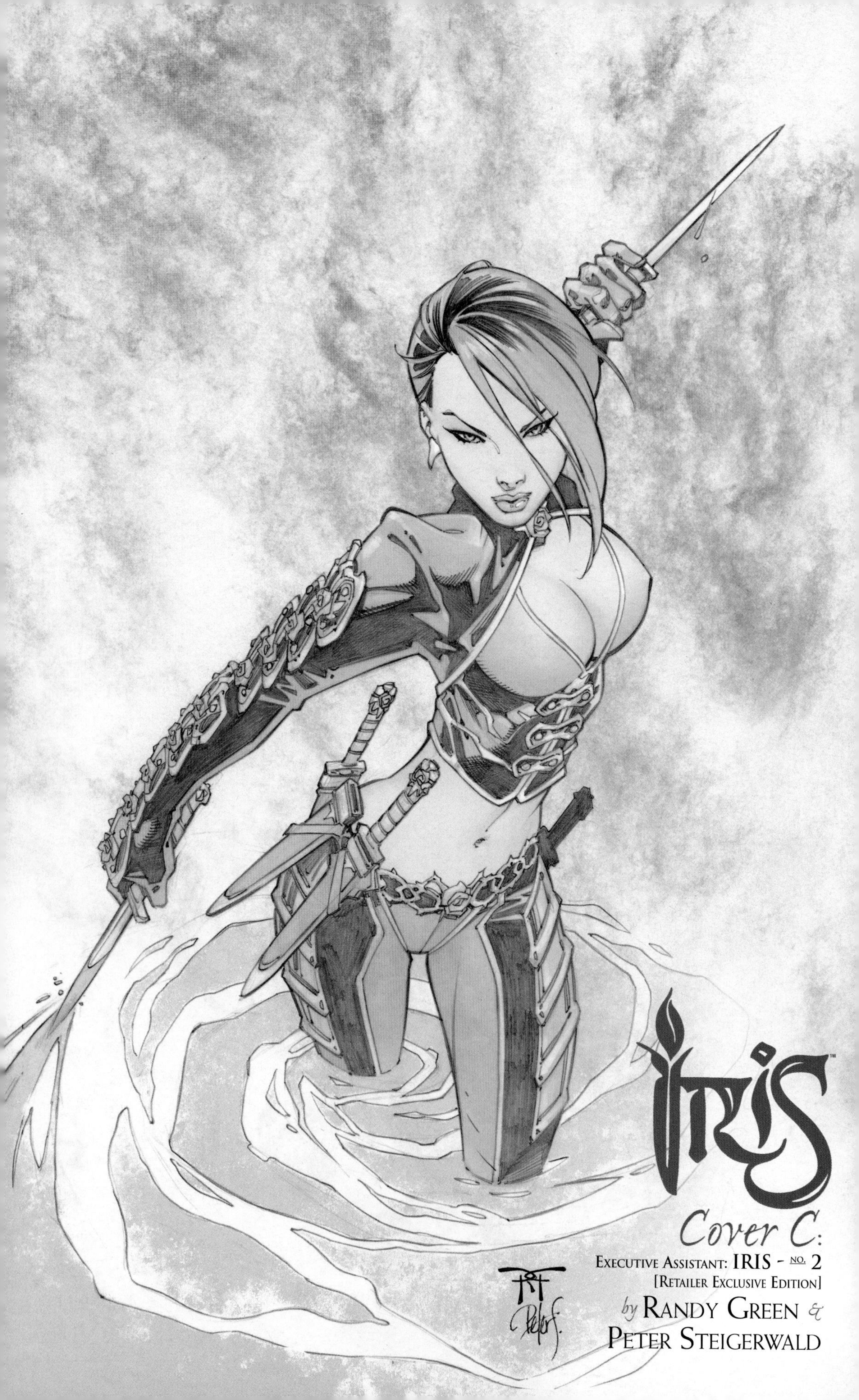
IRIS™
Cover C:
Executive Assistant: IRIS - No. 2
[Retailer Exclusive Edition]
by Randy Green &
Peter Steigerwald

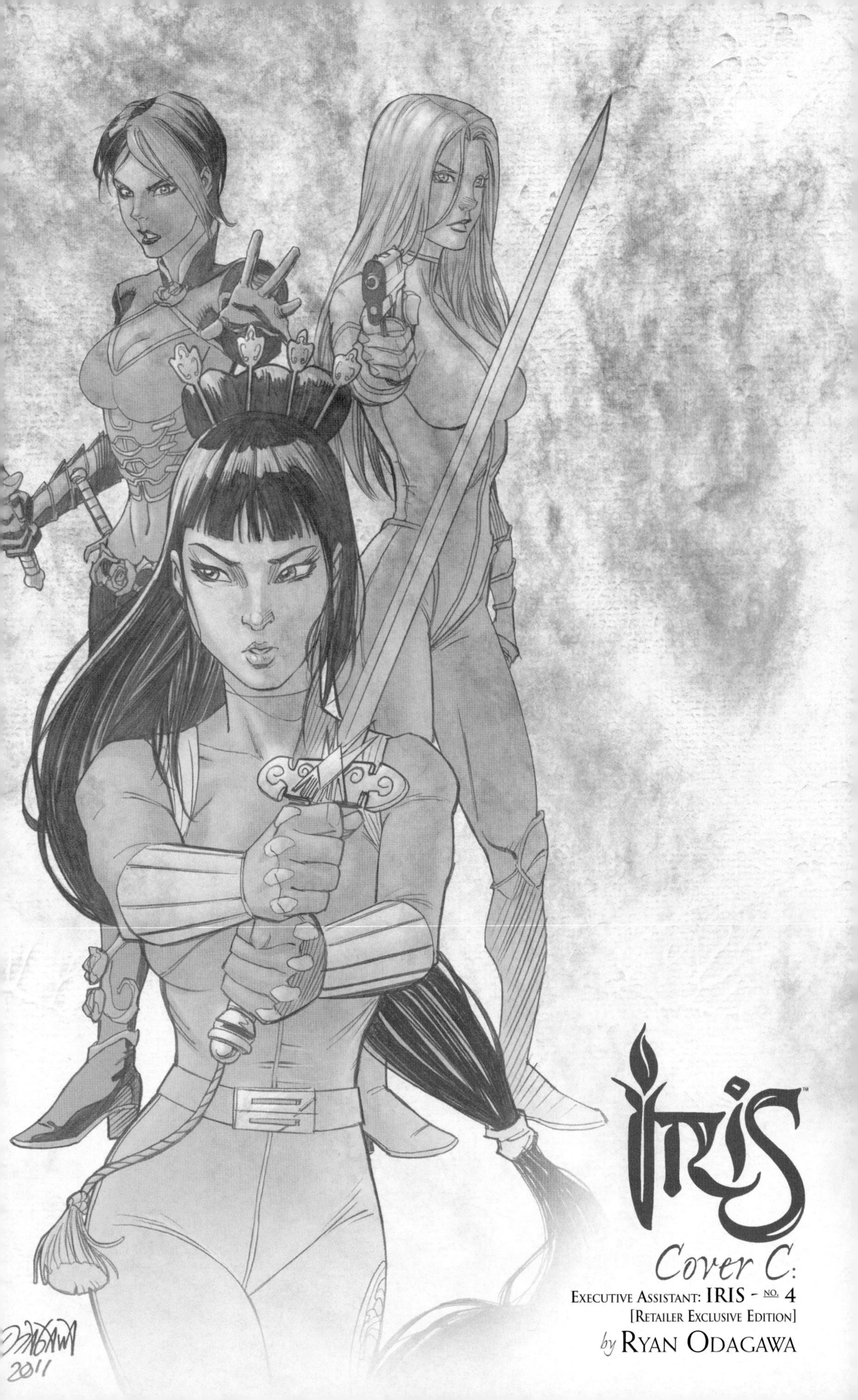
IRIS™
Cover C:
Executive Assistant: IRIS - No. 4
[Retailer Exclusive Edition]
by Ryan Odagawa

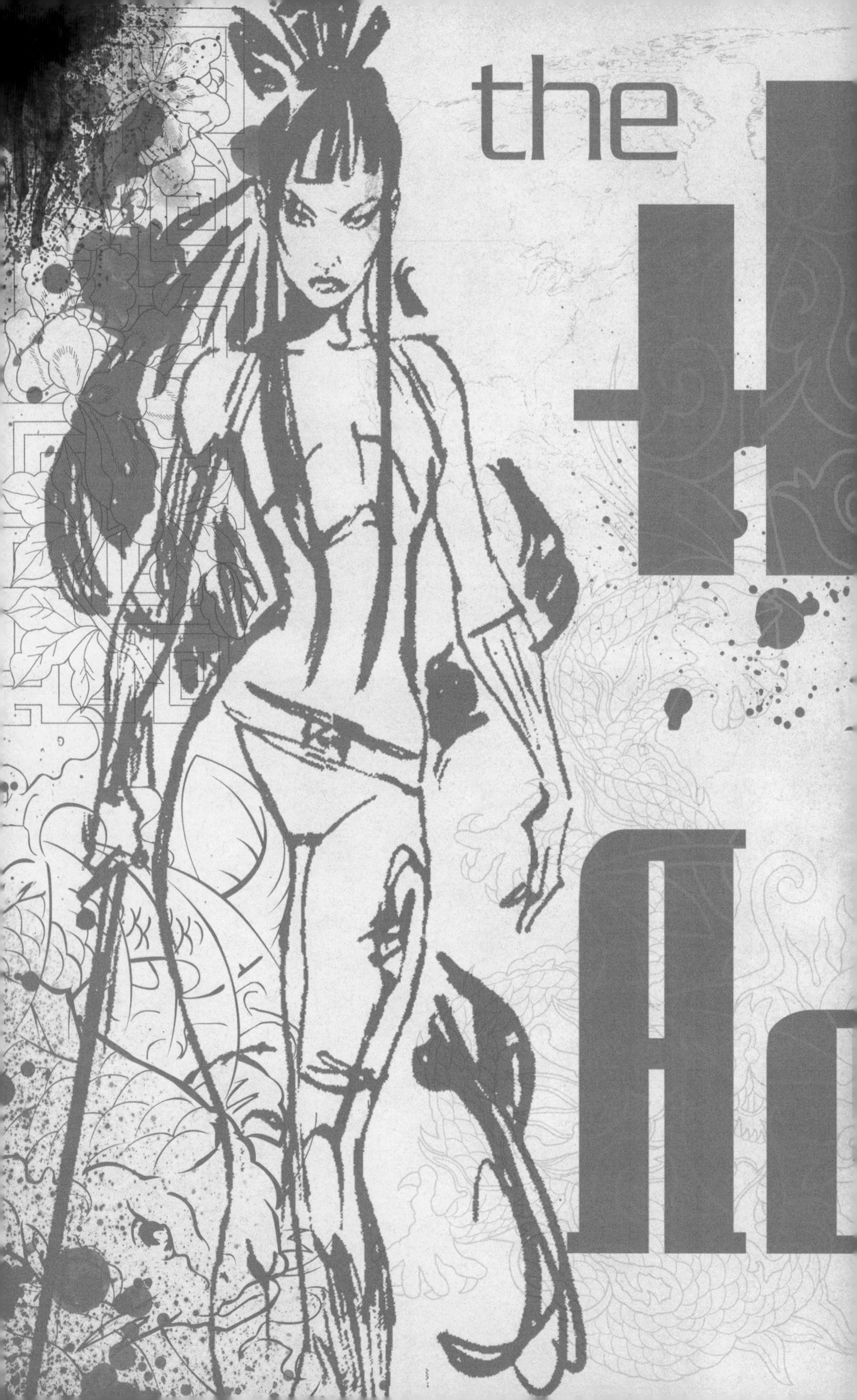
the

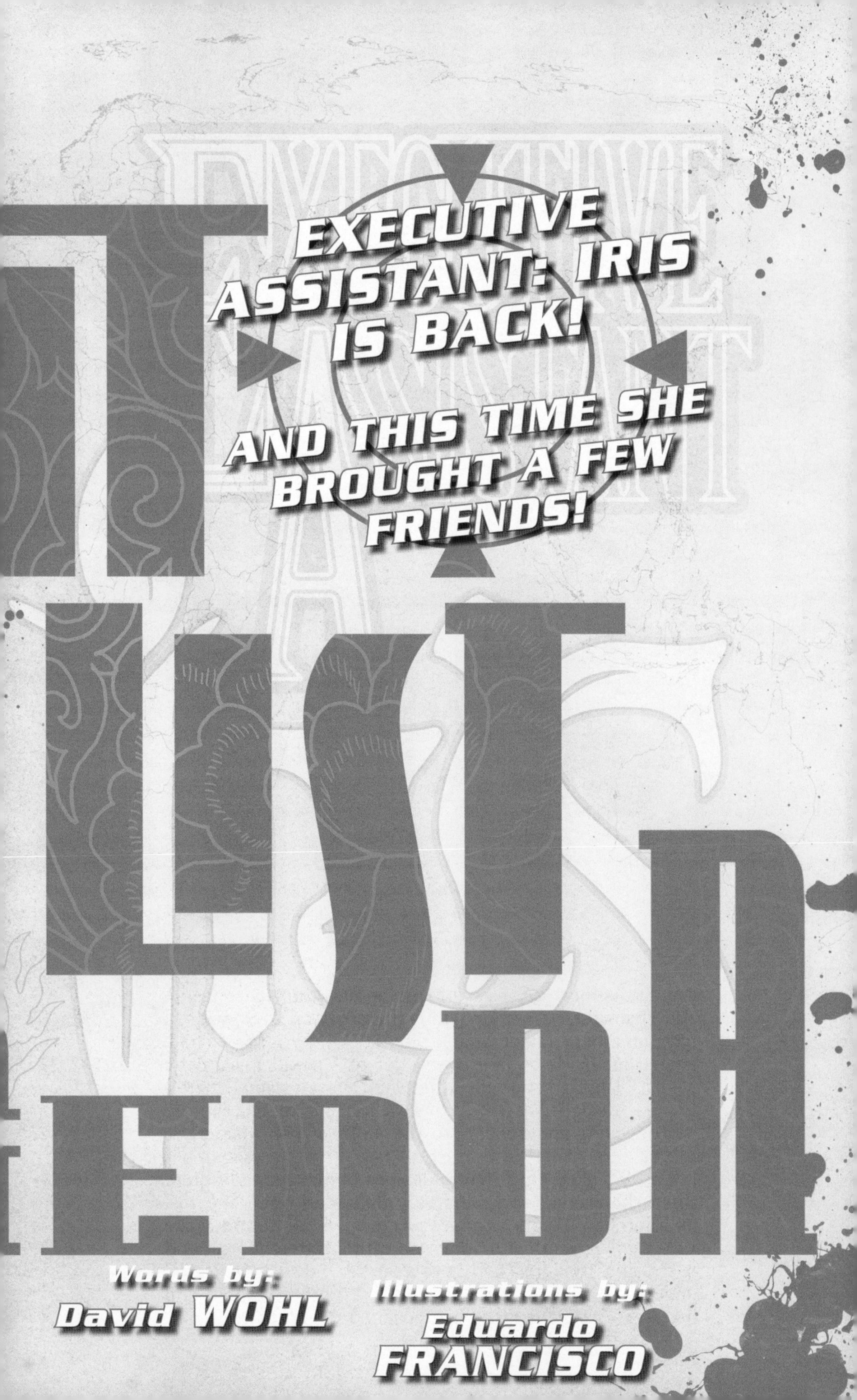
EXECUTIVE ASSISTANT: IRIS IS BACK!
AND THIS TIME SHE BROUGHT A FEW FRIENDS!
Words by:
David WOHL
Illustrations by:
Eduardo FRANCISCO

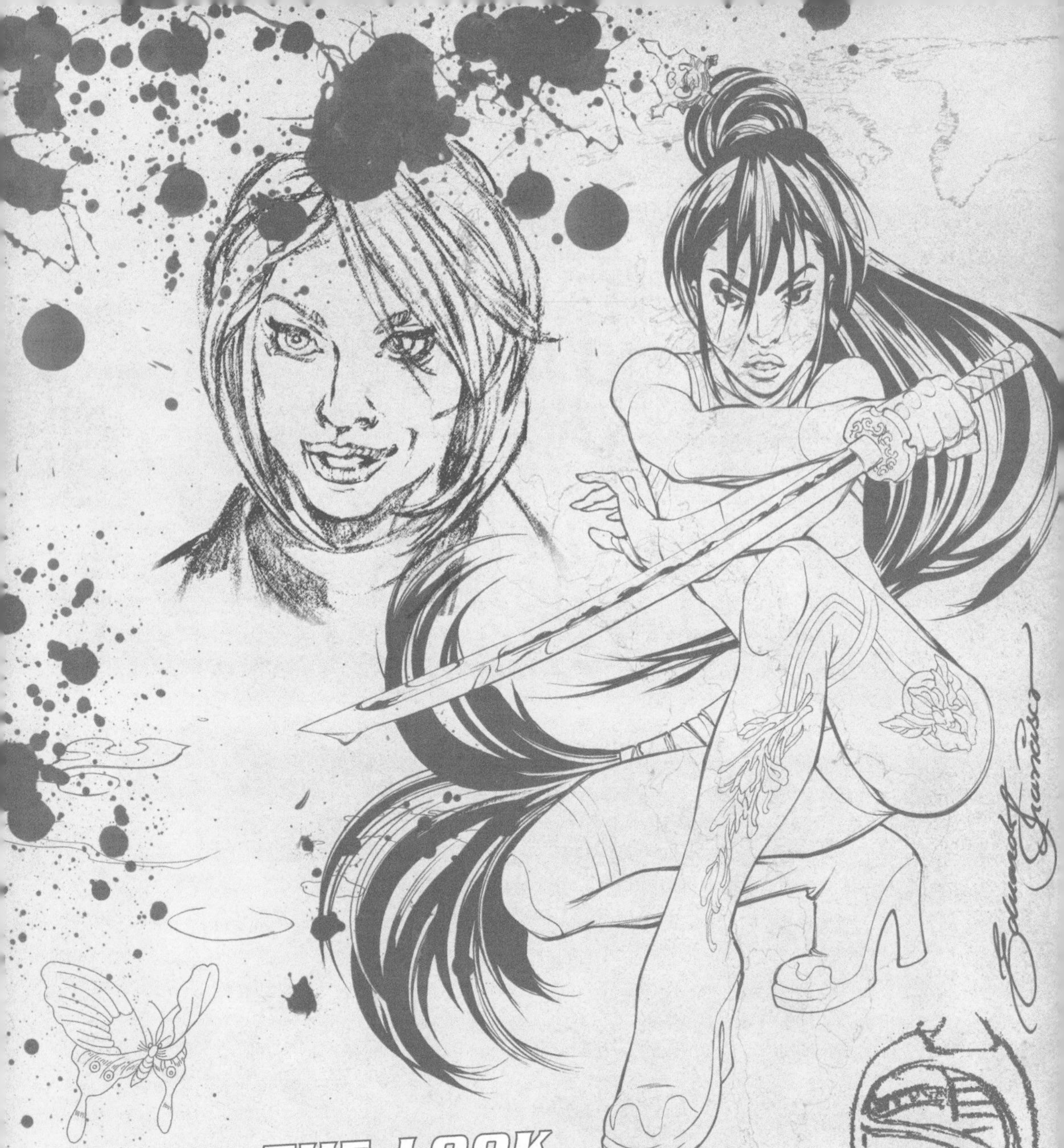

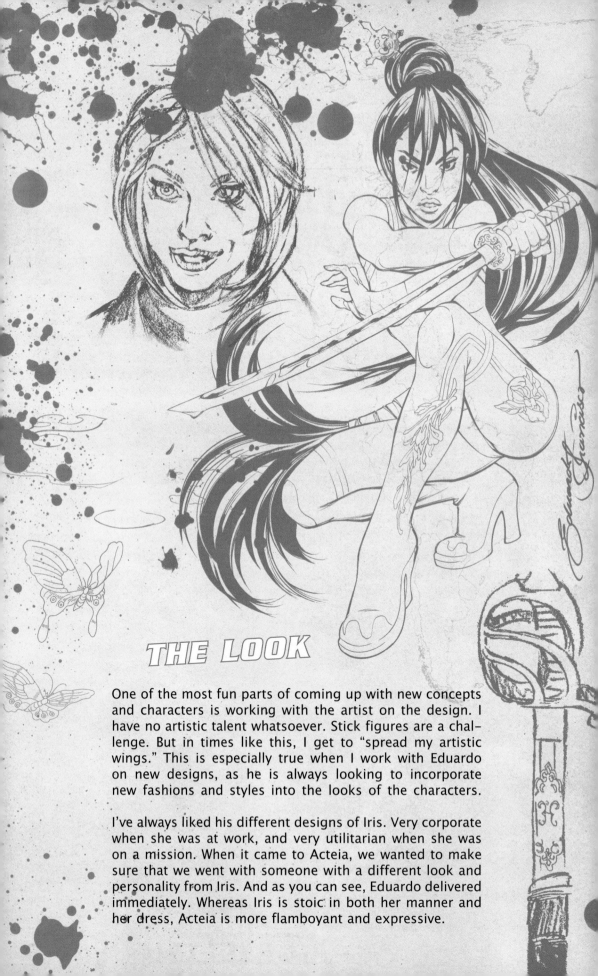

THE LOOK

One of the most fun parts of coming up with new concepts and characters is working with the artist on the design. I have no artistic talent whatsoever. Stick figures are a challenge. But in times like this, I get to "spread my artistic wings." This is especially true when I work with Eduardo on new designs, as he is always looking to incorporate new fashions and styles into the looks of the characters.

I've always liked his different designs of Iris. Very corporate when she was at work, and very utilitarian when she was on a mission. When it came to Acteia, we wanted to make sure that we went with someone with a different look and personality from Iris. And as you can see, Eduardo delivered immediately. Whereas Iris is stoic in both her manner and her dress, Acteia is more flamboyant and expressive.

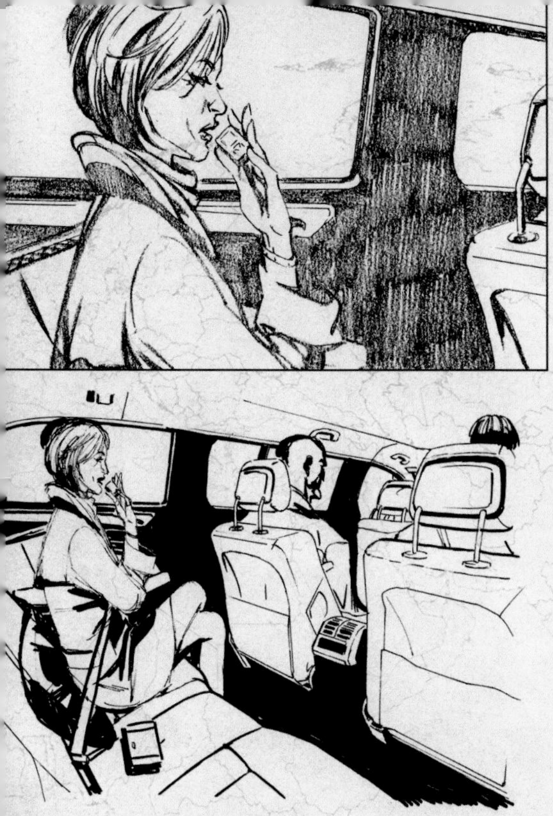

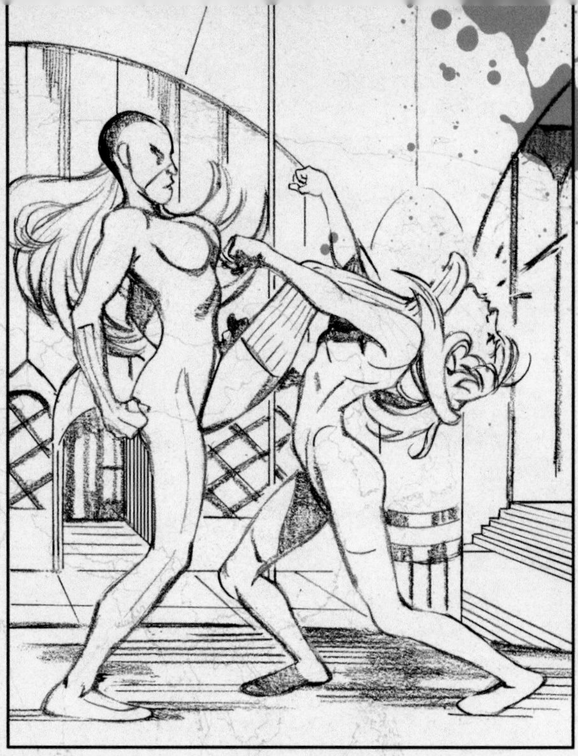

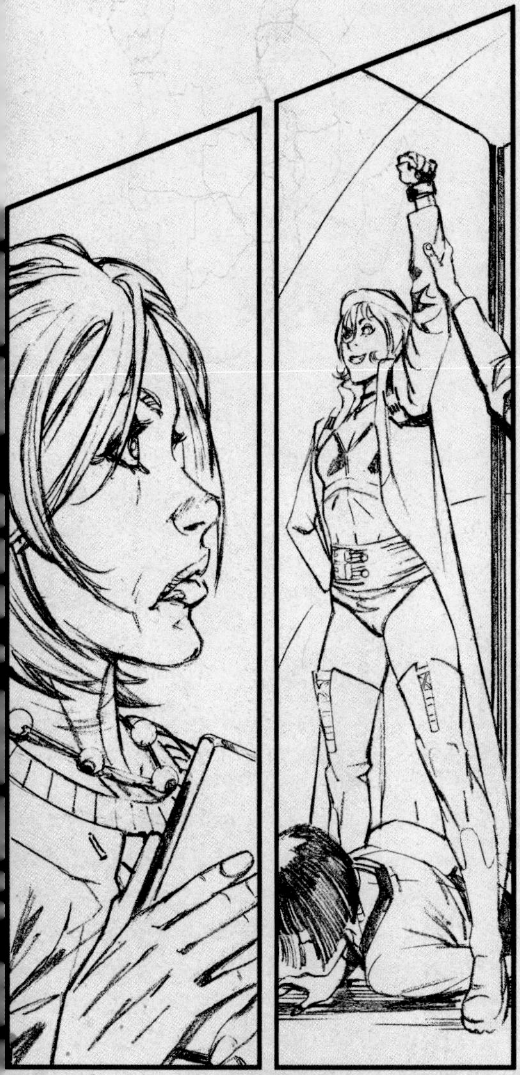

THE FOCUS

One thing we've always tried to put across is that, as much as possible, the Executive Assistant should reflect the personality of their employer. Even when they're doing the choosing, the prospective "owners" will gravitate toward certain Executive Assistants. We quickly establish the kind of woman Diane Coverdale is. She's no-nonsense and willing to fight for what she believes in, so that tends to get her into trouble. She's also extremely stylish. For her obviously, protection is the number one concern, but she also wanted someone who would fit in her glamorous Hollywood lifestyle. Iris would probably stand out like a sore thumb when TMZ is snapping photos. But Acteia not only would fit right in, she'd smile for the camera...before breaking it.

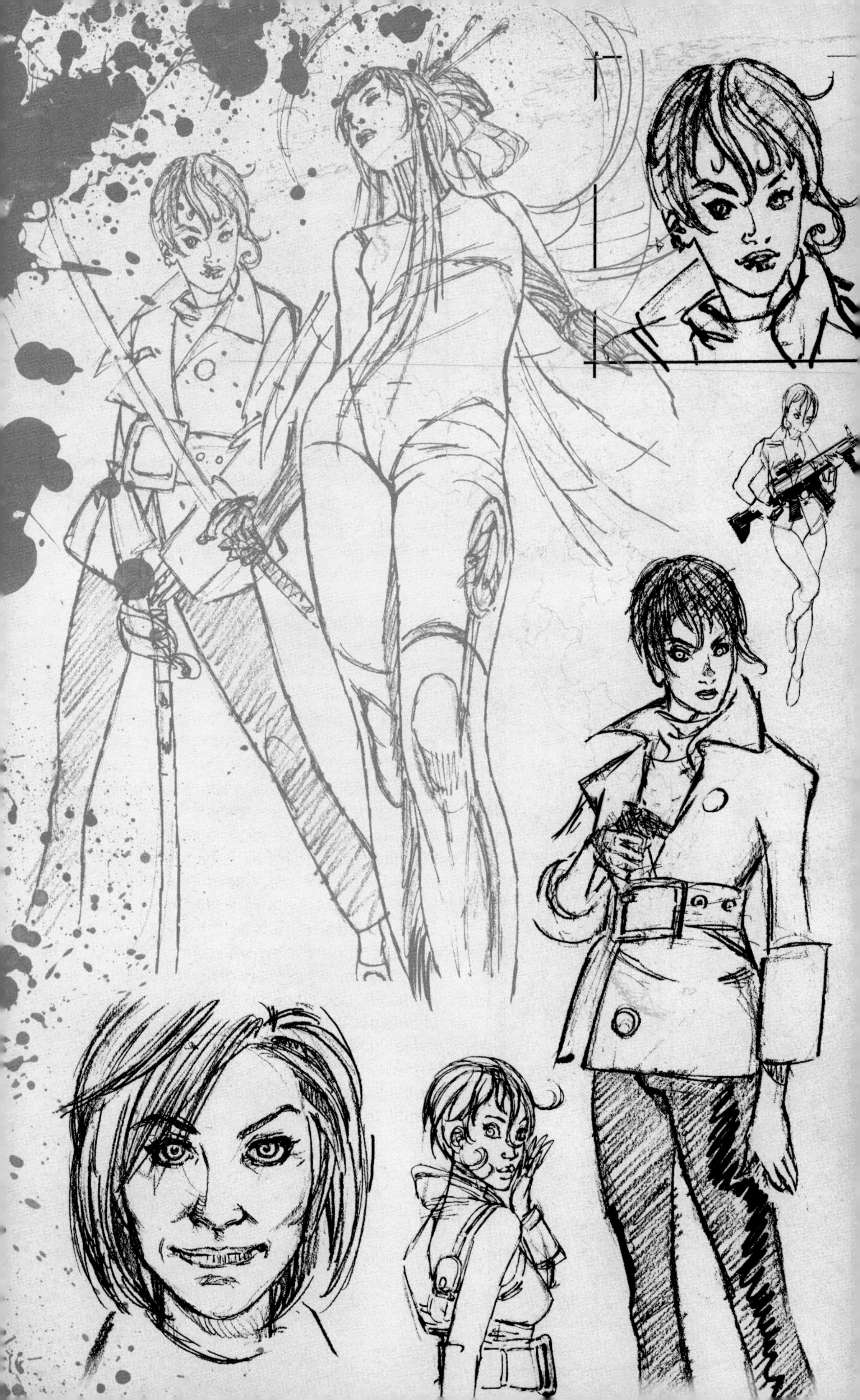

THE FOCUS

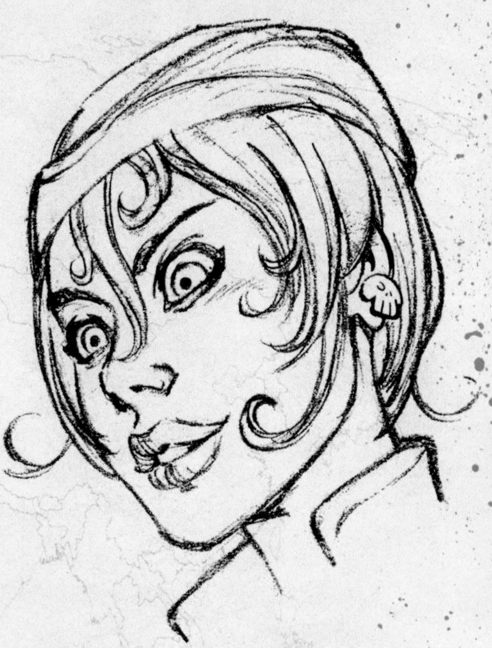

I believe that the Hit List Agenda is the natural evolution of the Executive Assistant series. The first time around, we introduced readers to the world of Iris and showed where she came from. But we only scratched the surface of the mythology and the universe. As people will quickly see, Acteia and Iris may both ultimately have the same goals--to protect and serve their employers--but they go about that service in very different ways. One thing they have in common is that they can kick serious ass when called upon to do so. The difference is, Iris would prefer to solve problems by other means while Acteia has no problem using her fists, or a sword, or an assault rifle to solve her problems. Over the course of the series though, Iris and Acteia will find that they have more in common than they ever realized.

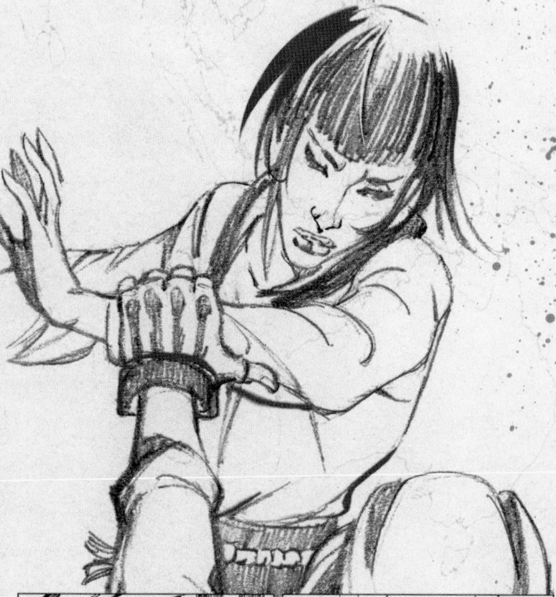

To bring this big world to life, we've been fortunate to be able to work with some very talented creators, each of them bringing their own unique vision to the crossover. First, of course, there's my buddy Eduardo, who worked with me on the original Iris series and has returned to stay on the new series. Then we have one of my oldest friends in comics, Scott Lobdell. Oh wait, maybe that didn't come out right. Sorry, Scott. Anyway, Scott is working with Micah Gunnell on Executive Assistant: Orchid. This is a part of the story that I wish I was able to tell myself. Orchid is employed by a Mexican gangster, and the events in her story have a feel right out of a Quentin Tarantino film. Meanwhile, Aspen's own Editor in Chief and master scribe Vince Hernandez and the awesome Oliver Nome embark on a completely different kind of Executive Assistant tale of political intrigue and global stakes in Executive Assistant: Lotus. And then we have the renowned Marc Andreyko teaming up with another old friend, Pop Mhan, in Executive Assistant: Violet, which is a James Bond-ish tale of espionage in the U.K.

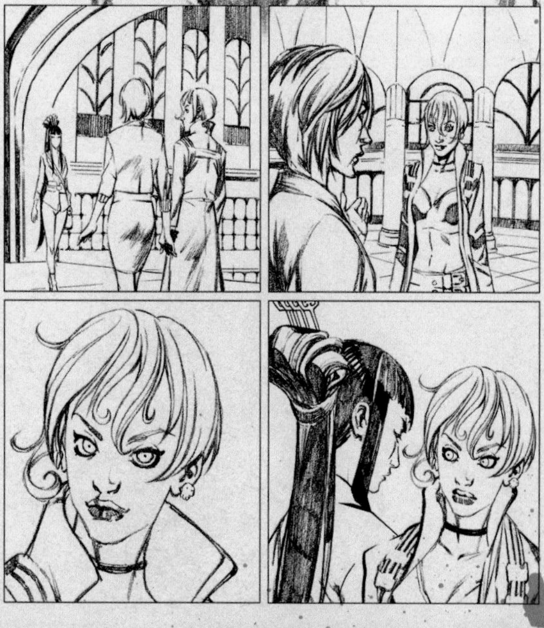

THE RESULT

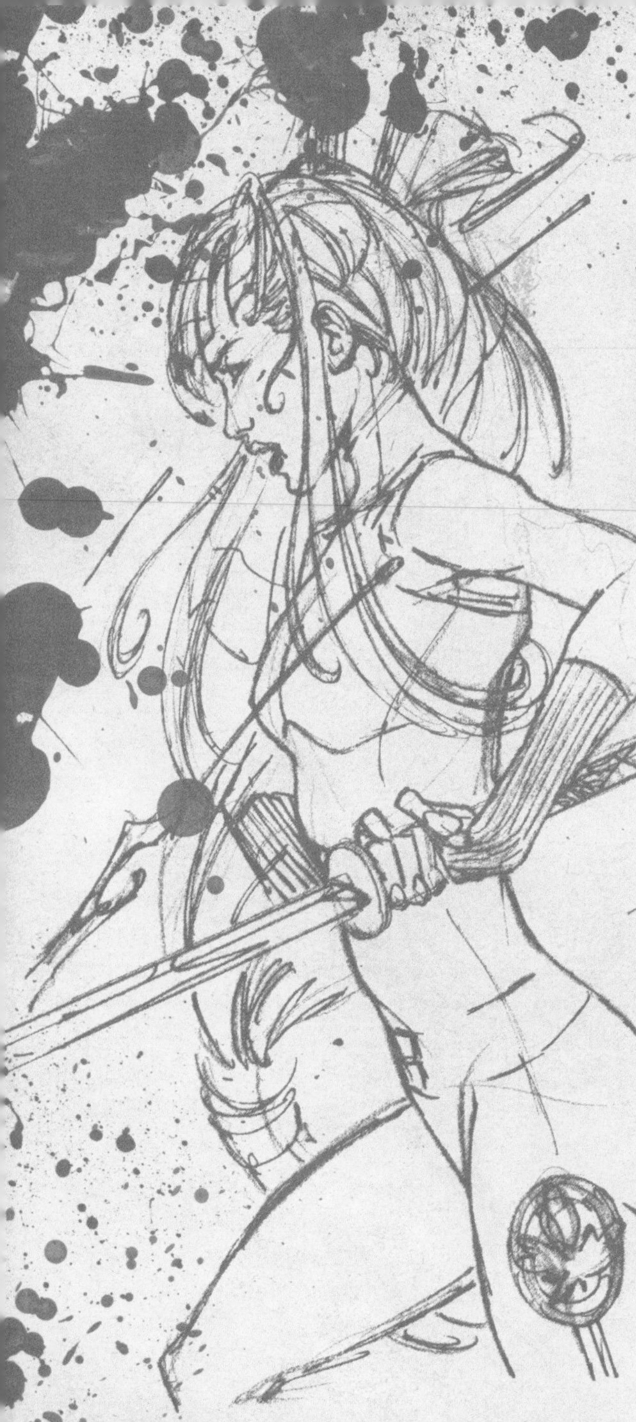

I must say that it's been a pleasure working with these great creators. Everyone brings their own expertise and story sense to the crossover, and this allows each of the different titles to have it's own special, unique style and flavor. But beneath that, we're all heading in the same direction, working on one big, explosive story that will bring all of these extraordinary characters together.

Doing an ambitious crossover like this isn't easy, but it's very rewarding when you see the final product.

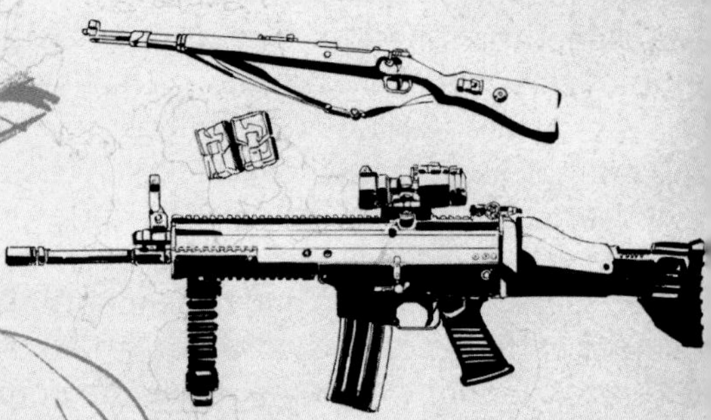

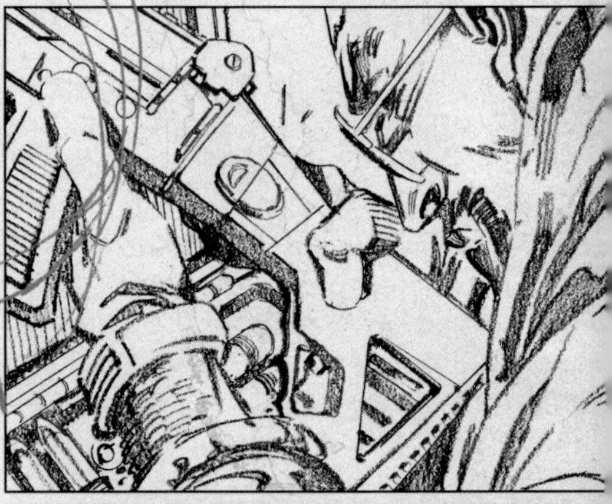

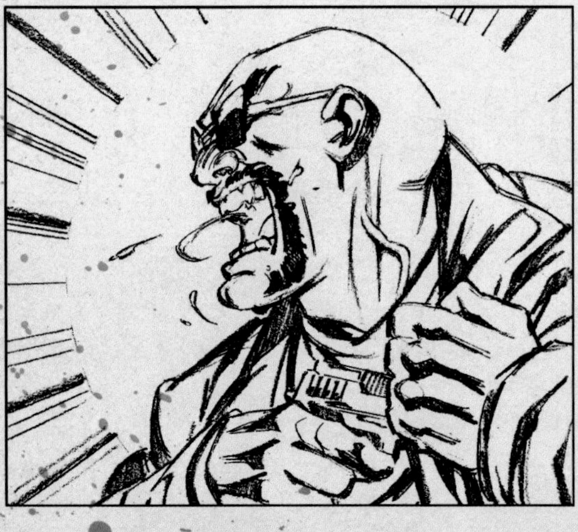

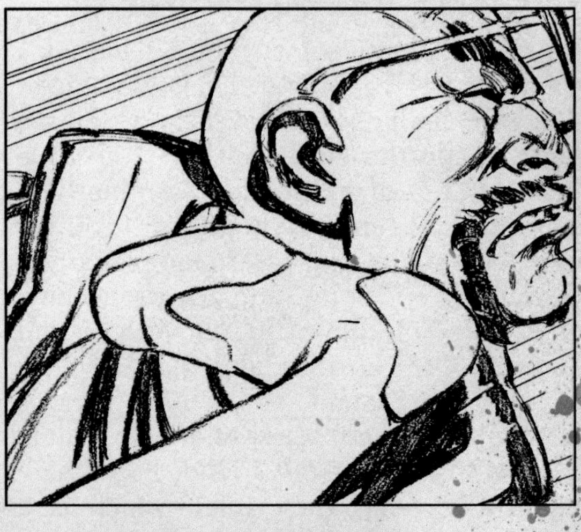

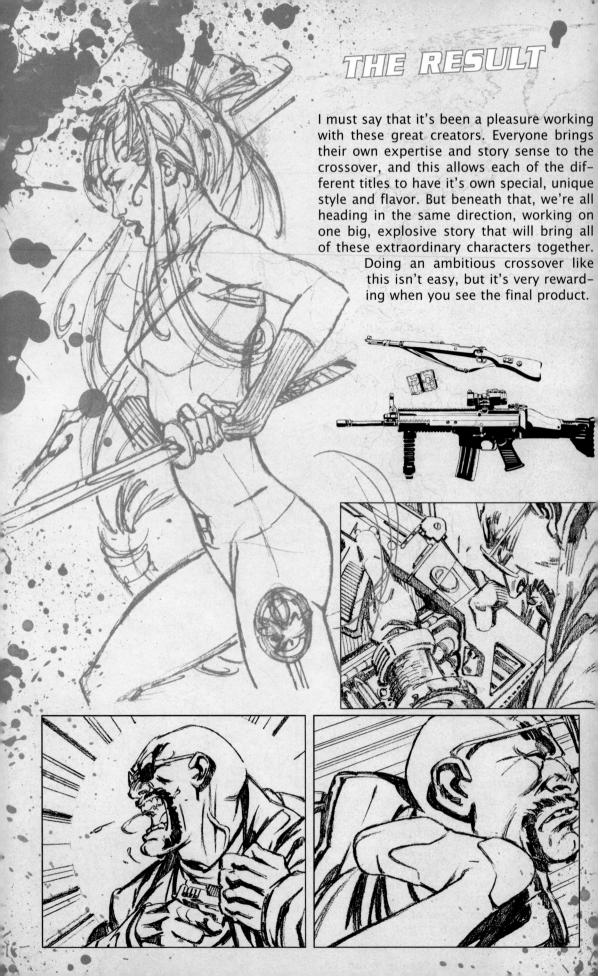

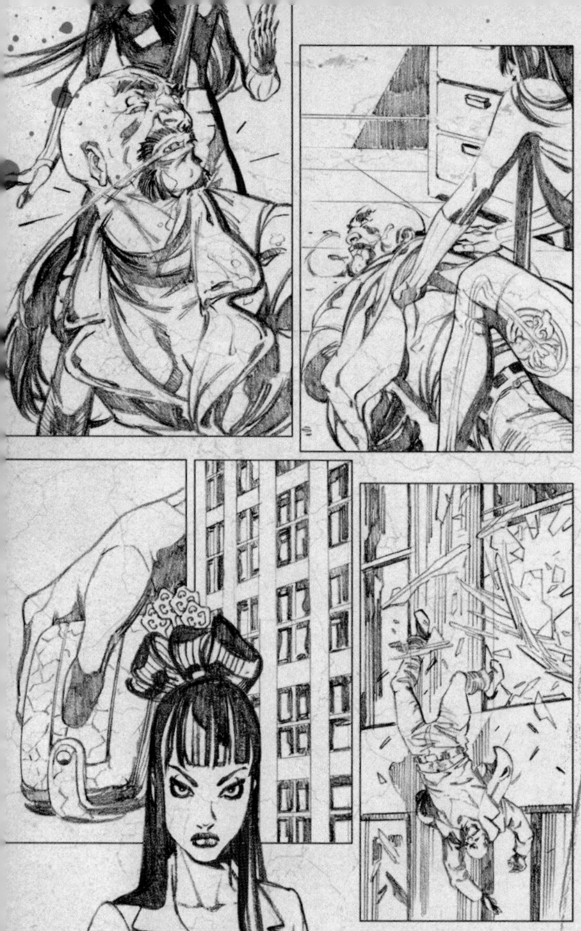

THE REWARD

And it's even more rewarding when the books are finally on the stands, and you get to read and experience what we've been toiling over for months. And then, hopefully at some convention down the line, or on the message boards or on Facebook or Twitter or any of the other hundreds of ways one has to communicate these days, you'll let us know what you think of our baby, The Hit List Agenda!!!!

David Wohl

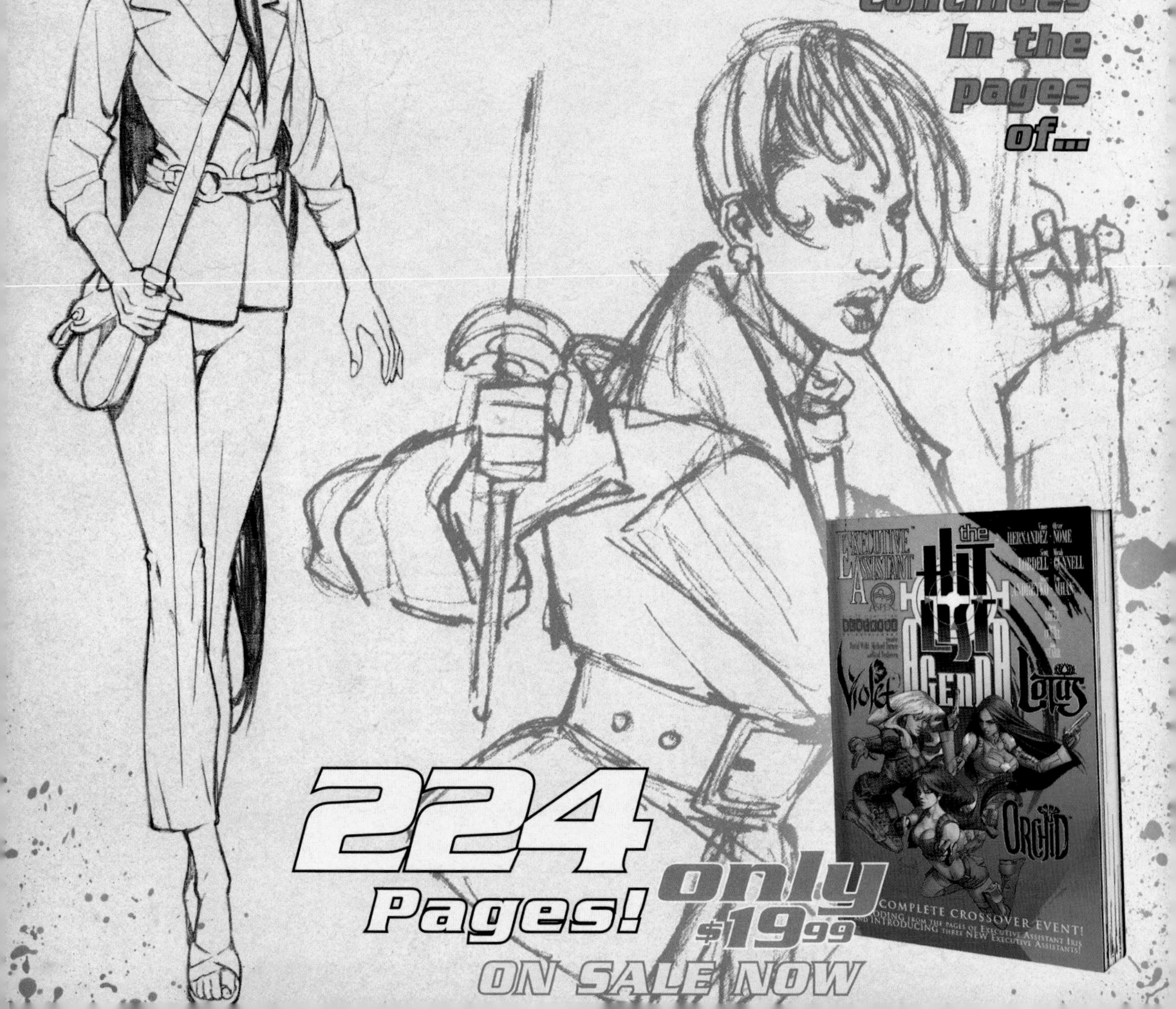

Executive Assistant
the Hit List Agenda
Violet
Lotus
Orchid
COMPLETE CROSSOVER EVENT!
224 Pages!
only $19.99
ON SALE NOW

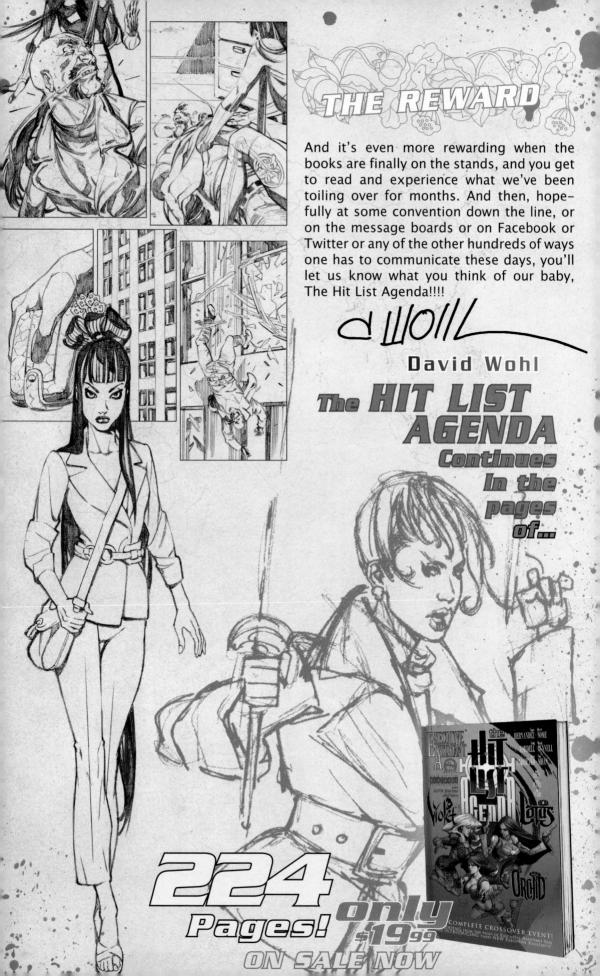

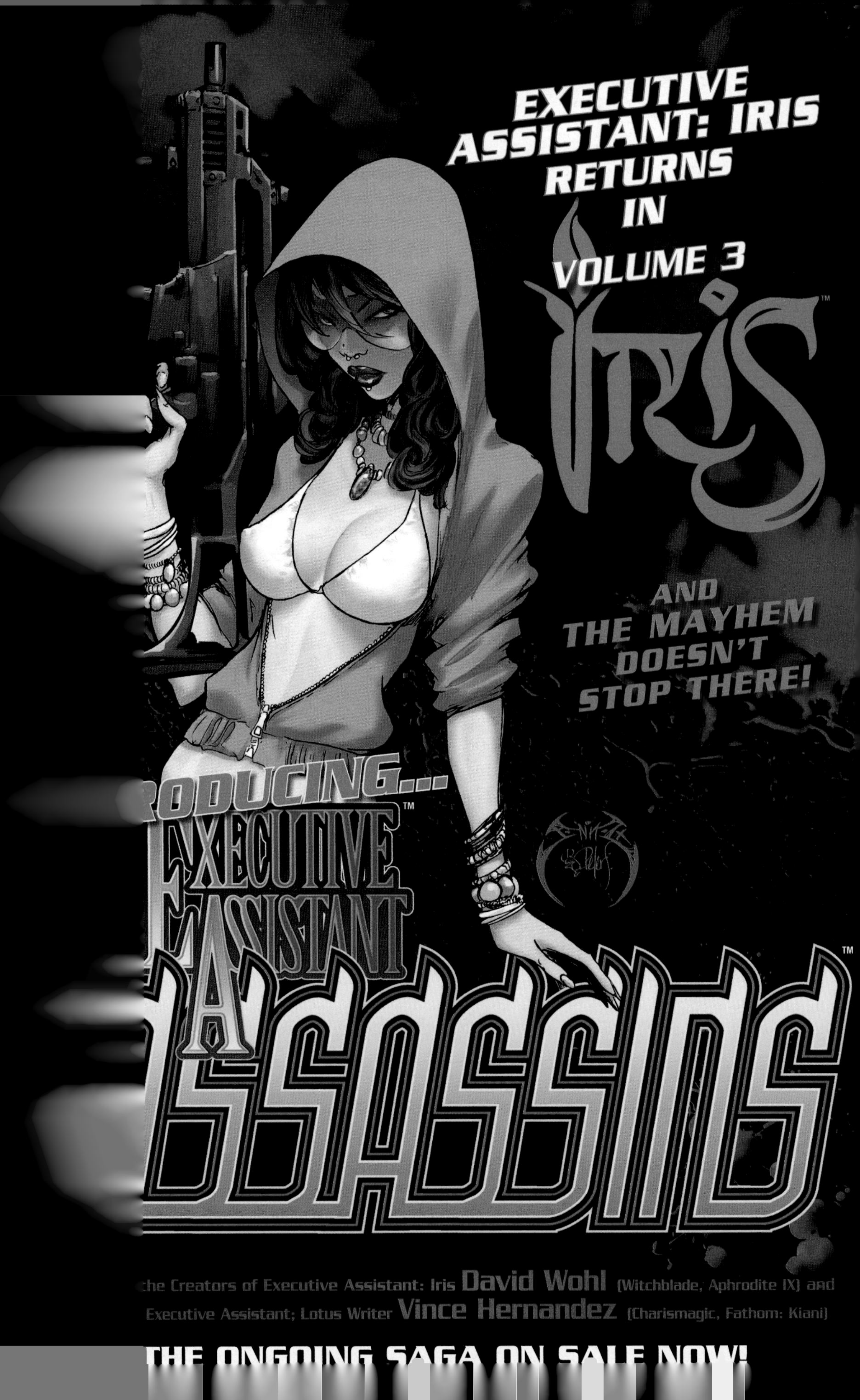
EXECUTIVE ASSISTANT: IRIS RETURNS IN VOLUME 3
IRIS™
AND THE MAYHEM DOESN'T STOP THERE!
RODUCING...
EXECUTIVE ASSISTANT™
ASSASSINS™
the Creators of Executive Assistant: Iris David Wohl (Witchblade, Aphrodite IX) and
Executive Assistant; Lotus Writer Vince Hernandez (Charismagic, Fathom: Kiani)
THE ONGOING SAGA ON SALE NOW!

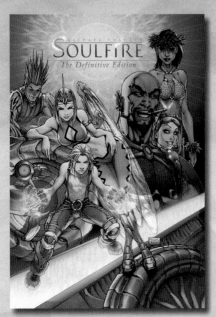

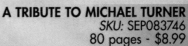

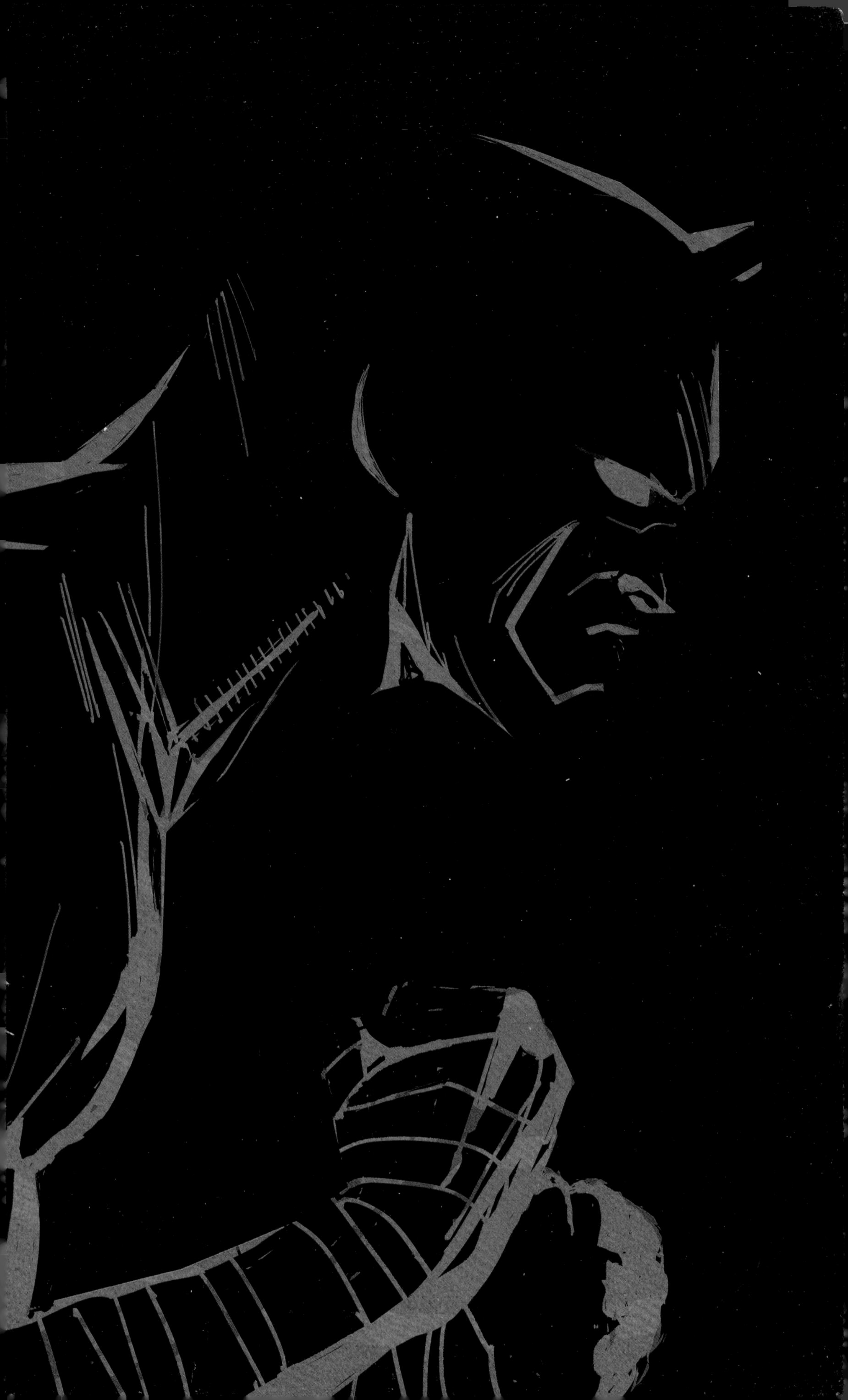

WHEN MATT MURDOCK WAS A KID, HE LOST HIS SIGHT IN AN ACCIDENT INVOLVING
A TRUCK CARRYING RADIOACTIVE CHEMICALS. THOUGH HE COULD NO LONGER SEE,
THE CHEMICALS HEIGHTENED MURDOCK'S OTHER SENSES AND IMBUED HIM WITH AN
AMAZING 360-RADAR SENSE. NOW MATT USES HIS ABILITIES TO FIGHT FOR HIS CITY.
HE IS THE *MAN WITHOUT FEAR.* HE IS...*DAREDEVIL*!

MATT MURDOCK BECAME A FAMOUS DEFENSE ATTORNEY BUT WAS EVENTUALLY
FORCED TO PUBLICLY REVEAL HE WAS DAREDEVIL. HE HAS MYSTERIOUSLY FOUND A
WAY TO KEEP HIS SECRET FROM THE WORLD AGAIN AND HAS NOW BECOME A
PROSECUTOR FOR THE CITY OF NEW YORK. AS DAREDEVIL, HE MENTORS A
YOUNG VIGILANTE NAMED **BLINDSPOT**, A.K.A. SAMUEL CHUNG.

DAREDEVIL
DARK ART

CHARLES SOULE
WRITER

RON GARNEY
ARTIST

MATT MILLA
COLOR ARTIST

VC's CLAYTON COWLES
LETTERER

RON GARNEY & MATT MILLA
COVER ART

CHRIS ROBINSON
ASSISTANT EDITOR

MARK PANICCIA
EDITOR

COLLECTION EDITOR **JENNIFER GRÜNWALD**
ASSISTANT EDITOR **CAITLIN O'CONNELL**
ASSOCIATE MANAGING EDITOR **KATERI WOODY**
EDITOR, SPECIAL PROJECTS **MARK D. BEAZLEY**
VP PRODUCTION & SPECIAL PROJECTS **JEFF YOUNGQUIST**
SVP PRINT, SALES & MARKETING **DAVID GABRIEL**
BOOK DESIGNER **ADAM DEL RE**

EDITOR IN CHIEF **AXEL ALONSO**
CHIEF CREATIVE OFFICER **JOE QUESADA**
PUBLISHER **DAN BUCKLEY**
EXECUTIVE PRODUCER **ALAN FINE**

DAREDEVIL: BACK IN BLACK VOL. 3 — DARK ART. Contains material originally published in magazine form as DAREDEVIL #10-14. First printing 2017. ISBN# 978-1-302-90297-1. Published by MARVEL WORLDWIDE, INC., a subsidiary of MARVEL ENTERTAINMENT, LLC. OFFICE OF PUBLICATION: 135 West 50th Street, New York, NY 10020. **Printed in Canada.** ALAN FINE, President, Marvel Entertainment; DAN BUCKLEY, President, TV, Publishing & Brand Management; JOE QUESADA, Chief Creative Officer; TOM BREVOORT, SVP of Publishing; DAVID BOGART, SVP of Business Affairs & Operations, Publishing & Partnership; C.B. CEBULSKI, VP of Brand Management & Development, Asia; DAVID GABRIEL, SVP of Sales & Marketing, Publishing; JEFF YOUNGQUIST, VP of Production & Special Projects; DAN CARR, Executive Director of Publishing Technology; ALEX MORALES, Director of Publishing Operations; SUSAN CRESPI, Production Manager; STAN LEE, Chairman Emeritus. For information regarding advertising in Marvel Comics or on Marvel.com, please contact Vit DeBellis, Integrated Sales Manager, at vdebellis@marvel.com. For Marvel subscription inquiries, please call 888-511-5480. **Manufactured between 12/30/2016 and 2/6/2017 by SOLISCO PRINTERS, SCOTT, QC, CANADA.**

10 9 8 7 6 5 4 3 2 1

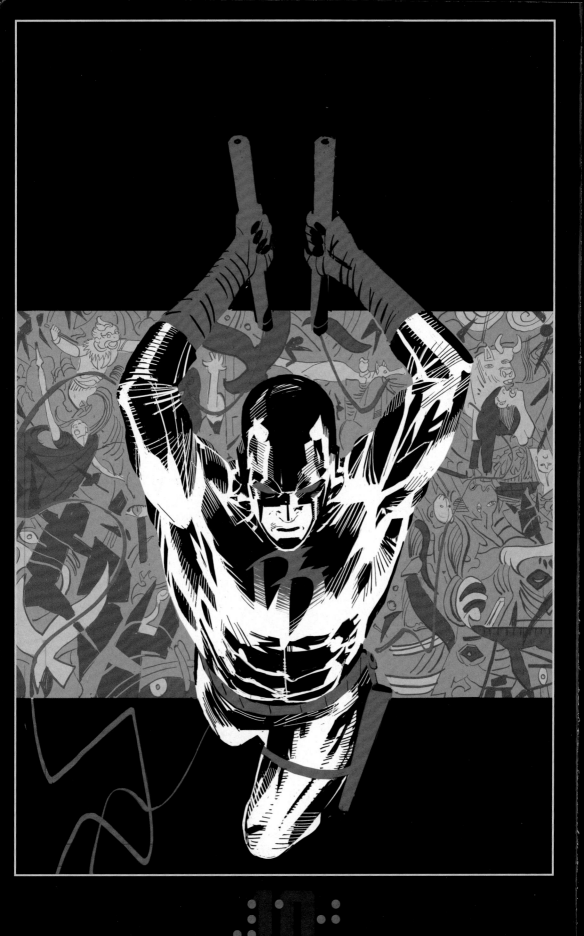

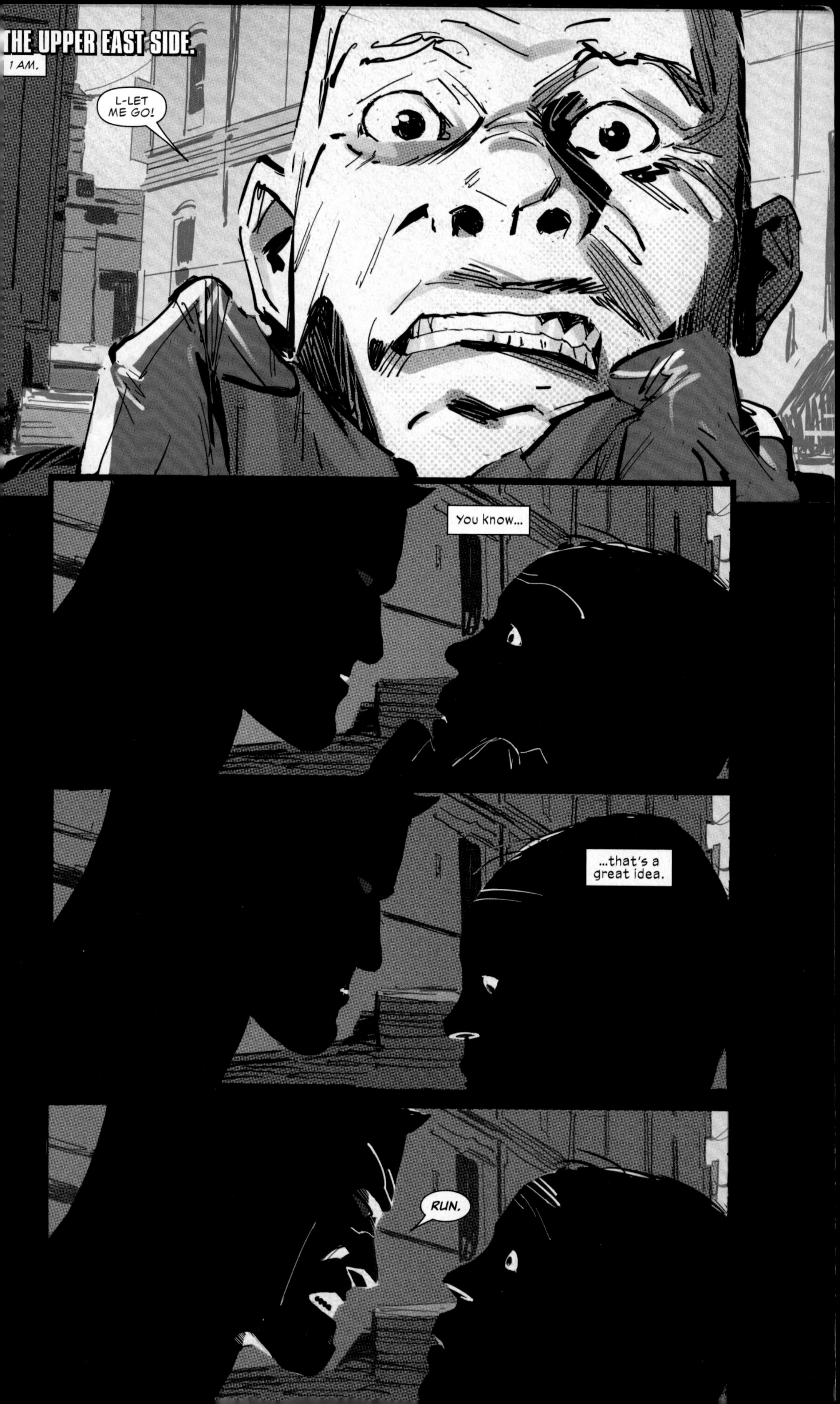

THE UPPER EAST SIDE.
1 AM.
L-LET ME GO!
You know...
...that's a great idea.
RUN.

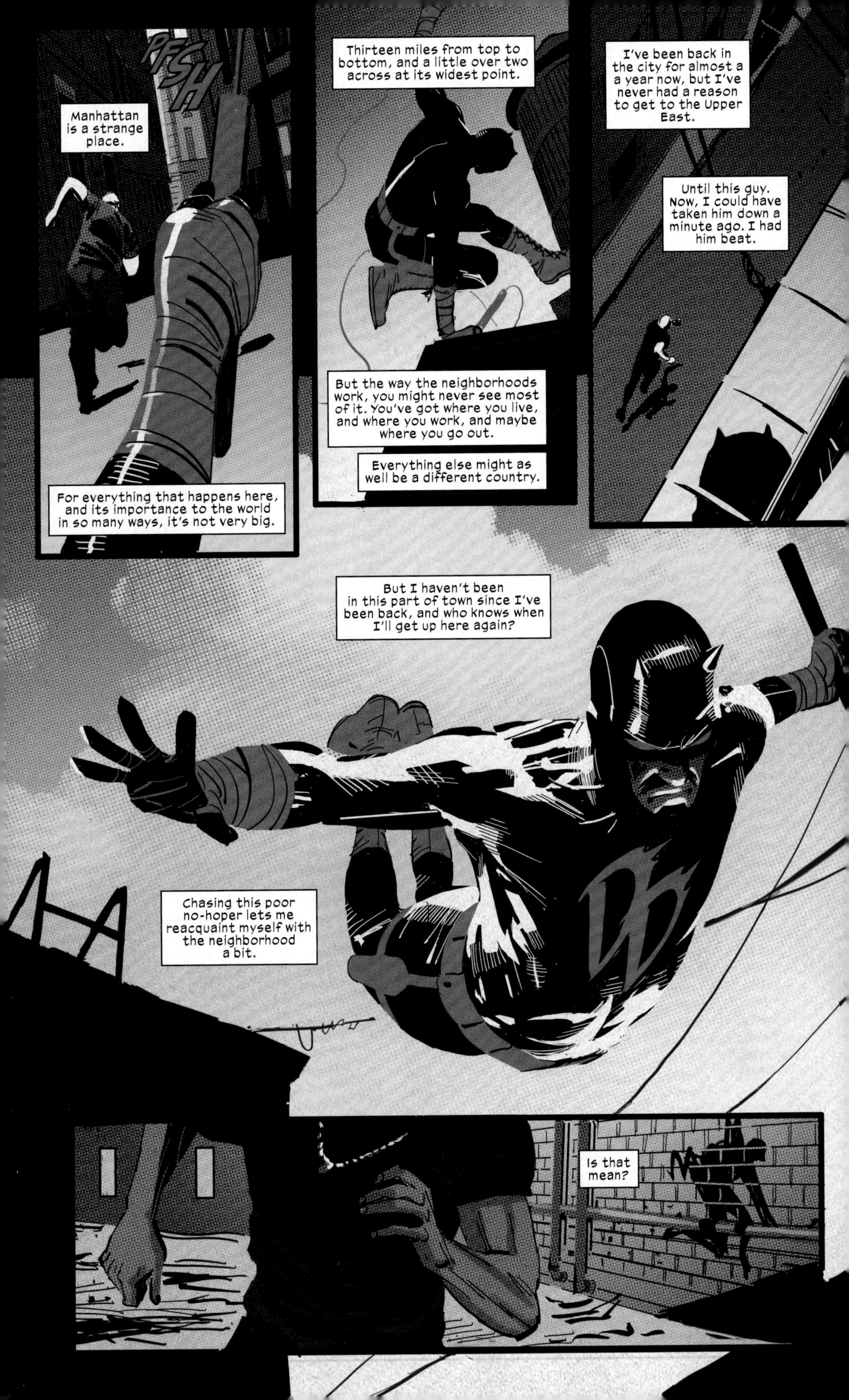
PFSH
Manhattan is a strange place.
For everything that happens here, and its importance to the world in so many ways, it's not very big.
Thirteen miles from top to bottom, and a little over two across at its widest point.
But the way the neighborhoods work, you might never see most of it. You've got where you live, and where you work, and maybe where you go out.
Everything else might as well be a different country.
I've been back in the city for almost a a year now, but I've never had a reason to get to the Upper East.
Until this guy. Now, I could have taken him down a minute ago. I had him beat.
But I haven't been in this part of town since I've been back, and who knows when I'll get up here again?
Chasing this poor no-hoper lets me reacquaint myself with the neighborhood a bit.
Is that mean?

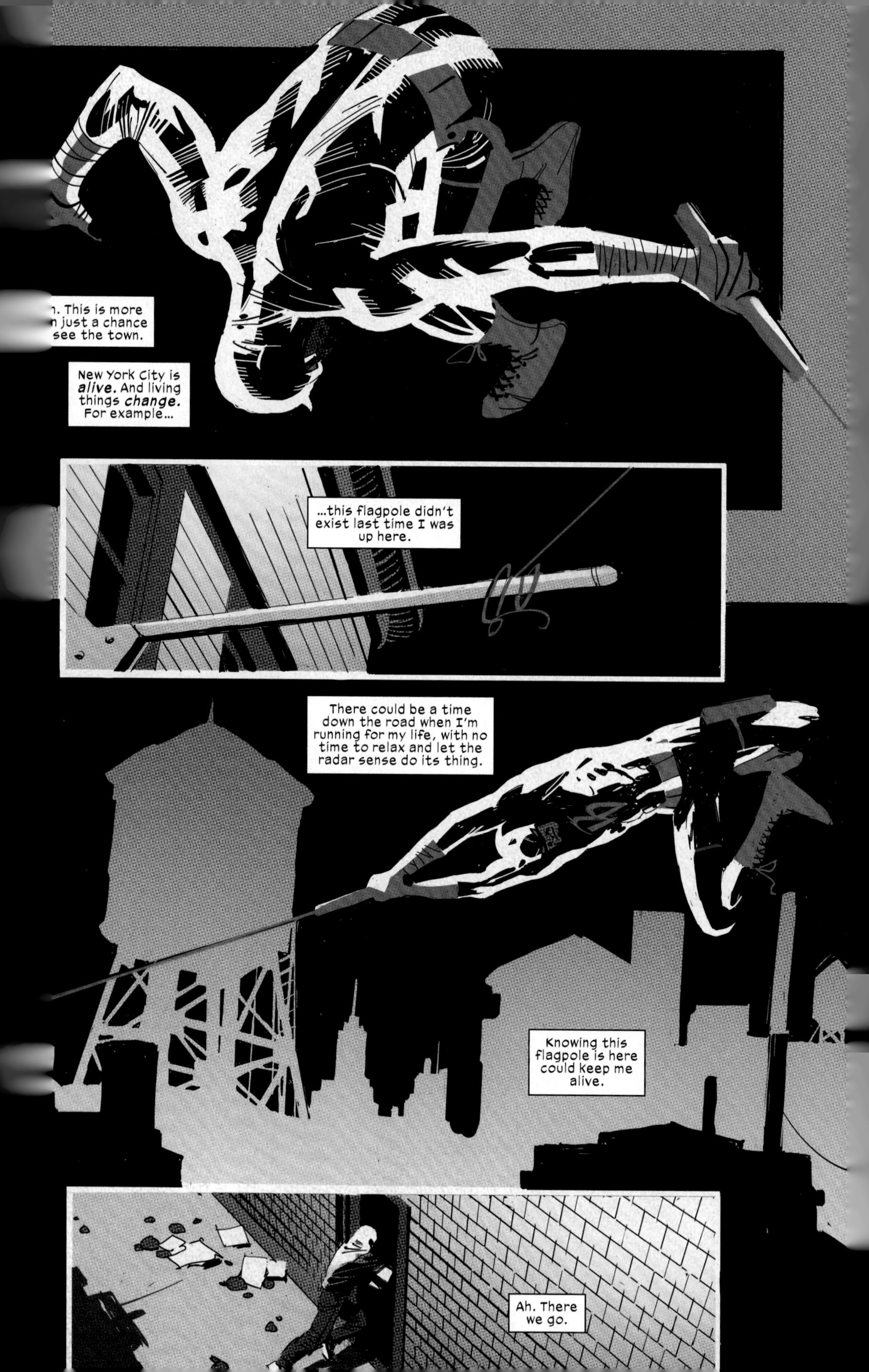

.. This is more
.. just a chance
.. see the town.
New York City is *alive.* And living things *change.* For example...
...this flagpole didn't exist last time I was up here.
There could be a time down the road when I'm running for my life, with no time to relax and let the radar sense do its thing.
Knowing this flagpole is here could keep me alive.
Ah. There we go.

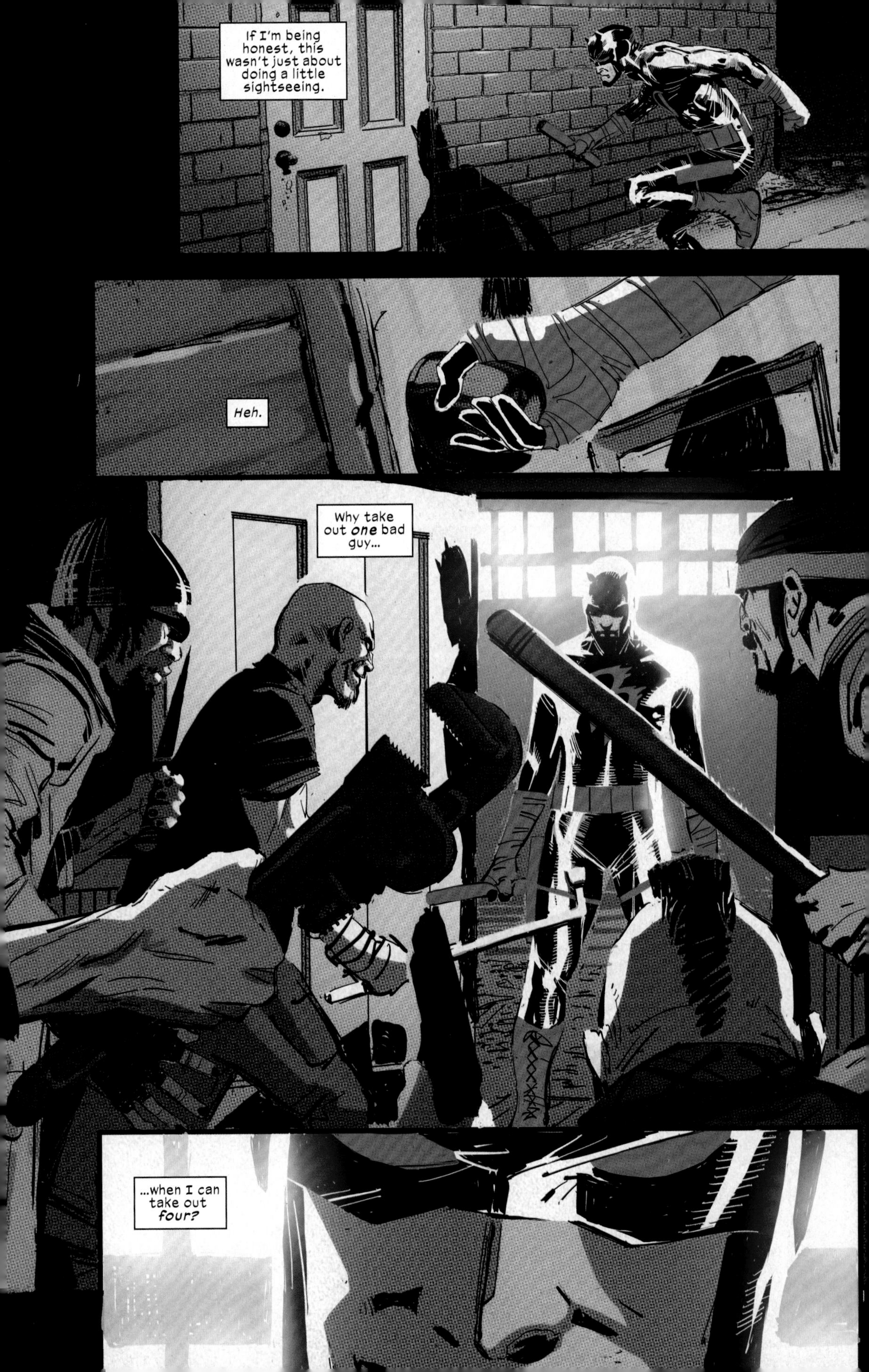
If I'm being honest, this wasn't just about doing a little sightseeing.
Heh.
Why take out *one* bad guy...
...when I can take out *four?*

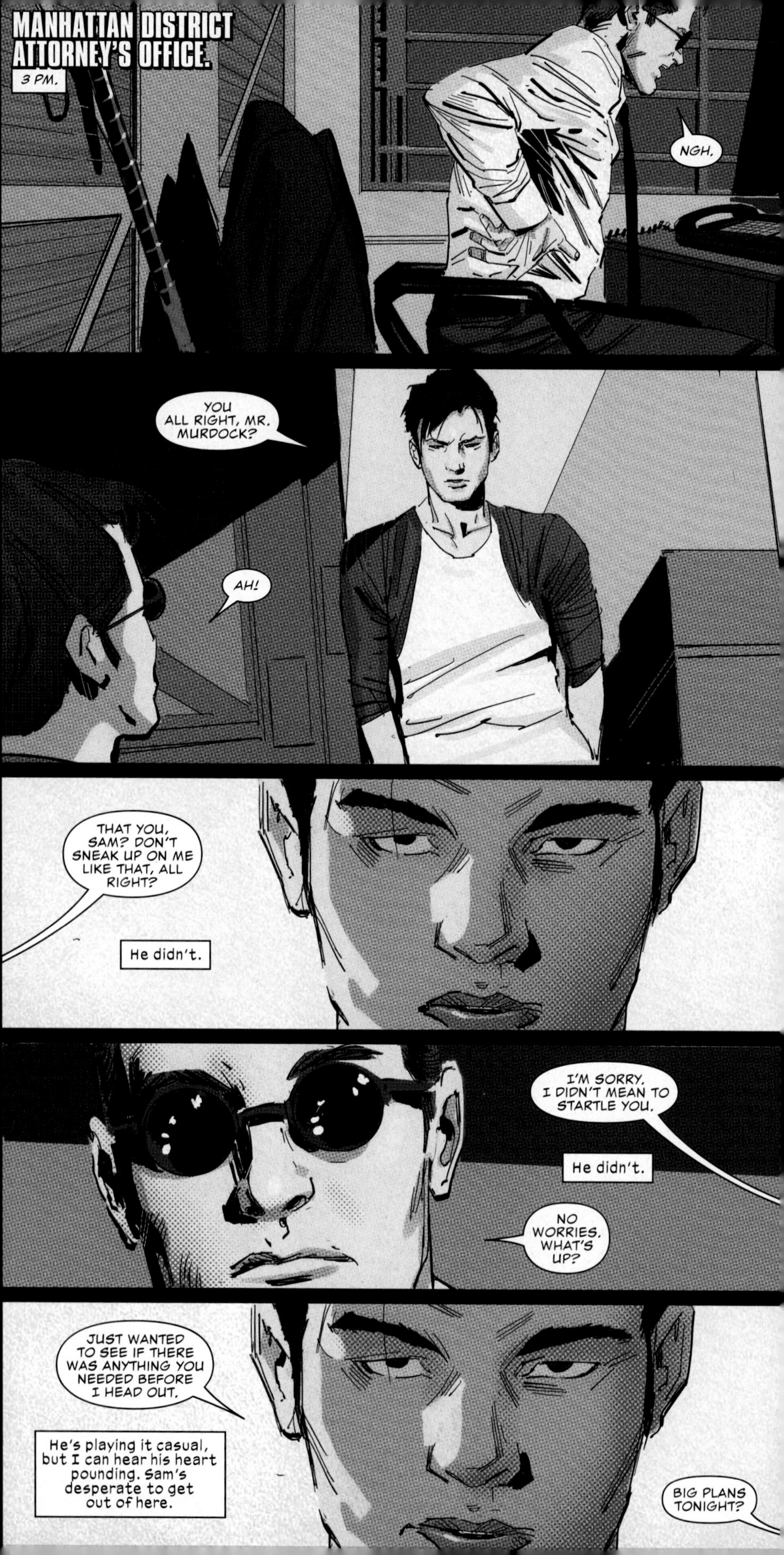
MANHATTAN DISTRICT ATTORNEY'S OFFICE.
3 PM.
NGH.
YOU ALL RIGHT, MR. MURDOCK?
AH!
THAT YOU, SAM? DON'T SNEAK UP ON ME LIKE THAT, ALL RIGHT?
He didn't.
I'M SORRY. I DIDN'T MEAN TO STARTLE YOU.
He didn't.
NO WORRIES. WHAT'S UP?
JUST WANTED TO SEE IF THERE WAS ANYTHING YOU NEEDED BEFORE I HEAD OUT.
He's playing it casual, but I can hear his heart pounding. Sam's desperate to get out of here.
BIG PLANS TONIGHT?

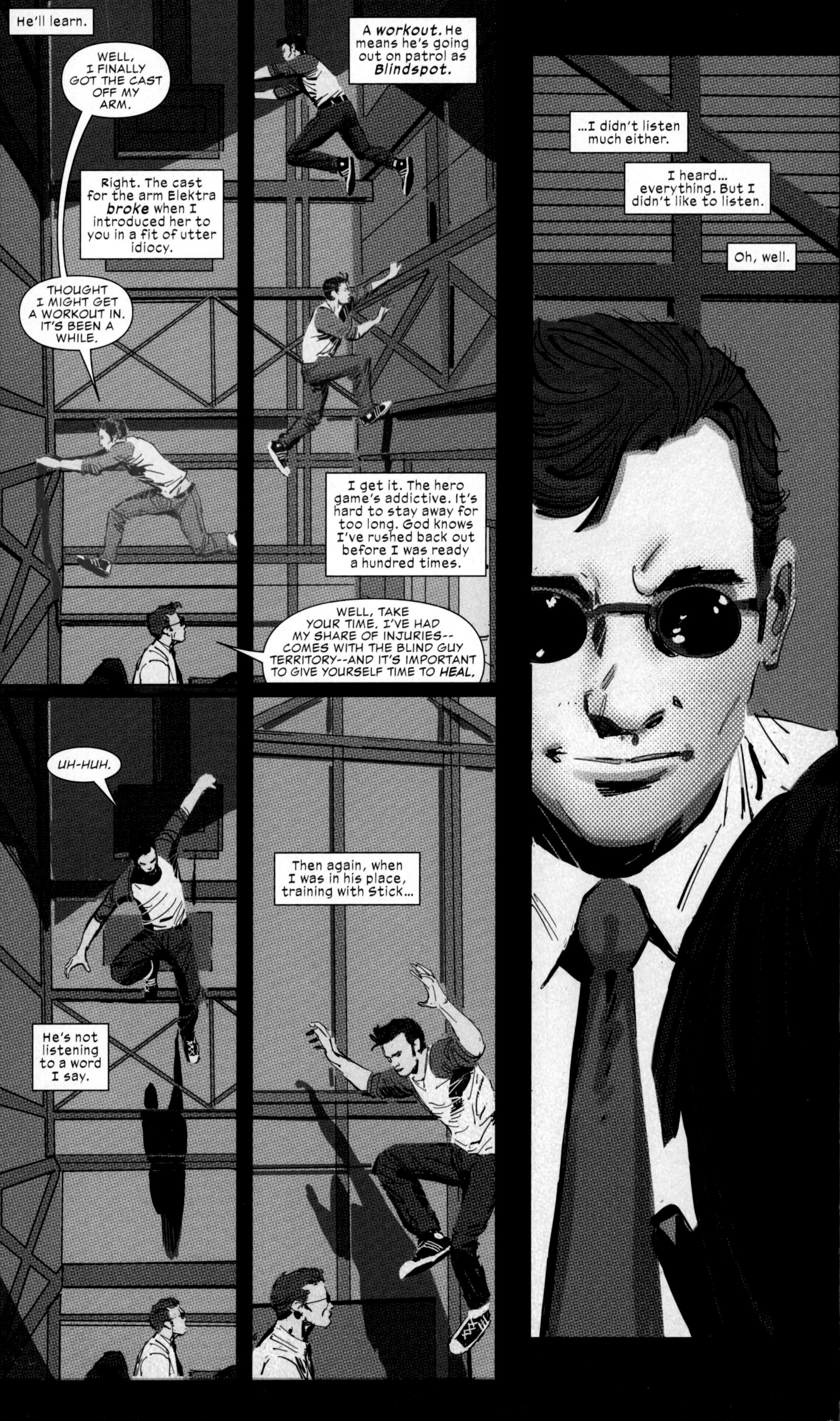
He'll learn.
WELL, I FINALLY GOT THE CAST OFF MY ARM.
Right. The cast for the arm Elektra broke when I introduced her to you in a fit of utter idiocy.
THOUGHT I MIGHT GET A WORKOUT IN. IT'S BEEN A WHILE.
A workout. He means he's going out on patrol as Blindspot.
I get it. The hero game's addictive. It's hard to stay away for too long. God knows I've rushed back out before I was ready a hundred times.
WELL, TAKE YOUR TIME. I'VE HAD MY SHARE OF INJURIES--COMES WITH THE BLIND GUY TERRITORY--AND IT'S IMPORTANT TO GIVE YOURSELF TIME TO HEAL.
UH-HUH.
He's not listening to a word I say.
Then again, when I was in his place, training with Stick...
...I didn't listen much either.
I heard... everything. But I didn't like to listen.
Oh, well.

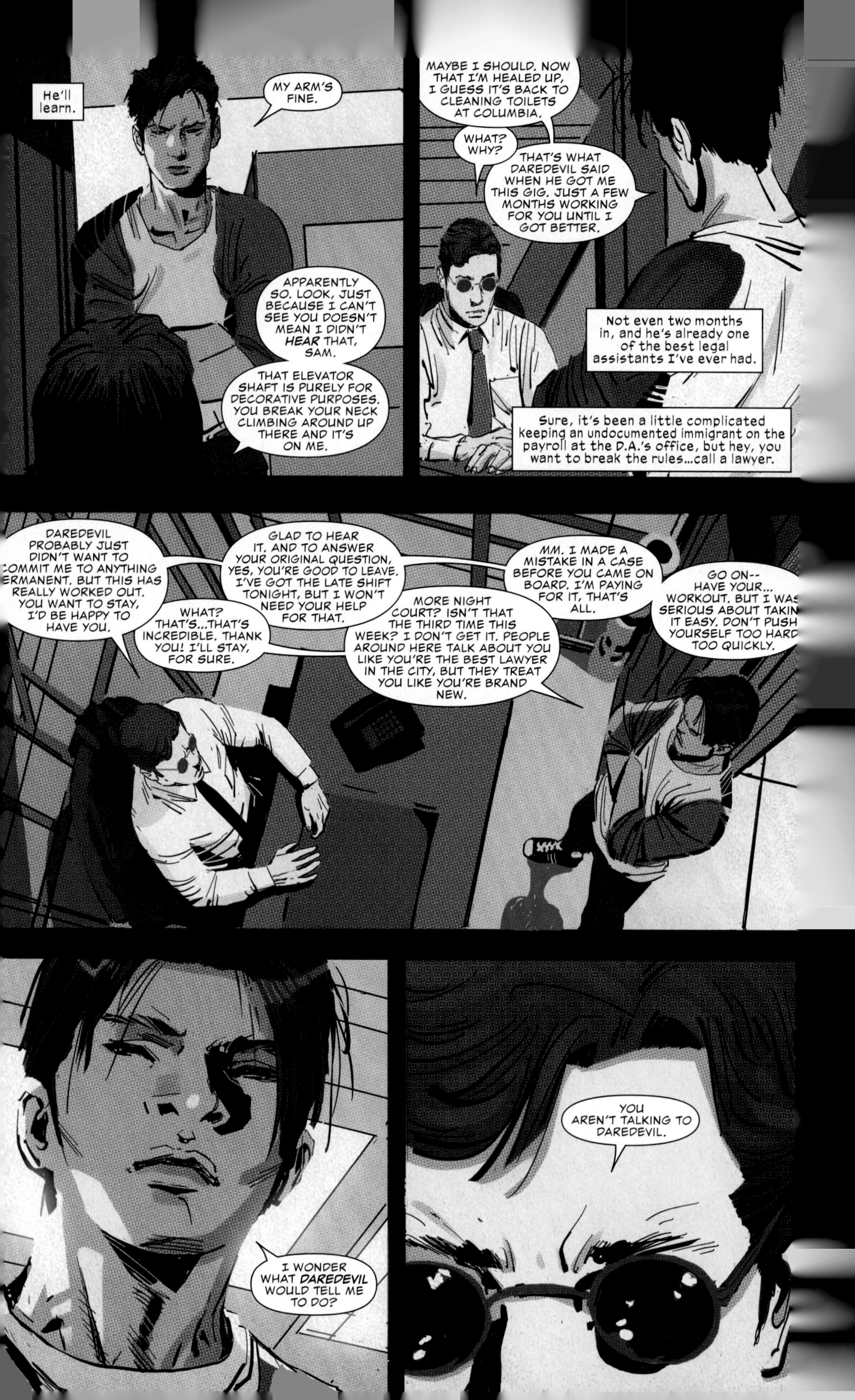

He'll learn.
MY ARM'S FINE.
APPARENTLY SO. LOOK, JUST BECAUSE I CAN'T SEE YOU DOESN'T MEAN I DIDN'T HEAR THAT, SAM.
THAT ELEVATOR SHAFT IS PURELY FOR DECORATIVE PURPOSES. YOU BREAK YOUR NECK CLIMBING AROUND UP THERE AND IT'S ON ME.
MAYBE I SHOULD. NOW THAT I'M HEALED UP, I GUESS IT'S BACK TO CLEANING TOILETS AT COLUMBIA.
WHAT? WHY?
THAT'S WHAT DAREDEVIL SAID WHEN HE GOT ME THIS GIG. JUST A FEW MONTHS WORKING FOR YOU UNTIL I GOT BETTER.
Not even two months in, and he's already one of the best legal assistants I've ever had.
Sure, it's been a little complicated keeping an undocumented immigrant on the payroll at the D.A.'s office, but hey, you want to break the rules...call a lawyer.
DAREDEVIL PROBABLY JUST DIDN'T WANT TO COMMIT ME TO ANYTHING PERMANENT. BUT THIS HAS REALLY WORKED OUT. YOU WANT TO STAY, I'D BE HAPPY TO HAVE YOU.
WHAT? THAT'S...THAT'S INCREDIBLE. THANK YOU! I'LL STAY, FOR SURE.
GLAD TO HEAR IT. AND TO ANSWER YOUR ORIGINAL QUESTION, YES, YOU'RE GOOD TO LEAVE. I'VE GOT THE LATE SHIFT TONIGHT, BUT I WON'T NEED YOUR HELP FOR THAT.
MORE NIGHT COURT? ISN'T THAT THE THIRD TIME THIS WEEK? I DON'T GET IT. PEOPLE AROUND HERE TALK ABOUT YOU LIKE YOU'RE THE BEST LAWYER IN THE CITY, BUT THEY TREAT YOU LIKE YOU'RE BRAND NEW.
MM. I MADE A MISTAKE IN A CASE BEFORE YOU CAME ON BOARD. I'M PAYING FOR IT, THAT'S ALL.
GO ON-- HAVE YOUR... WORKOUT. BUT I WAS SERIOUS ABOUT TAKING IT EASY. DON'T PUSH YOURSELF TOO HARD TOO QUICKLY.
I WONDER WHAT DAREDEVIL WOULD TELL ME TO DO?
YOU AREN'T TALKING TO DAREDEVIL.

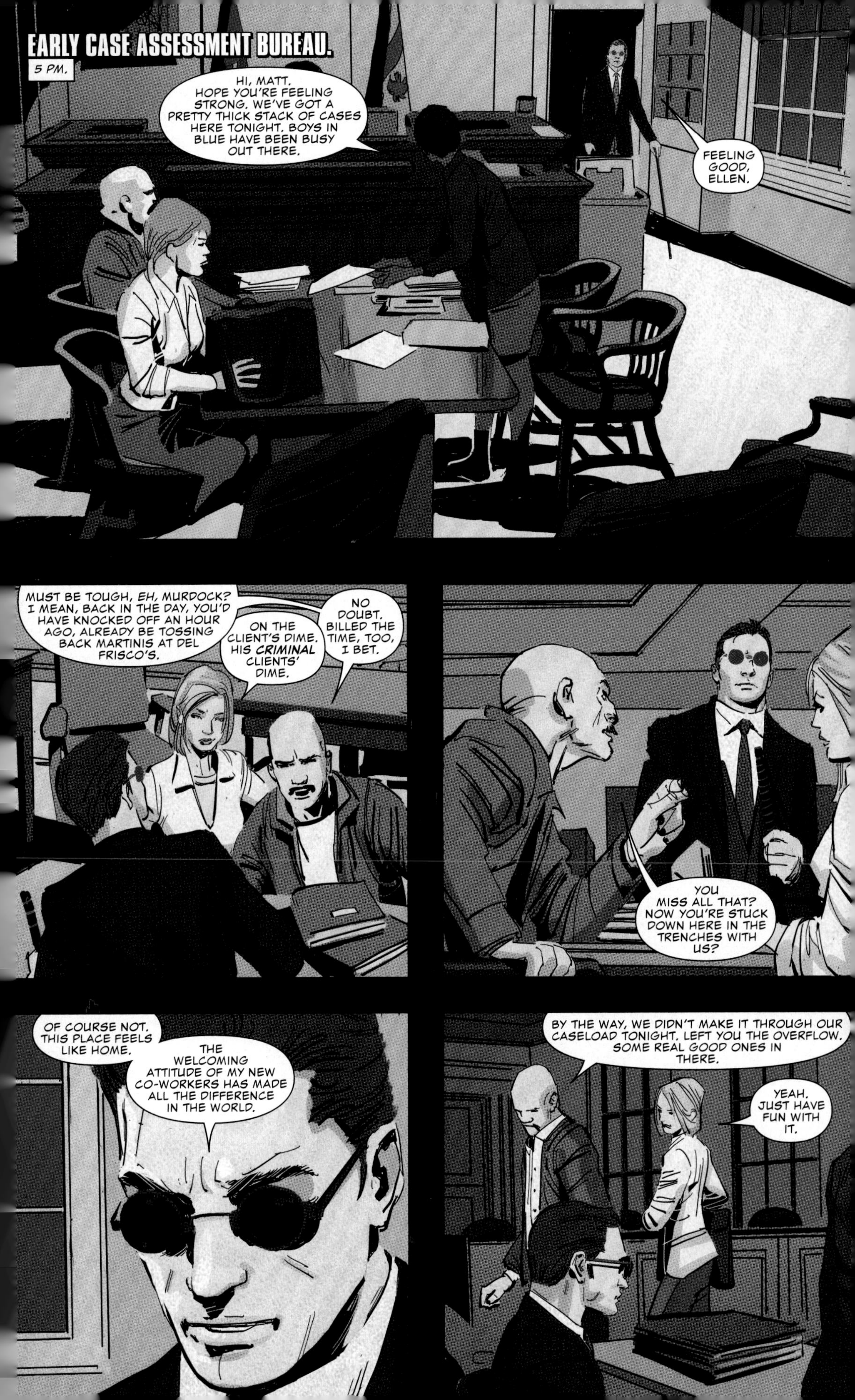

EARLY CASE ASSESSMENT BUREAU.
5 PM.
HI, MATT. HOPE YOU'RE FEELING STRONG. WE'VE GOT A PRETTY THICK STACK OF CASES HERE TONIGHT. BOYS IN BLUE HAVE BEEN BUSY OUT THERE.
FEELING GOOD, ELLEN.
MUST BE TOUGH, EH, MURDOCK? I MEAN, BACK IN THE DAY, YOU'D HAVE KNOCKED OFF AN HOUR AGO, ALREADY BE TOSSING BACK MARTINIS AT DEL FRISCO'S.
ON THE CLIENT'S DIME. HIS CRIMINAL CLIENTS' DIME.
NO DOUBT. BILLED THE TIME, TOO, I BET.
YOU MISS ALL THAT? NOW YOU'RE STUCK DOWN HERE IN THE TRENCHES WITH US?
OF COURSE NOT. THIS PLACE FEELS LIKE HOME.
THE WELCOMING ATTITUDE OF MY NEW CO-WORKERS HAS MADE ALL THE DIFFERENCE IN THE WORLD.
BY THE WAY, WE DIDN'T MAKE IT THROUGH OUR CASELOAD TONIGHT. LEFT YOU THE OVERFLOW. SOME REAL GOOD ONES IN THERE.
YEAH. JUST HAVE FUN WITH IT.

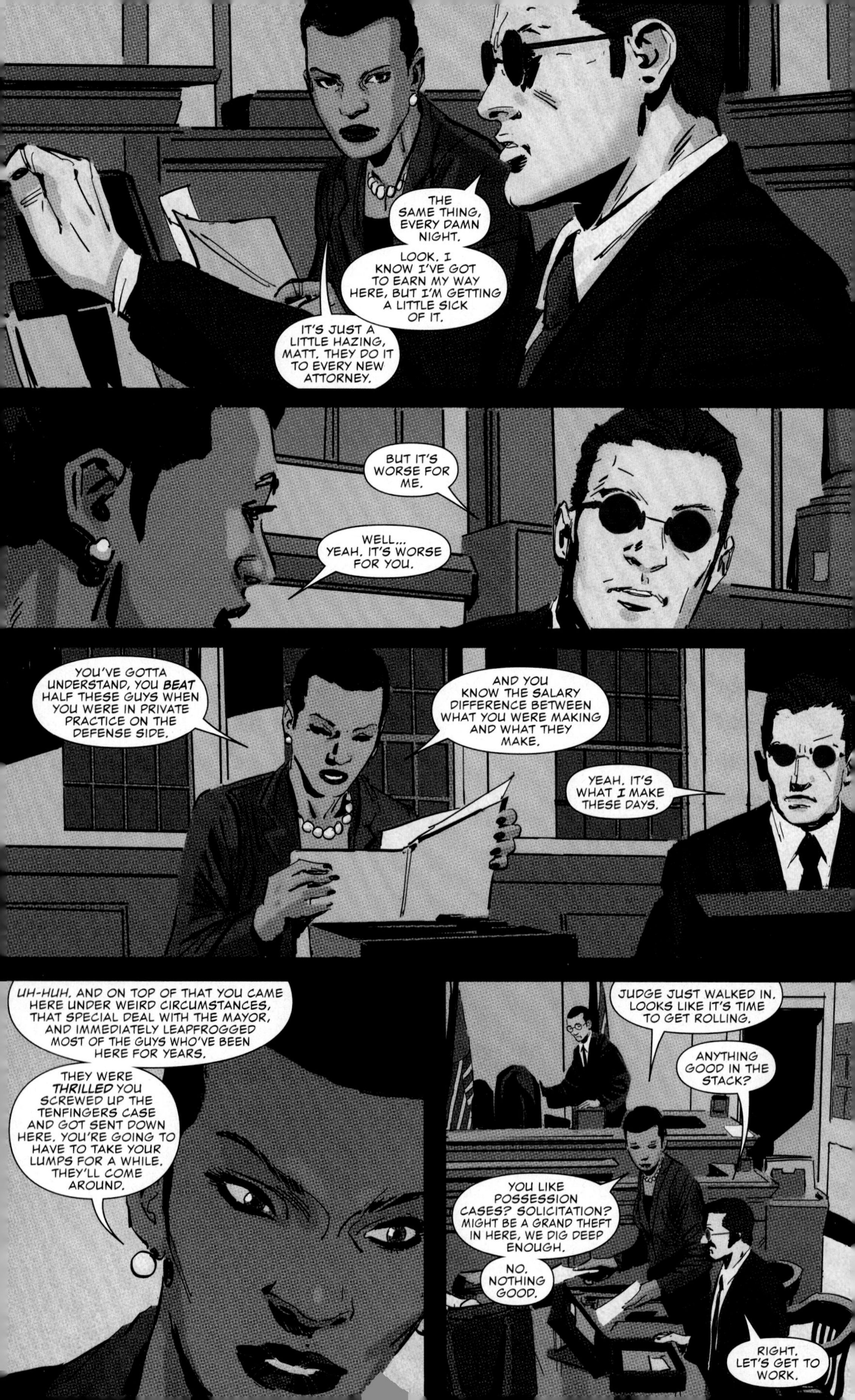
THE SAME THING, EVERY DAMN NIGHT.
LOOK. I KNOW I'VE GOT TO EARN MY WAY HERE, BUT I'M GETTING A LITTLE SICK OF IT.
IT'S JUST A LITTLE HAZING, MATT. THEY DO IT TO EVERY NEW ATTORNEY.
BUT IT'S WORSE FOR ME.
WELL... YEAH. IT'S WORSE FOR YOU.
YOU'VE GOTTA UNDERSTAND, YOU BEAT HALF THESE GUYS WHEN YOU WERE IN PRIVATE PRACTICE ON THE DEFENSE SIDE.
AND YOU KNOW THE SALARY DIFFERENCE BETWEEN WHAT YOU WERE MAKING AND WHAT THEY MAKE.
YEAH. IT'S WHAT I MAKE THESE DAYS.
UH-HUH. AND ON TOP OF THAT YOU CAME HERE UNDER WEIRD CIRCUMSTANCES, THAT SPECIAL DEAL WITH THE MAYOR, AND IMMEDIATELY LEAPFROGGED MOST OF THE GUYS WHO'VE BEEN HERE FOR YEARS.
THEY WERE THRILLED YOU SCREWED UP THE TENFINGERS CASE AND GOT SENT DOWN HERE. YOU'RE GOING TO HAVE TO TAKE YOUR LUMPS FOR A WHILE. THEY'LL COME AROUND.
JUDGE JUST WALKED IN. LOOKS LIKE IT'S TIME TO GET ROLLING.
ANYTHING GOOD IN THE STACK?
YOU LIKE POSSESSION CASES? SOLICITATION? MIGHT BE A GRAND THEFT IN HERE, WE DIG DEEP ENOUGH.
NO. NOTHING GOOD.
RIGHT. LET'S GET TO WORK.

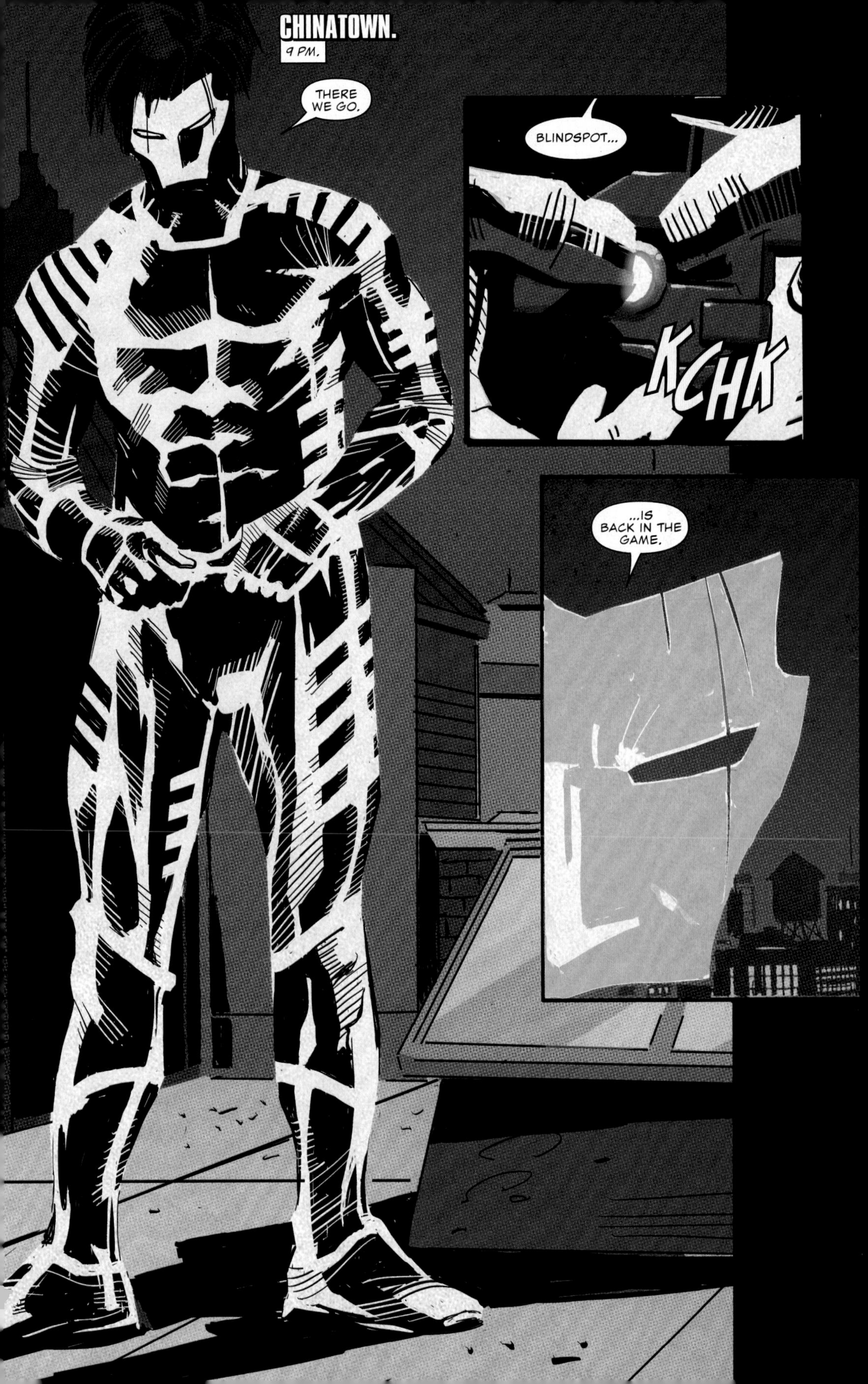
CHINATOWN.
9 PM.
THERE WE GO.
BLINDSPOT...
KCHK
...IS BACK IN THE GAME.

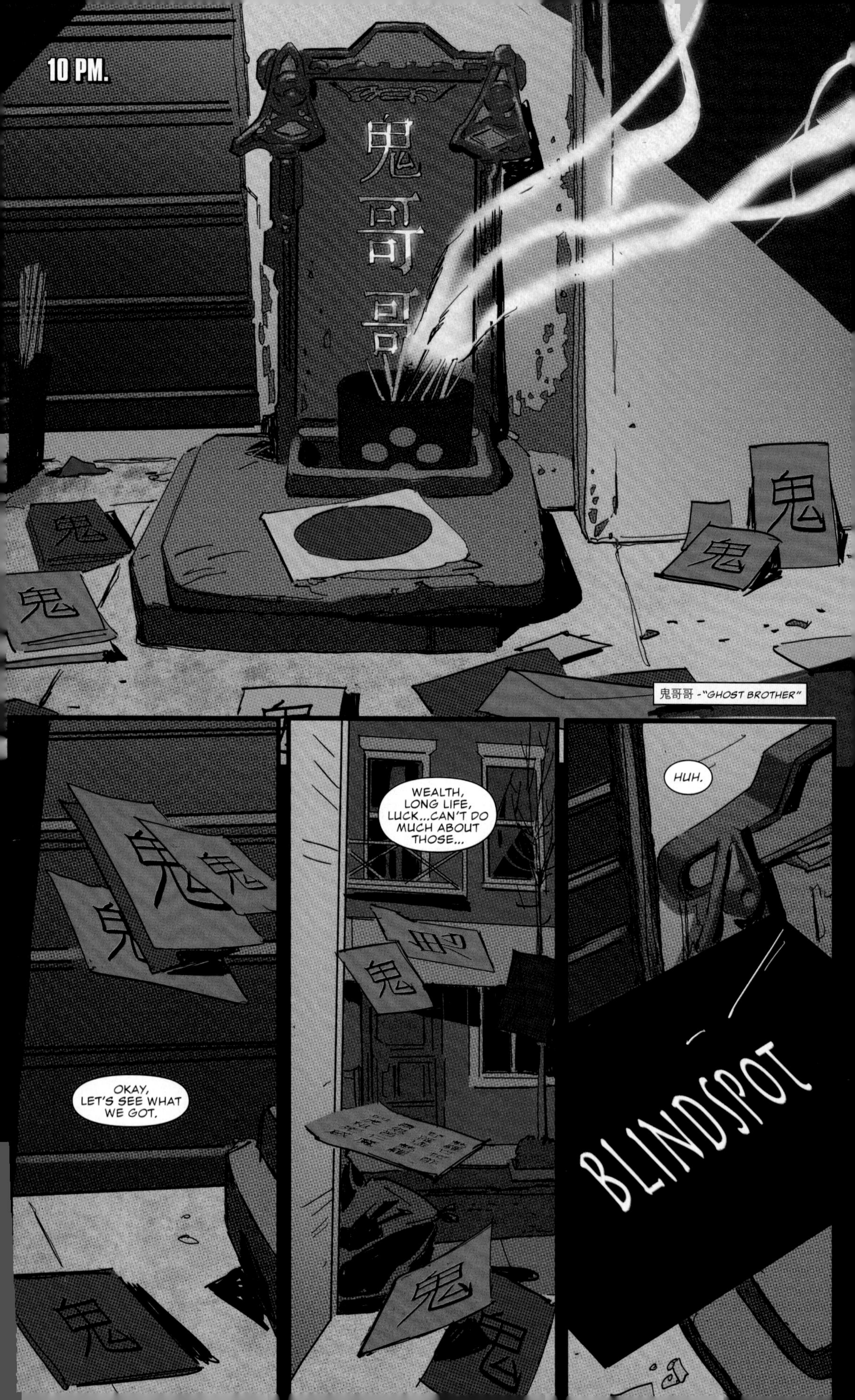
10 PM.
鬼哥哥
鬼哥哥 - "GHOST BROTHER"
OKAY, LET'S SEE WHAT WE GOT.
WEALTH, LONG LIFE, LUCK...CAN'T DO MUCH ABOUT THOSE...
HUH.
BLINDSPOT

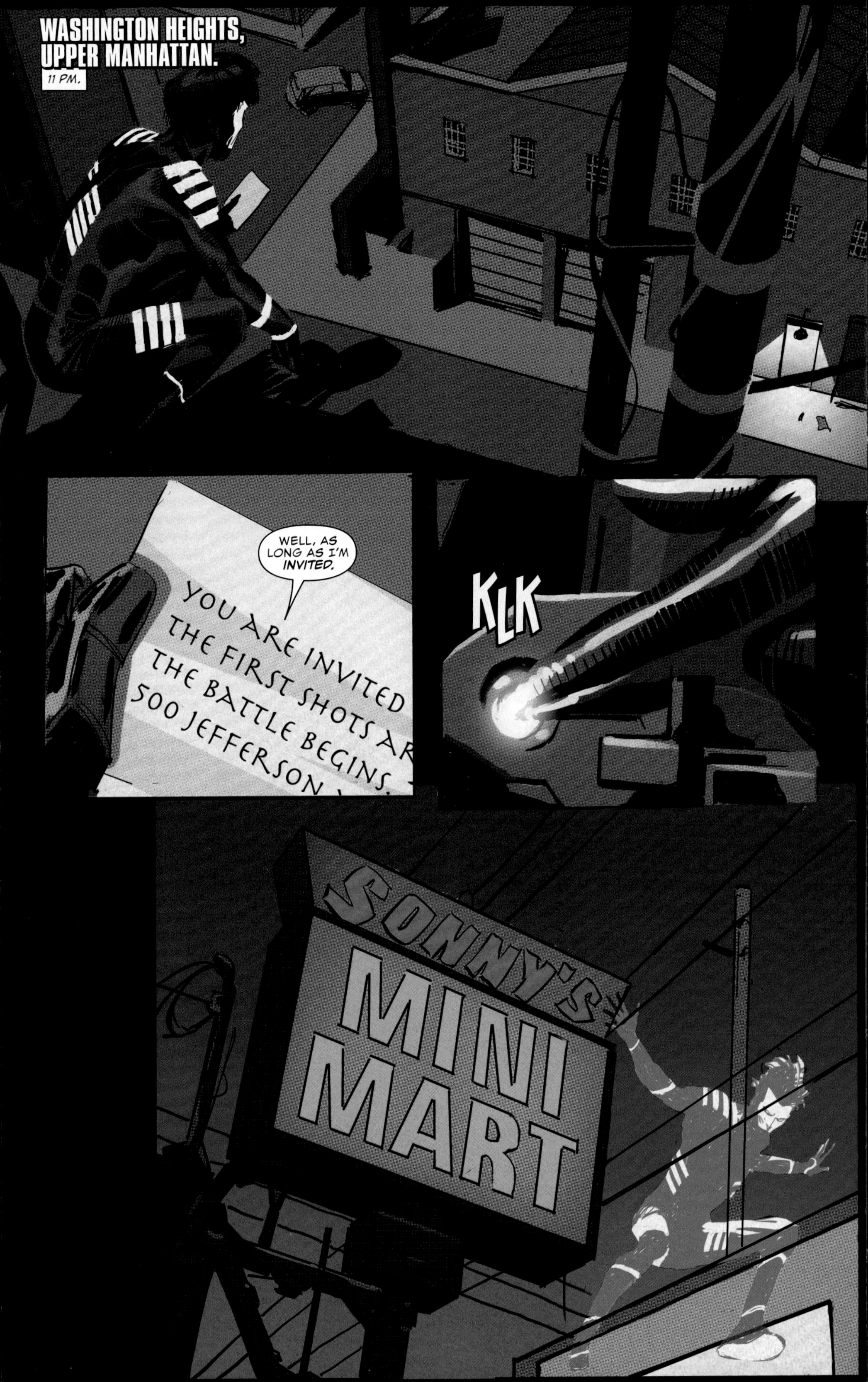
WASHINGTON HEIGHTS, UPPER MANHATTAN.
11 PM.
WELL, AS LONG AS I'M INVITED.
YOU ARE INVITED
THE FIRST SHOTS AR
THE BATTLE BEGINS.
500 JEFFERSON
KLK
SONNY'S
MINI MART

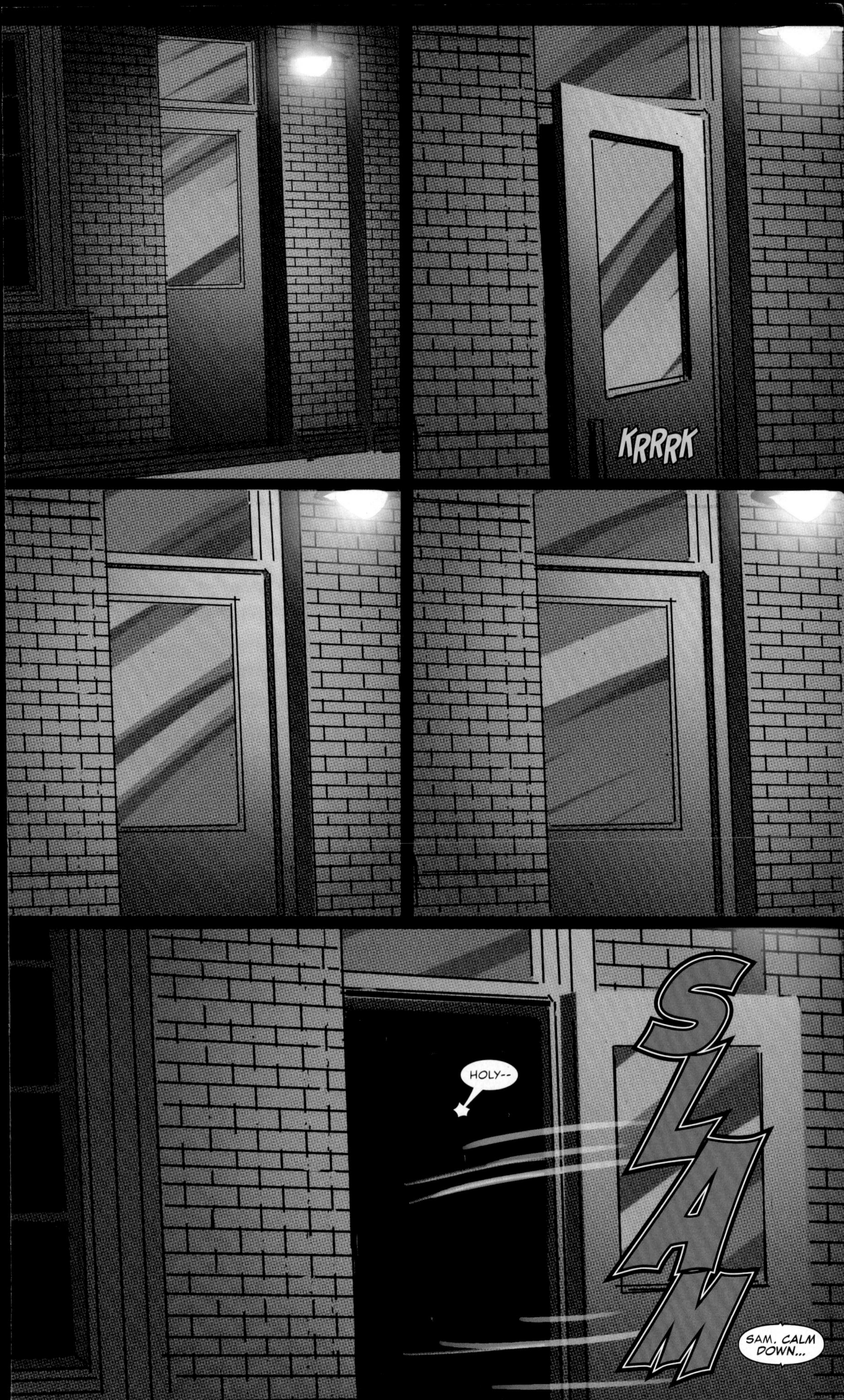
KRRRK
HOLY--
SLAM
SAM, CALM DOWN...

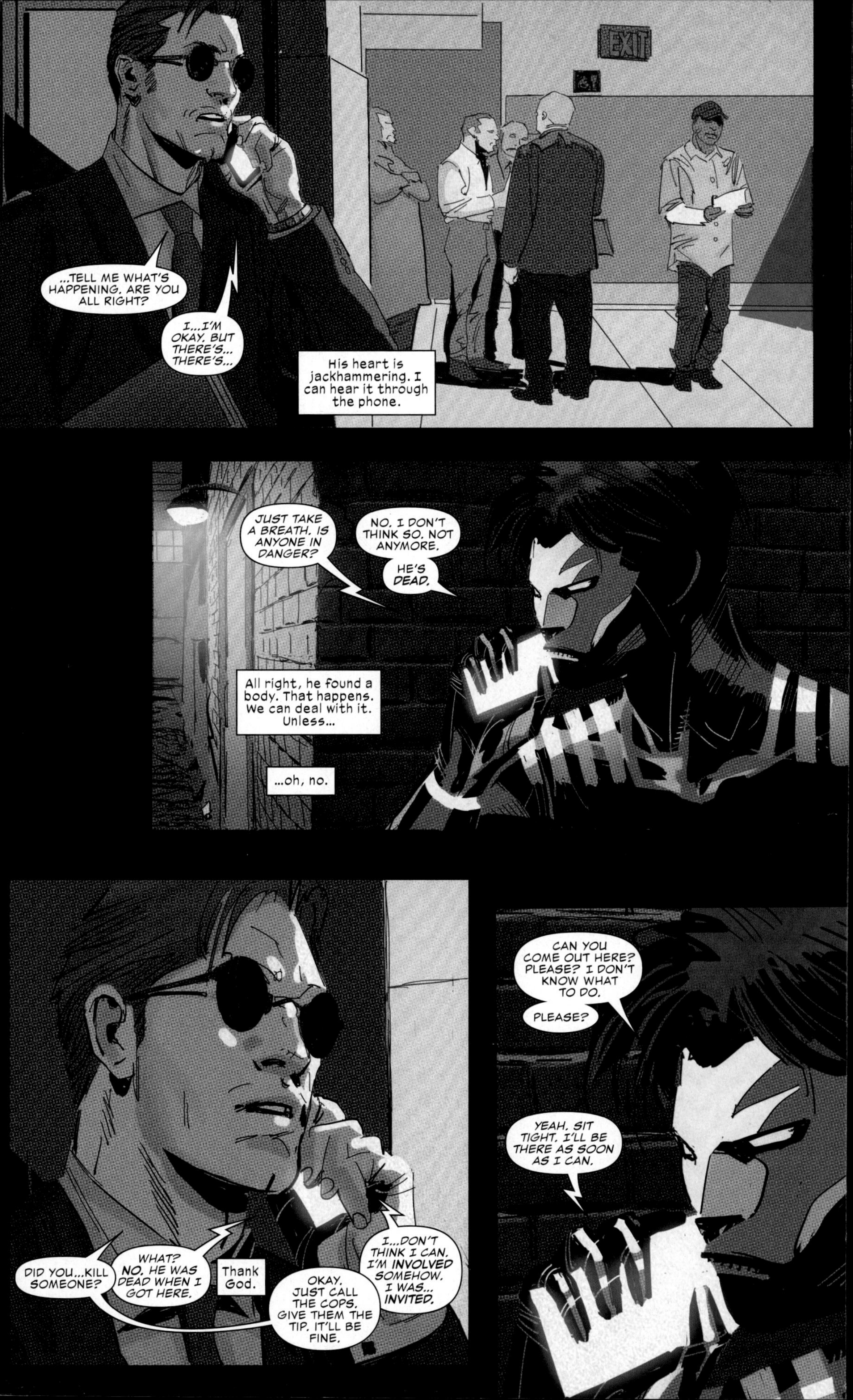

...TELL ME WHAT'S HAPPENING. ARE YOU ALL RIGHT?
I...I'M OKAY. BUT THERE'S... THERE'S...
His heart is jackhammering. I can hear it through the phone.
EXIT
JUST TAKE A BREATH. IS ANYONE IN DANGER?
NO. I DON'T THINK SO. NOT ANYMORE.
HE'S DEAD.
All right, he found a body. That happens. We can deal with it. Unless...
...oh, no.
DID YOU...KILL SOMEONE?
WHAT? NO. HE WAS DEAD WHEN I GOT HERE.
Thank God.
OKAY. JUST CALL THE COPS. GIVE THEM THE TIP. IT'LL BE FINE.
I...DON'T THINK I CAN. I'M INVOLVED SOMEHOW. I WAS... INVITED.
CAN YOU COME OUT HERE? PLEASE? I DON'T KNOW WHAT TO DO.
PLEASE?
YEAH. SIT TIGHT. I'LL BE THERE AS SOON AS I CAN.

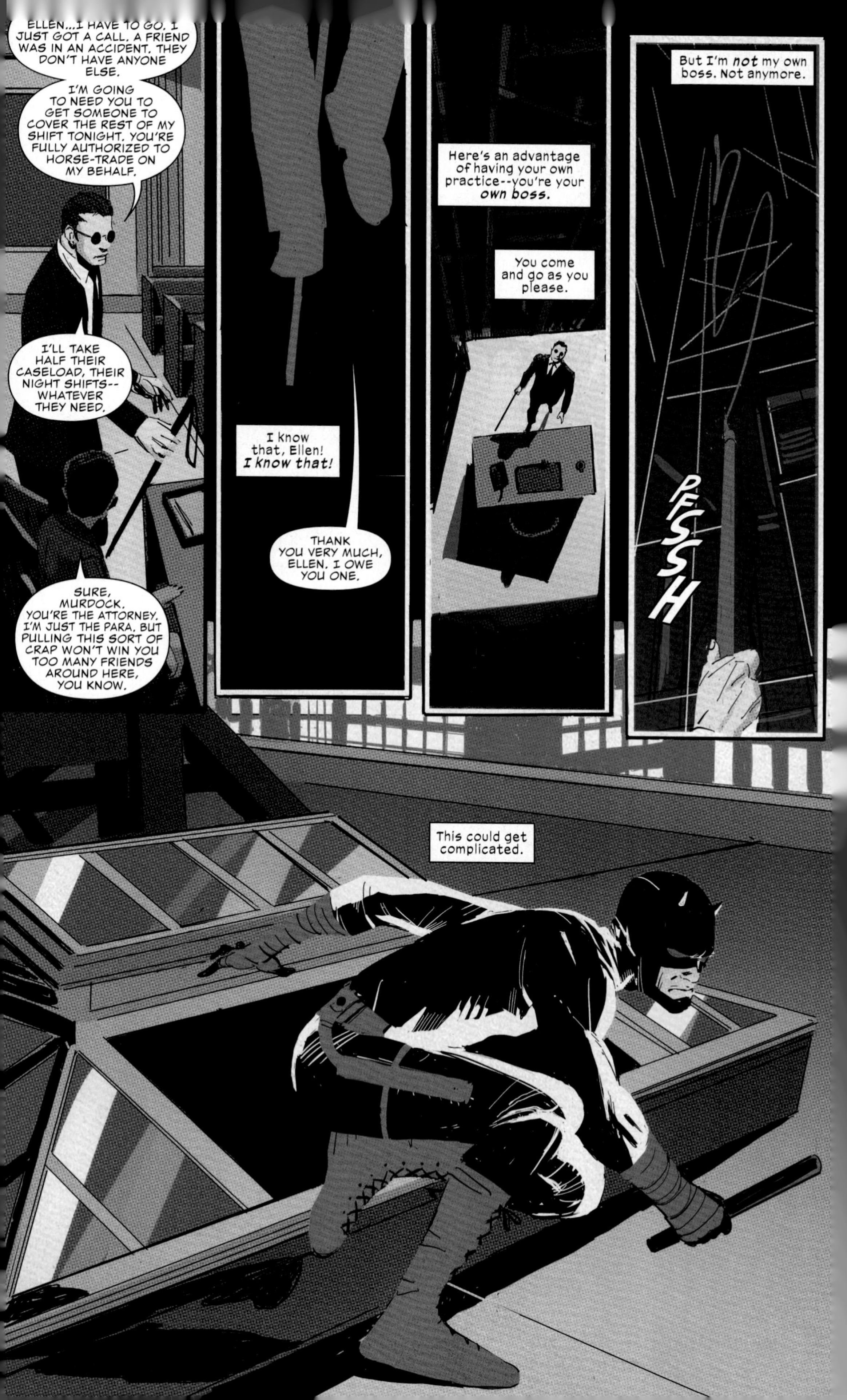
ELLEN...I HAVE TO GO. I JUST GOT A CALL. A FRIEND WAS IN AN ACCIDENT. THEY DON'T HAVE ANYONE ELSE.
I'M GOING TO NEED YOU TO GET SOMEONE TO COVER THE REST OF MY SHIFT TONIGHT. YOU'RE FULLY AUTHORIZED TO HORSE-TRADE ON MY BEHALF.
I'LL TAKE HALF THEIR CASELOAD, THEIR NIGHT SHIFTS--WHATEVER THEY NEED.
SURE, MURDOCK. YOU'RE THE ATTORNEY. I'M JUST THE PARA. BUT PULLING THIS SORT OF CRAP WON'T WIN YOU TOO MANY FRIENDS AROUND HERE, YOU KNOW.
I know that, Ellen! *I know that!*
THANK YOU VERY MUCH, ELLEN. I OWE YOU ONE.
Here's an advantage of having your own practice--you're your *own boss.*
You come and go as you please.
But I'm ***not*** my own boss. Not anymore.
PFSSH
This could get complicated.

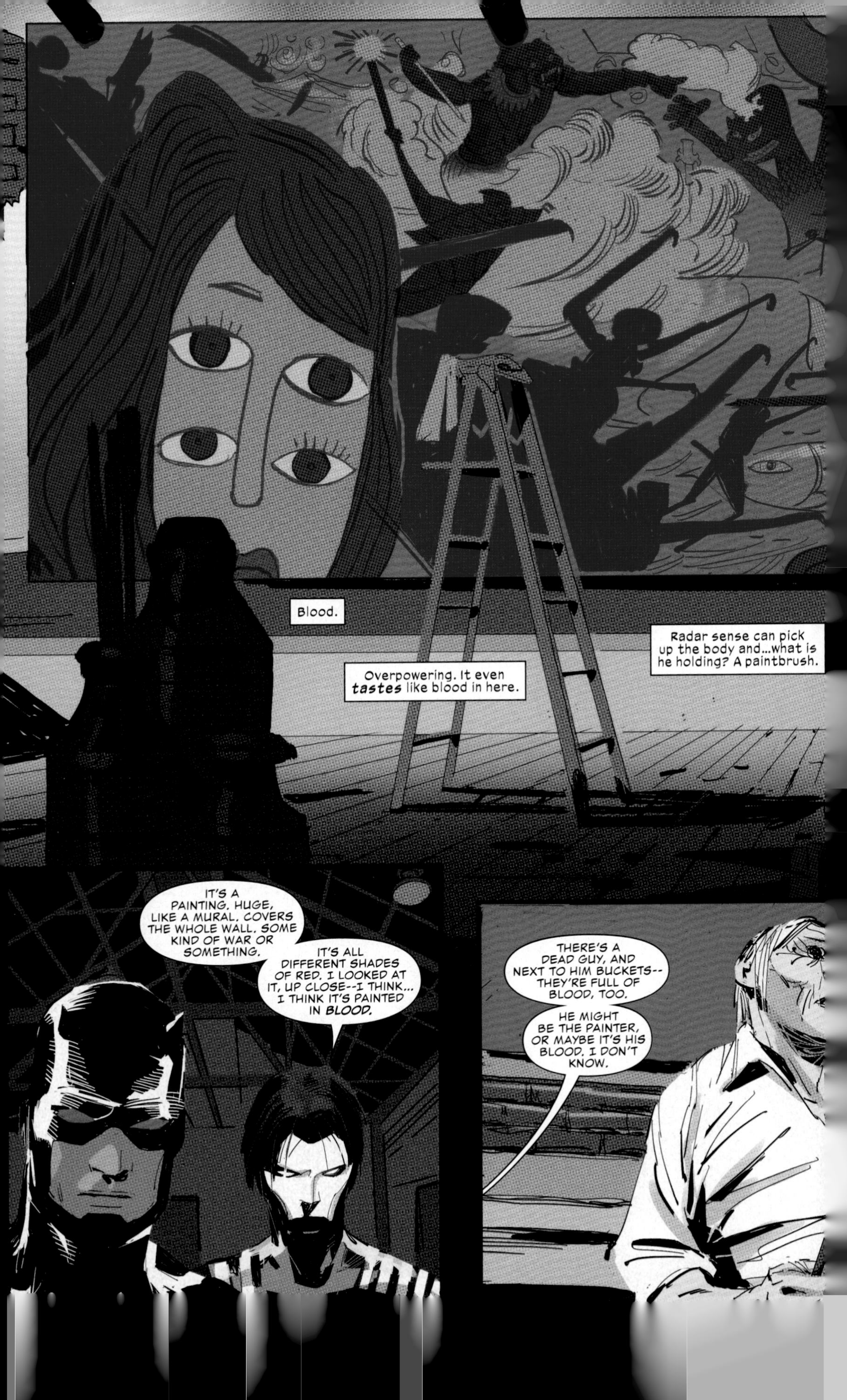
Blood.
Overpowering. It even *tastes* like blood in here.
Radar sense can pick up the body and...what is he holding? A paintbrush.
IT'S A PAINTING. HUGE, LIKE A MURAL. COVERS THE WHOLE WALL. SOME KIND OF WAR OR SOMETHING.
IT'S ALL DIFFERENT SHADES OF RED. I LOOKED AT IT, UP CLOSE--I THINK... I THINK IT'S PAINTED IN *BLOOD.*
THERE'S A DEAD GUY, AND NEXT TO HIM BUCKETS-- THEY'RE FULL OF BLOOD, TOO.
HE MIGHT BE THE PAINTER, OR MAYBE IT'S HIS BLOOD. I DON'T KNOW.

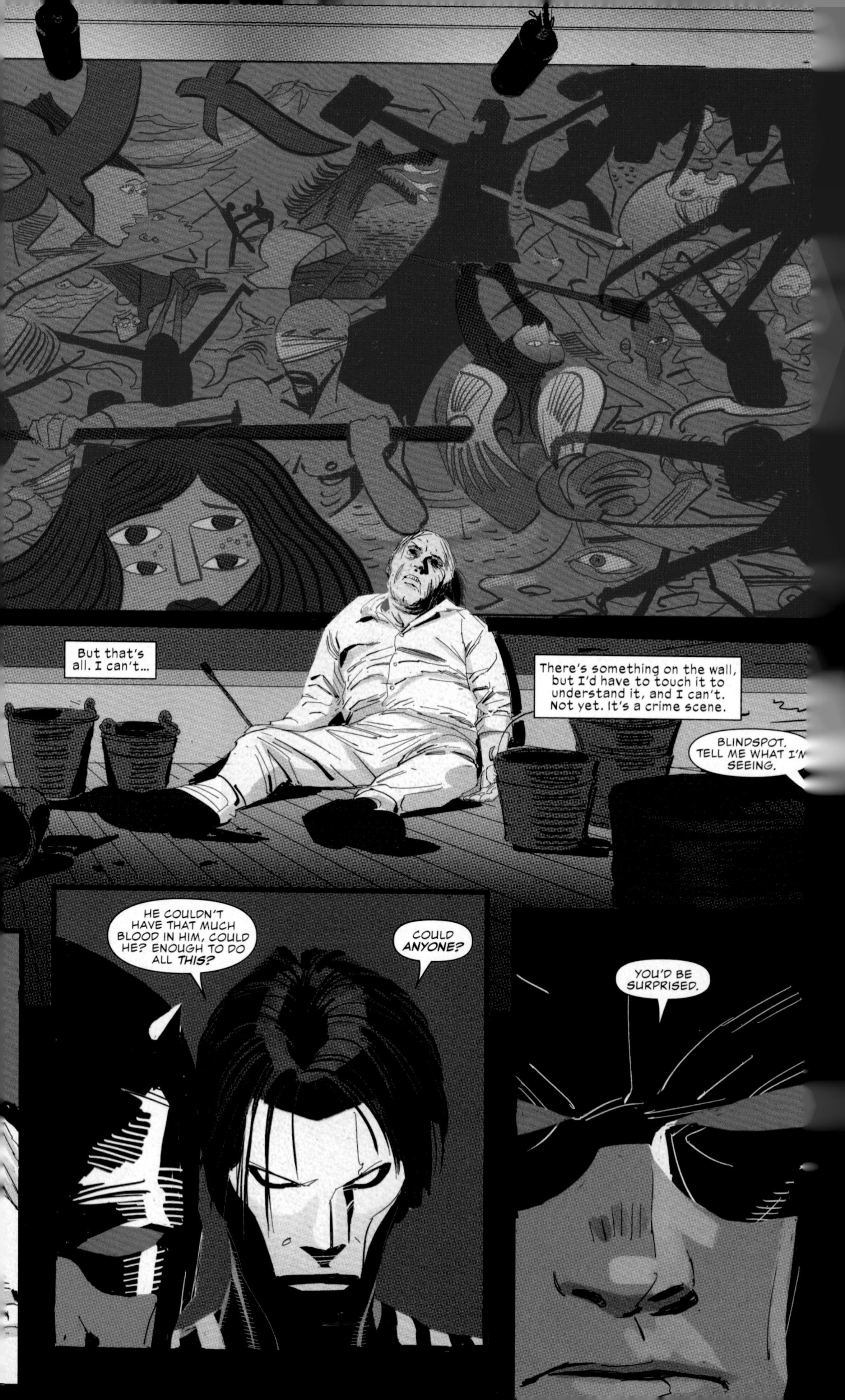

But that's all. I can't...
There's something on the wall, but I'd have to touch it to understand it, and I can't. Not yet. It's a crime scene.
BLINDSPOT. TELL ME WHAT I'M SEEING.
HE COULDN'T HAVE THAT MUCH BLOOD IN HIM, COULD HE? ENOUGH TO DO ALL THIS?
COULD ANYONE?
YOU'D BE SURPRISED.

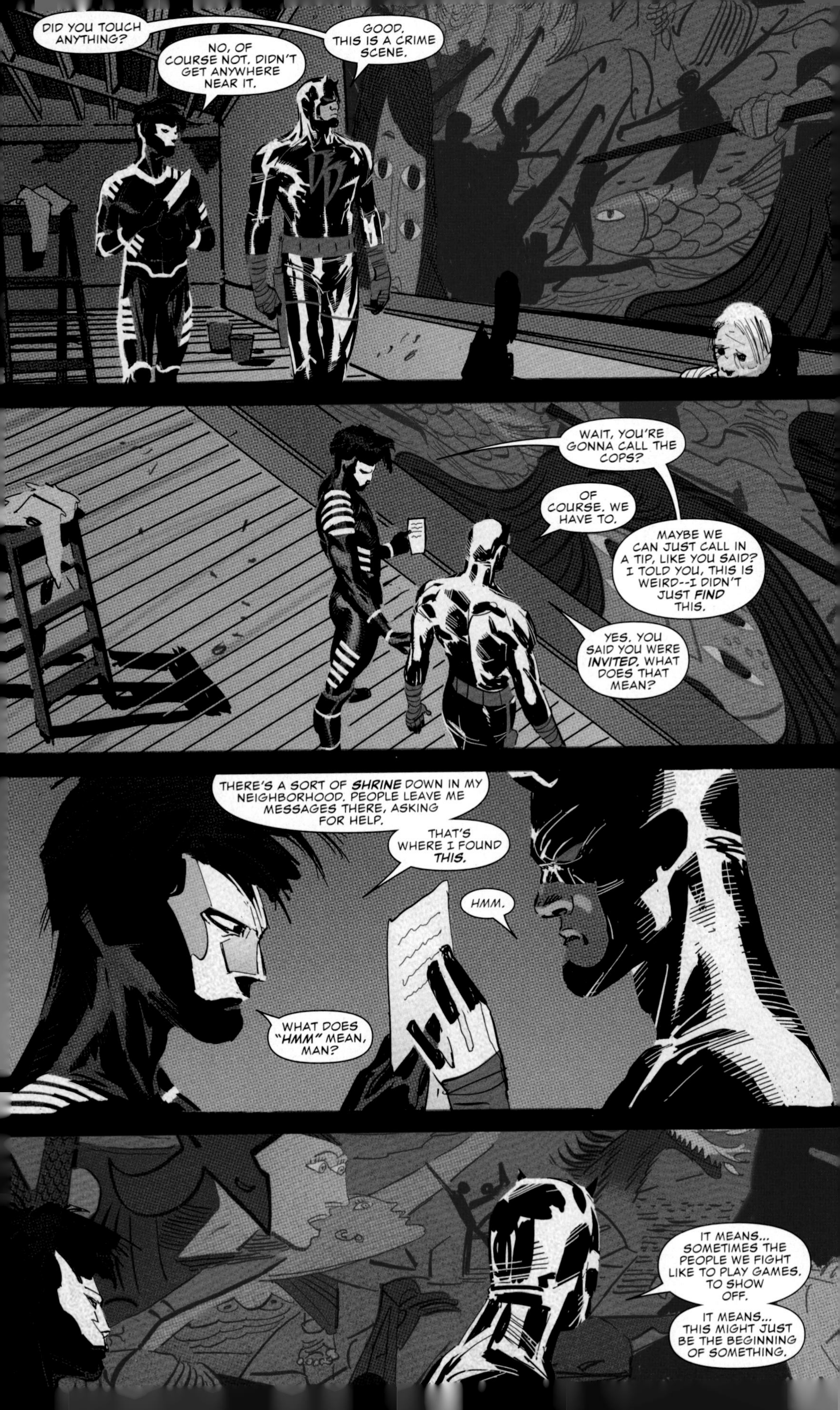
DID YOU TOUCH ANYTHING?
NO, OF COURSE NOT. DIDN'T GET ANYWHERE NEAR IT.
GOOD. THIS IS A CRIME SCENE.
WAIT, YOU'RE GONNA CALL THE COPS?
OF COURSE. WE HAVE TO.
MAYBE WE CAN JUST CALL IN A TIP, LIKE YOU SAID? I TOLD YOU, THIS IS WEIRD--I DIDN'T JUST FIND THIS.
YES. YOU SAID YOU WERE INVITED. WHAT DOES THAT MEAN?
THERE'S A SORT OF SHRINE DOWN IN MY NEIGHBORHOOD. PEOPLE LEAVE ME MESSAGES THERE, ASKING FOR HELP.
THAT'S WHERE I FOUND THIS.
HMM.
WHAT DOES "HMM" MEAN, MAN?
IT MEANS... SOMETIMES THE PEOPLE WE FIGHT LIKE TO PLAY GAMES. TO SHOW OFF.
IT MEANS... THIS MIGHT JUST BE THE BEGINNING OF SOMETHING.

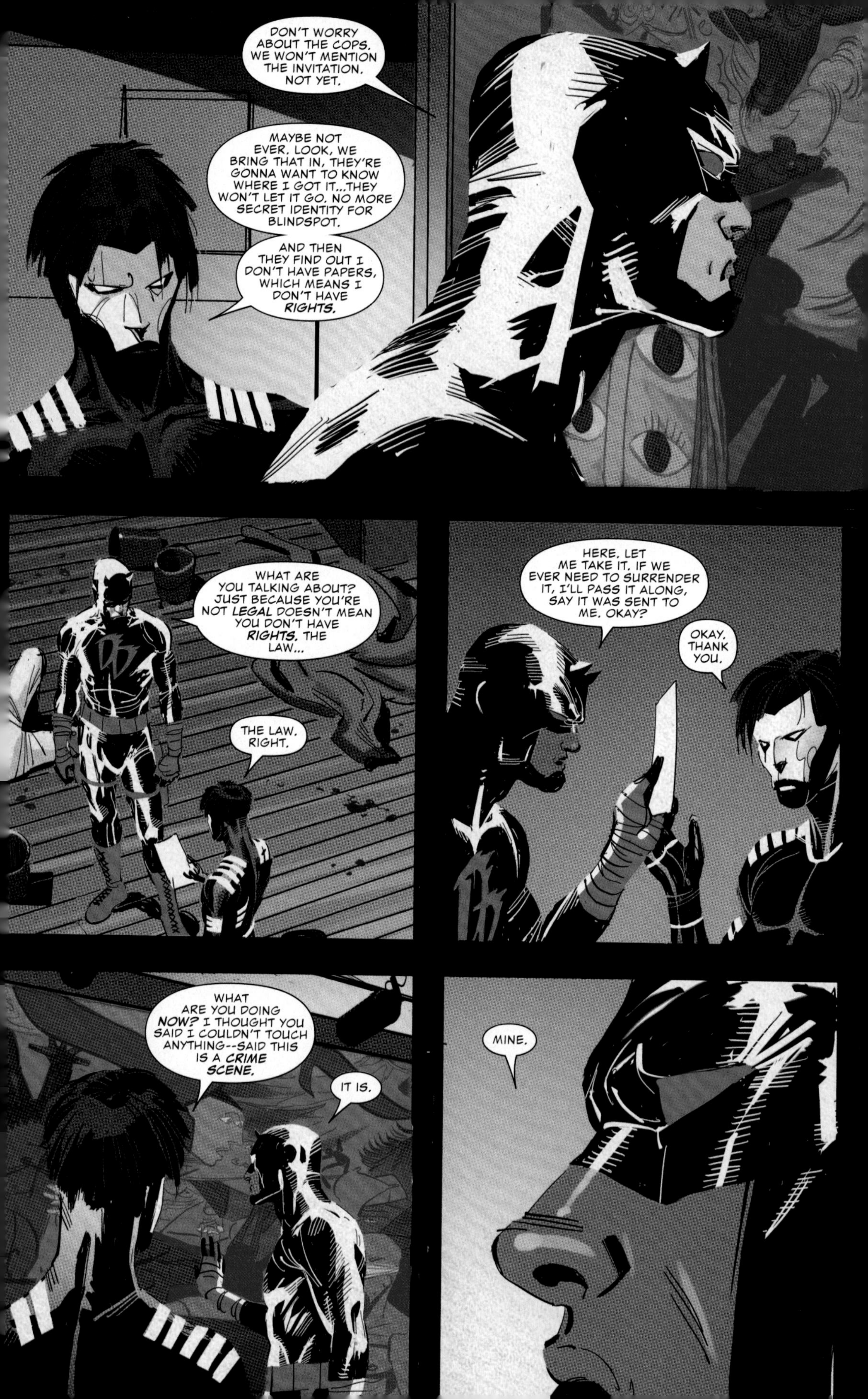
DON'T WORRY ABOUT THE COPS. WE WON'T MENTION THE INVITATION. NOT YET.
MAYBE NOT EVER. LOOK, WE BRING THAT IN, THEY'RE GONNA WANT TO KNOW WHERE I GOT IT...THEY WON'T LET IT GO. NO MORE SECRET IDENTITY FOR BLINDSPOT.
AND THEN THEY FIND OUT I DON'T HAVE PAPERS, WHICH MEANS I DON'T HAVE *RIGHTS.*
WHAT ARE YOU TALKING ABOUT? JUST BECAUSE YOU'RE NOT *LEGAL* DOESN'T MEAN YOU DON'T HAVE *RIGHTS.* THE LAW...
THE LAW. RIGHT.
HERE. LET ME TAKE IT. IF WE EVER NEED TO SURRENDER IT, I'LL PASS IT ALONG, SAY IT WAS SENT TO ME. OKAY?
OKAY. THANK YOU.
WHAT ARE YOU DOING *NOW?* I THOUGHT YOU SAID I COULDN'T TOUCH ANYTHING--SAID THIS IS A *CRIME SCENE.*
IT IS.
MINE.

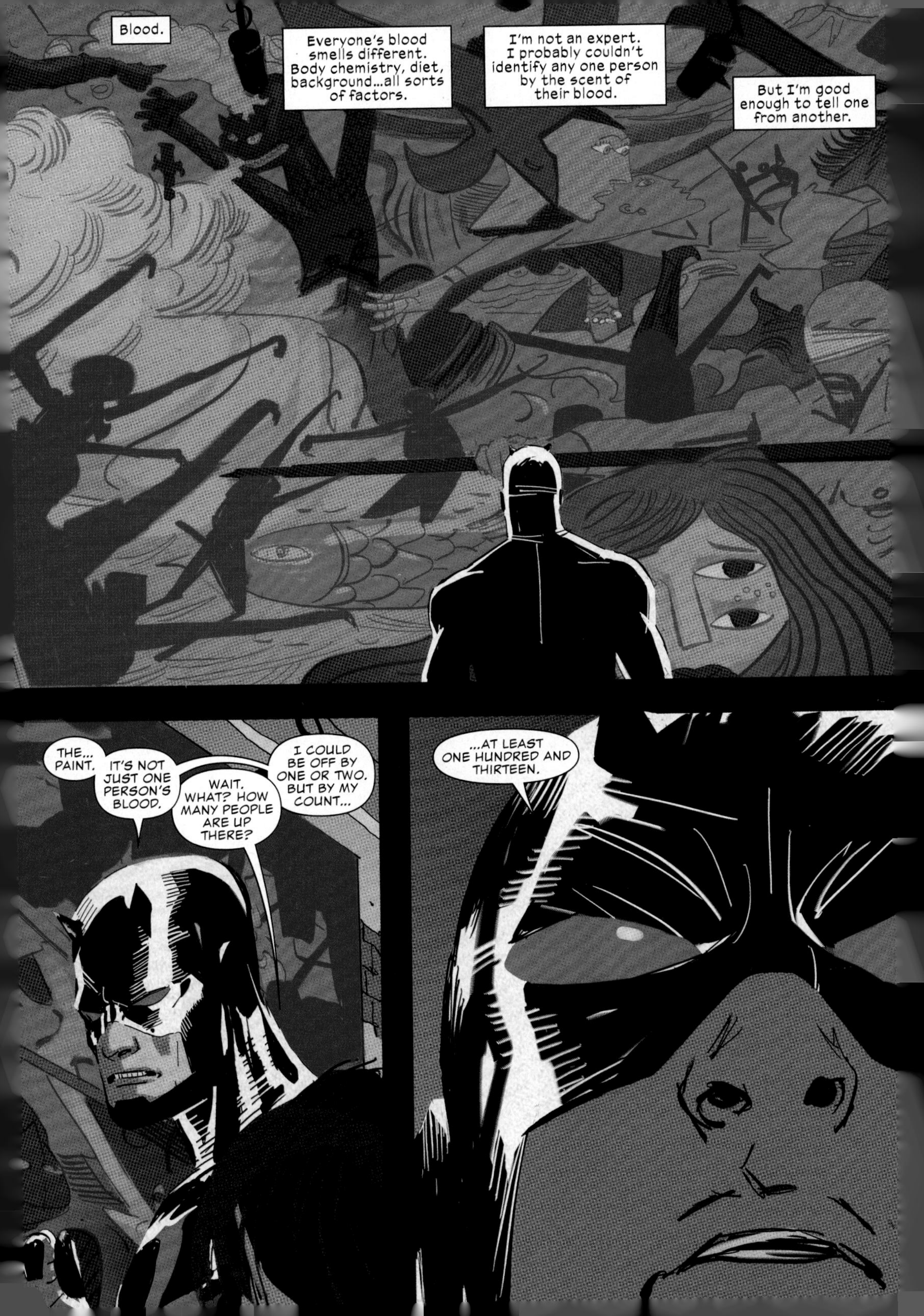

Blood.
Everyone's blood smells different. Body chemistry, diet, background...all sorts of factors.
I'm not an expert. I probably couldn't identify any one person by the scent of their blood.
But I'm good enough to tell one from another.
THE... PAINT.
IT'S NOT JUST ONE PERSON'S BLOOD.
WAIT. WHAT? HOW MANY PEOPLE ARE UP THERE?
I COULD BE OFF BY ONE OR TWO. BUT BY MY COUNT...
...AT LEAST ONE HUNDRED AND THIRTEEN.

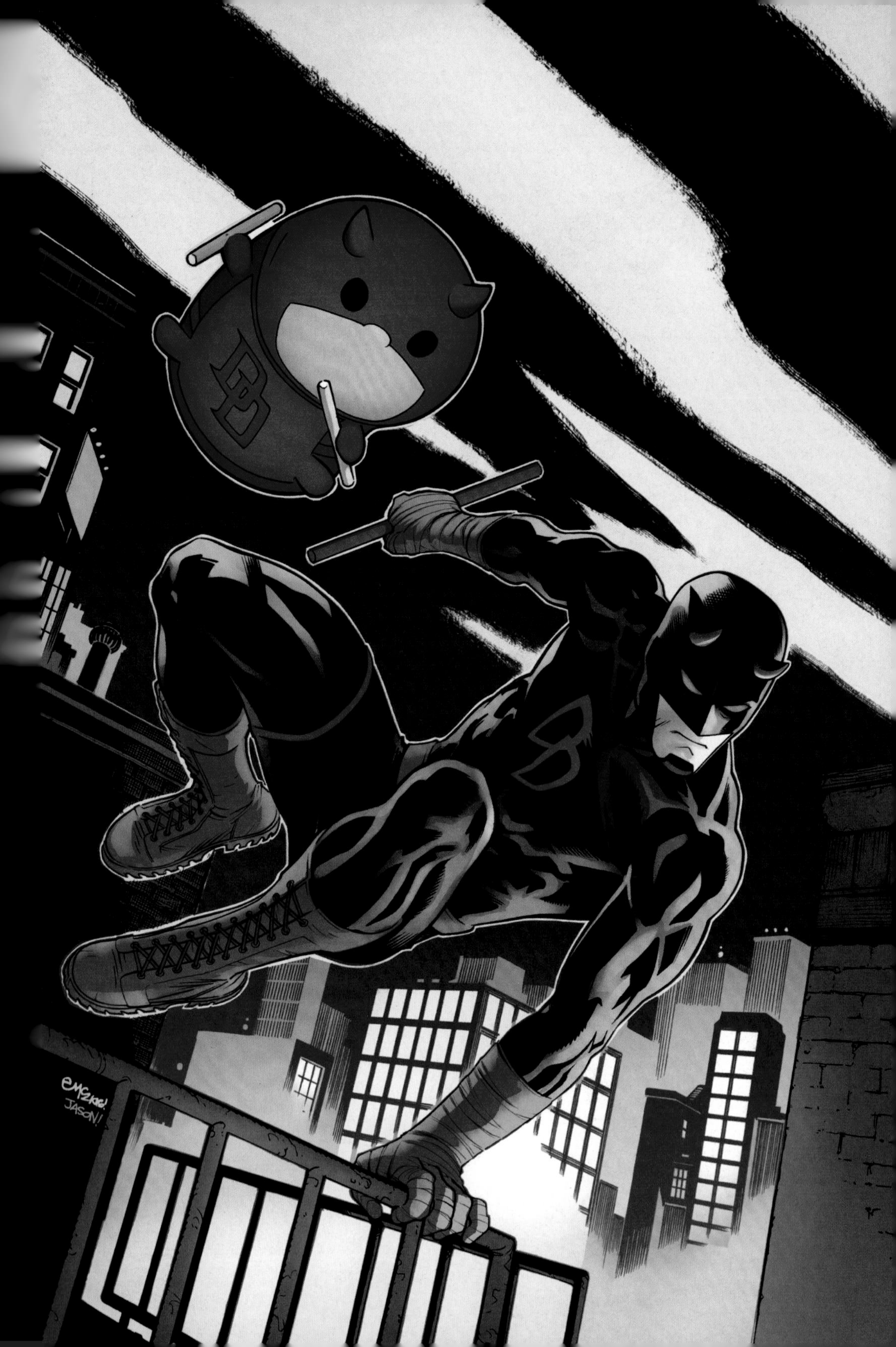

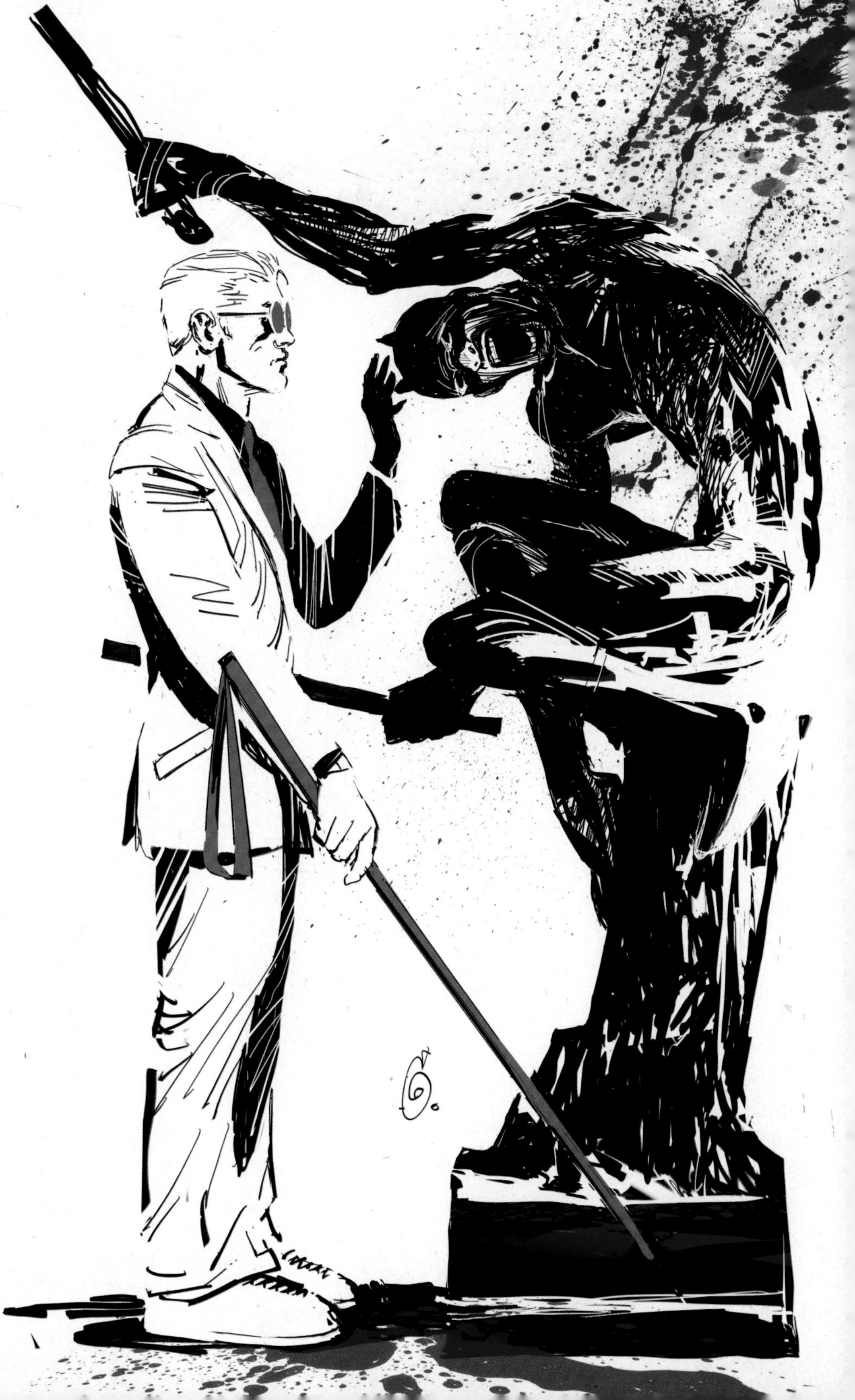

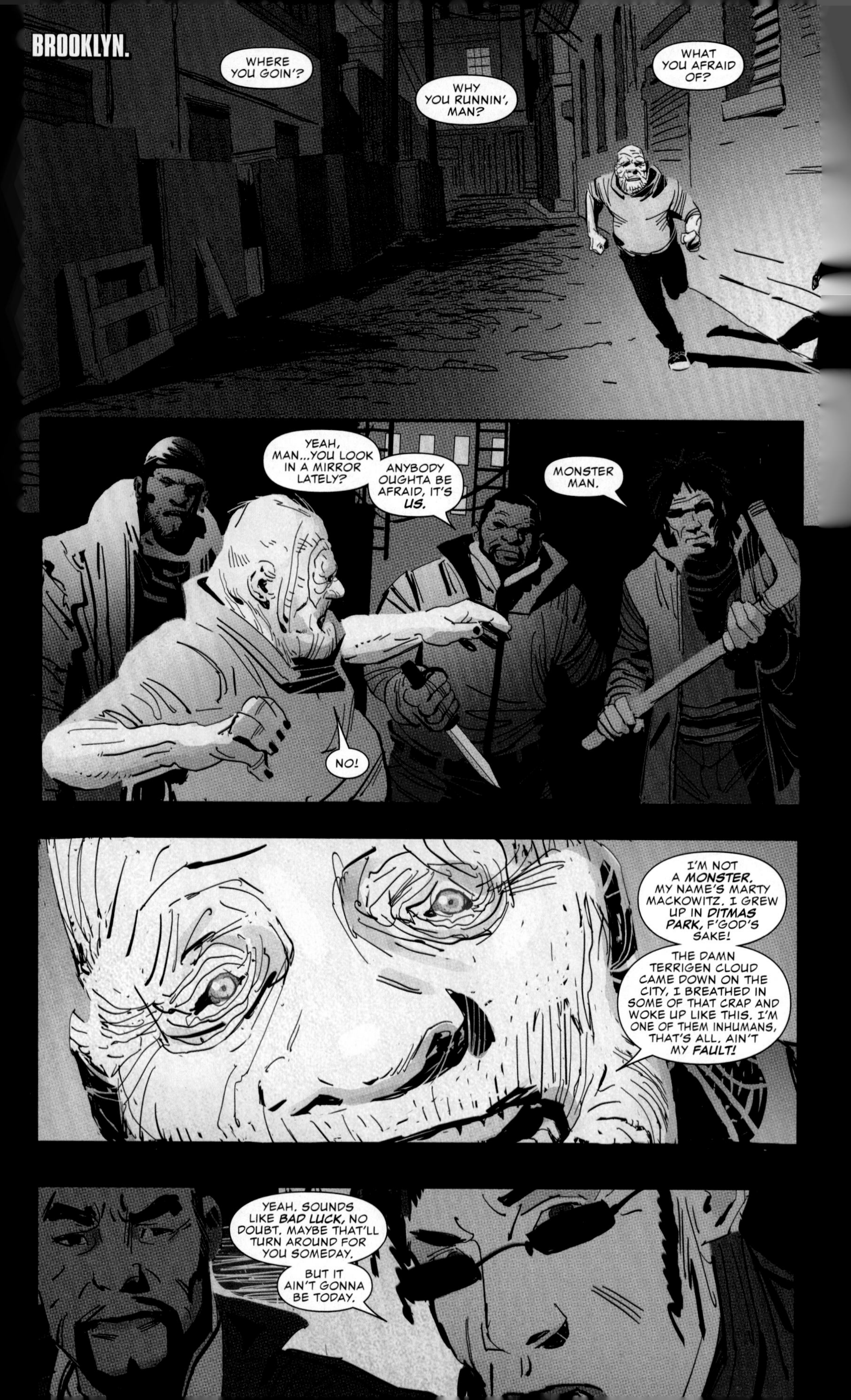
BROOKLYN.
WHERE YOU GOIN'?
WHY YOU RUNNIN', MAN?
WHAT YOU AFRAID OF?
YEAH, MAN...YOU LOOK IN A MIRROR LATELY?
ANYBODY OUGHTA BE AFRAID, IT'S US.
MONSTER MAN.
NO!
I'M NOT A MONSTER. MY NAME'S MARTY MACKOWITZ. I GREW UP IN DITMAS PARK, F'GOD'S SAKE!
THE DAMN TERRIGEN CLOUD CAME DOWN ON THE CITY, I BREATHED IN SOME OF THAT CRAP AND WOKE UP LIKE THIS. I'M ONE OF THEM INHUMANS, THAT'S ALL. AIN'T MY FAULT!
YEAH. SOUNDS LIKE BAD LUCK, NO DOUBT. MAYBE THAT'LL TURN AROUND FOR YOU SOMEDAY.
BUT IT AIN'T GONNA BE TODAY.

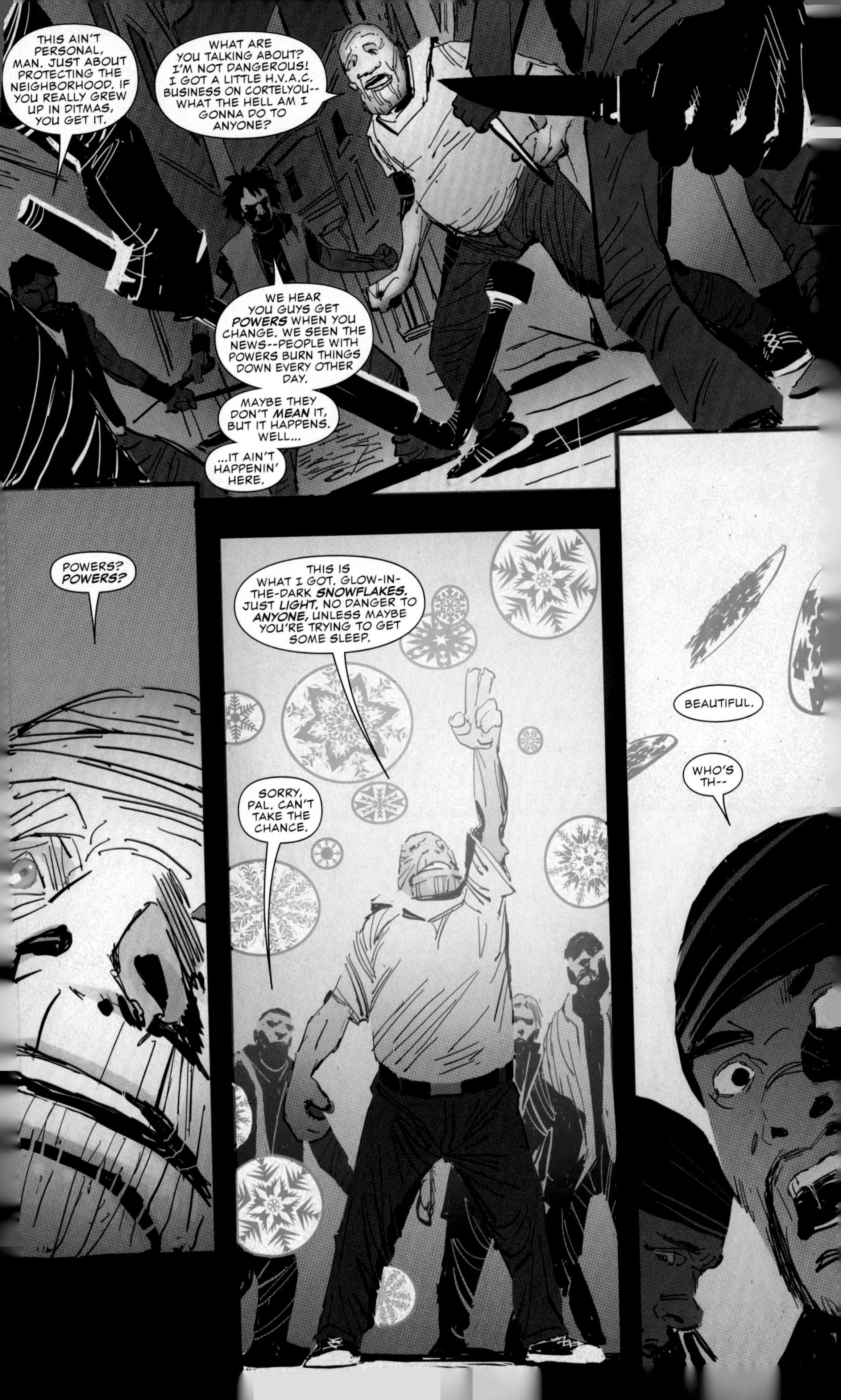
THIS AIN'T PERSONAL, MAN. JUST ABOUT PROTECTING THE NEIGHBORHOOD. IF YOU REALLY GREW UP IN DITMAS, YOU GET IT.
WHAT ARE YOU TALKING ABOUT? I'M NOT DANGEROUS! I GOT A LITTLE H.V.A.C. BUSINESS ON CORTELYOU-- WHAT THE HELL AM I GONNA DO TO ANYONE?
WE HEAR YOU GUYS GET POWERS WHEN YOU CHANGE. WE SEEN THE NEWS--PEOPLE WITH POWERS BURN THINGS DOWN EVERY OTHER DAY.
MAYBE THEY DON'T MEAN IT, BUT IT HAPPENS. WELL...
...IT AIN'T HAPPENIN' HERE.
POWERS? POWERS?
THIS IS WHAT I GOT. GLOW-IN-THE-DARK SNOWFLAKES. JUST LIGHT. NO DANGER TO ANYONE, UNLESS MAYBE YOU'RE TRYING TO GET SOME SLEEP.
SORRY, PAL. CAN'T TAKE THE CHANCE.
BEAUTIFUL.
WHO'S TH--

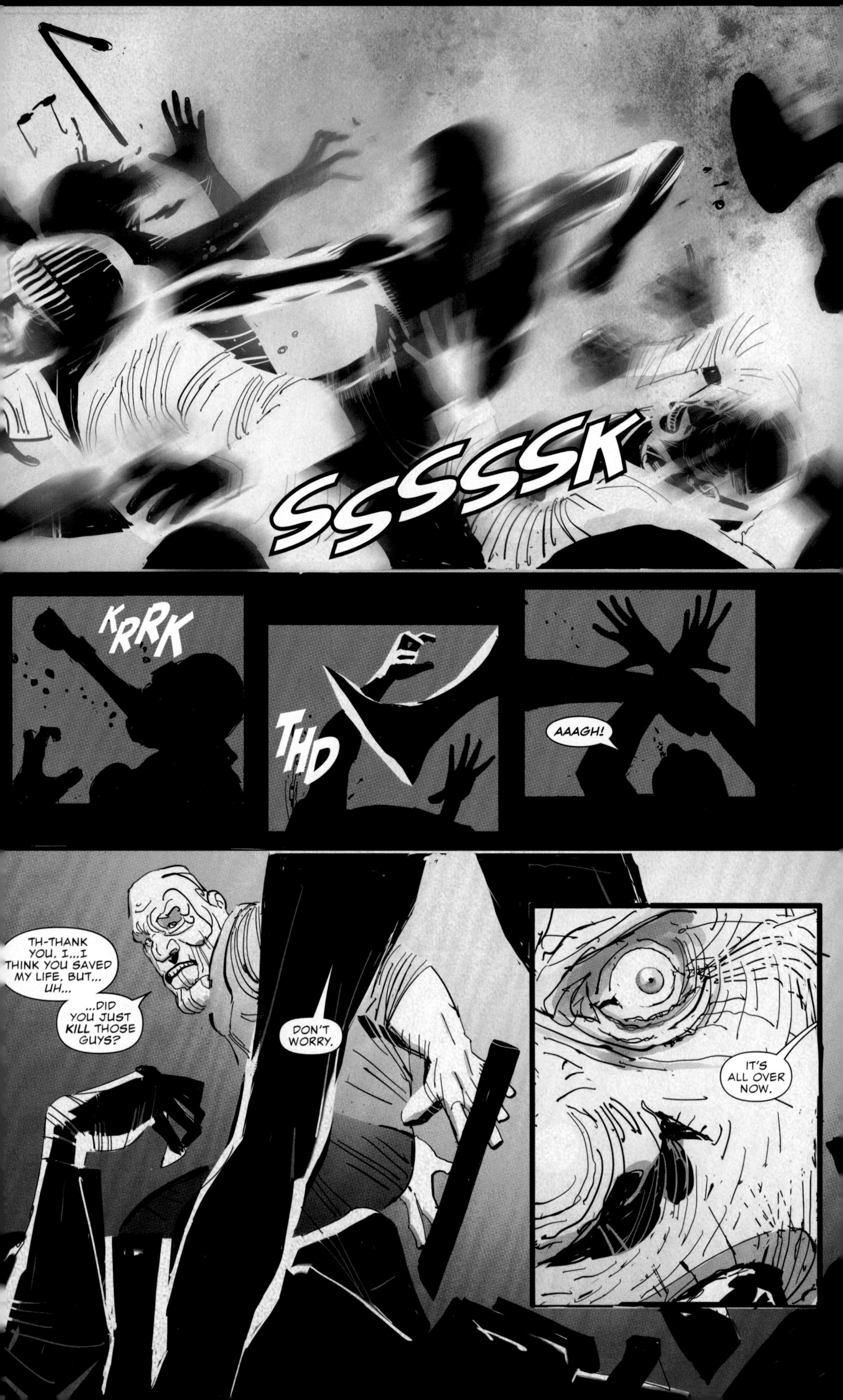
SSSSSK
KRRK
THD
AAAGH!
TH-THANK YOU. I...I THINK YOU SAVED MY LIFE. BUT... UH...
...DID YOU JUST KILL THOSE GUYS?
DON'T WORRY.
IT'S ALL OVER NOW.

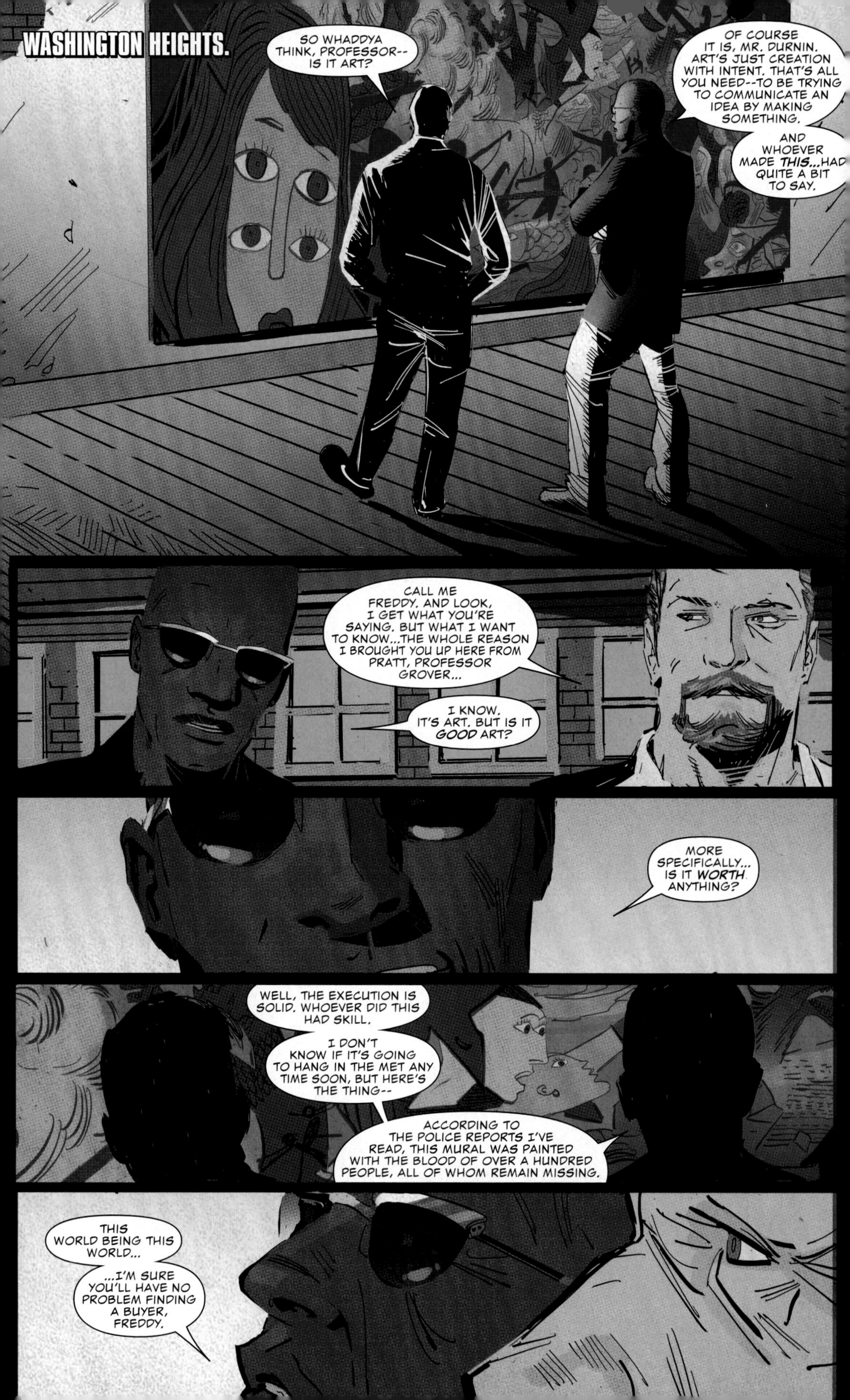
WASHINGTON HEIGHTS.
SO WHADDYA THINK, PROFESSOR-- IS IT ART?
OF COURSE IT IS, MR. DURNIN. ART'S JUST CREATION WITH INTENT. THAT'S ALL YOU NEED--TO BE TRYING TO COMMUNICATE AN IDEA BY MAKING SOMETHING.
AND WHOEVER MADE THIS...HAD QUITE A BIT TO SAY.
CALL ME FREDDY. AND LOOK, I GET WHAT YOU'RE SAYING. BUT WHAT I WANT TO KNOW...THE WHOLE REASON I BROUGHT YOU UP HERE FROM PRATT, PROFESSOR GROVER...
I KNOW. IT'S ART. BUT IS IT GOOD ART?
MORE SPECIFICALLY... IS IT WORTH ANYTHING?
WELL, THE EXECUTION IS SOLID. WHOEVER DID THIS HAD SKILL.
I DON'T KNOW IF IT'S GOING TO HANG IN THE MET ANY TIME SOON, BUT HERE'S THE THING--
ACCORDING TO THE POLICE REPORTS I'VE READ, THIS MURAL WAS PAINTED WITH THE BLOOD OF OVER A HUNDRED PEOPLE, ALL OF WHOM REMAIN MISSING.
THIS WORLD BEING THIS WORLD...
...I'M SURE YOU'LL HAVE NO PROBLEM FINDING A BUYER, FREDDY.

THAT'S WHAT I LIKE TO HEAR.

MAYBE I'LL GET YOU INVOLVED WHEN I THINK IT'S TIME TO SELL--YOU CAN HELP ME FIGURE OUT A PRICE. GET YOU A NICE LITTLE COMMISSION, TOO. HOW'S THAT SOUND?

FREDDY, NOW THAT THE F.B.I. AND N.Y.P.D. HAVE COMPLETED THEIR INITIAL INVESTIGATIONS, YOU CAN OBVIOUSLY DO WHAT YOU WANT.

BUT...AND IT'S REALLY NOT MY BUSINESS...DON'T YOU THINK THAT CHARGING ADMISSION TO SEE THIS, OR SELLING IT... IT'S A LITTLE GHOULISH?

I MEAN, PEOPLE MAY HAVE DIED IN THE CREATION OF THIS WORK. POSSIBLY MORE THAN 112 PEOPLE.

WELL... THAT AIN'T MY FAULT, IS IT?

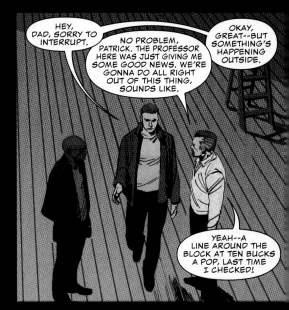

HEY, DAD, SORRY TO INTERRUPT.

NO PROBLEM, PATRICK. THE PROFESSOR HERE WAS JUST GIVING ME SOME GOOD NEWS. WE'RE GONNA DO ALL RIGHT OUT OF THIS THING, SOUNDS LIKE.

OKAY, GREAT--BUT SOMETHING'S HAPPENING OUTSIDE.

YEAH--A LINE AROUND THE BLOCK AT TEN BUCKS A POP, LAST TIME I CHECKED!

NAH, NOT THAT. THERE'S SOME LADY MAKING A LOT OF NOISE OUT THERE--AND SHE BROUGHT THE COPS.

AH, WHATEVER. I CHECKED WITH MY LAWYER, THIS IS PRIVATE PROPERTY. I CAN DO WHAT I WANT. COPS CAN'T DO A DAMN THING.

LET HER IN. LONG AS SHE PAYS HER TEN BUCKS, WHAT DO I CARE WHAT SHE THINKS?

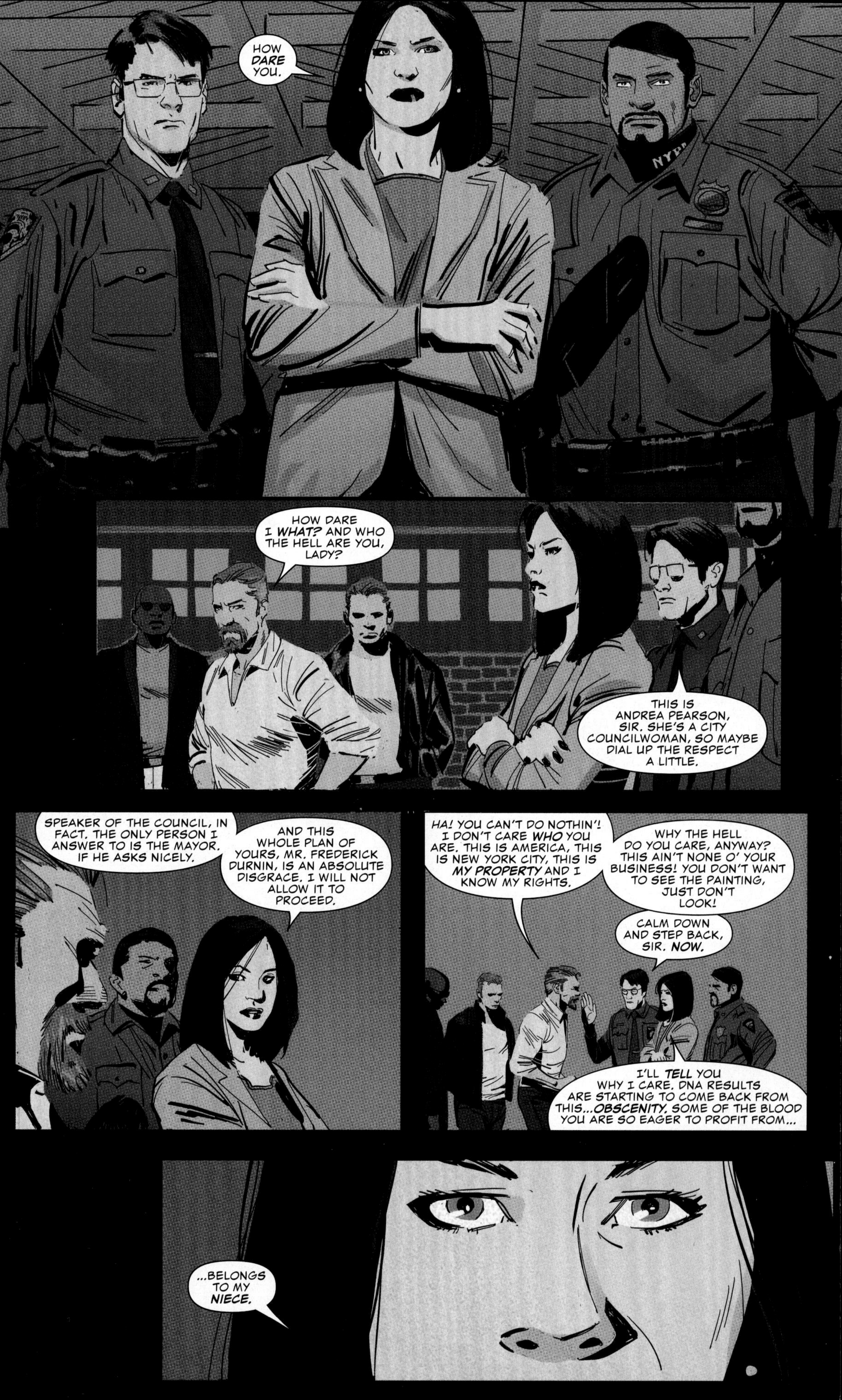

HOW DARE YOU.
HOW DARE I WHAT? AND WHO THE HELL ARE YOU, LADY?
THIS IS ANDREA PEARSON, SIR. SHE'S A CITY COUNCILWOMAN, SO MAYBE DIAL UP THE RESPECT A LITTLE.
SPEAKER OF THE COUNCIL, IN FACT. THE ONLY PERSON I ANSWER TO IS THE MAYOR. IF HE ASKS NICELY.
AND THIS WHOLE PLAN OF YOURS, MR. FREDERICK DURNIN, IS AN ABSOLUTE DISGRACE. I WILL NOT ALLOW IT TO PROCEED.
HA! YOU CAN'T DO NOTHIN'! I DON'T CARE WHO YOU ARE. THIS IS AMERICA, THIS IS NEW YORK CITY, THIS IS MY PROPERTY AND I KNOW MY RIGHTS.
WHY THE HELL DO YOU CARE, ANYWAY? THIS AIN'T NONE O' YOUR BUSINESS! YOU DON'T WANT TO SEE THE PAINTING, JUST DON'T LOOK!
CALM DOWN AND STEP BACK, SIR. NOW.
I'LL TELL YOU WHY I CARE. DNA RESULTS ARE STARTING TO COME BACK FROM THIS...OBSCENITY. SOME OF THE BLOOD YOU ARE SO EAGER TO PROFIT FROM...
...BELONGS TO MY NIECE.

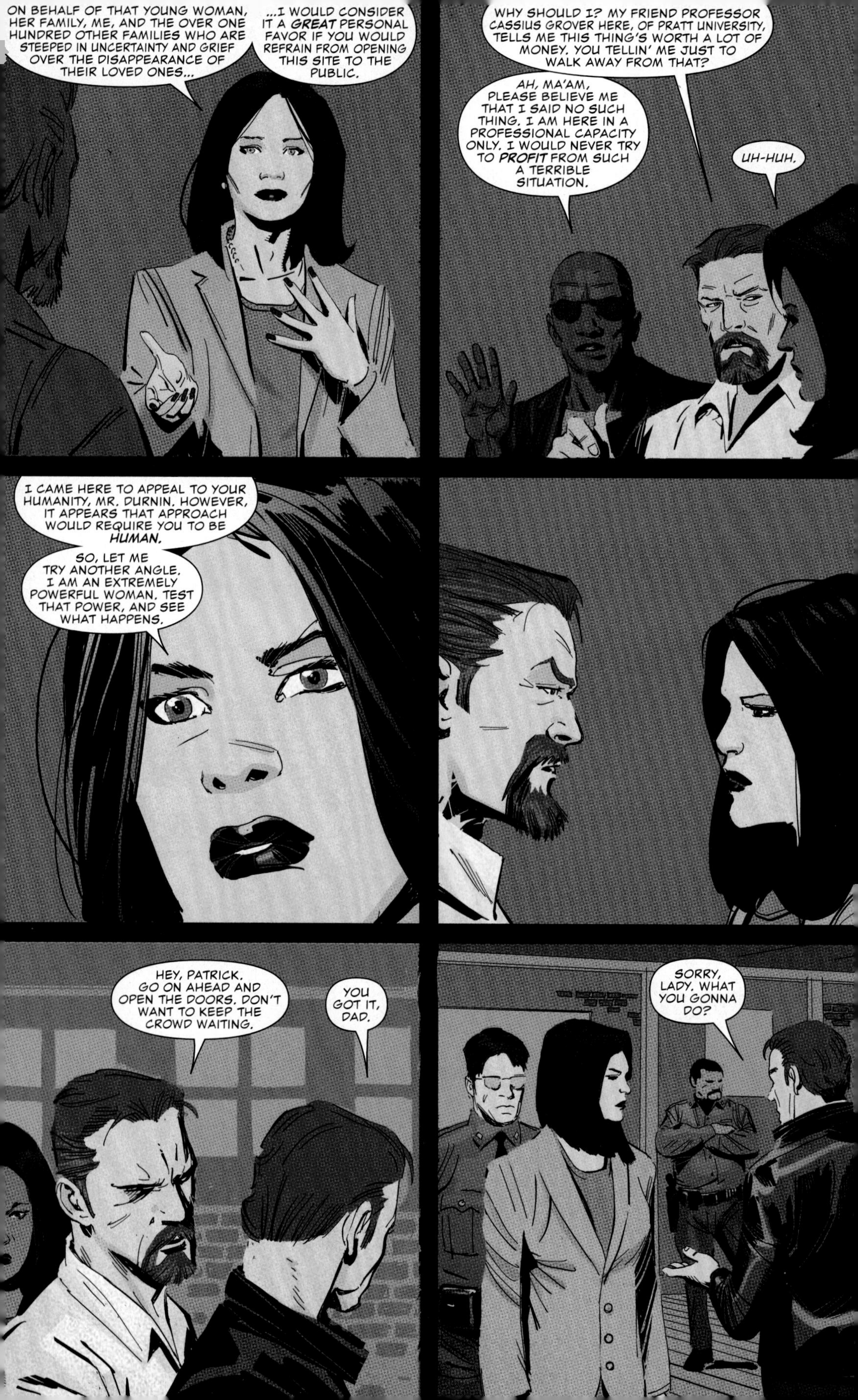
ON BEHALF OF THAT YOUNG WOMAN, HER FAMILY, ME, AND THE OVER ONE HUNDRED OTHER FAMILIES WHO ARE STEEPED IN UNCERTAINTY AND GRIEF OVER THE DISAPPEARANCE OF THEIR LOVED ONES...
...I WOULD CONSIDER IT A GREAT PERSONAL FAVOR IF YOU WOULD REFRAIN FROM OPENING THIS SITE TO THE PUBLIC.
WHY SHOULD I? MY FRIEND PROFESSOR CASSIUS GROVER HERE, OF PRATT UNIVERSITY, TELLS ME THIS THING'S WORTH A LOT OF MONEY. YOU TELLIN' ME JUST TO WALK AWAY FROM THAT?
AH, MA'AM, PLEASE BELIEVE ME THAT I SAID NO SUCH THING. I AM HERE IN A PROFESSIONAL CAPACITY ONLY. I WOULD NEVER TRY TO PROFIT FROM SUCH A TERRIBLE SITUATION.
UH-HUH.
I CAME HERE TO APPEAL TO YOUR HUMANITY, MR. DURNIN. HOWEVER, IT APPEARS THAT APPROACH WOULD REQUIRE YOU TO BE HUMAN.
SO, LET ME TRY ANOTHER ANGLE. I AM AN EXTREMELY POWERFUL WOMAN. TEST THAT POWER, AND SEE WHAT HAPPENS.
HEY, PATRICK. GO ON AHEAD AND OPEN THE DOORS. DON'T WANT TO KEEP THE CROWD WAITING.
YOU GOT IT, DAD.
SORRY, LADY. WHAT YOU GONNA DO?

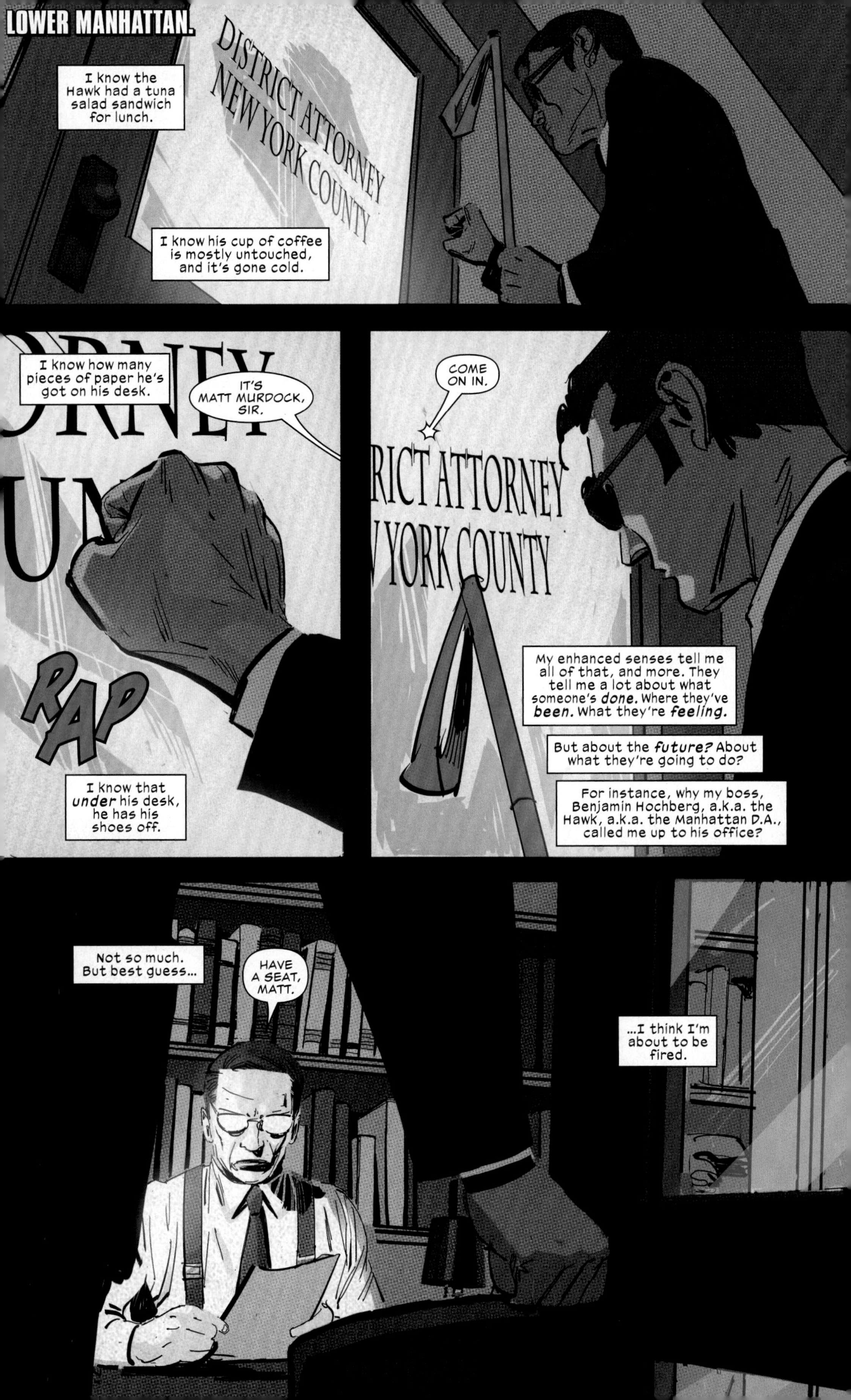
LOWER MANHATTAN.
DISTRICT ATTORNEY NEW YORK COUNTY
I know the Hawk had a tuna salad sandwich for lunch.
I know his cup of coffee is mostly untouched, and it's gone cold.
I know how many pieces of paper he's got on his desk.
IT'S MATT MURDOCK, SIR.
RAP
I know that *under* his desk, he has his shoes off.
COME ON IN.
My enhanced senses tell me all of that, and more. They tell me a lot about what someone's *done*. Where they've *been*. What they're *feeling*.
But about the *future?* About what they're going to do?
For instance, why my boss, Benjamin Hochberg, a.k.a. the Hawk, a.k.a. the Manhattan D.A., called me up to his office?
Not so much. But best guess...
HAVE A SEAT, MATT.
...I think I'm about to be fired.

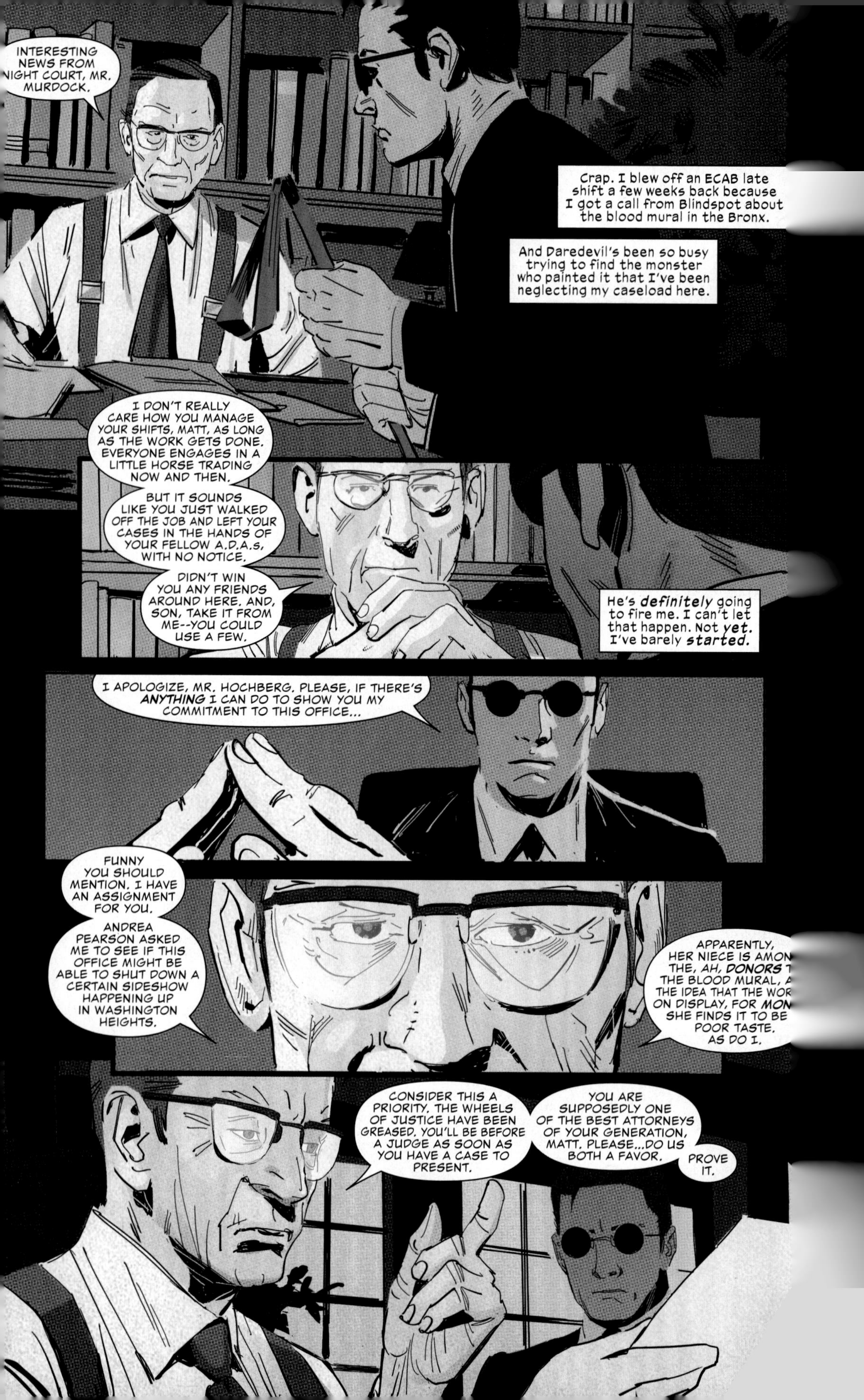
INTERESTING NEWS FROM NIGHT COURT, MR. MURDOCK.
Crap. I blew off an ECAB late shift a few weeks back because I got a call from Blindspot about the blood mural in the Bronx.
And Daredevil's been so busy trying to find the monster who painted it that I've been neglecting my caseload here.
I DON'T REALLY CARE HOW YOU MANAGE YOUR SHIFTS, MATT, AS LONG AS THE WORK GETS DONE. EVERYONE ENGAGES IN A LITTLE HORSE TRADING NOW AND THEN.
BUT IT SOUNDS LIKE YOU JUST WALKED OFF THE JOB AND LEFT YOUR CASES IN THE HANDS OF YOUR FELLOW A.D.A.s, WITH NO NOTICE.
DIDN'T WIN YOU ANY FRIENDS AROUND HERE. AND, SON, TAKE IT FROM ME--YOU COULD USE A FEW.
He's *definitely* going to fire me. I can't let that happen. Not ***yet.*** I've barely ***started.***
I APOLOGIZE, MR. HOCHBERG. PLEASE, IF THERE'S ***ANYTHING*** I CAN DO TO SHOW YOU MY COMMITMENT TO THIS OFFICE...
FUNNY YOU SHOULD MENTION. I HAVE AN ASSIGNMENT FOR YOU.
ANDREA PEARSON ASKED ME TO SEE IF THIS OFFICE MIGHT BE ABLE TO SHUT DOWN A CERTAIN SIDESHOW HAPPENING UP IN WASHINGTON HEIGHTS.
APPARENTLY, HER NIECE IS AMON THE, AH, ***DONORS*** T THE BLOOD MURAL, A THE IDEA THAT THE WOR ON DISPLAY, FOR ***MON*** SHE FINDS IT TO BE POOR TASTE. AS DO I.
CONSIDER THIS A PRIORITY. THE WHEELS OF JUSTICE HAVE BEEN GREASED. YOU'LL BE BEFORE A JUDGE AS SOON AS YOU HAVE A CASE TO PRESENT.
YOU ARE SUPPOSEDLY ONE OF THE BEST ATTORNEYS OF YOUR GENERATION, MATT. PLEASE...DO US BOTH A FAVOR.
PROVE IT.

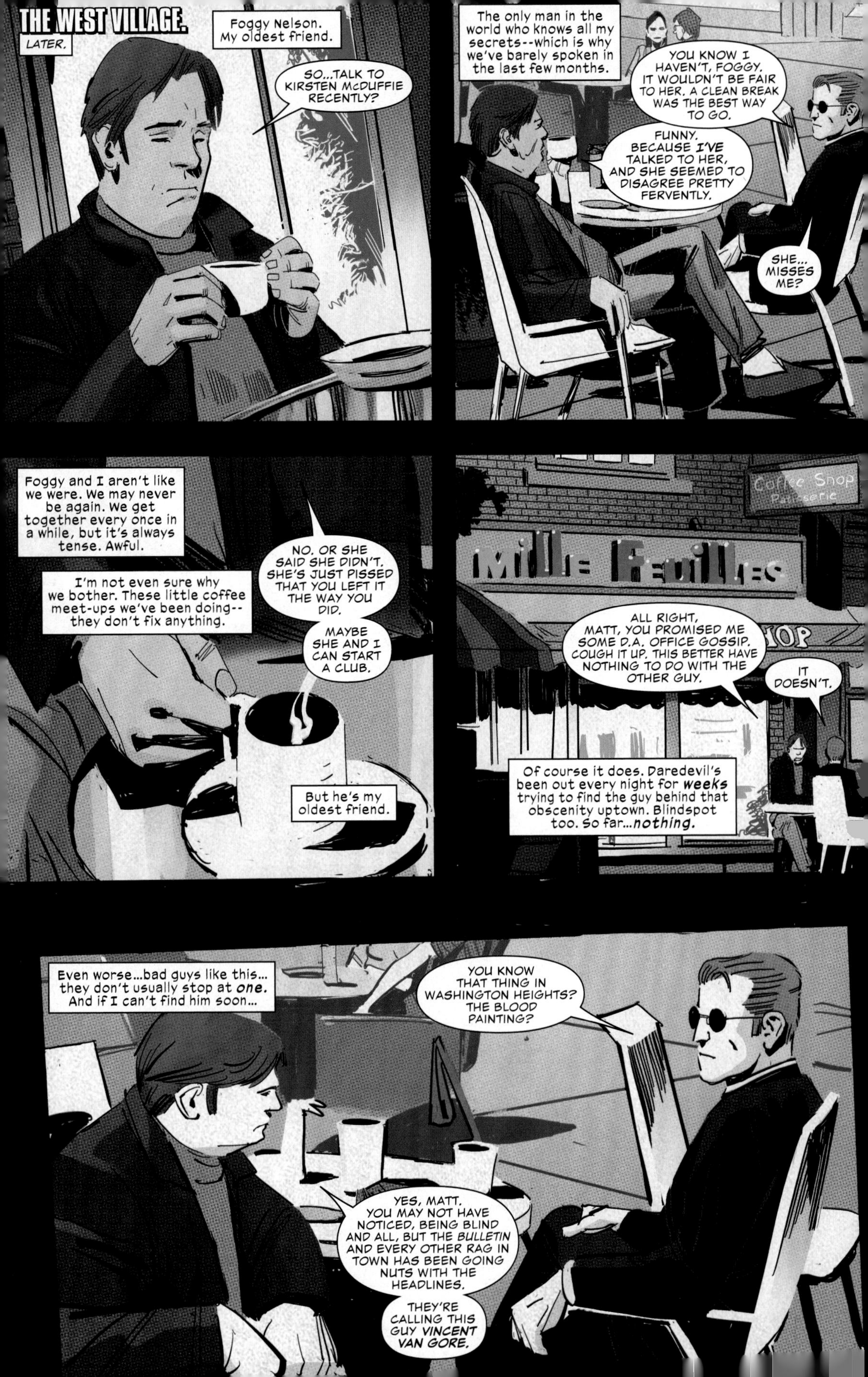
THE WEST VILLAGE.
LATER.
Foggy Nelson. My oldest friend.
SO...TALK TO KIRSTEN McDUFFIE RECENTLY?
The only man in the world who knows all my secrets--which is why we've barely spoken in the last few months.
YOU KNOW I HAVEN'T, FOGGY. IT WOULDN'T BE FAIR TO HER. A CLEAN BREAK WAS THE BEST WAY TO GO.
FUNNY. BECAUSE I'VE TALKED TO HER, AND SHE SEEMED TO DISAGREE PRETTY FERVENTLY.
SHE... MISSES ME?
Foggy and I aren't like we were. We may never be again. We get together every once in a while, but it's always tense. Awful.
I'm not even sure why we bother. These little coffee meet-ups we've been doing--they don't fix anything.
NO. OR SHE SAID SHE DIDN'T. SHE'S JUST PISSED THAT YOU LEFT IT THE WAY YOU DID.
MAYBE SHE AND I CAN START A CLUB.
But he's my oldest friend.
Coffee Shop
Patisserie
ALL RIGHT, MATT, YOU PROMISED ME SOME D.A. OFFICE GOSSIP. COUGH IT UP. THIS BETTER HAVE NOTHING TO DO WITH THE OTHER GUY.
IT DOESN'T.
Of course it does. Daredevil's been out every night for weeks trying to find the guy behind that obscenity uptown. Blindspot too. So far...nothing.
Even worse...bad guys like this... they don't usually stop at one. And if I can't find him soon...
YOU KNOW THAT THING IN WASHINGTON HEIGHTS? THE BLOOD PAINTING?
YES, MATT. YOU MAY NOT HAVE NOTICED, BEING BLIND AND ALL, BUT THE BULLETIN AND EVERY OTHER RAG IN TOWN HAS BEEN GOING NUTS WITH THE HEADLINES.
THEY'RE CALLING THIS GUY VINCENT VAN GORE.

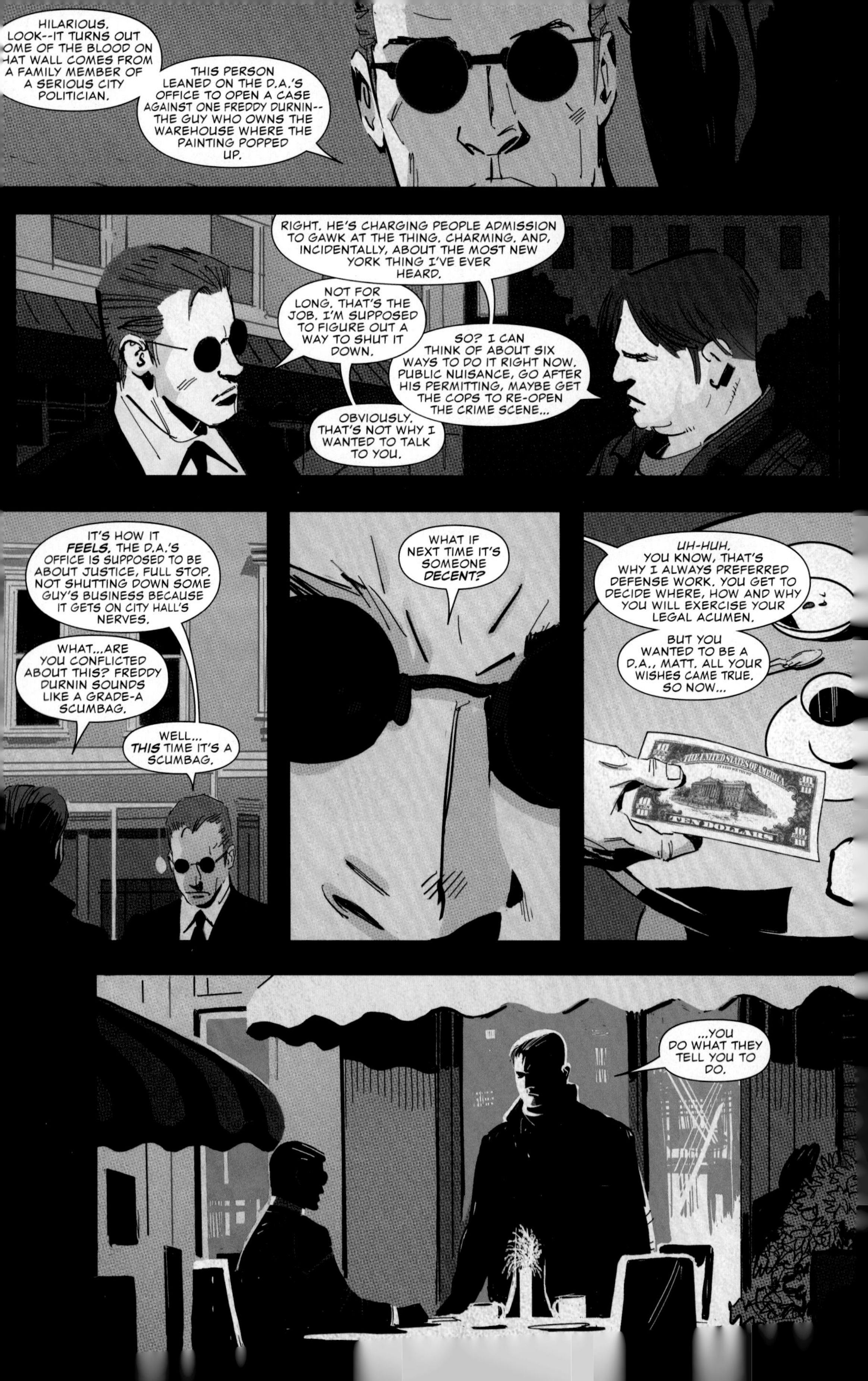
HILARIOUS. LOOK--IT TURNS OUT OME OF THE BLOOD ON HAT WALL COMES FROM A FAMILY MEMBER OF A SERIOUS CITY POLITICIAN.
THIS PERSON LEANED ON THE D.A.'S OFFICE TO OPEN A CASE AGAINST ONE FREDDY DURNIN-- THE GUY WHO OWNS THE WAREHOUSE WHERE THE PAINTING POPPED UP.
RIGHT. HE'S CHARGING PEOPLE ADMISSION TO GAWK AT THE THING. CHARMING. AND, INCIDENTALLY, ABOUT THE MOST NEW YORK THING I'VE EVER HEARD.
NOT FOR LONG. THAT'S THE JOB. I'M SUPPOSED TO FIGURE OUT A WAY TO SHUT IT DOWN.
SO? I CAN THINK OF ABOUT SIX WAYS TO DO IT RIGHT NOW. PUBLIC NUISANCE, GO AFTER HIS PERMITTING, MAYBE GET THE COPS TO RE-OPEN THE CRIME SCENE...
OBVIOUSLY. THAT'S NOT WHY I WANTED TO TALK TO YOU.
IT'S HOW IT FEELS. THE D.A.'S OFFICE IS SUPPOSED TO BE ABOUT JUSTICE, FULL STOP. NOT SHUTTING DOWN SOME GUY'S BUSINESS BECAUSE IT GETS ON CITY HALL'S NERVES.
WHAT...ARE YOU CONFLICTED ABOUT THIS? FREDDY DURNIN SOUNDS LIKE A GRADE-A SCUMBAG.
WELL... THIS TIME IT'S A SCUMBAG.
WHAT IF NEXT TIME IT'S SOMEONE DECENT?
UH-HUH. YOU KNOW, THAT'S WHY I ALWAYS PREFERRED DEFENSE WORK. YOU GET TO DECIDE WHERE, HOW AND WHY YOU WILL EXERCISE YOUR LEGAL ACUMEN.
BUT YOU WANTED TO BE A D.A., MATT. ALL YOUR WISHES CAME TRUE. SO NOW...
THE UNITED STATES OF AMERICA
TEN DOLLARS
...YOU DO WHAT THEY TELL YOU TO DO.

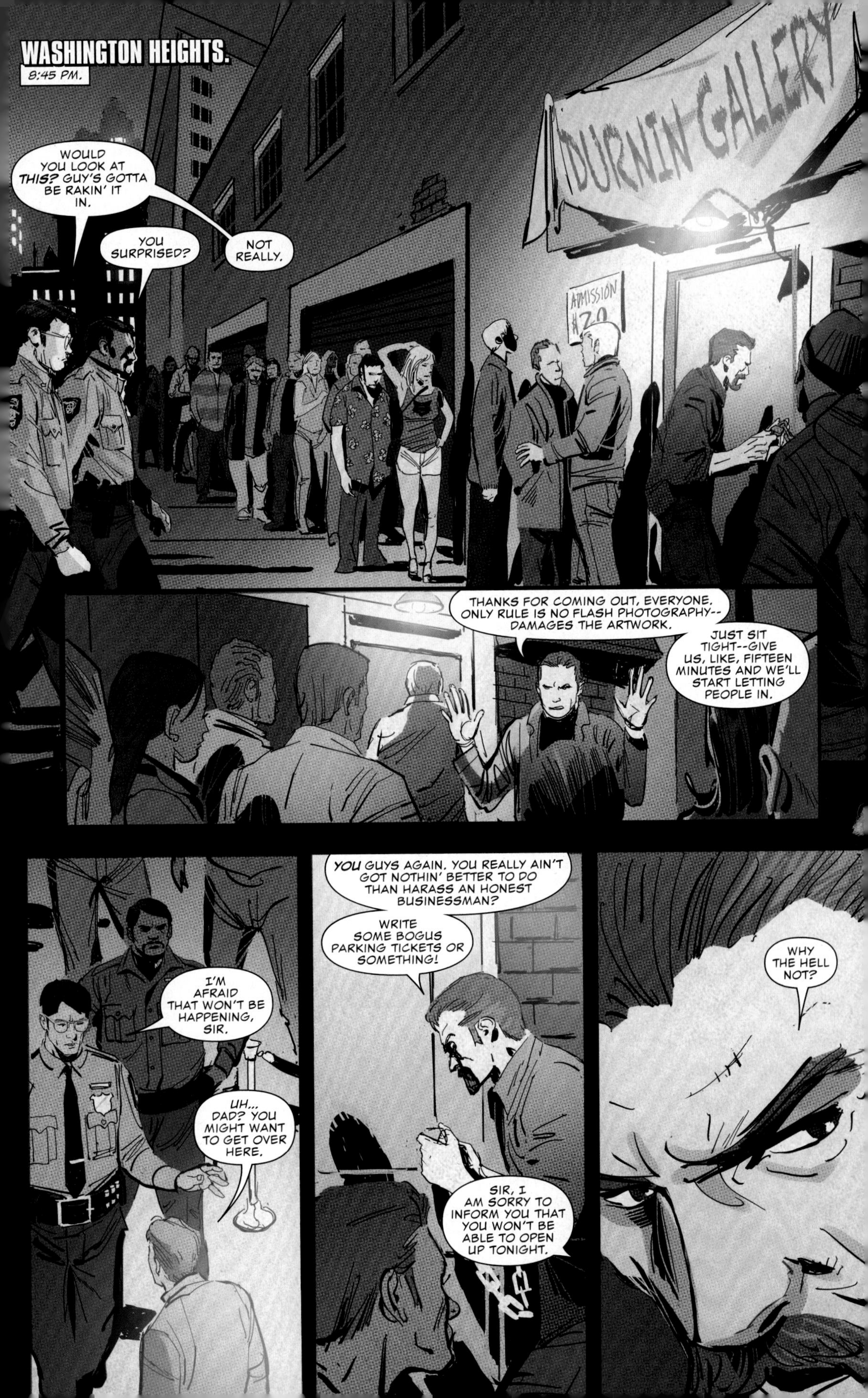
WASHINGTON HEIGHTS.
8:45 PM.
WOULD YOU LOOK AT THIS? GUY'S GOTTA BE RAKIN' IT IN.
YOU SURPRISED?
NOT REALLY.
DURNIN GALLERY
ADMISSION $20
THANKS FOR COMING OUT, EVERYONE. ONLY RULE IS NO FLASH PHOTOGRAPHY-- DAMAGES THE ARTWORK.
JUST SIT TIGHT--GIVE US, LIKE, FIFTEEN MINUTES AND WE'LL START LETTING PEOPLE IN.
YOU GUYS AGAIN. YOU REALLY AIN'T GOT NOTHIN' BETTER TO DO THAN HARASS AN HONEST BUSINESSMAN?
WRITE SOME BOGUS PARKING TICKETS OR SOMETHING!
I'M AFRAID THAT WON'T BE HAPPENING, SIR.
UH... DAD? YOU MIGHT WANT TO GET OVER HERE.
SIR, I AM SORRY TO INFORM YOU THAT YOU WON'T BE ABLE TO OPEN UP TONIGHT.
WHY THE HELL NOT?

COURT ORDER.
PRELIMINARY INJUNCTION? WHAT THE HELL IS THAT?
IT MEANS THAT BY LAW, YOU ARE PREVENTED FROM OPERATING THIS ESTABLISHMENT AS AN ART GALLERY UNTIL SUCH TIME AS A COURT MAKES A FINAL RULING ON THE LEGALITY OF WHAT YOU'RE DOING HERE.
OH...SON OF A...IT'S THAT LADY, ISN'T IT? MISS "I'M SO POWERFUL." SICCED THE D.A.'S OFFICE ON ME. MATT MURDOCK... WHOEVER THE HELL THAT IS.
SORRY, FOLKS! LOOKS LIKE THE CITY THINKS YOU'RE ALL A BUNCH OF BABIES WHO DON'T DESERVE TO SEE AN IMPORTANT WORK OF ART.
SIR, LET'S JUST TAKE IT DOWN A NOTCH...
NOW YOU'RE GONNA STEP ON MY FREEDOM OF SPEECH, TOO?
WHAT'RE YOUR NAMES--MENENDEZ AND SCOTT? I'M GONNA REMEMBER THAT. I GOT A REAL GOOD MEMORY. MAYBE I'LL SUE YOU GUYS, TOO. WHY NOT? THIS IS AMERICA.
ANYBODY CAN SUE ANYBODY.
MR. DURNIN, WE HAVE TO ENFORCE THIS INJUNCTION. YOU CAN'T LET THESE PEOPLE IN.
I AIN'T LETTIN' ANYONE IN--BUT THIS IS MY PLACE. YOU GONNA TELL ME I CAN'T GO INTO MY OWN PLACE?
DON'T THINK SO--
AWW, CRUD.

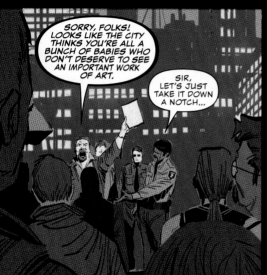

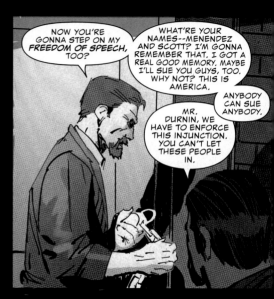

youre only as good as your last performance
1602 EAST 171ST
I'M GONNA NEED A FULL FORENSICS TEAM UP AT 500 JEFFERSON IN THE HEIGHTS. WE'VE HAD A DEVELOPMENT.
SOMEONE SEEMS TO HAVE DEFACED THE BLOOD MURAL. ADDED A MESSAGE.
BOTH OF YOU, BACK OUTSIDE. NOW!
OH, MAN.

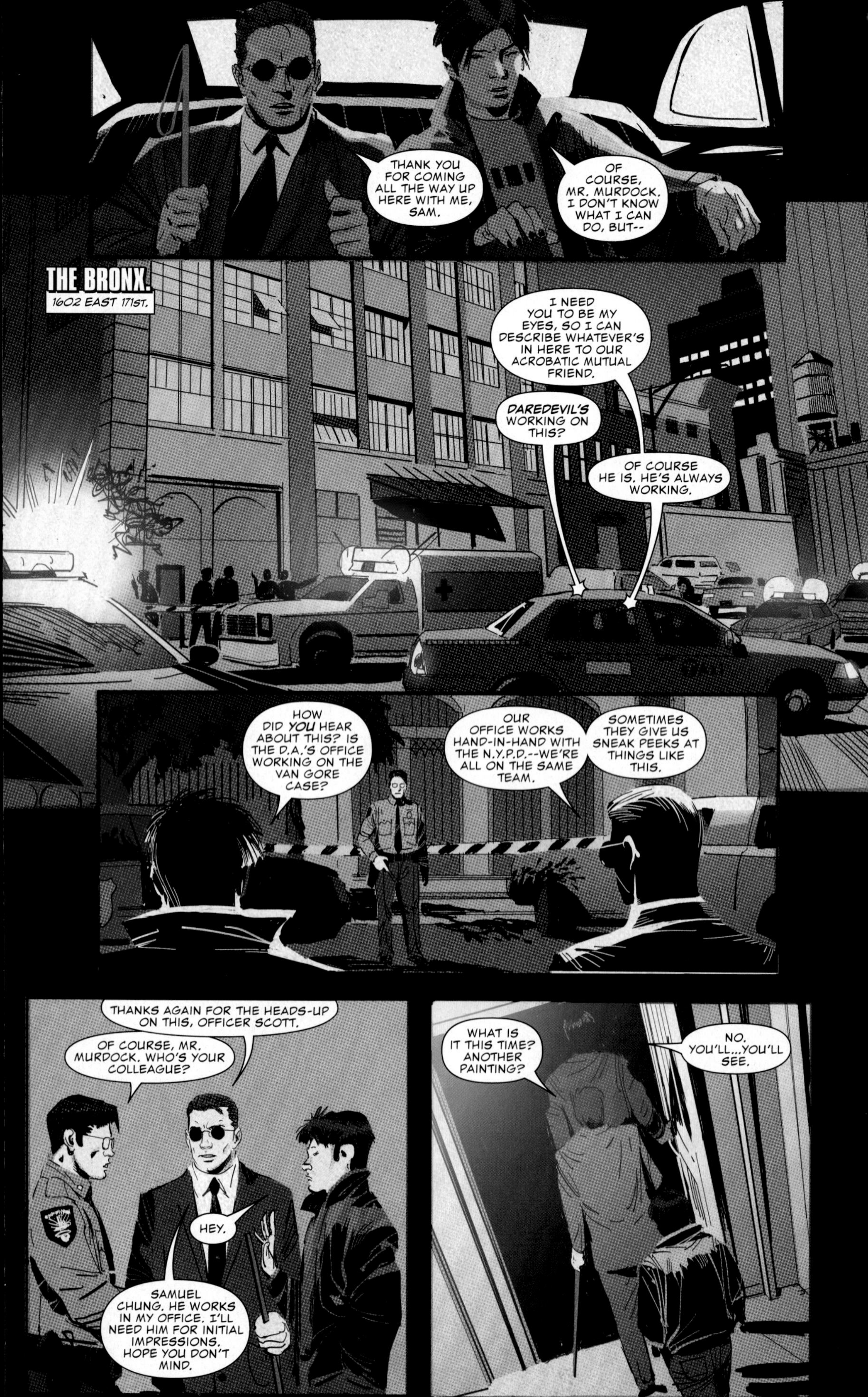
THANK YOU FOR COMING ALL THE WAY UP HERE WITH ME, SAM.
OF COURSE, MR. MURDOCK. I DON'T KNOW WHAT I CAN DO, BUT--
THE BRONX.
1602 EAST 171ST.
I NEED YOU TO BE MY EYES, SO I CAN DESCRIBE WHATEVER'S IN HERE TO OUR ACROBATIC MUTUAL FRIEND.
DAREDEVIL'S WORKING ON THIS?
OF COURSE HE IS. HE'S ALWAYS WORKING.
HOW DID YOU HEAR ABOUT THIS? IS THE D.A.'S OFFICE WORKING ON THE VAN GORE CASE?
OUR OFFICE WORKS HAND-IN-HAND WITH THE N.Y.P.D.--WE'RE ALL ON THE SAME TEAM.
SOMETIMES THEY GIVE US SNEAK PEEKS AT THINGS LIKE THIS.
THANKS AGAIN FOR THE HEADS-UP ON THIS, OFFICER SCOTT.
OF COURSE, MR. MURDOCK. WHO'S YOUR COLLEAGUE?
HEY.
SAMUEL CHUNG. HE WORKS IN MY OFFICE. I'LL NEED HIM FOR INITIAL IMPRESSIONS. HOPE YOU DON'T MIND.
WHAT IS IT THIS TIME? ANOTHER PAINTING?
NO. YOU'LL...YOU'LL SEE.

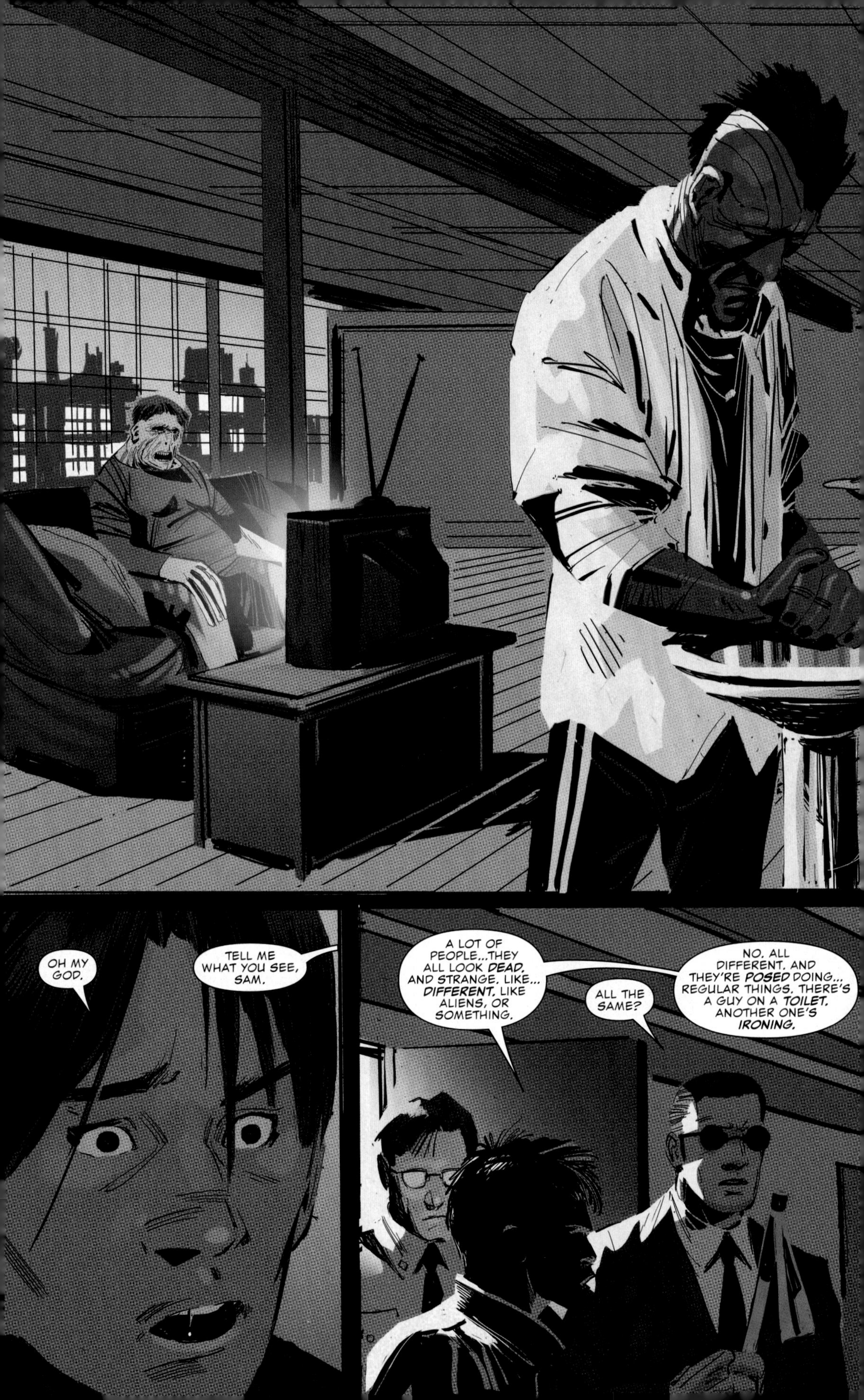
OH MY GOD.
TELL ME WHAT YOU SEE, SAM.
A LOT OF PEOPLE...THEY ALL LOOK DEAD. AND STRANGE. LIKE... DIFFERENT. LIKE ALIENS, OR SOMETHING.
ALL THE SAME?
NO. ALL DIFFERENT. AND THEY'RE POSED DOING... REGULAR THINGS. THERE'S A GUY ON A TOILET. ANOTHER ONE'S IRONING.

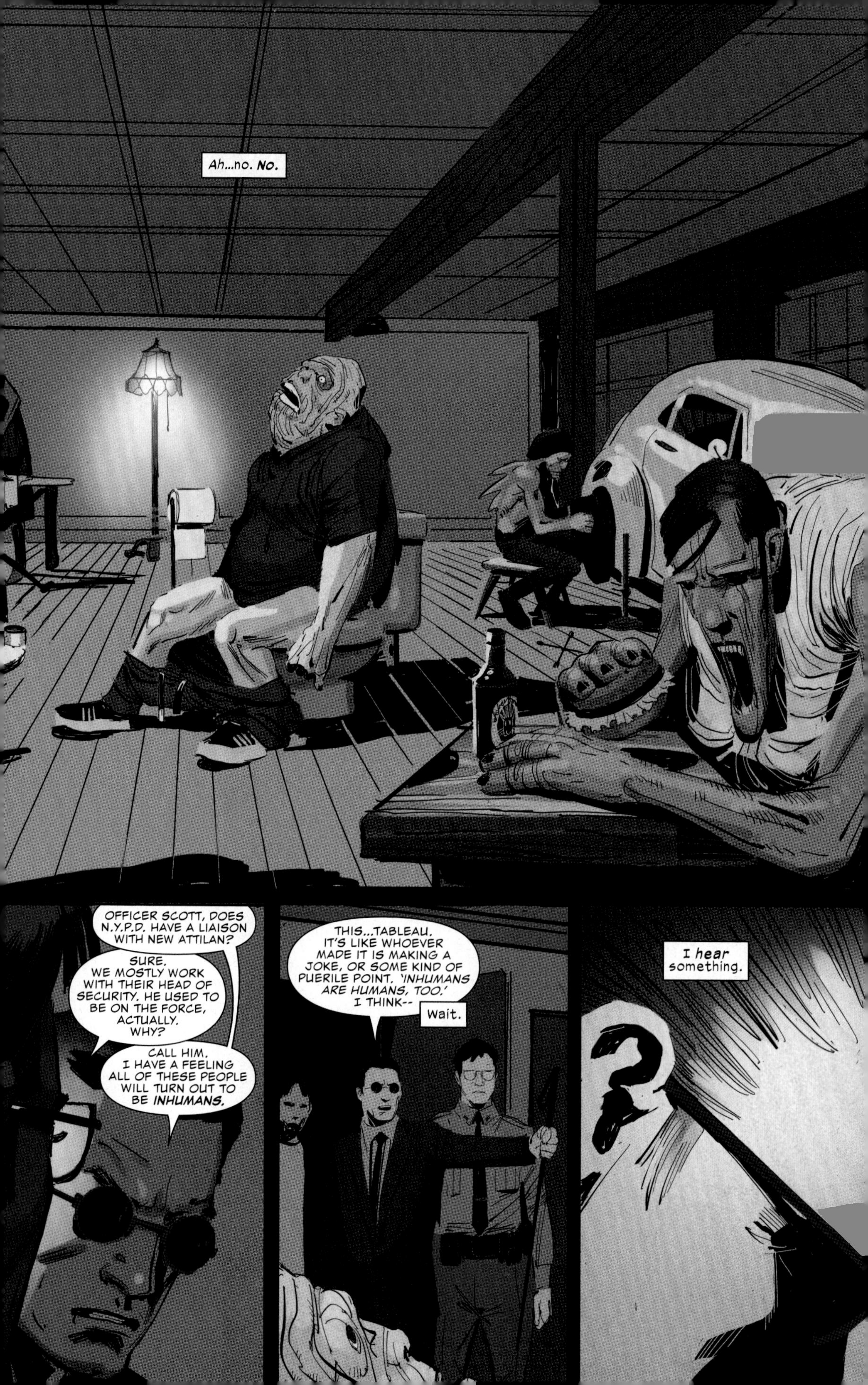
Ah...no. NO.
OFFICER SCOTT, DOES N.Y.P.D. HAVE A LIAISON WITH NEW ATTILAN?
SURE. WE MOSTLY WORK WITH THEIR HEAD OF SECURITY. HE USED TO BE ON THE FORCE, ACTUALLY. WHY?
CALL HIM. I HAVE A FEELING ALL OF THESE PEOPLE WILL TURN OUT TO BE INHUMANS.
THIS...TABLEAU. IT'S LIKE WHOEVER MADE IT IS MAKING A JOKE, OR SOME KIND OF PUERILE POINT. 'INHUMANS ARE HUMANS, TOO.' I THINK--
Wait.
I hear something.

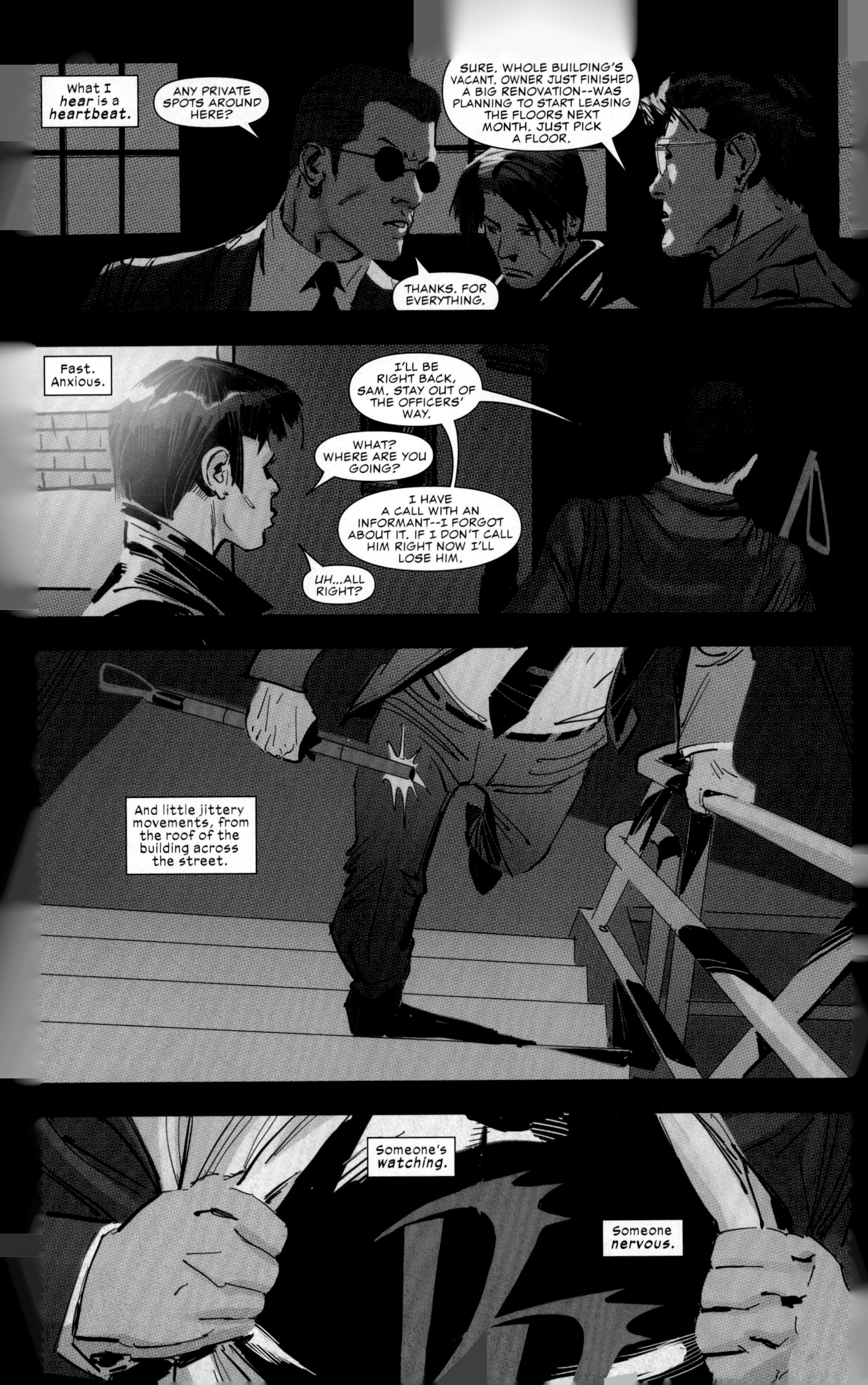
What I *hear* is a *heartbeat.*
ANY PRIVATE SPOTS AROUND HERE?
SURE. WHOLE BUILDING'S VACANT. OWNER JUST FINISHED A BIG RENOVATION--WAS PLANNING TO START LEASING THE FLOORS NEXT MONTH. JUST PICK A FLOOR.
THANKS. FOR EVERYTHING.
Fast. Anxious.
I'LL BE RIGHT BACK, SAM. STAY OUT OF THE OFFICERS' WAY.
WHAT? WHERE ARE YOU GOING?
I HAVE A CALL WITH AN INFORMANT--I FORGOT ABOUT IT. IF I DON'T CALL HIM RIGHT NOW I'LL LOSE HIM.
UH...ALL RIGHT?
And little jittery movements, from the roof of the building across the street.
Someone's *watching.*
Someone *nervous.*

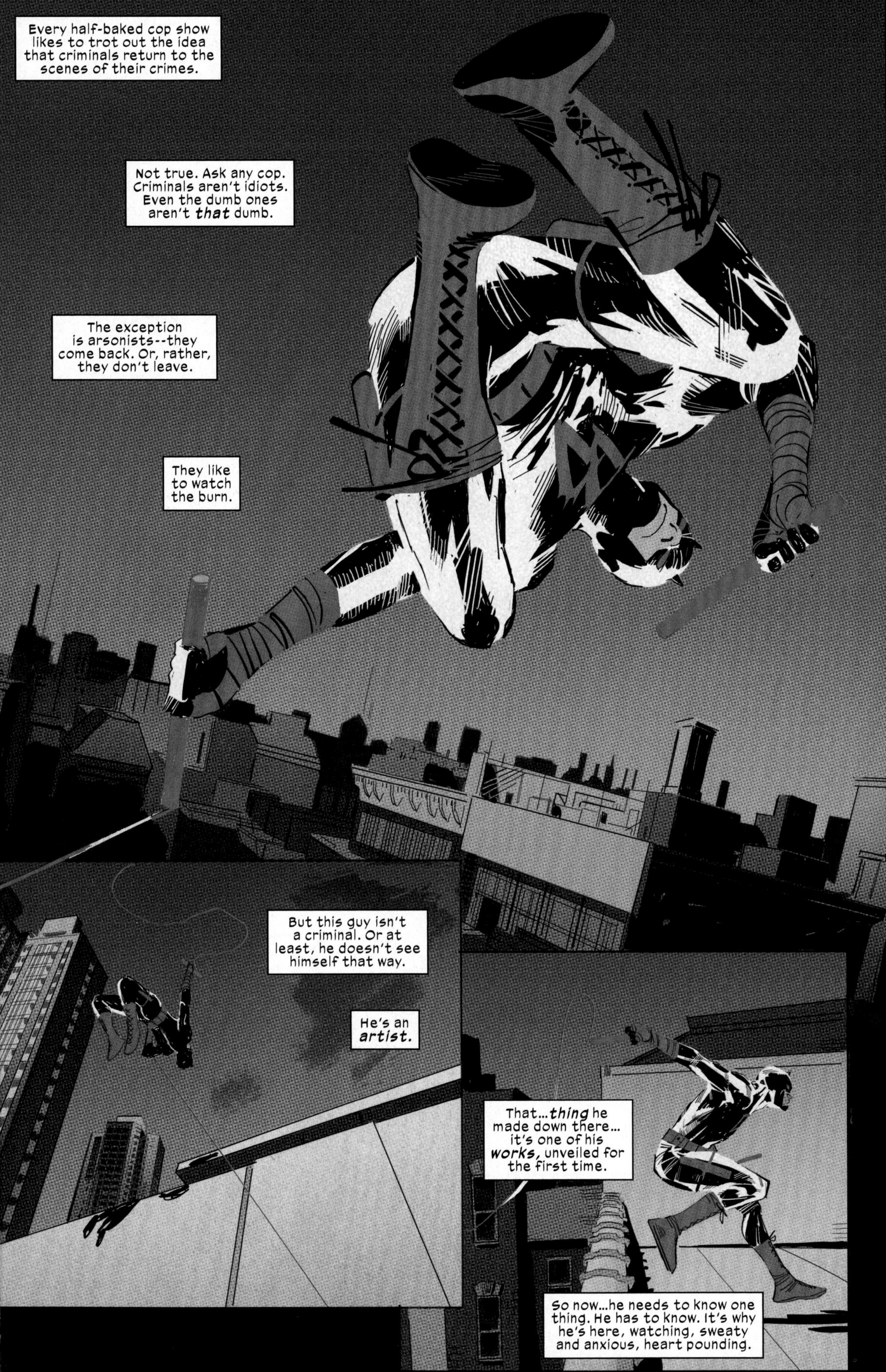
Every half-baked cop show likes to trot out the idea that criminals return to the scenes of their crimes.
Not true. Ask any cop. Criminals aren't idiots. Even the dumb ones aren't *that* dumb.
The exception is arsonists--they come back. Or, rather, they don't leave.
They like to watch the burn.
But this guy isn't a criminal. Or at least, he doesn't see himself that way.
He's an *artist.*
That...*thing* he made down there... it's one of his *works,* unveiled for the first time.
So now...he needs to know one thing. He has to know. It's why he's here, watching, sweaty and anxious, heart pounding.

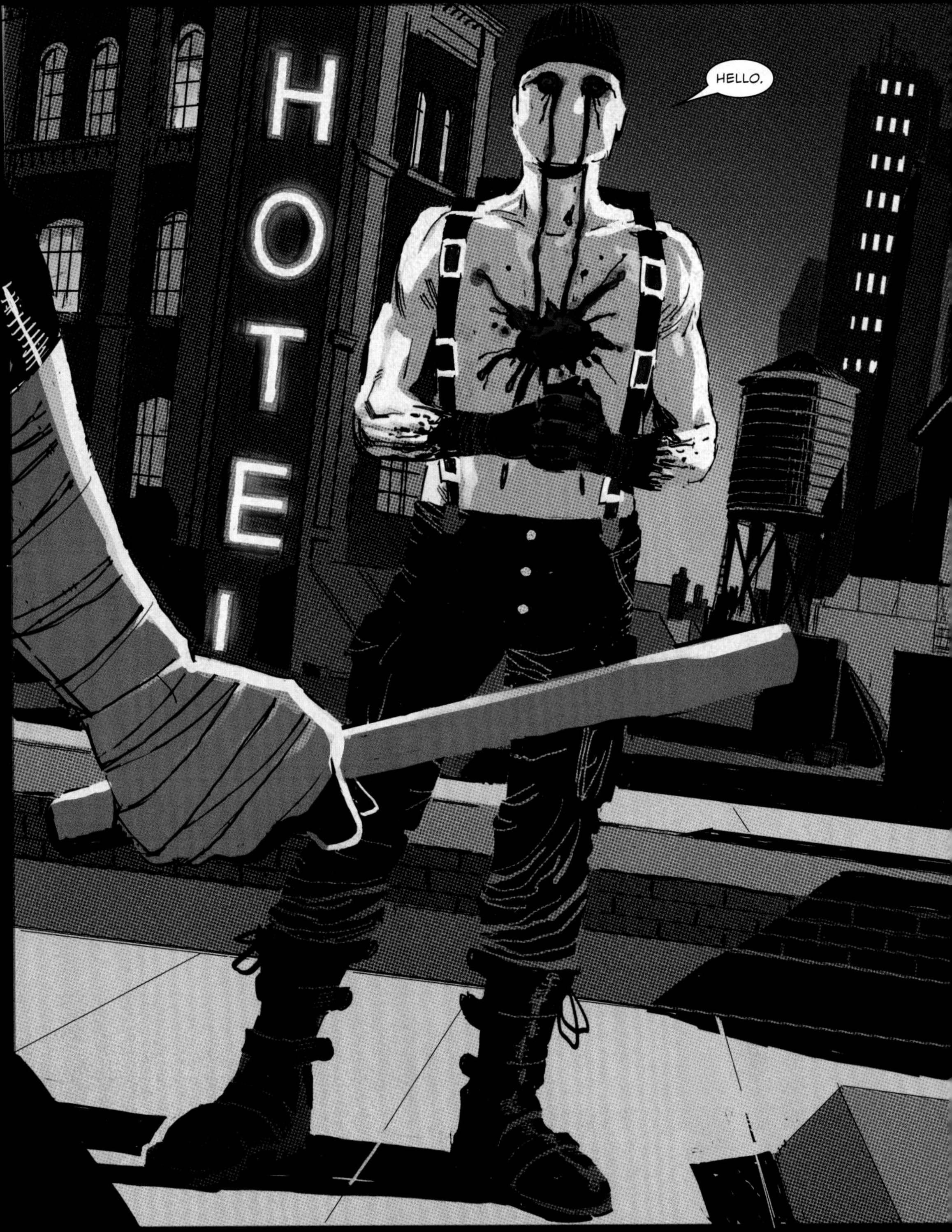
HELLO.
HOTEL

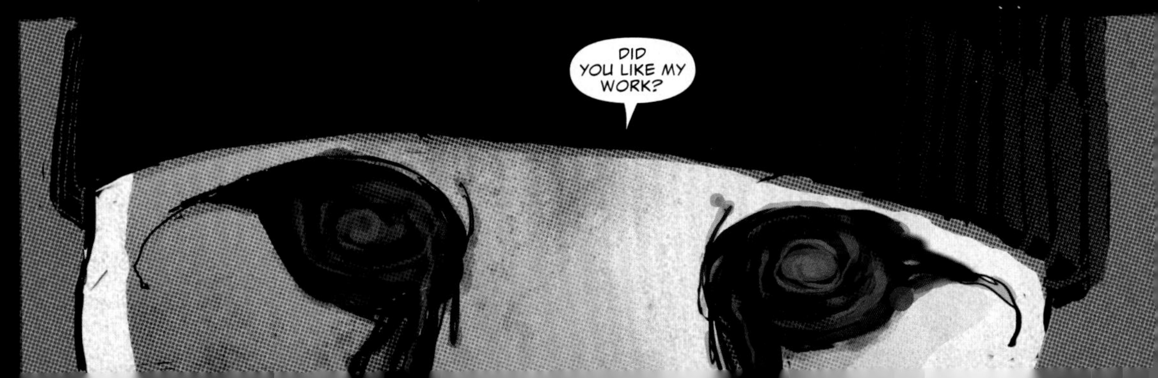
DID YOU LIKE MY WORK?

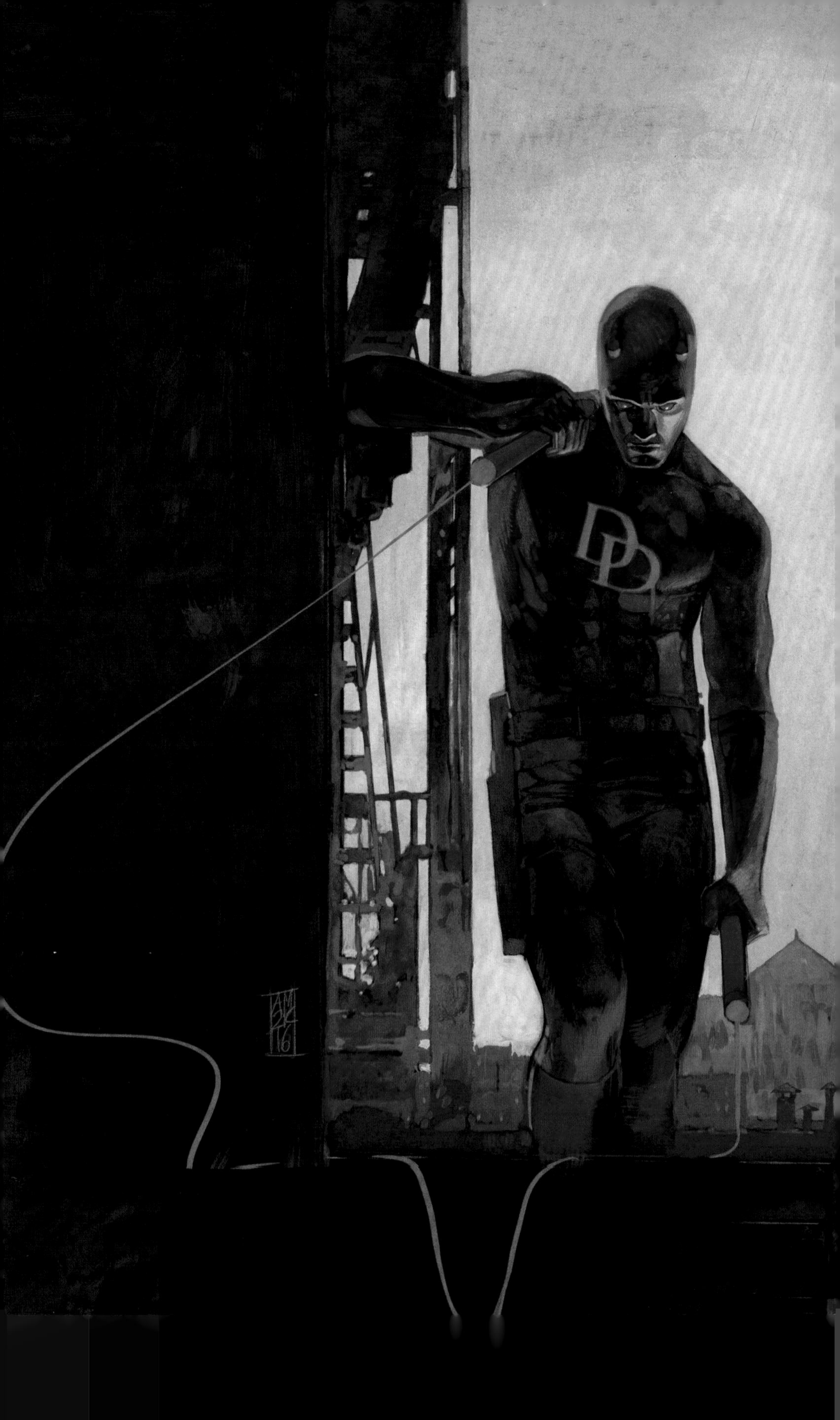

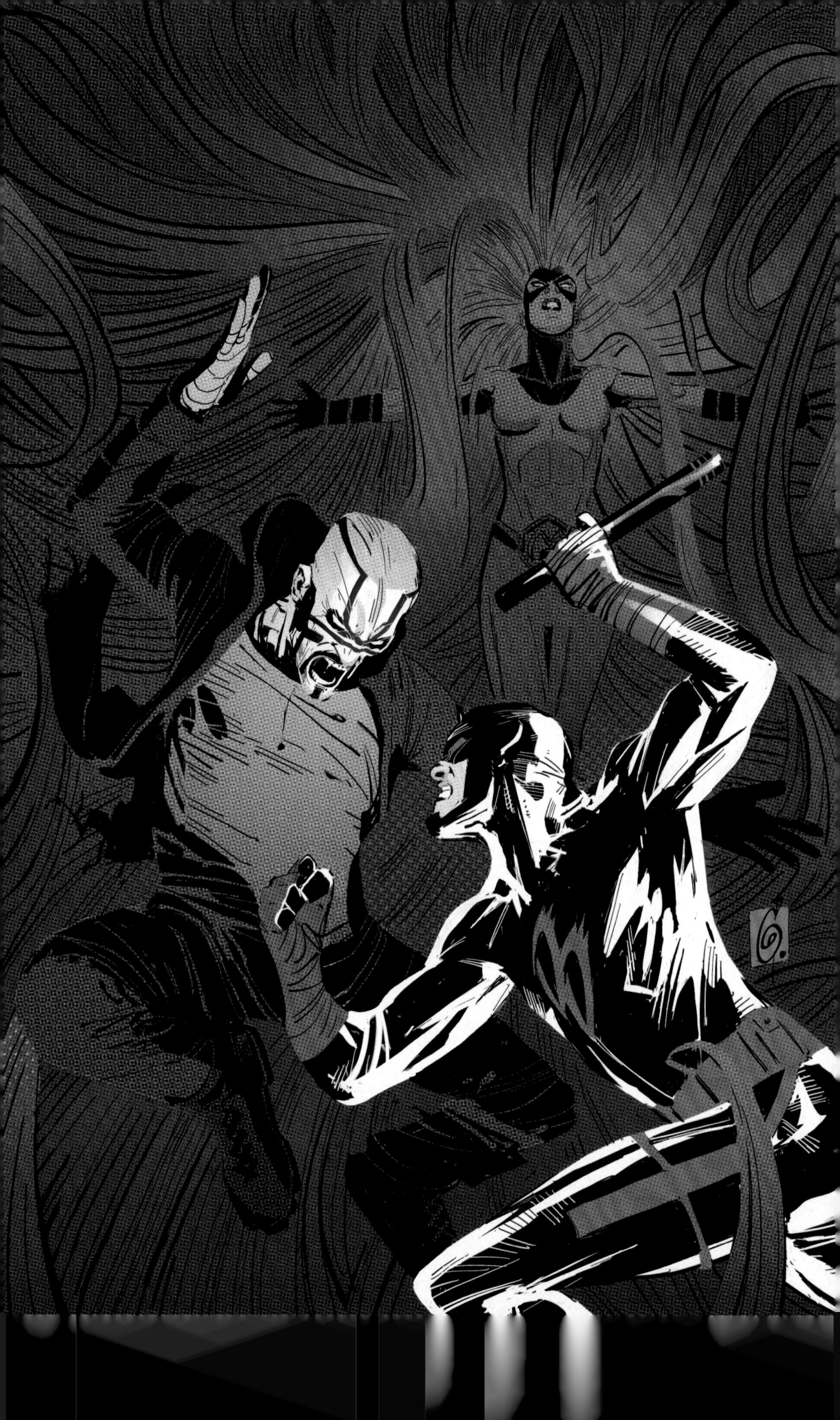

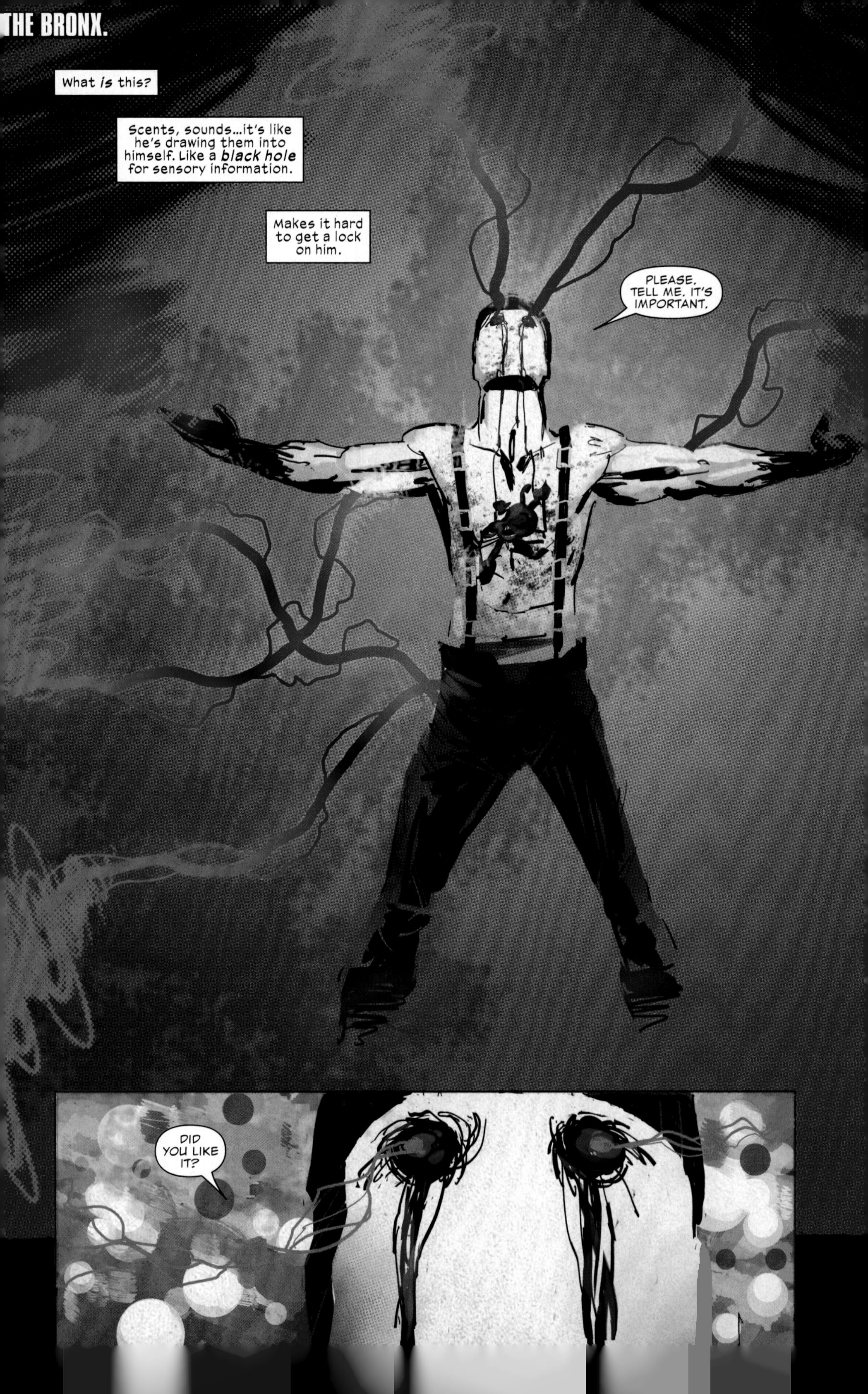
THE BRONX.
What *is* this?
Scents, sounds...it's like he's drawing them into himself. Like a *black hole* for sensory information.
Makes it hard to get a lock on him.
PLEASE. TELL ME. IT'S IMPORTANT.
DID YOU LIKE IT?

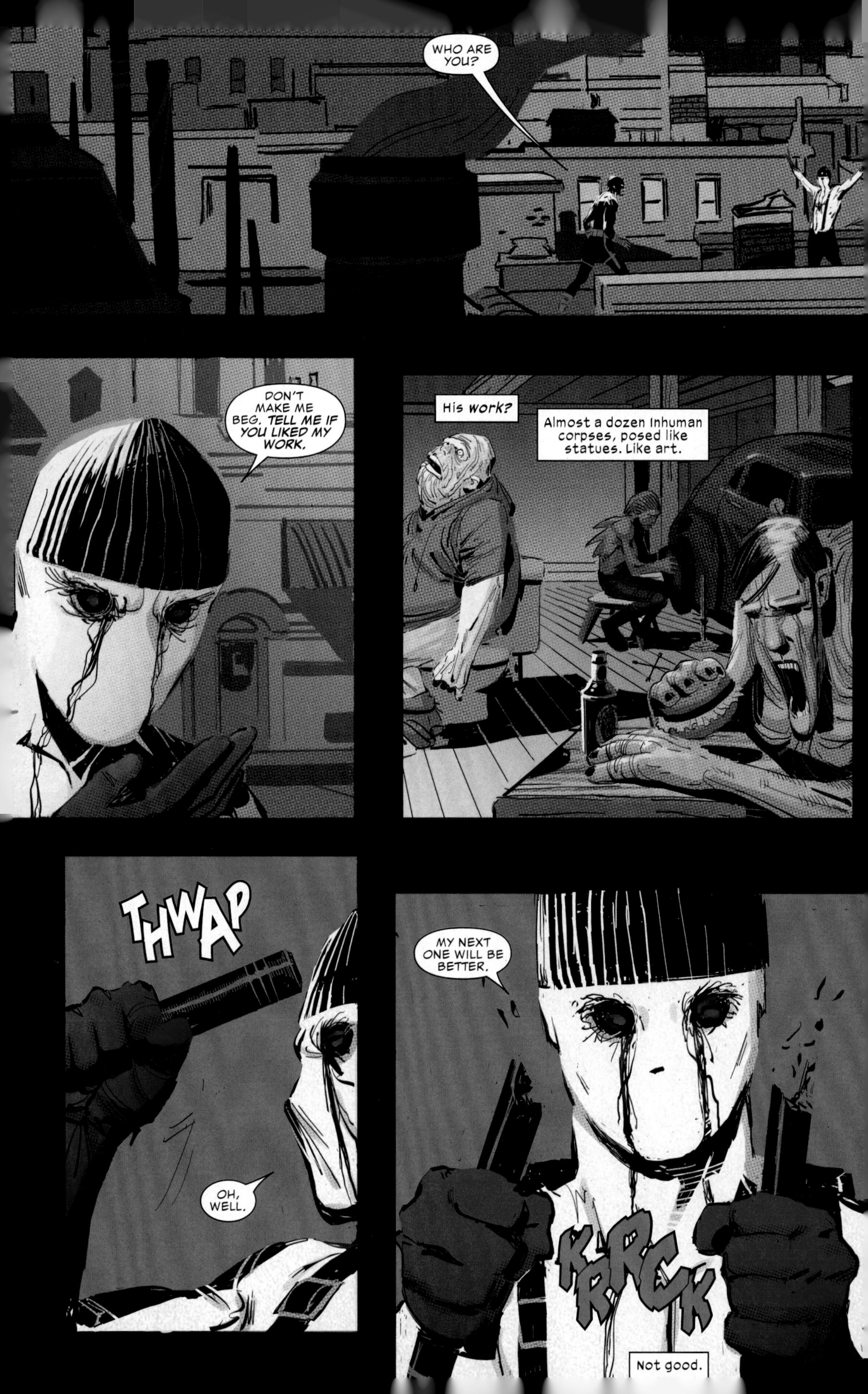
WHO ARE YOU?
DON'T MAKE ME BEG. TELL ME IF YOU LIKED MY WORK.
His work?
Almost a dozen Inhuman corpses, posed like statues. Like art.
THWAP
OH, WELL.
MY NEXT ONE WILL BE BETTER.
KRRCK
Not good.

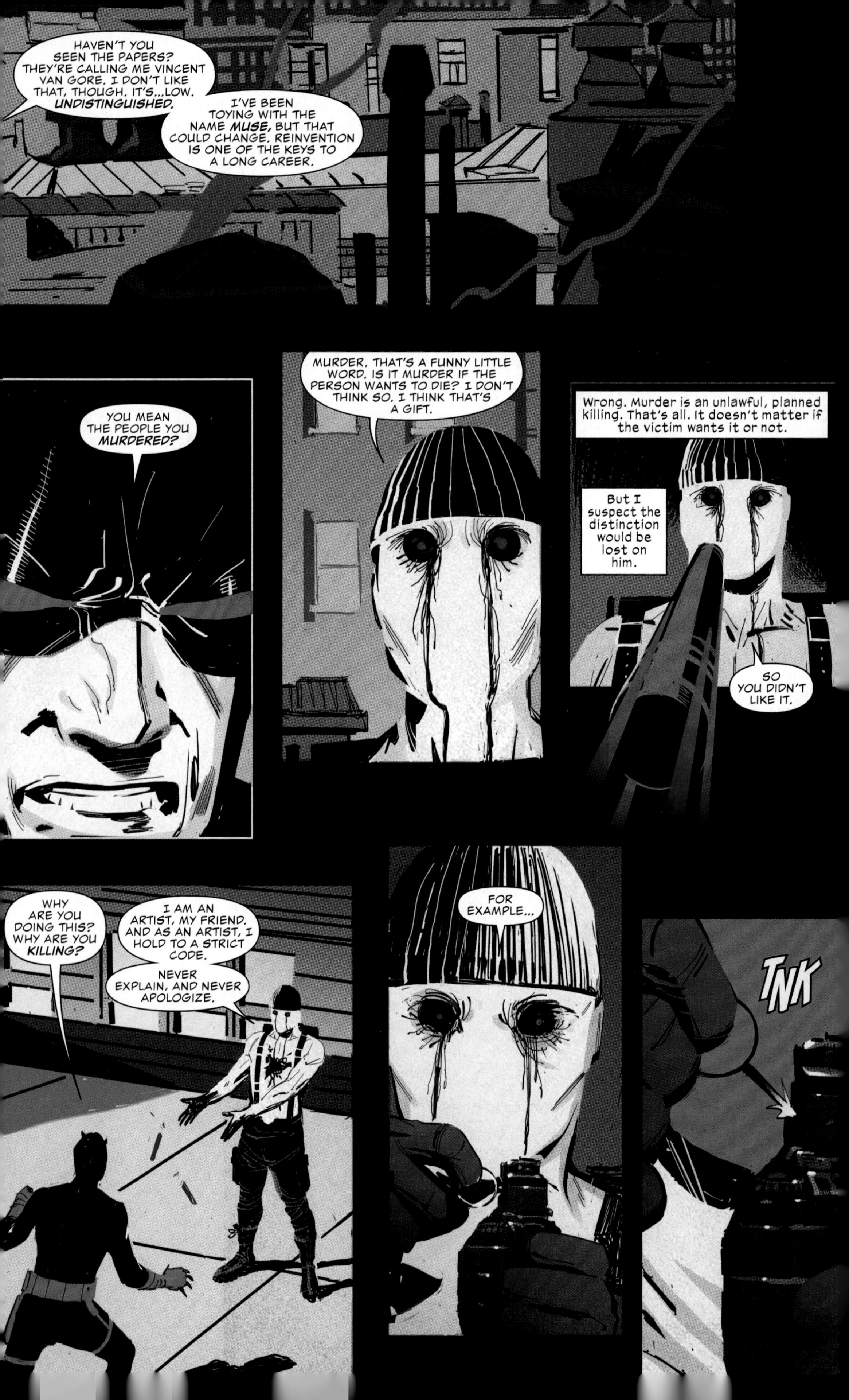
HAVEN'T YOU SEEN THE PAPERS? THEY'RE CALLING ME VINCENT VAN GORE. I DON'T LIKE THAT, THOUGH. IT'S...LOW. UNDISTINGUISHED.
I'VE BEEN TOYING WITH THE NAME MUSE, BUT THAT COULD CHANGE. REINVENTION IS ONE OF THE KEYS TO A LONG CAREER.
YOU MEAN THE PEOPLE YOU MURDERED?
MURDER. THAT'S A FUNNY LITTLE WORD. IS IT MURDER IF THE PERSON WANTS TO DIE? I DON'T THINK SO. I THINK THAT'S A GIFT.
Wrong. Murder is an unlawful, planned killing. That's all. It doesn't matter if the victim wants it or not.
But I suspect the distinction would be lost on him.
SO YOU DIDN'T LIKE IT.
WHY ARE YOU DOING THIS? WHY ARE YOU KILLING?
I AM AN ARTIST, MY FRIEND. AND AS AN ARTIST, I HOLD TO A STRICT CODE.
NEVER EXPLAIN, AND NEVER APOLOGIZE.
FOR EXAMPLE...
TNK

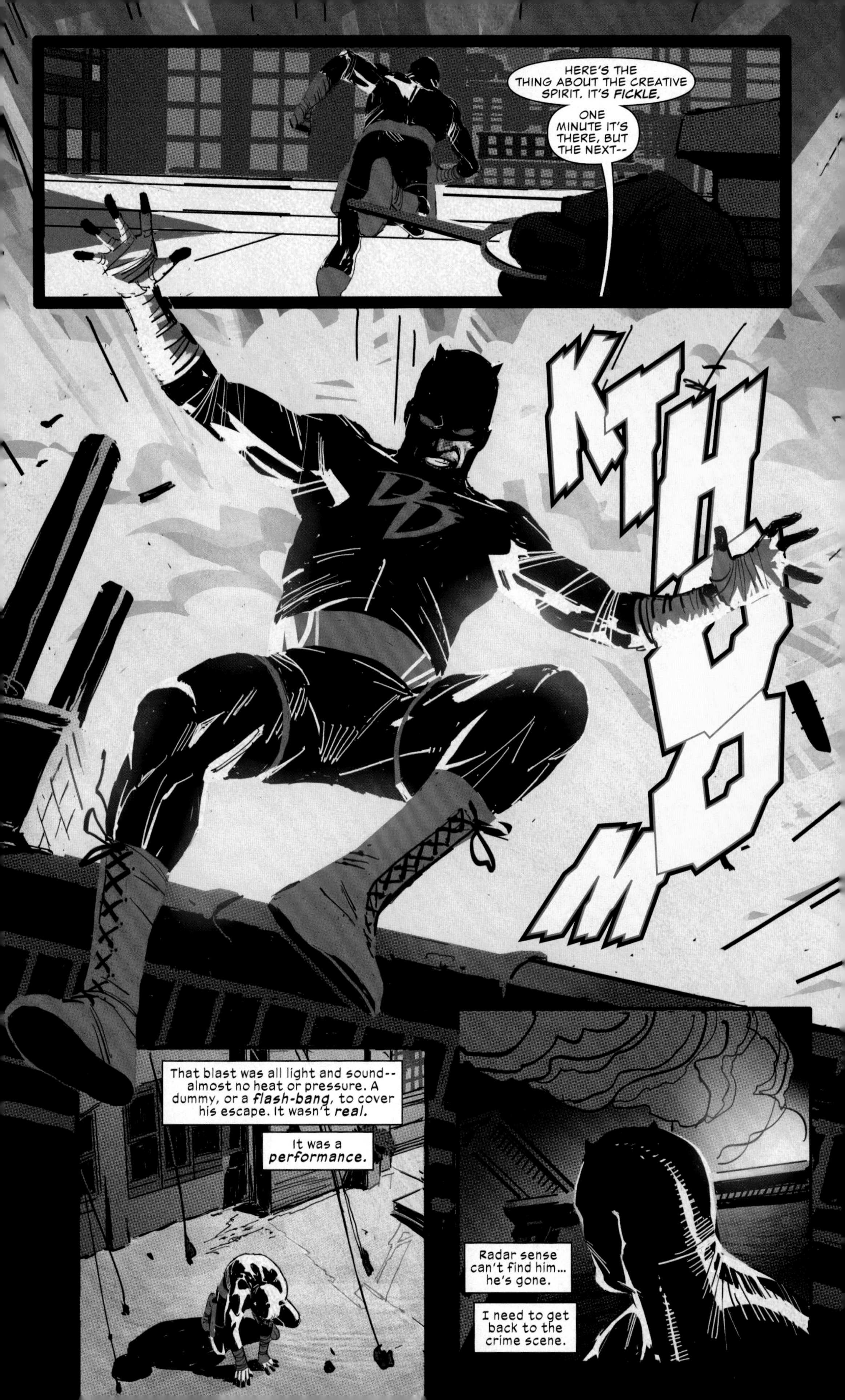
HERE'S THE THING ABOUT THE CREATIVE SPIRIT. IT'S *FICKLE.*
ONE MINUTE IT'S THERE, BUT THE NEXT--
KTHOOM
That blast was all light and sound--almost no heat or pressure. A dummy, or a *flash-bang*, to cover his escape. It wasn't *real.*
It was a *performance.*
Radar sense can't find him... he's gone.
I need to get back to the crime scene.

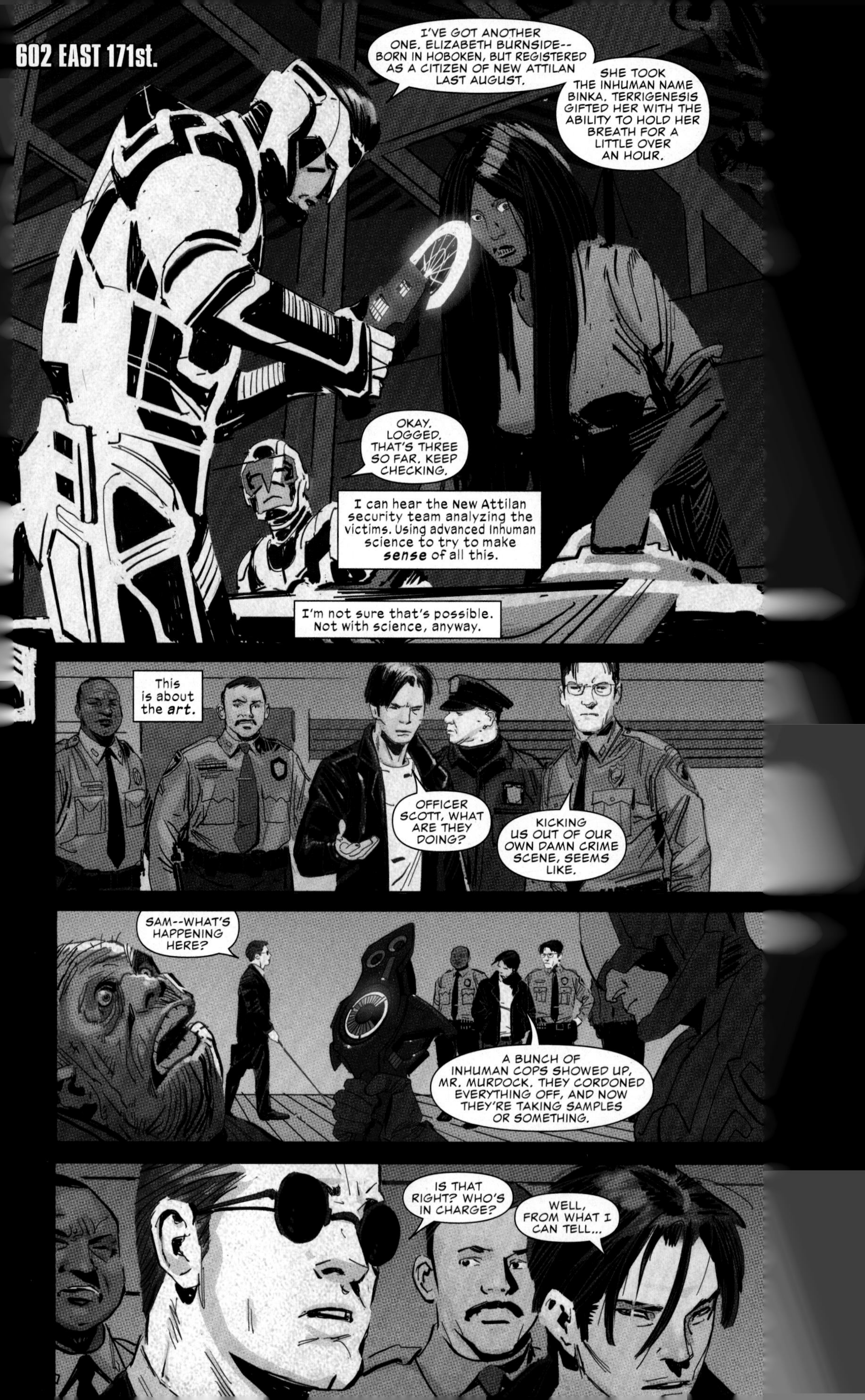
602 EAST 171st.
I'VE GOT ANOTHER ONE. ELIZABETH BURNSIDE--BORN IN HOBOKEN, BUT REGISTERED AS A CITIZEN OF NEW ATTILAN LAST AUGUST.
SHE TOOK THE INHUMAN NAME BINKA. TERRIGENESIS GIFTED HER WITH THE ABILITY TO HOLD HER BREATH FOR A LITTLE OVER AN HOUR.
OKAY. LOGGED. THAT'S THREE SO FAR. KEEP CHECKING.
I can hear the New Attilan security team analyzing the victims. Using advanced Inhuman science to try to make *sense* of all this.
I'm not sure that's possible. Not with science, anyway.
This is about the *art*.
OFFICER SCOTT, WHAT ARE THEY DOING?
KICKING US OUT OF OUR OWN DAMN CRIME SCENE, SEEMS LIKE.
SAM--WHAT'S HAPPENING HERE?
A BUNCH OF INHUMAN COPS SHOWED UP, MR. MURDOCK. THEY CORDONED EVERYTHING OFF, AND NOW THEY'RE TAKING SAMPLES OR SOMETHING.
IS THAT RIGHT? WHO'S IN CHARGE?
WELL, FROM WHAT I CAN TELL...

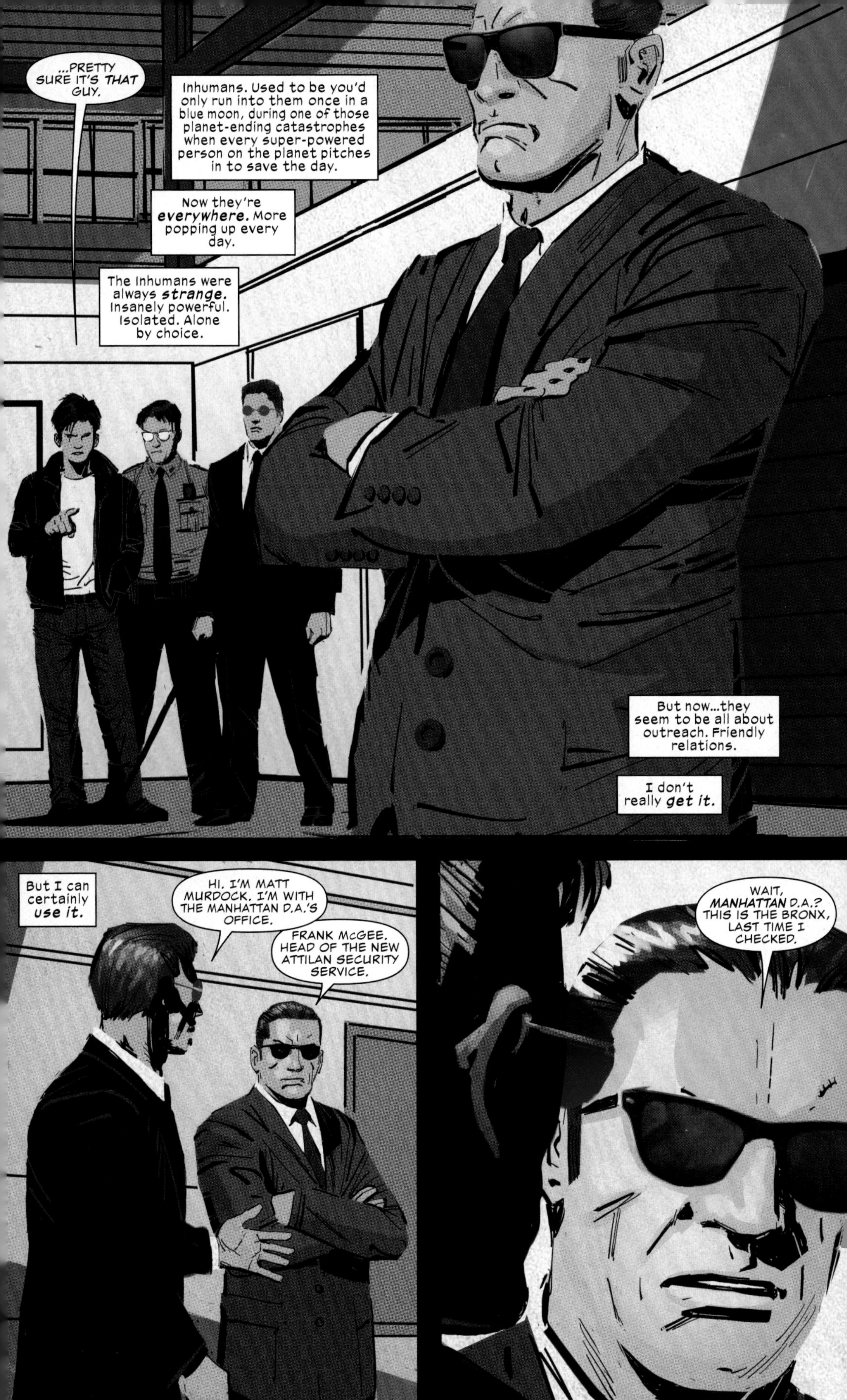
...PRETTY SURE IT'S THAT GUY.
Inhumans. Used to be you'd only run into them once in a blue moon, during one of those planet-ending catastrophes when every super-powered person on the planet pitches in to save the day.
Now they're everywhere. More popping up every day.
The Inhumans were always strange. Insanely powerful. Isolated. Alone by choice.
But now...they seem to be all about outreach. Friendly relations.
I don't really get it.
But I can certainly use it.
HI. I'M MATT MURDOCK. I'M WITH THE MANHATTAN D.A.'S OFFICE.
FRANK McGEE. HEAD OF THE NEW ATTILAN SECURITY SERVICE.
WAIT, MANHATTAN D.A.? THIS IS THE BRONX, LAST TIME I CHECKED.

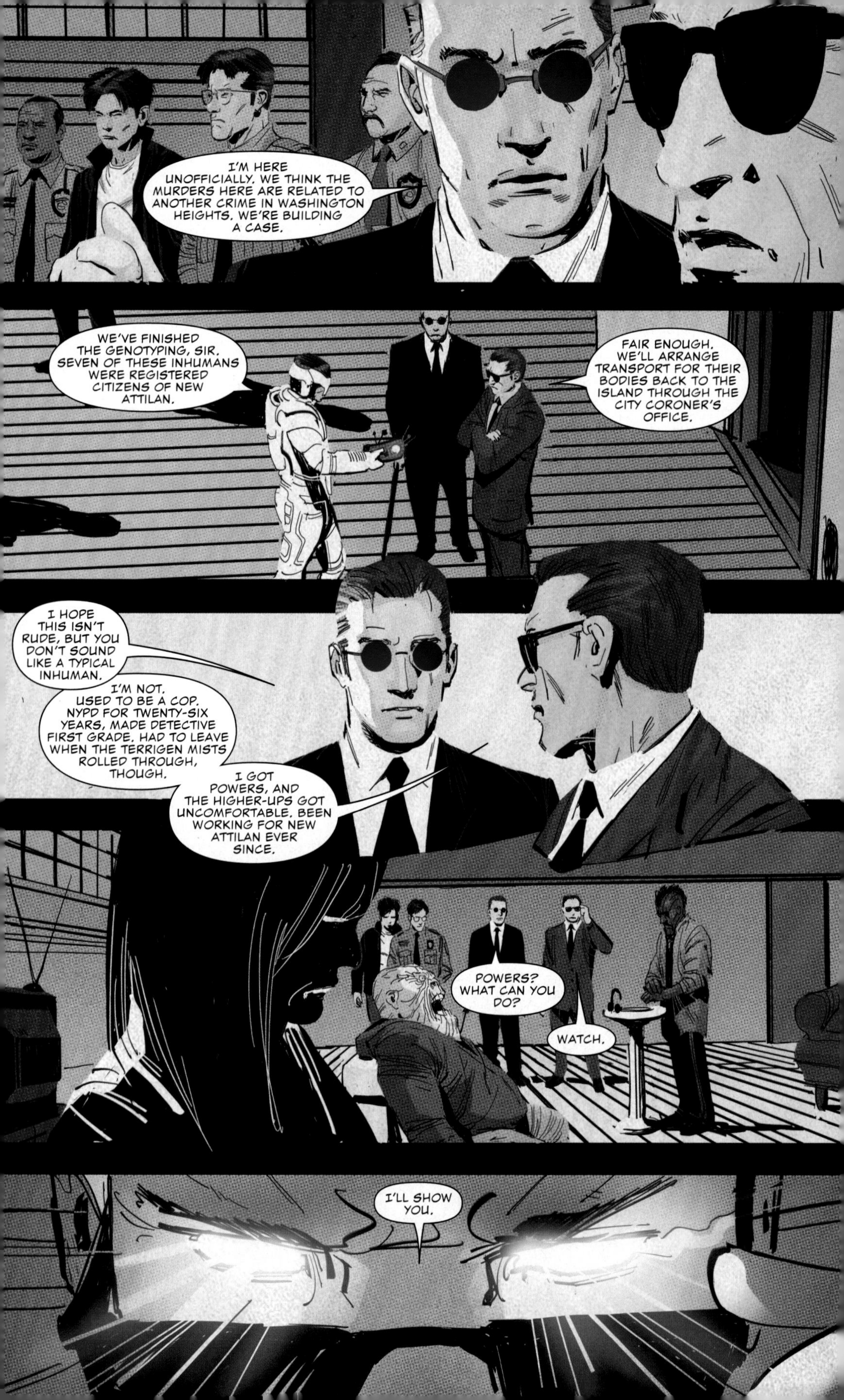
I'M HERE UNOFFICIALLY. WE THINK THE MURDERS HERE ARE RELATED TO ANOTHER CRIME IN WASHINGTON HEIGHTS. WE'RE BUILDING A CASE.
WE'VE FINISHED THE GENOTYPING, SIR. SEVEN OF THESE INHUMANS WERE REGISTERED CITIZENS OF NEW ATTILAN.
FAIR ENOUGH. WE'LL ARRANGE TRANSPORT FOR THEIR BODIES BACK TO THE ISLAND THROUGH THE CITY CORONER'S OFFICE.
I HOPE THIS ISN'T RUDE, BUT YOU DON'T SOUND LIKE A TYPICAL INHUMAN.
I'M NOT. USED TO BE A COP. NYPD FOR TWENTY-SIX YEARS, MADE DETECTIVE FIRST GRADE. HAD TO LEAVE WHEN THE TERRIGEN MISTS ROLLED THROUGH, THOUGH.
I GOT POWERS, AND THE HIGHER-UPS GOT UNCOMFORTABLE. BEEN WORKING FOR NEW ATTILAN EVER SINCE.
POWERS? WHAT CAN YOU DO?
WATCH.
I'LL SHOW YOU.

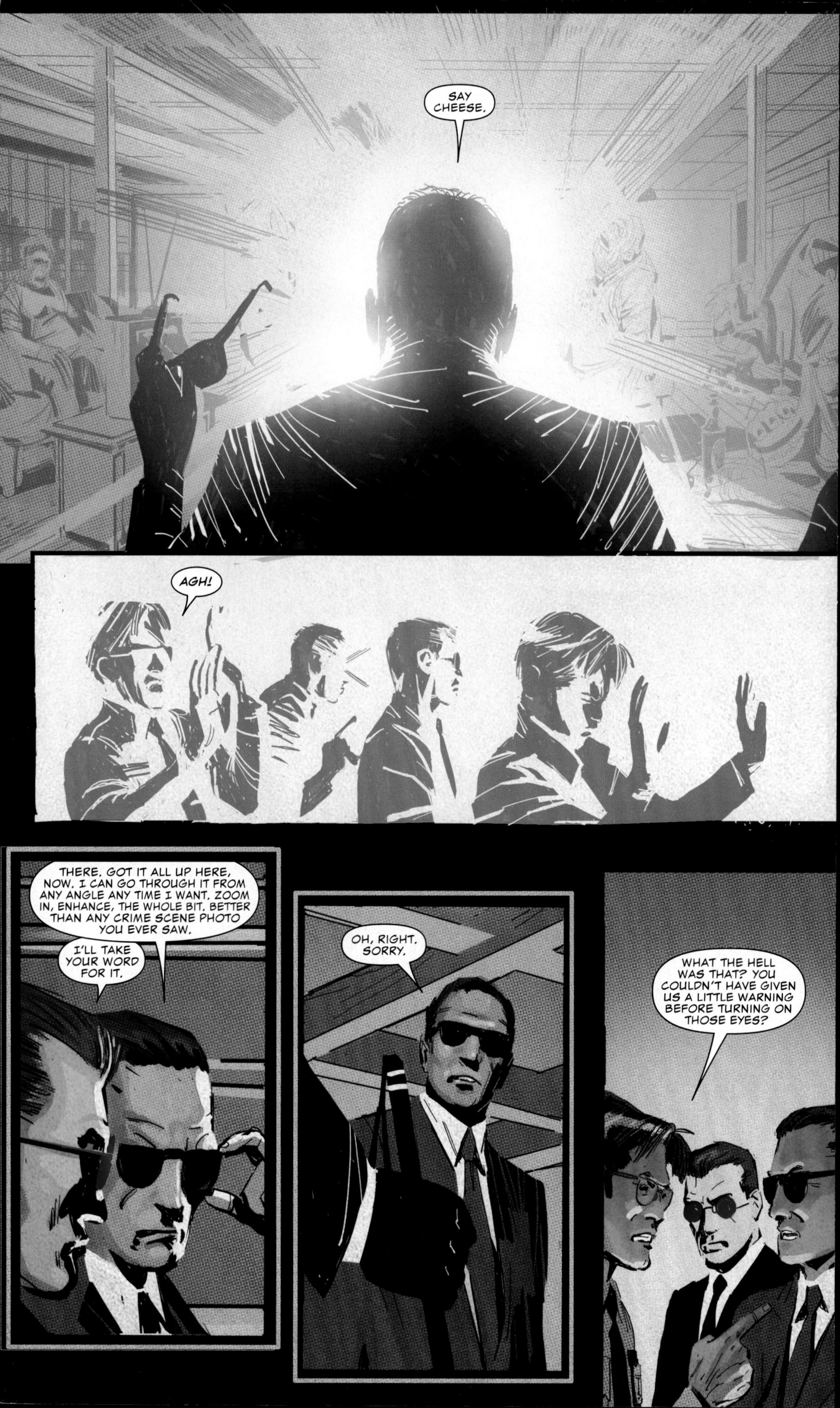
SAY CHEESE.
AGH!
THERE. GOT IT ALL UP HERE, NOW. I CAN GO THROUGH IT FROM ANY ANGLE ANY TIME I WANT. ZOOM IN, ENHANCE, THE WHOLE BIT. BETTER THAN ANY CRIME SCENE PHOTO YOU EVER SAW.
I'LL TAKE YOUR WORD FOR IT.
OH, RIGHT. SORRY.
WHAT THE HELL WAS THAT? YOU COULDN'T HAVE GIVEN US A LITTLE WARNING BEFORE TURNING ON THOSE EYES?

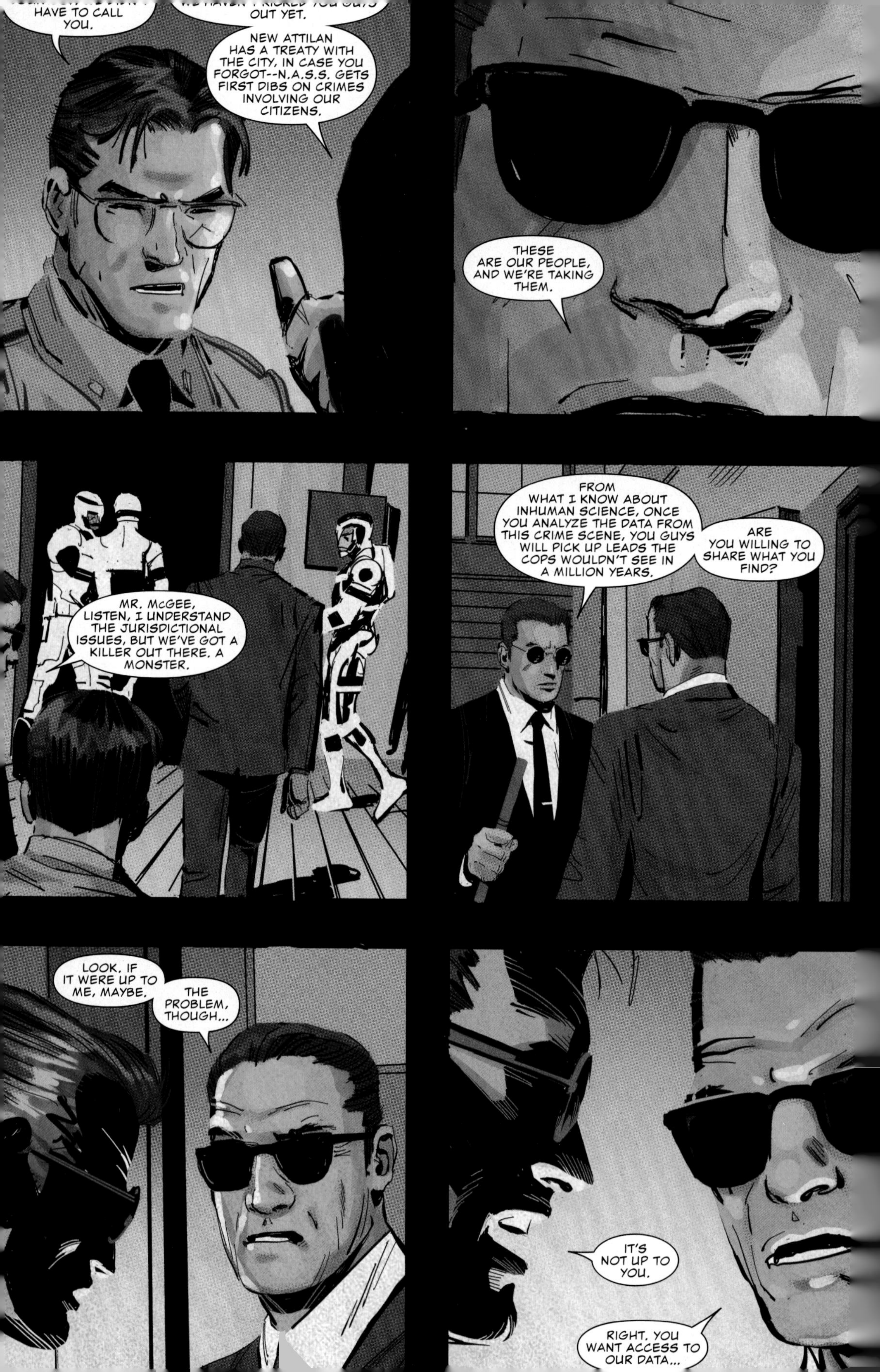
HAVE TO CALL YOU.
OUT YET.
NEW ATTILAN HAS A TREATY WITH THE CITY, IN CASE YOU FORGOT--N.A.S.S. GETS FIRST DIBS ON CRIMES INVOLVING OUR CITIZENS.
THESE ARE OUR PEOPLE, AND WE'RE TAKING THEM.
MR. McGEE, LISTEN, I UNDERSTAND THE JURISDICTIONAL ISSUES, BUT WE'VE GOT A KILLER OUT THERE. A MONSTER.
FROM WHAT I KNOW ABOUT INHUMAN SCIENCE, ONCE YOU ANALYZE THE DATA FROM THIS CRIME SCENE, YOU GUYS WILL PICK UP LEADS THE COPS WOULDN'T SEE IN A MILLION YEARS.
ARE YOU WILLING TO SHARE WHAT YOU FIND?
LOOK, IF IT WERE UP TO ME, MAYBE.
THE PROBLEM, THOUGH...
IT'S NOT UP TO YOU.
RIGHT. YOU WANT ACCESS TO OUR DATA...

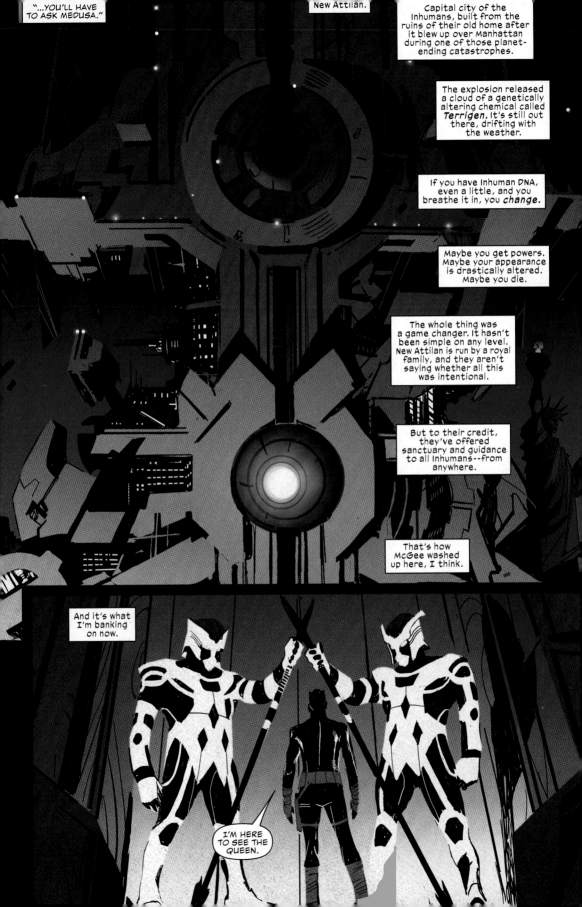

"...YOU'LL HAVE TO ASK MEDUSA."

New Attilan.

Capital city of the Inhumans, built from the ruins of their old home after it blew up over Manhattan during one of those planet-ending catastrophes.

The explosion released a cloud of a genetically altering chemical called *Terrigen.* It's still out there, drifting with the weather.

If you have Inhuman DNA, even a little, and you breathe it in, you *change.*

Maybe you get powers. Maybe your appearance is drastically altered. Maybe you die.

The whole thing was a game changer. It hasn't been simple on any level. New Attilan is run by a royal family, and they aren't saying whether all this was intentional.

But to their credit, they've offered sanctuary and guidance to all Inhumans--from anywhere.

That's how McGee washed up here, I think.

And it's what I'm banking on now.

I'M HERE TO SEE THE QUEEN.

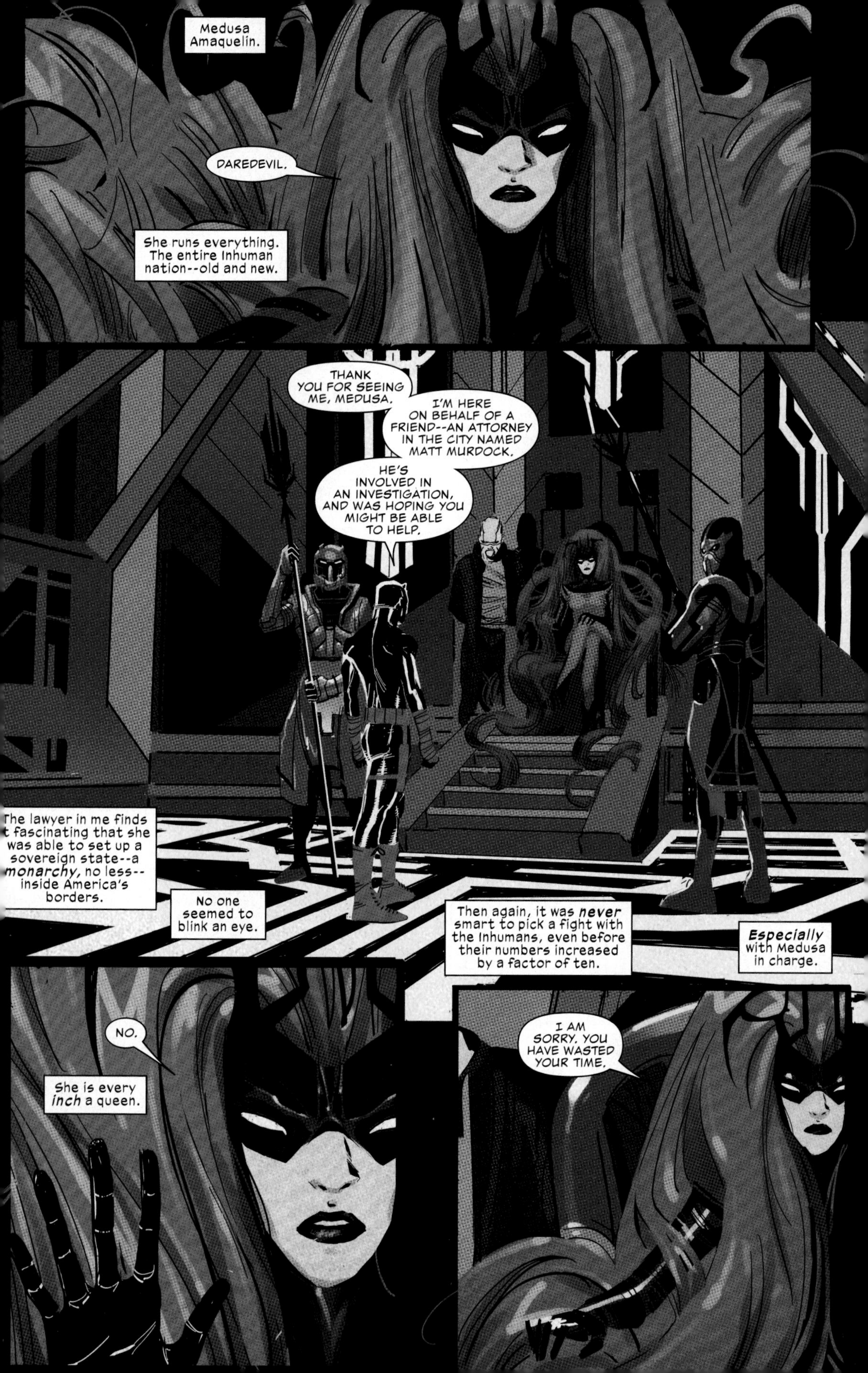

Medusa Amaquelin.
DAREDEVIL.
She runs everything. The entire Inhuman nation--old and new.
THANK YOU FOR SEEING ME, MEDUSA.
I'M HERE ON BEHALF OF A FRIEND--AN ATTORNEY IN THE CITY NAMED MATT MURDOCK.
HE'S INVOLVED IN AN INVESTIGATION, AND WAS HOPING YOU MIGHT BE ABLE TO HELP.
The lawyer in me finds it fascinating that she was able to set up a sovereign state--a *monarchy,* no less--inside America's borders.
No one seemed to blink an eye.
Then again, it was *never* smart to pick a fight with the Inhumans, even before their numbers increased by a factor of ten.
Especially with Medusa in charge.
NO.
She is every *inch* a queen.
I AM SORRY. YOU HAVE WASTED YOUR TIME.

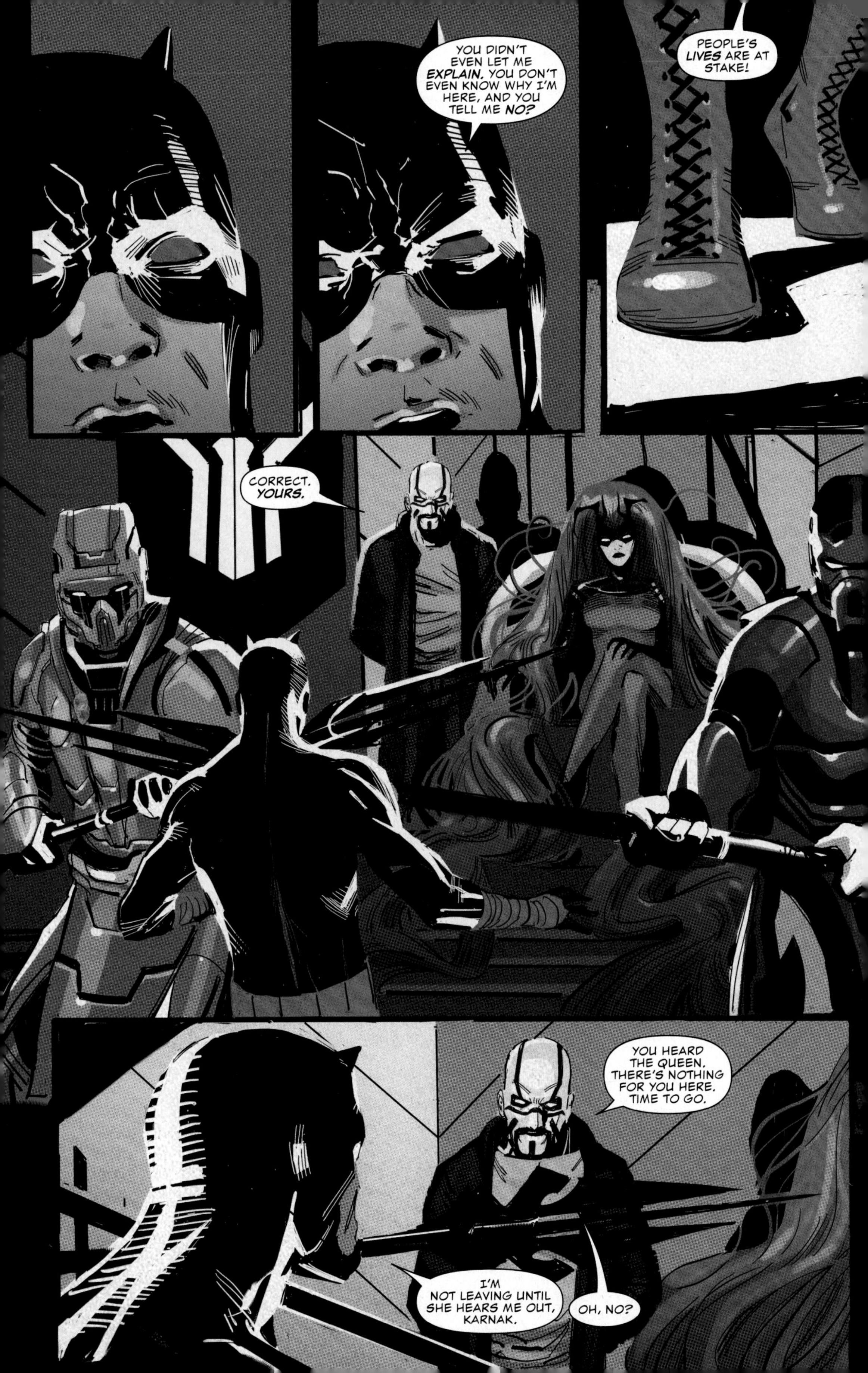

YOU DIDN'T EVEN LET ME EXPLAIN. YOU DON'T EVEN KNOW WHY I'M HERE, AND YOU TELL ME NO?
PEOPLE'S LIVES ARE AT STAKE!
CORRECT. YOURS.
YOU HEARD THE QUEEN. THERE'S NOTHING FOR YOU HERE. TIME TO GO.
I'M NOT LEAVING UNTIL SHE HEARS ME OUT, KARNAK.
OH, NO?

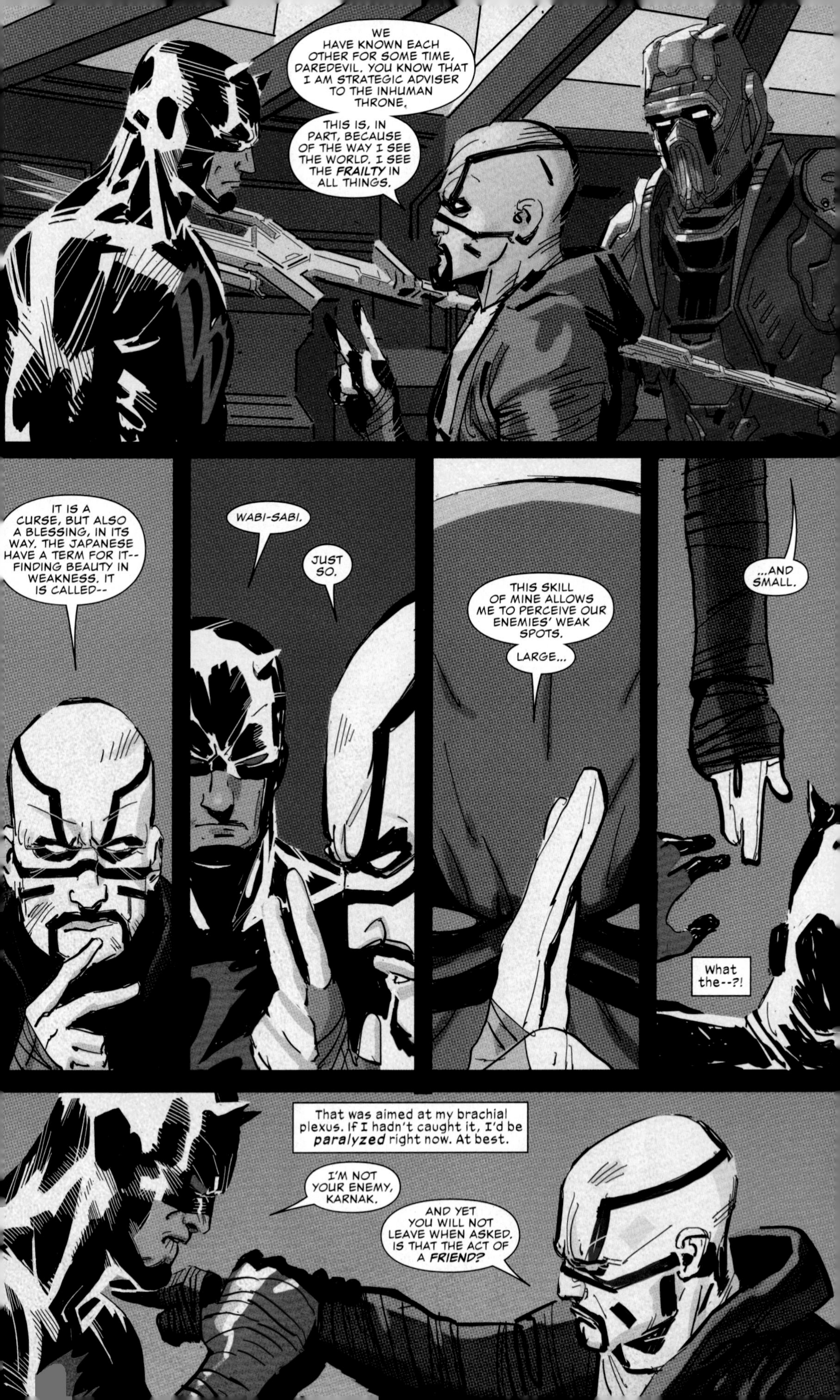
WE HAVE KNOWN EACH OTHER FOR SOME TIME, DAREDEVIL. YOU KNOW THAT I AM STRATEGIC ADVISER TO THE INHUMAN THRONE.
THIS IS, IN PART, BECAUSE OF THE WAY I SEE THE WORLD. I SEE THE *FRAILTY* IN ALL THINGS.
IT IS A CURSE, BUT ALSO A BLESSING, IN ITS WAY. THE JAPANESE HAVE A TERM FOR IT-- FINDING BEAUTY IN WEAKNESS. IT IS CALLED--
WABI-SABI.
JUST SO.
THIS SKILL OF MINE ALLOWS ME TO PERCEIVE OUR ENEMIES' WEAK SPOTS.
LARGE...
...AND SMALL.
What the--?!
That was aimed at my brachial plexus. If I hadn't caught it, I'd be *paralyzed* right now. At best.
I'M NOT YOUR ENEMY, KARNAK.
AND YET YOU WILL NOT LEAVE WHEN ASKED. IS THAT THE ACT OF A *FRIEND?*

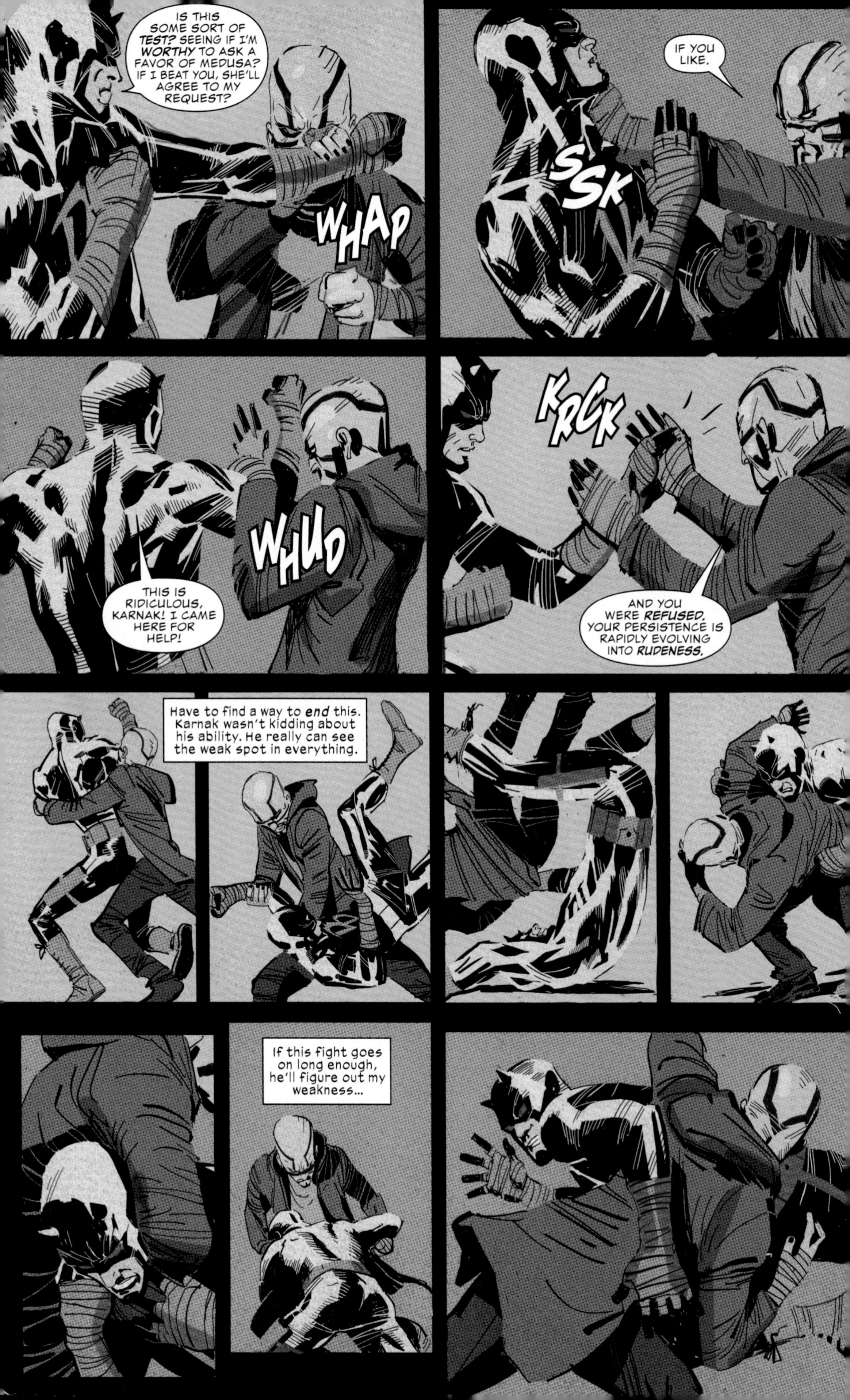
IS THIS SOME SORT OF TEST? SEEING IF I'M WORTHY TO ASK A FAVOR OF MEDUSA? IF I BEAT YOU, SHE'LL AGREE TO MY REQUEST?
WHAP
IF YOU LIKE.
SSK
WHUD
THIS IS RIDICULOUS, KARNAK! I CAME HERE FOR HELP!
KRCK
AND YOU WERE REFUSED. YOUR PERSISTENCE IS RAPIDLY EVOLVING INTO RUDENESS.
Have to find a way to end this. Karnak wasn't kidding about his ability. He really can see the weak spot in everything.
If this fight goes on long enough, he'll figure out my weakness...

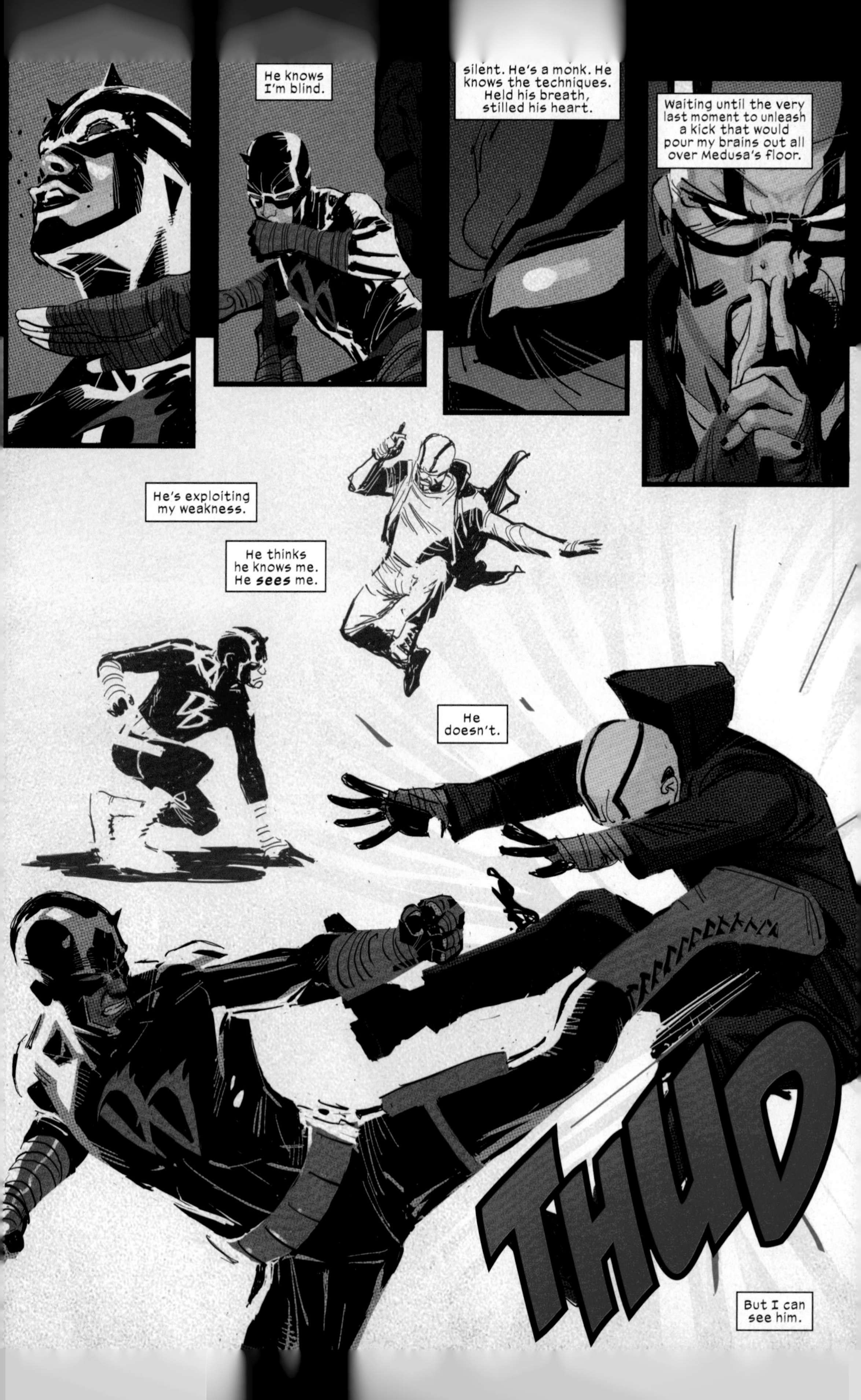
He knows I'm blind.
silent. He's a monk. He knows the techniques. Held his breath, stilled his heart.
Waiting until the very last moment to unleash a kick that would pour my brains out all over Medusa's floor.
He's exploiting my weakness.
He thinks he knows me. He *sees* me.
He doesn't.
THUD
But I can see him.

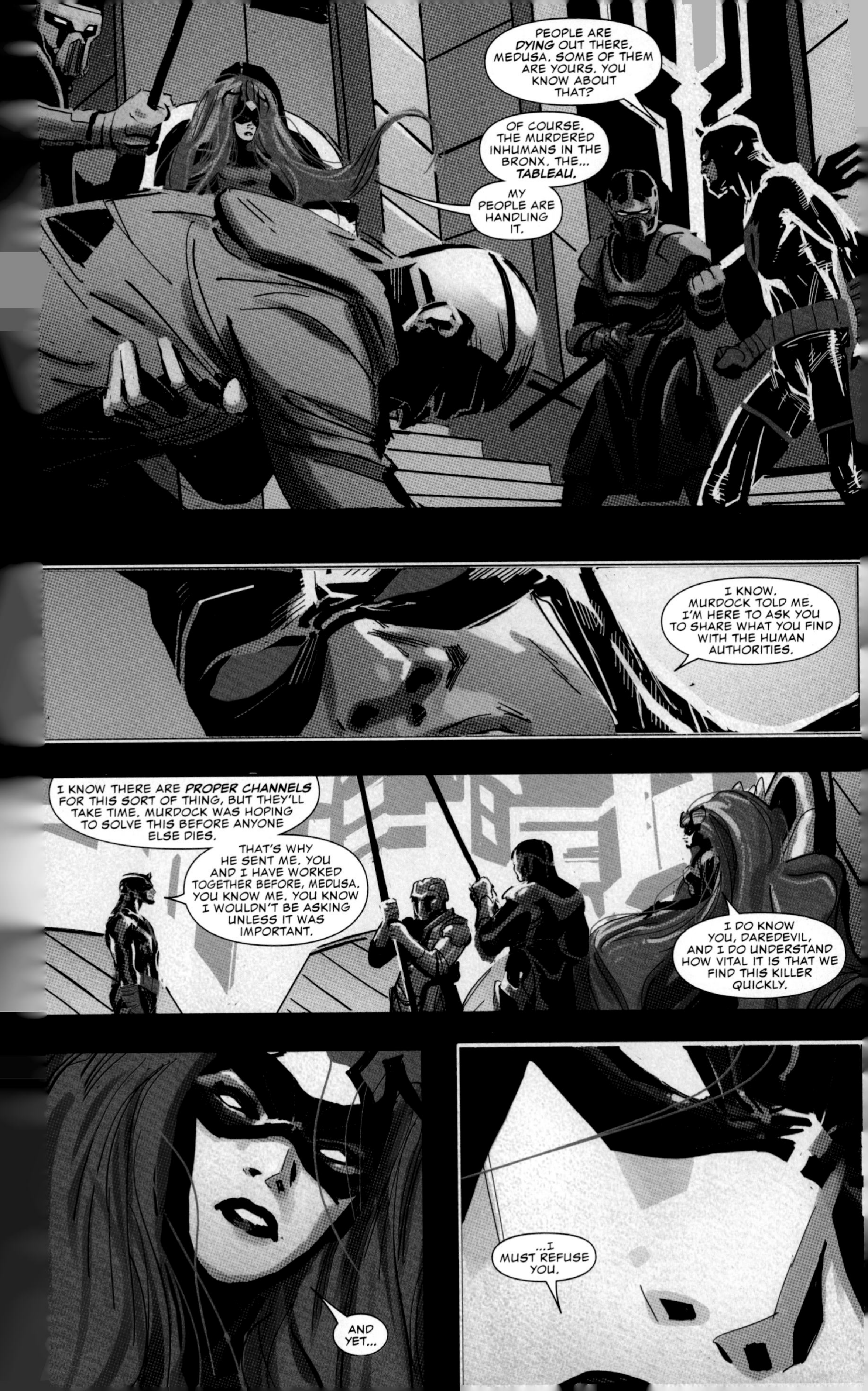
PEOPLE ARE DYING OUT THERE, MEDUSA. SOME OF THEM ARE YOURS. YOU KNOW ABOUT THAT?
OF COURSE. THE MURDERED INHUMANS IN THE BRONX. THE... TABLEAU.
MY PEOPLE ARE HANDLING IT.
I KNOW. MURDOCK TOLD ME. I'M HERE TO ASK YOU TO SHARE WHAT YOU FIND WITH THE HUMAN AUTHORITIES.
I KNOW THERE ARE PROPER CHANNELS FOR THIS SORT OF THING, BUT THEY'LL TAKE TIME. MURDOCK WAS HOPING TO SOLVE THIS BEFORE ANYONE ELSE DIES.
THAT'S WHY HE SENT ME. YOU AND I HAVE WORKED TOGETHER BEFORE, MEDUSA. YOU KNOW ME. YOU KNOW I WOULDN'T BE ASKING UNLESS IT WAS IMPORTANT.
I DO KNOW YOU, DAREDEVIL, AND I DO UNDERSTAND HOW VITAL IT IS THAT WE FIND THIS KILLER QUICKLY.
AND YET...
...I MUST REFUSE YOU.

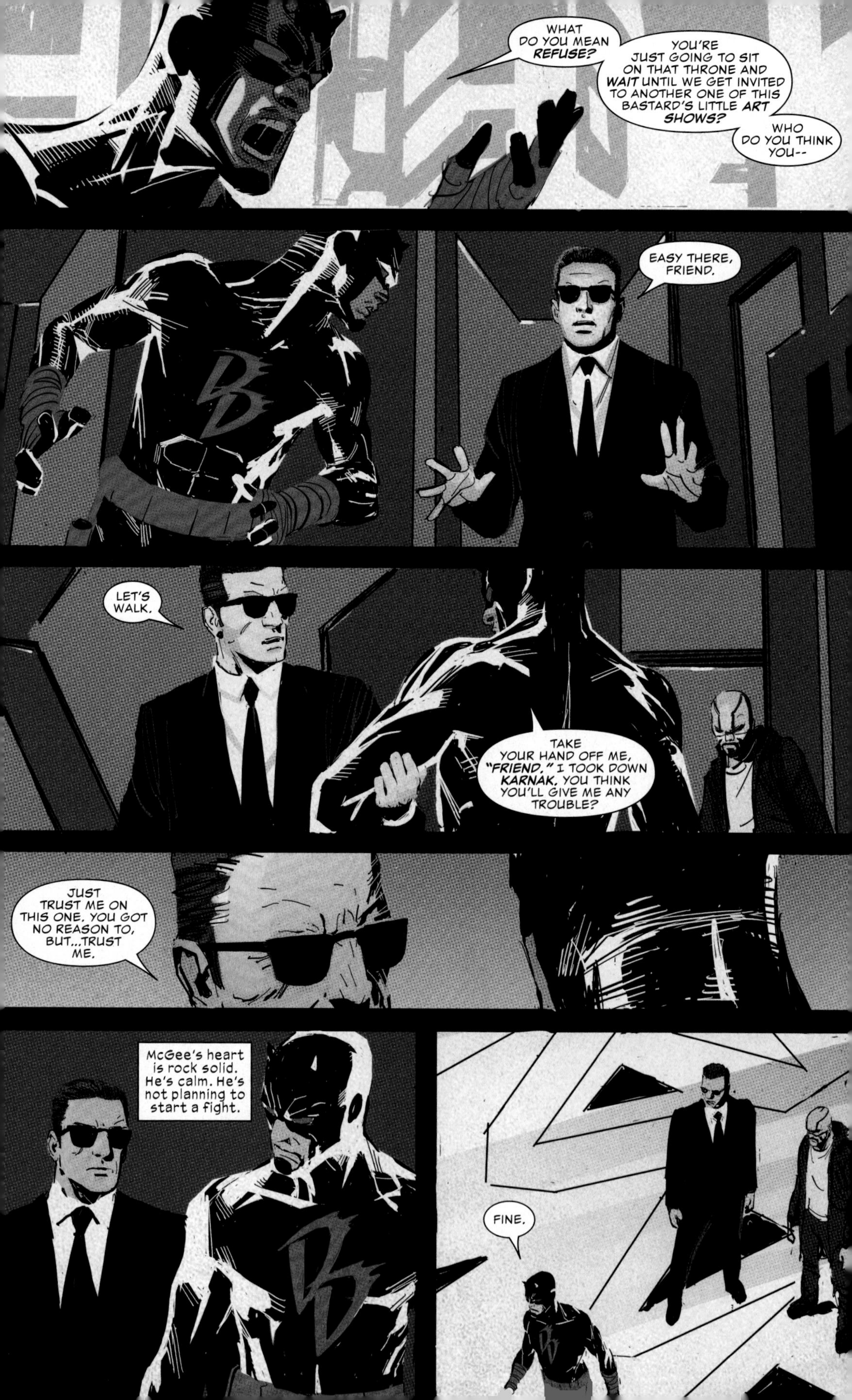
WHAT DO YOU MEAN REFUSE?
YOU'RE JUST GOING TO SIT ON THAT THRONE AND WAIT UNTIL WE GET INVITED TO ANOTHER ONE OF THIS BASTARD'S LITTLE ART SHOWS?
WHO DO YOU THINK YOU--
EASY THERE, FRIEND.
LET'S WALK.
TAKE YOUR HAND OFF ME, "FRIEND." I TOOK DOWN KARNAK. YOU THINK YOU'LL GIVE ME ANY TROUBLE?
JUST TRUST ME ON THIS ONE. YOU GOT NO REASON TO, BUT...TRUST ME.
McGee's heart is rock solid. He's calm. He's not planning to start a fight.
FINE.

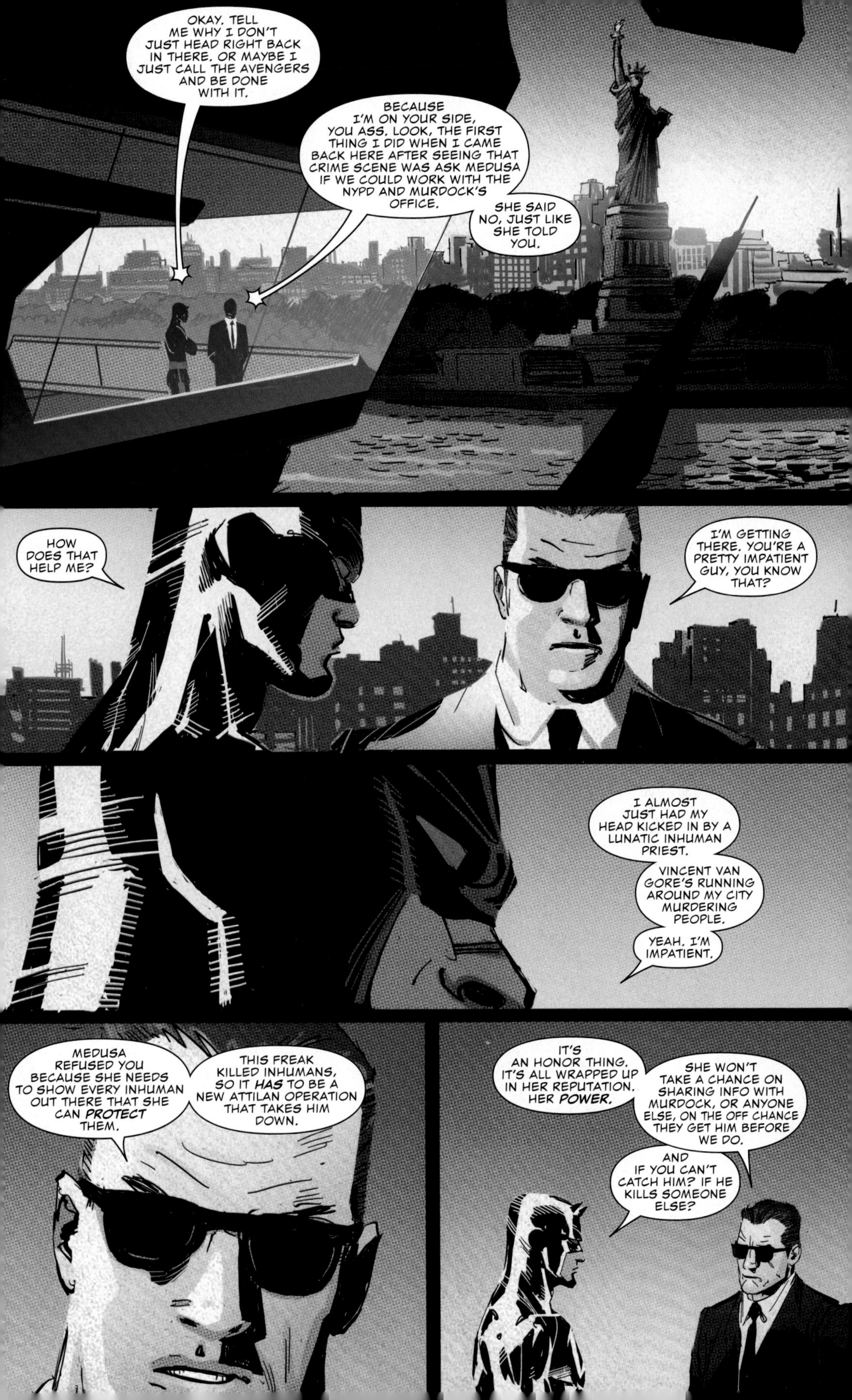
OKAY. TELL ME WHY I DON'T JUST HEAD RIGHT BACK IN THERE. OR MAYBE I JUST CALL THE AVENGERS AND BE DONE WITH IT.
BECAUSE I'M ON YOUR SIDE, YOU ASS. LOOK, THE FIRST THING I DID WHEN I CAME BACK HERE AFTER SEEING THAT CRIME SCENE WAS ASK MEDUSA IF WE COULD WORK WITH THE NYPD AND MURDOCK'S OFFICE.
SHE SAID NO, JUST LIKE SHE TOLD YOU.
HOW DOES THAT HELP ME?
I'M GETTING THERE. YOU'RE A PRETTY IMPATIENT GUY, YOU KNOW THAT?
I ALMOST JUST HAD MY HEAD KICKED IN BY A LUNATIC INHUMAN PRIEST.
VINCENT VAN GORE'S RUNNING AROUND MY CITY MURDERING PEOPLE.
YEAH. I'M IMPATIENT.
MEDUSA REFUSED YOU BECAUSE SHE NEEDS TO SHOW EVERY INHUMAN OUT THERE THAT SHE CAN *PROTECT* THEM.
THIS FREAK KILLED INHUMANS, SO IT *HAS* TO BE A NEW ATTILAN OPERATION THAT TAKES HIM DOWN.
IT'S AN HONOR THING. IT'S ALL WRAPPED UP IN HER REPUTATION. HER *POWER.*
SHE WON'T TAKE A CHANCE ON SHARING INFO WITH MURDOCK, OR ANYONE ELSE, ON THE OFF CHANCE THEY GET HIM BEFORE WE DO.
AND IF YOU CAN'T CATCH HIM? IF HE KILLS SOMEONE ELSE?

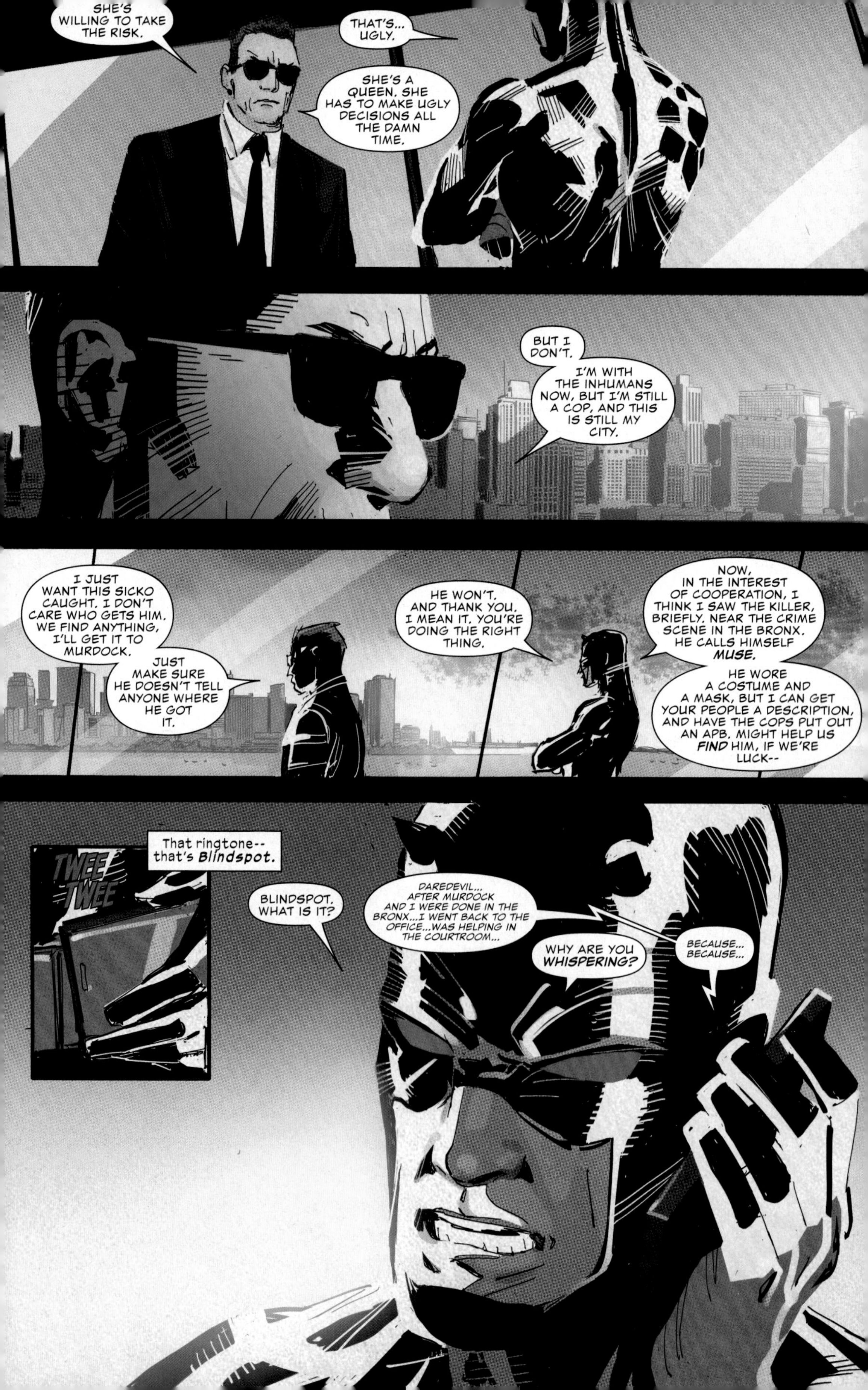
SHE'S WILLING TO TAKE THE RISK.
THAT'S... UGLY.
SHE'S A QUEEN. SHE HAS TO MAKE UGLY DECISIONS ALL THE DAMN TIME.
BUT I DON'T.
I'M WITH THE INHUMANS NOW, BUT I'M STILL A COP, AND THIS IS STILL MY CITY.
I JUST WANT THIS SICKO CAUGHT. I DON'T CARE WHO GETS HIM. WE FIND ANYTHING, I'LL GET IT TO MURDOCK.
JUST MAKE SURE HE DOESN'T TELL ANYONE WHERE HE GOT IT.
HE WON'T. AND THANK YOU. I MEAN IT. YOU'RE DOING THE RIGHT THING.
NOW, IN THE INTEREST OF COOPERATION, I THINK I SAW THE KILLER, BRIEFLY. NEAR THE CRIME SCENE IN THE BRONX. HE CALLS HIMSELF MUSE.
HE WORE A COSTUME AND A MASK, BUT I CAN GET YOUR PEOPLE A DESCRIPTION, AND HAVE THE COPS PUT OUT AN APB. MIGHT HELP US FIND HIM, IF WE'RE LUCK--
TWEE TWEE
That ringtone-- that's Blindspot.
BLINDSPOT. WHAT IS IT?
DAREDEVIL... AFTER MURDOCK AND I WERE DONE IN THE BRONX...I WENT BACK TO THE OFFICE...WAS HELPING IN THE COURTROOM...
WHY ARE YOU WHISPERING?
BECAUSE... BECAUSE...

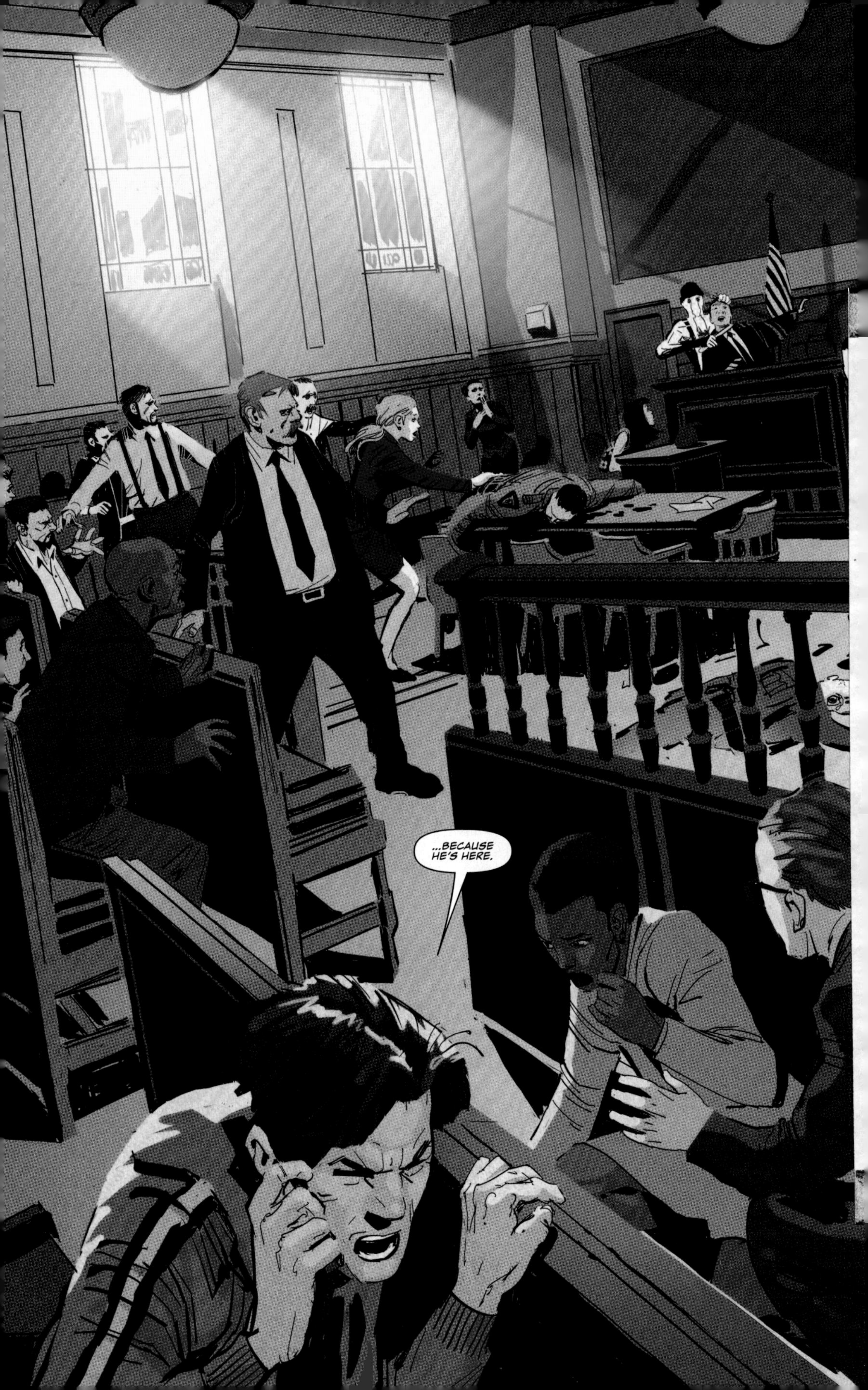
...BECAUSE HE'S HERE.

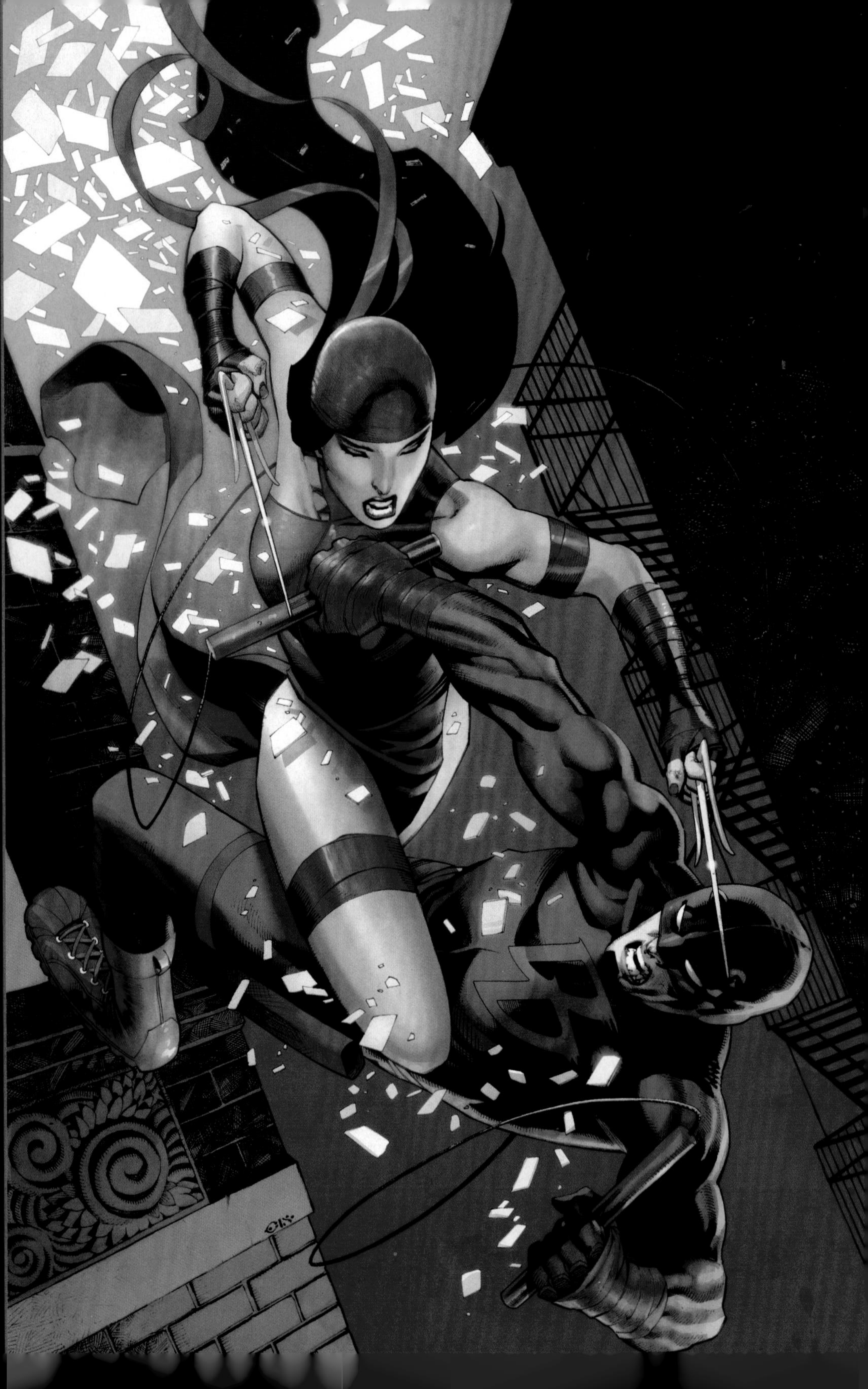

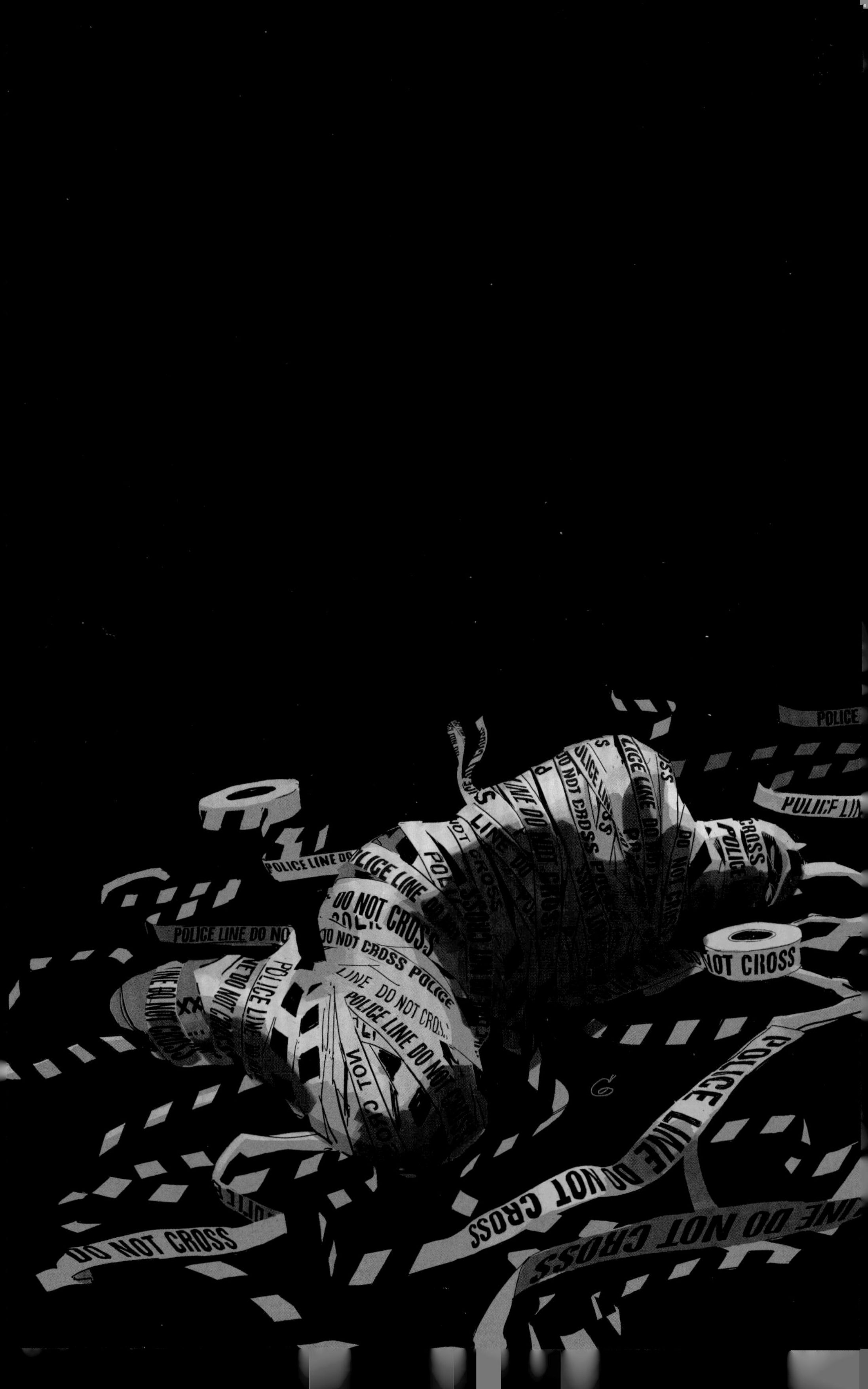
POLICE
POLICE LINE
POLICE LINE DO
POLICE LINE DO NO
DO NOT CROSS
NOT CROSS
POLICE LINE DO NOT CROSS
DO NOT CROSS
LINE DO NOT CROSS

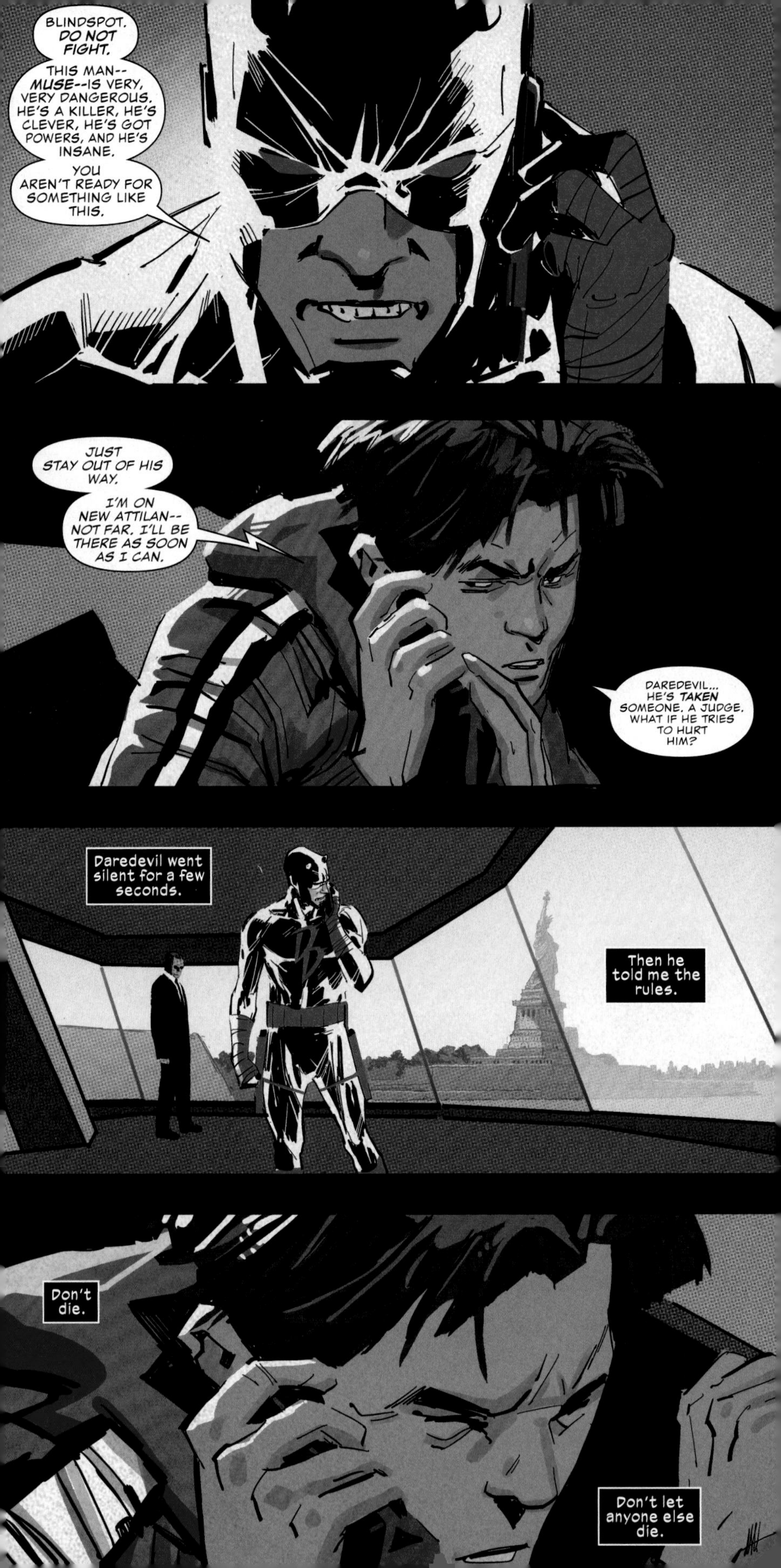

BLINDSPOT. DO NOT FIGHT.
THIS MAN-- MUSE--IS VERY, VERY DANGEROUS. HE'S A KILLER, HE'S CLEVER, HE'S GOT POWERS, AND HE'S INSANE.
YOU AREN'T READY FOR SOMETHING LIKE THIS.
JUST STAY OUT OF HIS WAY.
I'M ON NEW ATTILAN-- NOT FAR. I'LL BE THERE AS SOON AS I CAN.
DAREDEVIL... HE'S TAKEN SOMEONE. A JUDGE. WHAT IF HE TRIES TO HURT HIM?
Daredevil went silent for a few seconds.
Then he told me the rules.
Don't die.
Don't let anyone else die.

You follow both if you can.

But there will come a time when you can only follow one.

It's inevitable. Part of the job.

When it does, you make your choice, and you live with it.

DO YOU LIKE MY KNIFE? I CARVED IT MYSELF.

I BELIEVE YOU CAN FIND BEAUTY INSIDE JUST ABOUT ANYTHING.

Or you don't.

FOR INSTAN... MY KNIFE ONCE INSIDE NAMED CA... STRING

NOT A VERY *ATTRAC* LADY, IT HAS TO

BUT JUST LOOK AT HER NOW.

LOSE THE KNIFE! NOW!

SURE THING.

AGH!

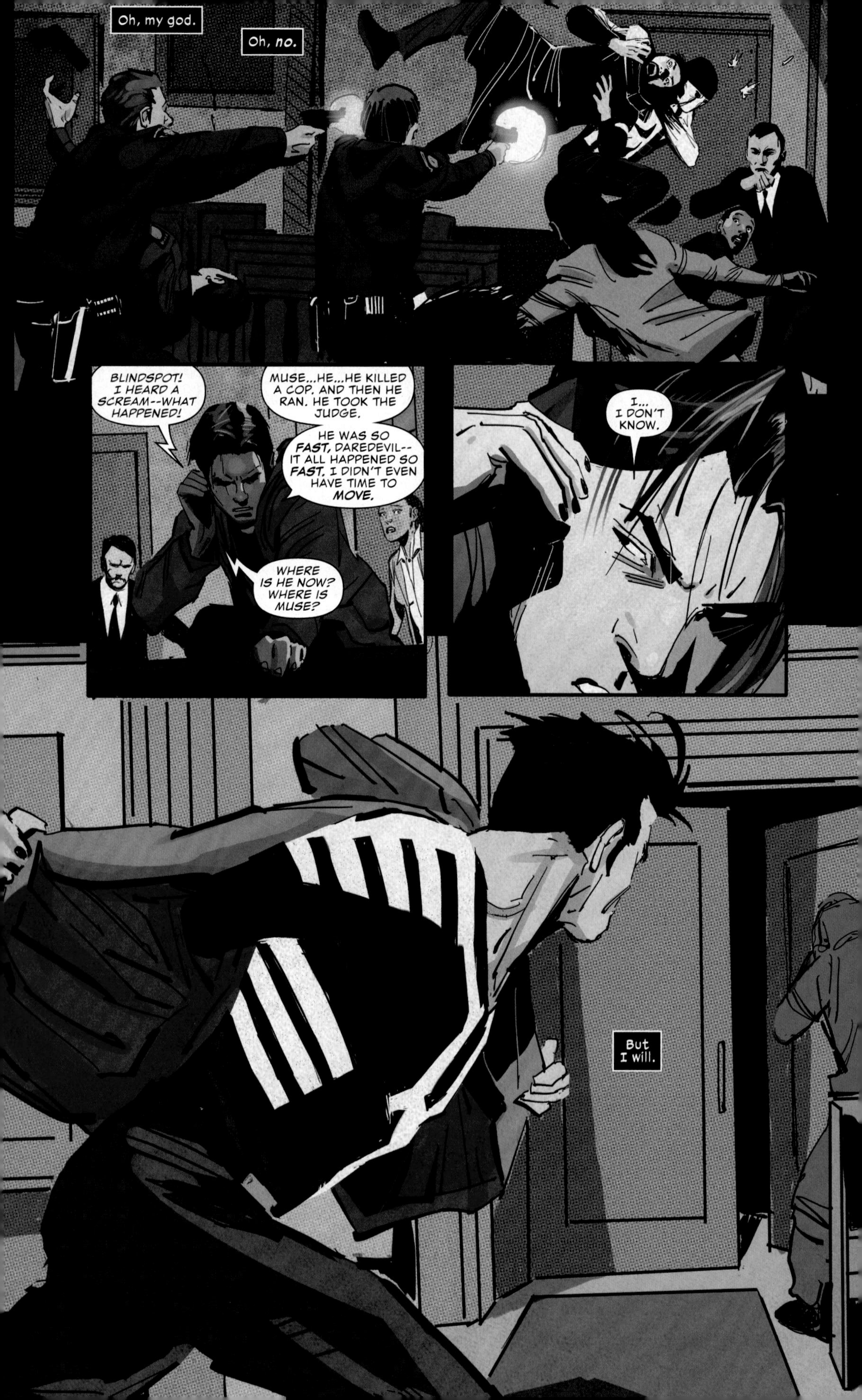

Oh, my god.
Oh, no.
BLINDSPOT! I HEARD A SCREAM--WHAT HAPPENED!
MUSE...HE...HE KILLED A COP. AND THEN HE RAN. HE TOOK THE JUDGE.
HE WAS SO FAST, DAREDEVIL-- IT ALL HAPPENED SO FAST. I DIDN'T EVEN HAVE TIME TO MOVE.
WHERE IS HE NOW? WHERE IS MUSE?
I... I DON'T KNOW.
But I will.

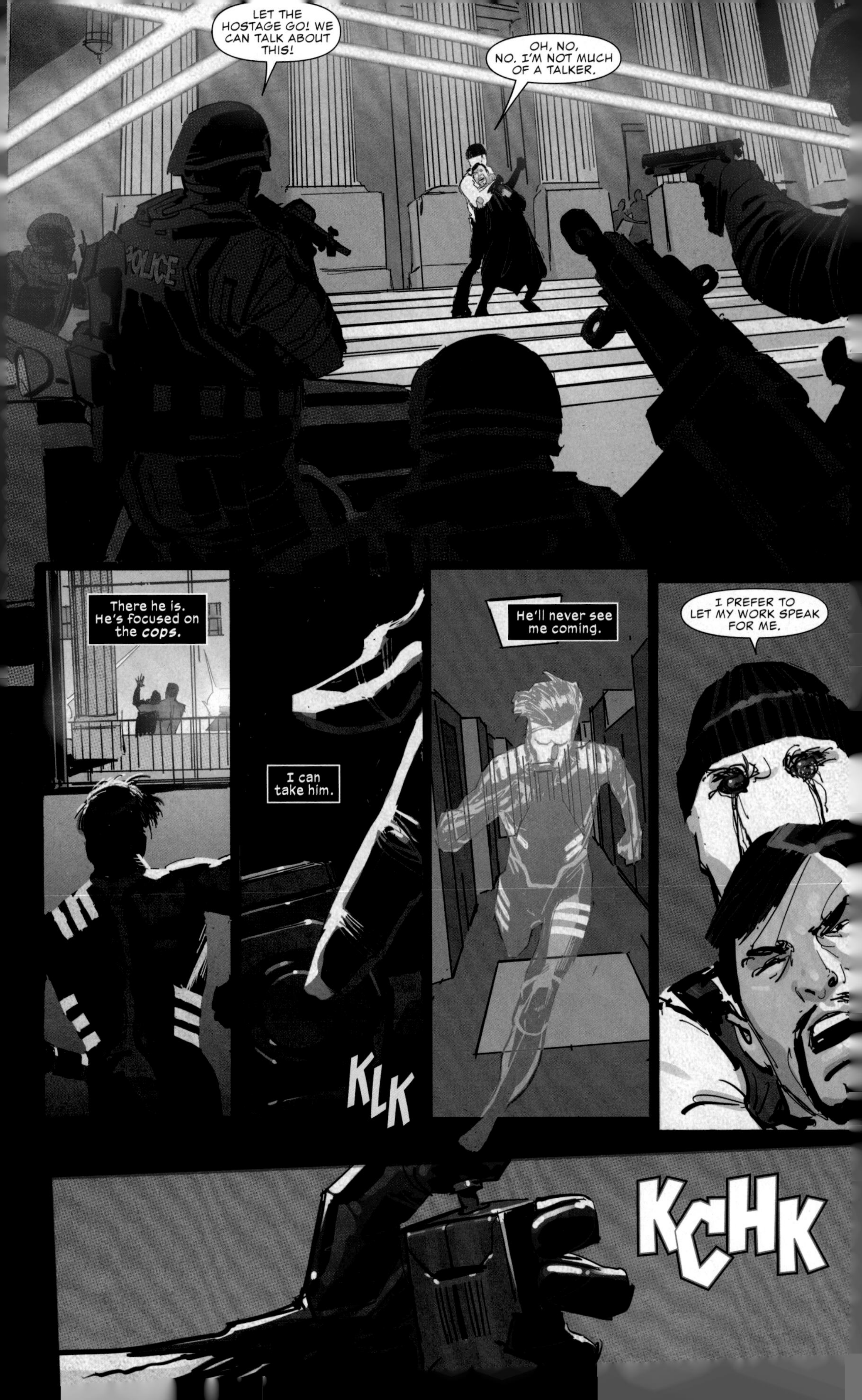
LET THE HOSTAGE GO! WE CAN TALK ABOUT THIS!
OH, NO, NO. I'M NOT MUCH OF A TALKER.
POLICE
There he is. He's focused on the *cops.*
I can take him.
KLK
He'll never see me coming.
I PREFER TO LET MY WORK SPEAK FOR ME.
KCHK

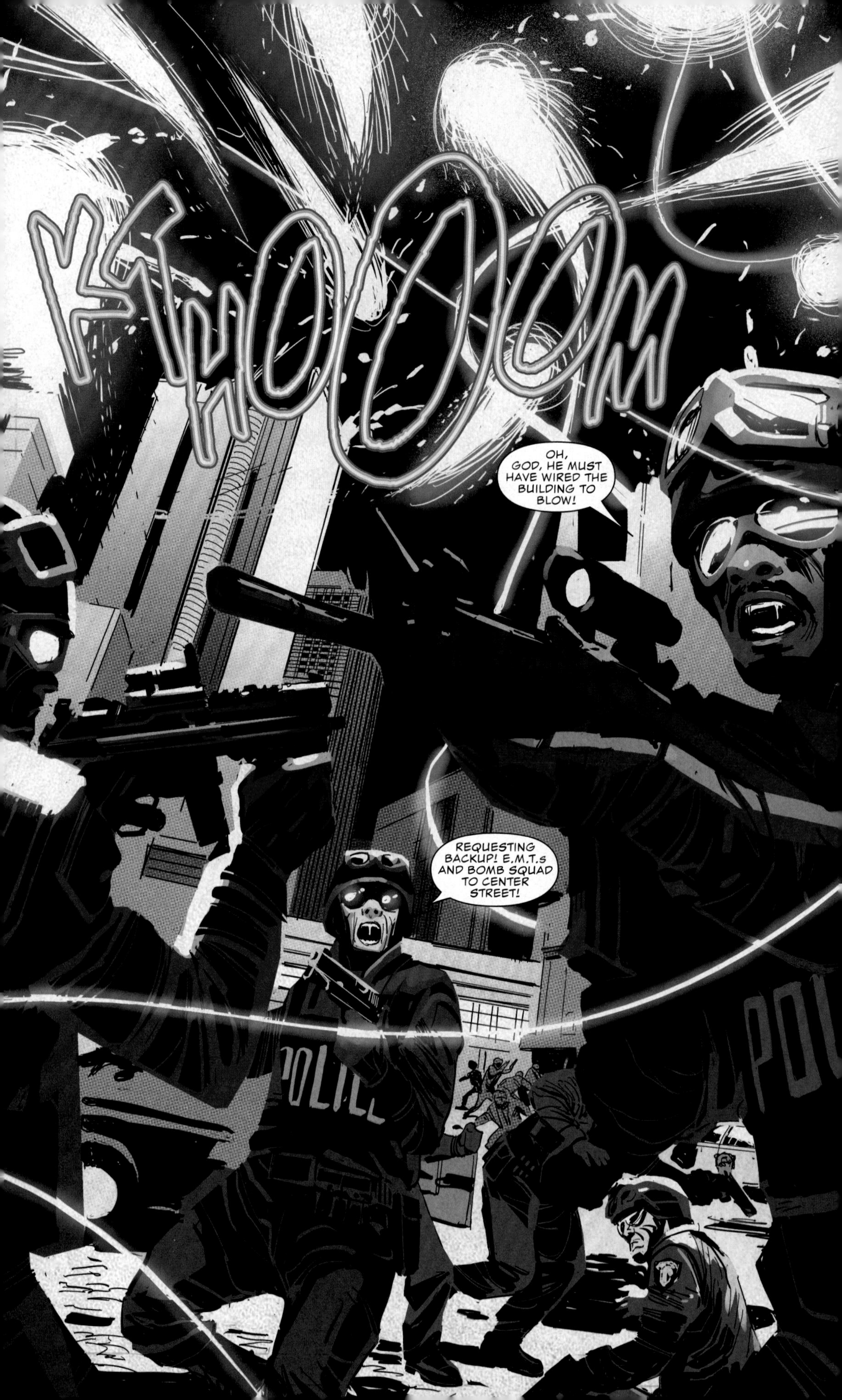
KATHOOOOM
OH, GOD, HE MUST HAVE WIRED THE BUILDING TO BLOW!
REQUESTING BACKUP! E.M.T.s AND BOMB SQUAD TO CENTER STREET!
POLICE

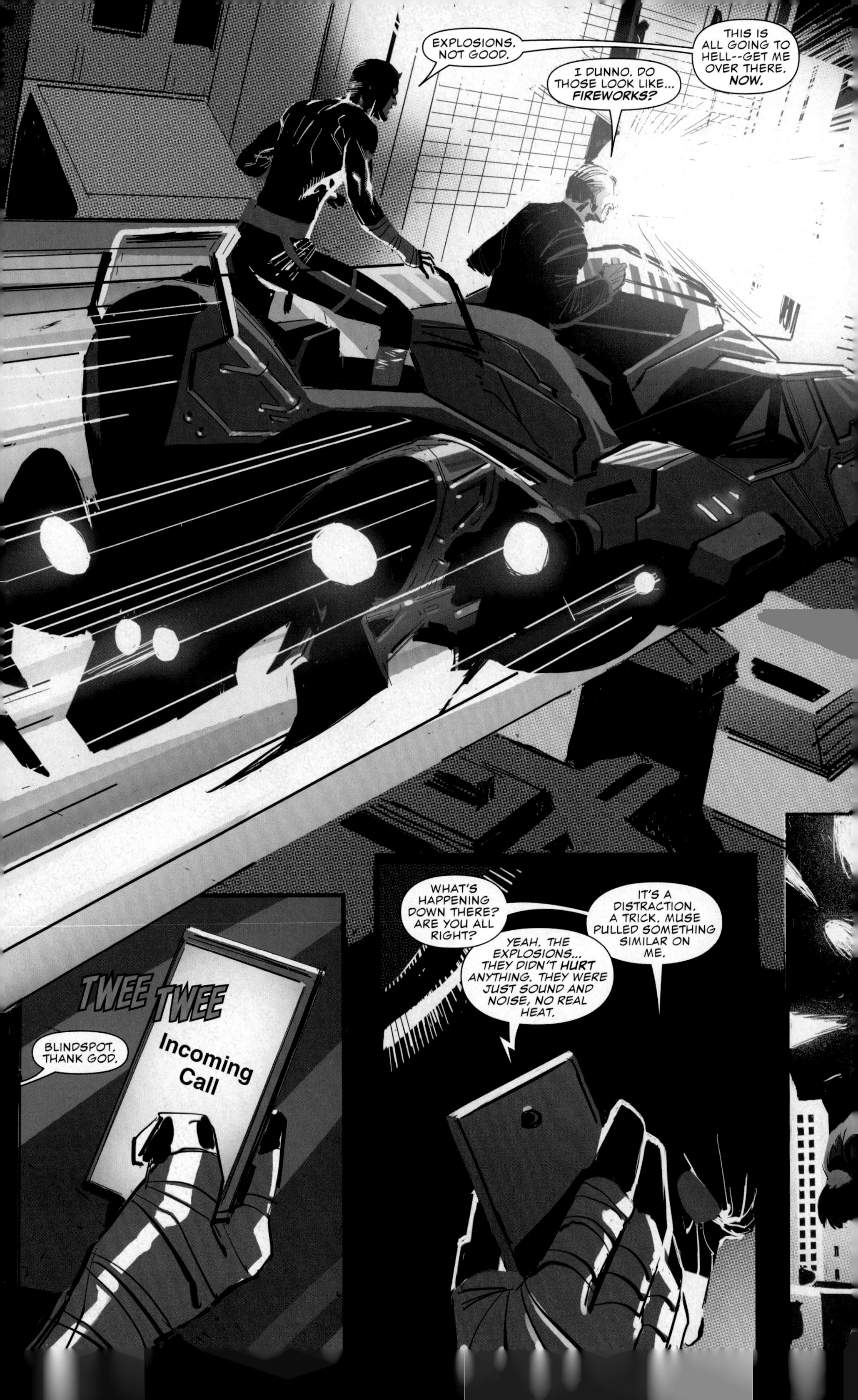
EXPLOSIONS. NOT GOOD.
THIS IS ALL GOING TO HELL--GET ME OVER THERE. NOW.
I DUNNO. DO THOSE LOOK LIKE... FIREWORKS?
TWEE TWEE
Incoming Call
BLINDSPOT. THANK GOD.
WHAT'S HAPPENING DOWN THERE? ARE YOU ALL RIGHT?
IT'S A DISTRACTION. A TRICK. MUSE PULLED SOMETHING SIMILAR ON ME.
YEAH. THE EXPLOSIONS... THEY DIDN'T HURT ANYTHING. THEY WERE JUST SOUND AND NOISE, NO REAL HEAT.

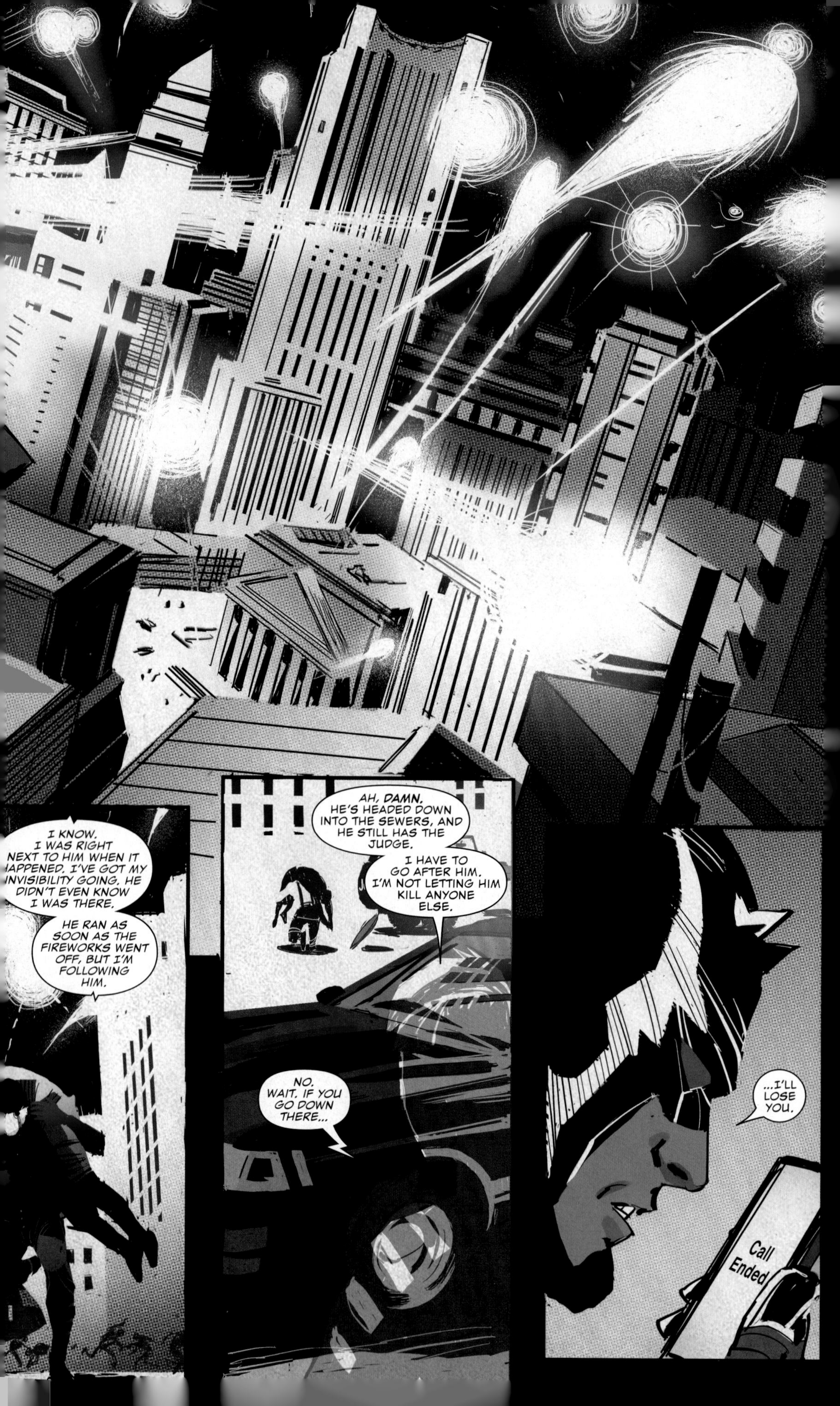
I KNOW. I WAS RIGHT NEXT TO HIM WHEN IT HAPPENED. I'VE GOT MY INVISIBILITY GOING. HE DIDN'T EVEN KNOW I WAS THERE.
HE RAN AS SOON AS THE FIREWORKS WENT OFF, BUT I'M FOLLOWING HIM.
AH, DAMN. HE'S HEADED DOWN INTO THE SEWERS, AND HE STILL HAS THE JUDGE.
I HAVE TO GO AFTER HIM. I'M NOT LETTING HIM KILL ANYONE ELSE.
NO. WAIT. IF YOU GO DOWN THERE...
...I'LL LOSE YOU.
Call Ended

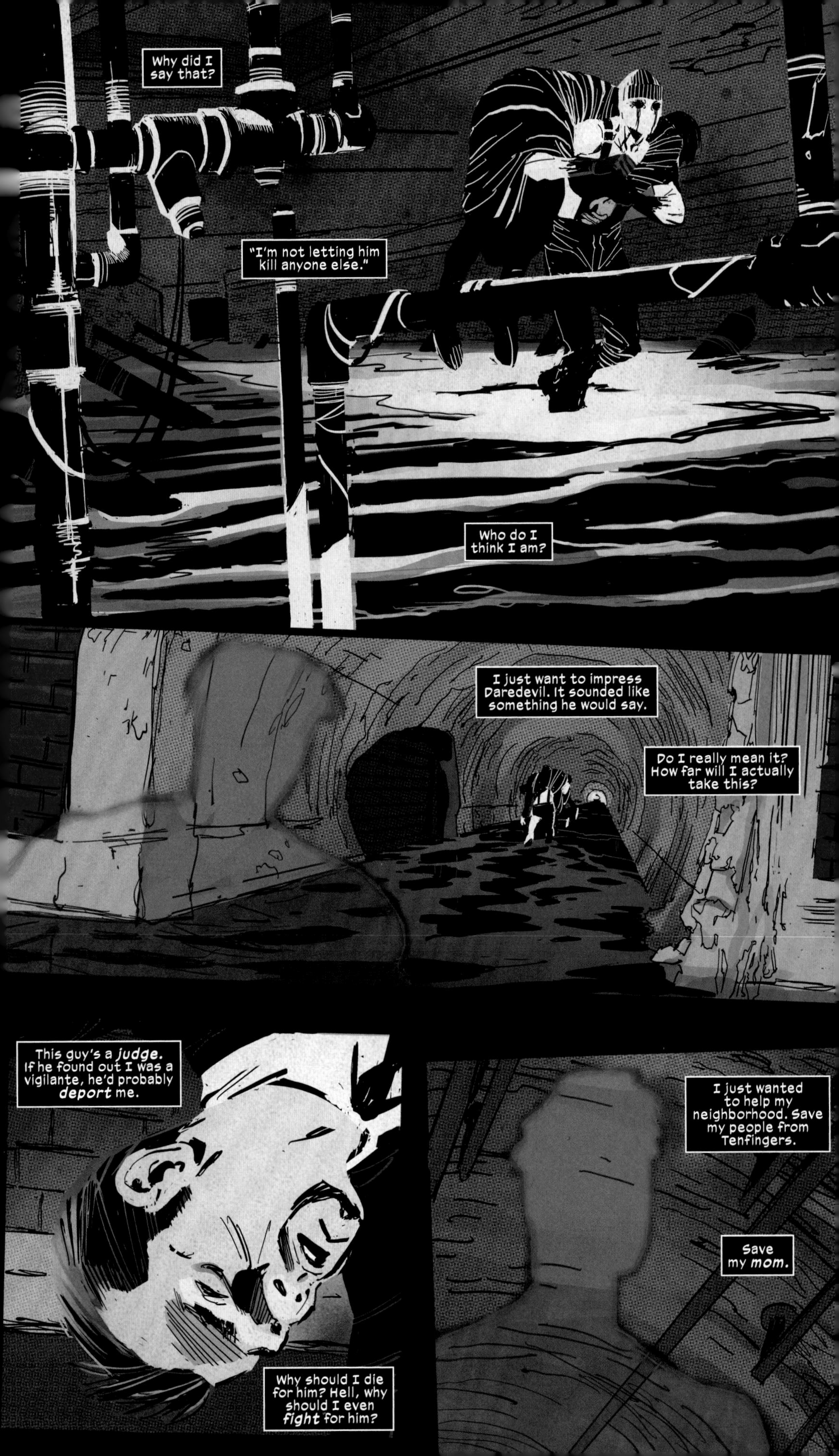

Why did I say that?
"I'm not letting him kill anyone else."
Who do I think I am?
I just want to impress Daredevil. It sounded like something he would say.
Do I really mean it? How far will I actually take this?
This guy's a *judge.* If he found out I was a vigilante, he'd probably *deport* me.
Why should I die for him? Hell, why should I even *fight* for him?
I just wanted to help my neighborhood. Save my people from Tenfingers.
Save my *mom.*

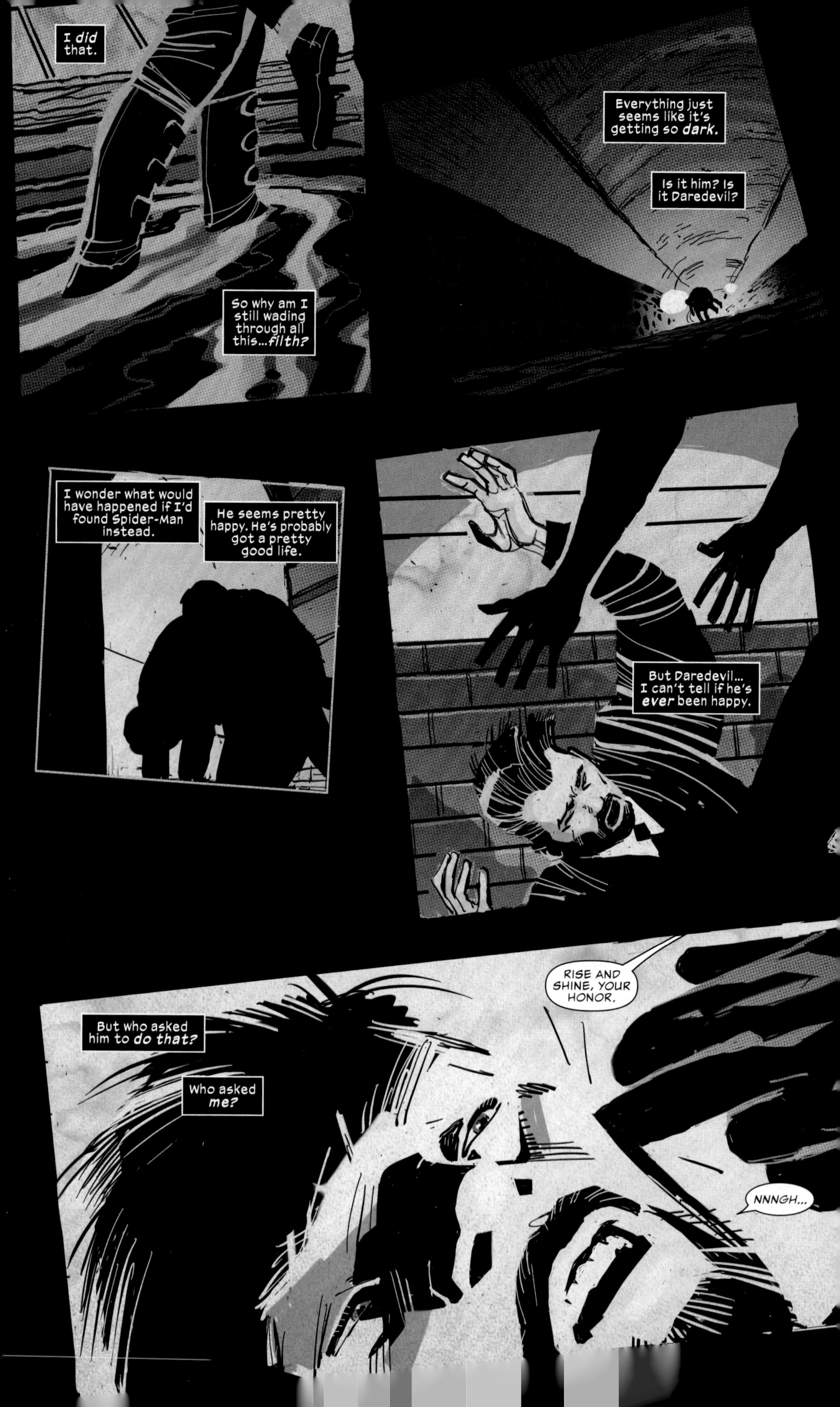

I *did* that.
So why am I still wading through all this... *filth?*
Everything just seems like it's getting so *dark.*
Is it him? Is it Daredevil?
I wonder what would have happened if I'd found Spider-Man instead.
He seems pretty happy. He's probably got a pretty good life.
But Daredevil... I can't tell if he's *ever* been happy.
But who asked him to *do that?*
Who asked *me?*
RISE AND SHINE, YOUR HONOR.
NNNGH...

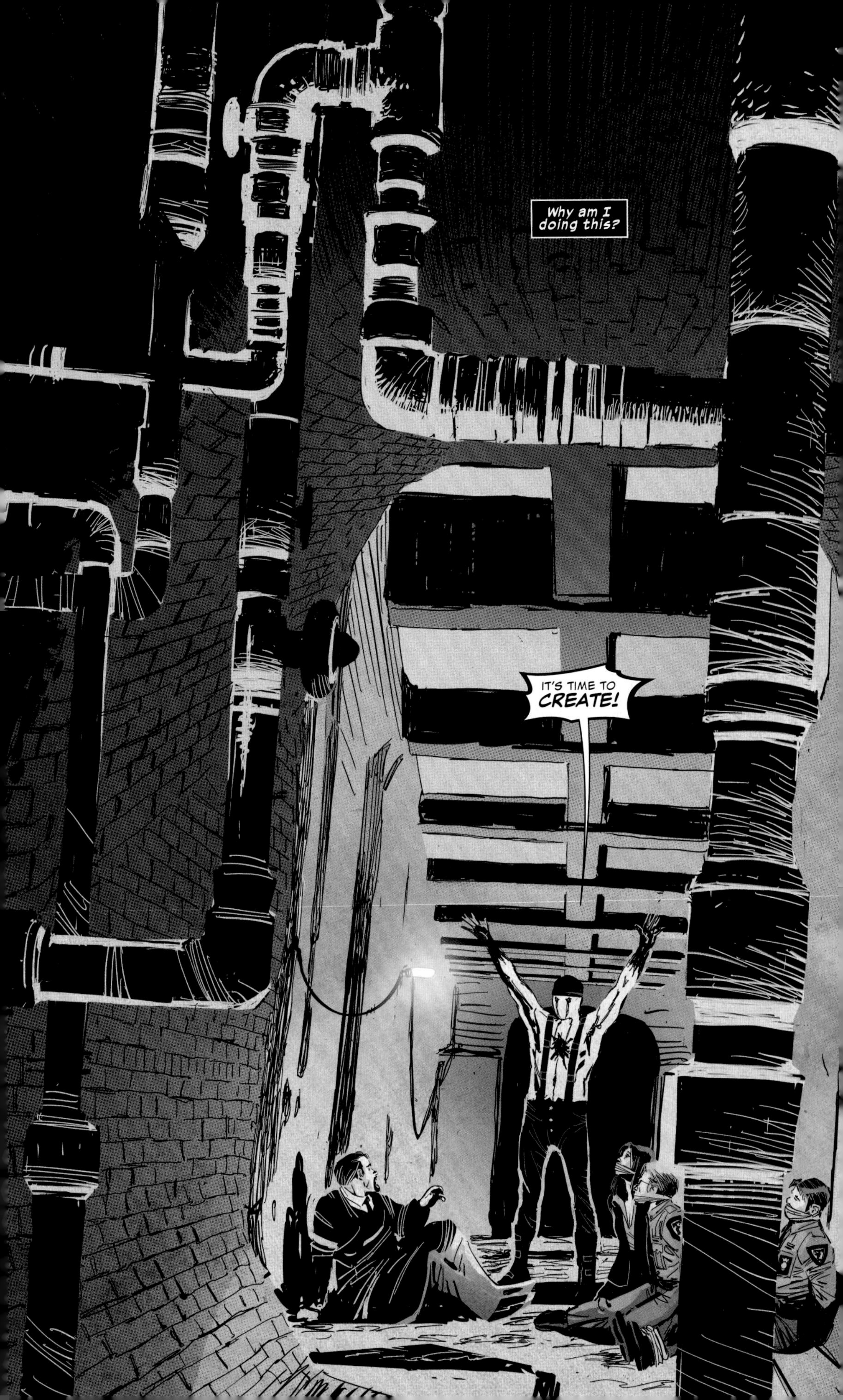
Why am I doing this?
IT'S TIME TO CREATE!

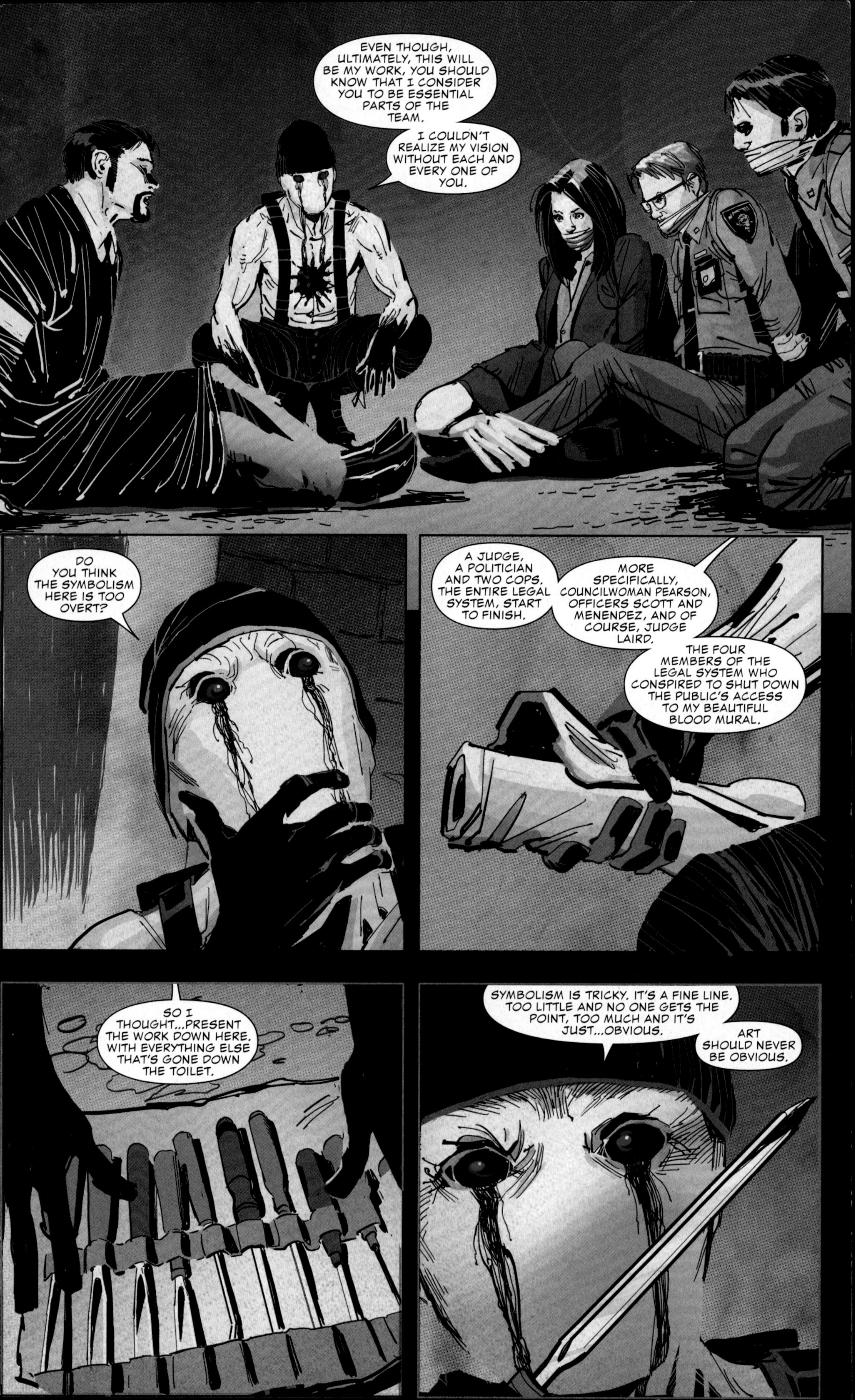

EVEN THOUGH, ULTIMATELY, THIS WILL BE MY WORK, YOU SHOULD KNOW THAT I CONSIDER YOU TO BE ESSENTIAL PARTS OF THE TEAM.
I COULDN'T REALIZE MY VISION WITHOUT EACH AND EVERY ONE OF YOU.
DO YOU THINK THE SYMBOLISM HERE IS TOO OVERT?
A JUDGE, A POLITICIAN AND TWO COPS. THE ENTIRE LEGAL SYSTEM, START TO FINISH.
MORE SPECIFICALLY, COUNCILWOMAN PEARSON, OFFICERS SCOTT AND MENENDEZ, AND OF COURSE, JUDGE LAIRD.
THE FOUR MEMBERS OF THE LEGAL SYSTEM WHO CONSPIRED TO SHUT DOWN THE PUBLIC'S ACCESS TO MY BEAUTIFUL BLOOD MURAL.
SO I THOUGHT...PRESENT THE WORK DOWN HERE, WITH EVERYTHING ELSE THAT'S GONE DOWN THE TOILET.
SYMBOLISM IS TRICKY. IT'S A FINE LINE. TOO LITTLE AND NO ONE GETS THE POINT, TOO MUCH AND IT'S JUST...OBVIOUS.
ART SHOULD NEVER BE OBVIOUS.

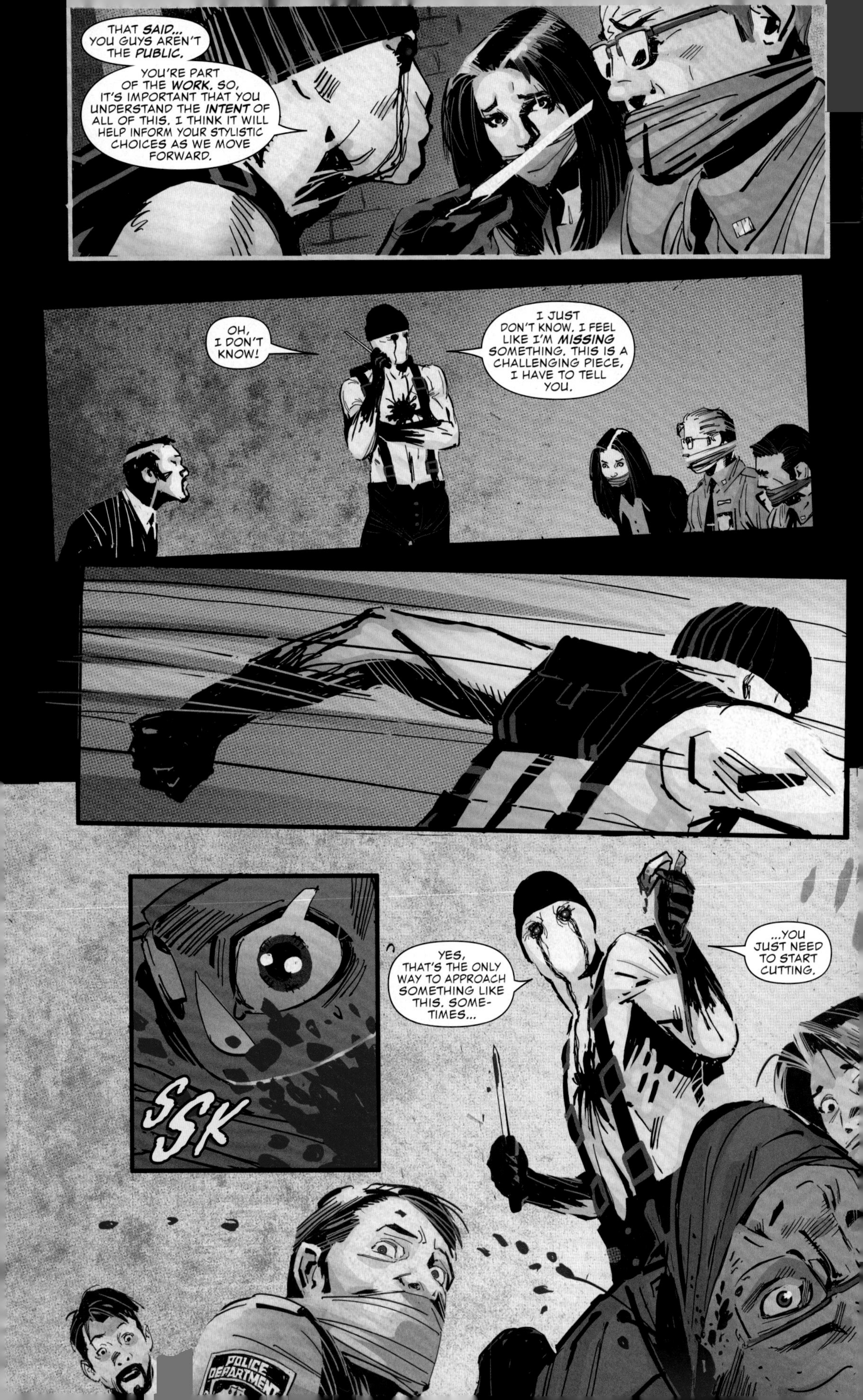

THAT SAID... YOU GUYS AREN'T THE PUBLIC.
YOU'RE PART OF THE WORK. SO, IT'S IMPORTANT THAT YOU UNDERSTAND THE INTENT OF ALL OF THIS. I THINK IT WILL HELP INFORM YOUR STYLISTIC CHOICES AS WE MOVE FORWARD.
OH, I DON'T KNOW!
I JUST DON'T KNOW. I FEEL LIKE I'M MISSING SOMETHING. THIS IS A CHALLENGING PIECE, I HAVE TO TELL YOU.
SSK
YES, THAT'S THE ONLY WAY TO APPROACH SOMETHING LIKE THIS. SOME-TIMES...
...YOU JUST NEED TO START CUTTING.
POLICE DEPARTMENT

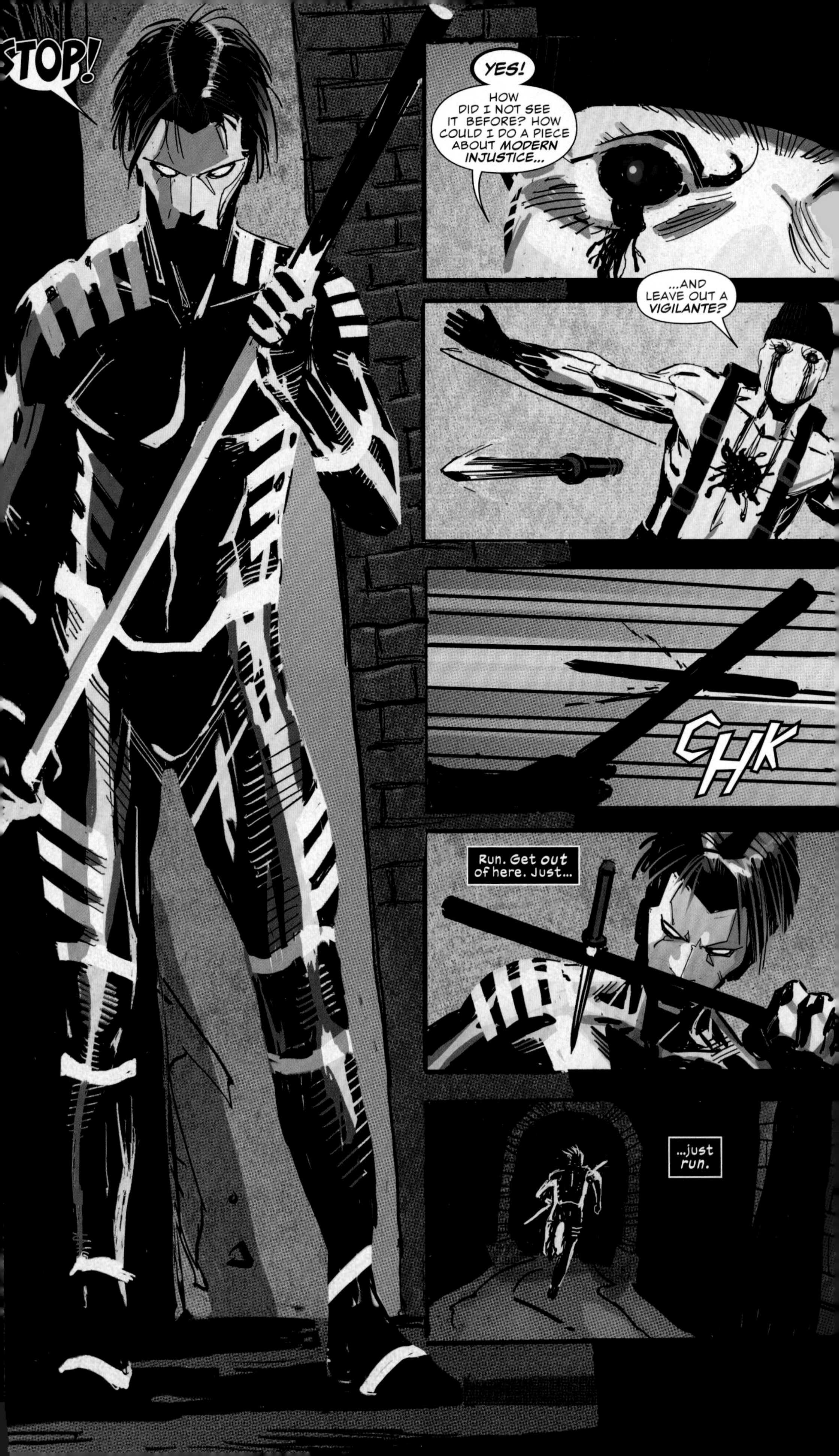
STOP!
YES!
HOW DID I NOT SEE IT BEFORE? HOW COULD I DO A PIECE ABOUT MODERN INJUSTICE...
...AND LEAVE OUT A VIGILANTE?
CHK
Run. Get out of here. Just...
...just run.

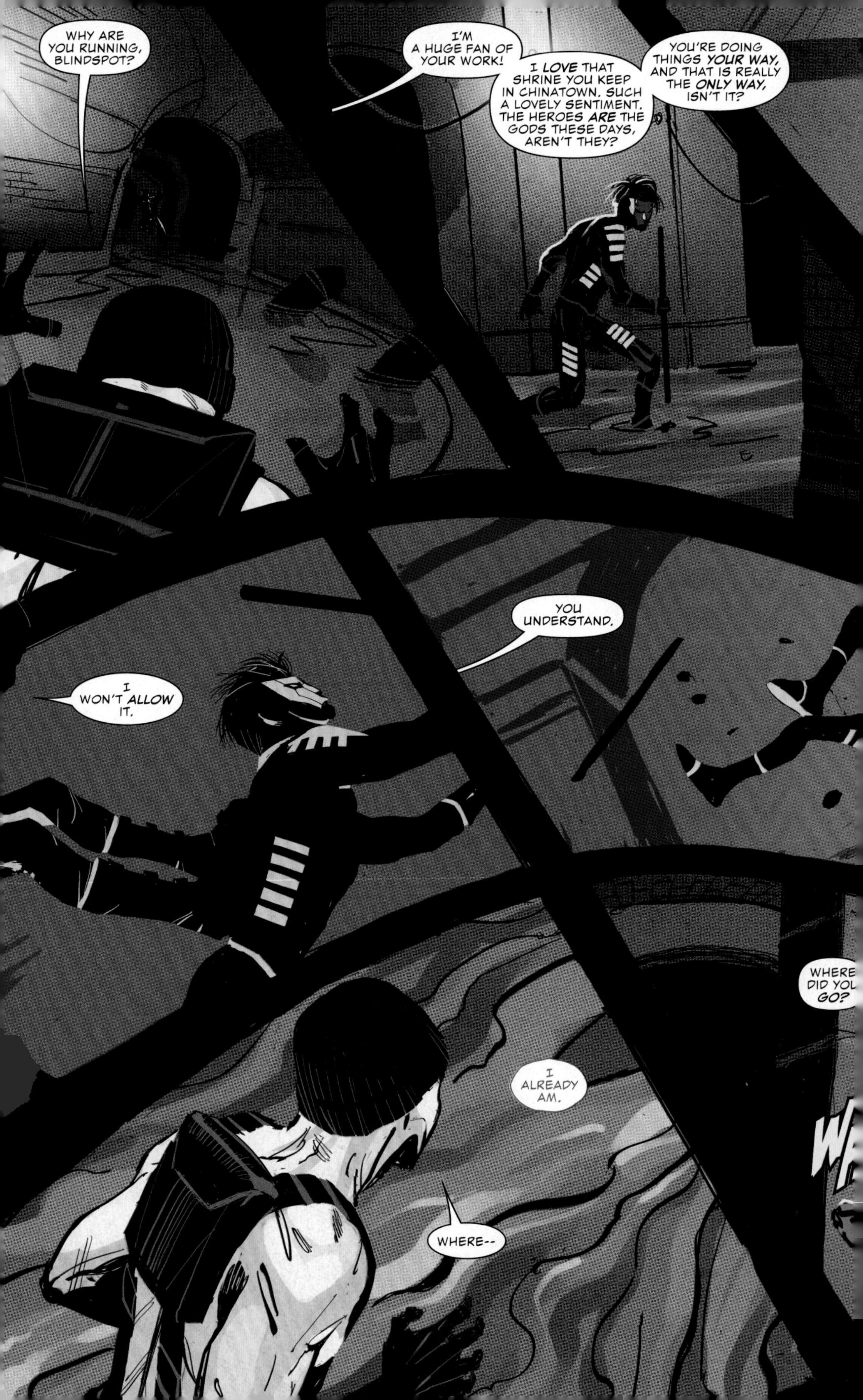

WHY ARE YOU RUNNING, BLINDSPOT?
I'M A HUGE FAN OF YOUR WORK!
I LOVE THAT SHRINE YOU KEEP IN CHINATOWN. SUCH A LOVELY SENTIMENT. THE HEROES ARE THE GODS THESE DAYS, AREN'T THEY?
YOU'RE DOING THINGS YOUR WAY, AND THAT IS REALLY THE ONLY WAY, ISN'T IT?
YOU UNDERSTAND.
I WON'T ALLOW IT.
WHERE DID YOU GO?
I ALREADY AM.
WHERE--

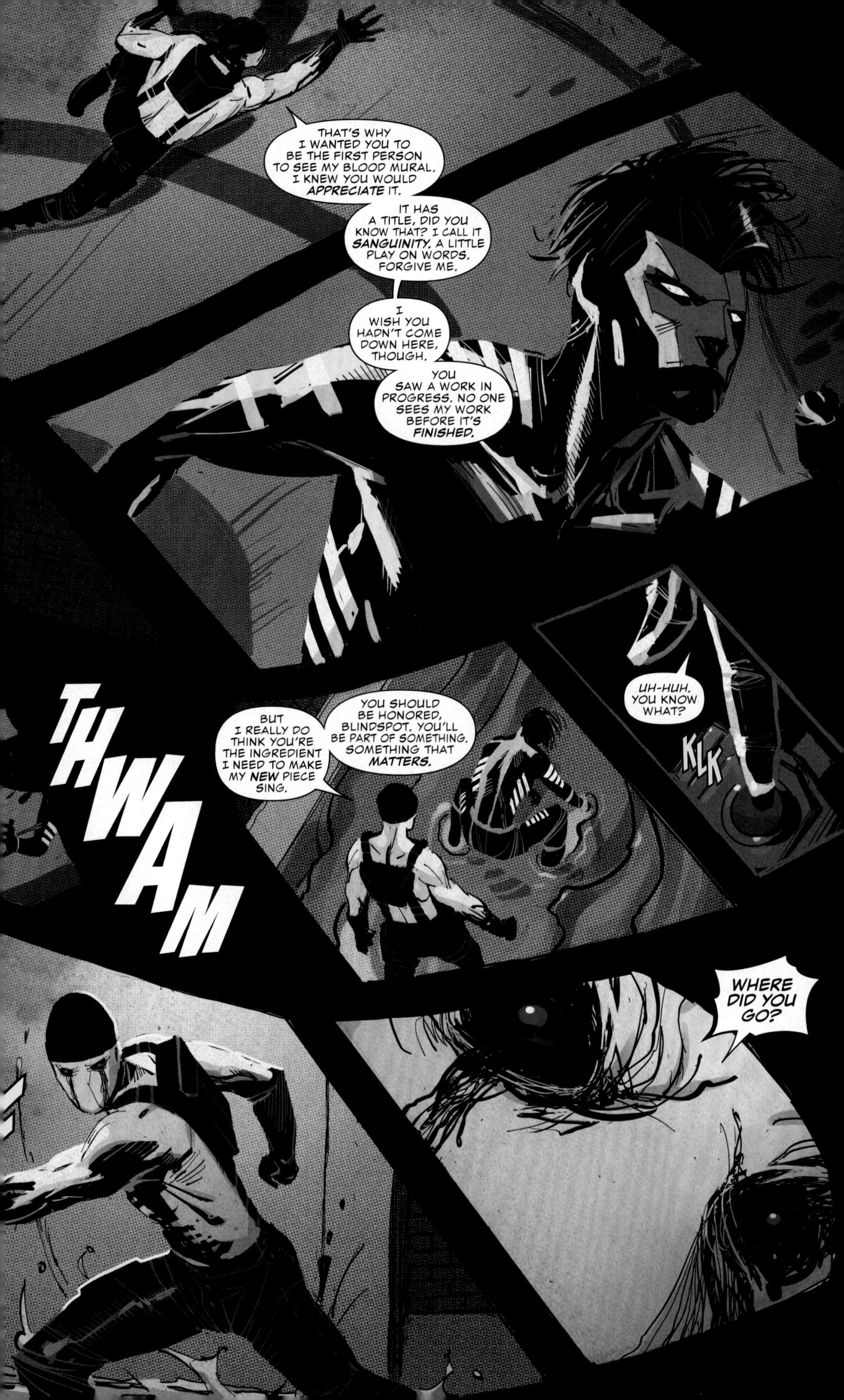
THAT'S WHY I WANTED YOU TO BE THE FIRST PERSON TO SEE MY BLOOD MURAL. I KNEW YOU WOULD APPRECIATE IT.
IT HAS A TITLE, DID YOU KNOW THAT? I CALL IT SANGUINITY. A LITTLE PLAY ON WORDS. FORGIVE ME.
I WISH YOU HADN'T COME DOWN HERE, THOUGH.
YOU SAW A WORK IN PROGRESS. NO ONE SEES MY WORK BEFORE IT'S FINISHED.
UH-HUH. YOU KNOW WHAT?
KLK
YOU SHOULD BE HONORED, BLINDSPOT. YOU'LL BE PART OF SOMETHING. SOMETHING THAT MATTERS.
BUT I REALLY DO THINK YOU'RE THE INGREDIENT I NEED TO MAKE MY NEW PIECE SING.
THWAM
WHERE DID YOU GO?

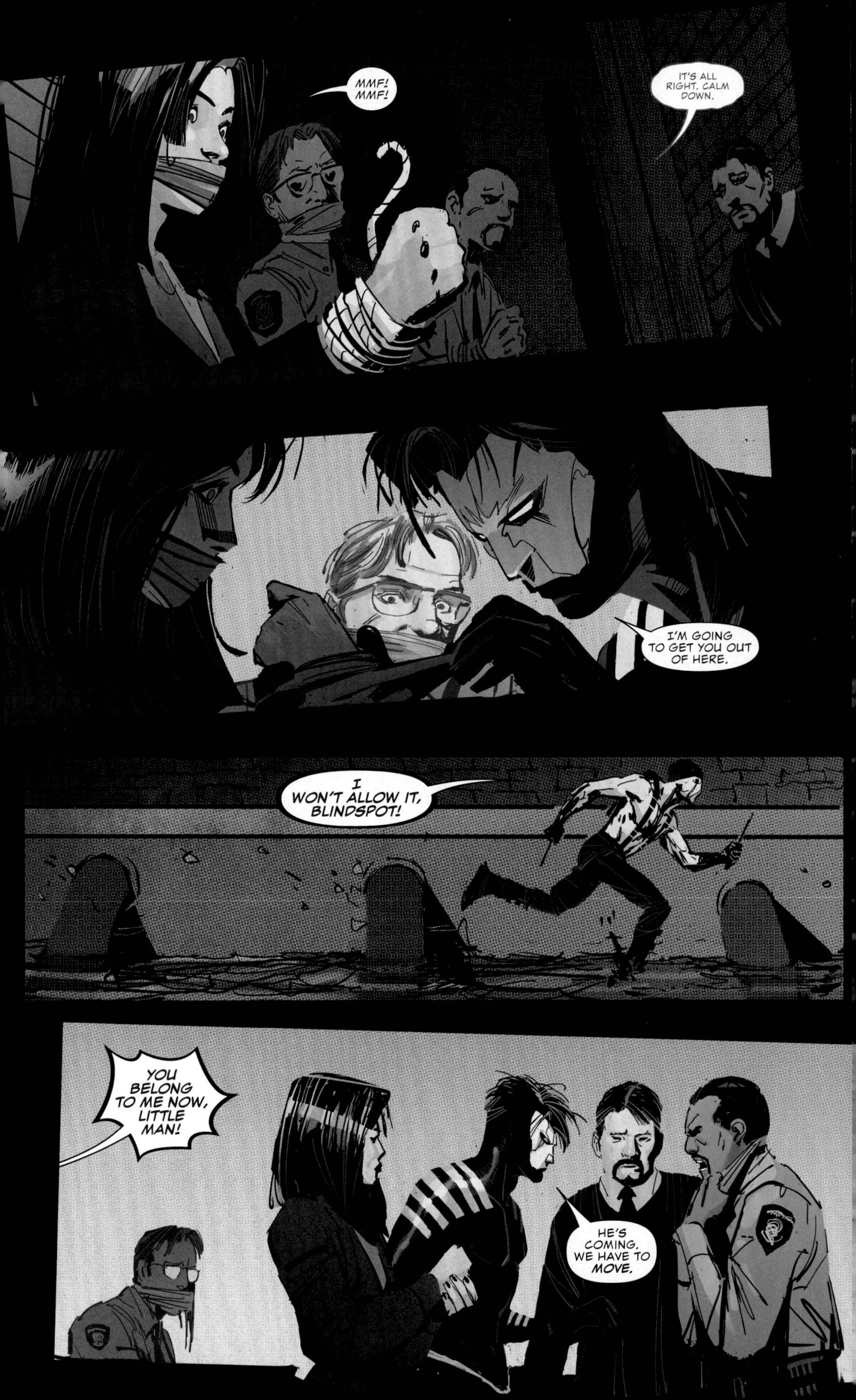
MMF! MMF!
IT'S ALL RIGHT. CALM DOWN.
I'M GOING TO GET YOU OUT OF HERE.
I WON'T ALLOW IT, BLINDSPOT!
YOU BELONG TO ME NOW, LITTLE MAN!
HE'S COMING. WE HAVE TO MOVE.

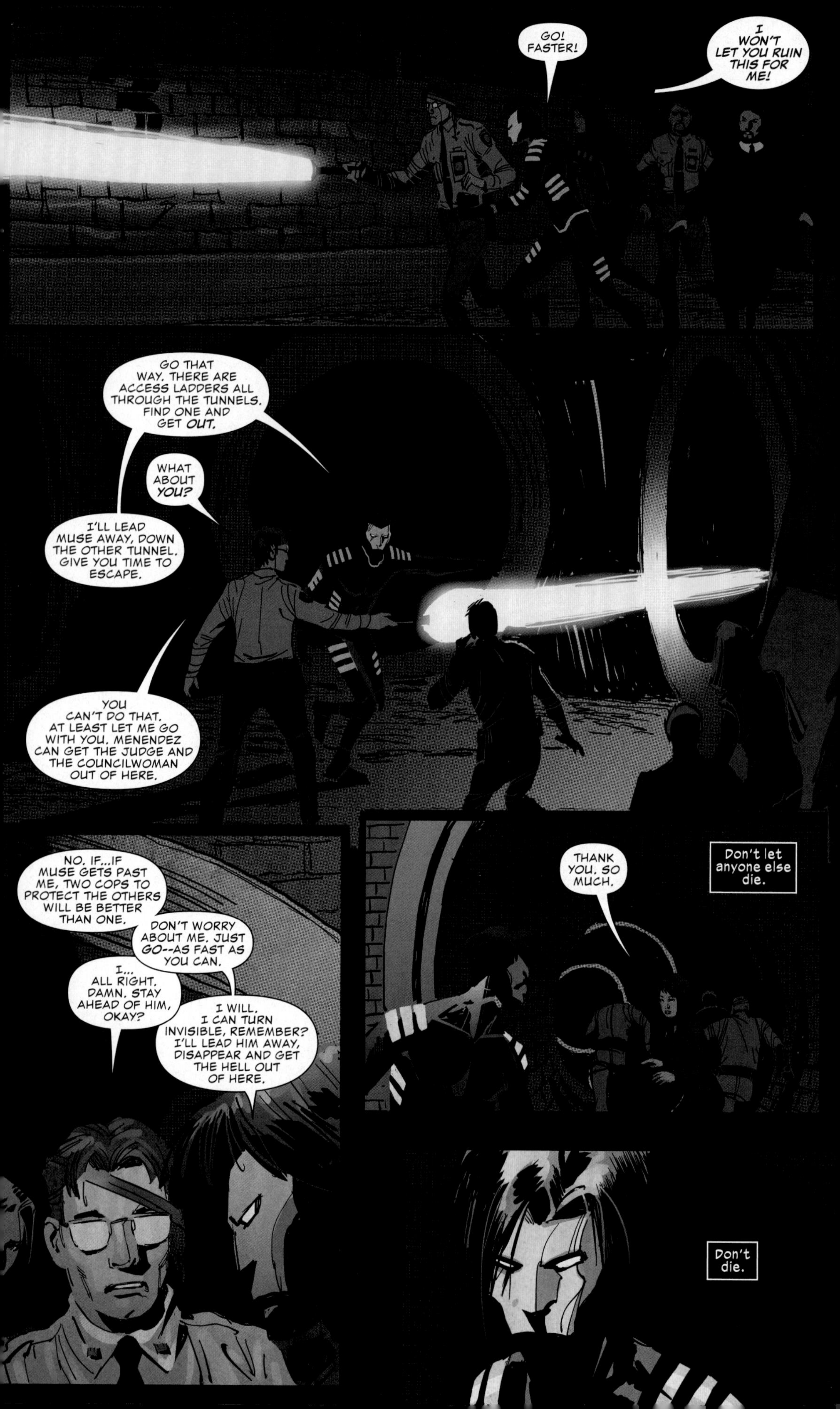
GO! FASTER!
I WON'T LET YOU RUIN THIS FOR ME!
GO THAT WAY. THERE ARE ACCESS LADDERS ALL THROUGH THE TUNNELS. FIND ONE AND GET OUT.
WHAT ABOUT YOU?
I'LL LEAD MUSE AWAY, DOWN THE OTHER TUNNEL. GIVE YOU TIME TO ESCAPE.
YOU CAN'T DO THAT. AT LEAST LET ME GO WITH YOU. MENENDEZ CAN GET THE JUDGE AND THE COUNCILWOMAN OUT OF HERE.
NO. IF...IF MUSE GETS PAST ME, TWO COPS TO PROTECT THE OTHERS WILL BE BETTER THAN ONE.
DON'T WORRY ABOUT ME. JUST GO--AS FAST AS YOU CAN.
I... ALL RIGHT. DAMN. STAY AHEAD OF HIM, OKAY?
I WILL. I CAN TURN INVISIBLE, REMEMBER? I'LL LEAD HIM AWAY, DISAPPEAR AND GET THE HELL OUT OF HERE.
THANK YOU. SO MUCH.
Don't let anyone else die.
Don't die.

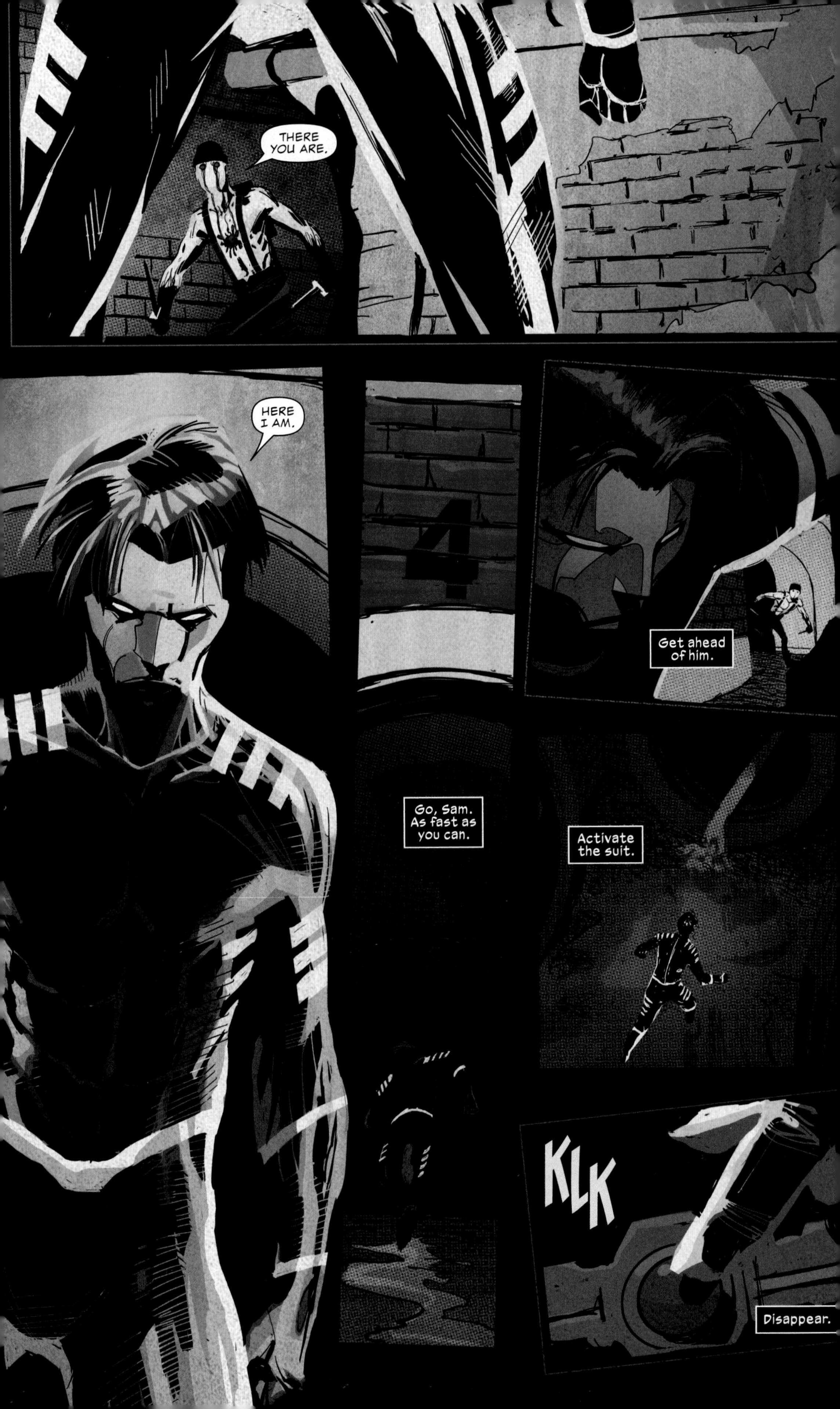
THERE YOU ARE.
HERE I AM.
Get ahead of him.
Go, Sam. As fast as you can.
Activate the suit.
KLK
Disappear.

Oh, no.

The *batteries...*

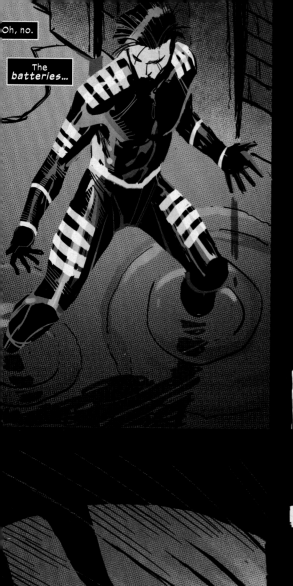

...dead.

KLNG

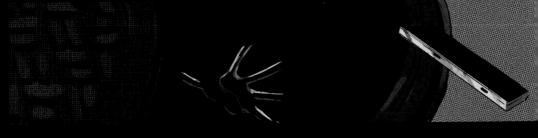

Calling Daredevil

Call in Progress 0:00

BLINDSPOT? WHERE ARE YOU?

PLEASE...

Call in Progress

0:10

...TALK TO ME.

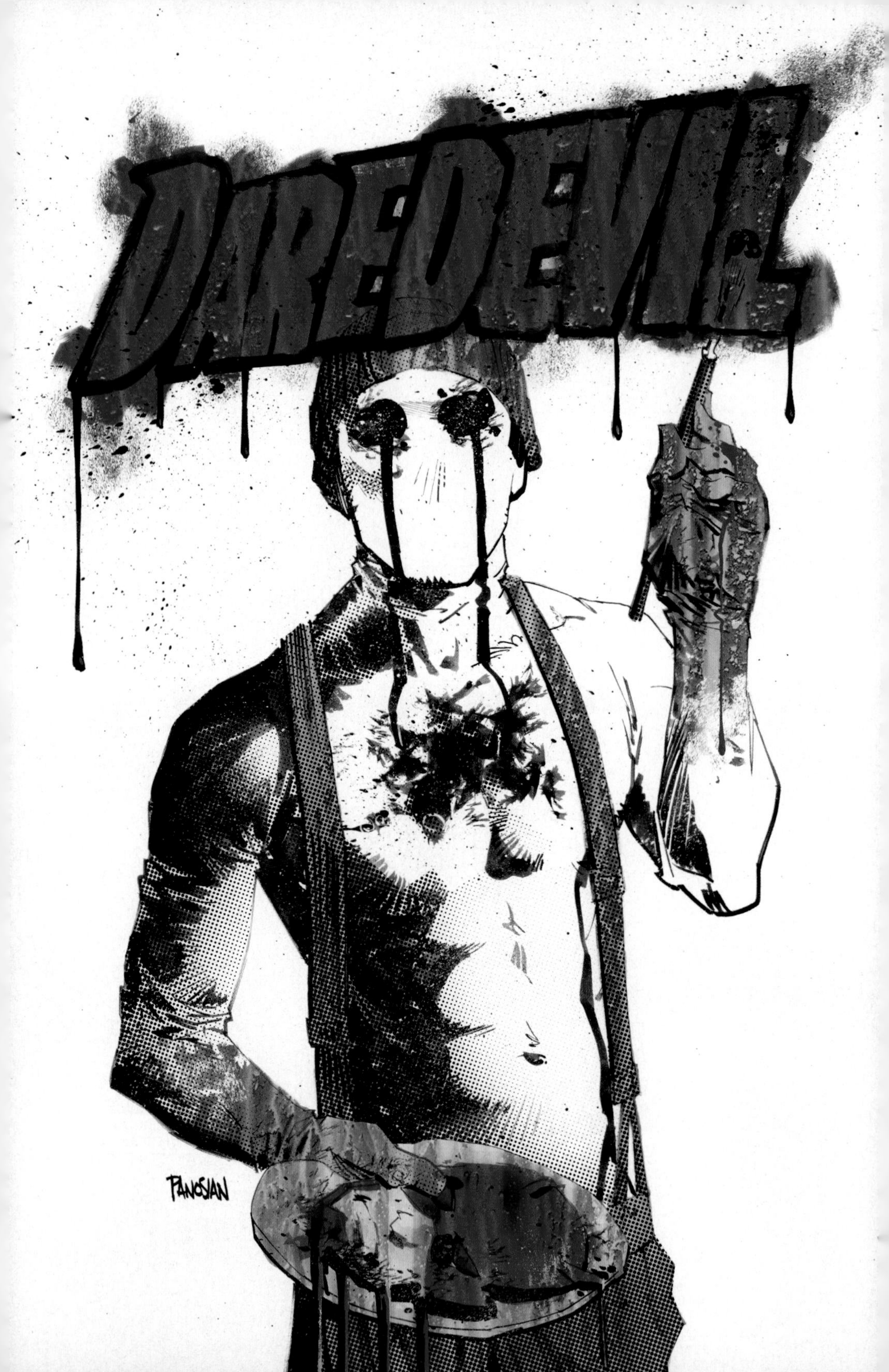
DAREDEVIL
PANOSIAN

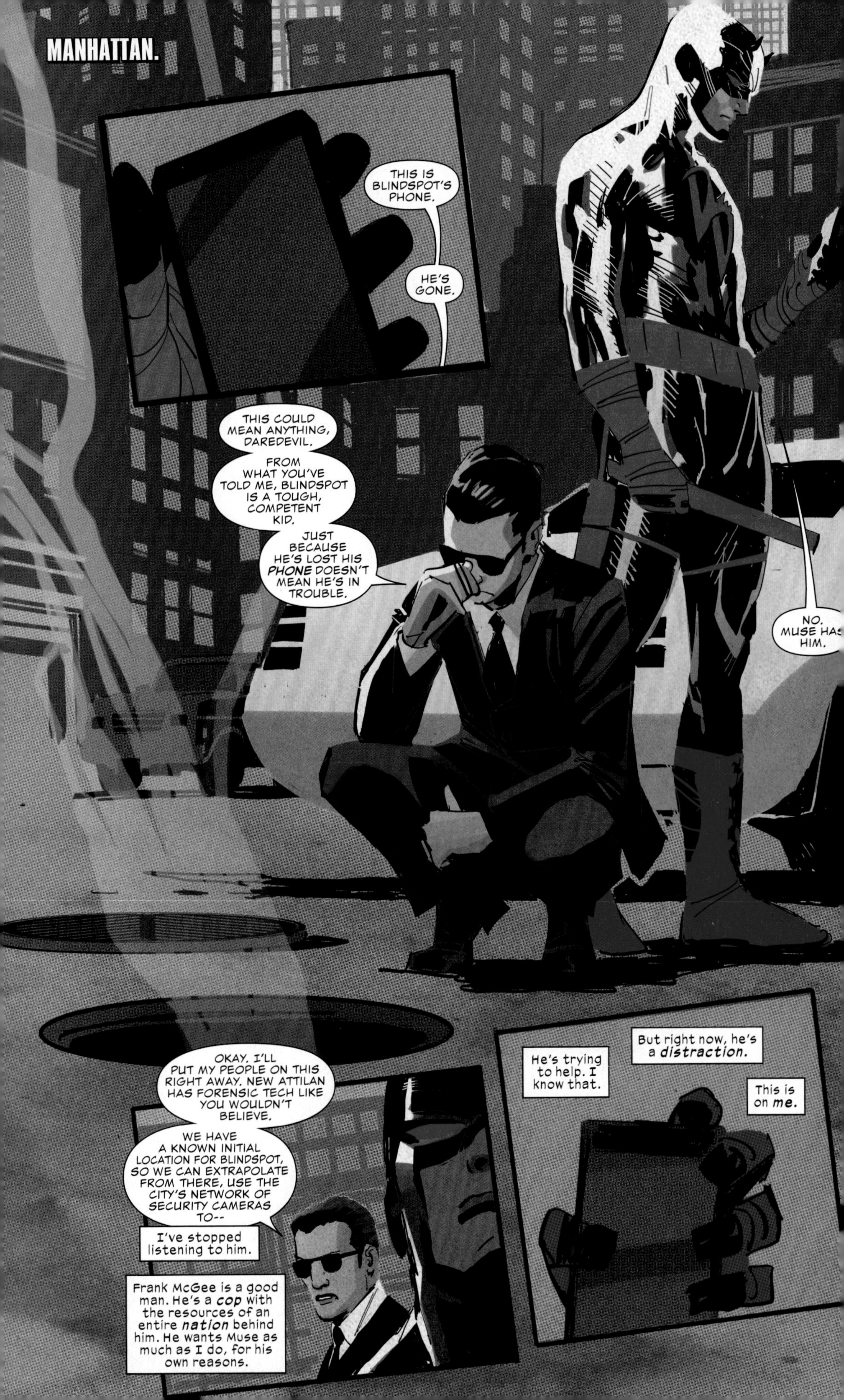

MANHATTAN.
THIS IS BLINDSPOT'S PHONE.
HE'S GONE.
THIS COULD MEAN ANYTHING, DAREDEVIL.
FROM WHAT YOU'VE TOLD ME, BLINDSPOT IS A TOUGH, COMPETENT KID.
JUST BECAUSE HE'S LOST HIS PHONE DOESN'T MEAN HE'S IN TROUBLE.
NO. MUSE HAS HIM.
OKAY. I'LL PUT MY PEOPLE ON THIS RIGHT AWAY. NEW ATTILAN HAS FORENSIC TECH LIKE YOU WOULDN'T BELIEVE.
WE HAVE A KNOWN INITIAL LOCATION FOR BLINDSPOT, SO WE CAN EXTRAPOLATE FROM THERE, USE THE CITY'S NETWORK OF SECURITY CAMERAS TO--
I've stopped listening to him.
Frank McGee is a good man. He's a cop with the resources of an entire nation behind him. He wants Muse as much as I do, for his own reasons.
He's trying to help. I know that.
But right now, he's a distraction.
This is on me.

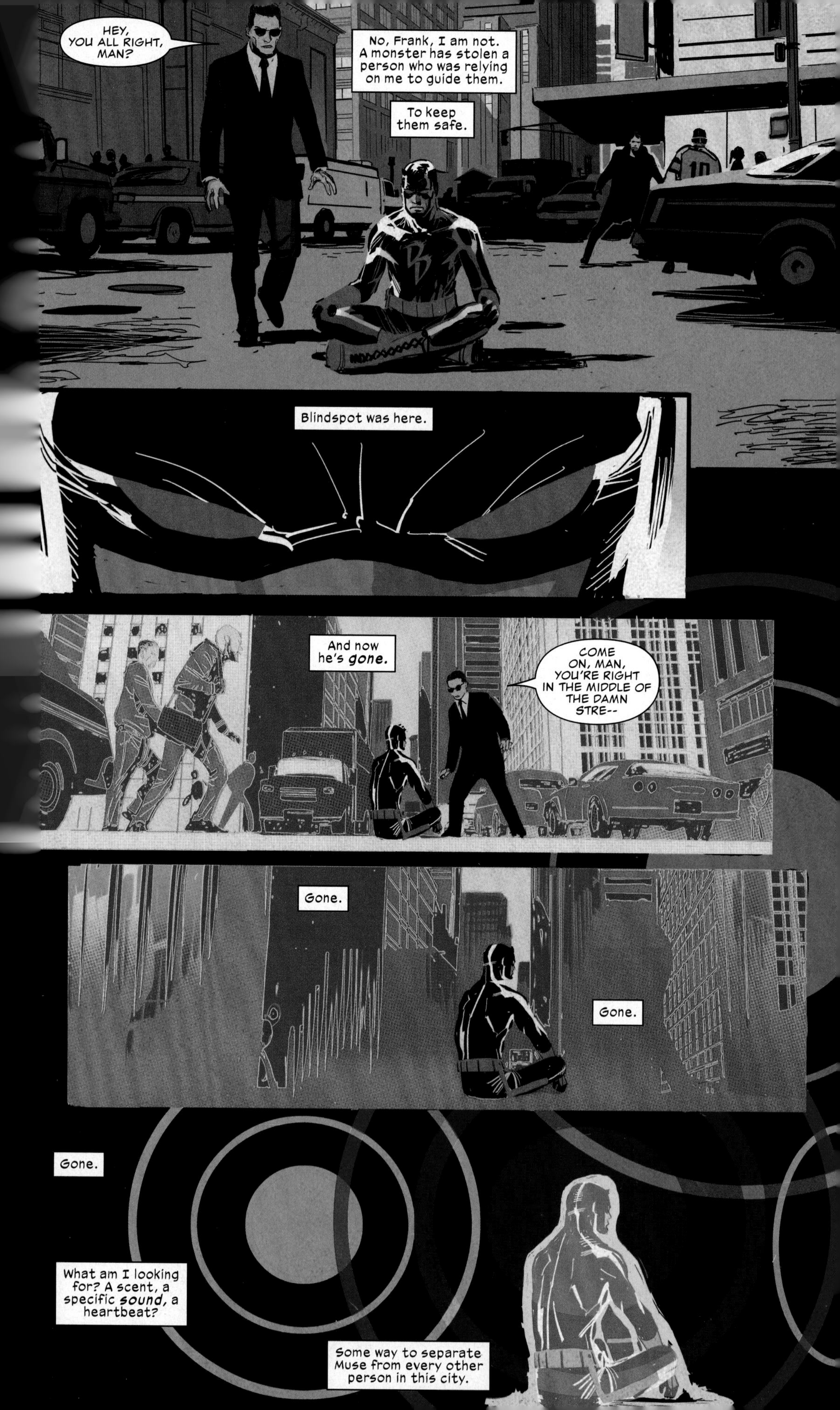
HEY, YOU ALL RIGHT, MAN?
No, Frank, I am not. A monster has stolen a person who was relying on me to guide them.
To keep them safe.
Blindspot was here.
And now he's *gone.*
COME ON, MAN, YOU'RE RIGHT IN THE MIDDLE OF THE DAMN STRE--
Gone.
Gone.
Gone.
What am I looking for? A scent, a specific *sound*, a heartbeat?
Some way to separate Muse from every other person in this city.

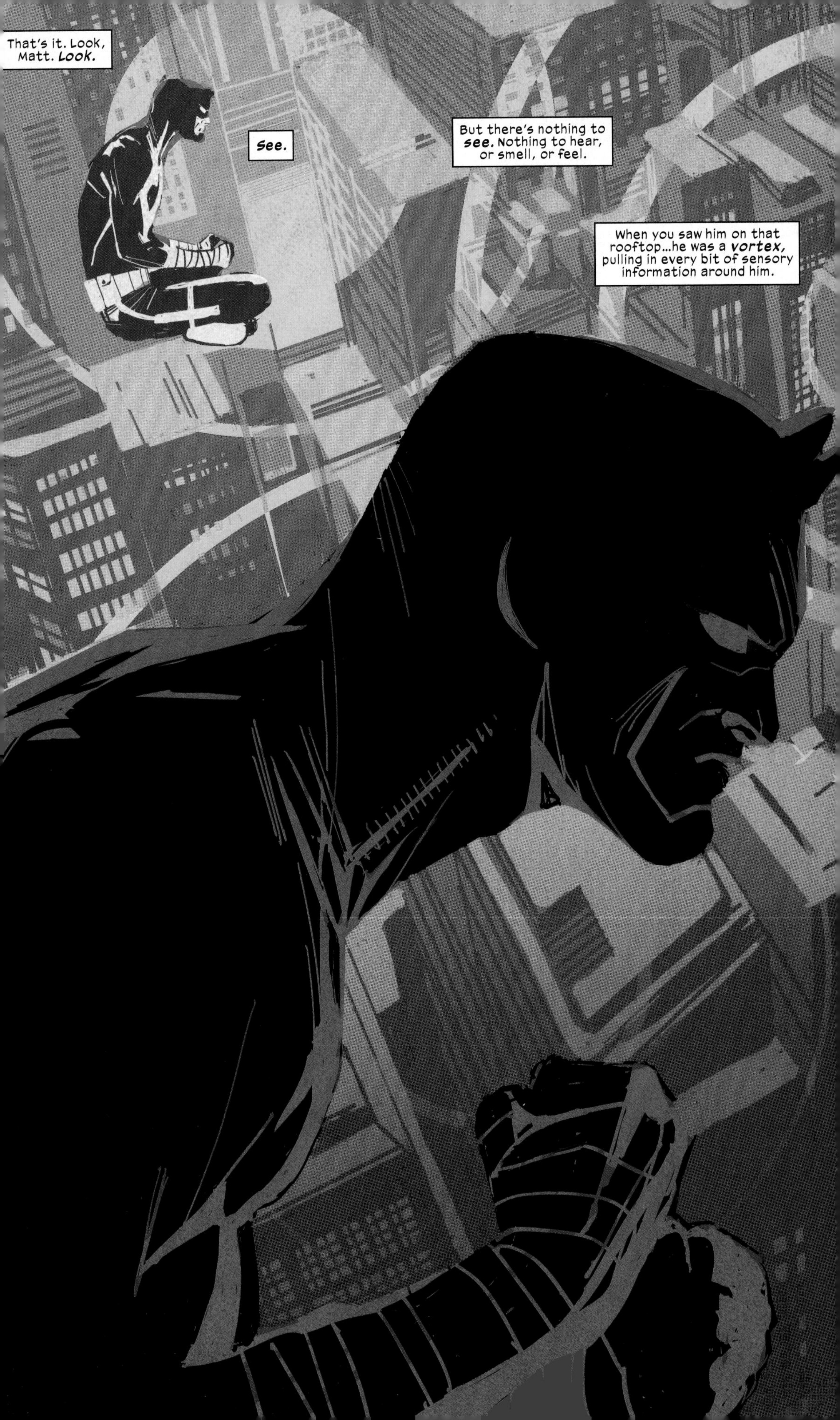
That's it. Look, Matt. *Look.*
See.
But there's nothing to *see.* Nothing to hear, or smell, or feel.
When you saw him on that rooftop...he was a *vortex,* pulling in every bit of sensory information around him.

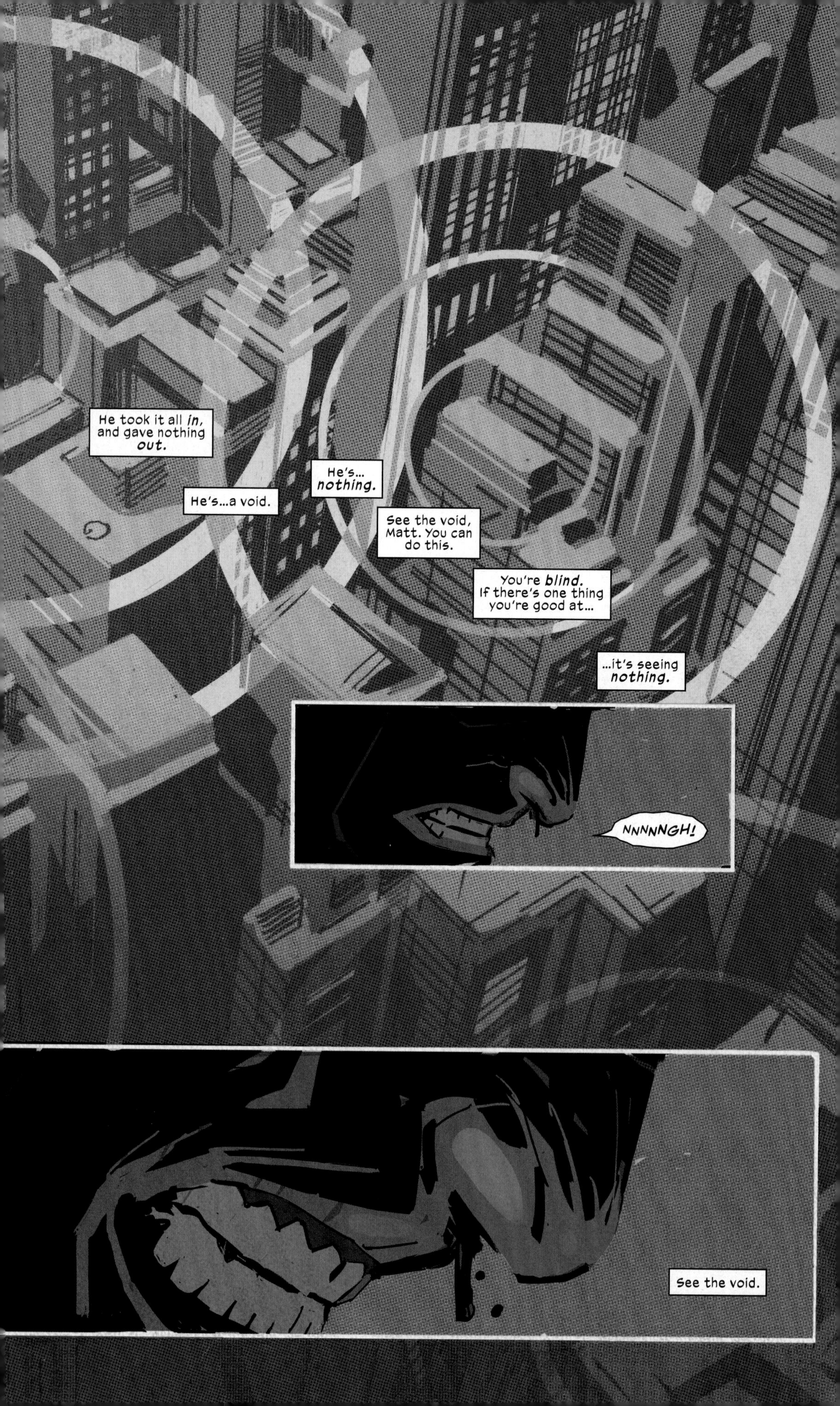

He took it all *in*, and gave nothing *out*.
He's...a void.
He's... *nothing*.
See the void, Matt. You can do this.
You're *blind*. If there's one thing you're good at...
...it's seeing *nothing*.
NNNNNGH!
See the void.

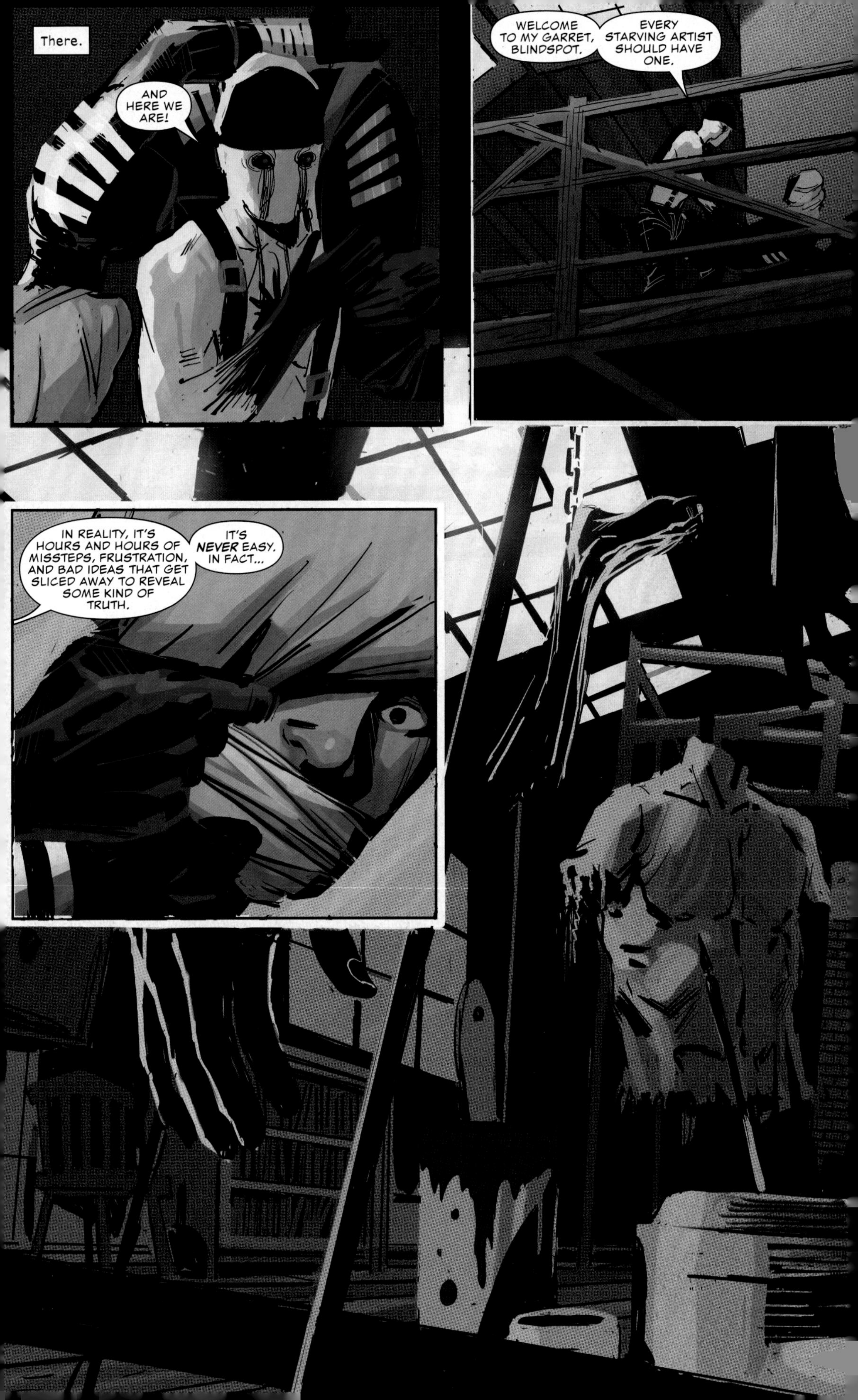
There.
AND HERE WE ARE!
WELCOME TO MY GARRET, BLINDSPOT.
EVERY STARVING ARTIST SHOULD HAVE ONE.
IT'S NEVER EASY. IN FACT...
IN REALITY, IT'S HOURS AND HOURS OF MISSTEPS, FRUSTRATION, AND BAD IDEAS THAT GET SLICED AWAY TO REVEAL SOME KIND OF TRUTH.

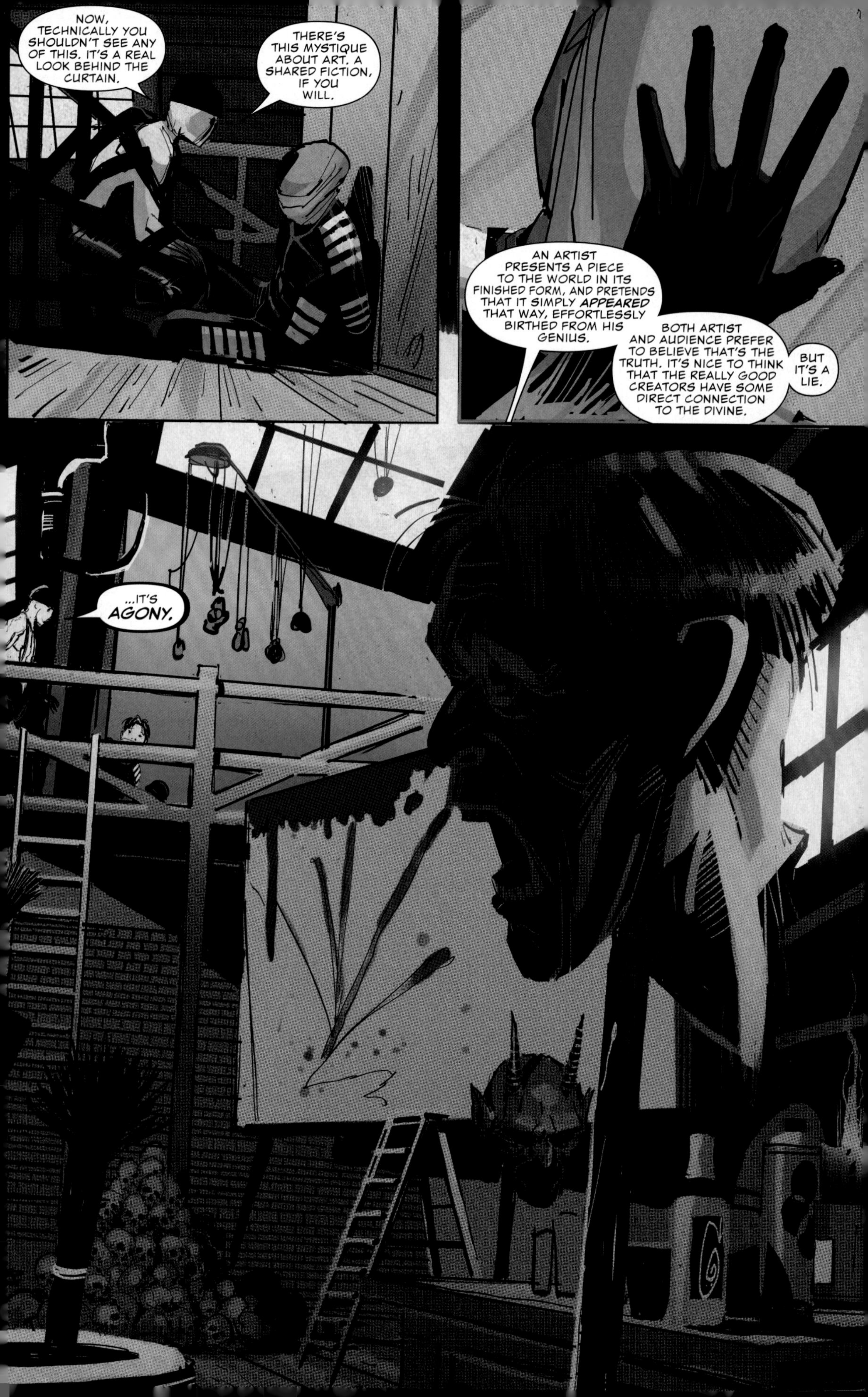
NOW, TECHNICALLY YOU SHOULDN'T SEE ANY OF THIS. IT'S A REAL LOOK BEHIND THE CURTAIN.
THERE'S THIS MYSTIQUE ABOUT ART. A SHARED FICTION, IF YOU WILL.
AN ARTIST PRESENTS A PIECE TO THE WORLD IN ITS FINISHED FORM, AND PRETENDS THAT IT SIMPLY *APPEARED* THAT WAY, EFFORTLESSLY BIRTHED FROM HIS GENIUS.
BOTH ARTIST AND AUDIENCE PREFER TO BELIEVE THAT'S THE TRUTH. IT'S NICE TO THINK THAT THE REALLY GOOD CREATORS HAVE SOME DIRECT CONNECTION TO THE DIVINE.
BUT IT'S A LIE.
...IT'S **AGONY.**

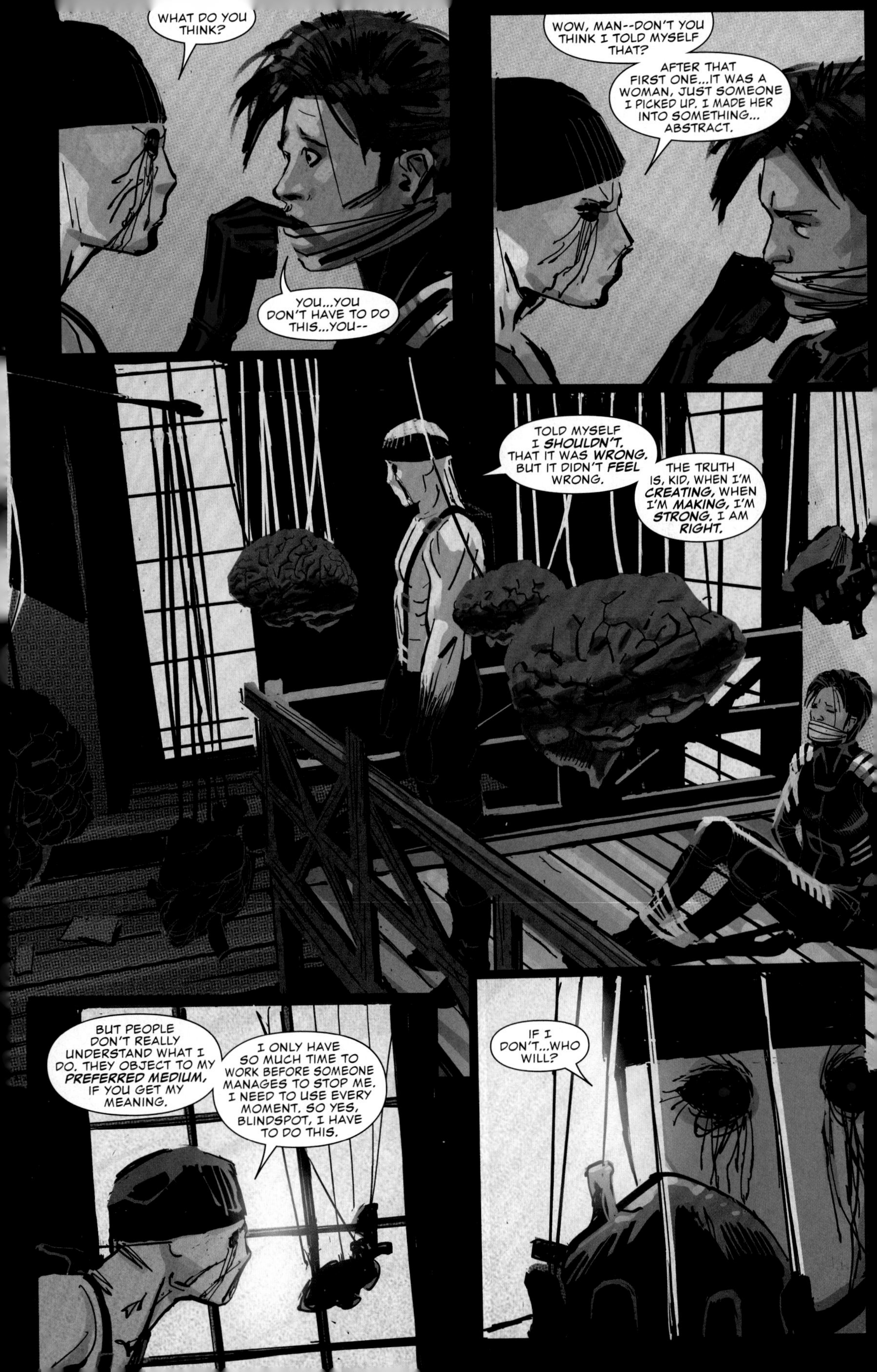
WHAT DO YOU THINK?
YOU...YOU DON'T HAVE TO DO THIS...YOU--
WOW, MAN--DON'T YOU THINK I TOLD MYSELF THAT?
AFTER THAT FIRST ONE...IT WAS A WOMAN, JUST SOMEONE I PICKED UP. I MADE HER INTO SOMETHING... ABSTRACT.
TOLD MYSELF I SHOULDN'T. THAT IT WAS WRONG. BUT IT DIDN'T FEEL WRONG.
THE TRUTH IS, KID, WHEN I'M CREATING, WHEN I'M MAKING, I'M STRONG. I AM RIGHT.
BUT PEOPLE DON'T REALLY UNDERSTAND WHAT I DO. THEY OBJECT TO MY PREFERRED MEDIUM, IF YOU GET MY MEANING.
I ONLY HAVE SO MUCH TIME TO WORK BEFORE SOMEONE MANAGES TO STOP ME. I NEED TO USE EVERY MOMENT. SO YES, BLINDSPOT, I HAVE TO DO THIS.
IF I DON'T...WHO WILL?

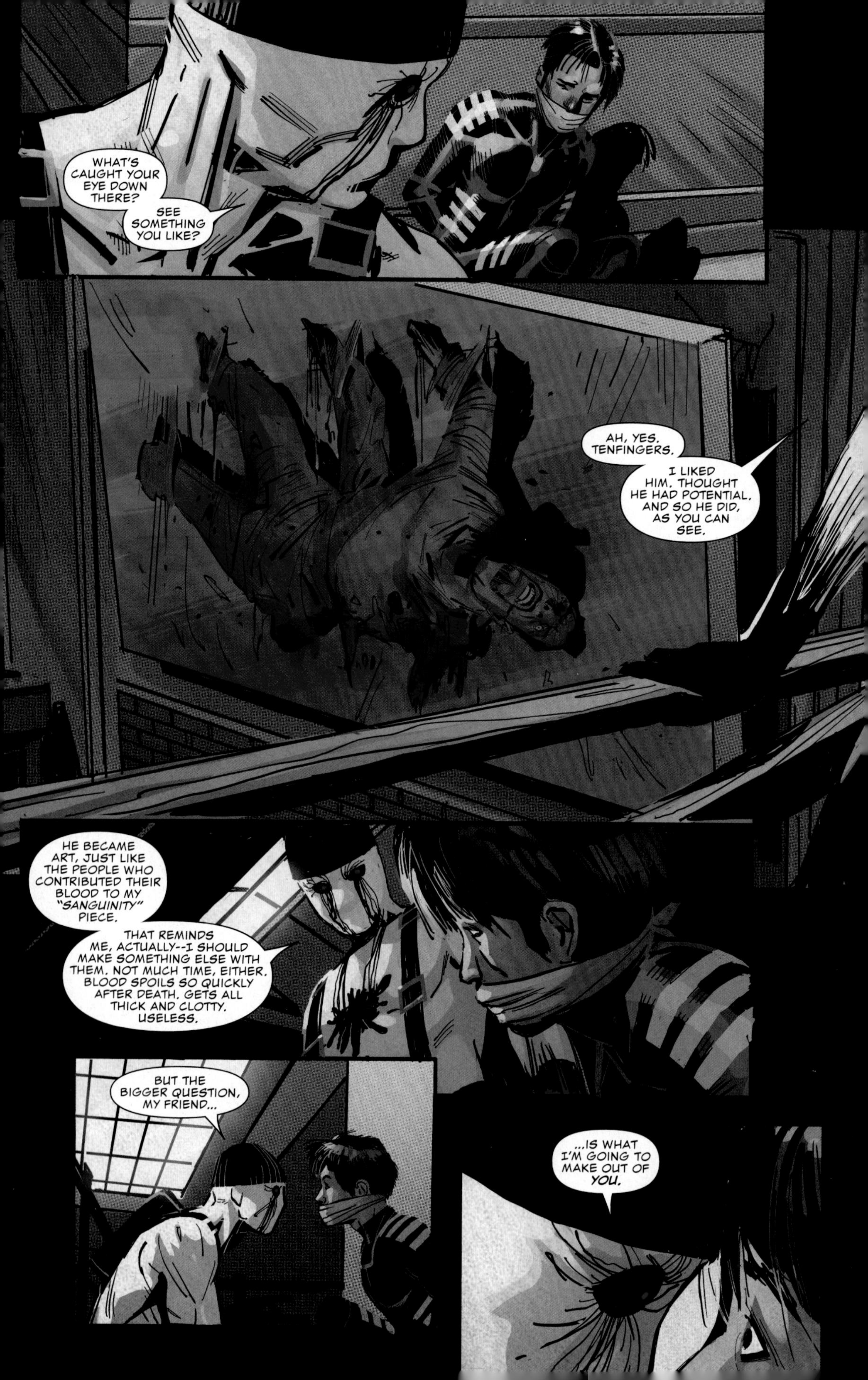
WHAT'S CAUGHT YOUR EYE DOWN THERE?
SEE SOMETHING YOU LIKE?
AH, YES. TENFINGERS.
I LIKED HIM. THOUGHT HE HAD POTENTIAL. AND SO HE DID, AS YOU CAN SEE.
HE BECAME ART, JUST LIKE THE PEOPLE WHO CONTRIBUTED THEIR BLOOD TO MY "SANGUINITY" PIECE.
THAT REMINDS ME, ACTUALLY--I SHOULD MAKE SOMETHING ELSE WITH THEM. NOT MUCH TIME, EITHER. BLOOD SPOILS SO QUICKLY AFTER DEATH. GETS ALL THICK AND CLOTTY. USELESS.
BUT THE BIGGER QUESTION, MY FRIEND...
...IS WHAT I'M GOING TO MAKE OUT OF YOU.

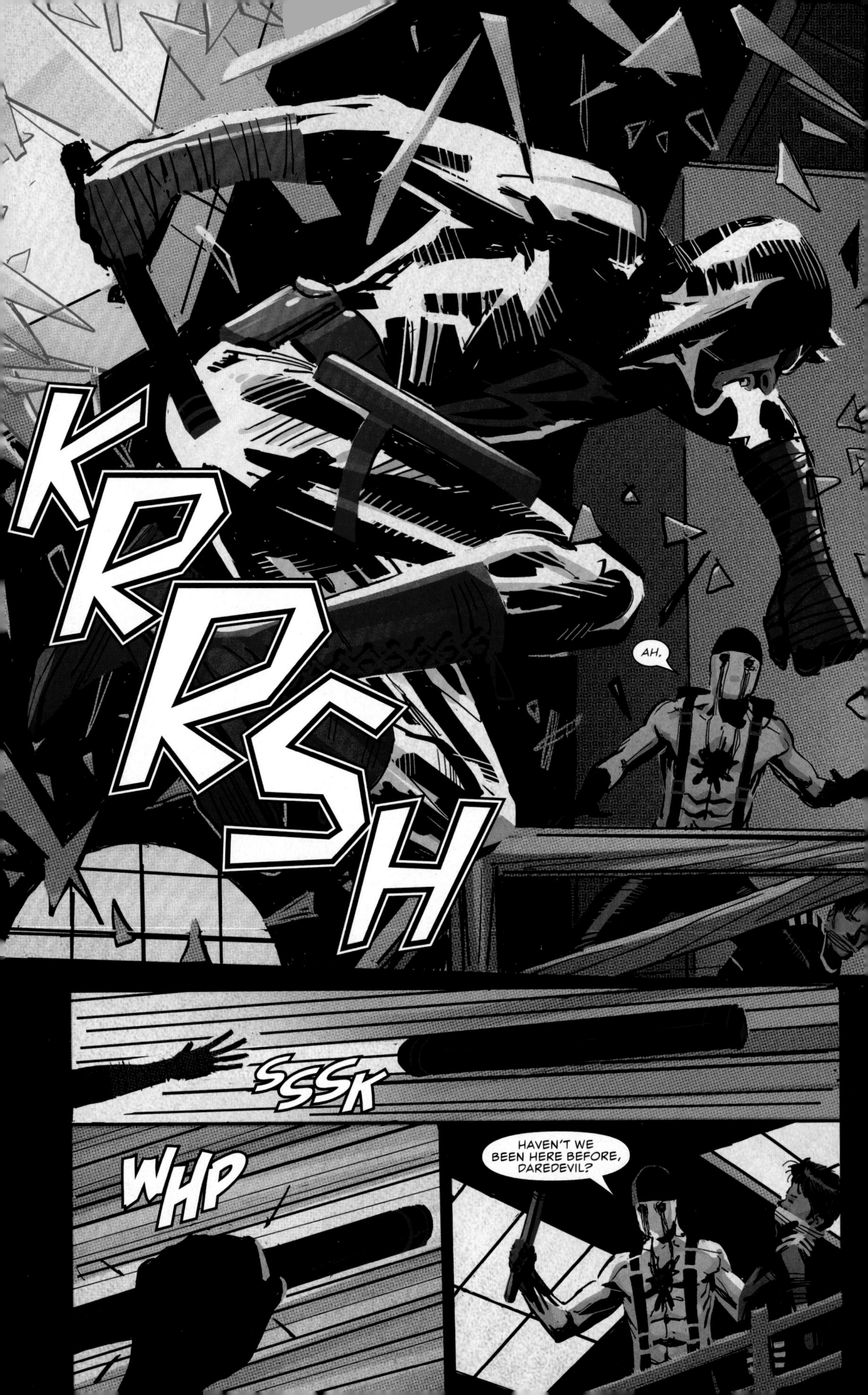
KRRSH
AH.
SSSK
WHP
HAVEN'T WE BEEN HERE BEFORE, DAREDEVIL?

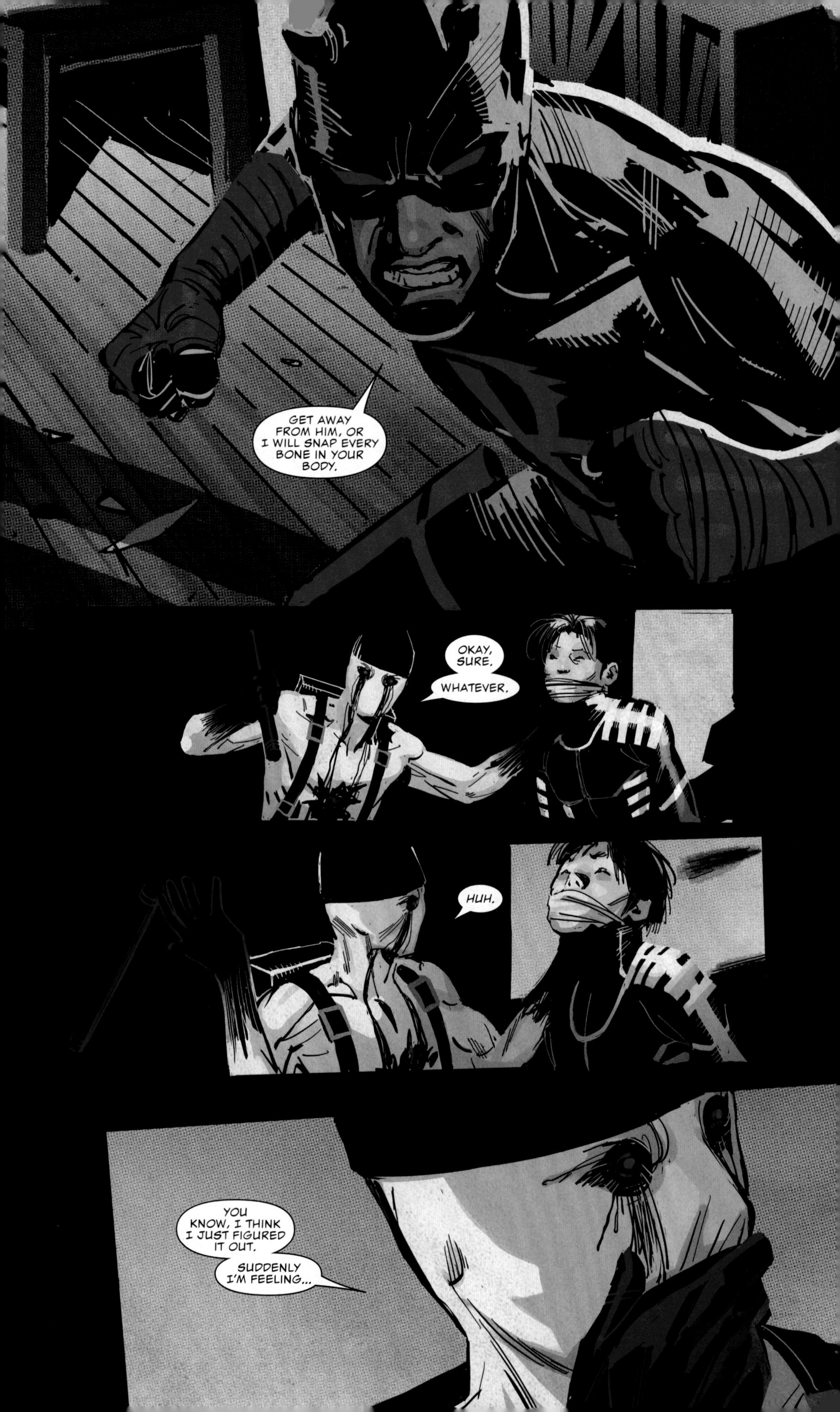
GET AWAY FROM HIM, OR I WILL SNAP EVERY BONE IN YOUR BODY.
OKAY, SURE.
WHATEVER.
HUH.
YOU KNOW, I THINK I JUST FIGURED IT OUT.
SUDDENLY I'M FEELING...

...INSPIRED.
NO!
YOU SEE IT, DON'T YOU?
BLINDSPOT.
JUST BEAUTIFUL.

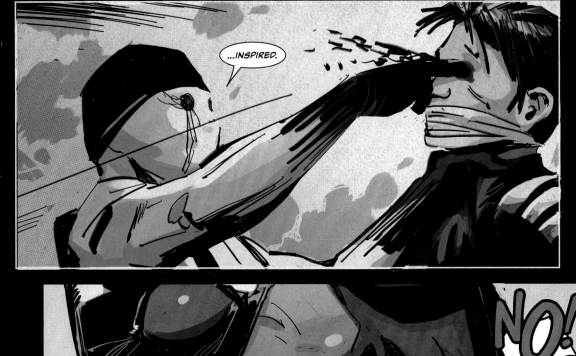

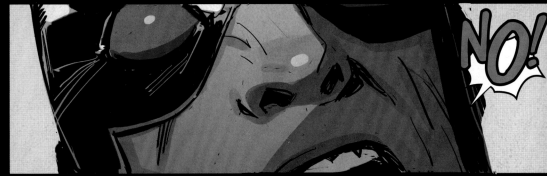

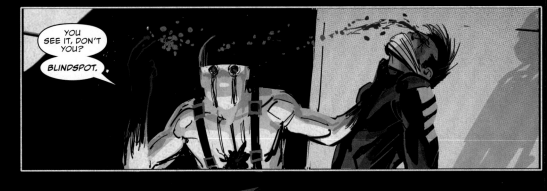

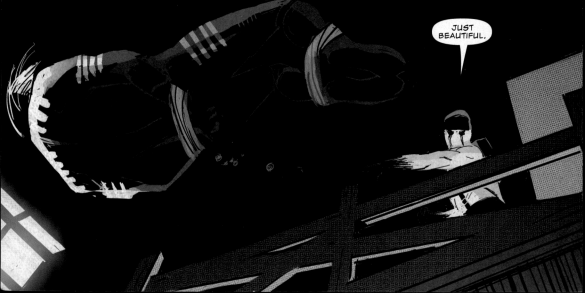

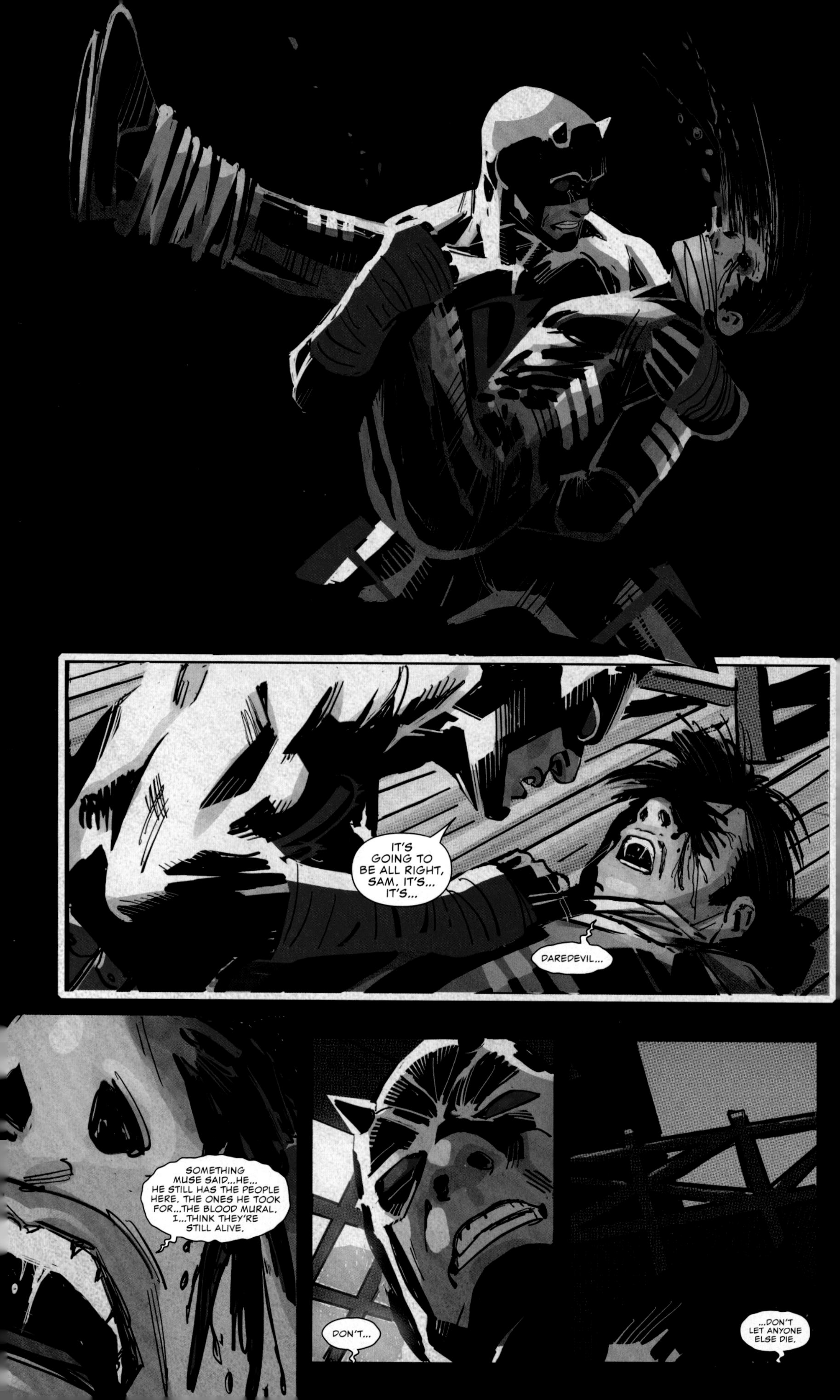
IT'S GOING TO BE ALL RIGHT, SAM. IT'S... IT'S...
DAREDEVIL...
SOMETHING MUSE SAID...HE... HE STILL HAS THE PEOPLE HERE. THE ONES HE TOOK FOR...THE BLOOD MURAL. I...THINK THEY'RE STILL ALIVE.
DON'T...
...DON'T LET ANYONE ELSE DIE.

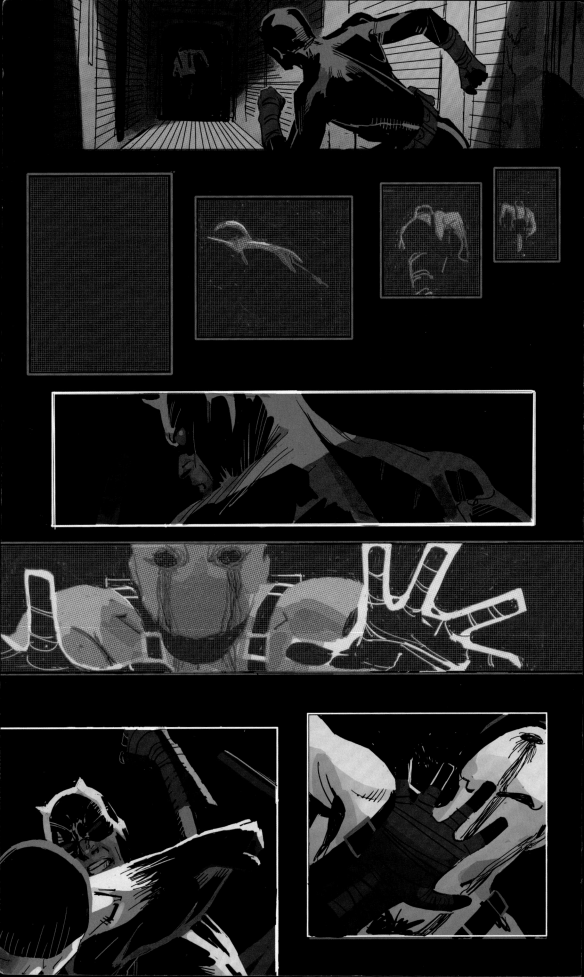

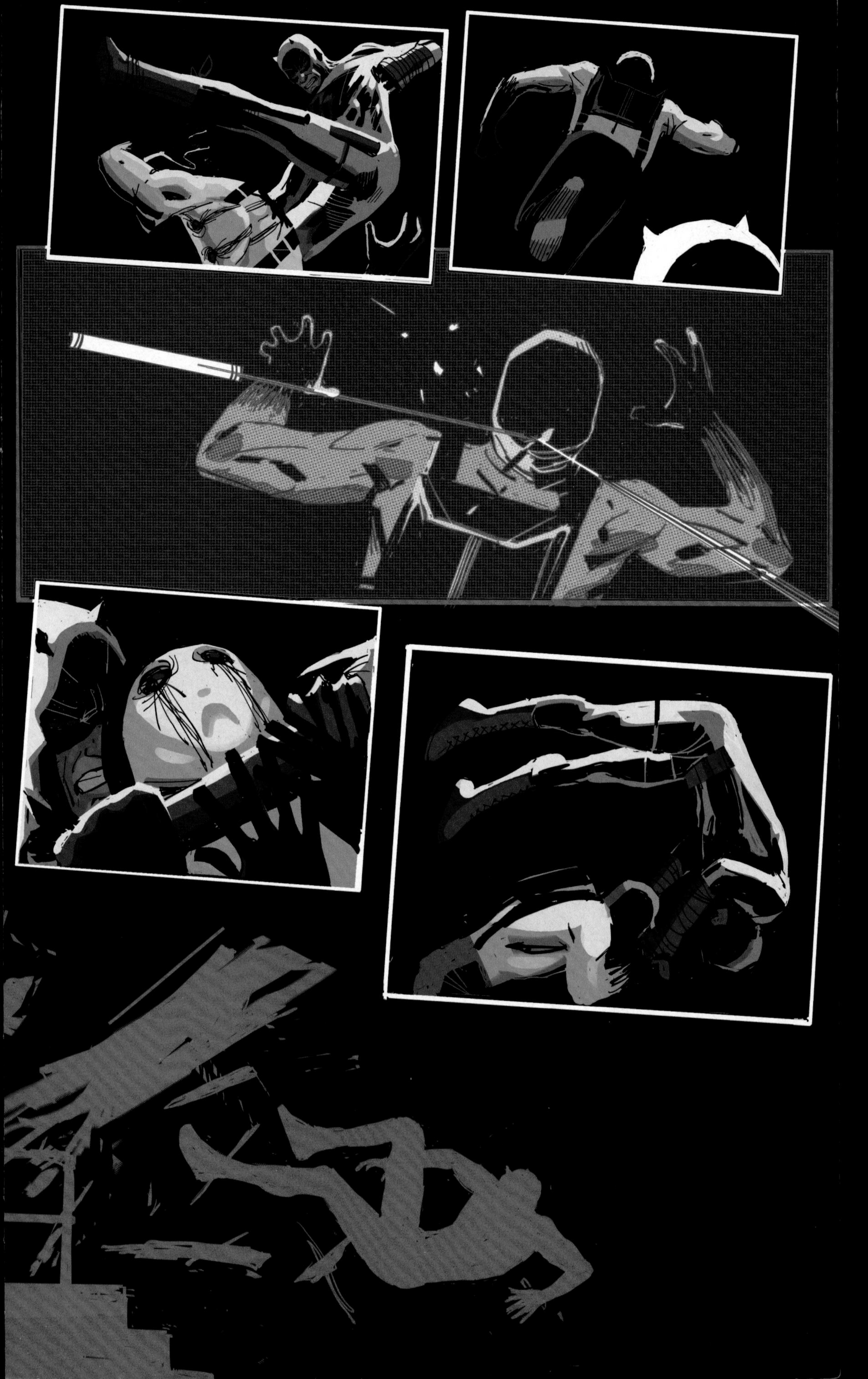

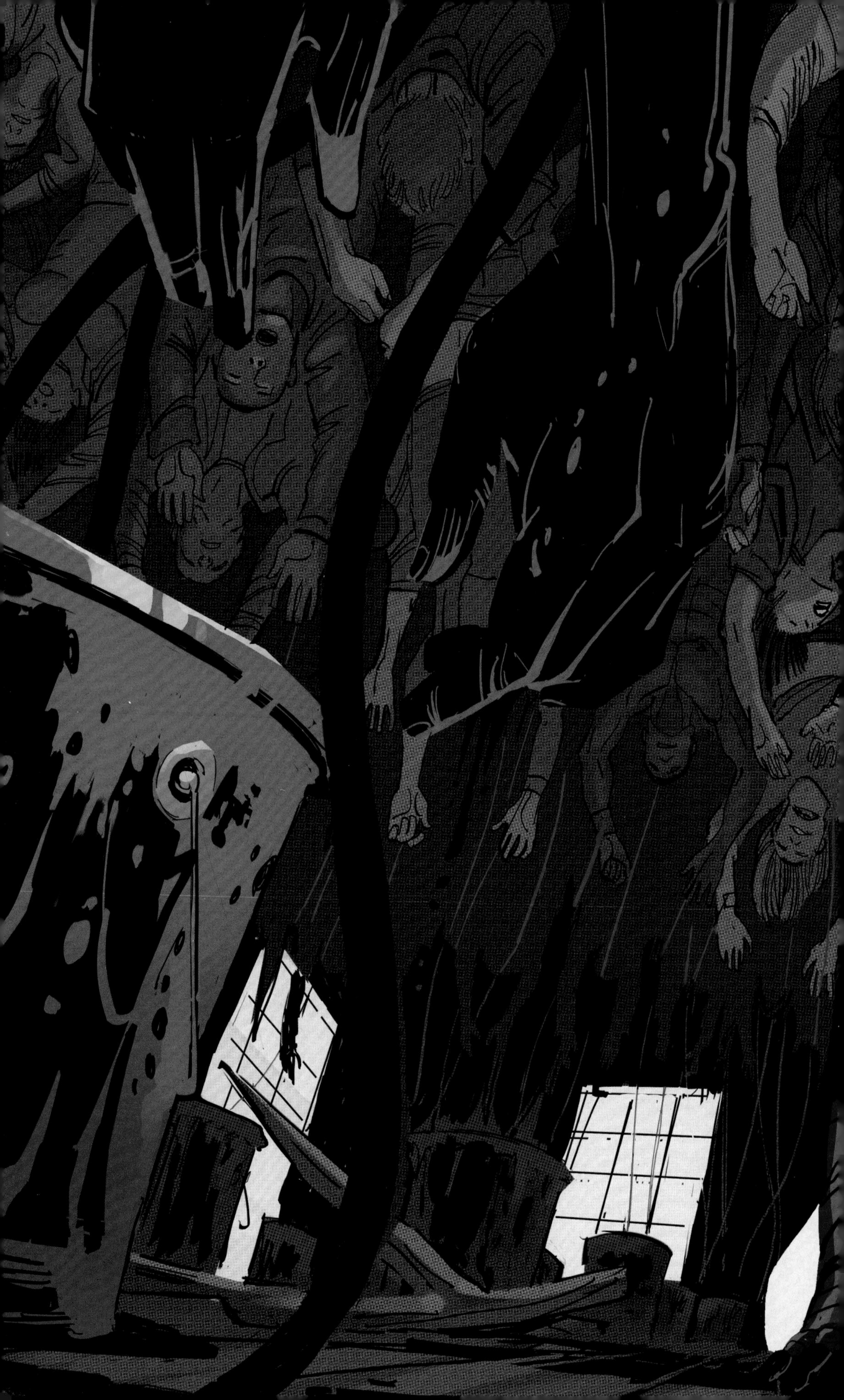

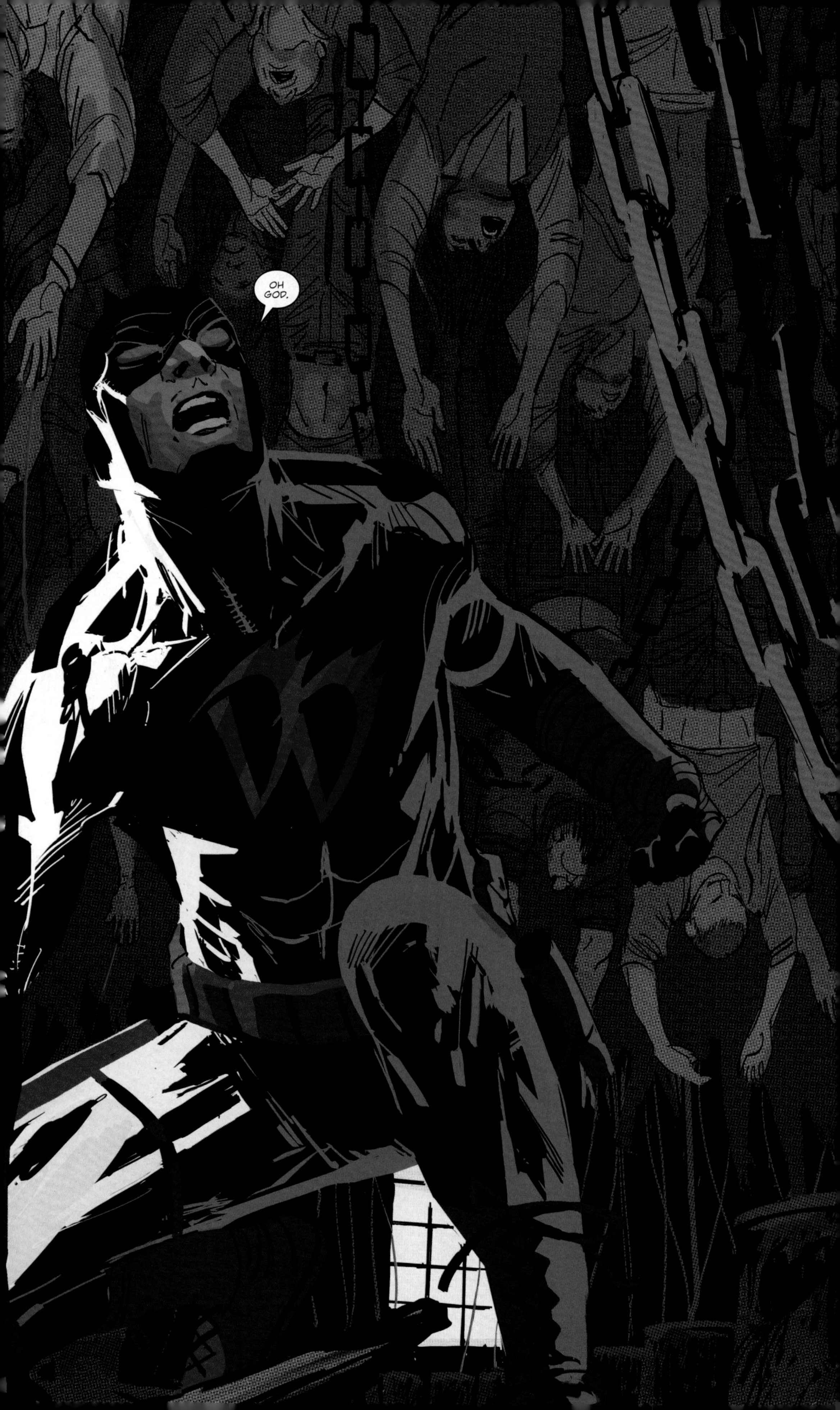
OH GOD.

WHY DO YOU CARE ABOUT THESE PEOPLE?

DON'T YOU REALIZE THEY'RE BETTER OFF? THEIR LIVES MEAN SOMETHING NOW. IT DOESN'T MATTER IF THEY DIE HERE.

THEY'RE IMMORTAL, I MEAN--

EH. YOU'LL NEVER GET IT.

KTHNK

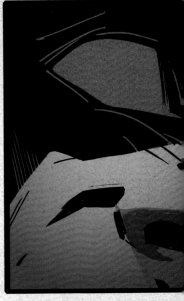

Oh, my god.

THD

I'm losing him.

THWP

I'm losing him.

ARRGH!

No more. No more.

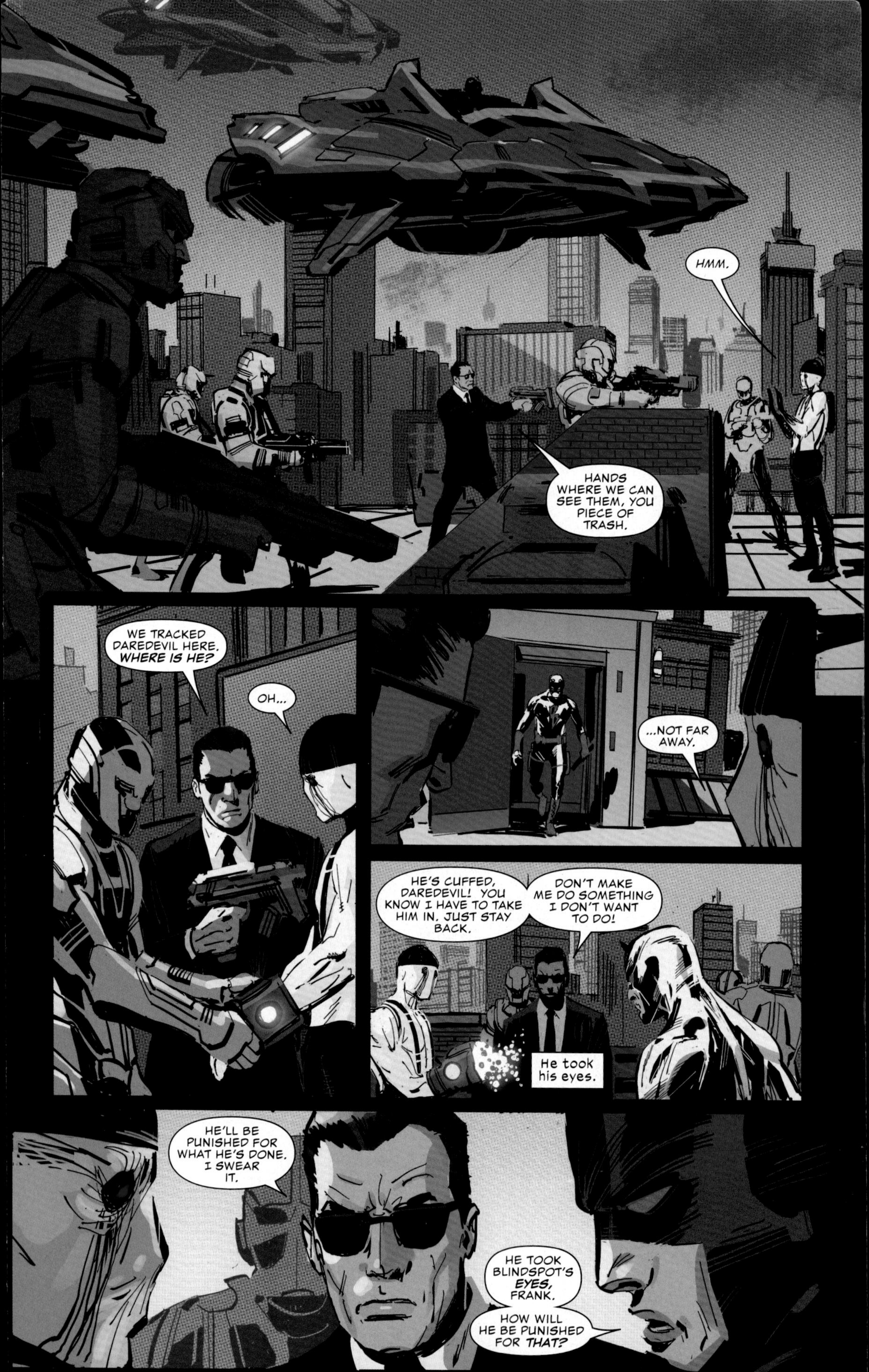
HMM.
HANDS WHERE WE CAN SEE THEM, YOU PIECE OF TRASH.
WE TRACKED DAREDEVIL HERE. *WHERE IS HE?*
OH...
...NOT FAR AWAY.
HE'S CUFFED, DAREDEVIL! YOU KNOW I HAVE TO TAKE HIM IN. JUST STAY BACK.
DON'T MAKE ME DO SOMETHING I DON'T WANT TO DO!
He took his eyes.
HE'LL BE PUNISHED FOR WHAT HE'S DONE. I SWEAR IT.
HE TOOK BLINDSPOT'S *EYES,* FRANK.
HOW WILL HE BE PUNISHED FOR *THAT?*

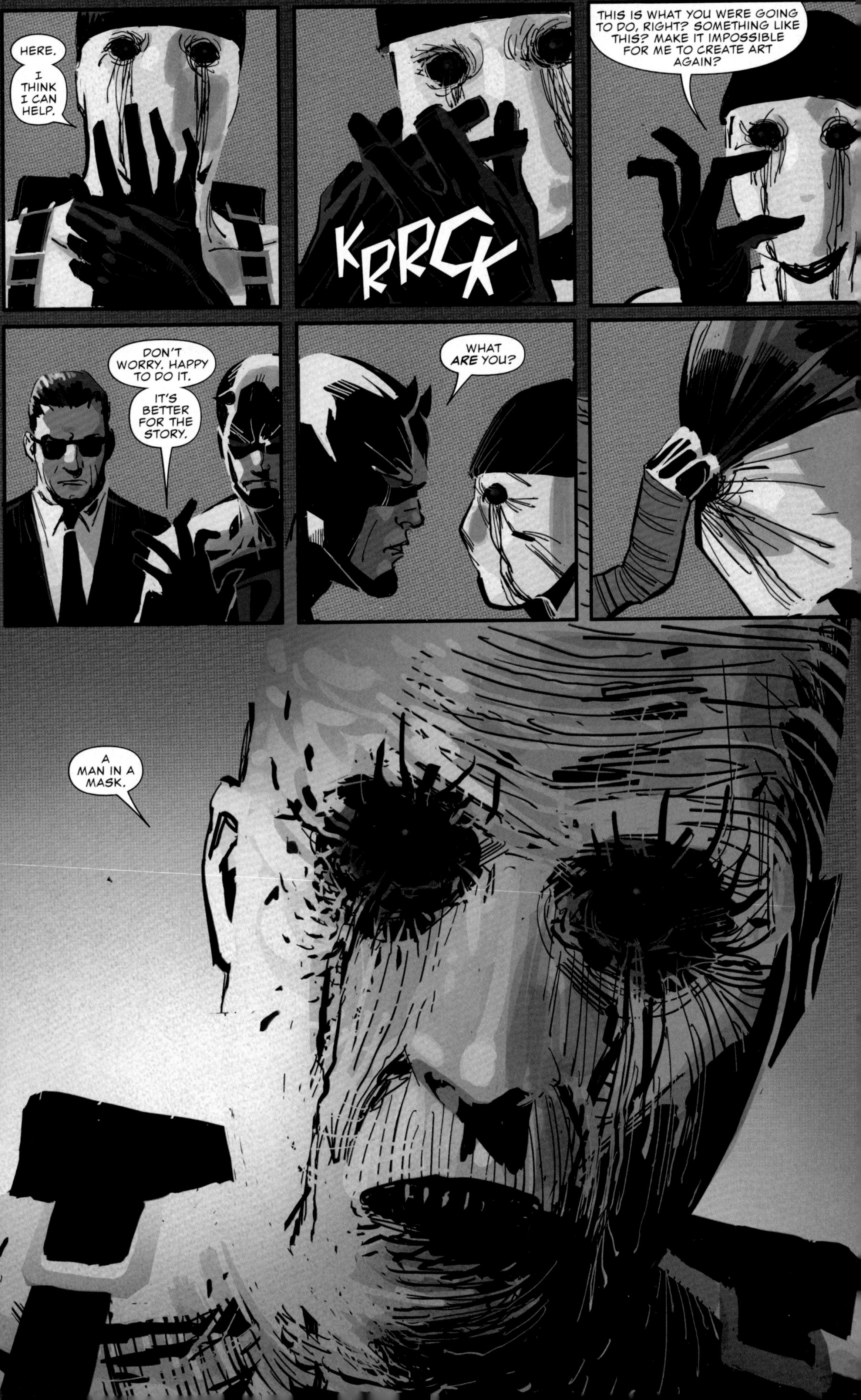
HERE.
I THINK I CAN HELP.
KRRCK
THIS IS WHAT YOU WERE GOING TO DO, RIGHT? SOMETHING LIKE THIS? MAKE IT IMPOSSIBLE FOR ME TO CREATE ART AGAIN?
DON'T WORRY. HAPPY TO DO IT.
IT'S BETTER FOR THE STORY.
WHAT ARE YOU?
A MAN IN A MASK.

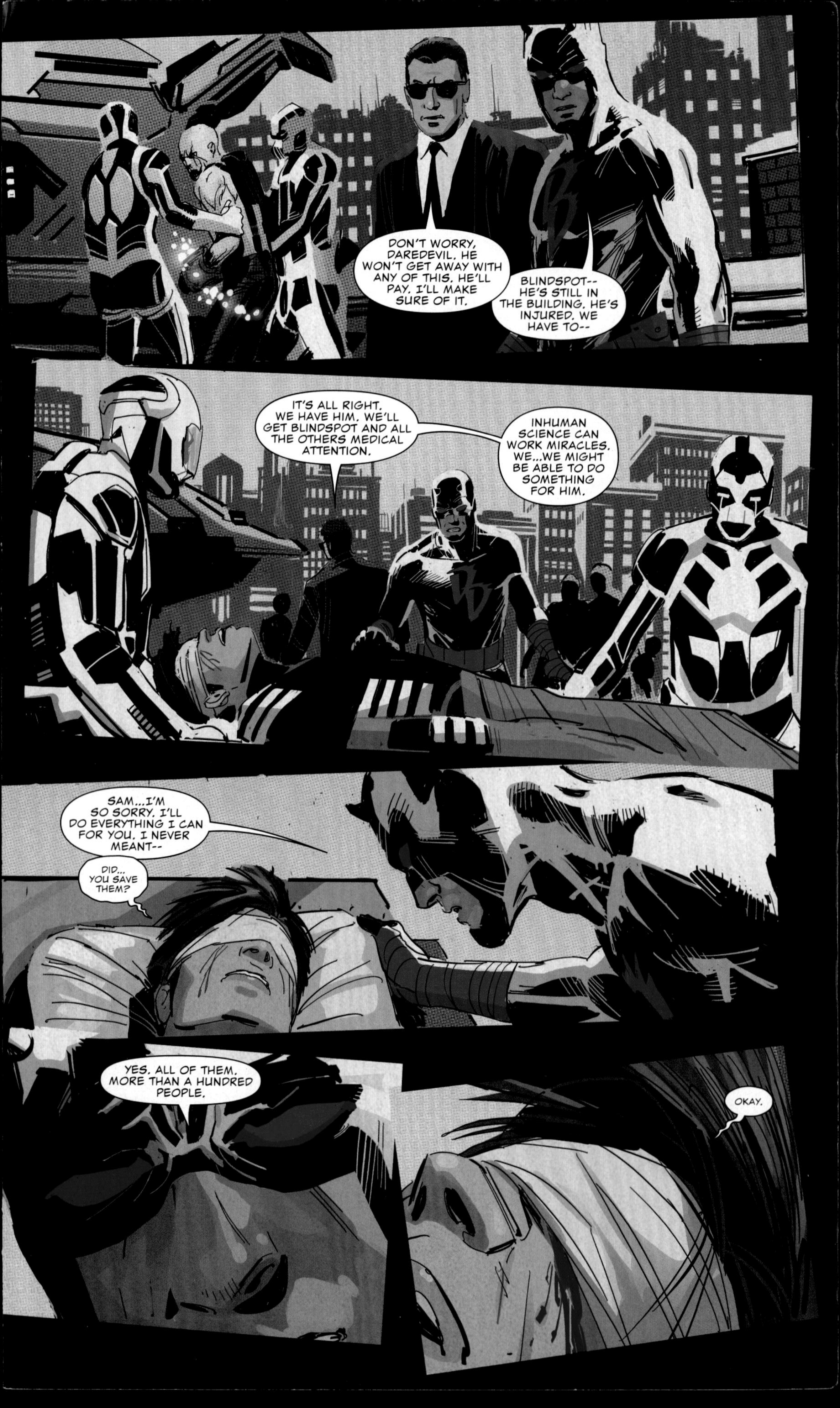
DON'T WORRY, DAREDEVIL. HE WON'T GET AWAY WITH ANY OF THIS. HE'LL PAY. I'LL MAKE SURE OF IT.
BLINDSPOT-- HE'S STILL IN THE BUILDING. HE'S INJURED. WE HAVE TO--
IT'S ALL RIGHT. WE HAVE HIM. WE'LL GET BLINDSPOT AND ALL THE OTHERS MEDICAL ATTENTION.
INHUMAN SCIENCE CAN WORK MIRACLES. WE...WE MIGHT BE ABLE TO DO SOMETHING FOR HIM.
SAM...I'M SO SORRY. I'LL DO EVERYTHING I CAN FOR YOU. I NEVER MEANT--
DID... YOU SAVE THEM?
YES. ALL OF THEM. MORE THAN A HUNDRED PEOPLE.
OKAY.

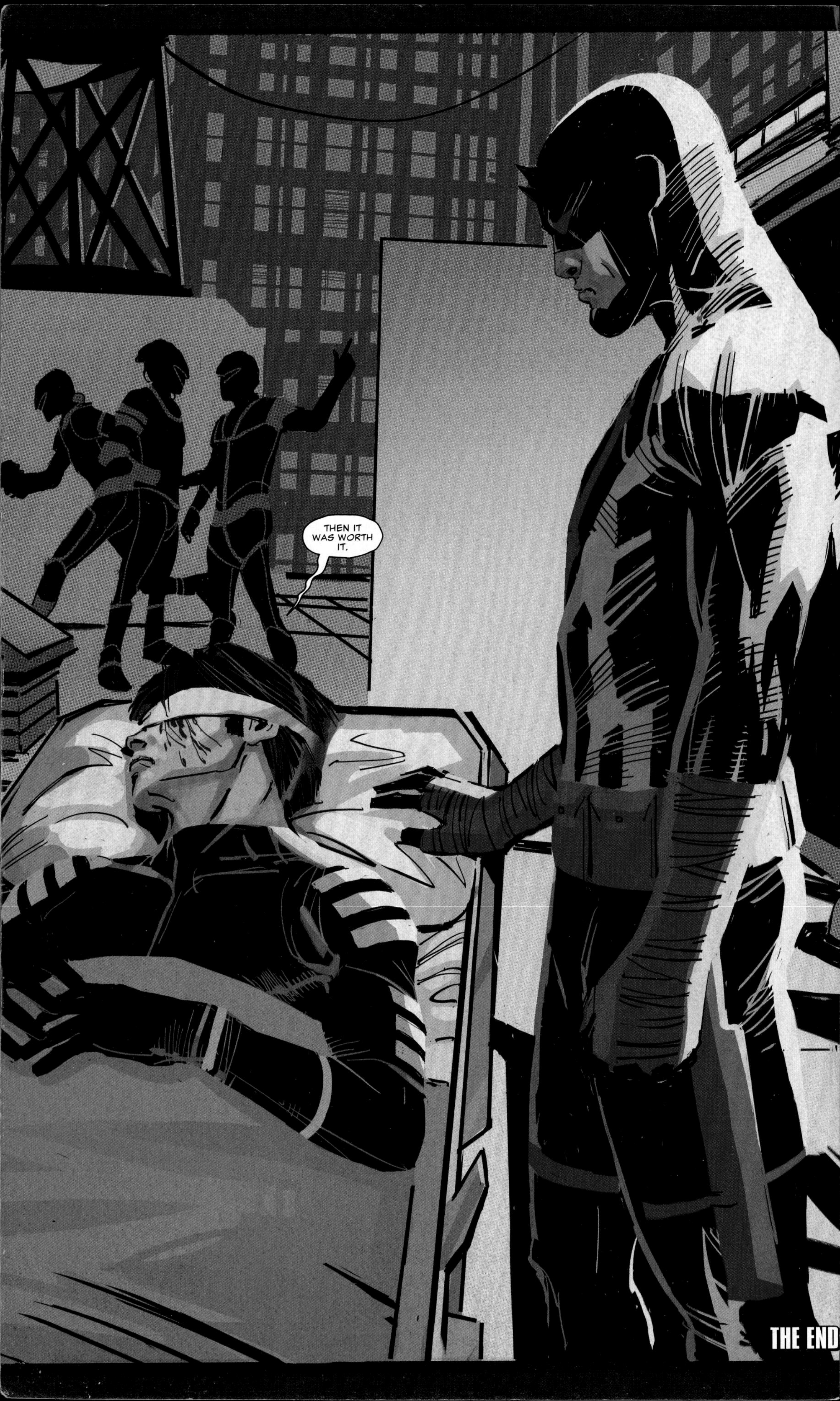
THEN IT WAS WORTH IT.
THE END

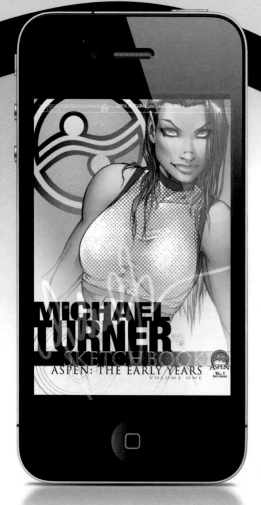
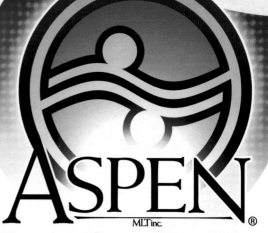